BASIC REAL ESTATE APPRAISAL: PRINCIPLES AND PROCEDURES

SEVENTH EDITION

Richard M. Betts, ASA, MAI, SRA
Certified General Real Estate Appraiser
and
Real Estate Instructor, Economist

Silas J. Ely, RECI
Certified General Real Estate Appraiser
and
Community College Instructor/Consultant
Real Estate Education

Dennis McKenzie
Series Editor

SOUTH-WESTERN
CENGAGE Learning

Australia • Brazil • Japan • Korea • Mexico • Singapore • Spain • United Kingdom • United States

SOUTH-WESTERN
CENGAGE Learning™

Basic Real Estate Appraisal: Principles and Procedures, Seventh Edition
Richard M. Betts and Silas J. Ely

VP/Editor-in-Chief: Dave Shaut

Executive Editor: Scott Person

Associate Acquisitions Editor: Sara Glassmeyer

Developmental Editor: Arlin Kauffman,
    LEAP Publishing Services, Inc.

Editorial Assistant: Adele Scholtz

Senior Marketing Manager: Mark Linton

Senior Marketing Communications Manager:
    Jim Overly

Content Project Manager: Patrick Cosgrove

Managing Technology Project Manager:
    Matt McKinney

Senior Manufacturing Coordinator:
    Charlene Taylor

Production House: LEAP Publishing Services, Inc.

Compositor: Jouve

Art Director: Linda Helcher

Cover Designer: KeDesign

For product information and technology assistance, contact us at
Cengage Learning Customer & Sales Support, 1-800-354-9706

For permission to use material from this text or product,
submit all requests online at **www.cengage.com/permissions**
Further permissions questions can be e-mailed to
permissionrequest@cengage.com

Library of Congress Control Number: 2007930276

Package: Student Edition:
ISBN 13: 978-0-324-65261-1
ISBN 10: 0-324-65261-5

Student Edition (core text only):
ISBN 13: 978-0-324-65262-8
ISBN 10: 0-324-65262-3

South-Western Cengage Learning
5191 Natorp Boulevard
Mason, OH 45040
USA

Cengage Learning is a leading provider of customized learning solutions with office locations around the globe, including Singapore, the United Kingdom, Australia, Mexico, Brazil, and Japan. Locate your local office at **www.cengage.com/global**

Cengage Learning products are represented in Canada by Nelson Education, Ltd.

To learn more about South-Western, visit **www.cengage.com/southwestern**

Purchase any of our products at your local college store or at our preferred online store **www.cengagebrain.com**

Printed in the United States of America
2 3 4 5 13 12 11

CONTENTS

CHAPTER 5
Real Estate Economics and Value

CHAPTER 6
Property Inspection and Analysis: The Site

CHAPTER 7
Property Inspection and Analysis: The Improvements

CHAPTER 8
The Sales Comparison Approach

CHAPTER 9
Analyzing and Adjusting Comparable Sales

CHAPTER 10
Valuing the Site

CHAPTER 11
Introducing the Cost Approach

CHAPTER 12
Estimating Loss in Value: Accrued Depreciation

CHAPTER 13
The Income Approach

CHAPTER 14
Income Capitalization: Rates and Techniques

CHAPTER 15
Reconciling the Value Estimates

CHAPTER 16
Reporting Appraisal Opinions

CHAPTER 17
Appraising Special Ownerships and Interests

CHAPTER 18
The Professional Appraiser

MEETING THE AUTHORS

Richard M. Betts

Mr. Betts is a California Certified General Real Estate Appraiser and consultant in Oakland, California. He was educated at the University of California, Berkeley, where he earned B.S. and M.B.A. degrees in business administration, with emphasis in real estate. Subsequent educational work includes a Real Estate Certificate; AIREA courses/exams I, II, IV, and VIII; and SREA Course 301. Mr. Betts has extensive experience as a fee appraiser, including expert witness appraisal before various superior courts and assessment appeal boards.

He has taught numerous times for Merritt Community College; the University of California, Berkeley, Extension Division; AIREA; SREA; and the Appraisal Institute. He also taught for IAAO (Courses, 1, 2, and 3); the University of Southern California; and the University of California, Berkeley, School of Business. Mr. Betts holds the professional designations MAI, SRA, and ASA (Real Estate), and is a past president of both the Northern California Chapter 11 of AIREA and the East Bay Chapter 54 of SREA. For some years, Mr. Betts served on national committees of AIREA, including the National Editorial Board, *The Appraisal Journal*. Mr. Betts is president of REAMUG, the appraisers' computer user group. He coauthored *The Essentials of Real Estate Economics*, 5th ed., published by South-Western Cengage Learning in 2006.

The late Silas J. Ely

Mr. Ely was a California Certified General Real Estate Appraiser, instructor, and educational consultant. He passed away in 2006 at his residence in San Luis Obispo County, California. He was a graduate of the University of California at Los Angeles, where he earned a B.A. degree in political science and a certificate in real estate. He also held a full-time California Community College instructor credential. For many years, Mr. Ely was a principal appraiser and regional manager for the Los Angeles County Assessor. Most recently an instructor at the College of the Canyons, Mr. Ely was an appraisal instructor at both Los Angeles Valley and Santa Monica Colleges, where he taught appraisal courses for over 20 years. Also, he was a senior faculty member in appraisal for the University of Southern California College of Continuing Education. Mr. Ely was the 1978 chairman of the California Association of Real Estate Teachers and a past president of the Los Angeles County Chapter of the IAAO. A Director Emeritus of the California Real Estate Education Association and long-time member of the Real Estate Educators Association, Mr. Ely held the RECI designation of the former group. He was a recipient of the Teacher of the Year Award for 1979 from the California Association of Real Estate Teachers. A continuing author of the *California Community College Instructor and Student Guides for Real Estate Appraisal*, Mr. Ely also authored a continuing education course in land use and development for the California Department of Real Estate in 1993. In recent years he had been an educational consultant for the American Society of Appraisers, authoring the 1997–98 instructor and student manuals used in their Course RP201, *Introduction to Real Property Valuation*. He has been a major contributor to the teaching of real estate appraisal and really will be missed.

PREFACE

This seventh edition of *Basic Real Estate Appraisal: Principles and Procedures* is a thorough outline of current appraisal theory and practice. It provides a practical guide to real estate appraisal for students, real estate professionals, and consumers. The recent Scope of Work changes of the Appraisal Standards Board have received special attention. Importantly, this text covers all of the topics listed in the educational requirements for state licensing, including the 2008 Appraisal Qualification Board changes for the first two courses.

Crafted to build upon the classical appraisal process, *Basic Real Estate Appraisal: Principles and Procedures* describes how this important valuation model has been refined and made more explicit in recent years by the Uniform Standards of Professional Appraisal Practice. Web sites of representative services and resources are included in the text.

Basic Real Estate Appraisal: Principles and Procedures has been written for easy reader comprehension. Both simple and complex subjects are covered, in terms that are easy to understand, yet accurate. Throughout, typical appraisal tasks and problems are described and illustrated. Charts and currently used appraisal forms are presented where useful.

Each chapter is subdivided into sections. The chapter starts with a preview paragraph and statement of learning objectives. These should help the reader identify the important elements in the chapter. The major sections of the text material follow. Each chapter concludes with a comprehensive summary and a list of important terms and concepts. A group of chapter review questions is provided to help the reader review his or her understanding. The answers to these questions are provided at the end of the book. Finally, there are end-of-chapter exercises, leading to production of a full appraisal report using the Bradford ClickFORMS appraisal software program provided on CD with the book.

The appraisal concepts and techniques covered in this book are important tools that are useful to people in every field of real estate. We hope that our presentation will provide many helpful ideas and skills for use in your own real estate endeavors.

Richard M. Betts

ClickFORMS

ClickFORMS Appraisal Software is a complete solution to your residential appraising needs. It is the only appraisal software that is Microsoft Certified, which means that it is Windows Vista-Ready. This translates to fewer things going wrong—so downtime is virtually eliminated. You can expect productivity right out of the box because it's the fastest to learn and the easiest to use. ClickFORMS is simplicity at its best, productivity at its highest.

Bradford Technologies—Committed to Customer Satisfaction and Product Quality

Bradford Technologies, Inc., formerly known as Bradford and Robbins, has developed and sold software for the real estate appraisal industry since 1987. We are located in California's Silicon Valley, the world center of high technology innovation. This enables our company to hire experts to develop software solutions and provide quality customer service. Our dedication to producing high-quality software is equally matched by our commitment to providing the best customer support. Our success depends on your success!

ACKNOWLEDGMENTS

This edition is dedicated to the memory of my coauthor, the late Silas Ely. He has played a major role in every edition until this one. This edition has also benefited from the very thorough review by David W. Johnson, MAI, CCIM, Downey, California, and instructor for UCLA.

Over the years, many people have played a part in the preparation of this book. To each one we express our deep appreciation. Valued technical contributions were made by Alfred Watts, MAI, instructor at Merritt College; Carol Chirpich, SRA, instructor at Saddleback College; Neil Olson, president, and Steve Costello, marketing director, both formerly of the California Market Data Cooperative (a service known best as "CMDC") in Irvine, California; Lowell Anderson, department chairman of real estate, Cerritos College; Marjory Reed, former coordinator of real estate programs, San Diego Community College District; Dr. Stanley S. Reyburn, instructor at UCLA and several California community colleges; Robert Mason, MAI, consulting appraiser, Mason & Mason; James Goodhue, MAI; Noland Cavey, SRA, supervising real property appraiser, Sacramento County Assessor's Office; and James Palmer, MAI.

Many other people have helped in the formulation of *Basic Real Estate Appraisal: Principles and Procedures*—the students in our appraisal classes who have shared their insights with us over the years, the appraisal colleagues and friends with whom we have exchanged and debated ideas, the authors of earlier appraisal texts from which we have learned, and the lecturers at the appraisal courses and seminars at which we have been students. Our special thanks go to the many instructors of real estate appraisal classes who have participated with us at instructor workshops, sponsored by the California Community College Real Estate Education Center and the California Real Estate Education Association. We hope that we have adequately incorporated and passed along all of their good ideas.

R. M. B.

CHAPTER 1
REAL ESTATE APPRAISAL AND YOU

PREVIEW

Well-founded appraisals are a vital part of most real estate decisions, particularly those that involve the listing, financing, sale, or purchase of real estate. What is an appraisal? If you have had previous courses in real estate, or have worked in this dynamic field, you will know that an appraisal can be simply defined as an opinion or estimate of value.

Most of us make decisions in our everyday lives that use appraisal skills, whether in buying consumer goods or in serving as real estate professionals.

The goal of this book is to help you develop appraisal skills in your own chosen field of real estate, while at the same time gaining a better understanding of the appraisal techniques and standards used by professional appraisers.

This first chapter will explain what an appraisal is, who prepares appraisals, and how appraisals are developed, reported, and used in our society. A brief introduction to the *Uniform Standards of Professional Appraisal Practice* (USPAP) is included in this chapter, and will be expanded on in future chapters.

OBJECTIVES

When you have completed this chapter you should be able to:

1. Define the term *appraisal.*
2. Explain the difference between a formal and an informal appraisal, and between an appraisal and an appraisal report.
3. List the main uses of appraisals.
4. Outline the Ethics Standards of USPAP.
5. List several important reasons for studying appraisal.

1.1 What Is an Appraisal?

Very simply, an appraisal is the preparation of an estimate or opinion of **value** of some object or thing. It is defined this way because it is neither a statement of value nor a fixing of value. An appraisal of value is only one person's opinion, based on whatever skills, training, data, dedication, and/or objectivity that person possesses. What do we mean by value? Value means the **worth**, usefulness, or utility of an object to someone for some purpose. Under this definition, the so-called value of any object can vary, depending on the purpose for which it is to be used or the person seeking to use it. Thus, there are actually many different types of "values," each appropriate to a particular appraisal problem. Several distinctly different types of value will be defined and discussed in Chapter 3.

Note that this text is on the appraisal of real estate (defined in Chapter 2). An appraisal can be performed on any object, whether real or personal property, or a combination.

However, the purpose of most real estate appraisals is to form an opinion of what is known as *market value.* While several formal definitions are used, market value is most easily defined as the *most probable selling price* of a property in a competitive and open market. Accurately estimating what real estate should sell for is the focus of this book.

Informal Appraisals

Have you ever estimated what price to pay for an object at a garage sale or an auction? If you have, then you have made a type of appraisal. Such an informal appraisal is a common part of our lives. Whenever we buy groceries, household appliances, or automobiles, we usually make an informal appraisal to judge if the prices are reasonable. We do this by consciously or unconsciously comparing one product with another, or by matching the price of one item against that of a similar one. As we become more experienced in comparing items and prices, we develop an intuitive understanding of the value of things. Such an intuitive knowledge of value can also be applied to real estate.

Informal appraisals are routinely made by almost everyone working in the field of real estate. For example, the "market analysis" made by brokers and salespeople when listing or selling a given property sometimes is best described as an informal appraisal. Very experienced sales agents on occasion can closely estimate the eventual selling price of a house after only a quick walk-through. To be reliable, however, informal appraisals like these depend on an active and competitive market in the particular kind and location of property being analyzed. Most importantly, they also require a high level of skill and judgment that only experience and knowledge can provide.

Formal Appraisals

Historically, both consumers and practitioners have always relied upon expert advice to estimate the value of anything that they have little experience buying or selling. This was particularly true in the case of real estate. The intuitive value judgment used in informal appraisals could not be relied upon when there had been little or no market experience at that time. In the absence of expert advice, there are only three alternatives to estimating the value of real estate without direct experience: 1) to rely on inadequate intuition, 2) to settle for poor advice, or 3) to deliberately develop and analyze the kind of information needed to make reliable value estimates. The third of these choices best describes the logical system that underlies what is now referred to in the industry as a formal appraisal.

A **formal appraisal** is a means of reaching an opinion of value by the methodical collection and analysis of relevant market data. Most often reported in writing, formal appraisals are usually made by people who are specially trained for this work. Since a formal appraisal involves a value conclusion that is based on an analysis of factual material, a client or disinterested party can easily review the appraisal report and understand how the conclusion was reached. This is in contrast to an **informal** appraisal, in which factual material may be absent or sketchy, and the value conclusion was reached by using intuition, past experience, and general knowledge. None of these can be easily reviewed. To better understand the difference between formal and informal appraisals, see Figure 1-1.

In practice, formal and informal appraisals share some common ground. Although formal appraisals are based primarily on supporting data, in practice, they must also rely to a degree on the appraiser's judgment and intuition. On the other hand, informal appraisals are based mainly on intuition, but may also include some data that supports the value estimate. Appraisals by professional appraisers are

Figure 1-1 Formal and Informal Appraisals.

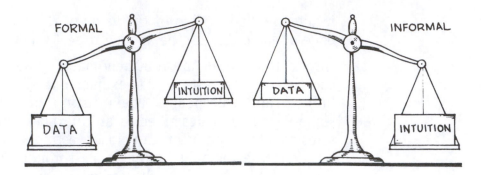

usually more formal, while those by experienced salespeople are more often intuitive and informal.

The Appraisal Report

The results of formal appraisals are communicated to the client by what is known as the **appraisal report**. Appraisal reports may be either oral or written. Written reports may vary in length, from a short form or letter to a detailed narrative document. The length of an appraisal report does not necessarily reflect the complexity or quality of the appraisal itself. Instead, the form and content of reports are to a large extent governed by professional and legal standards now relied upon by professional appraisers. Formal appraisal reports will be described in more detail in the chapters that follow.

1.2 How Appraisals Are Used

Appraisals serve two important functions in our society. The first function is to assist the public by advising them on questions of property value. Many people do not have the skills, the time, or the knowledge to make good value estimates on their own; instead, they turn to professionals for formal or informal appraisals.

The second social function that appraisals perform is to provide an unbiased independent and disinterested opinion of value, where total objectivity is required by business practice or by provision of law. Appraisals in such situations must be formal and credible. Like the notes of the certified court reporter or the signature of the notary public, the formal appraisal and report, made by an unbiased and objective appraiser, is an important instrument in business and legal affairs.

Occasions Requiring Appraisals

In our complex society, there are countless occasions when formal or informal appraisals are needed. Such occasions can be divided into two major categories: market transactions and legal transactions. As we will see, parties to these transactions might include buyers, sellers, agents, lenders, landlords, and tenants, as well as various agencies of government.

Market Transactions

Most of the *market transactions* requiring appraisals are connected with the sale, purchase, finance, management, and use of real estate. As we have already seen, buyers, sellers, and sales agents need formal or informal appraisals to guide them in establishing the price and terms of the real estate transaction being contemplated. When the terms are finally agreed on, some financing is typically involved. This usually means that a formal appraisal will also be required, to support the loan approval. In cases where there are multiple buyers and sellers (as with some investment properties), several separate appraisals may be involved in a single transaction.

Various kinds of appraisals are also required in the management and use of real estate. For example, an appraisal is sometimes needed to estimate the proper rent level at the time a new lease is negotiated. Usually, an appraisal is also needed to estimate the values of properties being exchanged. Or one may be required to estimate proper insurance coverage, based on the kind of coverage in the insurance contract. Appraisals may also be used to see whether the cost of proposed remodeling is justified, considering the probable increase in a property's value. Finally, an appraisal may be necessary to estimate which of several possible uses of a vacant land parcel will prove to be the *highest and best use*, that is, the most profitable use of the land.

Legal Transactions

By *legal transactions*, we mean various government actions involving real estate and those private actions that take place in legal settings or are otherwise regulated by law. When appraisals are required, they usually must be formal and often in writing.

Government actions requiring appraisals are mainly in two areas of public control: eminent domain (the right to acquire private property for a public purpose) and the various forms of taxation. Under the laws of eminent domain, condemnation appraisals estimate what "just compensation" or payment to the owner should be made for any property acquired for public use or in the public interest. Condemnation appraising is a highly specialized field, to be further discussed in Chapter 17.

Property taxation is perhaps the largest area of public control involving appraisals. In thousands of jurisdictions across the country, the property tax appraiser, or assessor, must estimate a value to be used as the basis for the property tax. In turn, the taxpayer may have the property privately appraised, to see if the agency valuation is reasonable or whether it should be appealed. (Appraisals for property tax purposes will be discussed later in this book.) Public or governmental appraisals may also be necessary to establish the basis for inheritance, estate, or gift taxes.

Various types of appraisals are made in conjunction with income tax reporting or appeal. For example, appraisals may be required to support an income tax claim for a casualty loss. An appraisal may be needed to allocate the purchase price of property between the land and the improvements, in order to set up income tax depreciation deductions. On occasion, appraisals are needed to establish historical values, so that capital gains since the earlier date can be calculated. As the various tax laws become more complicated, tax-related formal appraisals may come into even greater demand.

Personal and corporate actions in a variety of legal settings also give rise to appraisals. For example, there is an occasional need for appraisals to accompany environmental impact reports, required in many property use and development situations. Both fire insurance and title insurance claims frequently require a formal appraisal, in order to establish the amount of the claim, depending on the wording of the insurance policy. Appraisals are often needed to set the value of property involved in divorce situations. When lawsuits between building owners and tenants revolve around questions of property value or rental amounts, appraisals may also be required. Additionally, legal actions arising over damages to real estate may require appraisals, usually to estimate the loss in value from such damages.

Another occasion for appraisals arises when loans are in default. Here, lenders need to know the market value of any real estate security, in preparation for commencing the foreclosure process. Bankruptcy actions may also call for appraisals. If real estate is offered as security for bail bonds, appraisals might be required, too. Appraisals for legal purposes often require the appraiser to act as an expert witness. Such assignments are among the most challenging work appraisers undertake.

The most common occasions requiring appraisals are shown in the following list.

1. Market Transactions
   a. Purchase, sale, and exchange
   b. Financing
   c. Leasing
   d. Management
   e. Insurance coverage
   f. Remodeling and development
   g. Feasibility and highest and best use studies
   h. Exercise of purchase or lease options

2. Legal Transactions
    a. Eminent domain—condemnor and condemnee
    b. Property tax assessment and tax appeals cases
    c. Estate, inheritance, and gift taxes
    d. Income tax—casualty loss, depreciation basis, and capital gains reporting
    e. Personal and corporate legal actions
    f. Environmental impact reports
    g. Fire or title insurance claims
    h. Marital and partnership dissolutions
    i. Landlord-tenant and property damage lawsuits
    j. Loan foreclosures
    k. Company liquidation or merger
    l. Bankruptcy
    m. Security for bail bonds

1.3 Standards of Appraisal Practice

We can see that appraisals and appraisal reports are an important part of the social, business, legal, and governmental fabric of our society. How is the public protected against nonprofessional or unethical appraisal practice?

Professional appraisal groups have long sponsored and promoted strict standards of ethics and practice among their members. Several groups continue to award professional designations to those members who distinguish themselves with knowledge, experience, and demonstrated ability. Examples include the MAI designation of the Appraisal Institute and the ASA designation of the American Society of Appraisers, discussed further in Chapter 18.

In 1987, nine leading appraisal groups banded together to formulate uniform *appraisal standards*. These were eventually recognized by professional appraisal organizations throughout the United States and North America. Now published and maintained by The Appraisal Foundation, the *Uniform Standards of Professional Appraisal Practice*, known informally as USPAP, is now required and followed by most state and federal regulatory agencies. The brief overview of USPAP provided in this book is intended to be introductory in nature. Those who intend to pursue a career in either real estate appraisal or real estate finance are urged to purchase and maintain a current copy of USPAP from The Appraisal Foundation (http://www.appraisalfoundation.org).

USPAP imposes both ethical obligations and minimum appraisal standards that must be adhered to by all professional appraisers.

Ethics Rule

The *Ethics Rule* of USPAP places ethical obligations on the appraiser in the following general areas of practice.

Conduct. Requires that the appraiser perform all assignments ethically and competently, in accordance with USPAP, and do so with impartiality, objectivity, and independence, and without accommodation of personal interests.

Management. Prohibits the payment of any undisclosed fees or commissions in connection with obtaining an appraisal assignment. Any compensation for developing an opinion of value that is contingent upon the value conclusion is also generally forbidden.

Confidentiality. Requires that the appraiser not reveal confidential factual data obtained from the client, or the results of an assignment, to anyone other than: (1) the client and those he/she has authorized; (2) state licensing agencies and third parties authorized by law; and (3) a duly authorized professional peer review committee.

Record Keeping. Requires that the appraiser prepare and keep a comprehensive work file for each assignment for at least five years after preparation, and also at least two years after final disposition of any judicial proceeding where testimony was given.

In addition to the ethics standards imposed upon the appraiser, USPAP includes four other rules (discussed in more detail in Section 18.4):

1. The *Competency Rule* requires that appraisers accept only that work that they have the experience necessary to perform, either individually, or, if needed, in association with others.

2. The *Scope of Work Rule* states that "the appraiser must identify the problem to be solved; determine and perform the scope of work necessary to develop credible assignment results; and disclose the scope of work in the report."

3. The *Jurisdictional Exception Rule* declared that "if any part of USPAP is contrary to the law or public policy of any jurisdiction, only that part shall be void and of no force or effect in that jurisdiction."

4. The *Supplemental Standards Rule* covers added requirements issued as policy or regulation by government agencies or similar bodies.

Appraisal Standards

USPAP contains the following general standards for real estate appraisers:

> *Standard 1: Real Property Appraisal Development.* In developing a real property appraisal, an appraiser must identify the problem to be solved, determine the scope of work necessary to solve the problem, and correctly complete research and analyses necessary to produce a credible appraisal.
>
> Source: *Uniform Standards of Professional Appraisal Practice*, 2006 ed., The Appraisal Foundation, Washington, D.C.: 2006, p. 17.
>
> *Standard 2: Real Property Appraisal Reporting.* In reporting the results of a real property appraisal, an appraiser must communicate each analysis, opinion, and conclusion in a manner that is not misleading.
>
> Source: *Ibid*, page 23.

More information on professional appraisal groups and the standards of professional appraisal practice are provided in Chapters 16 and 18 of this text. The procedures and techniques presented in this book are intended to reflect the appraisal standards presented in USPAP. These standards are modified when a new edition is released (now to be every two years). Appraisers must try to keep current with these changes.

Appraiser Licensing and Certification

State and federal laws that were enacted in 1993 require that appraisals made in support of certain federally related financial real estate transactions (federally insured loans, for example) must meet special requirements. Only appraisals that are in excess of a minimum amount must comply. One requirement is that the appraisals must be performed by licensed or certified appraisers. Such appraisals and their reports must conform to the USPAP standards referred to above. State license and certification requirements are outlined in Chapter 18.

1.4 Developing Appraisal Skills

We believe that appraisal skills are important to everyone who is, or wants to be, involved with real estate in any way! These skills are particularly important to real estate agents, who have a special responsibility to their clients. Improved appraisal skills can help salespeople improve their listing skills. For example, suggesting a reasonable asking price can avoid the problems associated with either too high, or too low, asking prices. High listing prices, for example, could result in no sale, an unhappy client, or a waste of otherwise productive time.

It is also important for people working in other real estate areas to study appraisal and develop appraisal skills. For example, investors must use appraisal skills to estimate the right price at which to buy or sell property. Lenders rely on appraisal skills every day, when reviewing loan appraisal reports, to ensure that each loan has adequate security.

A second important reason for studying appraisal is to acquire basic knowledge and terminology that will help you in any future real estate course. Beginning and advanced real estate finance, real estate investment analysis, and advanced appraisal courses all rely on the information and ideas presented in this book.

Third, studying this book can also help you pass the real estate sales agent's or broker's license test, or prepare for appraiser licensing and certification exams.

Finally, a fourth reason for studying appraisal is to improve your understanding of the way appraisers work and talk. This will help you communicate with appraisers, intelligently evaluate their work, and improve your understanding of appraisals and appraisal reports. Learning how to explain appraisal principles and procedures to your clients is another important benefit.

How Will the Format of This Book Help You?

The format of this book has been developed to assist your study of the material presented. First, each chapter has a brief preview that introduces the material to be covered and points out key learning objectives. At the end of each chapter, there is a summary, so that you can review what you have read and reinforce your understanding. The chapter summary is followed by a list of important terms, to help you develop an appraisal vocabulary and remember which terms are important. Review questions at the end of each chapter are designed to test and reinforce your understanding of the material covered. Answers to these questions are provided at the end of the book, along with a glossary and an index!

We have also provided a series of practical home appraisal exercises at the end of most chapters, using the well-known URAR loan appraisal report form. A copy of the ClickFORMS report-generating program has been included with this book, courtesy of Bradford Technologies, Inc. However, other programs can also be used.

Of course, the learning objectives, chapter summary, and review questions will help you the most if you put them to work. So take the time to read each chapter carefully and thoughtfully. When you finish, if you can answer the questions without looking back, you are doing fine. If you do need to look back, don't feel upset; looking up the answers will aid your learning considerably. Remember, you only get back from a book what you put into it. Appraisal skills can measurably contribute to your success, so your effort will be rewarded.

The Chapters Ahead

This book outlines the entire formal ***appraisal process*** and explains the various skills that are involved. In general, the sequence of the chapters matches the steps in the appraisal process. Chapters 2 and 3 introduce the vocabulary and define the terms that you must be familiar with before the actual appraisal starts. An overview of the entire appraisal process is also provided.

Chapters 4 and 5 outline the major forces that influence value and point out how these forces can be interpreted. Chapters 6 and 7 detail the tasks of the actual property inspection. Chapters 8 through 15 show you the analytical techniques that are considered when valuing the property. Chapter 16 outlines the structure of the appraisal report, explains the report format alternatives, and details information that needs to be included in order to satisfy USPAP. Chapter 17 introduces a number of advanced appraisal topics to help you build upon your basic appraisal skills, as well as prepare you for an advanced appraisal course. Chapter 18 turns your attention to appraising as a profession. It details the typical education and experience requirements for state licensing and certification of appraisers. Chapter 18 also lists several leading national appraisal organizations and describes their activities. The chapter closes with a brief description of professional appraisal work.

SUMMARY

In this chapter, we found that an appraisal is simply an estimate of value. Value generally means the worth or ***usefulness*** of something to someone for some purpose. Although there are many types of value, the purpose of most appraisals is to form an opinion of market value, or the price at which something should sell.

Estimating the selling price of things is a process that everyone performs at one time or another. People do this by relying on their prior experiences with selling or buying an item. Such a value estimate is an informal or ***intuitive appraisal***. When people have accumulated a lot of experience buying or selling an object, close to the time of the value estimate, their intuitive appraisals may be very good. However, it is difficult for someone else to judge whether an intuitive appraisal is accurate or not.

Many people do not have the experience or judgment that is needed to make good intuitive real estate appraisals. They can nevertheless learn to logically gather and analyze data that is relevant to market value. Once acquired, such skills can be used to make formal appraisals. The quality of formal appraisals does not depend on intuition to the degree that informal appraisals do. Reports of formal appraisals also have the advantage of presenting data and analyses that can be reviewed easily.

This allows a client or reviewer to consider objectively whether the appraisal estimate seems reasonable. However, in practice, the appraisal report does not always contain all of the information and calculations that were developed during a formal appraisal. Hence, the length of the report does not necessarily reflect the complexity or quality of the appraisal.

Appraisals are a vital part of real estate. Every real estate transaction involves informal appraisals by the buyer and seller. One or more formal appraisals may also be needed, especially to meet the lender's requirements. In addition, the legal framework of our society requires many appraisals, including appraisals for eminent domain, insurance claims, and various taxation purposes, and for use as evidence in civil lawsuits involving real property. Most real estate appraisals and reports must now conform to what is known as the *Uniform Standards of Professional Appraisal Practice*, referred to by most appraisers as USPAP. Published and maintained by The Appraisal Foundation, USPAP has now been adopted, and its use is required, by most state and federal regulatory agencies. The purpose is to ensure professionalism in appraisals, and to protect the public interest in receiving reliable appraisal reports. The appraisal procedures and techniques presented in this book are meant to reflect USPAP standards.

The study of real estate appraisal is important to all involved in real estate. Whether you are a real estate consumer or real estate professional, having appraisal skills will make your real estate decisions better, more profitable, and more error-free. Another reason for studying real estate appraisal is that this material can assist you in taking future real estate courses or in preparing for real estate sales, broker, or appraiser licensing exams. Studying appraisal also enables you to communicate better with appraisers. By learning their language and techniques, you will be able to review their work intelligently. If you are a real estate professional, knowledge of appraisal skills also helps you to explain to others how your own value decisions are reached.

IMPORTANT TERMS AND CONCEPTS

Appraisal (formal and informal)

Appraisal process

Appraisal report

Appraisal standards

Competency Rule

Ethics Rule

Intuitive appraisal

Jurisdictional Exception Rule

Legal transactions

Market transactions

Scope of Work Rule

Supplemental Standards Rule

Uniform Standards of Professional Appraisal Practice

Usefulness

Value

Worth

REVIEWING YOUR UNDERSTANDING

1. The general term *value* means:
   a. The function of an object
   b. The average use of an object to all people
   c. The worth, usefulness, or utility of an object to someone for some purpose
   d. A good buy

2. The goal of an appraisal is:
   a. A fixing of value
   b. An estimate or opinion of value
   c. A statement of value
   d. A value determination

3. The two types of real estate appraisals are:
   a. Formal and informal
   b. Informal and intuitive
   c. Structural and formal
   d. None of the above

4. Informal appraisals are performed:
   a. Only by appraisers
   b. Only by skilled real estate people
   c. By all consumers
   d. Without the use of instinct

5. Informal appraisals rely mostly on:
   a. Intuition and experience
   b. Facts and figures
   c. Supporting data
   d. A value formula

6. Formal appraisals rely primarily on:
   a. A secret value formula
   b. Intuition and experience
   c. Analysis of supporting data
   d. Facts and figures

7. Besides assisting the public by advising them on questions of value, appraisals serve to:
   a. Provide unbiased and objective opinions of value
   b. Make market transactions conform to economics
   c. Prove or disprove value estimates made by others
   d. None of the above

8. Legal transactions that often require appraisals include all of the following except:
   a. Income tax casualty loss estimates
   b. Property damage lawsuits
   c. Company stock buy-backs
   d. Loan foreclosure
   e. Private feasibility studies

9. Some of the important reasons for studying appraisal are:
   a.   To improve your value estimation skills
   b.   To help you pass real estate agent, broker, or appraiser examinations
   c.   To help you understand other real estate courses
   d.   To improve your ability to communicate with appraisers
   e.   All of the above

10. USPAP standards must be adhered to by state licensed and certified appraisers when performing and reporting appraisals of real estate except when:
    a.   The appraisal is federally related
    b.   The client requires such standards not be followed
    c.   The appraiser is allowed by law or regulation not to comply
    d.   Appraising commercial property

PRACTICAL APPLICATIONS

This series of exercises, at the end of most chapters, is intended to give you a better understanding of the art of appraising! The exercises will lead you through the steps of preparing an appraisal and report, using a property that you select.

The first step is to install the software in a computer that you will be able to have regular access to. If you do not have regular access to a computer, you can obtain printed blank forms and use them to complete the exercises.

Next, start up the software program and get familiar with how it works. If you have questions, go to http://www.bradfordsoftware.com, click on "Services" at the upper right of the home page, and then on "ClickFORMS Training Programs" in the middle of the "Services" page. See the free online training section!

Note that these exercises will give you the opportunity to 1) fill out the complete URAR appraisal form, used by nearly all lenders for full appraisal reports, 2) prepare a sketch of the building being appraised, using the included sketcher program, 3) prepare a location map for the subject property and the comparable sales, and 4) insert digital photos that you take into the report.

CHAPTER 2
LEGAL CONSIDERATIONS IN APPRAISAL

PREVIEW

In Chapter 1, we described what an appraisal is, and how it is used in our society. We pointed out that having knowledge of appraisal principles is important to people working in all areas of real estate. Before proceeding to the actual appraisal process, we need to carefully define real estate and real property, and describe their physical and legal characteristics. In this chapter, we also describe, explain, and give examples of the three basic types of legal descriptions that are commonly used in real estate transactions. Finally, the chapter ends with a discussion of real estate contracts.

OBJECTIVES

When you have completed this chapter you should be able to:

1. Define real estate, real property, and personal property; give examples of these; and describe their differences.

2. Define and give examples of the bundle of rights.

3. Explain and provide examples of the three broad categories of restrictions on the use of real property.

4. Define the four governmental restrictions on the private ownership of all property.

5. List and provide examples of the major types of legal descriptions.

6. List and explain the five requirements for a valid contract.

2.1 Physical and Legal Characteristics of Real Estate

What is real estate? What rights are involved in its ownership? Understanding the physical and legal characteristics of real estate is not as simple as it sometimes seems. People involved with real estate transactions can see, walk on, or go through the physical property in which they are interested. But the property itself may or may not be what they are buying! This is because the documents that buyers get convey only those rights to the physical property that are described in the documents and defined by our legal system.

Real Estate, Real Property, and Personal Property

In order to understand the meaning of real estate, we must first define **property**. Property consists of rights that have value, or, in more legal terms, "valuable rights held to the exclusion of others." For example, the right to occupy a house is a valuable property right. When property rights concern physical objects, such as a house or a car, the rights to these objects are called **tangible property**. If there are no physical objects but just valuable rights or obligations, these rights are called **intangible property**. A company's trademarks constitute one example of intangible property; a patent for an invention is another example.

Tangible property is further divided into either **real property** or **personal property**. Real property generally refers to the land and everything that is permanently fastened to the land. Personal property consists of property that is movable; more accurately, it refers to all property that is not real property.

Originally, the term *real property* referred only to the rights that one gained by owning land. In many states, real property by statute now includes the physical object (that is, the land itself), as well as the rights that go with it. In other states, the physical object is still described by the old technical term, **real estate**. Today, *real estate* and *real property* are usually used interchangeably, which is how they will be used in this book.

The Components of Real Property

The term real property refers to more than just the land. Actually, real property can have four components, as shown in the following list.

1. The land.
2. Objects permanently affixed to the land.

**Figure 2-1
Definition of Real
Estate (Courtesy of
the California
Department of Real
Estate).**

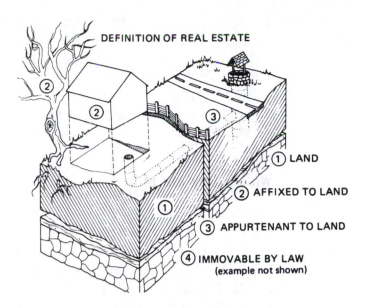

3. That which is appurtenant to, or legally accompanies, the land.

4. That which is immovable by law.

Components that define real property and real estate are shown in Figure 2-1.

The Land

The land includes the surface, the soil and rocks beneath, and the space above. In the past, these rights extended "for an indefinite distance upward as well as downward." Now, however, ownership of the space over the land—the airspace—has been limited to that which the landowner can reasonably use and enjoy. Similarly, the ownership of liquids and gases (oil, natural gas, water, steam, and so on) below the surface has also been limited in several ways. Since these liquids and gases move naturally through the ground, they do not belong to a particular parcel of land, even if located under it, until they are physically "seized" by the landowner (e.g., by being pumped out). How rights to underground liquids and gases are determined is especially complex and is not covered in this book.

Permanently Affixed Objects

When an object is permanently fastened to the land, it is legally considered to be a part of the land and thus a part of the real estate. Clearly, objects such as trees, bridges, or buildings are commonly thought of as permanently attached to the land and are easily identified as real property. Objects such as doors, which are permanently attached to a building, are also real estate. However, when objects are not clearly attached to the land in a permanent way, their classification as either real or personal property can be difficult. A garden statue is an example. To make things even more complicated, objects that had been personal property can become permanently affixed objects. When this happens, the object is called a *fixture* and becomes part of the real estate. The courts have developed a series of tests to determine whether items of personal property have become fixtures. These are listed in the section below. In addition, state legislatures have adopted rules for deciding if an object is to be classified as a fixture or as personal property in different circumstances.

Appurtenant Rights

The third component of real property consists of appurtenant rights, or appurtenances. An *appurtenance* is a right giving the owners of one property (called the *dominant tenement*) a right to use some or all of another property (called the *servient tenement*) in a specific way that benefits their property. One type of appurtenance would be the continued rights to enjoy the benefit of natural features (such as water courses or drainage channels) that extend beyond the property. Another category consists of an appurtenant *easement*, which may be established by an agreement between the property owner and the easement owner-user, or by other legal means. The most common easement is for an access right-of-way across another owner's land. Other easements may protect a view or protect exposure to sunlight. A third category of appurtenance is the occasional situation in which ownership of a mutual, or community, water or telephone company is appurtenant to the land. In this instance, the shares of company stock are tied to the land and can only be sold with the land. They cannot be sold separately, as normal stock shares can.

That Which Is Immovable By Law

Items that are immovable by law make up the fourth component of real property. Objects that fit into this category are those that have been declared to be real property by a specific law or court action. Often found in your local state civil or business code, such items are part of the real estate, whether or not they meet the strict requirements of permanent attachment. The classification of these objects as being real or personal property is up to the legislature and courts.

A Closer Look at Fixtures

Real estate cannot and/or may not be moved. It is permanently fixed in its location. Personal property, on the other hand, is movable. Fixtures are personal property items that have become attached to the real estate and converted into real estate.

The Law of Fixtures

Generally, the courts have established five tests to determine whether an object is a fixture or personal property. These five tests are to be weighed collectively. They relate to the **intention of the parties**, the **degree of attachment**, whether the item is uniquely **adapted to the land or building**, existence of any **agreement between the parties**, and the **relationship of the parties**.

1. The intention of the person incorporating the personal property into the land. If there is clear evidence that, for example, a dining room chandelier installed by a tenant had previously been installed in and removed from the tenant's prior residence, this might be convincing evidence of the tenant's intention to remove it from the current residence at the end of the lease. This would make the chandelier personal property.

2. How permanently the property is attached to the land and building. A built-in stove is considered real property because it is clearly attached; a freestanding stove can be judged as personal property. The courts sometimes refer to this test as the degree of annexation.

3. The extent to which the property is uniquely adapted to be used with the land. A loose throw rug, if cut to fit an odd-shaped room, might well become a fixture. However, a standard rectangular throw rug, even if tacked down, probably would not be considered a fixture. Adaptation to use is commonly tested by the object's function. For example, a chalkboard attached to the wall of a classroom serves as a necessary functional part of the building and thus should be classified as a fixture; however, the same chalkboard in a home might not be.

4. The existence of any agreement between the parties involved that defines ownership of the property and whether it is to be considered as real estate. Many leases contain such provisions.

5. The relationship between the person putting in the personal property and any other person with a claim to the real estate. For example, in a legal dispute, the courts might classify an object differently, depending on whether the dispute is between an owner and tenant or owner and lender.

Using the Fixture Law in Appraisals

Why should we be concerned with fixture definitions? Because real estate appraisals require us to decide which objects to include in the appraisal, and which to exclude. When unusual items are found in or on the property, this decision can be quite difficult. Quite often, there is a pending sale or lease of the property being appraised. In these cases, it can be helpful to find out what items the building occupants expect to remove as their personal property when they vacate. When ownership of any item is found to be in dispute, you may want to obtain lists from opposing parties (e.g., the owner and the tenant) and compare them. Finally, any questionable items may then be individually classified as either real property or personal property by using the five fixture tests cited earlier. In difficult cases, it is advisable for the appraiser to specify exactly which fixtures are being included in the evaluation. If the assignment requires that any personal property (e.g., furnishings) be included in the appraisal, such personal property must of course be clearly described, and usually given a separate value allocation. A variety of problems can crop up when you are trying to decide whether a particular object is real or personal property. Here are a few examples:

Carpets, drapes, and blinds: Classification depends on the intentions of the parties who installed the items, whether they were cut or tailored to fit, how they are fastened, and in the case of carpeting, whether there is a finished floor or just subflooring underneath.

Cabinets and kitchen equipment: These items are generally held to be *realty* (i.e., real property) when they are built into residential structures. They may qualify as *personalty* (i.e., personal property) in commercial situations, depending on the agreement or intentions of the parties. (See trade fixture examples, below.)

Chandeliers: Classification may depend on the intentions of the parties and who installed the chandeliers. Valuable antiques are often considered personalty.

Garden decorations (driftwood, statuary, stone lanterns, and so on): Resolution of questionable items may depend on intentions, how the objects are fastened down, and whether they were modified for use in the specific location. These are often held to be personalty.

Trade Fixtures: These are items of personal property that are owned and attached to rented space by the tenant. When used in the conduct of a business, such fixtures usually remain personal property by law and by common practice. Trade fixture examples include shelving, counters, display cases, restaurant equipment, and cash registers.

Real Property Rights

As noted above, the term *real estate* originally referred to the object itself: the land and what was attached to it. As time went by, a second term, *real property*, was added to refer primarily to the ownership *rights* that may attach to real estate.

Fee Ownership

The highest form of ownership one can have in real property is variously called the *fee*, the *fee simple*, or the *fee simple absolute estate*. As we will see, all ownership forms are subject to the applicable zoning laws, as well as the other restraints imposed by government. Property owned in *fee simple qualified* means that its use is also subject to certain conditions or limitations, such as deed restrictions.

The Bundle of Rights

Historically, property ownership rights have been compared to a large bundle of sticks, with each stick representing a different portion of the rights of ownership. From this concept came the phrase **bundle of rights**. Today, we recognize that the so-called bundle of rights to the ownership of land actually consists of many different rights. Examples include (1) the right to occupy the property, (2) the right to sell it, (3) the right to exclude others from it, (4) the right to borrow against it, and (5) the right to convey ownership by inheritance or gift. The right to refuse to exercise any of these rights is often cited as another example within the bundle of rights!

When the bundle of rights theory was further developed to allow property rights to be divided between various owners, without breaking up the physical property itself, the idea was originally called "breaking up the bundle of sticks." Now, the property rights created are known as **partial interests** (see Figure 2-2).

Partial Interests

Partial interests are created when an owner decides to keep certain property rights, but to give or sell other rights to another party. For example, a tenant with a lease has been granted the right to occupy or possess the real estate for the stated term of the lease. This amounts to a partial interest, and it is referred to as a **leasehold estate**. The partial interest that is remaining with the landlord is called a **leased fee estate,** or a fee title that is subject to a lease.

Figure 2-2
(a) Dividing the Property.
(b) Dividing the Rights.

(a)　(b)

A property owner may also keep the right of possession, but surrender the right to "will" the property away. In this event, the rights that the owner retained are called a **life estate.** A life estate is the right to live on the property or control its occupancy during the lifetime of the named person only. The owner of the property has agreed to surrender the property to another (called the remainderman, or **remainder estate**), upon the owner's death, but without involving an inheritance or a will.

Real property rights may be shared in other ways. One common way is by borrowing money that is secured by a deed of trust or a mortgage. The owner retains an interest called the **equity.** Another example is the common area of a condominium project, usually including the parking, storage, and recreation areas, which are legally shared and jointly owned. For each ownership unit, such "undivided interests" are typically joined with the fee ownership of a defined "airspace," to form the total ownership unit. The sharing of property rights may take many legal forms. Condominiums and other types of ownership will be discussed in Chapter 17.

Examples of Partial Interests

Here are examples of partial interests, including those that we have already cited. Check the Glossary in the back of the book if you have questions about any of these:

1. Leased fee estate
2. Leasehold estate
3. Life estate and remainder interest
4. Undivided interest in commonly held property
5. Easement appurtenant to other properties
6. Timeshare
7. Cooperative
8. Ownership subject to financial obligation
9. Air rights

This concept of real property, as a collection of rights and of partial interests in real estate, is important to real estate evaluation. Ownerships that include all the property rights are obviously worth more than those that include only a portion of these rights. It is vital, then, to define the particular property ownership rights to be valued in an appraisal, and also to clearly identify any rights that are to be excluded.

Because ownership rights are created by a document—a deed referring to a legal description—the laws of contracts are part of the legal setting for all real estate. Contracts are discussed further in Section 2.4.

2.2 Use Restrictions

Meaning and Importance

When people want to acquire real estate, it is obviously not just the physical object that they desire to own. Instead, buyers and other consumers want the many benefits that can accompany property ownership and use. In any given case, such benefits may come from an immediate use, from some anticipated future use, or from a combination of these. In other words, the acquisition of real estate is motivated by the expectation of some productive or beneficial use, now and in the future.

Realistically, which property uses are available to an owner or a tenant? The uses of a property are not determined just by an owner's plans and motivations. Instead, the possible uses are dictated by a large number of public and private restrictions that affect property. It is particularly important that use restrictions be understood in appraisals, because they affect what are available uses, and therefore property values. Remember: Value means worth, usefulness, or utility!

Categories of Use Restrictions

Use restrictions fall into three broad categories: *government*, *private*, and *market*. Each will be discussed here (see Figure 2-3).

Government Restrictions

The authority of government to impose public restrictions exists because, historically, all private ownership of real estate originated

Figure 2-3
Types of Restrictions.

from a grant of title given in the name of the king, **sovereign**, or sovereign body—the person or organization that was the central or principal authority of a country. It is interesting to note here that the word *real estate* is said to have Latin origins; loosely interpreted, it means *standing in the kingdom*.

In the United States, the sovereign body is "we, the people," collectively acting through our government. So, the laws of our country limit private ownership rights, in similar fashion to the limitations imposed historically by grants from the king.

Four specific rights are retained by the "sovereign." Thus, every aspect of one's right to use any property is limited by these four restrictions. (As a way to remember these four powers, think of the name PETE, which has the first letter of each power: Police, Eminent domain, Taxation, and Escheat.)

Government Restrictions on the Use of Property

1. *Police power*. The sovereign body has the right to regulate property, as necessary to promote the safety, health, morals, and general welfare of the public. The Police Power forms the basis of the controls that directly restrict the use of all property in nearly every location in this country.

2. *Power of eminent domain*. The sovereign body may take the property back at any time, if it is in the public interest to do so (such as for roads, schools, etc.). When this is done, the sovereign body must pay the owner a "just compensation."

3. *Power of taxation*. The sovereign body may impose any level of taxes needed to raise funds, so long as the taxes are fairly imposed.

4. *Power of escheat*. The sovereign body will take back the title to the property, if the owner dies or disappears and leaves no relatives or heirs.

How Police Power Affects Real Estate

Of the four government restrictions listed, police power has the most obvious effect on the use and value of real estate. Under authority of the police power, local government agencies adopt zoning ordinances, which specify where various land uses can be located, as well as the type and density of occupancy allowed. Zoning can regulate the height and size of buildings; the extent of yards, decks, parking, and other features; and the appearance, exterior materials, and architectural detailing of buildings. Zoning ordinances can also regulate noise levels allowed; hours that stores can operate; the amount of light, vibration, or odor that is permissible; and even the type and size of business signs.

Under its police power, the government can also pass building, housing, electrical, and plumbing codes. These codes define in great detail the minimum room sizes and ceiling heights, restrictions on the materials used, and floor-plan layouts. The types of heat may be defined, as well as allowable systems for plumbing, waste, and electricity. These ordinances extend to regulating types and sizes of windows and doors, as well as types of finish. Minimum maintenance standards are often set by these codes, usually with penalties for violations. In short, almost no detail of a building is exempt from some form of control, regulation, or prohibition under the police power.

Here are some examples:

Air and water pollution controls

Building, housing, and electrical codes

Coastal preservation zones

Condominium conversion ordinances

Endangered species acts

Environmental controls

Flood zones

Historical preservation acts

Master plans

Park dedications

Rent control

Seismic safety study areas

Sign abatement ordinances

Solid waste disposal laws

Strip mining rehabilitation acts

Subdivision requirements

Underground utility requirements

Wild river protection acts

Zoning ordinances

The importance and effect of government restrictions will be further discussed in Chapter 6.

Private Restrictions

The government is not alone in restricting the use of land. When people sell real estate, they sometimes impose conditions that restrict the future owners or users. For example, at one time, many properties were sold with a clause prohibiting the sale of alcoholic beverages on the property forever. More recently, most condominiums and planned unit developments with common areas utilize recorded CC&Rs (Conditions, Covenants, and Restrictions) to regulate their use, operation, and control. Usually, the existence of CC&Rs, or other private deed restrictions connected with the property, is revealed in a preliminary title report or title search. It is often advisable, and for a few appraisals, essential, to inquire about the possible effects of such restrictions and, if necessary, to review the actual documents.

Restrictions on the use of property can also be imposed by private easements and contracts. For example, the owners could grant to another party an easement for an electric power transmission line, which could restrict building any structures under the power lines. An easement for a buried gas pipeline could bar future owners of the land from building any structures over the pipeline. A view easement granted to a neighbor might limit the height of any building, perhaps to one story with a flat roof. A lease could restrict the use of the property to a specific purpose (e.g., a high-priced retail shoe store). A mortgage note, mortgage, or deed of trust document could also contain provisions limiting the uses of the property. In other words, nearly every contract that a real property owner signs that involves the property can impose limits on its use. The importance of private restrictions will be further discussed in Chapter 6.

Market Restrictions

In an economic sense, neither the government nor the property owner really determines the ultimate use of land. Instead, the eventual use of land depends on the restrictions imposed by the market, which operates within the limits set by the government and by private restrictions.

How does the market restrict the use of land? Each proposed land use must appear to be financially satisfactory, or investors will not choose that use. Proposed uses of land must earn enough money, or create enough benefits at that location, to justify the cost of the land and buildings. Thus, the market encourages uses of land that are *economically feasible*, that is, those uses that are able to pay at least all the costs of using the site and any necessary improvements. If a use is economically feasible, but forbidden by zoning and/or deed restrictions, there is an economic incentive for someone to have the restrictions removed. Otherwise, nothing will be done with the land until some allowable use becomes economically feasible.

Potential Use and Value

The combination of the three types of restrictions—**government restrictions**, **private restrictions**, and **market restrictions**—determines how land will be used, and thus ultimately determines its value. The government limits uses by zoning and other laws; private owners limit uses through various types of contracts; and the marketplace dictates what uses are economically feasible at a particular location. The real estate appraiser needs to be aware of all three sets of restrictions and their impact on current use, as well as their possible impact on future uses of land and buildings. Knowing how real estate can be used is vital to the appraisal of real estate.

2.3 Property Descriptions

When real estate is sold, leased, or borrowed against, legal documents must spell out the transaction. In each case, the property involved will be identified in these documents by its **legal description**.

Many people do not realize the importance of accurate legal descriptions. However, one small error in a legal description could conceivably cause a prospective buyer to look at a different property than the one listed. What may be *bought* is the property actually described! What was *wanted* was the property actually looked at! In other words, what you see may not always be what you get.

Most of the time, minor errors in legal descriptions can easily be corrected. On occasion, however, an error can result in confusion and ultimately a lawsuit. In one instance, a contractor actually built an office building on the wrong lot! Everyone in the real estate industry should know how to read the various types of legal descriptions, and how to compare them with the physical property observed. Such knowledge can resolve many common questions such as: Who owns the vacant lot next door? Who owns the common driveway between the houses? Who owns that overgrown area at the rear of the lot?

Three Basic Types of Legal Descriptions

There are three basic types of legal descriptions: (1) the **recorded lot, block, and tract description**, (also known as the **recorded map** or **subdivision map**), (2) the **metes and bounds** description, and (3) the **government survey** (or *rectangular survey*) description. Some valid legal descriptions use combinations of these types. It should be noted that the common Assessor's Book, Page, and Parcel identification typically is *not* a valid legal description!

Recorded Lot, Block, and Tract

Recorded maps can include *boundary maps*, *parcel maps* by licensed surveyors, and other maps that legally serve to subdivide the property. In most states, however, the most common type of legal description is based on *subdivision maps* that divide the land into *lots, blocks, and tracts*. When a developer buys acreage and subdivides it into lots and streets, the responsible level of local government in the process of giving its approval, requires that a map of the division be drawn by a

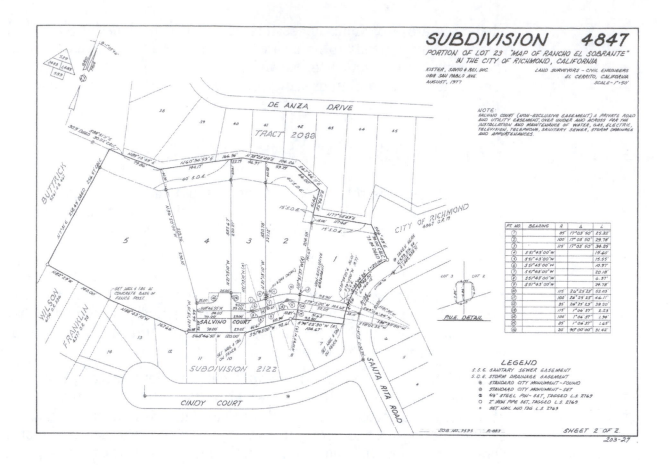

**Figure 2-4
An Example of a
Subdivision Map.**

licensed surveyor. The surveyor first checks the legal descriptions used in prior transfers of this parcel and the parcels around it, to be sure that they do not have conflicting boundaries. Next, the surveyor stakes out the new subdivision boundary lines, using established government survey markers in the area as starting points. Existing markers from previous surveys of the property or a nearby property may be used instead. Finally, the surveyor produces a scale map drawing that satisfies local agency requirements. Figure 2-4 is an example of a subdivision map.

The subdivision map divides the property into lots and, for larger subdivisions, into blocks of lots. Each block and each lot is labeled on the map with a number or letter. The map itself is identified, usually with the name or number of the subdivision and is registered in the public records of the local government (usually the county). Public Recorders' maps are usually indexed by volume, book, and page.

With a recorded map on file, a written legal description of a lot need contain only the lot number, the block number if any, the subdivision name or number, and the map record volume, book, and page number. With this legal description, another surveyor, years later, can look up the map and, by a field survey, accurately stake out the boundaries of the described lot. The legal descriptions of subdivision maps (also called *tract maps*) are among the shortest and easiest to understand. A sample might read:

> Lot 37 of block A of Greenhill Estates, Tract 2314, as recorded November 11, 1946, in Book 23 of Maps, Page 318, official records of Washington County.

Metes and Bounds

The earliest legal descriptions of property were by metes and bounds. Many legal descriptions today are also of this type, particularly descriptions of large and irregular parcels. A metes and bounds description simply gives the distance and direction of each boundary line of the property. It starts at a point of beginning and goes around the perimeter of the property, back to the point of beginning. Early metes and bounds descriptions often started at a well-known natural feature, such as "a large oak tree by the Jones farm," and went from tree to rock to boulder to tree. Figure 2-5 contains the actual wording from such a deed. As the trees died of old age and the rocks were bulldozed away, such descriptions became unusable. Today, more durable legal descriptions usually start at governmental or private **survey monuments**, or other known points, and proceed by very accurate direction bearings and distances around the property and back to the point of beginning. Any parcel, even a lot in a recorded subdivision,

Figure 2-5 From a Deed Recorded in the *Book of Deeds*, Book C-1, Page 462, on the 6th Day of March, 1907, with the Office of the Registrar of Deeds, in Ashe County, North Carolina.

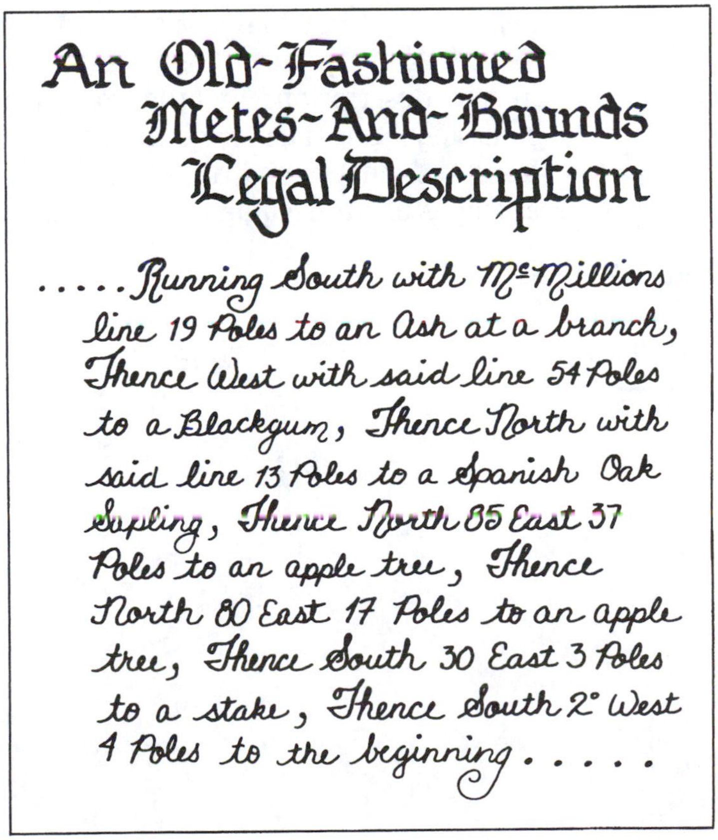

An Old-Fashioned Metes-And-Bounds Legal Description

..... Running South with Mc Millions line 19 Poles to an Ash at a branch, Thence West with said line 54 Poles to a Blackgum, Thence North with said line 13 Poles to a Spanish Oak Sapling, Thence North 85 East 37 Poles to an apple tree, Thence North 80 East 17 Poles to an apple tree, Thence South 30 East 3 Poles to a stake, Thence South 2° West 4 Poles to the beginning.....

could be described by a metes and bounds description. An example of such a description of a 75 by 100-foot lot follows.

> Beginning at a point on the southerly line of Henry Street, 100 feet east of the southeast corner of Henry Street and 35th Avenue; running then due south 100 feet; then due east 75 feet; then due north and parallel to the first course 100 feet to the southern line of Henry Street; then due west along the southern line of Henry Street, 75 feet to the point of beginning.

Modern metes and bounds legal descriptions can describe lines that do not run exactly north, east, south, or west (e.g., "a line north 1 degree, 46 minutes, 30 seconds west 209.71 feet"). The exact bearing is described relative to north, south, east, or west, with 90 degrees separating each direction. Such descriptions can also define lines that curve: ("then along the arc of a curve to the right, of radius 203.3 feet, for a distance of 37.63 feet"). From this combination, a parcel of almost any shape can be described. However, metes and bounds descriptions can be pages long. They can sometimes be difficult to understand. Typing errors are an occasional problem as well. Despite these disadvantages, metes and bounds descriptions are necessary for some parcels and are a valuable cross-check for others.

Today, appraisers can calculate the area of a parcel by typing the metes and bounds description into a program in a personal computer. The computer program can also be used to simulate a survey around the perimeter or boundary of the property, to see if the description ends at exactly the point of beginning. If it does not, there may be an error in the description. In order to have an unquestionable description, some legal documents will include both the parcel or tract map description and the metes and bounds description. Figure 2-6 shows an example of an irregular parcel map.

**Figure 2-6
An Example of an
Irregular Parcel Map.**

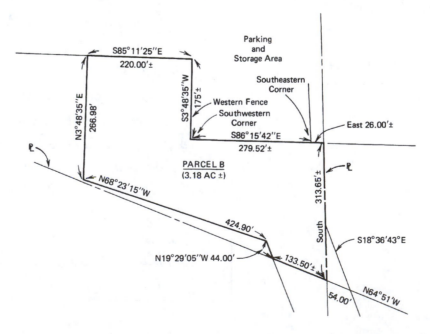

Government Survey

Much of the rural land in this country was first surveyed by U.S. government surveyors. Their basic survey system became the foundation for the third type of legal description, which is really just another type of map system. Government (or rectangular) survey legal descriptions start with reference points, often a point on a large mountain. For example, there are three different reference points in California, labeled Humboldt, Mount Diablo, and San Bernardino. A north-south line, called the ***principal meridian line***, goes through each reference point. An east-west line, called the ***base line***, goes through the reference point as well. Figure 2-7 shows the reference points, meridians, and base lines in California.

A series of ***range lines***, spaced six miles apart, parallel the principal meridian. ***Township lines*** run parallel to the base line and are also six miles apart. The series of intersecting township lines and range lines, as shown in Figure 2-8, set up a pattern of six-mile squares of land, each one, two, three, or more lines east or west and north or south of the reference point. Each six-mile square is called a ***township*** and is identified by counting from the reference point. One sample township would be identified as "township 3 north, range 2 east, San Bernardino Base and Meridian." In Figure 2-8, this sample township is identified by an "X" in the proper township square.

**Figure 2-7
California Base Lines
and Meridians
(Courtesy of the
California
Department of Real
Estate).**

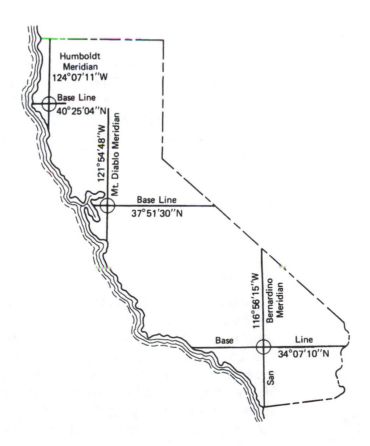

**Figure 2-8
Map of Township
Lines(Courtesy of
the California
Department of Real
Estate).**

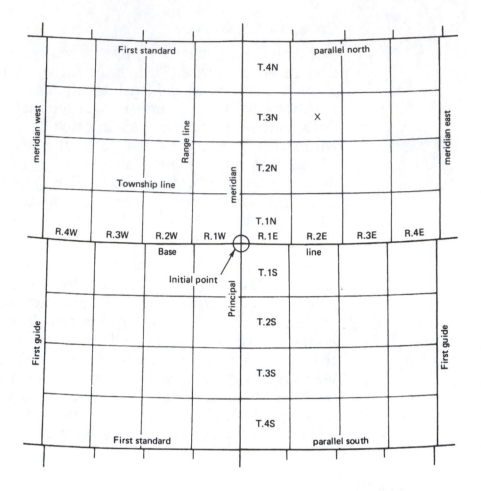

Each six-mile-square township is further subdivided. North-south and east-west lines, one mile apart, divide the township into 36 parcels, each part being one mile square. These are called **sections**. Each section is numbered, in a back-and-forth or serpentine system, as shown in Figure 2-9. Thus, each section is described by its number and the appropriate township description.

A section is one mile in each direction, with an area of one square mile, or 640 acres. Sometimes, it is necessary to describe smaller portions of a section. This is usually done by dividing the section into halves or quarters, or lesser amounts. Figure 2-10, on page 34, shows how the section could be subdivided and how the parts would be labeled.

As precise and predictable as the government survey may look, there are two complications. The first complication is that the survey grid is square but the earth is round. Consequently, parallel sets of range lines and base lines must be tapered to match the shape of the earth. This taper causes the north six-mile boundary of each township to be about 50 feet shorter than the south boundary (in the Northern hemisphere). Thus, each township north of the reference point shrinks in width by 50 feet, and each to the south grows by 50 feet. To compensate for

**Figure 2-9
Map of a Township
(Courtesy of the
California
Department of Real
Estate).**

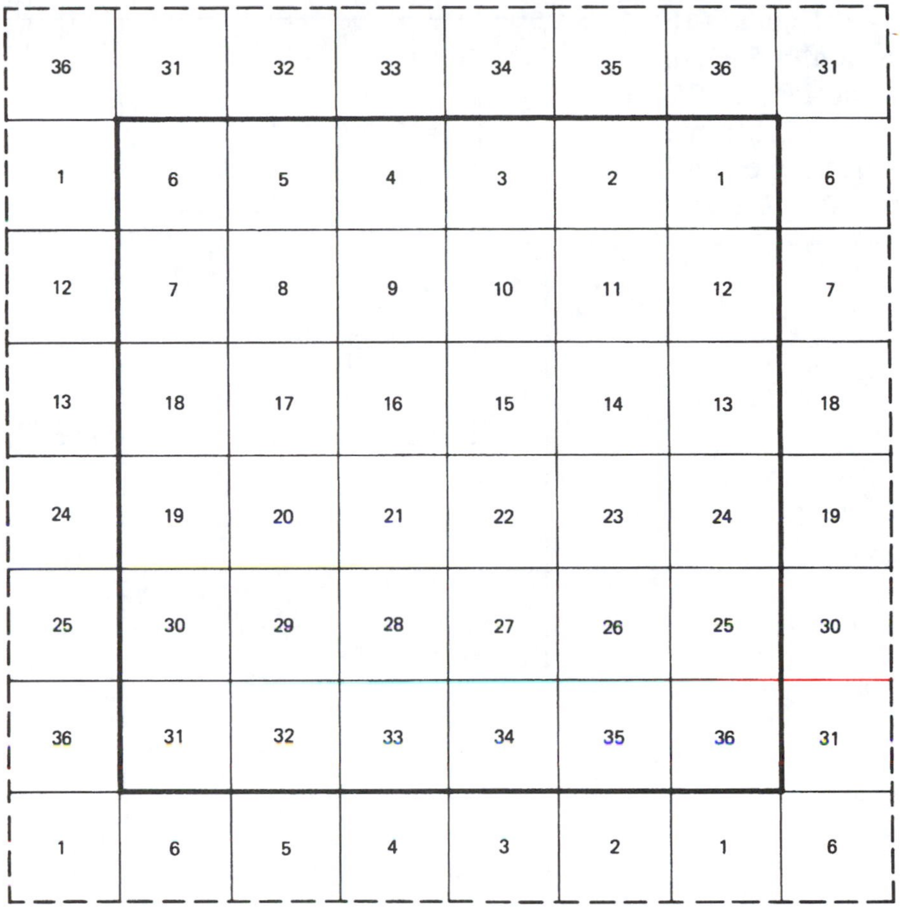

36	31	32	33	34	35	36	31
1	6	5	4	3	2	1	6
12	7	8	9	10	11	12	7
13	18	17	16	15	14	13	18
24	19	20	21	22	23	24	19
25	30	29	28	27	26	25	30
36	31	32	33	34	35	36	31
1	6	5	4	3	2	1	6

this, correction lines, both north-south and east-west, are run every 24 miles from the reference point. The result is that the actual dimensions and acreage area of a particular section can vary considerably from the standard one-mile-square section. The second complication is that some early surveys contained errors! Between the two types of problems, a given section in the real world might be quite different in size from what it should be!

Because of the importance of identifying the property being studied, real estate professionals must be able to read and understand the legal descriptions of property. Otherwise, neither they nor their clients will know for sure what property they are considering.

2.4 Real Estate Contracts

Contracts are essential to nearly all aspects of real estate. Since they are legal documents, their interpretation depends on attorneys and, ultimately, the courts. Nevertheless, as a practical matter, appraisers often read contracts to learn their impact upon the property and

**Figure 2-10
Map of a Section
(Courtesy of the
California
Department of Real
Estate).**

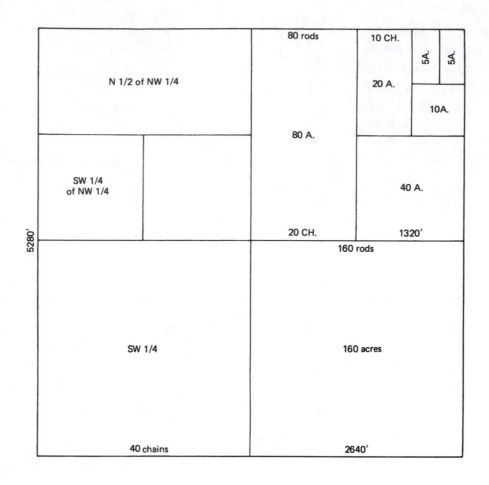

upon the appraisal. So, understanding the basics of contracts is part of what appraisers need to know.

It is important to recognize that contract law is very complex. Appraisers can encounter situations where a contract issue is so important to a particular assignment that an attorney's interpretation will be desirable. This section is only intended to introduce this complex material.

Definition and Essential Elements of a Contract

A **contract** is defined as:

> An agreement between two or more persons which creates an obligation to do or not to do a particular act.
>
> Source: *Black's Law Dictionary*, 6th ed., West Publishing Co., St. Paul, 1990.

So, a contract is an *agreement*, involving more than one *party*, creating an *obligation*, to do a *particular act*.

Essential Elements of a Contract

Every contract comes into existence because of specific elements. These elements are:

1. The offer
2. The acceptance
3. The consideration

Each of these elements must be present for a contract to be valid. The *offer* must spell out the specific details of the agreement: the act or acts to be performed, who will do which, and the timetable for performance. Usually, the offer is only valid for a defined time. The *acceptance* must be timely, and must agree to the entire offer, without exceptions or changes. And there must be *consideration*—each party must expect to get some benefit if the contractual agreement is carried out as expected.

Importance of Contracts to Real Estate

When real estate is simply occupied by the owner for many years, with no remaining loans secured by the real estate, there are no recent contracts to be understood. If the property is listed for sale, subject to an offer, or sold, then contract issues are present. If the property has a tenant, or an option to rent, contract issues are present. If there is a loan secured by the real estate, or the prospect of obtaining one or refinancing the existing loan, then contract issues are present.

From another perspective, consider that Section 2.1 analyzed the importance of real estate rights, which exist through contracts and are transferred by contracts. And Section 2.2 focused on governmental, private, and market influences on property use. Private restrictions exist solely through the contracts that created them. Finally, Section 2.3 analyzed property descriptions, which are essential elements of every contract impacting real estate.

Requirements for a Valid Contract

There are five elements that are required to create a valid contract. The first element is that the parties must be competent to enter into the contract. Generally, *competent parties* means that the parties are legally adults and without mental disability, incapacity, intoxicated, or convicts.

The second element is that the contract must have a subject, an act, or acts to be performed. The subject of the contract must be defined enough to be understood by all parties, and must not involve illegal acts if it is to be a valid contract.

The third element of a valid contract is that there must be a legal consideration—some legal benefit that each party reasonably expects to obtain from performance of the contract. It could be money, some act to be performed by the opposing party, or some consideration of love, affection, or duty.

If Party A promises to pay money to a stranger, Party B, for no good reason, perhaps there is no contract to pay, because of a lack of consideration!

The fourth element is a "meeting of the minds"—a *mutual obligation* or agreement by all parties as to the elements of the contract. If the contract simply refers to a street address, it might not be valid, if the seller only intended to sell the home and its lot, but not the second lot next door—but the buyer intended to buy both!

And the fifth element of a valid contract is the obligation of both parties to comply with the contract, sometimes called the mutuality of obligation. If one party is obligated to perform, but the other only has to perform "if," then there is no mutual commitment to perform, and the contract is an option until "if" occurs.

Statute of Frauds

The first statute of frauds was adopted in England in 1677. Similar laws have since been passed in nearly every state in the United States. It is particularly important in relation to contracts involving real estate.

The primary provision of interest is the requirement that certain classes of contracts must be evidenced by a note or memorandum or other writing for the contract to be enforceable. (If the courts will not enforce performance of a contract, or penalties for its non-performance, then performance of the contract effectively is up to just the good will of the parties.)

The exact definition of the classes of contracts depends upon the laws of the various states. However, the general categories are: 1) contracts for the sale of goods priced over an amount, say, $500; 2) contracts for the sale of real estate; 3) contracts which explicitly will take longer than a year to perform; and 4) contracts to guarantee the debt of another. Thus, all real estate sales, long-term loans, permanent private restrictions, and easements or leases for a year or longer involve contracts that are subject to the **Statute of Frauds**. This means that the contract itself must be in writing to be enforceable, or there must be a memo setting forth the details of the contract, signed by the party who is being sued for non-performance of the contract.

However, there are some exceptions to the Statute of Frauds. For example, if the parties to an oral contract complete all or most of the contractual duties, a court might find the oral contract binding.

The bottom line is this: Contracts are very common occurrences in real estate, and thus in real estate appraising. Not every contract is binding, or enforceable. Appraisers benefit from understanding something about the elements of a contract, what constitutes a valid contract, and when a contract might need to be in writing. At the very least, this awareness helps an appraiser understand when it might be desirable to speak to an attorney!

SUMMARY

In this chapter, we explained the distinction between real estate and real property. When making an appraisal, it is not enough just to look at a property and appraise what you see. Rather, you must first establish what legal rights exist for the property and then identify which rights are to be included in the appraisal.

Real estate is defined as the physical object, whereas real property refers to the rights gained by owning the object. However, increasingly, the two terms are used interchangeably. Personal property includes all objects on the property that are not real property. Real property is made up of four elements: the land, the objects permanently affixed to the land, the rights that are appurtenant to the land, and that which is immovable by law.

When personal property has been permanently affixed to the land, it changes into a category of permanently affixed real property called a fixture. Determining whether a particular object is a fixture depends on legislative statute and five different court-applied tests. These are: (1) the intention of the person installing the object, (2) the permanence of the installation, (3) the unique adaptation of the object to fit or work with the real estate, (4) any agreement of the parties, and (5) the type of relationship (one created by a lease or a mortgage, etc.) between the parties interested in owning the object. Numerous problems concerning fixtures and personal property can arise in an appraisal, unless appraisers are careful to distinguish one from the other and define what is being appraised.

Next, the chapter noted that real property refers to the many rights associated with real estate. The fact that this "bundle" of rights may be broken up, with different parties holding different parts of the bundle, or different rights, is very important. Partial rights to a property, such as those established by leases and mortgages, are very common. Thus, there are many occasions when an appraiser may have to examine or appraise portions of the bundle of rights.

The chapter went on to point out that the value of land depends on its potential and logical use. Property use is restricted by three types of limitations: government, private, and market. The government limitations consist of four restrictions: police power, eminent domain, taxation, and escheat. Most governmental restrictions on land use, such as zoning and building codes, are based on the police power. Private restrictions, often in the form of deed restrictions (or CC&Rs), are encountered less often than government restrictions, but on occasion they are also significant to the appraiser. Market restrictions have a powerful influence on value, since only economically feasible uses—ones that have a strong enough market demand—can be financially successful.

Next, we noted that the buyer does not really buy the physical object; rather, he or she buys specified rights to the property that are legally described in the purchase documents. The legal description of the property is needed to identify, with certainty, what real estate to appraise; hence, it is important to understand each form of description. The three common types of legal description—recorded lot, block, and tract; metes and bounds; and government surveys—were explained and illustrated. With a good understanding of legal descriptions, you will be able to review a particular legal description, have its accuracy checked, and use it to calculate land areas or dimensions.

This chapter also introduced you to real estate contracts. Nearly every appraisal assignment will involve reading one or more contracts. A contract is an agreement between two or more persons which creates an obligation to do or not to do a particular act. The essential steps in creating a contract are an offer, an acceptance, and the transfer of a consideration. In order for a contract to be valid, the parties must be competent to enter into it; the subject matter must be set forth; there must be a legal consideration; the parties mutually agree to the content of the contract; and the parties are mutually bound to comply with the contract. Oral contracts can be just as binding as written ones. However, the Statue of Frauds generally requires written evidence of a contract where the contract involves the sale of goods for more than, say, $500; the sale of land; a guarantee of the debt of another; or a matter that by definition will take a year or more to perform. Clearly, this requires many real estate contracts to be in writing.

IMPORTANT TERMS AND CONCEPTS

Acceptance	*Bundle of rights*
Adapted to the land or building	*Competent parties*
Agreement between the parties	*Consideration*
Appurtenance	*Contract*
Base line	*Degree of attachment*

Dominant tenement
Easement
Equity
Fixture
Government restrictions
Government survey
Intangible property
Intention of the parties
Leased fee estate
Leasehold estate
Legal description
Life estate
Market restrictions
Metes and bounds
Mutual obligation
Offer
Partial interests
Personal property
Police power
Power of eminent domain
Power of escheat
Power of taxation

Principal meridian line
Private restrictions
Property
Range lines
Real estate
Real property
Recorded lot, block, and tract description
Recorded map
Relationship of the parties
Remainder estate
Sections
Servient tenement
Sovereign
Statute of Frauds
Subdivision map
Survey monuments
Tangible property
Township
Township lines
Tract maps
Trade fixtures

REVIEWING YOUR UNDERSTANDING

1. What are the two categories of tangible property?
   a. Real property and personal property
   b. Intangible property and real property
   c. Real estate and intangible property
   d. None of the above

2. Real property includes all the following except:
   a. The land and objects permanently affixed to the land
   b. Bank accounts for purchase of land
   c. Appurtenant rights
   d. That which is immovable by law

3. List and define the five tests for a fixture.

4. Types of use restrictions include all the following except:
   a. Government
   b. Fee simple
   c. Private
   d. Market

5. The sovereign holds four specific rights relative to all private real estate:
   a. Appurtenances, eminent domain, police power, and escheat
   b. Police power, taxation, ordinances, and bundle of rights
   c. Taxation, escheat, police power, and eminent domain
   d. None of the above

6. Give six examples of government regulations based on the police power.

7. The three common types of legal descriptions are:
   a. Metes and bounds; recorded lot, block, and tract; and government survey
   b. Government survey, private survey, and county survey
   c. Metes and bounds, acreage blocks, and government survey
   d. Legal, informal, and house number

8. What is the shape, size, and area of a standard section?

9. What is the shape, size, and area of a standard township?

10. How many sections are there in a township?
    a. 48
    b. 36
    c. 360
    d. 100

11. Which of the following is not necessarily required for a valid contract?
    a. Competent parties
    b. In writing
    c. Mutual agreement
    d. Mutual obligation

PRACTICAL APPLICATIONS

If you did not carefully read the introduction to these exercises at the end of Chapter 1, please go back and read that first, before continuing here. Each of these exercises will build on the prior work! The result will be a completed appraisal and URAR report form on a residence.

Now that you have installed the program and gotten a bit familiar with how it works, the next step is to select the subject property! This could be a home that your instructor selected, for the entire class to use. It also could be a property that you select. We will talk about this second possibility.

Any residence will do! If you live in a home, a condo, a cooperative, or an apartment unit, you could use that! This is easiest, because you can take your time when measuring and doing your property inspection. (If you live in an apartment or a cooperative unit, for this exercise, treat it as if it was a condominium, and state that as a *hypothetical condition* in your report! See Chapter 3 to read about hypothetical conditions.)

Next, start up the software program and select the form that you are going to use for your report. If you will be appraising a detached home or a row house or townhouse, select the URAR, also known as the FNMA 1004. If you will be appraising a condo, co-op, or apartment unit, select the FNMA 1073 form. (Note that a correct appraisal of a cooperative or apartment would need to be on a different form, but this is beyond the scope of this text!)

Next, start to fill out the information about the property and yourself in the form. This would include your name, the property address, and other information that you know. *Do not* enter information in the neighborhood, lot, or improvement sections of the report at this time —wait until you get to the chapter that covers that topic! However, it is a good idea to look ahead at the coming sections of the form, so that you start thinking about the information that you will need to gather!

If you have questions about the program itself, please be sure to review the manuals and help information that was included with the program CD. Also, at anytime, you can go to http://www.bradfordsoftware.com, click on "Services" at the upper right of the home page, and then on "ClickFORMS Training Programs" in the middle of the "Services" page. See the free online training section!

CHAPTER 3
THE FORMAL APPRAISAL PROCESS

PREVIEW

This chapter outlines the four steps in the formal appraisal process, stressing the systematic and orderly procedure needed to meet the required appraisal standards. In particular, we stress the six elements that define the appraisal problem. The three traditional approaches to value are introduced here, along with a formal definition of *market value*, as the term is used by federally regulated financial institutions.

OBJECTIVES

When you have completed this chapter you should be able to:

1. Explain the four steps in the *appraisal process*.

2. Name the six elements that *define the appraisal problem*.

3. Define the term *scope of work*.

4. Explain the difference between *value in use* and *value in exchange*.

5. Define the term *market value*, and explain how it differs from *market price*.

6. Outline the three approaches to value, and explain how they are used in appraisals.

3.1 The Appraisal Process

The four-step *appraisal process* is the orderly procedure that appraisers use to help solve a valuation problem. The ability to diagnose a problem and propose a reasonable means to find a solution is a key skill of an appraiser. The ground rules for this process have been developed by professional appraisers over a period of many years. However, this classical appraisal process has in recent years been refined, modified, and made more explicit by the *Uniform Standards of Professional Appraisal Practice* (USPAP).

Conformity with USPAP Requirements

In its Standards 1 and 2, USPAP defines the appraisal process in terms of (1) how an appraisal should be developed, and (2) how it should be reported.

For many years, the traditional appraisal process was described by the following six steps:

1. Clearly define the appraisal problem.
2. Formulate an efficient appraisal plan.
3. Collect and analyze the pertinent data.
4. Apply the appropriate value approaches.
5. Arrive at a conclusion of value.
6. Report the conclusion of value.

The Appraisal Process

Now, it is increasingly common to consider the appraisal process as it is currently presented in USPAP, consisting of these *four* steps:

1. Identify the appraisal problem to be solved.
2. Identify appropriate solutions.
3. Execute the appropriate scope of work.
4. Report the findings and conclusions reached.

The modern view places equal emphasis on each of the four steps. Each is *equally* important in producing a good solution to the client's problem. The four steps in the appraisal process are shown in Figure 3-1. They are described in detail in the discussion that follows.

Figure 3-1 The Four Steps in the Appraisal Process.

I. Identify the Appraisal Problem
1. The client and any other intended users
2. The intended use of the appraisal and report
3. The type and definition of value
4. The effective date of the opinions and conclusions
5. The subject property and its relevant characteristics
6. Any assignment conditions

II. Identify Appropriate Solutions—The Scope of Work
1. The extent of property identification
2. The extent of property inspection
3. The type and extent of data researched
4. The type and extent of analysis employed

III. Execute the Appropriate Scope of Work
1. Collect information on the subject property
2. Sales comparison approach
3. Cost approach
4. Income approach
5. Reconciliation

IV. Report Findings and Conclusions
1. Type of report
2. Format of report

Step 1: Define the Appraisal Problem: The Six Elements

The beginning of any formal appraisal starts with obtaining a clear understanding of what question the appraisal seeks to answer. By clearly defining the question to be answered, the appraiser establishes a basis for defining the scope of work, planning the appraisal, and seeking the exact information required for the appraisal assignment.

In order to properly **define the appraisal problem**, the first step in the appraisal process, the appraiser must identify and define six critical elements, set forth in the Scope of Work Rule of USPAP. The six elements that need to be defined are:

1. The **client** and any other intended users

2. The intended use of the appraiser's opinions and conclusions

3. The type and definition of value

4. The effective date of the appraiser's opinions and conclusions

5. The **subject of the assignment** and its relevant characteristics

6. Any assignment conditions

(Note that one could divide the first element into two, and the sixth into two or more!) Each of these six elements *must* be defined very early in the assignment. In addition, all but the relevant characteristics of the subject property *must* be determined jointly by the appraiser and the client, based on the intended use of the appraisal and report.

What does it mean, ". . . must be determined jointly by the appraiser and the client. . . . "? The appraiser is trying to reach agreement on the assignment with the client. The appraiser cannot do much work until these elements are determined, so the decision is needed very early in the assignment. And the client and the appraiser must agree on them. Otherwise, the client will be expecting one assignment to be performed, and the appraiser will be preparing another—not a good idea!

The relevant characteristics of the subject property will be estimated by the appraiser, based upon the

- intended use of the appraisal and report
- what the appraiser finds out about the property
- what is important to the buyers of such property

1. Identification of the Client and Any Other Intended Users

This is the first of the six elements of defining the appraisal problem. The type of appraisal—as well as the type and content of the appraisal report to be produced—depends on its *intended users*. This means that the appraiser *must* identify the client and other intended users, in order to properly develop and report the appraisal. (If the client wishes to remain anonymous, the person or company need not be named in the report; however, it must at least be noted in the appraiser's workfile.) Note carefully that the client is *not* necessarily the party that pays for the appraisal, but rather is defined as the party that *engages* or hires the appraiser.

The appraiser must also identify the intended users—people other than the client who, the appraiser and client agree, will be relying on the appraisal conclusions. For example, for a home loan appraisal, the law might require the lender to give a copy of the *appraisal report* to the borrower. However, neither lender nor appraiser is providing a report that is intended to be clear and understandable to the borrower. The condensed format of the typical loan form report makes that clear. Therefore, the borrower typically would not be an intended user.

Often, the intended use of the appraisal report helps define who the intended users need to be. For example, an appraisal report for an estate might be viewed by the executor, the attorney or accountant preparing any estate or probate filing or tax return, the probate court, heirs, and tax authorities. However, the intended users usually would be the executor and the attorney or accountant. The probate court and the tax authorities would not be intended users as defined by USPAP. The real estate agent who handles the future sale of the property, the prospective buyer, or the lender for the buyer's loan would definitely not be intended users (unless the client specifically requested them).

The three key points for selecting the intended user(s) are these: 1) it is a decision reached between the client and the appraiser at the start of the assignment; 2) it only includes parties directly involved in the intended use of the appraisal and report; and 3) it includes *only* those parties to whom the appraiser is responsible for communicating clearly and adequately. Others might—by chance or practice—see the report, but the report does not have to be written to be clear and understandable to them, nor meet their expectations regarding content, procedures, and so on. Please note that the concept of "intended user" is relatively new and is likely to be revised in the future!

2. Intended Use of the Appraisal

The second element of defining the assignment is its ***intended use***. Buyers and sellers, banks, institutions, and public agencies each use appraisals for their own unique purposes, whether for sale, financing, taxation, or public acquisition. These different users have different requirements as to the type of appraisal and report needed, and the information required. If the appraisal and report are to be used in a federally insured loan transaction, for example, it must conform to USPAP and also to the rules of the federal agency regulating the lender. Identification of the intended use of the appraisal opinions and conclusions allows the appraiser to decide on the necessary scope of work to be completed and the level of information to be provided in the appraisal report.

The intended use may suggest the information needed in the report and therefore the appropriate type of report. The three choices set forth in USPAP are the Self-Contained, Summary, and Restricted Use reports. Also, the intended use must be determined in order to select a report format that will not be misleading for that use! Reporting options will be discussed in more detail later in this chapter. It is important to recognize and communicate to clients that an appraisal and report prepared for one intended use may not be valid or useable for some other use! For example, a report prepared for an estate almost certainly would not be useable for the future buyers' bank loan, according to federal rules.

3. Type and Definition of Value

The usual ***type of value*** to be estimated in an appraisal assignment is ***market value***. A market value estimate is most often needed for the sale and financing of a home or other real estate. However, appraisals can be made for many other purposes; for example, to estimate the replacement cost or perhaps the liquidation value of a property. Other appraisals may seek to estimate the insurable value, "going concern" value, assessed value, or rental value of a property. Types of value are discussed further in Section 3.3.

Whatever type of value is to be developed, it must be selected by the appraiser and client at the start of the assignment. Often, it is determined by the intended use of the appraisal. The appraiser should state in the report what the exact definition is, and its source. Also, if an opinion of market value is to be based on unusual financing that is likely to influence sales prices, the terms of such financing must be clearly identified and judged as to their influence on value. Adjusting for financing terms is discussed in Chapter 9 of this text.

When estimating market value, USPAP requires that the appraiser form an opinion of the reasonable *exposure time* on which the value opinion is based. Exposure time means the length of time the property was assumed to be exposed to the market, prior to the date of value. A common type of property might sell in an active market in a short time. A very unusual property might sell in a slow market only after a long exposure time.

Marketing time is defined as the time it would take to sell the property, assuming that marketing started on the date of value. USPAP does not require that this be estimated. However, this information may be valuable to the client, especially when the market is changing rapidly.

4. The Effective Date of the Appraisal

The fourth element, the *effective date* of the appraiser's opinions and conclusions, pinpoints the date to which the value estimate applies. A specific effective date is important, because real estate values are constantly changing. An appraisal conclusion is valid only as of a particular point in time. For this reason, the date of value must be agreed upon in advance between the appraiser and the client! When a current value is sought, the date of the appraiser's last field inspection is often selected, by custom, as the effective date of the value estimate. Thus, there can be **three** possible dates: the effective date of value, the date of the inspection, and the date of the report.

Sometimes, appraisals are needed to estimate value as of a past or even a future date. Appraisals for inheritance tax, divorce, eminent domain, and other legal purposes often must estimate value as of an earlier date than the date the appraisal was developed (the date of the report). On occasion, the assigned date of value may coincide with a future event, for example, the completion of a construction project. When either a *retrospective* (date in the past) or *prospective* (date in the future) appraisal is made, the report must clearly specify the exact historical or future date of value, so as not to mislead the reader into thinking that the stated value is the *current* market value! (See Figure 3-2.)

5. The Subject Property and Its Relevant Characteristics

Next, the fifth element of defining the assignment is the subject property. USPAP requires that the property be identified. Most properties are identified by the address and legal description. Although a

Figure 3-2 Title Page of a Historical Appraisal Report.

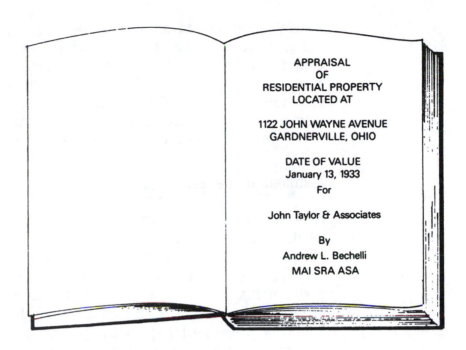

APPRAISAL
OF
RESIDENTIAL PROPERTY
LOCATED AT

1122 JOHN WAYNE AVENUE
GARDNERVILLE, OHIO

DATE OF VALUE
January 13, 1933
For

John Taylor & Associates

By
Andrew L. Bechelli
MAI SRA ASA

complete legal description is generally preferred, any combination of the legal description, property address, map reference, survey, plat map, property sketch, and/or photographs may be used. If the legal description is not used, the appraiser must be careful to define with the client what property to appraise. (Is the vacant lot next door included?) Comments in the report noting the key physical attributes of the property are helpful. Here is an example of a very brief property identification that might be used:

> The property being appraised is known as 1714 Mountain View Road, Atlanta, Georgia. It consists of a 50 x 100 foot parcel of land, improved with a single-family residence and garage. A plat map showing the shape and dimensions is enclosed.

A summary of the characteristics of the property that are relevant to the assignment should be provided, before considering the appropriate scope of work. If any personal property is included in the appraisal, it also must be clearly identified and reported. When available, the sales agreement should be reviewed, as it usually will list any personal property included in the purchase. If the personal property is not considered significant to the overall value of the property, the personal property need not be separately valued. There does not appear to be any definition of "significant" in this context! Certainly, less than 1 percent and probably 2 percent would not be considered significant.

The appraiser must also define with the client at the start of the assignment the real property rights (discussed in Chapter 2) to be appraised. This would include any known easements, restrictions, or special assessments affecting the property. One common appraisal assignment is to value all the rights of ownership of a property, commonly referred to as the *fee simple*, or *fee simple estate*. However, appraisals involving less than all the property rights are common. Examples of such assignments include appraisals of the leased fee, the leasehold estate, subsurface mineral rights, and other partial interests. The appraisal of partial interests is discussed in Chapter 17.

6. Assignment Conditions

Finally, the sixth element of defining the assignment is identifying what assignment conditions apply. Every appraisal assignment involves compliance with one or more **assignment conditions**, imposed by law, the client, or the intended use or users. For example, most appraisal assignments are taken with the understanding that the appraisal and report will be performed in compliance with the requirements set forth in USPAP. Thus, defining the assignment conditions that apply is a key part of the agreement between the appraiser and the client. A practical way to group these conditions is as follows:

- USPAP
- Supplemental Standards
- Jurisdictional Exceptions
- Extraordinary Assumptions
- Hypothetical Conditions
- Regular Assumptions and Conditions
- Contractual Conditions

a. Uniform Standards of Professional Appraisal Practice

As noted above, most appraisal assignments have compliance with USPAP as a condition to the assignment. Every appraisal performed in a federally related transaction must comply. Such transactions usually involve federally regulated lenders, or government agencies such as the Federal Housing Administration (FHA), or Veterans Administration (VA). In addition, the appraiser licensing law in some states, including California, requires that all licensed or certified appraisers comply with USPAP in *every* appraisal assignment. Further, appraisers who are members of the leading professional appraisal organizations have committed to comply with USPAP in every appraisal assignment.

There are some exceptions to the federal rules. Federally regulated lenders are able to use non-compliant appraisals if the transaction amount is below a certain threshold, currently $250,000. Sometimes, real estate brokers or others, without an appraisal license, perform these assignments. Usually, such loans are difficult for the lender to sell in the secondary loan market, due to the lack of a good formal appraisal and report.

b. Supplemental Standards

A *supplemental standard* is defined in USPAP as a requirement issued by a governmental agency, which *adds* to the requirements in USPAP for the development and/or reporting of appraisals. These refer *only* to published requirements, rules, regulations or policies, which apply to all properties or assignments. Requirements that are only in the contract for a specific appraisal are not considered to be supplemental standards.

For example, most appraisals that are performed for federally regulated lenders *must* comply with published supplemental standards. Appraisals for pension funds or other private lenders are not *required* to comply, but the client might require compliance, as part of the assignment agreement with the appraiser. Such appraisal compliance might make it easier for the lender to sell the loan in the secondary loan market.

Another example consists of the requirements for property tax appraisals that are set forth in the laws and regulations of most states. Another set of requirements applies to eminent domain appraisals, as detailed in federal or state laws and court cases, depending on which set of rules applies to the particular appraisal assignment (see Chapter 17).

Still another example involves appraisals performed for federal land acquisitions. Here, supplemental standards are imposed by *Uniform Appraisal Standards for Federal Land Acquisitions*, adopted by the Federal Interagency Land Acquisition Conference, and widely known as "the yellow book." The current version was adopted in 2000 and was subsequently published by the Appraisal Institute.

c. Jurisdictional Exceptions

A *jurisdictional exception* is defined in USPAP as a law, or a public policy, that *blocks* the application of one or more parts of USPAP. (Again, a requirement in an appraisal assignment contract by a government agency or a request from an attorney does not *by itself* establish a jurisdictional exception.) For example, for eminent domain appraisals, many states have adopted laws with very detailed appraisal standards, a few of which might conflict with USPAP. Many states do not allow the use of listings, offers, or option contracts as comparable market evidence, even though there probably are times when an appraiser could conclude that such less-reliable evidence is a better measure of a property's value than the available conventional sales data.

When a jurisdictional exception blocks compliance with some requirement of USPAP, the appraiser needs to establish that fact with the client early in the assignment. The appraiser must obtain the source of the particular law and its exact wording. When a jurisdictional exception applies, the appraiser must state in any report what "part or parts of USPAP were disregarded, and the legal authority justifying this action."

Source: *USPAP*, 2006 ed., Jurisdictional Exception Rule.

d. Extraordinary Assumptions

An *extraordinary assumption* is defined in USPAP as an assumption that is directly related to a specific assignment, and if found to be *not true*, could change the result of the appraisal. Information used in an appraisal, however thoroughly researched, can turn out to be in error. And it is rarely either practical, or expected, to research information as thoroughly as humanly possible. Some information, moreover, cannot be known at the time of the appraisal.

For example, the market rents at the time of completion of a proposed building can only be estimated approximately. This is an assignment where one or more extraordinary assumptions might be in order: date of completion, market rents and building expenses upon completion, loan interest rates, and competitive property sales price being likely ones!

Inspection of a home from the street (known as a "drive-by") might require an extraordinary assumption about the charm, condition and remodeling in the interior, and the rear yard. A desk appraisal (one performed without *any* inspection of the subject property) would require an extraordinary assumption about the existence, nature and condition of the property, and the characteristics of the neighborhood not shown in the available neighborhood data.

USPAP allows an extraordinary assumption to be used in an assignment only if:

1. It is required to properly develop credible opinions and conclusions.

2. The appraiser has a reasonable basis for the extraordinary assumption.

3. Use of the extraordinary assumption results in a *credible analysis*, and the appraiser complies with the disclosure requirements set forth in USPAP. Extraordinary assumptions must be disclosed in the report.

e. Hypothetical Conditions

USPAP defines a *hypothetical condition* as:

> that which is contrary to what exists but is supposed for the purpose of analysis.

> Source: *USPAP*, 2006 ed., The Appraisal Foundation, 2006.

A hypothetical condition may be used in an appraisal *only* if it is required for legal purposes or for reasonable analysis or comparison.

It also must be clearly set out in any report. And, in any case, the use of a hypothetical condition must result in a *credible analysis*.

One common hypothetical condition is the appraisal of a proposed new building, as if it already exists on the date of value. Another common example is the appraisal of a property, with a serious defect, as if the defect were not there. Note the importance of *clearly* communicating such a hypothetical condition!

f. Regular Assumptions and Conditions

Appraisers have listed "Standard Assumptions and Limiting Conditions" in their contracts and reports for many years. The *Statement of Assumptions and Limiting Conditions* section of the commonly used URAR loan appraisal form in Figure 3-3 illustrates many of the more common **limiting conditions**. Generally, these are intended to spell out the limits of the knowledge of an appraiser, in dealing with something as complicated as real property. It is important to recognize and communicate to clients and intended users the limitations on the knowledge of the appraisal, the appraisal process, and the data used. In some cases, the appraiser can only produce a credible appraisal and report if experts in other areas provide information needed by the appraiser. This might include the legal meaning of some document affecting title to the property, the cause and repair costs for noticeable foundation cracking or settlement, and similar legal or physical problems with the property.

g. Contractual Conditions

The client may propose any condition desired for the appraisal or the report. The appraiser must not accept any condition that blocks producing a *credible appraisal and report*, given the intended use and intended users that have been spelled out. However, when the proposed condition in the contract allows for a credible appraisal and report, the appraiser is free to accept the condition (recognizing that it may change the fee charged, and the delivery time for the appraisal report).

If the client wants twelve bound copies of the report, with individual 6-by-8-inch photos of each room, most appraisers would answer: "Sure!" But the fee and delivery almost certainly would be affected. Contractual conditions, as noted earlier, cannot require the appraiser to violate USPAP, any jurisdictional exception, or a supplemental standard. Generally, contractual conditions should be reported or discussed in the report.

Clearly, most assignment conditions must be established at the start of the assignment, and most need to be established by agreement with the client. It makes no sense to perform an appraisal when the client expects one set of conditions, but the appraiser plans to perform something else. Of course, not everything about the assignment can be

Figure 3-3
Assumptions and
Limiting Conditions
Section, FNMA URAR
Appraisal Form.

Uniform Residential Appraisal Report   File

This report form is designed to report an appraisal of a one-unit property or a one-unit property with an accessory unit; including a unit in a planned unit development (PUD). This report form is not designed to report an appraisal of a manufactured home or a unit in a condominium or cooperative project.

This appraisal report is subject to the following scope of work, intended use, intended user, definition of market value, statement of assumptions and limiting conditions, and certifications. Modifications, additions, or deletions to the intended use, intended user, definition of market value, or assumptions and limiting conditions are not permitted. The appraiser may expand the scope of work to include any additional research or analysis necessary based on the complexity of this appraisal assignment. Modifications or deletions to the certifications are also not permitted. However, additional certifications that do not constitute material alterations to this appraisal report, such as those required by law or those related to the appraiser's continuing education or membership in an appraisal organization, are permitted.

SCOPE OF WORK: The scope of work for this appraisal is defined by the complexity of this appraisal assignment and the reporting requirements of this appraisal report form, including the following definition of market value, statement of assumptions and limiting conditions, and certifications. The appraiser must, at a minimum: (1) perform a complete visual inspection of the interior and exterior areas of the subject property, (2) inspect the neighborhood, (3) inspect each of the comparable sales from at least the street, (4) research, verify, and analyze data from reliable public and/or private sources, and (5) report his or her analysis, opinions, and conclusions in this appraisal report.

INTENDED USE: The intended use of this appraisal report is for the lender/client to evaluate the property that is the subject of this appraisal for a mortgage finance transaction.

INTENDED USER: The intended user of this appraisal report is the lender/client.

DEFINITION OF MARKET VALUE: The most probable price which a property should bring in a competitive and open market under all conditions requisite to a fair sale, the buyer and seller, each acting prudently, knowledgeably and assuming the price is not affected by undue stimulus. Implicit in this definition is the consummation of a sale as of a specified date and the passing of title from seller to buyer under conditions whereby: (1) buyer and seller are typically motivated; (2) both parties are well informed or well advised, and each acting in what he or she considers his or her own best interest; (3) a reasonable time is allowed for exposure in the open market; (4) payment is made in terms of cash in U. S. dollars or in terms of financial arrangements comparable thereto; and (5) the price represents the normal consideration for the property sold unaffected by special or creative financing or sales concessions* granted by anyone associated with the sale.

*Adjustments to the comparables must be made for special or creative financing or sales concessions. No adjustments are necessary for those costs which are normally paid by sellers as a result of tradition or law in a market area; these costs are readily identifiable since the seller pays these costs in virtually all sales transactions. Special or creative financing adjustments can be made to the comparable property by comparisons to financing terms offered by a third party institutional lender that is not already involved in the property or transaction. Any adjustment should not be calculated on a mechanical dollar for dollar cost of the financing or concession but the dollar amount of any adjustment should approximate the market's reaction to the financing or concessions based on the appraiser's judgment.

STATEMENT OF ASSUMPTIONS AND LIMITING CONDITIONS: The appraiser's certification in this report is subject to the following assumptions and limiting conditions:

1. The appraiser will not be responsible for matters of a legal nature that affect either the property being appraised or the title to it, except for information that he or she became aware of during the research involved in performing this appraisal. The appraiser assumes that the title is good and marketable and will not render any opinions about the title.

2. The appraiser has provided a sketch in this appraisal report to show the approximate dimensions of the improvements. The sketch is included only to assist the reader in visualizing the property and understanding the appraiser's determination of its size.

3. The appraiser has examined the available flood maps that are provided by the Federal Emergency Management Agency (or other data sources) and has noted in this appraisal report whether any portion of the subject site is located in an identified Special Flood Hazard Area. Because the appraiser is not a surveyor, he or she makes no guarantees, express or implied, regarding this determination.

4. The appraiser will not give testimony or appear in court because he or she made an appraisal of the property in question, unless specific arrangements to do so have been made beforehand, or as otherwise required by law.

5. The appraiser has noted in this appraisal report any adverse conditions (such as needed repairs, deterioration, the presence of hazardous wastes, toxic substances, etc.) observed during the inspection of the subject property or that he or she became aware of during the research involved in performing this appraisal. Unless otherwise stated in this appraisal report, the appraiser has no knowledge of any hidden or unapparent physical deficiencies or adverse conditions of the property (such as, but not limited to, needed repairs, deterioration, the presence of hazardous wastes, toxic substances, adverse environmental conditions, etc.) that would make the property less valuable, and has assumed that there are no such conditions and makes no guarantees or warranties, express or implied. The appraiser will not be responsible for any such conditions that do exist or for any engineering or testing that might be required to discover whether such conditions exist. Because the appraiser is not an expert in the field of environmental hazards, this appraisal report must not be considered as an environmental assessment of the property.

6. The appraiser has based his or her appraisal report and valuation conclusion for an appraisal that is subject to satisfactory completion, repairs, or alterations on the assumption that the completion, repairs, or alterations of the subject property will be performed in a professional manner.

known in advance, so a change to the agreement regarding the assignment conditions can be needed at any time. But when it occurs, the appraiser must advise the client of the problem and obtain the client's consent to the proposed change in the agreement. It is important to consider if any different contractual conditions apply, at the start of any assignment.

At all times, the appraiser must remember the USPAP obligation to prepare a **credible appraisal** and report, given the intended use and the intended users. The word *credible* is defined in USPAP, 2006 edition, as meaning "worthy of belief," with the added comment: "Credible assignment results require support, by relevant evidence and logic, to the degree necessary for the intended use."

In the Scope of Work section of USPAP, the appraiser is reminded that an acceptable scope of work

> ". . . must meet or exceed: the expectations of parties who are regularly intended users for similar assignments; and what an appraiser's peers' actions would be in performing the same or a similar assignment."
>
> Source: *USPAP*, 2006 edition.

Step 2: Identify Appropriate Solutions

The second of the four steps in the appraisal process is to identify appropriate solutions to the appraisal problem, that is, to develop an appraisal plan. This plan is called the *scope of work*.

The **scope of work** refers to the type and extent of research and analyses needed to develop a credible result in an assignment. Note that USPAP currently does not consider the report to be a part of the scope of work.

The scope of work includes the following four issues:
- The extent of identification of the property
- The extent of property inspection
- The type and extent of data researched
- The type and extent of analysis employed to reach a conclusion

The scope of work decision must be consistent with 1) the expectations in the market (the client and similar users) and 2) the actions of the appraiser's peers, when performing similar assignments that are designed to meet the requirements of USPAP. Needless to say, the scope of work required for an appraisal depends on the intended use and intended users of the appraisal and the report. However, the appraiser should be prepared to support the decision to exclude any step, information, or procedure that would likely be relevant to an intended user relying on the appraisal and the report.

The extent of the data collection process can also vary with the type of property being appraised. Consider an assignment to estimate the market value of an income property for purposes of a lease renewal. This assignment might require a detailed analysis of each tenant space, and more data than is usually required. The appraisal of a unique property, such as a large resort hotel, could involve a search for comparables reaching over a broad region around the subject property. An eminent domain appraisal could require a detailed narrative report, reporting the analysis of the subject property from several perspectives, depending on the type of public acquisition involved. When the scope of work is defined and the extent of the data collection process is fully outlined, the appraisal can be planned more efficiently.

1. The Extent of Property Identification

The first issue in the scope of work is to consider how much information is needed in order to clearly identify the property being appraised —the *subject property*. How is the property to be identified for the appraisal and in the report? By the full legal description, the street address, or some other description? It has been identified, in defining the assignment, but more information may need to be developed in performing the appraisal.

A legal description (discussed in Chapter 2) has the advantage of being the most accurate and unambiguous. A street address often does not exist for vacant land. And the street address will not help the appraiser define whether an undeveloped rear area is part of the property, or whether the vacant lot next door is to be included in the appraisal!

The appraiser must be concerned with identifying the physical property to be appraised. Also, what legal rights to that property are to be included? As discussed in Chapter 2, buyers do not get the physical object they saw. Instead, they get a document giving them certain rights to the property legally described in the document. It is important for the client and appraiser to understand and agree on the rights to be appraised. Depending on the intended use of the appraisal and report, it might be necessary to *ignore* an existing lease (other than reporting it), or to base the value analysis primarily on it!

2. The Extent of Property Inspection

The second issue in the scope of work is this: How is the appraiser to view the subject property? Usually, appraisers walk through the living areas, basement, decks, and garage of homes. (Inspections will be discussed further in Chapters 6 and 7.) Similar areas would be viewed for other types of property. In some cases, however, the intended use of the appraisal calls for viewing the property from the street, once called a "curbstone," and now known as a "drive-by." Rarely, the intended use of the appraisal will call for *no* viewing, known as a "desk-top" appraisal. An example might be an appraisal of the security for each of the mortgages in a loan pool being purchased. In all cases, the extent of property viewing must be agreed upon with the client in advance. (In some cases, a preliminary inspection may be desirable, if the appraiser is not familiar with the neighborhood and the type of property.)

Also, a drive-by inspection might have been requested by the client, but the appraiser might find that there is too little information available on the subject property to produce a credible appraisal. For example, the property has not been sold for many years, so there is no old MLS listing describing the property. And the loan was paid off years ago and not renewed or refinanced; so there is no information from a past loan appraisal in the online databases. And the property tax assessor in the jurisdiction does not release any information about the improvements. In this case, a full inspection must be carried out!

Note that some of the above paragraphs used the word "view," instead of "inspect." The traditional word has been "inspect" for many decades. However, today, "inspect" increasingly refers to the work of "property inspectors," people trained to identify many possible physical problems with property. Appraisers do not have these skills, leading to confusion between the roles of appraisers and property inspectors. It is important for appraisers to be clear about what they do and what they don't do!

3. The Type and Extent of Data Researched

The third issue in defining the scope of work is to decide what types of data to research. In addition, for each type of data, the appraiser must decide how thoroughly—to what extent—to research the data. This topic will be explored more fully in later chapters. As we learned in Chapter 1, a formal appraisal is not simply an informed estimate of value. Rather, a formal appraisal is an estimate of value based on, and supported by, information and facts gathered in the real estate market. These market-derived facts are commonly called *market data*, and they form the backbone of all formal appraisals. Data sources available to the appraiser are noted in many of the following chapters. Most market value appraisals require the following:

1. General data on the region, city, and neighborhood. These include data on population, employment, income, price levels, and market conditions, as well as data on the availability of financing and on construction costs. Sometimes, very detailed city data will be needed, as when estimating the rent-up time for a vacant building.

2. Specific data on the subject property. These include detailed legal and physical data on the land and all existing buildings, as described in Chapters 6 and 7.

3. Specific data on comparable properties. These include detailed legal and physical data on comparable sites and buildings that sold

or were rented, as well as detailed information on the sales prices and terms of sale of the comparable properties considered. The number of transactions in part depends on the similarity of the comparable sales to the subject property and the methods of analysis to be used. One or two transactions would not be enough in nearly all cases, but five to ten often would be desirable.

Highest and Best Use Analysis. As already suggested, the kind of data required for any appraisal depends in large part on what is known as a *highest and best use analysis* (which will be more fully discussed in Chapter 6). A highest and best use analysis is a study of how well-suited the improved property is to its physical, legal, and economic environment. This means that the general and specific data described above should include an analysis of legally permitted uses of the property under local zoning laws, as well as any private restrictions on the use of the property. Once the highest and best use has been estimated, the collection of more detailed data can begin. Figure 3-4 points out one aspect of a highest and best use analysis.

How Much Information Is Needed? The amount and kinds of data required in an appraisal depend on the type of property being appraised and the intended use of the appraisal and report.

The type of property and the intended use of the appraisal and report may suggest the most appropriate value approaches, and therefore the amount and kinds of data needed. Income property appraisals often require data to support two or all three approaches to value, whereas a single-family home being appraised for a loan might require only the data needed for the sales comparison approach. Of course, appraisals made for legal purposes may require more supporting detail than those

Figure 3-4 Highest and Best Use?

made for purchase and sale. The scope of work plan examines what type of property data to obtain, how much data to obtain on each property, and what is likely to be the best data source.

Regardless of the type of property, most appraisals require sales information on comparable properties, fitting the general description of the property being appraised. However, the actual amount of market data that is needed varies with each appraisal. For instance, assume that several nearly new three-bedroom, approximately 1,800 sq. ft. homes in the same neighborhood have recently sold for prices ranging from $200,000 to $250,000. Then, a newly constructed three-bedroom property might be valued by comparing it with these sales. Specific data on the size, quality, age, and general amenities of the comparable homes could suggest a reasonable value for the subject property.

However, it would be logical and prudent to consider additional data before settling on a conclusion of value. What if the sold properties had better financing than is currently available? What if market conditions have changed since these sales, as a result of a serious increase in unemployment in the community? What if the new house being appraised recently cost the owner $300,000 to develop, including land and building? Should this cost govern the estimate of value? Each question suggests a need for additional data. As noted above, complex assignments, such as the appraisal of income or commercial properties, normally require more types of market data than single-family home appraisals. Techniques for locating and analyzing the general and specific data required for appraisals will be discussed in subsequent chapters.

4. The Type and Extent of Analysis Employed

This is the fourth and final issue in the scope of work decision. What types of data analyses are likely to be useful in reaching a credible conclusion? And does the intended use of the appraisal and report impact that decision?

There are three approaches—actually families of approaches—that can be used to analyze the value of property. When used to estimate market value, all rely on one or another form of market-derived data. Traditionally, appraisers selected an analysis from one or more of the approaches, depending on the type of property, economic conditions in the market for such property, and the intended use of the appraisal and report. Later chapters will analyze each approach and when each is more likely to be useful. However, it is also possible to perform more than one analysis of the same set of data, and then reconcile the two estimates.

For example, in estimating the value of vacant land zoned for apartment use, the appraiser might examine the sale price of properties per square foot of land area, per potential dwelling unit, or per square foot of allowable building area. As will be illustrated later, there are also different techniques that the appraiser could use to analyze these sales. Should the appraiser use only one technique to study the sales, or does the scope of work call for more?

Step 3: Execute the Appropriate Scope of Work

The third of the four steps in the appraisal process is to perform the scope of work that was developed in Step 2. You must remember that performing the work will not go exactly as planned! Everything is subject to change as more information is collected.

Even the original definition of the assignment, as agreed upon with the client, can change. The appraiser might uncover information that changes the rights to be appraised, the date of value, or the appraisal conditions. On occasion, the appraiser might identify something that would cause the client to cancel the appraisal, with the appraiser being paid just for the time to date. An example, when appraising a home for a lender, might be to find indications of major earth movement.

The appraiser must collect, analyze, and apply the appropriate data for each valuation approach selected. A quick summary of the three approaches follows (see Figure 3-5).

The **sales comparison approach** uses data on sales of comparable properties. The prices people are willing to pay are usually a good indication of the market value of any commodity. The **cost approach** relies on the appraiser's estimate of the amount required to buy vacant land

Figure 3-5 Flow of Market Data.

and the cost to construct the existing or proposed buildings or structures on it. Any loss in value from age or other causes is subtracted. Last, the ***income approach*** analyzes the income-producing capability of rental investment property to indicate its market value.

In most assignments, only the approach or approaches that clearly appear to be pertinent to performing a credible analysis need be applied. In the report itself, the exclusion of any value approach should of course be explained. An outline of the three value approaches is included in Section 3.3.

In executing the scope of work, the appraiser must reach a decision regarding the value conclusion. When two or more approaches have been used, the appraiser next reviews the estimates produced by the approaches and arrives at a final conclusion. This procedure is referred to as the ***reconciliation*** process. Three primary considerations are involved:

1. Review the appropriateness of each approach, considering the type of property, the market, and the intended use of the appraisal and report.

2. Consider the adequacy and reliability of the data and the validity of any assumptions made in its analysis.

3. Consider the range of indicated values and the position of each value within that range.

If the purpose of the appraisal is to estimate market value, the sales comparison approach is often the most persuasive, because it most directly reflects the actions of the market. In single-family residential appraisals, the sales comparison approach is most often emphasized, because market data are usually available, relatively reliable, and adequate in number. Where there are unique property characteristics or insufficient sales data, the cost and/or income approach may be emphasized, depending on the type of property.

Often, each approach is used as a check on the others. The value conclusion is rarely based on a simple averaging of the three value estimates. Reconciliation will be studied in depth in Chapter 15.

Step 4: Report the Findings and Conclusions Reached

The fourth and last step in the appraisal process is to report the appraisal opinion or conclusion. On occasion, only an oral report is required, but most often the client wants some form of written report. Written appraisal reports are traditionally transmitted on paper. However, electronically transmitted reports are becoming commonplace. Regardless of the method of transmittal, the content of appraisal reports must meet the requirements of one of the reporting options defined in USPAP.

1. Types of Written Reports

The three types of written reports set forth in USPAP are the **Self-Contained Appraisal Report**, the **Summary Appraisal Report**, and the **Restricted Use Appraisal Report**. These are detailed in Chapter 16. In brief

- The Self-Contained Appraisal Report contains *all* of the information needed for solution of the appraisal problem. The report *describes* the data and analyses, giving the client a full picture.

- The Summary Appraisal Report contains only a *summary* of the information used to prepare the appraisal.

- The Restricted Use Appraisal Report contains only a *brief statement* of the information used.

The appropriate reporting option must be decided on, in advance, between the appraiser and the client. The choice should be based on the intended use of the appraisal, the intended users of the report and their knowledge of the property to be appraised, and the degree of disclosure needed in the report. Once the reporting option has been selected, a statement as to the type of report used must appear in the appraisal report itself.

If a Restricted Use Appraisal Report is chosen, it must include a prominent *use restriction clause* that restricts any reliance on the report to the client alone. Also, a reference must be made to the specific information that is available in the appraiser's files and that is the support for the value conclusion. The file itself must still contain all of the information required to produce a self-contained appraisal report.

2. Formats of Appraisal Reports

There are three traditional formats for written reports: the letter report, the form (or short-form) report, and the narrative report. The report format to be used depends on the amount of information and detail required by the client, the intended use, and the appraisal standards to be met. Thus, the format chosen depends largely on the reporting option decided on (Self-Contained, Summary, or Restricted Use Report). A brief description of reporting formats follows. An expanded discussion will be presented in Chapter 16.

The Letter Report. Usually only one to five pages long, the letter report is the least formal of the formats. Historically, it simply contained the conditions of the assignment, a summary of the nature and scope of the appraiser's investigation, and an opinion of value. Now, it must also identify the extent of the appraisal process that was performed. The letter format is most suited to the Restricted Use Appraisal Report. However, an expanded letter report could have the proper content to qualify as a Summary Appraisal Report. The letter report is used most often when the client and the intended users are familiar with the property.

The Form Report. As the name implies, the form report uses a printed or computer-generated sheet to organize and standardize the appraisal report content. A checklist is often used to describe and rate property characteristics. While the form report is a logical choice for the Summary Report option, it can be expanded into a Self-Contained Report by using report addenda.

Institutions and government agencies that handle large quantities of appraisal reports use report forms that are designed to suit their special needs. Standard forms are usually available for all the major property classifications—that is, single family residential, multifamily residential, commercial, industrial, and so on. The form report is by far the most common type of report used for home loan appraisals.

The Narrative Report. The narrative appraisal report is often the longest and most formal of the appraisal formats. It allows for a step-by-step presentation of the facts used by the appraiser to arrive at a value estimate. This format also allows a detailed discussion of the methods used to analyze these facts. Narrative appraisal reports are preferred when the client needs to review each step taken by the appraiser. They are the logical format for Self-Contained Reports. However, the narrative format is frequently used for Summary or Restricted Use Reports, as well. Narrative reports are typical for appraisals performed for government agencies, and those reporting the value of major investment properties.

3.2 Types of Value

In this section, we will discuss the various meanings and types of value, the basic economic ways of measuring value, and finally, the market value concept itself.

Why Value Concepts Differ

While *value* is generally defined as the dollar **worth** of a thing, it is a word that has many different meanings. For example, the value of a parcel of real estate may be different to a particular buyer or seller than to a lender, an insurance adjuster, or an accountant. This difference exists because value can be very subjective.

For example, some real estate buyers and sellers have a tendency to measure value only by their personal desires and needs. On the other hand, the lender's concept of property value is most often related to an objective view of the market, where value is related to the listing and sales prices of similar properties and the most likely selling price of the subject property. The insurance adjuster's idea of value (depending on the policy) might be strictly related to the cost of replacing the improvements, in case of fire or other insured disaster. The accountant may think of value in terms of the original acquisition cost, the *cost basis*, or so-called *book value* of the property.

In the examples given, each interested party has in mind a different concept of value, each of which is quite limited in its usefulness and in definition. There are literally dozens of value types and concepts, each carrying its own identifying name. Here are some of the value labels you might encounter:

Assessed value	Leased value
Book value	Liquidation value
Capitalized value	Listing value
Cash value	Loan value
Depreciated value	Market value
Economic value	Nuisance value
Exchange value	Potential value
Face value	Rental value
Fair value	Salvage value
Going concern value	Use value
Inheritance tax value	Value in foreclosure
Insurance value	Value in place

Contrasting Value in Use and Value in Exchange

Economic theory suggests that most types of value fit into one of two basic categories. These categories are known as *value in use* and *value in exchange*.

Value in use refers to the value of an item or object to a particular user. For example, a single-family home that is located next to a local bakery might have a higher value to the family operating the bakery than to the public in general. Its higher value is a unique value to that user. This is often described as a *subjective value* concept.

Value in exchange describes the value of a thing to people in general. This can be termed *objective value*. Value in exchange can be estimated only for items or properties that are commonly bought and sold in the market, that is, "exchanged" for money or its equivalent (see Figure 3-6).

Figure 3-6 Market Value = Value in Exchange.

Almost 2,400 years ago, Aristotle said:

> All things which are exchanged must be comparable to one another. Money measures and compares; it states whether and by how much the value of one thing exceeds another.

The vast majority of real estate holdings are indeed bought and sold on the open market, at prices that are measured and compared by that market. Under the right conditions, we refer to this kind of price as market value.

Defining Market Value

Most formal appraisals are made for the purpose of estimating market value, as opposed to the other types of value discussed above. It is important to understand how market value differs from other types of value and why it is sought in appraisals.

Market value is broadly understood to mean "what property should normally sell for, assuming a willing buyer and a willing seller." However, economic and legal definitions for market value have been developed that imply some important additional criteria. As defined by our federal financial institutions (and required for appraisals made in connection with federally related real estate transactions), market value means:

> . . . the most probable price which a property should bring in a competitive and open market under all conditions requisite to a fair sale, the buyer and seller each acting prudently, knowledgeably, and assuming the price is not affected by undue stimulus.

Implicit in this definition is the completion of a sale as of a specified date, and the passing of title from seller to buyer where: 1) buyer and seller are typically motivated; 2) both parties are well informed or well advised, and each is acting in what he or she considers his or her own best interest; 3) a reasonable time is allowed for exposure in the open market; 4) payment is made in cash in U.S. dollars, or in terms of financial arrangements comparable to cash; and 5) the price represents the normal consideration for the property sold, unaffected by special or creative financing or sales concessions granted by anyone associated with the sale.

In other words, market value is a price arrived at in the market under certain prescribed conditions, regarding 1) *the terms of sale*, 2) *market exposure*, and 3) *informed parties*, not under duress. Each condition is explored in the following sections.

Please note that there are many different definitions of market value, usually with only minor differences. Often, it will be important to have the exact wording appropriate to the intended use of the appraisal, along with the source of the definition.

Terms of the Sale

There is a saying in real estate that the price depends on the terms: how much cash down and how much per month. Another famous saying is: "You can set the price, if I can set the terms!" Two identical houses will probably sell at different prices if each "deal" involves markedly different financing. This teaches us that *price* differences do not necessarily indicate *value* differences. If prices of comparables are to be considered as good indicators of value, the financing terms must be considered. Terms of sale will be discussed further in Chapter 9. For many appraisal assignments, the terms of sale are defined as all cash or cash to a new third-party loan.

Market Exposure

Market exposure means making many potential buyers of a property aware that the property is available for sale. A sign on the property might be adequate in a hot market, but some form of MLS listing or media advertising might be needed in a slow market. Ample market exposure is necessary to meet this condition of sale. In our new "computer age," property listings on the Internet are a rapidly growing option. Figure 3-7 shows such a listing. When we say that a property was "sold on the open market," we mean that it had good exposure to prospective buyers, and sold to an unrelated party as a result of that exposure.

Prices that result when sales lack adequate *open market exposure* are not typical of the market and therefore do not represent market value. Family transfers are usually not "open" or "arm's length" transactions. Not only are they not advertised, but family sales are often available to only a select few family members or at favorable prices or financing. Lack of adequate market exposure also invalidates some forced sales that result from job transfer, threat of foreclosure, or family breakup. What is adequate market exposure? There is no set standard! However, it is generally assumed that unique properties require a greater market exposure, because they are of interest to fewer buyers, and thus have a narrower market. For example, a rambling five-bedroom house may take two or three times as long

Figure 3-7 An Example of Market Exposure via the Internet.

to sell as a standard three-bedroom house in the same neighborhood. Adequate market exposure also is defined by the state of the local market, as properties selling in a hot market can get multiple offers just by the rumor of their availability!

Informed Parties

For a parcel of real estate to command a price matching its utility and value, the property's uses and purposes must be known to the potential buyers and sellers. Even in a normal market, buyers and sellers sometimes lack adequate information about the property. However, the seller is often more familiar with the specific features of the sale property than the prospective buyer. Without expert advice from real estate brokers, salespeople, and appraisers, parties on both sides of a given transaction may have a mistaken view of the property, and the price agreed on may not represent market value.

We can also say that these informed parties cannot be under duress to act. If they are, the sale does not qualify as involving *typical* motivation! What is duress? Perhaps the seller must close rapidly, or else face foreclosure or an involuntary bankruptcy. Or the buyer might have tried to buy several properties without success, and now very favorable first-time buyer financing is about to expire.

The concept of market value is important in appraisals, because it clearly distinguishes between *price* and *value*. Price reflects not only the terms and conditions of the particular sale, but also the unique and sometimes subjective motives of buyers and sellers. Most appraisal purposes are best served by relating value to a more precise standard than price alone. Thus, market value refers to the value of real estate to people *in general*, in terms of *money*, between informed and *knowledgeable people* who are buying and selling on the *open market*. In summary, then, market value can be understood as the most likely sale price when the conditions referred to above have been met.

3.3 The Classical Approaches to Value

As indicated in Section 3.1, the appraisal process requires the application of one or more of the three classical approaches to value. The sales comparison, cost, and income approaches are considered classical in the appraisal field, because they incorporate logical, time-tested techniques for valuing real estate. In early appraisal theory, all three approaches were required in every formal appraisal! Today, a particular approach is usually required only if needed to produce a credible conclusion for the value problem at hand. Each approach has its own unique importance. The three approaches are briefly outlined below and covered in greater detail in later chapters.

The Sales Comparison Approach

The sales comparison approach, also known as the market or direct comparison approach, is the most direct of the three approaches and often the most reliable. Simply stated, the sales comparison approach compares the property being appraised to similar properties that have sold on the open market at a time close to the date of value. From the prices paid, the appraiser estimates a probable selling price or value for the subject property, by making a careful analysis of differences in sale conditions and property characteristics. This process is introduced here. Example 3-1 illustrates the sales comparison approach.

Steps in the Sales Comparison Approach

In application, the sales comparison approach involves four basic steps:

1. Investigate sales of comparable properties; identify motives of buyers and sellers; collect information about the properties; and seek out the conditions of the sale: date, price, terms, and market exposure.

2. Analyze and compare the sales with the subject property, considering the time of sale, location, and other factors affecting market value.

3. Judge how the observed differences between the properties affect the prices paid. These differences are normally treated as "adjustments" to the prices paid for the comparables.

4. Arrive at a conclusion of value for the subject property, based on the most comparable sales.

EXAMPLE 3-1 The Sales Comparison Approach

Assume that the subject property is a medium-quality, 20-year-old, three-bedroom home, with a two-car garage. The home has 1,800 square feet of finished heated living area. The appraiser locates three similar homes that have sold in the neighborhood after adequate market exposure. All have similar square footage areas and numbers of rooms.

A. Comparables:

Data	Comparable A	Comparable B	Comparable C
Price paid	$250,000	$240,000	$200,000
Location	Better than subject property	Equal to subject property	Worse than subject property
Lot size	Equal to subject property	Larger than subject property	Smaller than subject property
Overall condition	Better than subject property	Equal to subject property	Worse than subject property

B. Dollar Adjustment Factors Indicated by Market Study:

For illustration purposes, assume that analysis of the sales suggests the following adjustments:

Location difference	$25,000
Lot size difference	$15,000
Overall condition difference	$10,000

C. Adjustments:

Data	Comparable A	Comparable B	Comparable C
Price paid	$250,000	$240,000	$200,000
Location	- 25,000	0	0
Lot size	0	- 15,000	+ 15,000
Overall condition	- 10,000	- 0	+ 10,000
Adjusted price	$215,000	$225,000	$225,000

D. Conclusion:

Subject property's indicated value is about $220,000.

How to Compare Sales

Comparing the sales of comparable properties with the subject property first involves listing any desirable features of the comparable properties that are not present in the subject property. Then, the estimated dollar value contribution of each missing feature must be *subtracted* from the respective selling prices of the comparables. Next, features of the subject property that are not present in the comparable properties must be noted. The estimated dollar value contribution of these features must be *added* to the prices of the comparables, to make them more like the subject property. It is important to remember that the appraiser must adjust the sale to be more like the subject. Another way to say it is to "adjust *from* the sale, *to* the subject."

In deciding how much to adjust for differences in the properties being compared, appraisers often rely on techniques "borrowed" from the cost (or even income) approach. For example, a new house with a fireplace might be appraised at $5,000 more than a comparable sale lacking this feature, if that amount represents the cost of installing a fireplace. Some adjustments can be estimated by comparing sales of properties with and without the issue being studied. Sales comparison approach techniques will be more fully discussed in Chapters 8 and 9.

The Cost Approach

The cost approach is based on the principle that property is worth what it would cost in money to replace the improvements as of the date of value (see Figure 3-8). Adjustments to cost are made to allow for any loss in value due to age, condition, and other factors that reduce market appeal. This is referred to as accrued depreciation. Thus, the cost approach involves adding the *depreciated replacement cost* of the improvements to the value of the land, as estimated from a market or economic study.

Steps in the Cost Approach

Applying the cost approach requires an appraiser to follow these five steps:

1. Estimate the market value of the land on the date of value, as if it were vacant and available for use at its highest and best use.

Figure 3-8 Value Is Related to the Cost of Development.

Source: Photograph Courtesy of Doug Frost.

2. Estimate the total cost to build a duplicate of the existing structure, figured at construction prices in effect on the date of value.

3. Estimate the appropriate amount to allow for accrued depreciation, that is, the loss in market value of the subject building when compared to a new structure.

4. Subtract the estimated depreciation from the cost of the hypothetical new structure. The answer is a depreciated cost estimate.

5. Add the value of the land to the depreciated replacement cost of the new structure. The result is the indicated property value by the cost approach.

Since the cost approach requires an estimate of depreciation, or loss in value, it is less reliable where buildings show major losses in value (because of old age or substantial obsolescence). Preparing realistic estimates of value loss from these causes can be very difficult. The cost approach is normally given more weight in the appraisal of new buildings and also service-type or special-use properties which are not frequently bought or sold (e.g., schools). Example 3-2 illustrates the cost approach. This approach will be explored further in Chapters 10, 11, and 12.

The Income Approach

The income approach (or capitalized income approach) is used to appraise commercial, industrial, and residential income properties, to reflect their ability to produce net income. Where the cost and sales comparison approaches are being emphasized in an appraisal, the income approach is sometimes used to test the results. The building in Figure 3-9 is a typical income-producing property.

Steps in the Income Approach

Example 3-3 illustrates the income approach, which involves estimating what the market will pay for the property's expected future income. Six steps are involved in estimating the value of the fee simple interest:

1. Obtain an annual rent schedule or income statement for the subject property as of the date of value and compare the rents with those of the competition, to arrive at a projection of *gross potential income*—the amount of rent when all available spaces or units are occupied and paying rent.

2. Estimate annual *vacancy and collection losses*.

3. Subtract these from the gross income, to arrive at the *effective gross income*.

4. Estimate the *annual operating expenses*, and subtract them from the effective gross income to arrive at the net income. Net income is often called *net operating income*.

EXAMPLE 3-2 The Cost Approach

A. Given:

Cost new:

Home:	$78 per sq. ft.
Garage:	$30 per sq. ft.

Depreciation:

Analysis of recent comparable sales prices suggests a value decline of about 0.5% for each year of age. Present age is 20 years.

Land Value:

$120,000, based on recent comparable sales

B. Value Estimate Using the Cost Approach:

Replacement cost

Building:	Width in feet	60	
Times:	Depth in feet	x 40	
Equals:	Area in sq. ft.	2,400	
Times:	Cost per sq. ft.	x $78	
Equals:	Cost of home		$187,200
Garage:	Width in feet	20	
Times:	Depth in feet	x 20	
Equals:	Area in sq. ft.	400	
Times:	Cost per sq. ft.	x $30	
Equals:	Cost of garage		+ $12,000
Total improvement replacement cost			*$199,200*
Less:	Depreciation: Age in years	20	
Times:	Annual depreciation	x 0.5%	
Equals:	Total percent depreciation	10%	
Times:	Total cost new	x $199,200	
Equals:	Depreciation amount		- 19,920
Equals:	Replacement cost less depreciation		$179,280
Plus:	Land value		+ 120,000
Equals:	*Indicated value by the cost approach (rounded)*		*$299,000*

---

5. Analyze comparable investments, in order to arrive at a capitalization method and rate.

6. Capitalize the projected net income into an estimate of value.

There are a number of capitalization methods in common usage, each designed to handle a specific type of appraisal problem. In the case

Figure 3-9 Example of an Income-Producing Property.

EXAMPLE 3-3 The Income Approach

A. Given:

A 20-unit apartment building has market rents of $800 per unit per month, or $192,000 per year. There is no rent control in this market, and all tenants are on month-to-month tenancies. There is no other income generated by the property. The estimated factor for vacancies and collection losses is 6% of the potential gross income. Projected annual operating expenses are

Property taxes	$15,000
Insurance	3,500
Management	10,500
Utilities	6,500
Maintenance and miscellaneous	+ 7,000
Total	$42,500

The appraiser selected the direct capitalization method and a 10% capitalization rate, based on the market data analyzed.

B. Solution, Using the Income Approach:

Potential gross annual income	$192,000
Less: Vacancies and collection loss	- 11,520
Equals: Effective gross income	$180,480
Less: Annual operating expenses	- 42,500
Equals: Net operating income	$137,980
Divided by: Capitalization rate	÷ 0.10
Equals: Indicated value by income capitalization (rounded)	$1,380,000

of single-family homes, the gross income multiplier method is often used, instead of income capitalization. Both income capitalization and the gross income multiplier method will be defined and discussed in Chapters 13 and 14.

SUMMARY

In Standards 1 and 2, USPAP defines the appraisal process and report, suggesting how an appraisal should be developed and how it should be reported. The steps in the appraisal process are to:

1. Identify the appraisal problem to be solved

2. Identify appropriate solutions

3. Execute the appropriate scope of work

4. Report the findings and conclusions reached

The first step in the appraisal problem is to *define the problem*. Six elements must be identified. Most require agreement with the client, in light of the intended use of the appraisal and report, as well as the intended users. All elements (except some aspects of element number 5) generally must be selected prior to the start of the appraisal. And all selections must be made with the intent of producing a credible appraisal and report. The six elements of defining the appraisal problem are:

1. The client and any other intended users

2. The intended use of the appraisal and report

3. The type and definition of value

4. The effective date of the appraiser's opinions and conclusions

5. The subject of the assignment and its characteristics

6. Any assignment conditions

The client is the person or entity with whom the appraiser has an agreement to prepare an appraisal and report. Intended users are those people that the appraiser and client agree are to receive, understand, and rely on the report. It is important to know the intended users in order to write a report that will be clear to them.

The intended use of the appraisal and report is critical, as it can determine the rights to be appraised, the type and definition of value, the date of value, the methods to be used, and the content of the report. The correct type of value must be selected and its definition reviewed. The date of value—the effective date of the conclusions—must be determined.

Next, the appraiser and the client must identify what *property and property rights* are to be appraised. A legal description of the property is the most precise, but sometimes only a property address is used. In either case, the correct description of the rights involved is needed. Is the appraisal to be of the fee simple interest, the leased fee, or some other set of rights? The client and the appraiser must clearly establish this.

The final step in defining the assignment is for the appraiser and the client to determine if there are any particular *assignment conditions* to be met. For example, most appraisals are to be performed in compliance with the conditions imposed by USPAP. A *supplemental standard*, imposed by law or regulation, may also apply to a particular assignment, requiring the appraiser to go beyond the requirements of USPAP. Or there may be a *jurisdictional exception*, a law or regulation that blocks application of some aspect of USPAP for some assignments. And the assignment may call for use of an *extra-ordinary assumption*, something that is assumed to be true but capable of changing the appraisal results if not true. Some assignments may also call for use of a *hypothetical condition*—something that is known to be untrue but is assumed for purposes of analysis. For example, the appraisal of a property with a defect can call for an analysis without the defect as a first step. Next, each appraisal is limited by the standard conditions that apply to every appraisal. Finally, the client may impose additional contract conditions, as long as they do not block the appraiser from producing a credible appraisal and report.

After the assignment has been defined, the second step in the appraisal process is to *identify the appropriate solutions*—the scope of work that will lead to a credible conclusion! The scope of work includes four issues:

1. The extent of property identification
2. The extent of property inspection
3. The type of data researched and the extent of research
4. The types and extent of data analyses used to reach the conclusion

In order to produce a credible result, the scope of work must be consistent with the expectations of similar clients, and the actions of the appraiser's peers, when performing similar assignments. The scope of work selected will be heavily influenced by the intended use of the appraisal.

How is the subject property to be identified? It has been identified in defining the assignment, but obtaining a better description may need to be an element of the scope of work. This would include obtaining more or better information on lot size and zoning, building age, size and features, a copy of the property tax bill or leases for the spaces in the building, and so on.

What type of property inspection is to be performed? It might be only from the appraiser's desk, or the street in front of the property, or a regular exterior and interior inspection. And the appraiser has to allow for the possibility of a change in the type of inspection, if needed to produce a credible appraisal and report!

Turning to the data, the scope of work plan must include what types of data to research. In part, this will depend on the type of property, the intended use of the report, and what these indicate about which appraisal methods might be useful. Data on sales of similar properties are often a key part of the search. Land sales, rental transactions, or expense information could also be needed. In some cases, extensive city and neighborhood information may be needed. One example would be when estimating how long it would likely take to sell all of the units in a new or converted condominium building.

The type of data to collect is not the only data question. The second question is the extent of the data. This includes both the *amount* of information collected on each property researched, and also how *many* properties to research.

In researching home sales, the sale date, terms, age, size, features, and condition are most important. However, the more that you know about the sale, the better. So, the scope of work includes where to access the needed data, and which data source has the most properties of the desired type and the most information on each property.

The scope of work step in the appraisal process ends with selecting the type and extent of data analysis to be used to reach the conclusion. Which of the three approaches (or which combination of approaches) appears to be useful, considering the property type, the intended use of the appraisal, and the data that is reasonably available? And exactly which methods or techniques should be applied? Each of the three approaches has more than one technique or method of analysis that might be useful.

After defining the scope of work, the third step in the appraisal process is to *perform the appropriate scope of work*. The appraiser must be alert to new information—about the property or the data—that suggests the intended scope of work must be modified.

Finally, the appraiser must consider the estimates of value that were reached by each approach or method used. This process is called *reconciliation*. The appraiser reviews the appropriateness of each approach to the appraisal problem, as well as the likely adequacy and reliability of the data used.

The fourth and last step in the appraisal process is to *report the findings and conclusions reached*. On occasion, an oral report is used. Most often, however, a written report is called for. USPAP provides for three types of written appraisal reports: Self-Contained, Summary, and Restricted Use. The type of report suggests the amount of detail included. If a Restricted Use Report is chosen, a use restriction clause must clearly restrict reliance on the report to just the client, because of the limited amount of detail included.

Generally, appraisal reports are either narrative in style, or are on specialized forms. The forms tend to be used primarily for loan appraisals and only for homes and small apartments. Narrative reports are used for appraisals of larger commercial properties and for appraisals for litigation.

An estimate of market value is the object of most appraisals. Market value differs from other types of value primarily in that it attempts to measure *value in exchange* rather than *value in use*. *Value in exchange* means value to people in general rather than to a specific user.

The common formal definition of market value attempts to remove any element of subjectivity (or personal bias) from the value question, by requiring that the price paid be 1) in terms of money, 2) after adequate market exposure, and 3) between knowledgeable parties not under pressure or duress.

Three classical approaches are used for valuing real estate: sales comparison, cost, and income. The sales comparison approach is often the most reliable because it is the most direct. It involves comparing the property being appraised with similar properties that have sold close to the date of value. The cost approach estimates the value of a property by adding its land value to the estimated cost to replace the existing structures, as of the date of value, less depreciation. The cost approach tends to be more relevant to the appraisal of newer properties or single-purpose properties. It is based on the principle that property is worth what it would cost in money to duplicate. The income approach compares the income-producing capability of the property with that of properties that have been sold. The net income projected for the subject property is then translated into an indication of value by a process known as capitalization. The income approach is used to appraise property that generates, or can generate, income. For single-family homes, an alternate gross income multiplier method can be used.

IMPORTANT TERMS AND CONCEPTS

Appraisal process	*Limiting conditions*
Appraisal report	*Market exposure*
Assignment conditions	*Market value*
Client	*Marketing time*
Cost approach	*Narrative report*
Credible appraisal	*Reconciliation*
Definition of the appraisal problem	*Restricted Use Appraisal Report*
Effective date of value	*Sales comparison approach*
Exposure time	*Scope of work*
Extraordinary assumption	*Self-Contained Appraisal Report*
Form report	*Subject of the assignment*
Hypothetical condition	*Summary Appraisal Report*
Income approach	*Supplemental standard*
Intended use of the report	*Type of value*
Intended users	*Value in exchange*
Jurisdictional exception	*Value in use*
Letter report	*Worth*

REVIEWING YOUR UNDERSTANDING

1. The appraisal process involves four steps, the first of which is to:
   a. Choose an appropriate value approach
   b. Define the appraisal problem
   c. View the property
   d. None of the above

2. The intended user of an appraisal report includes:
   a. Only the client
   b. All parties likely to receive a copy
   c. Those the appraiser intends to rely on it
   d. All parties not explicitly excluded

3. In appraisals, the effective date of value is:
   a. The date of the property inspection
   b. The date agreed on in advance with the client
   c. The day the appraisal is completed
   d. The date the appraisal is signed

4. One common appraisal assignment is to appraise the:
   a. Value of the mining rights
   b. "Fee simple" ownership
   c. Value subject to an existing loan
   d. Life estate

5. Assignment conditions include:
   a.   Hypothetical conditions
   b.   Extraordinary assumptions
   c.   Supplemental standards
   d.   All of the above

6. The amount and kind of data needed to prepare an appraisal depend upon:
   a.   The "highest and best use" analysis
   b.   The type of appraisal being performed and its intended use
   c.   The type of property being appraised, and the intended user of the appraisal
   d.   All of the above

7. The appraiser's conclusion of value should be based on:
   a.   An averaging of the three value conclusions indicated by the three approaches to value
   b.   A weighing of the values indicated by each of the three approaches according to their appropriateness and the reliability of the data used in each
   c.   The most recent selling price
   d.   None of the above

8. When a standard form is used to report an appraisal, it is most likely to be a:
   a.   Self-Contained Appraisal Report
   b.   Summary Appraisal Report
   c.   Limited Report
   d.   Restricted Use Report

9. The concept of market value in appraisal practice does not include:
   a.   Most probable price
   b.   Competitive and open market
   c.   A good buy
   d.   Buyer and seller each acting prudently

10. The cost approach is normally given more weight in the appraisal of:
    a.   Old and substantially obsolete buildings
    b.   Single-family tract houses over 10 years old
    c.   New buildings and special-use buildings
    d.   None of the above

PRACTICAL APPLICATIONS

If you did not carefully read the introduction to these exercises at the end of Chapter 1, please go back and read that first, before continuing here. Also review the exercise at the end of Chapter 2, and the work that you have performed to date.

This assignment involves defining the appraisal, which was the major topic in this chapter. The form itself is not set up to allow you to record each of the components in a logical order! Instead, make a list of the elements in defining the assignment, as set forth in this chapter. You can make this list by hand, typewriter, or computer!

Once the list is completed, referring to the text, try to fill in the pertinent information for each step that you have listed. Make sure that your list has all of the items noted in the text. After you have completed filling out the information, you can consider which items will need to be transferred to the form!

Next, start up the software program and open the file that you saved after the Chapter 2 assignment. Consider which information about the assignment should be transferred from your list over to the form. You may have to hunt to find where to enter some information, such as the date of value! Note that you have already entered the basic information about the property! And much of the information about "assignment conditions" is already specified in the Limiting Conditions section of the form.

As noted last time, *do not* enter information in the neighborhood, lot, or improvement sections of the report at this time—wait until you get to the chapter that covers that topic! However, it is a good idea to look ahead at the coming sections of the form, so that you start thinking about the information that you will need to gather!

Reminder: If you have questions about the program itself, please be sure to review the manuals and help information that was included with the program CD. Also, at anytime, you can go to http://www.bradfordsoftware.com, click on "Services" at the upper right of the home page, and then on "ClickFORMS Training Programs" in the middle of the "Services" page. See the free online training section!

CHAPTER 4
FOCUS ON NEIGHBORHOOD, COMMUNITY, AND MARKET

PREVIEW

In the previous chapters, we explained the necessity of defining the appraisal problem and planning the scope of work for the appraisal. We now turn to the gathering of data for the appraisal. The first phase of the data program is to examine the neighborhood district or community around the property and to note the influences that have the most important effect on the property's value. Since property value must always be understood in the context of the market, this chapter concludes with an analysis of real estate markets.

OBJECTIVES

When you have completed this chapter you should be able to:

1. Describe the neighborhood concept and how neighborhood boundaries are defined.

2. Explain how you can use information from a neighborhood study in the appraisal process.

3. Explain how economics influences community origins and growth.

4. Name four different physical patterns of community land use.

5. Define a perfect market and explain why real estate markets are not perfect.

6. Discuss the real estate market actions that you should study and why.

4.1 Neighborhood Analysis

No other aspect of appraising is as difficult to define as neighborhood analysis. As a result, its meaning and usage have often been misinterpreted. Each person, community group, and organization has an idea what a neighborhood is and how it affects property values. People concerned about allegations of discrimination in housing have questioned how and why appraisers use neighborhood information. In fairness to all, it is essential for those in real estate to understand the concept of the neighborhood or district as it is used in appraisals, and be able to objectively analyze the neighborhood around a subject property. In this section, we shall explain the concept of the neighborhood and show how to use neighborhood information.

Defining the Neighborhood

The term **neighborhood** has been defined as follows:

> A neighborhood is a cluster of properties (most of which are) of relatively similar land use and value.*A group of complementary land uses; a congruous grouping of inhabitants, buildings, or business enterprises.**

> Source: *D. J. McKenzie and R. M. Betts, *The Essentials of Real Estate Economics,* 5th ed., South-Western Publishing, Mason, Ohio, 2006.

> Source: **The Dictionary of Real Estate Appraisal,* 4th ed., Appraisal Institute, Chicago, Ill., 2002.

More broadly, a neighborhood is an area whose occupants and users share some common ties or characteristics. Thus, some form of shared identity creates a neighborhood and binds it together. From this larger definition, we can see that one neighborhood may be residential, another commercial, another industrial, and so on. (Sometimes, the word *district* is used, when referring to an industrial, office, or retail neighborhood.)

What is the meaning of the term **shared identity**? The term refers to whatever neighborhood characteristics are shared in common, and thereby create a positive bond, or a so-called linkage, among the occupants. Shared identity can be defined economically, by the land uses; physically, by the buildings; or sociologically, by the occupants. There can be many types of **neighborhood bonds**, even among commercial property users. In an office neighborhood, for example, the bonds might include the sharing of a common work pool, similar surroundings, and accessibility to nearby services. Sometimes the nature of the bond is difficult to see. For example, in a very diverse residential-commercial neighborhood, the most powerful bond could be the desire to live in such a diverse and varied environment.

Greenwich Village in New York City has been considered such a neighborhood, as well as the Montrose area in Houston and others.

Boundaries of the Neighborhood

Neighborhood boundaries are influenced by a wide variety of factors, usually economic, physical, or legal in character. Economically, such boundaries are determined by where the benefits of the location seem to change. Evidence of such a boundary can be seen by changes in the types of buildings or land uses, or changes in the shared characteristics of the occupants. Physical features often more sharply define the boundaries of a neighborhood. Examples include rivers, lakes, and mountains, as well as freeways, railroads, and other human structures. City, school district, and/or zoning boundaries are commonly noted by appraisers as legal factors influencing neighborhood boundaries.

The boundaries of a neighborhood are not always obvious. Property features often change gradually, as one moves from one neighborhood to the next. When this is the case, neighborhood boundaries are difficult to establish. Sometimes, however, the neighborhood boundary can be very precise. For example, the boundaries of commercial neighborhoods are often precisely defined by zoning laws and by where the commercial buildings are located. Also, industrial neighborhoods often have boundaries that are precisely defined by zoning.

Adjacent neighborhoods may have similar characteristics. When adjacent neighborhoods lack noticeable physical boundaries and have important features in common, it is possible to combine them for study purposes and treat them as a *larger neighborhood*. On the other hand, almost every neighborhood can also be divided up into *smaller neighborhoods*, by emphasizing minor differences in the common bonds that define the neighborhood as a whole. So we can call the one the larger neighborhood and the other the immediate neighborhood.

In summary, neighborhood boundaries may be set by economic factors, physical features, or legal boundaries, or by changes in the characteristics of occupants, buildings, and/or uses.

Neighborhood Profile

The neighborhood analysis for an appraisal should begin with a factual description of the significant characteristics of the area. This may be in the form of a short profile of the location and the market trends. For example, the neighborhood section of the URAR form (see Figure 4-1) requires the appraiser to report on the following issues:

1. *Neighborhood Characteristics:*
   - Is the location urban, suburban, or rural?
   - Is the neighborhood built up over 75%, 25-75%, or under 25%?

**Figure 4-1
The Neighborhood
Section of the URAR
Form.**

Uniform Residential Appraisal Report

Property Address 831 S. Dona Marta St.	City Ventura	State CA Zip Code 930xx
Borrower Robert Burns	Owner of Public Record	County Ventura
Legal Description Lot 68, Tract 25xx, Map Book No. 84-81-xx		

Assessor's Parcel # 009-001-xx	Tax Year 200x-Oy	R.E. Taxes $ @. 1026
Neighborhood Name Mountain View Homes	Map Reference 48 C-x	Census Tract 246xx

Occupant ☒ Owner ☐ Tenant ☐ Vacant   Special Assessments $ None   ☐ PUD   HOA $ ☐ per year ☐ per month
Property Rights Appraised ☒ Fee Simple ☐ Leasehold ☐ Other (describe)
Assignment Type ☐ Purchase Transaction ☒ Refinance Transaction ☐ Other (describe)
Lender/Client   Sample Saving and Loan   Address   116 San Luis Blvd. Ventura, CA 930xx
Is the subject property currently offered for sale or has it been offered for sale in the twelve months prior to the effective date of this appraisal? ☐ Yes ☒ No
Report data source(s) used, offering price(s), and date(s).

Note: Race and the racial composition of the neighborhood are not appraisal factors.

Neighborhood Characteristics			One-Unit Housing Trends			One-Unit Housing		Present Land Use %	
Location ☐ Urban ☒ Suburban ☐ Rural			Property Values ☐ Increasing ☒ Stable ☐ Declining			PRICE AGE		One-Unit	60 %
Built-Up ☒ Over 75% ☐ 25–75% ☐ Under 25%			Demand/Supply ☐ Shortage ☒ In Balance ☐ Over Supply			$ (000) (yrs)		2-4 Unit	05 %
Growth ☐ Rapid ☒ Stable ☐ Slow			Marketing Time ☐ Under 3 mths ☒ 3–6 mths ☐ Over 6 mths			200 Low 0		Multi-Family	05 %
Neighborhood Boundaries This quiet rural neighborhood is bounded on the north by the coastal mountains;						350 High 30		Commercial	0 %
on the south by Main Street; on the east by Foothill Blvd; and on the west by the San Jon Barranca.						280 Pred. 22		Other	30 %

Neighborhood Description   The neighborhood enjoys an above-average prestige factor. Its natural setting, and overlook of the mountains are the
most favorable features. Municipal services are above average. City parks and recreation centers are within 1 mile, and elementary schools
are within 1/2 mile. Employment centers are within 2 miles, and unemployment rates here are below the state average.

Market Conditions (including support for the above conclusions)   After several years of moderate decline, the market prices in the subject neighborhood
have stabilized. No vacant houses are in evidence, and there are a typical number of 'for sale' signs seen. Marketing time has improved
from about 6 months, to a present average of 4 months.

- Is the growth rate rapid, stable, or slow?

2. *One-Unit Housing Trends (reflecting the form's use for appraisals of homes):*
   - Are property values increasing, stable, or declining?
   - Is supply/demand a shortage, in balance, or an oversupply?
   - Is marketing time under 3 months, 3–6 months, or over 6 months?

3. *For One-Unit Housing:*
   - What are the low, high, and predominant (most common) prices and ages of homes in the neighborhood?

4. *Present Land Use in Percent:*
   - One-unit residential structures
   - 2-4 unit residential structures
   - Multi-family structures (5+ units)
   - Commercial
   - Other

5. *Neighborhood Boundaries:* Explain if any market data is not within these boundaries!

6. *Neighborhood Description:* Is this a new subdivision, or an older commuter neighborhood? See how much you can say in the space available!

7. *Market Conditions:* This space gives the appraiser room to expand the discussion of issues that are particularly important to the analysis of this neighborhood and market.

Sources of Neighborhood Data

Neighborhood information is available from a number of sources. These include local government planning agencies, chambers of commerce, real estate brokers, and property management groups. In recent years, appraisers have also used online appraisal services and the Internet to locate neighborhood and community information. (See Chapter 8 for a discussion of data sources available to the appraiser.)

Factors Affecting Neighborhood Quality

Since every neighborhood offers different advantages to its inhabitants, neighborhoods are said to differ in quality. Although it may seem a complex idea, the quality of a neighborhood can best be judged in terms of the needs and standards of its occupants. For example, the desirable features of a residential district would be different from those of a commercial or an industrial district. Appraisers often rate the various aspects of a neighborhood by comparing them with features of **competing neighborhoods**.

The major factors that affect the quality of any neighborhood can be grouped as physical, economic, social, and political in nature.

Physical and Locational Factors

The physical factors that affect neighborhood desirability and quality include the natural features of a location, as well as those created by people. Natural features include topography, trees, lakes, and other visual amenities. Desirable views in a residential neighborhood are often the result of these features. Natural features that affect neighborhoods also include climate and geological conditions, such as weather, soil quality, and flood, slide, and earthquake zones. Examples of neighborhoods with negative value influences from such conditions include some in the fog belts in San Francisco and the flood zones of the central riverways of the country.

Physical features that have been created by people are also part of the locational attributes of a neighborhood. Thus, the desirability of a neighborhood depends in part upon how the occupants view its **present land uses**, development and **growth rate**, and the quality, age, condition, and style of its buildings. Other factors related to location could include:

1. Convenience to schools, employment, transportation routes, shopping, public health and medical facilities, and religious and recreation centers.
2. Adequacy of utilities and other public services.
3. General appearance and compatibility of properties.
4. Appeal to the market.

5. Absence of toxic wastes and other adverse environmental conditions.

Economic Factors

The first important economic factor to consider is whether the income level of the neighborhood occupants is sufficient to maintain existing structures. This strongly relates to employment opportunities available, as well as the stability of existing employment.

In residential neighborhoods, for instance, we might study housing costs as a percent of household income. In commercial neighborhoods, we might study store **sales volume** per square foot of building floor area. Generally, the greater the economic strength, the greater the neighborhood quality will be.

Other economic factors to consider include those just described in the neighborhood profile: growth rate, **trend of property values**, supply and demand, marketing time for properties, and **land-use changes** in evidence.

Social Factors

Neighborhood desirability is influenced by the many social characteristics of the occupants. This is because people often seek to be in a neighborhood whose occupants have interests similar to theirs. This is true for industrial neighborhoods as well as residential ones. For example, people with young children often want to live in a residential neighborhood where there are children of the same age as their children. Significant social factors for residential neighborhoods include lifestyles or standards, education, occupations, ages, and family makeup of neighborhood occupants. The predominant occupancy (whether renters or owner-occupants) and the rate at which occupants move (the turnover rate) also affect how a neighborhood is viewed.

The presence of neighborhood groups and organizations that take an active role in community affairs can be an important factor. For example, homeowners' associations (such as those found in condominium and planned unit developments) can be a positive feature in a neighborhood, as can neighborhood watch organizations. Area industrial groups can strengthen industrial neighborhoods, by supporting issues and concerns that the occupants share. For commercial neighborhoods, merchant associations can be a significant favorable influence!

Neighborhood desirability is also dependent on the effort and money that neighborhood occupants put into the maintenance and modernization of buildings. Community support for the existing legal and political order is also a factor. Neighborhood attitudes can influence political decisions, such as the amount of city services provided, tax rates, and the quality of the schools. Another neighborhood attitude that the appraiser might study is how the occupants rate the desirability of their own neighborhood, relative to other neighborhoods.

Political Factors

The level of property taxes, assessment fairness, police and fire protection and other city services provided, public education, and protective zoning or planning all have an effect on neighborhood desirability. The reputation of the school district, or of a particular public school, may have a big impact on value. Governmental positions on air, soil, and water pollution, job safety, social programs, and noise, odor, and ecological controls can also be noted. Many political factors are the ultimate result of social attitudes, either in the neighborhood that the appraiser is studying, or in the city as a whole.

Neighborhoods and Change

Every neighborhood, regardless of land use, goes through a series of changes over the years. These changes usually follow a pattern. The first phase occurs when the vacant land is subdivided, streets and utilities are installed, and the first buildings are constructed. Over time, most of the available land is built upon. This first phase in the life cycle of a neighborhood is called the *development phase.*

The second phase gradually begins as development slows down. It is called the mature or *stable phase.* The most significant feature of this phase is the relative stability of the existing buildings and occupants. This phase usually lasts for an extended period of time.

During the stable years, building maintenance and renovation generally keep up with the normal deterioration caused by weather and usage. In time, however, neighborhood occupants may postpone needed repairs. Then, the third phase, the *decline phase* or decay, begins. Regardless of the type of building or use, the effects of age continually attack the stability that is apparent in the second phase. The elements, insects, pollution, and human use of the building all cause wear and tear to the interior and exterior of structures. Over time, there is competition from newer neighborhoods and from new building designs, decorative finishes, or building layouts, which make the older neighborhood less desirable. The degree of neighborhood decline varies, as does the length of time until the beginning of the fourth phase.

The fourth phase of neighborhood change is called the renewal or *renaissance phase*: the transition to a new sequence of life for the neighborhood. Neighborhood renaissance can occur slowly or rapidly, and may have either private or government sponsorship or a mixture of the two. The renaissance phase will involve either of the following events:

1. Demolition or relocation of the existing buildings and development of the land with new buildings, often for different uses.

2. Major renovation of the existing buildings to correct maintenance problems and obsolete features. The buildings may continue in the same uses or be converted to new uses.

The four phases of neighborhood change, shown in Figure 4-2, form a life cycle that occurs over time in every type of neighborhood. In older, more stable cities, there is evidence to suggest that this cycle in some neighborhoods has been repeated several times. Sometimes, it even involves renovating the same buildings for similar uses over and over again for centuries! Georgetown, in Washington, D.C., is one such neighborhood.

Evidence of Neighborhood Change

Figure 4-2
The Four Phases of
Neighborhood
Change:
(a) Development.
(b) Stable.
(c) Decline.
(d) Renaissance.

As a neighborhood passes through each of the four phases of the *neighborhood cycle*, there are clear signs of transition. The transition from the growth phase to the stable phase, for example, is identified by a reduction in available vacant land and a decline in the rate of construction of new buildings—the *development rate*.

(a)

(c)

(b)

(d)

The transition from the stable phase to the declining phase is identified by gradual but marked changes in existing buildings. One common change is a decrease in the amount of building maintenance, with increasing deterioration visible. Often, there will be a change in the density of use, with more people occupying the same space. In commercial or industrial property, this increase in density often means that there will be smaller firms occupying a given building than in earlier years.

When the transition to neighborhood renaissance is marked by the renovation of individual structures, improved maintenance and increased remodeling are noted first at scattered locations, and then gradually spread throughout the neighborhood.

Sometimes, the transition into the renaissance phase is marked first by changes in the uses of existing buildings. As the new, higher-priced uses begin to prosper, some deteriorated buildings will be demolished and replaced. Substantial physical deterioration must be present if this phase is to be carried out by private capital, because well-maintained structures are usually too valuable to be demolished.

Neighborhoods as Barometers of Change

Why should you learn about the neighborhood cycle or about neighborhood changes? The reason is that the value of a property is influenced by the neighborhood around it. So, we study neighborhood changes in order to understand how and why a property's value is changing. Often, some other location in a neighborhood will show value changes *before* the changes actually reach the property being appraised.

The immediate neighborhood has the most impact on the value of the subject property. For most land uses, this immediate area will include the properties in the same block, on both sides of the street, plus those "across the back fence" and even those on the cross streets. Figure 4-3 shows the neighborhood locations that are likely to have the greatest impact on the property being appraised. Neighborhood locations that are farther away have a gradually diminishing impact on the value of a particular property.

Nothing is constant except change, so goes a common expression. Neighborhoods are always changing, no matter how stable they may seem. For example, normal wear and tear from age, the elements, and neglect continually act to reduce a declining neighborhood's condition, desirability, and value. However, as the neighborhood's occupants work to delay or halt such decay, they can often reverse the decline, thus improving the desirability and value of the location. So it is that all the positive and negative forces present in the neighborhood eventually lead either to the renovation of the existing structures, or to their decline and demolition.

**Figure 4-3
The Immediate
Neighborhood—One
Version.**

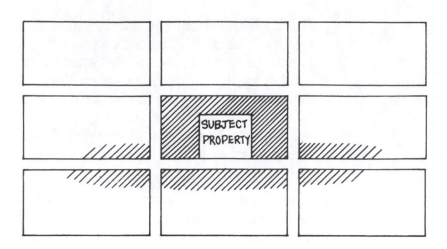

Cyclical changes in the neighborhood affect every property but usually at differing times. Noticeable change usually starts at the edge of a neighborhood, where land uses conflict with, or are different from, those of the adjoining neighborhood. Depending on the community reaction, the good or bad change may disappear, or may spread to the rest of the neighborhood. For this reason, appraisers look beyond the immediate area of the subject property, to the fringes of the neighborhood. They want to see what kinds of changes are occurring and how the neighborhood is meeting these changes. See Figure 4-4 for an example.

In summary, appraisers study a neighborhood in order to identify the various forces that are influencing and changing its character and desirability. These same forces are at work on the property being appraised, but often they are easier to see through their effect on other properties in the neighborhood. As we shall see, the appraiser uses this understanding of neighborhood change throughout the appraisal process.

Using Neighborhood Information

Why do appraisers need neighborhood information? The key reason is to define the geographic area that will be the center of the search for market data. Whether one looks for land sales, improved property sales, leases, costs, depreciation rates, or capitalization rates, the neighborhood around the property is almost always the starting point of the data search.

Another reason for studying neighborhoods is that it will assist you in defining what is referred to as the *highest and best use* of the property. While there are many possible uses of a property that may be legally and economically feasible, one particular use is considered the best. Recent history and trends in uses in a given neighborhood can tell the appraiser about the feasibility of various uses, as well as the

Figure 4-4
One Reason
for tudying
the Neighborhood.

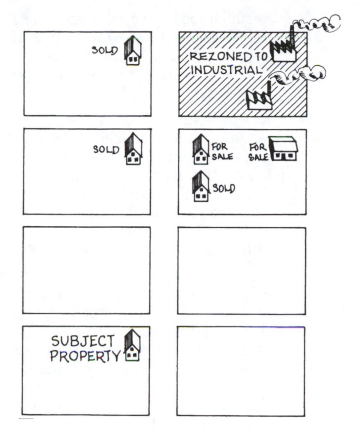

legal, social, and political constraints that may limit the success of a particular use. The term *highest and best use* will be more fully developed in later chapters.

The third reason for studying neighborhoods is really a part of the first reason. The neighborhood is the data source. It is here that the appraiser needs to find out whether, and by how much, to adjust the market data that have been gathered. Comparable sales might have occurred too many months ago to be useful without analysis, or might represent smaller or older structures than the subject property, or might be too far away. As a result, market data must often be adjusted to reflect such differences. The amount of such adjustment must be based on the importance of those differences in that particular market area or neighborhood.

In home sales, for example, the price of a property lacking a basement should probably be adjusted if the subject property does have a basement. This adjustment must be based on the importance of a basement in that market. In an industrial neighborhood, the amount of office area in a warehouse must be considered in light of warehouse office usage in that neighborhood. In considering the sale of a large house, the appraiser must keep in mind the general range of house sizes in the neighborhood, as well as trends in family sizes and incomes.

Neighborhood properties are rarely identical from one end of the neighborhood to the other. It is therefore important to understand how the various locations within the neighborhood may differ. Such knowledge helps the appraiser correctly use and adjust market information coming from different places within the neighborhood.

A significant problem arises when adequate information cannot be found within the subject neighborhood. When you lack sales of properties similar to the subject, you may need to use sales or information from other neighborhoods, communities, or even states. Then, you must try to understand each neighborhood, in order to adjust for the possible impact caused by the difference in location.

The Neighborhood Controversy

In the past, appraisers have been accused of using the process of neighborhood analysis to collect information that is entirely irrelevant to the appraisal, or is intended to prejudice. Some have even suggested that neighborhood analysis should be eliminated from the appraisal process. The controversy arises, it seems, from the failure of appraisers to define clearly how some neighborhood information is to be used. When its purpose is not clear, certain information collected may be challenged as irrelevant or no longer important. Reporting the race, creed, sex, handicap, familial status, or national origin of occupants is an example of information that is irrelevant to nearly all appraisal assignments.

In fact, the study of neighborhoods is at the heart of appraising and the estimation of market value. It is the study of the neighborhood that helps the appraiser discover what property characteristics are important to buyers and sellers in that location, and suggests the relative importance of such characteristics at any particular time.

4.2 Understanding Communities and How They Grow

All neighborhoods exist in relation to the social, economic, and political environment of a community. Understanding the origin, location, and layout of cities helps us understand the land uses within the community and the patterns of land use that tend to form. The factors that contribute to economic growth are especially important. As communities grow, they change in many ways. Community changes inevitably affect the values of individual properties.

Community Origins and Growth

Each community is located where it is for specific social, political, physical, or economic reasons. The town's original location in turn strongly influences its early physical layout. This early layout strongly influences how the town shape and layout change as it grows. For this reason, it is helpful for you to study **town origin** and growth.

Town Site Selection Factors

Historically, town locations were often selected because food and water were accessible, and the site could easily be defended against enemies. Some town sites were chosen for religious purposes. In America, most town sites were selected because of their commercial benefits. Often, the choice of a site was determined by the topography of the land, the availability of raw resources, and the transportation systems in use at the time.

Topography has always been one of the most important factors in the selection of a town site, because it usually determined where the existing transportation routes would be. In turn, these routes influence the accessibility of the land for habitation. Topography has particularly influenced the location of towns whose major function was to provide services along transportation routes.

The availability of raw resources has long been a major factor in choosing the location for some town sites. Resources with a low value for their bulk, such as copper ore, were usually processed near the mine, creating an industry. This processing industry often grew into a town site. Resources that had a high value per ton, or per unit of size, could be shipped without processing. Thus, some processing towns did not need to be as close to the mine. The total number of mines in an area also determined where processing was to take place, so the town site remained just a small mining town or else grew into a larger village.

Finally, the choice of location, especially for water-transport towns, depended on the form of transportation system in use at the time of the town's founding. If shallow-draft paddlewheel schooners were in use, a shallow, sheltered dock was sufficient for the site. When ocean-going steamers came into use, deep-water docks became necessary. Wind shelters were also critical for protection from storm waves. These examples show how the requirements for success as a town site constantly change.

Types of Towns

In America, towns and cities usually fit into one of three types, depending on the major functions that they serve. These are (1) the **central town**, (2) the **transportation-service town**, and (3) the **special-**

**Figure 4-5
Three Central Towns
in North Carolina and
Their Trade Areas
(From Urban Land
Use Planning,
Copyright 1979 by
Board of Trustees.
Used with
permission of the
University of Illinois
Press).**

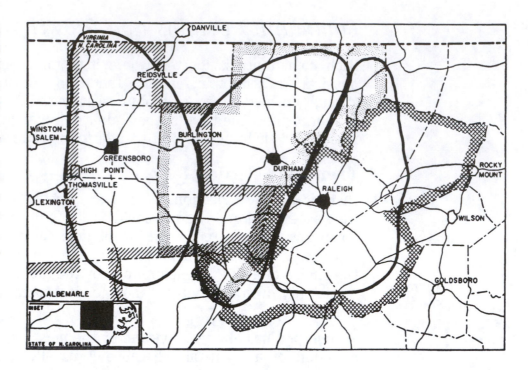

function town. Figure 4-5 shows a map of three central towns and their respective trade areas.

The central town is one that performs a variety of services for a surrounding area. The area is first developed, usually for farming, with widely scattered residences. The need for a place to buy supplies, and locate churches and schools, soon leads to the formation of a town. The town grows in population as a result of the expansion and profitability of the farming.

The transportation-service town is one that is selected to provide services along a transportation route, as noted above. Usually, these towns are situated at points called *nodes*. Nodes are points where transportation routes split or shift, or where a change in the type of transportation occurs. Typical nodes include ports, major rail intersections, freeway intersections, forks of navigable rivers, and mountain passes. San Francisco, California, is an example of a transportation-service town (see Figure 4-6). Early maps of this seaport town show existing buildings heavily clustered around the port area. Transport service towns may also develop at a place where transportation systems must be maintained. For example, a number of railroad water stops in the western United States have become cities, including San Bernardino, California, and Logan, Utah.

Special-function towns are those that concentrate on one special service or purpose, as does a mining town, a government seat, or a retirement community. Other examples include resort towns and university towns. Figure 4-7, on page 96, displays some examples of special-function towns.

(a)

(b)

Figure 4-6
Port of San Francisco:
(a) Golden Gate
Bridge; (b) Typical
Cargo Terminal.

Changes in City Function

As a town grows, it can change from one functional type to another. Pittsburgh, Pennsylvania, was founded at Fort Pitt, beside a major river fork, as a point of control over the commercial transportation in the area (then consisting entirely of riverboats). It was first a transportation-service town. Later, good coal and iron ore deposits were found nearby, so Pittsburgh became a resource-oriented iron mill town. The nearby iron and coal are now exhausted, but the workers' skills and the huge mills allowed Pittsburgh to continue for many years as a special-purpose, resource-oriented manufacturing town.

Economic Growth

Once a town comes into being, its continued existence depends on whether the town is an economic success. No town or community today is self-sufficient. The cars, electronics, food, and other commodities we use come from other towns, and we must pay for them. It follows that the many costs of imported goods and services must be paid for, with money earned by sales of the town's own products and services to other towns. Each town must perform some economic function: make products, mine a natural resource, or perform a service. Usually, whatever this economic function is, a portion of the product or service will be for sale or for use in the town. This is called *local production*. More important, however, is the surplus production that is sold to other towns and called *export production* (see Figure 4-8, on page 97). Export production forms the economic base of the town. The growth of towns, then, depends on the richness of the town's basic resources (e.g., ore bodies, timber stands, and agricultural fields) plus the skills, creativity, and industriousness of its workers.

Each community tends to develop a specialty, usually related to the town's origin. This specialty can be a product or a skill. When we

(a)

(b)

**Figure 4-7
Special-Function
Towns: (a) University
Town; (b)
Government Town;
(c) Retirement
Community.**

(c)

compare one town with another, or one region with another, we can see differences in the products that are made in each town or region and in how the population is employed. These differences reveal the special products or skills that provide the ***economic base*** for the town or region. We use this knowledge of the economic base activities to study the likelihood of population growth or decline, the relative stability of employment, or the future of particular neighborhoods economically tied to the area's exports.

Physical Patterns of the Community

As towns grow, the different land uses in the community form patterns. As we noted in our discussion of neighborhoods, each use often con-

Figure 4-8
Local and Export
Production.

centrates at one location, because the various users choose the most advantageous location for each use. The various uses compete for each location, and the use that gains the most from a particular location outbids the other uses, dominating that location.

Each site has unique advantages and disadvantages for each use. This forms the principle of **comparative advantage**. The various neighborhoods, each with their characteristic uses, make up the land-use pattern of the community. It should be remembered that the pattern may change over the years, in response to changing social and economic influences.

Major Factors in Land Use

A number of factors influence the **land-use patterns** and the locations of new buildings in a community. Four factors are especially important. Each, however, is to some extent connected to the other.

1. *Topography:* the shape and slope of the land and its natural features, such as rivers, swamps, and lakes. Topography usually determines transportation routes and good building sites.

2. *The town's origin:* where the town started and why. Both the functional origin and the physical point of origin of a community are determined by topography, transportation, and natural resources. In turn, the town's origin is a major factor in the subsequent development of the town site.

3. *Transportation systems:* how people and goods move around. Early transportation systems, such as walking, pack animals, and carts, allowed random movement in any direction, which contributed to the circular shape of towns. But as transportation systems became more sophisticated, the shape of towns changed. Of all four

factors, transportation is the most important in creating change in the pattern of land use, as you will see in our discussion of current trends in the following pages.

4. *Major existing uses:* the presence of major buildings, or concentrations of buildings, continues to attract people, even when the original reason for selecting the location of these buildings no longer exists.

Typical Patterns

The most common land-use pattern is the cluster of commercial uses at the intersection of major transportation routes (the *node* idea again). In small villages, commercial buildings at the crossroads become the downtown area. In towns larger than a small village, the number of land uses in the downtown area increases, to the extent that the area around the crossroads becomes divided up into different zones of uses. Although the prime commercial uses remain at the main intersection, the pressures of the town's growth eventually drive residences to the outskirts of town. High rents and values in the prime commercial area tend to cause offices, government buildings, schools and less profitable commercial uses to move away from the main intersection and gradually fill in the intermediate area of the town.

As this process continues, the town pattern begins to look like a series of rings around the downtown area. The prime commercial zone forms the inner ring, followed by a ring of office, government, and wholesale buildings. This ring, in recent years, has included a growing number of apartment buildings. The next ring contains older houses with some conversions to offices or boarding houses, and some new structures moving out from the second ring. The fourth ring consists of single-family residences, with the newer homes on the outer circumference. Figure 4-9 shows this pattern of concentric rings.

As **concentric rings** form around the downtown section of many cities, various factors often cause each ring to break into segments or become segmented. Depending on the existing uses and the topography of the ring, each segment will have some different uses from the other segments in the ring. Often service, some retail, wholesale, and manufacturing uses will concentrate in segments on one side of the downtown, with offices and higher-priced retail stores on the other. Particular segments on the outer rings will be favored for high-priced new homes, perhaps because of good views, favorable surroundings, or close proximity to older luxury homes. Mid-priced new homes will usually be located on the remaining segments of the outer ring. Usually, the high-priced commercial ring segment will line up with the high-priced home segment, as Figure 4-10, on page 100, demonstrates.

The concept of perfect concentric rings is somewhat oversimplified, but it still serves as a good analytical tool. Land-use patterns can be so

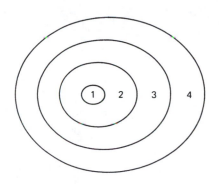

**Figure 4-9
Typical Patterns of
Land Use: Concentric
Rings(Dennis
J. McKenzie and
Richard M. Betts, The
Essentials of Real
Estate Economics,
5th ed., South-
Western Publishing,
Mason, Ohio, 2006).**

dominated by topography (as in the San Francisco Bay area) that the ring looks more like a cucumber! Economic-use patterns are also altered by personal motives. People sometimes hold on to their old family homes despite economic pressures to sell or to convert to commercial uses. In general, however, the pattern of land uses shows a strong concentric ring relationship, which is especially noticeable in small cities.

Current Trends

The early transport systems (walking or horse-drawn) were replaced by streetcars traveling on fixed lines, forming fixed linear routes. This change caused urban land-use patterns to change gradually from concentric to linear, as city growth began to follow the fixed-rail lines. Automobile transportation came next, and at first encouraged a return to the earlier patterns of random movement and circular cities. But arterial roads and freeways soon carried more traffic than regular city streets, and cities developed an even more linear pattern.

Now, as the arterial roads and freeways of large cities intersect, each major road intersection forms a node, where a commercial cluster often develops. In turn, small concentric rings often form about the cluster.

To summarize, in modern cities, locations for new developments are chosen more by proximity to transportation lines than by the distance from the downtown. Thus, the concentric circles that we discussed above are altered in larger cities that have freeways, thruways, expressways, arterials, streetcars, subways, and so on. Now, commercial uses often form linear strips instead of rings. Each major intersection develops its own minor ring. Service industries and warehouses often adjoin the linear strip or occupy districts far removed from the old warehouse district. So we can understand why the pattern of uses in most of the larger modern cities does not look like a series of concentric rings, but rather like an irregular spider web or a tangled pattern of yarn. The outline of the city itself, instead of being circular, is likely to look more like a star with a number of points. Figure 4-11 is an example.

**Figure 4-10
Segmented Rings
(Courtesy of the
California
Department of Real
Estate).**

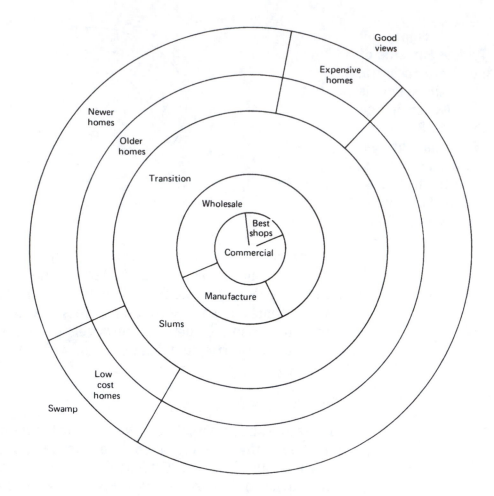

Using Information about Communities

As the appraiser looks at the community and region surrounding the property being appraised, the scope and amount of information may appear to be staggering. Countless data about political, social, economic, and physical aspects of the community might be collected. In order to select the most relevant information, the appraiser must have a clear concept of how and why this information is to be used.

The appraiser uses regional and community information for several reasons. The first is that some community forces and trends affect the trends in the neighborhood. For example, if the town is growing, residential neighborhoods close to downtown could be under pressure to become locations for stores or offices. Understanding these community trends helps you to interpret what is happening in the neighborhood, and possibly how to adjust sales from further away.

Second, some community trends can affect all the real estate markets in the community. For example, prices of all types of property in all neighborhoods in a town may decline if a dominant employer shuts down, or prices may increase if a large factory opens up. Understand-

**Figure 4-11
The Modern Star-
Shaped City(Dennis
J. McKenzie and
Richard M. Betts, The
Essentials of Real
Estate Economics,
5th ed., South-
Western Publishing,
Mason, Ohio, 2006).**

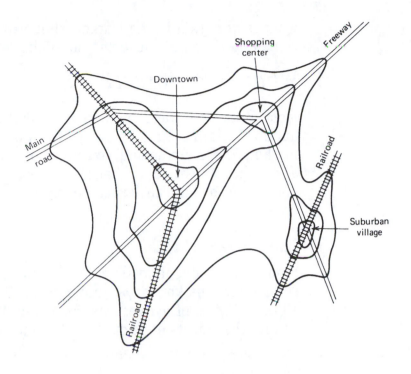

ing this second type of community trend helps you decide which sales occurred in market conditions that are similar to those on your date of value. For instance, in the case of an unexpected factory closure, sales prices for homes sold prior to the factory closing may differ from prices after the closing is announced.

In summary, understanding community origins and the patterns of growth helps the appraiser to analyze the economic and political factors affecting the subject property and its neighborhood. Some of these factors affect the entire community. Other influences may affect properties and values over a smaller area. Notice that as the area you study gets smaller, the focus on the community gradually changes to a neighborhood study, as discussed earlier in this chapter.

4.3 Real Estate Markets and Their Analysis

Since appraisals usually involve estimating market value, appraisers must understand real estate markets. Knowing the state or condition of the market will help you in different ways. It will help you when you select the market data to use in the appraisal. Sometimes the market data that are selected may have defects. Frequently, such defects are caused by market imperfections. If appraisers have a solid grasp of what is going on in the market, they can often detect these imperfections and thereby reduce the possibility of error.

What Is a Market?

Most of us have some impression of what a market is. We have seen an auction, a farmer's market, or pictures of the trading floor of the stock market. These are general examples of a market: a place where buyers and sellers meet to exchange goods or services. The concept of a market also has an exact technical definition, based on several criteria.

The Perfect Market

From the study of markets has come the concept of the perfectly competitive market, or **perfect market**. It is a standard against which all other types of markets are compared. The perfect market is defined as one that meets each of the following criteria:

1. There are numerous buyers and sellers.
2. All parties are knowledgeable.
3. All parties are free to trade or not trade.
4. All products are similar and interchangeable.
5. All products can be transported to better markets.
6. Items are small, inexpensive, and frequently purchased.
7. The government plays a very minor role in pricing.

Markets such as the stock market come close to being perfect markets. In such markets, prices move continuously, both up and down, and neither seller nor buyer can control the price movement.

Imperfect Markets

Many markets cannot meet the seven tests of a perfect market that we have listed. These markets are referred to as **imperfect markets**. For example, in some imperfect markets, such as for uncut diamonds, there are very few sellers. These sellers tend to fix prices, and there is little price fluctuation. A limited number of sellers is one type of problem that causes imperfect markets.

Another common feature of imperfect markets is the inadequate knowledge of buyers and/or sellers, either about the product itself or, more often, about true conditions in the market. The lack of adequate knowledge means that buyers and sellers are not able to make good decisions, so that when added information is finally obtained, price or location decisions turn out to have been wrong. When more information about a product becomes available, prices change. Some people get information ahead of the general market and use this information to their advantage and profit. When this occurs, the profits are made at the expense of those who lack full information.

Real Estate Markets

We can see, from reviewing the definition of a perfect market, that real estate markets are not perfect markets. In fact, real estate markets are often used by economists as examples of imperfect markets—the other extreme—because real estate markets do not meet any of the seven requirements for a perfect market.

At any one time in real estate markets, there are relatively few buyers and sellers for any one type, price range, and location of real property. Neither buyer nor seller is usually very knowledgeable, because the product, real estate, is complex and not as commonly bought and sold as other commodities. Both seller and buyer are often anxious to complete the deal, in order to get housing or to buy another property. Available properties are not very similar or interchangeable. Practically speaking, they cannot be transported to a better market, should the local market be poor. The properties are not small or inexpensive, and are not frequently purchased by most market participants. Surveys of buyer characteristics reveal that few people have made more than a half-dozen real estate purchases in their lifetimes. Finally, real estate pricing is strongly influenced by government actions. FHA financing and income tax benefits, for example, tend to help buyers; at the same time, property-use controls, such as development restrictions, zoning, building permits, and so on, tend to restrict the activity of buyers and sellers alike.

Because of the imperfection of the real estate market, prices for real estate do not rise or fall as smoothly or rapidly as do, for example, stock prices. Thus, in the real estate market, individual sales can occur well above or below the prices that would occur with a more perfect market. A unique price can result when there is a poorly informed buyer or seller, or when there is some unique characteristic of the property from the point of view of the typical buyer. To illustrate the latter, there are relatively few buyers willing to pay a proportionately high price for a large house (e.g., 3,500 square feet) if it has only one bedroom. To the right buyer, a relatively high price could be reasonable. To most buyers, however, the price would have to be considerably lower to be attractive.

Since real properties are so complex, many factors can influence prices. These factors vary in importance, depending on the place, time, or property type. Consequently, real estate markets are much more varied and unique than, say, bond markets.

In the real estate market, each subcategory of property is somewhat distinct from the others. Homes in Michigan may not sell at the same price as identical homes in California, for example. Within California, prices in the community of Alturas (in the northeast corner of the state in remote Modoc County) will have limited if any connection to prices in Sacramento, about 200 miles away.

Market Analysis and Interpretation

Why does the appraiser need to analyze and interpret the market? Fundamentally, it is to find out what is happening in the marketplace surrounding the subject property. In the appraisal process, the appraiser uses the knowledge and understanding of market activity in three critical ways: (1) to help decide what kinds of market data to collect and what adjustments to make, (2) to estimate a reasonable *marketing time* for the subject property, and (3) to report on current marketing conditions and trends that may affect future value, projected or forecasted income, and/or the absorption period for income-producing or multiple-unit properties.

For our study purposes, market behavior can be divided into three parts, namely, (1) *price levels*, (2) *price trends* or movement, and (3) the levels or volume of market activity.

Price Levels

The most obvious aspect of market activity to be examined is the level of prices. By comparing prices with current costs for new construction and lot prices, we can see how the market may eventually increase or deflate the value of older homes. We can also see whether this price change varies with the type of building, location, or market. Studying such market information helps us interpret the available market data.

We can also compare prices for other reasons. For example, within a neighborhood, we could compare prices and see the effects on sales prices of building age, size, an added half-bath, a swimming pool, or a view. On the other hand, by comparing prices paid for similar properties in different locations, we can learn how the market views the relative desirability of these locations.

Price Movements

The appraiser can learn even more by studying trends or price movements, rather than just price levels. In studying price movements, we see which way prices are changing, and how fast, and whether there are differences between various markets. The direction and speed of price movements tell us how strong or weak a particular market is. It tells us the state of *supply-demand balance*. We can also compare the strength of that market with our knowledge of the community's economy. This sharpens our understanding of what economic forces may be causing prices to change. For example, we might find that a city has two high-priced residential neighborhoods, but one has declining prices while the other has stable or increasing prices. As a result, data from these two markets will have to be interpreted differently. Upon further study, we may be able to develop an idea of why the difference is occurring. Perhaps the declining neighborhood previously catered to wealthy central-city commuters, who are now residing farther out. Perhaps the other neighborhood attracted local professionals who have not been as quick to move to the distant suburbs.

We might also want to compare the direction and speed of current price changes with past price changes, or with price movement in other price ranges and in other types of real estate. Is the rate of price change speeding up, slowing down, or staying the same? Answers to such questions may shed additional light on the appraisal problem at hand.

How do price changes compare with construction cost changes? If the price changes are greater, then we can see that either builder profits or land prices may be going up. If they are less, then land prices and builder profits may be under pressure.

This study of the direction and speed of price movements will demonstrate again and again a need to compare real estate trends to trends in the general economy. Are real estate prices going up faster than general prices? Than new construction costs? What about lot prices? Raw land prices? As we develop an understanding of the cost approach, we shall see that a change in the price of a completed house *must* involve changes in the prices of some or all of the elements that go into making up the house.

Levels of Activity

The appraiser should also study how active the market is. In real estate markets, we noted above that prices do not always respond smoothly to minor shifts in seller supply or buyer demand. Prices may move smoothly upward, as the general real estate price increases in many recent decades have demonstrated, or they may literally jump, as they did in many areas from 2003 to 2005. However, when real estate prices are under pressure to move downward, an irregular pattern is more typical.

When downward price pressures develop, what usually happens first is that buyers refuse to buy at the old prices. In a more perfect market, prices would slowly start to fall. In real estate markets, however, what often happens is that sellers try to wait this period out, hoping for an offer every day. Many eventually withdraw their property from the market, rather than sell for less. As a result, the volume of sales may fall off dramatically.

In a stagnant market, the first clue to where the market is heading is the declining number of sales, rather than a decline in prices. In time, either buyers will return to the market at old price levels, or the more anxious sellers will cut prices and entice a buyer into purchasing. If buyer resistance continues, then sellers may go through a wave of repeated cuts in listing prices without tangible results. When the sales finally do occur, they often will be a step lower than prior sales. Therefore, we might want to compare the current volume of sales with the volume in the past for that type of property. Is the volume up or down, and by how much? A key measure is how the sales volume compares to the number of listings! Has this relationship changed?

The patterns of listing activity can also help us decide what is happening in a market. How long is it taking to sell property? Are many listings expiring, unsold? Have there been many asking-price reductions for the current listings? Have owners of current listings received any offers? How low or high were the offers relative to the listing price?

Finally, we are interested in the buyer activity just as much as we are in the seller's listings. What is happening to the number of lookers? How many people are showing up for open houses, compared to earlier times? Are many people coming back for a second look?

There are several unusual patterns of activity levels of buyers or sellers that you might find. One pattern consists of increasing numbers of lookers, sometimes also with declines in the numbers of listings or with listings being withdrawn by the sellers. These signs can indicate a market condition in which an upward price jump could be forthcoming. This would be a different pattern of activity than for a stable market or one with smoothly moving gradual price changes.

The third pattern is the troubled market, as generally experienced starting in late 2006. As we observed above, when a real estate market turns downward, prices usually do not turn downward smoothly. Instead, list prices are often maintained at the old levels, while buyer activity declines, often substantially. When sales finally occur, they are often at lower prices. Such transitional markets are a challenging time for appraisers.

In the absence of sales close to the date of value, then, the appraiser may not want to use the earlier sales by themselves. What may be needed is a careful study of recent listing activity, and the reasons behind the absence of sales at that time. Activity levels are perhaps the most sensitive measure of the state of real estate markets.

SUMMARY

In the first section of this chapter, we discussed the concept of the neighborhood and its importance to appraisers. Although the neighborhood can be defined in a number of ways, it is, in general, an area whose occupants or users share some common ties or characteristics. Economically, neighborhood boundaries are set by where the characteristics and benefits of a location change. The neighborhood's quality depends on how well the neighborhood serves the land uses, and how the occupants maintain the neighborhood.

Neighborhoods go through a series of changes over the years, starting with the development of the initial buildings, then a phase of stability, which is followed by a third phase of decline. The fourth phase, called the renaissance, is the transition to a new life sequence, either by rehabilitation or by demolition.

Appraisers study the neighborhood because it leads to an understanding of the forces affecting the values of the subject property. The locations immediately around the property being appraised are the most important to study, because they will have the most direct impact on the subject property. However, locations at the periphery of the neighborhood are also important to study, because changes in a neighborhood tend to start at one edge and move inward. The neighborhood study is used to define the center of the market-data search area. It helps estimate the highest and best use of the property and establish what types of adjustments to the market data will be desirable.

This chapter then discussed community origins and growth. The influence that the town's origin plays in its future growth was first described. Origins of American communities were usually commercially motivated. Growth of the town depended on its commercial success in developing some resource, product, or skill to trade to other communities for goods which the local town could not produce.

As towns grow in size, predictable patterns emerge for the various land uses. The major influences affecting these patterns are the town's origin, its topography, the transportation systems in use, and the attraction of existing major buildings. The simplest pattern is the cluster of commercial uses at the main intersection. As towns become bigger, the cluster becomes a series of rings around the major downtown intersection, and the rings of similar uses then break up into different segments of slightly varied uses. Depending on transportation systems, the circles can be distorted by linear-strip commercial zones, making larger cities more star-shaped. This study of the community enables the appraiser to better understand trends in the community that are affecting property and its value.

The third section of the chapter focused on markets. First was a definition of the elements of a perfect market, followed by a description of the flaws that produce imperfect markets. Real estate markets were shown to be almost classic examples of imperfect markets.

The appraiser studies real estate markets for information to help interpret market data needed for the appraisal. Price levels, for example, are compared in order to estimate the price difference between properties of different sizes, ages, and so on. Price movements tell even more about the market. We can compare prices at different times, for different areas or types of property, or against changing prices in other parts of the economy. In some cases, levels of sales activity can be the most significant factor if there are no sales around the date of value. All this information helps the appraiser to correctly understand and adjust the many types of market data and to report on market trends and likely marketing time, as required for the appraisal report.

IMPORTANT TERMS AND CONCEPTS

Central town

Comparative advantage

Competing neighborhoods

Concentric rings

Decline phase

Development phase

Development rate

Economic base

Export production

Imperfect markets

Growth rate

Land-use changes

Land-use patterns

Local production

Marketing time

Neighborhood

Neighborhood bonds, or linkage

Neighborhood boundaries

Neighborhood cycle

Perfect market

Present land uses

Price levels

Price trends

Renaissance phase

Sales volume

Shared identity

Special-function town

Stable phase

Supply-demand balance

Topography

Town origin

Transportation-service town

Trend of property values

REVIEWING YOUR UNDERSTANDING

1. A neighborhood can be defined as:
   a.   A group of properties with very dissimilar land uses
   b.   An area in which the occupants and users share some common ties and characteristics
   c.   An area of a city that contains similar land uses within a defined location or boundary
   d.   Both (b) and (c)

2. "Shared identity" can mean:
   a.   Some characteristic of a neighborhood that is common to most of the inhabitants, land uses, or buildings
   b.   Some common characteristic of the occupants
   c.   Whatever shared characteristics create a common bond
   d.   All of the above

3. The boundaries of a neighborhood might be determined by:
   a.   An economic change in use
   b.   Physical features such as lakes, rivers, or freeways
   c.   Zoning or city limits
   d.   Two of the above
   e.   All of the above

4. The four phases of the neighborhood cycle are:
   a.   Development, stable, decline, and renaissance
   b.   Development, stable, demolition, and renaissance
   c.   Demolition, decline, renaissance, and stability
   d.   Renaissance, stability, decline, and demolition

5. The three most common types of towns and cities in America include all of the following except:
   a.   The central town
   b.   The shopping town
   c.   The transportation-service town
   d.   The special-function town

6. The factors that have the most influence on the patterns of land use of a community include all the following except:
   a.   The town's original location
   b.   The social systems
   c.   The transportation systems developed
   d.   The natural topography

7. A perfect market occurs when:
   a.   There are numerous buyers and sellers who are knowledgeable and are free to trade or not trade
   b.   All products are similar and interchangeable and can be transported to better markets
   c.   The items are small, inexpensive, and frequently purchased, and the government plays no role in pricing
   d.   Two of the above
   e.   All of the above

8. Real estate markets are imperfect because:
   a.   Real estate markets can be easily exchanged
   b.   They meet none of the criteria of a perfect market
   c.   They meet some of the criteria of a perfect market
   d.   Most real estate sales are resales of used property

9. Appraisers use all except one of the following to study and interpret market activity:
   a.   Price levels
   b.   Margin of profits
   c.   Price movements
   d.   Levels of market activity

10. Appraisers study neighborhoods:
    a. To define the geographic area that will be the center of the market data search
    b. To assist in the highest and best use study
    c. To understand how to adjust market data
    d. All of the above

PRACTICAL APPLICATIONS

As we will remind you at the start of each exercise, review the exercise at the end of the preceding chapter, and the work that you have performed to date.

The focus for this assignment is on the community and the neighborhood. As a starting point, review Figure 4-1, in this chapter, which shows you the neighborhood portion of the URAR form. Identify the information that you seek to find, in order to complete your own form. Next, consider what resources are available to you to obtain that information!

The "Neighborhood Characteristics" and "Present Land Use" checkboxes should be filled in based on your understanding of the area around your subject property. For the "One-Unit Housing Trends" checkboxes, you might review recent articles in the local newspapers, or ask a real estate agent in your neighborhood. The "One-Unit Housing" section, asking for price and age characteristics, could involve checking listings in the neighborhood on http://www.realtor.com, or other listing web sites. "Neighborhood Boundaries" ties back to the likely location of your comparable sales, which you have not selected yet. So, it would be desirable to define this widely enough to include where your comparable sales are to be found. The "Neighborhood Description" section is intended to be a short narrative description. See how much you can say, using as few words as possible! And the "Market Conditions" section allows you to expand, in narrative fashion, about the trends you have checked off above.

Finally, start up the software program and open the file that you saved after the prior chapter's assignment. Note that you have already entered the basic information about the property and the assignment! Now you want to fill in the neighborhood section, using the information that you have just gathered.

As we note at the end of each exercise, it is best not to get ahead of yourself! So, do not enter information in the later sections of the report until you have read the chapter(s) that covers that topic! However, it is a good idea to look ahead at the coming sections of the form, so that you start thinking about the information that you will need to gather! And it is certainly reasonable, and even desirable, for you to start collecting some of that information early, if you choose to do so!

Reminder: If you have questions about the program itself, please be sure to review the manuals and help information that were included with the program CD. Also, at anytime, you can go to http://www.bradfordsoftware.com, click on "Services" at the upper right of the home page, and then on "ClickFORMS Training Programs" in the middle of the "Services" page. See the free online training section!

CHAPTER 5
REAL ESTATE ECONOMICS AND VALUE

PREVIEW

Real estate is a basic and fundamental form of wealth. All of our material possessions can be traced to their beginnings in the land. We seek to understand how real estate is developed, adapted, distributed, and utilized in order to understand the economics of real estate. In turn, this gives insight into its value.

The value of real estate is created and modified by the many physical, economic, social, and political forces that act on it. In this chapter, we describe these basic forces, discuss economic trends affecting real estate, and outline the economic principles that govern appraisals.

OBJECTIVES

When you have completed this chapter you should be able to:

1. List the four basic elements of value.

2. List and give examples of the broad forces that affect value.

3. Define real estate cycles.

4. Name the major supply and demand factors that are involved in economic changes affecting real estate.

5. Describe the federal government's role in the economy.

6. Explain how the principles of value relate to the marketability and productivity of real estate.

5.1 The Real Estate Value Influences

Real estate has no *intrinsic* value. That means it has no value in and of itself. Instead, the monetary value of real estate is derived from the rights and benefits that come from its ownership, possession, and use.

As you learned in Chapter 2, such rights are referred to as real property rights. When real property rights are bought and sold in the market, the values of such rights are measured by the prices that are paid for them.

For any object to have market value, certain essential elements must be present. A review of these elements is necessary if we are to understand the basic forces that influence the value of real estate.

Four Essential Elements of Value

In the context of the market, there are only four basic elements behind the market value of any object. Sometimes referred to as prerequisites, these elements are:

1. *Utility*: usefulness; the ability to create a desire for possession.
2. *Scarcity*: in relatively short supply; a lack of abundance.
3. *Demand*: the desire to possess plus the ability to buy; *effective purchasing power*.
4. *Transferability*: the ability to change the owner or use; *marketable title*.

All of the listed elements must be present before an object can have value in the marketplace. An object must be useful, and at the same time scarce, for there to be any measurable benefits from owning it. For example, desert sand and ocean water are useful for certain purposes, but because they lack scarcity, they have little market value. Modern new houses and office buildings are extremely useful objects for human activity, but a serious oversupply of such buildings would without question reduce their market price. Why? Because oversupply is the opposite of scarcity.

Where does demand fit in? For any item to have value there must be people ready, willing, and able to buy it, at some price. Utility and scarcity cannot create a market unless there is demand, and the purchasing power to implement it. And if an object does not have transferability, the demand is ineffective. For example, a parcel of real estate that lacks marketable title can have no value in the market, because rights to its use cannot be transferred. In summary, utility, scarcity, demand, and transferability interact in combination to create

**Figure 5-1
Basic Elements
of Market Value.**

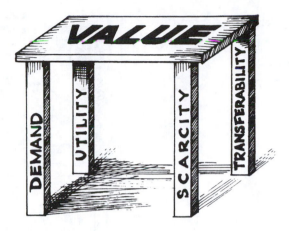

the condition that we refer to as **market value**, which is demonstrated in Figure 5-1.

Broad Forces Influencing Value

As we explained previously, real estate has market value when it meets the four criteria or tests listed. In turn, that market value is influenced by four broad groups of forces, acting to increase or decrease value. These forces are labeled as physical, social, economic, or political in nature (see Figure 5-2). In their many forms and combinations, these forces result from, or involve, all aspects of human behavior. The forces produce effects at both national, regional, community, and neighborhood levels. Understanding these forces and their activity at each level helps us to see why the nature and value of real estate are constantly changing.

Physical Forces

Because they are the most visible, the **physical forces** (or factors) affecting value are perhaps the easiest to understand. Some of them are natural and others are caused by people. Examples include:

1. *Natural resources:* the land itself, its topography, soil characteristics, access, and location; climate, air, and mineral resources (including water); plant and animal life; and scenic beauty and ecological balance.

2. *Developed resources:* the size and shape of land parcels; existing structures for human occupancy, commerce, and industry; public utilities, communications systems, and health and safety facilities; street and road improvements, highways, airports, waterways, and harbors; public transportation and recreation systems; and facilities for education and cultural pursuits.

**Figure 5-2
Forces Affecting
Value.**

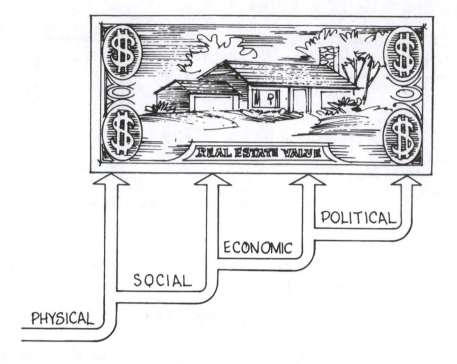

Social Forces

The *social forces* affecting value include all of the characteristics and customs of the people that make up the community. Here is a partial list:

1. *Demographics:* the distribution of family sizes, incomes, education levels, and age-groups in the various neighborhoods and communities.

2. *Neighborhood stability:* attitudes about property use and maintenance.

3. *Population:* growth, decline, or shifts at the community, regional, and national levels.

4. *Lifestyles and living standards:* often combined with other forces.

5. *Attitudes:* behavior, law enforcement, the role of government, and individual responsibility.

6. *Attitudes:* development, growth, environmental protection, and ecology.

7. *Attitudes:* public education.

Economic Forces

Our earlier discussion of the essential elements of market value mentioned interactions among utility, scarcity, and demand. These elements are, to a large extent, the products of our constantly changing economic climate, discussed further in Section 5.2. Thus, the major *economic forces* affecting real estate include:

1. *Income levels:* neighborhood and community residents.
2. *Employment:* opportunities and trends.
3. *Wages and jobs:* wage levels and types of jobs in the community.
4. *Money and credit:* availability and interest rate levels.
5. *Price levels* and the burdens imposed by property taxes and property insurance premiums.
6. *Personal savings:* levels and investment returns.
7. *General business activity.*
8. *Supply and demand for housing.*
9. *Production of goods and services.*

Real estate appraisers and analysts often study information from many of these areas to help identify economic trends. The importance of credit and interest rate levels to real estate values must be stressed.

Political Forces

In Chapter 2, you learned about the authority of the government to restrict the use of property, to impose taxes to fund government expenditures, and to regulate property to promote the safety and welfare of the general public. Besides the limitations and burdens placed on property by the police power and taxation, there are many government programs that stimulate private enterprise and help create a healthy business climate (see also Section 5.2). High employment, general economic stability, and business opportunity are partially the result of government involvement in our economy.

Whether regarded as positive or negative, the various government actions can be classified as ***political forces***. They have a far-reaching effect on the value of real estate. A partial list of political forces affecting value includes:

1. Zoning and land-use regulations.
2. Building and safety regulations.
3. Environmental protection laws.
4. Endangered species acts.
5. Police, fire, and health protection services.
6. Crime prevention, education, and recreation services.
7. Public works: power and water, (sometimes by private companies that are delegated authority by the government), transportation, sewers, and flood control.
8. Fiscal policy (discussed in Section 5.2) and taxation.
9. Monetary policy and controls (also discussed in Section 5.2).
10. Government-sponsored urban redevelopment and housing finance programs.
11. Regulation of industry and business.

In summary, the four great groups of forces that maintain, modify, or destroy real estate value are known as physical, social, economic, and political forces. As you can see, these forces overlap; many factors appear under more than one category. For example, "availability of money" is listed under economic forces. Note that this same factor is heavily influenced by what is called "monetary policy and controls," under the category of political forces. Even though the factors overlap and the forces interplay, carefully itemizing all relevant factors within each force can help the appraiser better understand the conditions affecting property to be appraised.

5.2 How Economic Trends Affect Real Estate

It is difficult to overstate the importance of real estate in the national economy. First, it represents approximately *two-thirds* of the net worth of the country. Second, it is an essential part of the production process, since money or rent is universally paid for its use. Third, real estate is a major employer. Real estate development, construction, finance, management, and brokerage provide employment for a large segment of the population, accounting for billions of dollars of national income.

It is obvious that real estate does not exist in a vacuum. In today's electronic age, national and international events can instantly change the social, economic, and political climate in which real estate functions. Economic trends and cycles are an important part of this climate.

Economic Trends and the Business Cycle

An economic *trend* is a pattern of changes, continuing in the same direction, in some aspect of the economy. A *cycle* is a pattern of up and down, repeating changes. The most important national economic trends and cycles are those that affect the supply of, and demand for, goods and services. Examples include the balance of foreign trade, commodity price levels, and change in the annual gross domestic product.

National trends and cycles in the economy often help explain trends or cycles that we can observe at local levels. Understanding economic trends and cycles at the regional, community, and neighborhood levels helps the appraiser interpret the market, cost, and income data that are pertinent to a particular appraisal. The local economic cycles or trends that are important to real estate involve such factors as plant production, employment, construction activity, deed recordings, and the general volume of business. Changes in employment, income, price levels, interest rates, and production have the greatest effect on real estate activity (see Figure 5-3).

Information relating to economic trends and cycles is available from many banks, savings and loans, trade associations, and private research organizations. However, most statistical information on the economy is obtained from government agencies, such as the Federal Reserve, the Department of Commerce, and the Bureau of the Census. Statistical information on the economy is also available from *Economic Trends*, a monthly publication of the Council of Economic Advisors of the U.S. President. (For a list of data resources on the Internet, see Chapter 8, Section 8.3.)

Cycles

Many important changes are cyclical in nature. This means a change that repeats itself. Some economic changes repeat in a seasonal pattern. Whether at the national, regional, or local levels, these usually are caused either by weather or social customs. For example, construction activity declines during the winter in many parts of the country. Travel and recreational activities typically increase during the summer. Retail sales volume often experiences a surge during the "back-to-school" and Christmas seasons.

Figure 5-3
All Employees on Nonfarm Payrolls 1990–2006 (Bureau of Labor Statistics, Current Employment Statistics survey, January 5, 2007).

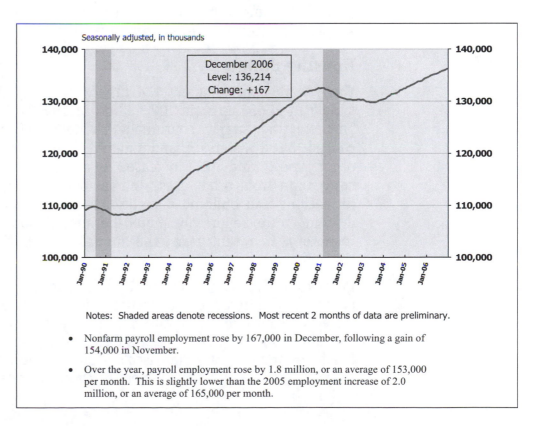

Notes: Shaded areas denote recessions. Most recent 2 months of data are preliminary.

- Nonfarm payroll employment rose by 167,000 in December, following a gain of 154,000 in November.

- Over the year, payroll employment rose by 1.8 million, or an average of 153,000 per month. This is slightly lower than the 2005 employment increase of 2.0 million, or an average of 165,000 per month.

The well-known **business cycles** are made up of expansions and contractions of general business activity. These cycles repeat on an average of every four years or so. Business cycles involve a series of stages. Prosperity increases to a point of stability, then declines, and a recession of the general economy follows. Finally, a recovery leads to growing prosperity, starting the cycle again. The length of the cycle is the time between one peak and the next.

The **real estate cycle** refers to the repeating changes noticeable in many areas of real estate, including the number of new subdivision lots, amount of new construction, and volume of sales. Some economists have contended that there are long real estate cycles, lasting about 18 years. Recently, however, recurrent changes in real estate seem to involve a shorter cycle of three or four years in duration. Although our understanding of real estate cycles is incomplete, we note that the short cycle often relates most directly to the cost and availability of money. Even so, a reduction in the cost of money does not always stimulate a lagging real estate market.

Real Estate Supply Factors

In order to understand the supply of real estate, we must study both existing and new facilities. This is a major difference from studying the supply of, say, strawberries or other perishables. Usually, we must consider residential property separately from commercial and agricultural property. Some of the more important factors in this supply are listed and briefly discussed here.

Housing Supply

There were approximately 124 million housing units in the national supply in 2005, up from 102 million in 1990, and 37 million in 1940. This existing supply continually changes because of (1) decreases caused by disasters, abandonment, demolition, and conversion to other uses, and (2) increases resulting from new construction, conversion from other uses, and remodeling. To allow for new family formations and building demolitions, the annual construction of new dwelling units reportedly should be approximately 3% of the existing inventory. In recent years, the annual net additions have been below this amount.

Protecting the supply of existing housing is a matter of national concern. Hundreds of neglected and abandoned inner-city homes have been brought back into use in recent decades by neighborhood revitalization programs, often subsidized by state and federal funds. Examples include San Francisco's Western Addition and the Pico and Normandy Redevelopment Project in the Los Angeles area.

New Construction Activity

The volume of new construction spending in the United States is a good measure of conditions in this industry and the changing supply of real estate. Since 1989, annual new construction spending (not adjusted for inflation) has increased from $477.5 billion to $1,143 billion in 2005, the latter amount representing about 9% of the value of all goods and services produced in the nation.

Historically, the cost of construction has followed general price levels, increasing during times of inflation and declining somewhat during recessions. Added costs for labor and materials that are used in energy-efficient heating, cooling, and insulating systems are causing an overall upward trend. Construction costs increased by about 8.2% per year between 1971 and 1981, but only by about 3% per year on average since that time. Product substitution (e.g., the trend toward replacing traditional wood framing material with less costly recycled wood, composites, and steel studs) plays a role in helping to keep costs under control. Higher construction costs tend to discourage development.

The Supply of Vacant Land

Political and social changes have greatly influenced the availability and cost of vacant land for real estate development. For example, as important as they were, many environmental protection and subdivision reform laws, starting with the Federal Clean Air Acts of the early 1970s, had the effect of decreasing the supply of buildable land. In turn, this decreased supply tended to increase the price. So did "open-space" and scenic easement agreements, wherein landowners agreed to restrict land to agricultural use in exchange for preferential property tax treatment in California and a number of other states. "No-growth" or limited-growth local planning, coupled with time-consuming public approval procedures, have also increased the cost and reduced the supply of subdivided lots in many areas.

Real Estate Demand Factors

Earlier in this chapter, we described *demand* as one of the essential elements of value. The two dominant demand factors that affect the real estate market are *population* and *purchasing power*. Although these two factors are obviously related, we shall try to look at them one at a time.

Population

All other things being equal, the demand for housing and other forms of real estate increases in direct relationship to any population growth. Since there is a limited supply of land on earth, an increase in demand for real estate usually results in higher land prices. Thus, population increases usually mean higher real estate values.

Our interest in population change is not just in the increase or decrease in numbers that may occur at a particular location. In projecting housing needs, we also study the composition and makeup of households. Thus, certain population characteristics like birthrates, age, sex, occupation, and family income are important. The study of such characteristics is known as **demography**. It is possible to estimate from this data the rate of formation of new families and the likely changes in household composition. In turn, knowing this information, we can predict specific future demands for various types of housing, in terms of size, desired features, and price range.

Americans are often on the move—from city to suburb, country to city, or city to country; North to South or East to West, and so on. Legal and illegal immigration also plays a role. The resulting migratory shifts continually affect the growth or decline of population in many communities. Population studies must therefore consider migration and immigration patterns, as well as the national population growth factors already mentioned.

Purchasing Power

Population increases mean higher real estate demand only to the degree that the population has purchasing power. One measure of purchasing power is the size of the national labor force. The Bureau of Labor Statistics (BLS) makes long-range predictions in this area. These are based on birthrates, mortality rates, migration and worker-participation rates, all of which can be estimated from the national census information and other statistical data. According to BLS figures, the U.S. civilian labor force grew from January 1989 to December 2005 in round numbers from 126 million to 150 million, showing an annual increase of about 1%. While this growth is significant, it represents a slowing from the higher rate of 2.5% per year for the period 1972–86, when unusually large numbers of both young people and women were entering the work force.

Another important influence on purchasing power is the annual change in the value of the **gross domestic product (GDP)**. A gauge of the strength of our economy, the GDP measures the value of all domestic goods and services produced in the country. After adjusting for inflation, the annual variations in the GDP ranged from a 2% decline to a 9% increase, in the years after World War II. Since 1996, the annual growth rate of the GDP has ranged between 3.4% and 4.2%, reflecting a very strong economy. Note that the growth rates are normally figured in constant dollars (i.e., adjusted for inflation). See Figure 5-4.

Statistics on employment, wage levels, and family income relate even more directly to the purchasing power of the American consumer. These figures allow economists to estimate the amount of money the average family has available to spend after paying taxes. This is often called "disposable income" or "per-capita spendable income." Since the major share of it is spent on living necessities, including housing, disposable income is significant to the potential demand for real estate. Other statistical figures used to study purchasing power include consumer-price-level indexes, land-use and city-growth figures, and industrial-expansion rates. Many economists pay close attention to the relative rates of increase of inflation and disposable income. When disposable income increases faster than inflation, the real estate demand tends to be strong.

Purchasing power is also very dependent on the availability of money for mortgage financing, usually arranged by mortgage brokers, savings and loan associations, banks, or insurance companies. The supply of money is largely dependent on the annual amount of personal savings, foreign investment in this country, and the general prosperity of the nation. As we shall see, the supply of money is also greatly affected by the monetary policy of the Federal Reserve System and the fiscal policy of government.

Federal Government Activity

Since real estate is our greatest national resource, the government makes use of programs that impact real estate, in order to pursue many of its social and economic goals. The areas of federal government activity that most directly affect privately owned real estate include housing and urban development, environmental protection and energy, monetary policy, and fiscal policy. We shall discuss these programs individually.

Housing and Urban Development Programs

The federal government has developed a number of programs that impact and promote real estate. Through the Department of Housing and Urban Development (HUD), the U.S. government encourages both low-rent housing and urban renewal projects. By stimulating new construction, the government helps to create jobs, trying to attack social and economic problems at the same time. Figure 5-5 is an example of a HUD program.

A number of federal agencies fall within the HUD sphere of influence, including the Federal National Mortgage Association (FNMA) and the Federal Housing Administration (FHA). FNMA (also known as Fannie Mae) is particularly significant. It is a private corporation, but sponsored and controlled by the government. FNMA buys mortgages from originating lenders, freeing up lender money to make more

PERCENT CHANGE FROM PRECEDING PERIOD IN REAL GROSS DOMESTIC PRODUCT

Line		1995	1996	1997	1998	1999	2000	2001	2002	2003	2004	2005
1	**Gross domestic product**	**2.5**	**3.7**	**4.5**	**4.2**	**4.5**	**3.7**	**0.8**	**1.6**	**2.5**	**3.9**	**3.2**
2	**Personal consumption expenditures**	2.7	3.4	3.8	5.0	5.1	4.7	2.5	2.7	2.8	3.9	3.5
3	Durable goods	4.4	7.8	8.6	11.3	11.7	7.3	4.3	7.1	5.8	6.4	5.5
4	Nondurable goods	2.2	2.6	2.7	4.0	4.6	3.8	2.0	2.5	3.2	3.6	4.5
5	Services	2.6	2.9	3.3	4.2	4.0	4.5	2.4	1.9	1.9	3.5	2.6
6	**Gross private domestic investment**	**3.1**	**8.9**	**12.4**	**9.8**	**7.8**	**5.7**	**- 7.9**	**- 2.6**	**3.6**	**9.8**	**5.4**
7	Fixed investment	6.5	9.0	9.2	10.2	8.3	6.5	- 3.0	- 5.2	3.4	7.3	7.5
8	Nonresidential	10.5	9.3	12.1	11.1	9.2	8.7	- 4.2	- 9.2	1.0	5.9	6.8
9	Structures	6.4	5.6	7.3	5.1	- 0.4	6.8	- 2.3	- 17.1	- 4.1	2.2	1.1
10	Equipment and software	12.0	10.6	13.8	13.3	12.7	9.4	- 4.9	- 6.2	2.8	7.3	8.9
11	Residential	- 3.2	8.0	1.9	7.6	6.0	0.8	0.4	4.8	8.4	9.9	8.6
12	Change in private inventories	—	—	—	—	—	—	—	—	—	—	—
13	**Net exports of goods and services**	—	—	—	—	—	—	—	—	—	—	—
14	Exports	10.1	8.4	11.9	2.4	4.3	8.7	- 5.4	- 2.3	1.3	9.2	6.8
15	Goods	11.7	8.8	14.3	2.2	3.8	11.2	- 6.1	- 4.0	1.8	9.0	7.5
16	Services	6.3	7.2	5.9	2.9	5.6	2.9	- 3.7	1.9	0.0	9.7	5.1
17	Imports	8.0	8.7	13.6	11.6	11.5	13.1	- 2.7	3.4	4.1	10.8	6.1
18	Goods	9.0	9.3	14.4	11.7	12.4	13.5	- 3.2	3.7	4.9	10.9	6.7
19	Services	3.3	5.5	9.4	11.4	6.9	11.1	-0.3	2.1	0.0	10.0	2.8
20	**Government consumption expenditures and gross investment**	**0.5**	**1.0**	**1.9**	**1.9**	**3.9**	**2.1**	**3.4**	**4.4**	**2.5**	**1.9**	**0.9**
21	Federal	- 2.7	- 1.2	- 1.0	- 1.1	2.2	0.9	3.9	7.0	6.8	4.3	1.5
22	National defense	- 3.8	- 1.4	- 2.8	- 2.1	1.9	- 0.5	3.9	7.4	8.7	5.9	1.7
23	Nondefense	- 0.4	- 0.7	2.6	0.7	2.8	3.5	3.9	6.3	3.4	1.2	1.1
24	State and local	2.6	2.3	3.6	3.6	4.7	2.7	3.2	3.1	0.2	0.5	0.5

Figure 5-4
Gross Domestic Product, Annual Percent Change, Real Dollars (U.S. Department of Commerce, Bureau of Economic Analysis).

loans. In turn, FNMA groups these mortgages into pools, and sells bonds and other securities backed by the pools of mortgages and paid off by mortgage loan payments. Originally, FNMA was a government body, set up to develop such a *secondary market* for loans. It was so successful that it was turned into a private entity.

As further evidence of its success, others followed. Most notable is Freddie Mac, chartered by Congress in 1970 as the Federal Home Loan

**Figure 5-5
Government Housing
Project Under
Construction.**

Source: Photograph Courtesy of Doug Frost.

Mortgage Corporation. Fannie Mae, Freddie Mac, and others have developed an extremely robust secondary market for loans. Now, thousands of loans are effectively traded every working day, allowing lenders ready access to more funds to loan.

Energy and the Environment

The federal government has vested authority in the Environmental Protection Agency (EPA) to enforce federal pollution standards. The government also attempts to control the quality of air, water, and coastal-zone ecology by the requirement of environmental impact studies for major proposed real estate developments and uses. State and local regulatory agencies sometimes carry out federal mandates in this area through their own elaborate regulatory activities. The Department of Energy was formed by Congress in 1977 to develop and carry out an overall plan to encourage the efficient use of existing energy sources and develop new ones. One of the more direct effects of the program has been felt in the housing industry, where solar-energy systems, electronic pilot lights, energy-efficient appliances, and minimum insulation standards were promoted. Income tax credits and preferential loan incentives have also been used, in order to increase the demand for energy-efficient homes.

Governmental Banking and Monetary Policy

The Federal Reserve System was established in 1913 as a semi-independent government agency. The function of the Federal Reserve Bank ("The Fed") is to regulate banking and the flow of money and credit. Today, the Federal Reserve System's goals are to stabilize the economy and control inflation, recession, and unemployment. The actions that the Federal Reserve Bank takes are called *monetary policy* actions.

An economic theory called the ***monetary theory*** holds that the supply of money in circulation influences the level of the economy—too much money leads to rapid economic expansion and resulting inflation; too little money causes an economic slowdown and recession or depression. The Federal Reserve Bank seeks to control the supply of money by buying or selling government securities, changing the *discount rate* (the interest rate the Federal Reserve Bank charges member banks for loans), and changing the amount of cash reserves that the Federal Reserve Bank requires member banks to hold. Because the Federal Reserve Bank controls the supply of money, the actions of the Fed affect the supply of money for financing real estate and change the cost of money—the interest rate. Changes in interest rates, in turn, change the market price of real estate. High interest rates tend to depress prices; low rates tend to increase them. The Federal Reserve Bank's Board of Governors and its Open Market Committee are constantly fine-tuning the money supply as they try to maintain a stable economy.

Another agency, the Federal Deposit Insurance Corporation (FDIC), insures most consumer deposits at banks. Similar smaller agencies insure most deposits at savings and loans and credit unions. In an indirect way, the regulatory activities of the FDIC help to assure the availability of funds from its member banks and thrifts and other covered lenders.

Fiscal Policy

Our government also uses its taxation and spending powers to moderate recession, inflation, and unemployment, and to further the aims of various social reform programs. This is called the ***fiscal policy*** of government. In recent years, the annual federal government expenditures exceeded two trillion dollars, up from a mere $479 billion in 1979. In times of recession, income taxes fall (as personal income declines). Lower income tax payments plus increased government spending means more money in the hands of consumers, acting to stimulate the economy and increase the demand for land, labor, and capital. During periods of a strong economy, often with inflation, reduced government expenditures and increases in income taxes tend to reduce consumer income and demand, thus reducing the pressure on prices and cooling inflation.

Real estate and business have long been favored areas for government programs designed to stimulate the economy. Home ownership has been encouraged by allowing the mortgage interest payments and property tax payments to be deducted for income tax purposes. Real estate and business investments sometimes benefit from various income tax advantages, including some interest and depreciation deductions for real estate holdings.

The fiscal policy of government works parallel to its monetary policy. For example, the government provides money for private real estate loans (through Federal Reserve money supply actions), besides insuring FHA loans and guaranteeing Department of Veterans Affairs (VA) loans. As the state of the economy dictates, our federal government modifies its fiscal policy in well-publicized "tax-reform" acts that have become a familiar part of our economic system. Since the government budget has generally operated at a deficit in the majority of recent years, fiscal policy has sometimes had inflationary effects, which monetary policy has attempted to counteract with varying degrees of success.

In summary, it might be said that our economic environment is increasingly the result of governmental laws, regulations, controls, and policies that are intended to benefit the general public and to promote social equality. Although economists may disagree on the effects, and therefore the desirability of such extensive government involvement, it appears that government laws and regulations will continue to shape and reshape our real estate economy.

5.3 The Economic Principles of Valuation

The economic principles of valuation are based on time-tested theories about real estate as both a *form* of and a *source* of wealth. As a form of wealth, real estate competes in the market with other goods and services that consumers might elect to spend money on. As a source of wealth, real estate combines with other economic forces and agents to produce income and other amenities for its users. Economic principles define and predict basic market patterns in both the use and development of real estate.

The principles of value covered in this section are the foundation for all appraisal methods and procedures. The principles apply collectively; none is independent. However, those that relate to real estate marketability especially help us understand the procedures and methods of the sales comparison and cost approaches. Those principles that relate to real estate productivity assist us primarily in understanding the various techniques of the income approach to value. Again, be aware that the principles are often interrelated, as are the three value approaches (see Chapter 3).

Principles of Real Estate Marketability

Real estate marketability is based on the following six principles:

1. *Principle of substitution*.
2. *Principle of conformity*.
3. *Principle of progression* and *principle of regression*.
4. *Principle of change*.
5. *Principle of supply and demand*.
6. *Principle of competition*.

Principle of Substitution

When a property easily can be replaced by another, the value of such a property tends to be set by the cost of acquiring an equally desirable substitute. A house listed at $250,000 will tend to sell in the range of $200,000, if there are others with the same amenities available for that lesser figure in the neighborhood. On the other hand, this same house might be worth only $185,000, if a similar one could be created nearby at that figure—including the cost of the lot and the construction—within a reasonable period of time. Because it is a tool for comparing market price, cost, or income, the principle of substitution is a basic concept behind each of the three approaches to value.

Principle of Conformity

In many markets, maximum value results when properties in a neighborhood are relatively similar in size, style, quality, use, and/or type. This depends primarily on local market attitudes, but is particularly true in a relatively stable area of average homes. The rule of conformity predicts that a five-bedroom home in a neighborhood of three-bedroom homes, for example, would probably be an *overimprovement*. This means that its value would be less than if it were in a neighborhood of similar five-bedroom homes.

For high-valued homes or other relatively unique types of properties, or in a higher-demand market, much less importance is placed on the conformity of physical features. Also, in some markets, a greater amount of conformity is demanded than in others.

Principles of Progression and Regression

Lower-valued properties generally benefit (increase in value) from close proximity to many properties of higher value. This illustrates the principle of progression. Conversely, higher-valued properties tend to suffer (decrease in value) when placed in close proximity with many lower-valued properties, following the principle of regression. The principles of progression and regression, which are related to the principle of conformity, assist us mainly in the analysis of sales in the sales comparison approach.

Principle of Change

Change is eternal. Changes in physical, social, economic, or political conditions constantly modify real estate use and value patterns. As suggested in Chapter 4, economists have a theory that neighborhoods, cities, and nations experience change in four stages, not surprisingly described as development, stability, decline (or old age), and renaissance (or rebirth).

The appraiser must always view real estate and its environment as in transition. Since important changes might be either sudden or gradual, current market conditions cannot always be measured by assuming that past trends will continue unchanged. All things change, even the rate of change!

Principle of Supply and Demand

Prices and rent levels increase when demand is greater than supply, and tend to decrease when supply exceeds demand. In real estate, a strong demand for housing, for example, if coupled with effective purchasing power, can logically lead to a short supply and higher prices. When builders and developers increase production to meet demand, the new supply tends to force prices back to "normal." If severe competition among builders occurs during the shortage, oversupply often results, leading to a weakening of prices. In time, attractively low prices serve to bolster demand, until the excess supply has been absorbed. Theoretically, when supply and demand are in balance, market prices reflect the cost of production, when a reasonable profit is included. As we saw earlier in this chapter, a large number of factors affect the supply and demand of real estate.

Principle of Competition

Market demand generates profits, and profits generate competition. When there is a strong demand for any form of real estate (as in houses, apartments, and commercial or industrial facilities), developers and builders will compete for the profits that are available by constructing new units for sale or rent. Competition usually holds down profits and keeps them stabilized. However, if excess profits are available, "ruinous" competition can result, which sometimes leads to oversupply and the collapse of prices.

Principles of Real Estate Productivity

The following five principles relate most closely to the productivity of real estate:

1. Agents of production.
2. Principles of surplus productivity, balance, and contribution.
3. Principle of increasing and decreasing returns.
4. Principles of highest and best use and consistent use.
5. Principle of anticipation.

Agents of Production

The benefits produced by real estate come in many forms. These may be intangible *amenities* (benefits not directly measured in money), as is true for certain benefits of home ownership, or they may be tangible, as in the case of dollar returns on real estate investments. In economic terms, all such benefits are considered as the returns on real estate production. Such production always requires the use of *labor*, *coordination*, *capital*, and *land*. These are known as the four agents (or factors) of production. The balance between these factors critically affects the ability of any property to serve the purpose for which it was intended. To understand the potential value of real estate, we must define the four *agents of production* and understand their economic priorities (see Figure 5-6).

Labor includes the cost of all operating expenses and all wages except management. In economic theory, it has the first claim on all money generated by production. *Coordination*, or management, includes charges for management and entrepreneurial effort. Such services have the second claim on returns of the enterprise. *Capital* includes

**Figure 5-6
The Agents
of Production.**

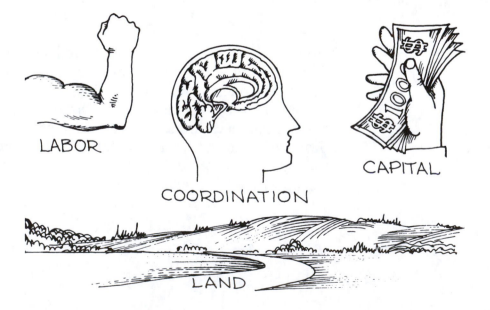

LABOR

COORDINATION

CAPITAL

LAND

all construction and equipment costs. Capital charges include return on, and repayment of, such investment monies. Capital charges have the third priority on production returns. **Land** includes the land, minerals, and airspace. Economically, it has the last claim on production revenues. This is why returns to the land are sometimes called "residual," because they refer to what is left over after all other claims have been satisfied. The concept of economic agents of production is the basis for many of the principles that follow.

Principles of Surplus Productivity, Balance, and Contribution

The net income or other benefits that remain after the cost of labor, coordination, and capital have been satisfied have been described as the "residual" returns to land. These same land returns are often referred to as the **surplus of productivity**. Since the value of land depends on its own earning power, the dollar amount of this surplus income becomes the basis for land value.

According to the **principle of balance**, a proper balance in the agents of production is required if the maximum value is to result from the costs invested. Consistent with the principle of conformity, an overly expensive home built on a marginal lot in a lower-income neighborhood probably could not be sold for the full amount invested. A less expensive home is more likely to sell for its full cost and would represent a better investment.

In a similar way, the value of any individual agent of production depends, not on its cost, but on how much it contributes to the value of the whole. This is the **principle of contribution**. For example, a swimming pool that adds $10,000 to the resale value of a home would only have a value of $10,000, even if it cost the owner $25,000 to construct.

The principle of surplus productivity forms the basis for the **principle of increasing and decreasing returns** and the **principle of highest and best use**.

Principle of Increasing and Decreasing Returns

It is possible to increase the value and potential income of real estate by adding appropriate improvements. However, there is a theoretical point of balance. Beyond that point, additional expenditures will not result in proportional added value or income. This general rule is important in understanding the economics of development and investment for profit. If a builder can make a 20% profit by developing a small tract of large houses, such a project would be preferred to a larger tract of small houses where only a 15% profit might be made. Even if the larger subdivision promised a greater dollar profit, the higher percentage profit would generally be favored. In actual practice, the investment decision would probably be based on a careful market study, and also on comparison with the other investments available to the builder. The classic illustration of decreasing returns is in farming, where added increments of fertilizer and labor do not result in equal increases in crop yield. After a point, no matter how much fertilizer is added, no added production can be obtained.

Applied to existing properties, the principle of increasing and decreasing returns helps property owners make decisions about adding improvements or remodeling. If the market value of a home can reasonably be expected to increase in proportion to the cost of a bedroom and bath addition, for example, the needed changes can be economically justified.

Principles of Highest and Best Use and Consistent Use

The highest and best use of a property means its most profitable or beneficial use. Such a use represents the theoretical balance between land and building investment. It results in the greatest present value of the land during the economic life of the improvements or structures. The principle of highest and best use is helpful in estimating land value and in making land-development feasibility studies.

In appraisal, the highest and best use should typically be estimated both for the land as if it were vacant, and also for the property as improved on the date of value. Whether the two uses are different or the same will have a major impact on all three value approaches, both as to the data selected and also how they are analyzed.

As a corollary to the principle of highest and best use, the **principle of consistent use** requires that land and improvements be appraised on the basis of the same use. As a matter of economic consistency, it might be improper, for example, to add the "value" of a single-family structure to the value of the lot as if vacant, where the lot in question has an obvious highest and best use as an apartment site. In reality, the home could even have a negative value, to reflect the cost to demolish it in order to redevelop the lot.

Principle of Anticipation

Property has value according to its expected or anticipated use, as measured by the benefits that should result from such use. A buyer with full knowledge of "the uses and purposes to which a property may be put" is concerned with the future use and not just the previous use. The price he or she is willing to pay, then, is said to be equal to the present worth of such future benefits. Some of the benefits may be in the form of intangible amenities, as in the case of home ownership and use, or they may be in the form of tangible benefits, such as rental income or capital gain. The **principle of anticipation** underlies the income approach to value.

SUMMARY

Although real estate is a basic and fundamental form of wealth, it has no intrinsic value. Its market value is a measure of the rights that the owners control, valued at prices set in the market. But in order to enter the market, the rights must have the four elements of *utility*, *scarcity*, *demand*, and *transferability*.

Four broad groups of forces maintain, modify, or destroy real estate value. These major forces are *physical*, *social*, *economic*, or *political* in nature. In their many combinations and forms, always changing, these broad forces account for the dynamic nature of real estate value.

National and international events constantly change the social, economic, and political climate of our country. An understanding of real estate and its position in the national economy can help us understand the effect of these events.

We know that real estate is affected by changing business conditions, such as employment, income and price levels, production volumes, and building construction costs. Thus, it is possible to analyze and better understand real estate by observing key supply and demand factors in the general economy. Economic trends often tend to be cyclical in nature.

We have seen that the federal government is heavily involved in areas vital to real estate. These include finance, housing and urban development, environmental protection, and energy.

In this chapter, we also discussed in detail the economic principles that form the basis of most of the methods and procedures we use in appraisal. The principles that relate primarily to the marketability of real estate include the following concepts:

Substitution

The value of any replaceable property tends to equal its cost of replacement. As a tool for comparing market prices, costs, or income, this principle underlies all three approaches to value.

Conformity

A reasonable degree of conformity is required for maximum value to result. A serious lack of market conformity in size, style, quality, or use type can be detrimental to value, particularly in single-family residential properties.

Progression and Regression

When a property does not conform in size or quality, its value tends to seek the level of the surrounding properties.

Change

Real estate values are constantly changed by the many social, economic, and political changes that occur in our society.

Supply and Demand

Real estate prices tend to increase when effective demand exceeds supply, and tend to decrease when supply is greater than demand.

Competition

Market demand creates profits, and profits generate competition. In turn, competition decreases profits, because new supply tends to overshoot the demand.

The valuation principles that relate mainly to the productivity of real estate primarily help the appraiser understand the income approach. They are summarized here.

Agents of Production

All real estate production depends on the use of the four agents of production: labor, coordination, capital, and land.

Surplus Productivity, Balance, and Contribution

Income that is available to land, after the other economic agents have been paid for, is known as the surplus of productivity. A proper balance of the agents maximizes the income available to land. The value of any agent is determined by its contribution to the whole.

Increasing and Decreasing Returns

Income and other benefits from real estate may be increased by adding capital improvements, but only up to the point of balance in the agents of production. Beyond that point, the increase in value tends to be less than the cost increase.

Highest and Best Use; Consistent Use

The most profitable, likely use of a property is its highest and best use. If the existing use does not qualify in this respect, consistency requires that the appraiser recognize this fact in the method used to value the existing structures.

Anticipation

Value is the present worth of future benefits, whether they are in the form of income or intangible amenities. The principle of anticipation is fundamental to the income approach to value.

Theory is no substitute for practical experience. But neither can any appraiser always expect his or her intuitive knowledge to suggest or recall just the right approach or procedure for every valuation problem.

When properly applied, the economic principles can suggest ways to solve the typical problems encountered by the real estate appraiser.

IMPORTANT TERMS AND CONCEPTS

Agents of production

Amenities

Business cycle

Demography

Economic forces

Fiscal policy

Gross domestic product (GDP)

Market value

Monetary policy

Monetary theory

Overimprovement

Physical forces

Political forces

Principle of anticipation

Principle of balance

Principle of change

Principle of competition

Principle of conformity

Principle of consistent use

Principle of contribution

Principle of highest and best use

Principle of increasing and decreasing returns

Principle of progression

Principle of regression

Principle of substitution

Principle of supply and demand

Purchasing power

Real estate cycle

Scarcity

Secondary market

Social forces

Surplus of productivity

Transferability

Utility

REVIEWING YOUR UNDERSTANDING

1. One of the essential elements of value is:
   a. Highest and best use
   b. Transferability
   c. Location
   d. Environmental control

2. Which of the following is ineffective without purchasing power?
   a. Utility
   b. Supply
   c. Demand
   d. Level of wages

3. The broad forces affecting value do not include:
   a. Physical
   b. Price trend
   c. Political
   d. Social

4. Political forces affecting value may include:
   a. Lifestyles and living standards
   b. Topography
   c. Education and recreation facilities
   d. None of the above

5. The real estate supply factors include:
   a. Housing supply
   b. New construction activity
   c. Both of the above
   d. None of the above

6. Environmental protection and changed subdivision laws that affect the availability and cost of vacant land include:
   a. The Federal Clean Air Acts of the early 1970s
   b. "Open-space" requirements
   c. Zoning changes to require larger lot size
   d. All of the above

7. Areas of government activity that directly affect privately-owned real estate include:
   a. Housing and urban development
   b. Environmental protection laws
   c. Monetary and fiscal policy
   d. All of the above

8. The fiscal policy of government is concerned primarily with:
   a. Urban development
   b. Interest rates
   c. The gross domestic product
   d. Government spending and taxation

9. The four agents of production do *not* include:
   a. Land
   b. Waste
   c. Coordination
   d. Labor

10. The principle that would prevent an appraiser from appraising a lot for its commercial value and the existing improvement for residential value is the:
    a. Principle of increasing and decreasing returns
    b. Principle of consistent use
    c. Principle of highest and best use
    d. Principle of anticipation

PRACTICAL APPLICATIONS

As we will remind you at the start of each exercise, review the exercise at the end of the preceding chapter, and the work that you have performed to date.

The focus for this assignment is on the economy and how it may be affecting the data that you will soon be collecting and analyzing. As a starting point, review Chapter 5 and think what you believe that you know about the economy of your community and the economics of your neighborhood. Consider what added information about the community or the neighborhood you could obtain to improve your understanding.

Review the information that you have filled in for the neighborhood, in performing the exercise for the last chapter. Review the discussion about that exercise at the end of that chapter.

Finally, start up the software program, and open the file that you saved after the Chapter 4 assignment. Note that you have already entered the basic information about the property and the assignment, as well as the neighborhood section. Review this information for accuracy.

Next, review what information will be needed to fill in the next section of the form, and start thinking where to get it.

As we note at the end of each exercise, it is best not to get ahead of yourself! So, do not enter information in the later sections of the report until you have read the chapter(s) that covers that topic. However, it is a good idea to look ahead at the coming sections of the form so that you can start thinking about the information that you will need to gather. And it is certainly reasonable, and even desirable, for you to start collecting some of that information early, if you choose to do so.

Reminder: If you have questions about the program itself, please be sure to review the manuals and help information that were included with the program CD. Also, at any time, you can go to http://www.bradfordsoftware.com, click on "Services" at the upper right of the home page, and then on "ClickFORMS Training Programs" in the middle of the "Services" page. See the free online training section!

CHAPTER 6
PROPERTY INSPECTION AND ANALYSIS: THE SITE

PREVIEW

This chapter takes you through the actual site inspection, describing how each step is performed. You will learn how to prepare for the inspection, why a highest and best use analysis is critical to the appraisal, and what site information usually is most important. Finally, this chapter shows how to calculate the area of lots and buildings, a skill that is essential for both site and building analysis.

This chapter may be seen as an introduction to the appraisal of the site, which is covered in Chapter 10.

OBJECTIVES

When you have completed this chapter you should be able to:

1. List three reasons for making site inspections.
2. List the four criteria for highest and best use.
3. List the three main categories of site information.
4. Calculate the area of a square, rectangle, triangle, trapezoid, and circle.

6.1 Preparing to Inspect the Site

Before performing the site inspection, you should ask yourself two questions: "Why am I inspecting the site?" and "What information do I need to gather?" Answering these questions in advance allows you to plan your site inspection, look for any special site problems, and perform the site inspection both faster and better.

Reasons for Inspecting and Analyzing the Site

Overall, there are three reasons for inspecting and analyzing the site.

1. To estimate the highest and best use.

2. To identify key features.

3. To seek to identify any legal or physical problems.

Highest and Best Use Estimate

The most important reason for inspecting and analyzing a site is to collect information that you will need in order to estimate the *highest and best use* of the land. Highest and best use is generally defined as:

> The reasonably probable and legal use, which is physically possible, appropriately supported, financially feasible and that results in the highest value.
>
> Source: *The Dictionary of Real Estate Appraisal*, 4th ed., The Appraisal Institute, 2002.

The importance of highest and best use, and techniques for its analysis, will be covered in Section 6.2. Before estimating the highest and best use, the appraiser must identify the key features of the property and gather other preliminary data.

Identify Key Features

The appraiser will want to identify and note all of the significant characteristics of the property to be appraised. Although there are many characteristics of a site to be considered, they may be grouped as follows:

1. *Physical characteristics.*

2. *Site location elements.*

3. *Public and private restrictions.*

These site characteristics will be discussed further in Section 6.3. They are key to estimating possible uses of the site, and to the selection and adjustment of comparable sales.

Identify Possible Legal or Physical Problems

Another reason for inspecting the site is to look for possible legal or physical problems that may be present. Appraisers are not trained to be experts in many problems that may exist; however, it is helpful to be aware of the most common site problems and to try to recognize clues to their existence. Any unresolved issues can then be referred to qualified experts for their analysis.

Site problems may be of a legal nature. For example, an apartment building located on land zoned for single-family homes clearly does not meet the zoning requirements, making it a nonconforming use. It might be either a legal or illegal nonconforming use (discussed later). The close proximity of a neighboring structure to the fence line of the subject could suggest an unauthorized encroachment. As we will see in Section 6.3, site problems could also be physical ones, such as flood risks, poor soils, or the existence of actual or potential environmental hazards (see Figure 6-1).

Real estate is subject to many problems that can have a negative effect on market value. While the appraiser is *not* expected to be an expert in most technical problems, the appraiser does have the responsibility of noting in the appraisal report any possible adverse conditions that are evident or that have been revealed during the appraisal. Estimating the effect of legal or highly technical land problems on market value, however, may not be possible without the advice of a trained specialist.

When serious problems are found in the course of an appraisal, the appraiser should notify the client and request that an expert's opinion

Figure 6-1 Identify Possible Problems (By Bill Shelly, from Retail Traffic Magazine, Penton Media, Inc. [formerly known as The Shopping Center World] May 1, 1980).

"Gentlemen, I have some bad news about your proposed site."

or study be furnished. If the client is unwilling to supply such a study, the appraiser must clearly note the problem in the report and comply with USPAP.

USPAP requires that the appraiser can only ignore a possible problem if: 1) the client agrees or 2) the report clearly identifies the possible problem and labels the decision to ignore it as a Hypothetical Condition or an Extraordinary Assumption (explored in Chapter 3). Appraisers can feel pressure from clients to ignore or minimize property problems. However, it is important for appraisers to resist this pressure. See Section 18.4 for more on this topic.

What Data and Tools Are Needed?

It is wise to gather certain basic information about the site before the actual inspection. Having information in advance can make the fieldwork more efficient and can prevent accidentally overlooking an important property detail during the inspection.

Sales History of Subject

Industry standards and USPAP require that a three-year sales history and any known lease, agreement of sale, option, or listing of the subject property around the date of value, be considered and analyzed by the appraiser. Such data might be collected either before or after the site inspection. However, if collected before, the appraiser will be able to use the inspection to follow up on the sale or listing information. (Refer to Chapters 8 and 10 for further discussion of this topic.)

Site and Neighborhood Data

Factual information about the site and its environs should be assembled for the inspection. The appraiser should plan to take a plat map or drawing of the site as an aid to the inspection. Such a map should show the location, boundary dimensions, and size and shape of the site. For improved parcels, the location of buildings and structures can be noted and sketched on the map for future reference.

When indicated, special flood and geologic maps should also be acquired and possibly taken to the field. It might be necessary to have the map during the inspection. For example, the boundary between two flood zone categories may not be clear, just from looking at the *flood map*. An aerial photo might be very useful as well. Many such maps or aerial photos can be obtained on the Internet.

Information on such legal characteristics as ownership, assessed value, zoning, and recorded *easements* and encumbrances should also be gathered in advance. Knowledge about the availability of *utilities* is also useful prior to inspection, particularly when a vacant site is being appraised. With such data, a more intelligent site inspection is possible.

Certain data on the neighborhood and city should also be known in advance. Examples include population demographics and the locations of schools, churches, and public offices. Appraisers often like to get an overall picture of the site and its surroundings. Driving several blocks in each direction around the site allows the appraiser to observe nearby shopping areas, major transportation routes, and areas of possible conflicting land uses.

Appraisers usually collect tentative market data prior to making a field inspection. When preliminary facts suggest the highest and best use, advance data could include vacant land sales, improved property sales, and/or market rent comparables. Collecting this information in advance allows comparables to be inspected on the same field trip as the inspection of the subject property. However, collecting the sales in advance is recommended only when the appraiser has an idea of the type of comparables that will be needed.

Data Sources

Relevant data for the site inspection can come from a number of sources. Lenders and other clients sometimes furnish the appraiser with a subject property profile acquired from a local title company. Such a profile can include a plat map, information on ownership, property taxes, recent sales, recorded easements, and encumbrances of record. Most of this information is also available from the Internet or city or county assessors' offices. Many appraisers subscribe to data services that provide similar public information on CD-ROM or by computer access to the Internet.

Official zoning information and pending public actions affecting the site may usually be acquired from city or county websites or planning offices; community demographics are available online or from printed census reports and chambers of commerce. Information on flood-prone areas is found in the maps showing areas of probable flooding within a 100-year period. These are produced for FEMA (the Federal Emergency Management Agency) and are available from city or county engineering departments as well as from various data services. Increasingly, appraisers obtain such data from the Internet.

Geologic and seismic-fault maps are produced by the national and state topographic and geologic agencies. The best place to inspect these maps is usually online, or at city and county engineering departments, safety offices, or permit bureaus. Information on **radon gas** and **toxic waste** is available from the local office of the state or federal Environmental Protection Agency. Other site data may be obtained from the various sources noted in Chapter 8.

Tools and Equipment

Since various tools and equipment are used during the inspection, it is desirable to prepare them in advance. Some appraisers use a standard inspection checklist to ensure that they collect all needed information during the inspection. Others use the actual form on which the appraisal is to be presented. Either the checklist or the report form might be on paper, or on a tablet computer or a pocket computer. The URAR (Uniform Residential Appraisal Report), also known as the Freddie Mac Form 70 or Fannie Mae 1004, is the most widely used home loan appraisal report form. A copy of the site description portion of the URAR is shown in Figure 6-2. These forms will be discussed later.

Here is a list of tools commonly used during the site inspection.

1. Checklist or appraisal form (on a clipboard, or a tablet or pocket computer).

2. A note pad or small recorder; sheets of graph paper for making sketches of the property, or a computer with a sketch program.

3. A measurement device, such as a reinforced cloth tape (usually 50 or 100 feet long). Some appraisers prefer a rolling wheel measuring tool. A shorter steel tape may also be useful. Laser measuring devices are becoming more common; some automatically transfer measurements to a computer sketch program, saving time and errors.

4. An ice pick in a sheath is a tool in some appraisers' field kits. It may be used to anchor the end of the measuring tape or to test for possible wood rot.

5. A camera to take photographs of the property, some intended for use in the report, and others for the appraiser's files, to document condition, quality, special features, or possible problems. Nearly all appraisers have switched to digital cameras.

6. A street map of the area and a plat map of the site, as described above.

In addition to a plat map of the subject site, other kinds of official maps may be helpful in the site inspection. County maps and United States Geological Survey quadrangle topographical maps are helpful in

Figure 6-2 Site Description Section of URAR Form.

Dimensions 90 X 145.2	Area 13,068 Sqft	Shape Rectangular	View Nominal

Specific Zoning Classification R-1-10	Zoning Description Single- family detached, 10,000 s.f. minimum lot size

Zoning Compliance ☒ Legal ☐ Legal Nonconforming (Grandfathered Use) ☐ No Zoning ☐ Illegal (describe)

Is the highest and best use of the subject property as improved (or as proposed per plans and specifications) the present use? ☒ Yes ☐ No If No, describe

Utilities	Public	Other (describe)		Public	Other (describe)	Off-site Improvements—Type	Public	Private
Electricity	☒	☐	Water	☒	☐	Street Asphalt	☒	☐
Gas	☒	☐	Sanitary Sewer	☒	☐	Alley None	☐	☐

FEMA Special Flood Hazard Area ☐ Yes ☒ No FEMA Flood Zone -------- FEMA Map # Not mapped FEMA Map Date --------

Are the utilities and off-site improvements typical for the market area? ☒ Yes ☐ No If No, describe

Are there any adverse site conditions or external factors (easements, encroachments, environmental conditions, land uses, etc.)? ☒ Yes ☐ No If Yes, describe

There were no adverse conditions observed. Site has a steep upslope beginning 25 feet from the back of the house.

rural areas. The latter shows land contours and other important geographic features and can help to locate the property. Often, rural appraisers now use geographic position equipment (GPS) to establish their location. As already mentioned, geologic maps can help you locate earthquake faults and other significant land features, and official flood maps can reveal whether the subject property is located in a flood hazard area.

6.2 Highest and Best Use Analysis

Whether land is improved or vacant, its value is economically a function of its highest and best use. As introduced in Section 6.1, the highest and best use represents that reasonable and probable use that will support the *highest* value as of the date of value. The *Uniform Standards of Professional Appraisal Practice* requires that all appraisals estimating market value must reach and report an opinion of highest and best use. This opinion should be based upon a careful analysis of the property and its surroundings.

In this section, we will cover: 1) the purpose of the opinion of highest and best use, 2) the alternative use assumptions the appraiser should consider, and 3) the criteria the appraiser reviews, in reaching an opinion of highest and best use.

Purpose

The opinion of highest and best use defines the use that will be the basis of both the data-collection process and the appraisal methodology. Let us look first at the question of data collection.

The collection of market data for an appraisal relies strongly on comparability. Because of complex market factors, land often has different values for different potential uses. For example, vacant land zoned for retail or office use often has a higher value than that zoned for single-family residential use.

Assume that you are appraising a small commercial building and that you intend to estimate land value in order to apply the cost approach. Realizing that land may have a different value for different uses, you can see that each of the vacant land comparable sales should have a potential use that agrees with the highest and best use of the subject land. When the market comparison approach is being applied in that same appraisal, the potential use of the underlying land in each *improved* sale should, for the same reason, be comparable to the potential use of the land of the subject property if it were vacant. Both examples show the importance of making an initial analysis of highest and best use *before* collecting market data.

The question of highest and best use also affects the appraisal methods to be used. For example, the cost approach would not be as reliable in the appraisal of a single-family home that has been developed on land now zoned commercial (the principle of consistent use). In all cases, the highest and best use analysis strongly suggests the value approach and appraisal method that should be emphasized.

Alternative Use Assumptions

The appraiser's opinion of highest and best use must recognize and address two alternative use assumptions:

1. The highest and best use of the land *as if vacant*.
2. The highest and best use of the property *as improved*.

The importance of estimating the highest and best use of land as if vacant derives from valuation theory. The value of land is presumed to be a function of its potential use, rather than its actual or present use (see Example 6-1). Most of the economic principles of valuation discussed in the previous chapter are based on this assumption. The appraiser's estimate of the highest and best use as if vacant requires consideration of the feasibility and profitability of alternative uses. When an opinion of the most profitable use is determined, that use forms the basis of value for the land. See Chapter 10 for further discussion.

The appraiser's opinion of the highest and best use of the property as improved recognizes that the land is committed, at least at the time of value, to the existing use. Existing improvements may contribute

---

EXAMPLE 6-1 Highest and Best Use As Improved

A. Given:
The property is a two-story older home, in good condition, on a lot now zoned for commercial use. There have been nearby sales of other homes with the same zoning. Some were sold for use as homes and some converted to offices. None were torn down. Sales of similar homes on residential sites suggest a value as a home of about $350,000. Total cost to convert the home to offices (including profit) is about $100,000, with a value when converted and occupied of about $450,000.

B. Analysis:
The highest and best use of the property as improved on the date of value is the use that produces the highest value for the property as it exists. One possible use is as residential, with a likely value of around $350,000. The other possible use is for conversion to offices, with a value before conversion of around $350,000. The two uses appear equally valuable. However, some houses are being bought for one use and some for the other.

C. Conclusion:
The appraiser must try to determine *why* some houses were bought for one use and some for the other. Next, the appraiser must try to determine which group the subject property fits into.

---

something to the property value, even when they don't represent the land's highest and best use as if vacant. Or the highest and best use of the property as improved might turn out to be demolition and redevelopment.

The appraiser should explore alternative uses and management methods that can be used to maximize the benefits or return on the improved property. Ultimately, the appraiser will reach an opinion of the ideal use or occupancy for the property as presently improved.

If the highest and best use as improved is different from the highest and best use as if vacant, it is often referred to as an ***interim use***. See Example 6-2. An interim use of the property means that the improvements are likely to be demolished, or massively remodeled, much sooner. In turn, the value contribution of the improvements as an interim use is likely to be much less. This means that estimating the depreciation deduction in a cost approach for an interim use will be much more complex.

Highest and Best Use Criteria

The appraiser's opinion of the highest and best use of a property should be based on careful consideration of all the physical, legal, and economic factors affecting the land and the property. Here are the four accepted tests (or criteria) of highest and best use. To be eligible, the suggested use must be:

1. Physically possible.
2. Legally permissible.

EXAMPLE 6-2 Analysis of an Interim Use

A. Given:
The subject property is an older home, in good condition, on a lot now zoned for commercial use. There are no sales of homes with commercial zoning. No commercial uses have been developed. Recent sales of similar homes, on residential sites, suggest a value of about $350,000. Analysis of these sales and of recent residential land sales suggests a building value contribution of $250,000. Commercial land sales on a parallel street indicate a land value as zoned of about $300,000.

B. Analysis:
The property cannot be worth more than the higher of 1) the value of the land as if it was vacant and 2) the value of the property as improved, with consistent zoning. Therefore, adding the building value contribution with consistent zoning, $250,000, to the commercial land value of $300,000, is in error as it violates the Principle of Consistent Use.

C. Conclusion:
The highest and best use of the property as improved is not clear, given the available data. The property's value is between a low of $300,000 and a high of $350,000, and very likely less than the maximum. No more certain answer can be obtained from the available evidence.

---

3. Economically feasible.

4. The most productive.

A projected use would be *physically possible* or practical, if the site's location, access, size, shape, topography, soil type, and other characteristics do not block such a use. Uses that require a larger or more level site than the subject, for example, can be eliminated from consideration.

A suggested use is *legally permissible* when the use is allowed under present zoning, reasonably expected future zoning, or other entitlement. However, if any required conditional use permit, variance, or environmental approval would likely be denied for a particular use, such a use would not qualify.

To be *economically feasible*, a projected use must be economically sound, given the balance between its cost and economic demand. For example, a suggested use should not involve excessive costs of development, either in terms of money or the time required for completion. If the acquisition and development costs are certain to exceed the value of the end product, the use would not be economically feasible. In a similar way, for a property use to be the highest and best use, it must be a use that is needed at that location and that would provide a fair return on the investment.

To be the *most productive* (maximally productive), a use must provide more return or income than any other use, i.e., the greatest net return to the land. To test this, a number of possible uses could be analyzed. Each must first pass the tests of physical, legal, and economic acceptability. In each case, the potential net income should be estimated, then that amount should be reduced by the income required for a fair return on the projected cost of the necessary improvements. The particular use that promises the greatest "residual" return to the land would be suggested as the highest and best use. Feasibility studies and the analysis of highest and best use are further discussed in Chapters 10 and 14.

6.3 Major Categories of Site Information

A good site inspection includes identifying and recording all significant aspects of the site and its surroundings. These aspects fall into three main categories (see Figure 6-3).

1. *Physical characteristics*.

2. *Site location elements*.

3. *Public and private restrictions*.

Figure 6-3 Aspects of a Site.

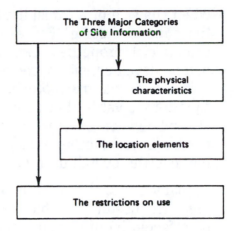

Important Physical Characteristics

The physical features most important to the site's overall utility should be carefully identified and noted during the site inspection. In this section, we will discuss the following seven different *site characteristics*, and show how each is important to the value of the land.

1. *Size and shape.*
2. *Topography, soil, and geology.*
3. *Drainage and flood hazards.*
4. *Environmental factors.*
5. *Form of ownership (a physical and legal feature).*
6. *Lot type and orientation.*
7. *On-site and off-site improvements.*

Size and Shape

Aside from location, the most important detail of the site is its overall size. First, most zoning laws require that a site meet certain minimum size requirements in order to qualify for development. In many jurisdictions, the size of the lot also determines the size of allowable construction, in terms of floor area, site coverage, and/or the number of residential or commercial units allowed. Thus, lot size greatly influences the site's utility and potential use.

The size, or area, of the lot is usually expressed in terms of square feet or acres, although other measurements are sometimes used. In countries using the metric system, appraisers most often measure land size in square meters, or hectares. One hectare is about two and one-half acres. Often, the area of a site is shown on the local property tax assessor's maps. If not, it can be calculated from the dimensions of the property as shown by the maps.

When the size of a parcel limits its utility, the disadvantage may sometimes be overcome. For example, in larger residential income and commercial properties, two or more small sites are often combined before development to create the desired size parcel. The process is referred to as **assemblage**, or **plottage**. Any increase in unit or square-foot value that results is often referred to as **plottage value**. The subdivision of large acreage parcels into smaller, more marketable parcels is yet another example of changing the size of land parcels to improve the overall utility and the value per unit.

In many cases, the **gross area** of a site is not as important as its **useful area**. The useful or usable area (sometimes called **net area**) of a lot can be affected by unfavorable topography or type of soil, as well as other physical features. It can also be affected by the setback requirements of local zoning laws. So it follows that subdivided lots also may have a useful area considerably smaller than the gross area. The area that the building sits on is referred to as the **building footprint**, sometimes expressed as a percent of the lot area and labeled the **coverage ratio**. This will vary depending on the zoning ordinance and specific use (see Figure 6-4).

Shape is a particularly important characteristic of the site. It can affect both the usable area of a site and its overall utility. **Lot shape** generally refers to the relationship between the parcel's width and **depth**. Some lots are too narrow for ideal use, and others are too shallow. Shape can also refer to the configuration of the lot. Property with an ideal shape on a map may be found upon inspection to have features that alter the

Figure 6-4 Be Sure to Check the Useful Area of the Lot.

shape of the usable area of the parcel, making it less valuable. This could be a bluff, a creek, or a swamp.

The length of the property's frontage should also be recorded. ***Frontage*** is the boundary or lot side that faces, or is adjacent to, a street or highway. The amount of frontage affects the utility and value of a site for many uses, especially retail, because it affects the exposure to the public and the ease of access.

The *depth of the parcel* is also significant. The projected use of a parcel can determine its ideal dimensions. A deep lot, that is, one that extends far back from the street, may be efficient for one type of use and not for another. When the rear portion of a lot is significantly less useful for a particular use than the front portion, the lot is described as having ***excess depth***.

The usefulness of depth in a parcel can vary not only from use to use, but also from time to time and from community to community. This makes it difficult to evaluate deeper parcels or very shallow ones. Over the years, studies have been conducted to see how lot values vary with depth. Some of these studies have produced depth tables. Used primarily for mass appraisal work, depth tables are available for general use. However, since depth tables have usually reflected only one time period, one land use, or one location, their reliability is generally limited by their lack of connection to the particular market under study. Nonetheless, some interesting ideas are presented.

One well-known older depth table suggests that for the standard depth lot in a particular location, 40 percent of the value lies in the first one-quarter of the depth, 30 percent of the value is in the second one-quarter of the depth (making 70 percent of the value in the first one-half of the depth), 20 percent for the third one-quarter, and 10 percent for the last, or back, one-quarter of the depth. If the standard depth in one community is 200 feet and the going market price for lots in this location is $100,000, a lot that is 50 feet deep would be considered to be worth 40% × $100,000, or $40,000. A lot that is 100 feet deep, or one-half of this standard depth, would be considered to be worth 70% (40% + 30%) × $100,000, or $70,000. Of course, the type of use projected, the legally required minimum lot size, and set-back requirements in a particular location are more likely to govern market demand, utility, and relative site value for depth than will published tables.

Topography, Soil, and Geology

After examining the size and shape of the parcel, the appraiser should look at the topography, soil, and geology of the site. ***Topography*** (or contour) refers to the surface of the parcel and its particular features. These features may include hills, valleys, creeks, ravines, cliffs, bluffs and slopes. Although land with irregular topography is generally more costly to build on, certain features can be assets or liabilities, depending on the use and size of the parcel and the location of roads and utilities. For instance, slopes may command a premium when developed to take advantage of a good view of the surrounding area. However, if they cause problems with providing utilities or gaining access for building materials during construction, slopes can cause substantial value penalties. The pros and cons of any land feature must be carefully evaluated and compared.

While looking at the topography of the parcel, the appraiser should also look at the surroundings. What might be an impressive view may soon be obstructed by a roof or tree on a neighbor's property. Usually, the highest knoll in the area has the greatest value as a homesite, because lower knolls may have others looking down on them. Do surrounding parcels pose threats of landslides or rock falls? This too can seriously affect the value of the subject property. View lots are further discussed later in the section "Lot Type and Orientation."

Soil and geology are also important aspects of land utility and value, particularly as these features affect the ability to support structures. A steep slope in rock is more stable than a steep slope in sand. Clays that expand when wet may make construction impossible without expensive foundation footings. Soils may be of such poor composition that deep pilings are necessary, or soil may be too dense or too moist for any needed septic tanks to work. Public maps may indicate that the site is situated in a slide, soil liquefaction, or earthquake hazard area. Certain geologic factors may preclude *any* building on the site!

Drainage and Flood Hazards

A feature closely related to topography and geology is *water drainage*. The topography of land creates its own drainage through natural systems of rainwater runoff, such as valleys, creeks, and rivers. People modify the natural runoff when the land is used or developed. Ideally, this is done by constructing properly engineered drainage systems, such as underground drains, culverts, and lined ditches. When inspecting the site, the appraiser should consider how present and future drainage systems will affect the planned use of the site. It may be found that the property is located in a mapped flood plain or flood zone, or that excessive soil erosion could result from uncontrolled water runoff. We will discuss this topic in more depth later.

Environmental Factors

A number of environmental factors may also limit building on the site. Of recent concern are areas of high concentrations of radon or methane gas, and/or proximity to toxic waste sites. **Radon** (radioactive) and **methane gas** (explosive) are odorless gasses occurring naturally in the soil. Methane gas can also be generated in buried garbage. Several areas across the country have been found to have dangerously high concentrations of radioactive radon gas, according to standards published by the federal Environmental Protection Agency. In the West, however, methane gasses are more commonly found than radon. Areas with hazardous levels of gasses or toxic wastes are currently being studied by local health services and environmental protection agencies.

Form of Ownership

Important site characteristics include the form of real estate ownership. We have grouped this with the physical characteristics of the lot because this is so apparent physically during the site inspection. The *form of ownership* refers to the physical and legal form of the parcel. Please note that some names or labels are from legal origins, some are physical descriptions, and some are trade names. The most common entity is the *conventional detached lot*, where the site is the entire lot with ownership in fee. Its frontage is on either a street or a permanent access easement.

A second common form of ownership involves a subdivided lot on which the improvements sit, plus an undivided interest in adjacent common areas. These common areas may include recreational facilities, parking areas, driveways, walks, lawns, open space, and so on. This second type of ownership or legal entity is known by a number of names. Perhaps the most common of these is the **Planned Unit Development (PUD)**, or Residential Planned Development (RPD), named after the zoning category under which it is often developed. The term **townhouse** is also sometimes applied, named after the townhouse building design style frequently used (see Figure 6-5). (In some cases, PUDs include regular detached homes.) In some jurisdictions,

Figure 6-5 An Example of Townhouse Building Design.

this second type of legal entity, what we refer to as the PUD, is referred to as a ***condominium***, or "condo." More commonly, the term condo is used to refer to the third type of legal entity, to be discussed next. Note that there are also regional differences in usage, making it important for the appraiser to understand the sales and use clear descriptions during interviews and in reports.

Condominiums, or airspace condominiums, involve the ownership of a defined block of airspace in a building, plus an undivided interest in the common areas. The difference between the townhouse planned unit development (PUD) type and the airspace condominium is that a townhouse PUD unit is built on a separate wholly owned lot, whereas in an airspace condominium, the dwelling is one of a number of units that share ownership of one piece of ground. Both the townhouse PUD and the airspace condominium typically include an undivided interest in common areas, as described earlier. Of course, airspace condominium unit ownership also includes an undivided interest in the structural support and the building systems, such as the pipes and drains necessary for the unit to function (see Figure 6-6).

Figure 6-6 Airspace Condominiums.

Source: Photograph Courtesy of Doug Frost.

Since both townhouse PUDs and airspace condominiums have common areas that are part of the total site, the appraiser's site inspection should review both the unit site and the common areas! Additionally, the various **association agreement** documents should be examined. The latter can reveal the property tax assessments and the annual budget, as well as the CC&Rs, bylaws, and articles of incorporation and reserves for future maintenance.

At one time, lenders and the Federal National Mortgage Association (FNMA) created a special category of PUD known as a *De Minimus PUD*. Used mainly to qualify certain projects for insured loans, the term described a PUD in which the owner 1) actually owned the fee title to the land; 2) was responsible for maintaining the unit interior and exterior; and 3) was motivated to purchase the unit primarily for housing needs, rather than for recreation benefits or other amenities. In 1990, FNMA eliminated these restrictions and dropped the term from its regulations, but appraisers still find people using the term.

Lot Type and Orientation

Another physical characteristic to consider is the **lot type** and its relationship to other lots and the streets that surround it. The major types of lots are shown in Figure 6-7. The most common type of lot is

Figure 6-7 Common Types of Lots (Courtesy of the California Department of Real Estate).

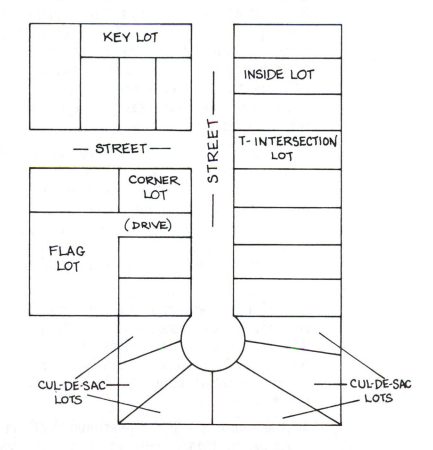

the *interior lot*. This is a lot that "fronts" on only one street. Another common type is the *corner lot*, which has frontage (and usually access) on two intersecting streets.

In the past, corner lots often sold at a premium over interior lots, because people with home offices (e.g., doctors and lawyers) needed a separate side entrance for the office. Today, residential corner lots often command a premium because of the easy access to the rear yard. Such access is very desirable in communities that prohibit parking motor homes or boat trailers on the street or in the front driveways of houses.

When residential lots have wide frontages, the corner premium may disappear. Side yards on such lots are sometimes wide enough to allow easy parking for recreational vehicles. However, commercial corner lots nearly always sell for a premium price because of the increased frontage or "showcase" space. In summary, corner premiums today depend on the local market, the use of the lot, its location, and its size.

A less common type of lot is the *key lot*. This is a lot that has several other lots backing onto its side yard. A key lot is often considered a less valuable lot than other types because of a loss of privacy.

A *cul-de-sac lot* is one that is located at the end of a dead-end street. Because most cul-de-sacs are now made with a curved turnaround, the lots taper and have very little street frontage. Although this may make guest parking difficult, the disadvantage is usually counterbalanced by large backyards, extra privacy, and reduced street traffic. Cul-de-sac lots are usually considered especially desirable for family housing because of the large rear play area and the relatively greater safety resulting from reduced auto traffic.

Another type of lot is the *flag lot*. This is a rear lot, behind other houses or lots, with a long narrow access. The lot and access route resemble a flag and flagpole. Flag lots usually have excellent privacy but may be inconvenient for visitors, since street numbers are hard to find. In snow country, the long driveway is a drawback. The flag lot is also less desirable than other lots for people who prefer that their attractive house be visible to the public.

Still another type of lot is the *T-intersection lot*, which is a lot at the end of a T intersection. In some cases, T-intersection lots suffer from the danger of speeding cars failing to turn the corner. However, T-intersection lots seldom sell for a lower price. They may even sell for a premium, because the site can be seen from a long distance down the intersecting street. This is particularly true of commercial parcels.

Just as important as the relationship of the lot to streets and other lots is its *orientation* to sun, wind, climate, views, and surrounding land features. For example, a lot with desirable views of land or sea commands a higher selling price. Generally, water views are worth more than land views. A wider view is generally worth more than a narrow view. A shallow view, over the roof of the house below, is generally worth less than a deep view.

Views and exposure may depend on whether a lot slopes uphill or downhill from the street access. But upslope lots are generally more expensive to build on than downslope lots, and therefore may sell for less, if there are no compensating factors.

Orientation to the sun is becoming more important as we consider the utilization of solar energy. For maximum solar efficiency in many areas, houses should have the glassed areas facing south and the windowless areas facing north. If the best views are to the north, however, only careful design will produce an energy-efficient house that also benefits from the good view.

The appraiser should check to see if any orientation advantages of an existing house or lot can be considered permanent. New construction on the lot across the street or the growth of vegetation may destroy advantages of view or of sun exposure. Protection is sometimes provided by view easements across adjacent properties, by tract restrictions that require regular tree topping, by a city ordinance, or simply by the natural topography of the land.

For any site to be utilized, it must have *convenient access*. Access depends on the type of lot, as well as the street and traffic patterns. Lots that are accessible only by long, complex travel routes normally sell for less than competing lots located on more direct routes.

Physical access is also affected by the topography of the area. Access routes in hilly, older neighborhoods or areas with banks, ravines, slopes, and creeks can be so winding and narrow as to block fire trucks or other emergency vehicles. In such neighborhoods, the narrow streets often increase the costs of new construction by limiting space for the delivery of lumber and other materials.

Some land parcels are completely inaccessible, surrounded by other parcels, and "landlocked." When physical access is sought for such a parcel, it is usually necessary to obtain an access easement and construct an access road. Access easements can be very expensive to purchase, develop, and maintain. Therefore, the appraiser should try to find out if the site has legal access.

On-Site and Off-Site Improvements

Improvements to the site represent another important part of the physical characteristics of a site. *On-site improvements* may consist of earth leveling, grading, filling, drainage, compaction, or excavation. These are normally appraised as part of the land. The property being appraised may be landscaped with trees, lawns, and shrubs, and may also have a sprinkler system. In addition, there may be retaining walls or fences, walks, paths, or patios. Because some of these features may eventually be appraised as improvements instead of as land, they must be inspected and noted in the same manner as the main building improvements (to be discussed in Chapter 7).

Adjacent *off-site improvements* include the width and paving of streets and the presence or absence of curbs, gutters, sidewalks, alleys, street lighting, and parking facilities. Some appraisal books include utilities as part of the off-site improvements. Here, utilities are considered as part of the characteristics of that location.

In some states, many of the off-site improvements in new subdivisions are financed by municipal bonds, to be paid off by special assessments imposed on the eventual owners. (California's so-called "Mello-Roos" law provides one method for such financing.) By this device, land developers are sometimes able to pass the costs of street improvements, utilities, and the like on to future buyers, without these costs directly increasing the selling prices. Bonded indebtedness assessments may not only increase the annual costs of ownership, but they can also reduce the purchase financing available. Appraisers need to identify and consider the source of funds for off-site improvements in new subdivisions. It may be necessary to adjust comparable sales if they differ in bonded indebtedness. This topic will be revisited in later chapters.

Analysis of Site Location Elements

There is a truism that there are only three important factors in the value of property: location, location, and location! In other words, to appraise any site, we must appraise its *location*. This is true regardless of the use of the site.

Analyzing the site location should be done in an organized way. First, a general evaluation should be made of the neighborhood where the site is located. Next, we need to look at the proximity of the neighborhood to earthquake fault zones, flood hazard areas, environmental hazards, and hazardous waste sites.

Evaluation of the Neighborhood

We will use a residential neighborhood as the focus of this discussion. Other land uses involve similar neighborhood issues. The desirability of a neighborhood depends in part on its convenience to transportation, schools, and community centers, and to the main centers of employment and shopping. Proximity to public health and medical facilities, and to religious and recreation centers, is also important. The market appeal of a residential neighborhood also depends on the quality, age, style, condition, and adequacy of its housing. As we learned in Chapter 4, an in-depth neighborhood study should also consider the social and economic demographics of the area and the local market conditions at the date of value.

Proximity to Earthquake, Flood, and Environmental Hazards

The analysis of a site's location should always include a look at its proximity to any earthquake and flood zones. Close proximity to an earthquake fault line is of concern to insurance companies and lenders in California and some other states, as well as to potential purchasers of land. As noted in Section 6.1, geologic and seismic fault maps are usually available in city and county engineering offices.

The proximity of a site to a flood hazard zone must be considered. If the appraised property is within a Special Flood Hazard Area (SFHA), as defined and mapped by the Federal Emergency Management Agency (FEMA), the flood zone map number, zone code, and date of the map may be required for completion of the Uniform Residential Appraisal Report. Federal regulations require that lenders, or appraisers acting under their direction, determine whether a building is within a flood hazard zone. This is discussed further in Chapter 16. Figure 6-8 shows a special form used for this purpose. More information on flood maps can be found at http://msc.fema.gov or at http://www.floodsmart.gov.

As mentioned earlier in this section, a number of environmental factors can impact the site location. On-site and off-site problems may include radon or methane gasses, lead-based paint, asbestos, and the proximity of toxic waste sites or former military locations where explosives may remain.

Comparison with Neighborhood Properties

In the analysis of the site, it is important to see how the site conforms to the average site characteristics in the neighborhood. Whatever the size, shape, topography, and overall utility of the property being appraised, it must be put into the scale of those characteristics in its own neighborhood. A one-acre site, for example, may pose a special appraisal problem when in a neighborhood of much smaller lots.

Consider the impact of the neighboring properties on the value of the subject property. How are they maintained, judging by the standards of the neighborhood? Is there evidence of renovation or remodeling? Does the immediate area have a history of high, average, or low crime rates or of family or civic disturbances? Obviously, you must also consider whether the past record may be changing.

When comparing the site to neighborhood properties, you should note whether there are nearby properties with conflicting uses. Are neighboring properties being used in such a way that they will interfere with the usefulness of the subject property? Use conflicts may result from unwanted noise, odors, or other negative characteristics referred to above. Next, note the property's amount of privacy. Privacy may be

Figure 6-8 Standard Flood Hazard Determination Form.

DEPARTMENT OF HOMELAND SECURITY FEDERAL EMERGENCY MANAGEMENT AGENCY **STANDARD FLOOD HAZARD DETERMINATION**	*See The Attached Instructions*	O.M.B. No. 1660-0040 *Expires October 31, 2008*

SECTION I - LOAN INFORMATION

1. LENDER NAME AND ADDRESS	2. COLLATERAL *(Building/Mobile Home/Personal Property* PROPERTY ADDRESS *(Legal Description may be attached)*

3. LENDER ID. NO.	4. LOAN IDENTIFIER	5. AMOUNT OF FLOOD INSURANCE REQUIRED $

SECTION II

A. NATIONAL FLOOD INSURANCE PROGRAM (NFIP) COMMUNITY JURISDICTION

1. NFIP Community Name	2. County(ies)	3. State	4. NFIP Community Number

B. NATIONAL FLOOD INSURANCE PROGRAM (NFIP) DATA AFFECTING BUILDING/MOBILE HOME

1. NFIP Map Number or Community-Panel Number (Community name, if not the same as "A")	2. NFIP Map Panel Effective/ Revised Date	3. LOMA/LOMR ☐ yes ___ Date	4. Flood Zone	5. No NFIP Map

C. FEDERAL FLOOD INSURANCE AVAILABILITY *(Check all that apply)*

1. ☐ Federal Flood insurance is available *(community participates in NFIP)*   ☐ Regular Program   ☐ Emergency Program of NFIP

2. ☐ Federal Flood insurance is not available because community is not participating in the NFIP.

3. ☐ Building/Mobile Home is in a Coastal Barrier Resources Area (CBRA) or Otherwise Protected Area (OPA), Federal Flood insurance may not be available.

   CBRA/OPA designation date: _____

D. DETERMINATION

IS BUILDING/MOBILE HOME IN SPECIAL FLOOD HAZARD AREA (ZONES CONTAINING THE LETTERS "A" OR "V")?   ☐YES   ☐NO

If yes, flood insurance is required by the Flood Disaster Protection Act of 1973.
If no, flood insurance is not required by the Flood Disaster Protection Act of 1973.

E. COMMENTS *(Optional)*

This determination is based on examining the NFIP map, any Federal Emergency Management Agency revisions to it, and any other information needed to locate the building/mobile home on the NFIP map.

F. PREPARER'S INFORMATION

NAME, ADDRESS, TELEPHONE NUMBER *(if other than Lender)*	DATE OF DETERMINATION

FEMA Form 81-93, DEC 05   **This form may be locally reproduced.**

measured simplistically by what other people hear or see of you and by what you hear or see of them. However, the standards of the local market will judge its importance. In some markets, privacy is more important to value than in others.

Utilities

The availability of utilities is another element to consider in rating a location. Costs, restrictions on service, reliability, and the sources for each utility are all pertinent considerations. The site analysis should focus not only on water supply, trash collection, and electricity service, but also on telephone, cable TV, and natural gas or propane service. High-speed internet service is also beginning to be important. The appraiser needs to find out whether the property uses a septic tank system or a public sewer. How storm runoff is handled is also an issue. The absence of a municipal water supply in an area would suggest a reliance on private wells. Observing the location of existing wells might give you an idea of the chances of drilling a successful well on the subject property. Similarly, the absence of nearby city sewer lines may mean that a sewer line extension is needed, or that a septic tank and drainfield must be installed before development can occur.

The appraiser usually cannot tell whether septic tanks will be permitted, unless an official percolation test has been performed and the site is large enough for any required drainfield. However, a check of public records for such permits issued nearby might be indicative, although certainly not conclusive, evidence. Note that the minimum lot size established by the health authority for a new septic system may be different from (usually larger than) the zoning minimum.

Since the services provided by many utility companies are available over wide areas, the appraiser may not need to research utility company information for each and every appraisal assignment. It is worth noting, however, that some assignments are of parcels that are located beyond municipal boundaries, where the availability or cost of utility services may need to be thoroughly investigated. When utility services are inadequate or absent, the possible cost of providing any required new services has a direct impact on land value, and therefore must be considered in the rating of site location.

Vacant sites are often considerably more difficult to analyze than improved parcels. The uncertainty and potential cost of obtaining utility service are major factors in this problem.

Transportation

The final element of site location is *transportation* and transportation access. In modern living, any site has value only if it can be connected to other sites where we live, work, shop, and play. Generally, the poorer the transportation and accessibility, the lower is the value of the property. When reviewing transportation, the appraiser should be sure to consider both public and private systems. With public transportation, check to see how close the property is located to public transportation systems and loading points. How well does the local system connect to the main travel points? Consider the cost of fares, the frequency of schedules, and the travel time between the property and the places to which users of this property might travel. Are there major seasonal changes?

The appraiser's concern for transportation services differs, depending on the type of property being appraised. With a residential site, for example, you should check the availability, cost, and convenience of the public transportation system for commuting and shopping. When appraising a commercial location, on the other hand, the concern is for midday shopping travel, easy access to working people, and access to those transferring between different transportation routes or lines.

In the review of transportation, there are other things to consider. How close is the subject property to freeways or major streets? How convenient is it to get on and off the freeway or throughway for this property? Is it convenient from both directions? Consider the time of travel and direction of travel the users of this property are likely to take. Travel time will vary, depending on the peak traffic hours and the destination of the commuters!

Public and Private Restrictions

Nothing can be more important to an appraiser than understanding the public and private restrictions on the use of property. As detailed in Chapter 2, such restrictions have a notable impact on value because they help to determine the highest and best use. To be able to compare properties and judge the feasibility of different uses, the appraiser's analysis of the site must therefore include an investigation of public and private restrictions. These form the second major complication when appraising vacant land!

Public Restrictions

Public restrictions on the use of land most often appear in the form of public easements, zoning regulations, subdivision laws, and building and safety codes. State and federal regulations designed to protect people and the environment also must be added to this list.

The most common public easements are those needed for public utilities, transportation, and communications. There could also be drainage easements, flood control easements, or avigation easements (that allow aircraft to fly low over the parcel while using a nearby airport). Government-controlled open space and scenic easements are also commonplace today.

Of the many government controls impacting real estate, *zoning regulations*—usually deriving from community and regional master plans—have the most obvious effect on land use and development. Common zoning regulations cover permitted uses, the density or intensity of use, setback, rear-yard and side-yard requirements, height restrictions, and parking requirements. Among such controls, use density seems to play the most familiar role in land development. Typical zoning regulations, for example, classify residential land in categories with labels such as R-1, R-2, R-3, and so on. Development is allowed in each category according to rules.

For residential zones, often these rules focus on the minimum square-foot land area required for each residential unit. On standard-sized lots, R-1 land generally allows only individual single-family homes; R-2 and R-3 zoned land may permit two or more units on such lots, with additional units allowed on larger sites. Residential income and commercial zoning usually includes parking requirements, which vary with the size, number, and type of units. Parking requirements often combine with the coverage requirements, in a way that further restricts the size of the project that can be built on any given lot or site.

Procedures for obtaining variances from zoning restrictions are different for each jurisdiction. However, variances are typically granted only where the strict application of the zoning ordinance deprives a property of privileges that are enjoyed by nearby properties. Zoning regulations will also vary in how they handle a *nonconforming use*. This term refers to a use that is not allowed under the zoning in effect at the time. If the use was legal on this site at the time the use started, before the effective ordinance was adopted, it is called a *legal nonconforming use*. If it was not legal then, it is an illegal nonconforming use and the city might try to shut it down. The appraiser should try to be familiar with zoning laws, and be alert to their impact on property values.

Subdivision laws regulate the division of land, and therefore restrict its use. State and local requirements for subdivision maps, off-site improvements, utilities, and public reports generally depend on the proposed use, the size and number of lots, and whether the new parcels will be offered for sale. Subdivision requirements are particularly important in the appraisal of vacant or under-improved land, as they greatly affect its highest and best use and value.

Building and safety regulations represent another category of public restriction. Municipal housing, building, plumbing, and electrical codes are examples. Because such codes differ from place to place, there can be circumstances in which a particular type of construction is economically feasible in one town and not in an adjacent town. As we have seen, such factors as soil type, local geology, and proximity to earthquake faults can also affect the legal and economic feasibility and type of construction for a site.

Another type of public limit on the use of property arises when the **right of access** to a property is restricted. A common example is when access rights alongside a freeway are purchased and extinguished. Adjacent lands must then rely on other access routes. Sometimes, access restrictions simply limit the location and/or number of driveways, restricting use and development of the property. Gas stations and drive-in restaurants are prime examples of properties that are materially impacted, if deprived of driveway access when new freeways or freeway ramps are built.

Since passage of state and federal environmental protection laws in the 1970s, the development of both public and private lands has been subject to many conditions. These are designed to protect against pollution and the destruction of wetlands and wildlife habitation. This means that an *environmental impact report (EIR)* and other special studies often must precede new development. Studies are also required when potential or actual environmental hazards exist. Examples of listed hazards include toxic wastes, methane or radon gas, and abandoned munitions or mines.

Local ordinances designed to protect or to preserve the environment may include temporary *moratoriums* on new water or sewer hookup permits. This can mean that construction is prohibited until problems with water supply or the quality or capacity of water or sewer treatment plants can be resolved. In some "slow-growth" areas, there is an increasing tendency to ration building permits, so that an owner might find the city has temporarily stopped issuing building permits, even for subdivided lots.

Federal flood zones can also severely affect the ability to use property. In other cases, however, several feet of relatively inexpensive fill can serve to "flood-proof" the property and restore the land's usefulness. Still another public restriction results from state or local *geologic hazard zones*. These can include earthquake fault-rupture zones, areas where soils are likely to slide or liquefy in the event of an earthquake, or areas where an earthquake could generate a tsunami (an earthquake-generated sea or tidal wave) that could endanger property. Building restrictions in such areas could vary from a total banning of development to moderate increases in structural strength requirements. Whatever the type or reason, public land-use restrictions can seriously impact the value of land.

Property Taxes

As a form of public restriction on the use of land, property taxes deserve special attention here, as they often can notably affect the value of a site.

Historically, property taxes in this country have been based on an *ad valorem*, or "according to value" formula. Property taxes are tied to each property's value. In theory, this makes the tax burden proportional to the benefits received. However, in some states, including California (via the well-known "Proposition 13"), a public revolt against county and municipal spending practices led to drastic property tax assessment reforms in the late 1970s.

Under California law, property tax assessments are now based not on the market value on the assessment valuation date, but on historic value. A 2% maximum annual increase is allowed for change in the consumer price index. Reassessments at market value are allowed only with 1) change of ownership, 2) a new long-term lease agreement, or 3) new construction. Because of the inequities between the tax burden of the newly acquired properties and those that have remained in the same ownership for a number of years, some lawmakers are now suggesting remedial reforms, but there is no easy solution!

Besides ad valorem taxes, direct (or special) assessments also affect the total property tax burden, and therefore the market value of land. Often collected with regular property taxes, direct assessments are increasingly imposed by local government entities to replace revenue lost to ad valorem tax limits. Municipal street lighting, roads, libraries, parks, water supply systems, sewage treatment plants, and public landfills may be financed by special assessments, as can flood and water runoff control services.

As mentioned in our earlier discussion of off-site improvements, direct assessments are sometimes imposed to reimburse developers of new subdivisions for the cost of streets, curbs, and utilities. If two properties are otherwise equal but one has a large annual special tax assessment to pay, it is logical that the one without the assessment would sell at a higher price. Special assessments are increasingly common. For this reason, it is sometimes useful for the appraiser to obtain a copy of the property tax bill in order to see what charges are listed.

Property tax exemptions and preferential property tax laws make the analysis of the property tax burden or cost even more complex. Religious and charitable exemptions have long shielded some properties from property taxation. Now, many laws provide reduced assessments to certain lands restricted to agriculture or recreational use, and also to land set aside as scenic corridors.

For the reasons cited above, the existing taxes on a property are not a good indication of the future tax burden for the property. The appraiser should become familiar with local property tax laws and practices and consider their effect on property value from one location to another.

Finally, another tax that is levied on property is the *property transfer tax*. At one time, this was a federal tax collected from revenue stamps placed on various types of deeds, and called a documentary tax or stamp tax. Transfer taxes are now imposed by local jurisdictions. The most common transfer tax is at the rate of $0.55 per $500 of cash consideration. In the usual ordinance, assumed trust deeds or mortgages are not included in the calculation of tax, whereas new mortgages and equity cash payments are considered. A number of cities are increasing transfer tax rates to raise revenues in support of local services. In some cases, appraisers must know the local transfer tax rate.

Private Restrictions

Private restrictions take many forms, ranging from simple *deed restrictions* to complex agreements between groups of owners (see Chapter 2). The most simple deed restriction may specify the minimum size of structures. For example, in a residential subdivision, houses may be required to have a certain minimum-sized living area. Some older deed restrictions prohibited the sale of alcoholic beverages. We have seen deed restrictions that forbid commercial use of the property and some that restrict the property to only commercial or industrial uses. (Restrictions against race, color, religion, sex, handicap, marital or familial status, age, or national origin are generally prohibited by law.)

The most complex private restrictions include those typical of planned unit developments and condominiums. These are known as association or community agreements. Here, each property is part of a larger group of parcels and is bound by the Conditions, Covenants, and Restrictions (CC&Rs) that apply to all properties within that association. Such agreements may mandate paint colors; degree of maintenance; type of landscaping; type of shades, awnings, and drapes; and so on. Association restrictions should be reviewed by the appraiser and discussed with the community association manager before a judgment is made as to their effect on the value of the property.

Private easements represent another common restriction on the use of land. These include ingress and egress easements, as well as easements for private utility lines and easements for light and air. Figure 6-9 shows a typical private road and utility easement. Clearly, such easements have an impact on the use and value of the affected properties.

Leases are another important example of private restrictions. Commercial and industrial property is commonly bought and sold, subject to existing leases. Depending on the length of the lease, the rent to be paid, and other terms, the impact on both the use and value of such property can be very significant. When an appraisal is of a property subject to a lease, the appraiser must consider all landlord and tenant agreements that affect the benefits received by the owner. This topic will be discussed further in Chapter 17.

As this section suggests, there are a large number of factors that might influence the value of a site. The appraiser seeks to be aware of them in order to properly consider those that are significant to the value of the specific property being appraised.

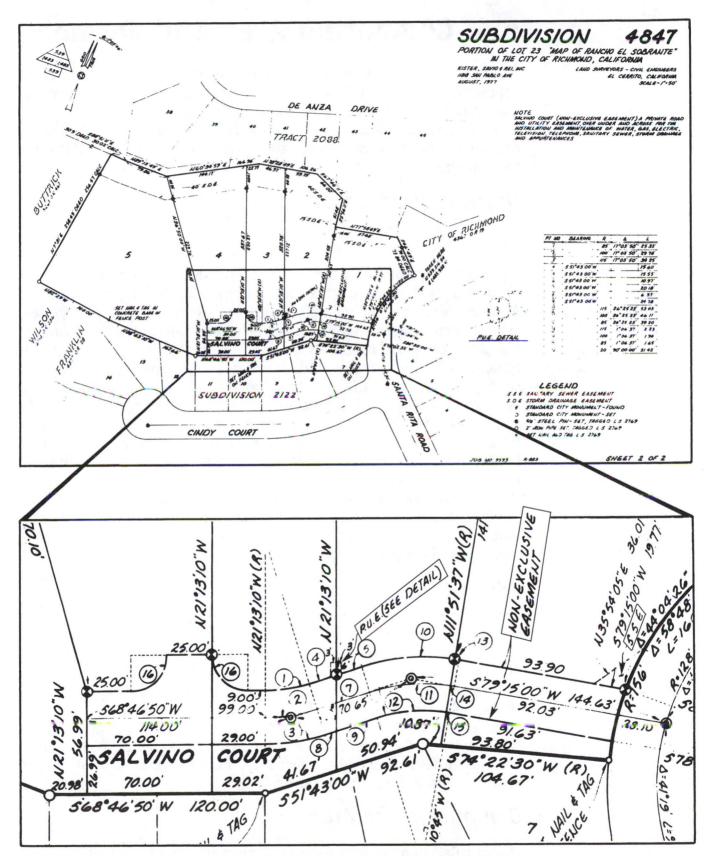

Figure 6-9 An Example of a Private Road and Utility Easement.

6.4 Computing Area and Volume

The ability to do basic arithmetic is one of the necessary skills of an appraiser. This section demonstrates how to make simple calculations that assist the appraiser in estimating lot and house areas, room sizes, and surface areas of walls, as well as measurements of volume. Area and volume measurements are often important in the sales comparison approach and also in the cost and income approaches to value.

Definition of Terms

Area

The *area* of an object is the space it occupies on a flat surface or a single flat level with just two dimensions, namely length and width. Area is calculated by multiplying these two measurements. In real estate, circumstances calling for the calculation of area include finding the area of a lot or parcel of land, and calculating the area of structures located on the land. Land areas are typically measured in square feet or acres. In larger land parcels, area could be described in sections (as discussed in Chapter 2) or even in square miles. In structures, area is most often calculated to find the floor space in a building in square feet. Examples include finding the livable area of a home, as well as the size of garages, basements, and porches. The size of individual rooms may also be needed. In income property appraisals, the average floor area per apartment unit is often important. Sometimes, the area of certain building components—such as the square foot area of the kitchen counters, or even the surface area of the roof cover—is important.

Volume

The *volume* relates to size in three dimensions, that is, to measuring a space with three dimensions. The most common example in real estate appraisal is calculating the airspace, or cubic volume, within a building. Volume is sometimes used in estimating construction costs. One can see, for example, that in calculating the cost to build a silo or a grain storage elevator, the cubic volume would be a helpful measure for cost calculations. Some complicated building code regulations also require calculation of the room volume in order to compare the volume with the square feet of usable window area. However, this is a calculation that an appraiser would not normally do.

Computing the Area

The calculation of an area requires 1) that only one system of measurement be used (all in feet, or all in yards, for example) and 2) that the proper formula be used for the shape or figure whose area is to be calculated. The importance of using only one measurement scale is that if one dimension is given in feet and another in yards, the two cannot be directly multiplied to give an answer either in square feet or in square yards. Consequently, the measurement in yards must be translated into feet, or the measurement in feet must be translated into yards, before the area can be calculated.

If the distance and direction of each perimeter line of a figure are known, one very modern method to compute an area is with a computer program. Here, the line values (distance and direction) are simply input as variables, and the area and/or diagram is produced automatically. The most common method of computing the square-foot or acre size of a figure is to prepare a scale drawing with a ruler or straightedge and calculate the area based on dimensions and shape.

Following are the formulas for calculating some of the more common figures or shapes that an appraiser might encounter. These include the square, the rectangle, the triangle, the trapezoid, and the circle. The formulas for other types of figures are not used as often. If needed, they can be located in a geometry text or mathematical reference book. An alternative is to use a survey computer program.

The Square

A *square* is defined as a closed figure (no gaps in any of the lines) with four equal sides and four right angles. A right angle is one-fourth of a full circle. The formula for the area of a square is as follows ("length" refers to the length of a side):

$$\text{Area of a square} = \text{length}^2 \text{ (or length} \times \text{length)}$$

The concept of multiplying a number times itself is called *the square of the number*. Thus, we could say that the area of a square equals the length squared. Let us calculate the area of a lot that is square in shape, with four equal sides and four right angle corners, having a street frontage of 100 feet and a depth of 100 feet. By using the given formula, the area is calculated to be 100 × 100, or 10,000 square feet. (Make sure that you have the right number of zeros in your answer!)

The Rectangle

A *rectangle* is defined as a closed four-sided figure with four right angles and with its opposite sides equal and parallel. The formula for the area of a rectangle is:

$$\text{Rectangle area} = \text{width} \times \text{length}$$

Thus, the area of a rectangular lot with a street frontage of 75 feet and a depth of 100 feet would be 75 × 100, or 7,500 square feet. Notice that a square is a special type of rectangle, and its area is the same using either formula.

The Triangle

A *triangle* is defined as any closed figure with three sides. We could create a triangle by first drawing a rectangle and then connecting any two opposite corners with a diagonal line. This allows us to see that the two triangles created must have the same total area as the area of the rectangle. The formula for the area of a triangle is as follows:

$$\text{Triangle area} = \text{height} \times \text{base} \times \frac{1}{2}$$

In calculating the area of a triangle, be sure to correctly define the base and the height. By convention, the base is taken as the lower or bottom line of the triangle; however, any of the three sides can be used as the base if it makes calculation easier. Height is defined as the length of the line that is perpendicular to (i.e., at right angles to) the base line, and connecting the base line with the opposite point of the triangle. See the examples shown in Figure 6-10.

The appraiser will find a variety of situations in which the formula for the area of a triangle can be used. The most common use is in calculating the area of a lot that is wider at the rear than at the front (or vice versa). Such lots are common at the end of cul-de-sac streets. The area of such lots can be calculated by dividing the lot into a series of rectangles and triangles. The area of each rectangle or triangle is calculated. If necessary, missing dimensions can be scaled on a map. The areas of the several rectangles and triangles are then totaled to give the area of the total parcel. This method is not as accurate as the calculations performed by surveyors or by modern computer survey programs, but is adequate for most appraisal purposes if more accurate calculations are not available.

The Trapezoid

The *trapezoid* is defined as a closed four-sided figure with two parallel sides. The two other sides are usually not parallel. From what you have already studied, a little doodling will show you that it is possible to calculate the area of a trapezoid by breaking the figure up into a rectangle and one or two triangles. Next, calculate the area of each, and add the areas together. However, it is quicker to use the formula for the area of a trapezoid, because it takes fewer calculations. The formula for the area of a trapezoid is:

$$\text{Trapezoid area} = [(\text{side 1} + \text{side 2}) \times \text{height}] / 2$$

Figure 6-10
Examples of
Triangles.

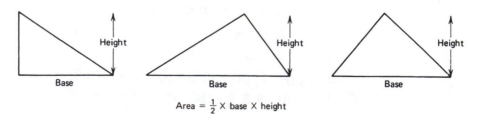

Area $= \frac{1}{2} \times$ base $\times$ height

Figure 6-11 The Area of a Trapezoid.

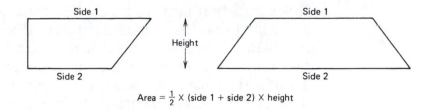

Area = $\frac{1}{2}$ × (side 1 + side 2) × height

In this formula, the two sides mentioned are the two parallel sides. The height is the perpendicular distance between them, just as in the formula for a triangle (see Figure 6-11). In a common real estate example, you might need to calculate the area of a lot that has a street frontage of 100 feet. Both sidelines go back at right angles to the street, with one sideline being 110 feet deep and the other 130 feet deep. The rear line, as you can see from the drawing in Figure 6-12, slants at a diagonal to the street, making the lot deeper at one back corner. This lot is in the shape of a trapezoid. The height (the perpendicular distance between the sides) is the 100-foot frontage on the street. The area would be $\frac{1}{2}$(110 + 130) × 100 = 12,000 square feet. Lots that are somewhat trapezoidal are common, so this is one formula that appraisers often use.

The Circle

The *circle* is defined as a curved line that forms a closed figure. The center of the figure is of equal distance from all points on the curved line. A straight line joining two points on the circle and passing through the center is called the *diameter*. A straight line joining the center point to any one point on the curve is called the *radius* of the circle and is, of course, one-half of the length of the diameter. The distance around the circle is called the *circumference*. The formula for the area of a circle is:

Circle area = *pi* × radius^2 (or *pi* × radius × radius)

Figure 6-12 Example of a Trapezoid-Shaped Lot.

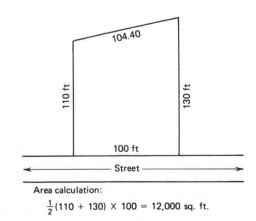

Area calculation:

$\frac{1}{2}$(110 + 130) × 100 = 12,000 sq. ft.

This calculation involves a new feature: the constant *pi*. A *constant* is something that has the same number value at all times. The value of *pi* is 3.1416+. Whenever you calculate the area of a circle, whether large or small, *pi* will always be the same (depending on how you round it), 3.1416. Remember that when a number is squared, it means that the number is multiplied by itself. A circle is shown in Figure 6-13.

If the appraiser is seeking to calculate the area of a house built as a geodesic dome, and finds that the distance across the house from one outside wall to the opposite outside wall is 100 feet, then the area of the structure would be 50 × 50 × 3.1416 = 7,854 square feet —a substantial floor space! The formula for the area of a circle is useful, not only under rare circumstances when you are appraising a geodesic dome, but also for homes that have half-circle bay windows. In this case, the area of the bay window would be one-half of the area of the circle. Similarly, there can be round swimming pools, round gazebos, round commercial buildings, and even half-circle sections of lots, where the appraiser can use the formula for the area of a circle.

Using Area Formulas

However irregular or unusual the shape of the object, the same procedure is used to calculate its area (assuming that you are not using a computer program). The first step is to prepare a scale diagram of the shape of the object. This might be taken from existing drawings or maps or might require measuring the object itself. The second step is to analyze the figure that is before you and decide how it can be broken down into a series of regular geometric shapes. These might be rectangles, triangles, trapezoids, half-circles, and so on. The third step is to estimate the dimensions of each of the subdivided shapes. This may require scaling the known distances on the map and using this calculation to estimate the length of unknown distances or lines.

Figure 6-13 The Area of a Circle.

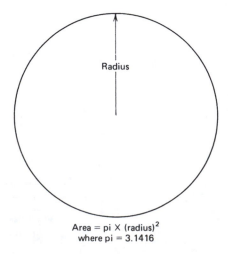

Radius

Area = pi × (radius)^2
where pi = 3.1416

In some cases it is also possible, using computer drawing programs or formulas in geometry books, to calculate some unknown distances from others that are known. The fourth step is to compute the area of each of the geometric shapes that were developed. The final step is to total the areas of each of the shapes. A practical example of this process is shown in Example 6-3.

Computing Volume

Volume is calculated by multiplying the three dimensions of an object. All three must be the same scale, that is, they must all be measured in feet, all in yards, or all in inches. The formula for calculating volume is as follows:

$$\text{Volume} = \text{area} \times \text{average height}$$

The use of this formula requires that the area be calculated first. Once the area is calculated, it is multiplied by the average height. In a building with flat ceilings or a flat roof, the average height would not be hard to determine. With pitched or sloping ceilings, however, the average height (the average of the lowest and highest height) must be calculated. In multiple-story buildings, the average height usually

---

EXAMPLE 6-3 Using Area Formulas

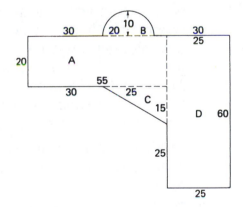

Steps:

1. Prepare a scale diagram.
2. Decide how to break it down into shapes.
3. Determine the dimensions of each shape.
4. Compute the area of each shape.
5. Total the areas of the shapes.

Shape A:	20 x 55 =	1,100
Shape B:	3.1416 x (10 x 10) x 1/2 =	157 (rounded)
Shape C:	15 x 25 x 1/2 =	188 (rounded)
Shape D:	25 x 60 =	+ 1,500
Total Area:		2,945 sq. ft.

is calculated using the distance from the floor level to the next floor level up.

For an example of the use of volume calculations in real estate appraisal, assume you are appraising a single-family residence with a living area of 2,340 square feet. The ceiling height is 10 feet, including the ceiling joists. You are using a cost manual that reports building costs only by the cost per cubic foot. For your building, the cost per cubic foot is $7.00. You calculate the cubic volume of the structure to be 2,340 × 10 = 23,400 cubic feet. Next, you multiply it by $7.00, to estimate its replacement cost new of $163,800. The use of cubic costs is less common now than it once was, so the calculation of volume is of less practical use today than earlier.

SUMMARY

The actual site inspection is one of the most important parts of the entire appraisal process. Therefore, the inspection should be planned well in advance.

The three major reasons for inspecting the property are:

1. To estimate the highest and best use of the site. The highest and best use generally means the legal and feasible use that will support the highest land value. The use must be physically possible, legally permitted, economically feasible, and maximally productive. The value of a property will vary depending on its use. An estimate of highest and best use is required by the *Uniform Standards of Professional Appraisal Practice* in almost all appraisals and written appraisal reports.

2. To identify the key site features. These may be grouped as physical characteristics, site location elements, and public and private restrictions.

3. To identify possible problems. Although you may not be experienced in all the areas in which a problem can exist, there are potential legal and physical problems that the appraiser might suspect are present.

It is desirable to have certain kinds of information before the actual site inspection begins. Data on the size and shape of the parcel, its legal characteristics, and the availability of utilities generally should be known beforehand. Information on comparable properties may also be useful. With this information, the site and comparables can be inspected on the same field trip.

The tools and equipment necessary to perform the inspection were then outlined. Many appraisers use a checklist during the actual inspection, to make certain that that they gather all the necessary information. A great variety of information about the site and its surroundings can be noted during the inspection. This information is divided into three categories.

1. The physical characteristics of the site.
2. The locational features of the site.
3. Public and private restrictions on the use of the site.

During the inspection, the appraiser should first investigate the physical characteristics of the site. These include the size, shape, frontage, and depth of the site. The topography, soil, and drainage of the site are also important. Land with irregular topography may be more costly to build on, but may contain desirable features such as a sweeping view. Is the soil of good quality? Will it support the uses being considered for this site? The water drainage or runoff systems, whether man-made or natural, should also be inspected.

Physical characteristics also include the form of ownership, type of lot, its orientation, and physical access. There are several forms of ownership, ranging from the conventional detached lot, to the planned unit development (PUD), to the airspace condominium. The conventional detached lot is a site that is the entire lot. The PUD is a site that involves ownership of a subdivided lot on which the owner's unit is built, plus an undivided ownership interest in the common areas. A condominium unit includes the fee ownership of a block of airspace (within which the unit sits), plus an undivided ownership in the common areas and the building's supporting walls.

There are a variety of lot types that you should be familiar with. These include the corner lot, the key lot, the cul-de-sac lot, and the flag lot. It is also important to note the lot's orientation to the sun, wind, and view. In recent years, utilization of the sun's energy has become more important.

The property must also be reasonably accessible. Properties situated in areas less accessible to large emergency vehicles, such as fire trucks, could face a reduction in value.

The improvements made to the site or on areas surrounding it should also be examined. Such improvements include landscaping, grading, excavation, and the width and paving of streets and sidewalks.

The second category of information to note during the site inspection is the location of the site. Analyzing the location involves three steps:

1. Compare the site to the properties around it.
2. Note the availability of utilities.
3. Examine the transportation systems that connect the site to nearby shopping and jobs.

The third category of information to consider during the site inspection includes public and private restrictions. Public restrictions are becoming more complicated and influential in our sophisticated society. Examples include zoning regulations, building and safety code regulations, and health and environmental protection laws. Another form of public restriction is the property tax. Property taxes are a burden on property, reducing the profitability of any use. While property taxes were historically imposed according to value, state and local laws and practices now vary as to the basis for property taxes. Related to the property tax are taxes collected by special assessment districts. Such taxes are used to pay for a particular public improvement, such as street lighting. Special assessments are generally based on the benefits that the project provides to the properties in the district.

A variety of private restrictions can affect the property's use. These range from simple deed restrictions to complex agreements between owners, as found in condominiums and in planned unit development projects. Since public and private restrictions have a direct influence on the use and value of real estate, it is important that they be carefully considered during the site inspection and analysis.

In Section 6.4, we discussed the importance of having some basic arithmetic skills. These mathematical skills are required throughout the appraisal process, in measuring the area of lots, building floor areas or volumes, and so on. Increasingly, appraisers now use computers to assist in these calculations.

Some buildings and lots have very irregular shapes, so that calculating their areas may seem impossible. However, complex shapes can usually be broken into a series of simple squares, rectangles, triangles, trapezoids, and circles (or half-circles). The area of each of these shapes is easily calculated using the proper formula. Alternatively, a computer area-calculating program can be used.

The volume, or cubic area, of a building can also be easily calculated by a formula. Such a volume calculation is sometimes used in the cost approach.

IMPORTANT TERMS AND CONCEPTS

Area	*Coverage ratio*
Assemblage	*Cul-de-sac lot*
Association agreement	*Depth*
Building footprint	*Easements*
Condominium	*Environmental impact report (EIR)*
Corner lot	*Excess depth*

Flag lot	*Planned Unit Development (PUD)*
Flood map	*Plottage*
Form of ownership	*Plottage value*
Frontage	*Private restrictions*
Gross area	*Public restrictions*
Highest and best use	*Radon gas*
Interim use	*Right of access*
Interior lot	*Site characteristics*
Key lot	*T-intersection lot*
Location	*Topography*
Lot shape	*Townhouse*
Lot type	*Toxic waste*
Methane gas	*Transportation*
Net area	*Useful area*
Off-site improvements	*Utilities*
On-site improvements	*Volume*
Orientation	

REVIEWING YOUR UNDERSTANDING

1. Before performing the site inspection, you should:
   a. Gather basic information about the site
   b. Be sure you know the reasons for the site inspection
   c. Have a map or drawing of the site
   d. All of the above

2. The first important reason for inspecting and analyzing the site is to:
   a. Estimate the highest and best use
   b. Note any unusual characteristics
   c. Find comparable sales
   d. None of the above

3. An appraiser should identify and record the physical characteristics, the public and private restrictions, and the locational elements of a site. Which of the following is considered an aspect of location?
   a. Topography
   b. Neighborhood conformity
   c. Deed restrictions
   d. Size and shape

4. Which best describes the site in a planned unit development?
   a.   Subdivided lot, plus appurtenant interest in the common areas
   b.   Defined block of airspace, plus an undivided interest in the common areas
   c.   Townhouse
   d.   None of the above

5. The criteria that define the highest and best use include all of the following except:
   a.   The use must be physically possible
   b.   The use must be legally permissible and economically feasible
   c.   The use must be low density
   d.   The use must be the most productive

6. Public restrictions on the use of land include all the following except:
   a.   Zoning regulations
   b.   Deed restrictions
   c.   Subdivision laws
   d.   Environmental protection laws

7. The appraiser's opinion of highest and best use should include:
   a.   The highest and best use as if vacant
   b.   The highest and best use as presently improved
   c.   Both a and b above
   d.   None of the above

8. A key lot is:
   a.   A lot that is shaped like a key
   b.   A lot that has several other lots backing onto its side yard
   c.   A lot that is located at the end of a dead-end street
   d.   None of the above

9. What is plottage value?
   a.   The value of land between the subject property and another property
   b.   The increase in value that may be obtained by combining parcels
   c.   The price of land per plot
   d.   The depth divided by the frontage

10. The formula for the area of a trapezoid is:
    a.   [(side 1 + side 2) x height] / 2
    b.   [(side 1 + side 2) x height] / 3
    c.   (side 1 + side 2 x height)
    d.   [(side 1 + side 2) x height] / 4

PRACTICAL APPLICATIONS

As we will remind you at the start of each exercise, review the preceding chapter exercise, and the work you have performed to date.

The focus for this assignment is on the site description section of the URAR Form and information that you need to collect. Review the copy of the site section shown in Figure 6-2. Consider what information you must obtain, and where you might be able to get it.

Some of the information consists of facts that you must find out. Site dimensions should be available from any website that has assessor records. Local title companies or your local government office may be able to help as well. For zoning, start with the local government. The engineering or public works office of your local government office can help you get answers to the utility questions or you may know from the monthly bills paid for utility service.

The remaining information calls for you to develop an opinion. For example, what is the highest and best use of the site if it were vacant? Read the section in the chapter covering this topic to refresh your memory. The same issues arise when faced with the question about adverse conditions or factors. Consider what you have read and then consider what you know about the subject property.

One practical problem will be faced by those students who live in a condo, an apartment, or a co-op. We suggested earlier that you might just appraise your individual unit as if it were a home. However, we are not describing the condo or co-op form in these exercises. What you need to do for the URAR is to either report the whole site as it really is or to make a hypothetical assumption, which you must include in your report, that you are appraising just a 50 by 100 foot portion of the lot. Only the dimensions and area would be hypothetical. Report all of the other information as it really is.

(Please note that you also could use the proper form if you choose. However, if your exercise is for submission in class, check with your instructor to see what should be done, as the instructor may want everyone "on the same form," to allow for a more efficient review.)

Finally, start up the software program and open the file that you saved after the prior chapter's assignment. Note that you have already entered the basic information about the property and the assignment, as well as the neighborhood section. Review this information. Next, enter the information about the site that you have collected.

As we note at the end of each exercise, it is best not to get ahead of yourself! Do not enter information in the later sections of the report until you have read the chapter(s) that covers that topic. However, it is a good idea to look ahead at the coming sections of the form so that you can start thinking about the information that you will need to gather. And it certainly is reasonable, and even desirable, for you to start collecting some of that information early, if you choose to do so.

Reminder: If you have questions about the program itself, please be sure to review the manuals and help information that were included with the program CD. Also, at anytime, you can go to http://www.bradfordsoftware. com, click on "Services" at the upper right of the home page, and then on "ClickFORMS Training Programs" in the middle of the "Services" page. See the free online training section!

CHAPTER 7
PROPERTY INSPECTION AND ANALYSIS: THE IMPROVEMENTS

PREVIEW

In the last chapter, we discussed the inspection and analysis of the site and its surroundings. Now we shall cover what is involved in the inspection and analysis of the improvements that are found on the site.

As used in appraisal terminology, improvements include everything attached to the vacant lot, that is, the building, swimming pool, shed, patio, walks, fence, and whatever other structures are to be found.

OBJECTIVES

When you have completed this chapter you should be able to:

1. Describe what tools are useful when making a field inspection of the improvements.

2. Describe the data emphasized in each of the three approaches to value.

3. Name the major items of a structure that the appraiser seeks to describe and rate.

4. Describe four construction classification types.

5. Explain what is meant by functional utility.

7.1 Planning the Building Inspection

Any inspection will go more smoothly if you prepare for it! This means assembling the tools necessary to perform the inspection, and planning what data to collect.

Equipment Needed

The building inspection usually requires a few special tools, in addition to the clipboard and pencil (or tablet or pocket computer), measuring tape, roller or laser measurer, ice pick or nail, and camera, which you have already assembled for the inspection of the site. The most important of these is an ***inspection checklist*** or appraisal form, for recording your data in an organized manner. Some appraisers use a specialized inspection form, while others enter data directly on the standard URAR appraisal forms. The property description section of the FNMA Uniform Residential Appraisal Report (often referred to as the ***URAR***) is shown in Figure 7-1. Methodical use of a standard checklist avoids having to return to the site for details that were overlooked! Some appraisers carry a pocket tape recorder and dictate building details for later transcription and completion of appraisal forms. Increasingly, appraisers take notes on a tablet or pocket computer.

To help in the building inspection, you may also want to carry a pocket flashlight for looking under houses and into dark corners. A marble can be handy for testing surfaces to see if they are level. Take along plot plans and blueprints if they are available. These plans can help you verify the location and dimensions of the improvements, and spell out important structural and mechanical details.

What Information Should You Collect?

The information collected for an appraisal varies with the type of property, the report format, the intended use of the report, the value definition, and any special conditions that may apply. Also, some unique or special data may be necessary to support the particular value approach that is being emphasized. Of course, the appraiser must always consider the degree of inspection called for by USPAP standards, by any state regulations that may apply, and any supplemental standards or client requirements.

Consider the Client's Intended Use of the Report

The client's intended use of the report and the appraisal largely determine the level of information to be provided in the appraisal. Building inspections required by lenders, for example, range from

**Figure 7-1
Improvement
Description Section
of the URAR Form.**

IMPROVEMENTS						
Units ☒ One ☐ One with Accessory Unit	☐ Concrete Slab ☒ Crawl Space	Foundation Walls Concrete	Floors Carpet/Good
# of Stories One	☐ Full Basement ☐ Partial Basement	Exterior Walls Stucco	Walls Plaster/VG
Type ☒ Det. ☐ Att. ☐ S-Det./End Unit	Basement Area N/A sq. ft.	Roof Surface C/Shingle	Trim/Finish Stock/Good
☒ Existing ☐ Proposed ☐ Under Const.	Basement Finish N/A %	Gutters & Downspouts Yes	Bath Floor Ceramic/Good
Design (Style) Contemp	☐ Outside Entry/Exit ☐ Sump Pump	Window Type Slid. Alum.	Bath Wainscot Tile Shower
Year Built 1981	Evidence of ☐ Infestation None Vis.	Storm Sash/Insulated Yes	Car Storage ☐ None
Effective Age (Yrs) 17	☐ Dampness ☐ Settlement	Screens Aluminium	☐ Driveway # of Cars
Attic ☒ None	Heating ☐ FWA ☐ HWBB ☐ Radiant	Amenities ☐ Woodstove(s) #	Driveway Surface Asphalt
☐ Drop Stair ☐ Stairs	☒ Other Fuel Gas	☒ Fireplace(s) # 1 ☒ Fence Wood	☒ Garage # of Cars 2
☐ Floor ☐ Scuttle	Cooling ☐ Central Air Conditioning	☒ Patio/Deck Concrete ☐ Porch	☐ Carport # of Cars
☐ Finished ☐ Heated	☐ Individual ☐ Other	☐ Pool ☒ Other Htd Spa	☒ Att. ☐ Det. ☐ Built-In

Appliances ☐Refrigerator ☒Range/Oven ☒Dishwasher ☒Disposal ☐Microwave ☐Washer/Dryer ☐Other (describe)

Finished area **above** grade contains:	6 Rooms	4 Bedrooms	2.00 Bath(s)	1,768 Square Feet of Gross Living Area Above Grade

Additional features (special energy efficient items, etc.) Kitchen and master bath have skylights. Master bath has mirrored double pullman basins. The rear yard improvements include a covered patio, and a 7 foot heated spa.

Describe the condition of the property (including needed repairs, deterioration, renovations, remodeling, etc.).
There are no physical, functional, or external inadequacies noted; the kitchen and baths were recently decorated.

Are there any physical deficiencies or adverse conditions that affect the livability, soundness, or structural integrity of the property? ☐ Yes ☒ No If Yes, describe
There are no adverse environmental conditions in evidence.

Does the property generally conform to the neighborhood (functional utility, style, condition, use, construction, etc.)? ☒ Yes ☐ No If No, describe

detailed interior and exterior inspections, to exterior inspections only. If the appraisal assignment requires an interior inspection and a self-contained report, the work would be very different from an assignment with only an exterior inspection.

A good example of special lender requirements was the national standard for FHA loan appraisals adopted in 1999 by HUD. In addition to the standard URAR form, HUD required the completion of a Valuation Condition (VC) form, to ensure that the property met the Department's Minimum Property Standards requirements. A detailed review of the property's condition and code conformity and a report of any safety problems were required. This form was dropped in 2005 when the revised URAR form was released.

It is easy to see that the client and the intended use of the appraisal report determine its form and content. If the appraisal report is to be used by the seller of a single-family dwelling to estimate a realistic price, a brief description of the building structure, design, and room count may be all that is needed, subject to the ethical requirements of USPAP. However, if the appraisal is being made for loan purposes, the lender will usually require completion of a detailed form, such as the URAR referred to previously. A description of the URAR and its requirements is found in Chapter 16. For some types of appraisals, such as relocation assignments, the appraiser must also review the personal property to be included in the transfer. When an appraisal report is prepared for court proceedings, more specialized information and added documentation are usually necessary.

The majority of appraisal reports are used for home loans. Even here, lender requirements vary, and may be relatively simple or quite detailed. Certain loans may require information on room sizes, door and window placement for cross ventilation, heating, plumbing, finish materials, storage, access, privacy, and so on. As you can see, physicall y measuring room sizes and noting door openings, if required, could take more time and effort than you might have allowed if you had just planned to perform a measurement of the outside dimensions.

Besides specific physical details, loan appraisals may require measured judgment on such factors as the property's conformity to the neighborhood, market acceptability of the property, compatibility with surrounding land uses, and the physical condition of the subject property. Ideally, dwellings should conform to the following requirements:

1. Safe, secure, healthful, and attractive living facilities.
2. Ease of circulation and housekeeping.
3. Visual and auditory privacy.
4. Appropriate light and ventilation.
5. Fire and accident protection.
6. Economy of maintenance.
7. Adequate sanitation facilities.
8. Accessory services.

Some lenders are now using an abbreviated version of the URAR form in conjunction with their own risk analysis programs for certain single-family home and condominium loans. **FNMA Form 2055** is used by lenders in an automated system called the **Desktop Underwriter Program**. This form allows the appraisal to be made with an exterior inspection only, referred to as a *drive-by*, if the critical physical characteristics of the property can be supplied using reasonably reliable sources. Another version, **FNMA Form 2075**, is now used for inspection and reporting purposes only and usually only for Freddie Mac loans. More information on these forms is presented in Chapter 16.

Consider the Value Definition

The purpose of most appraisals is to estimate market value. As suggested above, an inspection for this purpose usually requires a detailed and accurate description of the physical structures and an analysis of the acceptability of the property by local standards. Conformity to building codes, deed restrictions, and zoning regulations should also be reviewed, to the degree that the appraiser is able. In this regard, any apparent nonconformity should be carefully noted, so that its influence on market value can be considered.

Finally, the highest and best use of the property as presently improved should be analyzed. If the present use differs from the highest and best use of the site as if it were vacant, the building inspection should be designed to explore alternative uses. As suggested in Chapter 6, estimating the contribution of the improvements to the total property value is the appraiser's objective.

Appraisals made for purposes other than market value may demand more specialized data than that described above. For example, appraisals made to report an opinion of insurable value would logically require the appraiser to seek out the data needed to estimate construction costs, rate the structure's fire resistance, and report the physical condition of the building.

Special Conditions

The presence or absence of any special conditions, as established at the outset of an appraisal assignment, may also influence the detail required in a building inspection. For example, if an appraisal is being made subject to the completion of remodeling that is in progress, the exact nature and extent of the proposed changes to the improvements must be obtained in advance, and then kept in mind during the building inspection.

What Value Approaches Are To Be Emphasized?

The information that you gather during the visual inspection will be influenced by the value approaches you expect to emphasize. Consider the general data requirements for each approach.

The Cost Approach. Generally, the cost approach requires the most descriptive detail. Besides the appraiser's rating of the age, condition, and utility of the improvements, the data collected must be adequate to allow you to calculate the cost estimate. Cost estimates often rely on the use of published cost manuals. Here are some of the factors that cost manuals usually consider significant. These will be explored more fully in Chapter 11.

Significant Cost Issues

1. Design or use type.
2. Construction classification.
3. Rating of quality.
4. Size, shape, and height.
5. Special equipment.
6. Yard or site improvements.

Some cost-estimating methods, such as the segregated method that is an option in the Marshall Valuation Service, utilize detailed measurements of individual building components. This might call for the dimensions of the floors, exterior walls, interior partitions, storefronts, roof structure and cover, and so on. The rating for age, condition, and utility strongly affect the allowance for depreciation in the cost approach, so close attention to details of property maintenance and repair is also important.

The Sales Comparison Approach. This approach requires improvement details that can be compared with the features of similar properties that have sold. So, again, familiarity with the type of data to be compared is important, to avoid a second inspection to fill in the gaps. Here is a list of the typical property characteristics to be noted in single-family home appraisals. Most of these items are also included in the various computerized lists of residential sales used by appraisers.

Typical Characteristics of Single-Family Homes

Architectural style

Above- and below-grade finished areas

Construction type

Type of exterior

Type of roof covering

Number of stories

Floor plan

Overall quality

Condition

Year built

Number of bedrooms

Number of bathrooms

Total number of rooms

Square feet of living area

Basement area

Type of heating and cooling

Fireplace(s)

Built-ins

Any remodeling

Parking accommodations

Outside improvements (such as pools and patios)

The Income Approach. If the income approach is to be emphasized, the appraiser should be aware of the property characteristics that have the greatest effect on the income potential and the probable expenses. In most income properties, the following features would be among those sought:

Describing Income Property

Number and types of rentable units, and number of vacant units.

The ratio of useable tenant area to the total building area.

Quality of the tenant space.

Recreation areas, parking, services, and other amenities available.

Durability of the structure and materials.

Physical condition of the structure and equipment.

Now that we have assembled the necessary tools and made appropriate plans for the task, we are ready to begin the building inspection.

7.2 Performing the Building Inspection

The purpose of the building inspection is to identify the condition, quality, features, and functionality of the property being appraised, *to the degree practical*. It bears repeating that appraisers are not qualified to be construction, design, code, or defect inspectors. In this section, we shall describe the building inspection techniques most appraisers use. When you have your equipment in order, your checklist in hand, and have made an appointment with the owner, manager, or tenant of your subject property, you are ready to begin the building inspection.

Recording and Rating Improvement Characteristics

As you start noting the physical features of a property, be prepared to follow the checklist or appraisal form you have selected for the job. Most checklists suggest a logical sequence of observations which, if followed, can help you avoid missing important data. It is desirable to use correct construction terminology in your report, but your notes may use abbreviations or your own form of shorthand. Structural components and finish materials will be discussed in Section 7.3.

What to Inspect

As part of defining the Scope of Work, if an interior inspection is to be performed, the appraiser must consider what areas of the building (or buildings) to inspect. If the inspection is only from the street, then no interior inspection will be made.

In rare cases, the appraiser will be authorized to be on the property but will not be able to enter the building. One example is when it would not be safe to do so due to structural damage. Here, the appraiser typically would only inspect from the building exterior, and looking through any accessible windows, glass doors, and so on. (It is highly desirable to knock on the front door first, even if the building is reported to be vacant!)

What does an appraiser inspect when doing an interior inspection? It depends on the Scope of Work, but there are still some general statements that apply. For example, appraisers almost never go up on the roof of the building, but they do try to look at the roof from below, both to be able to report what type of roof cover is present, and also to see if there is obvious evidence of deterioration. If there is an accessible roof deck, however, they would usually go on it.

Inside the finished areas of the structure, appraisers typically would enter every room, opening every door (to avoid missing a bath or storage area). Sometimes, storage areas might only be viewed from the entry doorway. For apartment, hotel, mini-warehouse, retail, office and similar buildings, the same thorough inspection is made of any unit entered. However, the appraiser does not necessarily inspect each unit. This is an issue that should be discussed with the client as a necessary part of defining the Scope of Work! For industrial plants, usually all of the building(s) will need to be inspected, primarily because the construction details and finish often vary tremendously within the plant.

What about basements? Most often, appraisers inspect them. At the least, they need to be measured! The basement also often contains heating, cooling, water heating, and electrical equipment that the appraiser must see in order to write down the type and capacity information. There also might be a sump pump to be noted! In addition, portions of the basement might be finished or might be only crawl space. Appraisers rarely enter crawl space areas, as they do not have the training to 1) do so safely and 2) interpret what might be visible there. Appraisers also inspect the basement to see the type of foundation, if there are signs of water intrusion, and if there are foundation or floor cracks that should be noted.

Mezzanines are usually inspected: The type and quality of finish and ceiling heights can be much different from the rest of the building. Attics are more variable. If an attic is accessible by a stairway or a pull-down stair, appraisers probably at least view the space from the top of the stair. If it is large or finished, then a fuller inspection would be indicated. Caution is needed to make sure that one does not step on weak flooring and fall through to the floor below! The appraiser would need to note any skylights, dormers or other windows, any lighting, and the degree of finish. But if the attic is only accessible from a ceiling hatch, appraisers almost never inspect, even just by looking from the hatchway.

Exterior and Interior Features

The exterior is often inspected first, starting with the foundation and basement (if any), then the exterior finish, windows, doors, and finally the roof. Be sure to note the type, style, materials used, and condition of each of the parts of the exterior. Now, outside structures, walks, driveways, and landscaping should be described.

Next, the interior is inspected. The number and type of rooms and their arrangement are noted. The interior finish is rated as to type and condition of materials and quality of workmanship. Finally, the built-in kitchen equipment (such as range and oven), as well as the heating, air conditioning, and other systems, are inspected and their type and probable adequacy noted. The presence and adequacy of insulation in the roof, ceiling, walls, windows, and floor must be investigated to the degree that is practical, noting the R-factor, if available (see "Typical Residential Specifications" in Section 7.3). Also, note any special energy-efficient equipment, such as solar heating.

Lastly, some state and local laws require that all houses have (upon sale), or be retrofitted with, smoke detectors and/or water conservation devices. Earthquake retrofitting, gas water heater blankets and anchors, and gas seismic shutoff valves may also be required. Many laws now require safety glass in shower and patio doors. Try to identify and note the presence or absence of such items, as much as you are able!

Rating for Appeal and Marketability

As you walk through the building, you should be able to get some idea of the general marketability and appeal of the property. Try to be aware of the demands and tastes of the specific market in the neighborhood of the property. Do the features of this house fit in with others in the neighborhood? If you were buying here, would you like this house, and why?

It is generally agreed that the marketability and appeal of a single-family residential property depend on:

1. Construction quality of the materials and finishes.
2. Physical condition of the structure, exterior and interior finishes, and equipment.

3. Room sizes, layout, and privacy (both visual and noise).
4. Adequacy of closets and other storage areas.
5. Energy efficiency.
6. Adequacy and condition of plumbing and bath facilities.
7. Adequacy and condition of the electrical system.
8. Adequacy of heating equipment and any air conditioning.
9. The adequacy, condition, convenience, and quality of kitchen cabinets and equipment.
10. Type and adequacy of car storage facilities.
11. Landscaping and outdoor improvements.
12. General livability and appeal.

Every person has an ideal home in his or her imagination. While inspecting a residence, the appraiser tries to "wear the shoes" of the typical buyer of the particular property, in order to see its faults and advantages. A certain "quiet quality" may increase the marketability of a home far more than extra equipment, whereas other factors, such as a pervading musty odor in the bathrooms and closets, or a poor room arrangement, may seriously detract from the appeal of an otherwise sound building.

Evaluating Construction Quality

Quality can be a very subjective word. However, in appraising, it is used to describe the apparent quality of the basic structural integrity, materials, finishes, and special features of the building. The quantity and type of fixtures, cabinets, and built-in equipment are considered to be part of the quality rating, as is the level of overall workmanship.

Quality is also relative; that is, we can judge it only by comparison with a given standard. Most appraisers attempt to rate buildings according to typical specifications provided in published cost-estimating guides. Generally, these guides use the four ratings of 1) good, 2) average, 3) fair, and 4) poor. These quality ratings will be discussed in detail in Section 7.3.

Evaluating Physical Condition

Although the physical *condition* of a building is often closely related to its age, each aspect is of concern to the appraiser. Has the house generally been kept in good repair or allowed to run down? When rating a building for condition, any possible deferred maintenance or structural defects that are identified should always be examined and described. It is also appropriate for the appraiser to try to identify and note any probable asbestos-containing material. Asbestos-containing materials are most commonly found as insulating materials in older structures.

If the inspection suggests the possible presence of any of the environmental hazards described in Chapter 6 (lead-based paint or methane or radon gas, for example), they should be noted. An official environmental report could be requested from the client, or the property appraised under the clearly reported Extraordinary Assumption (see Chapter 3), that no hazards are present.

Note the condition of paint, floor and wall coverings, kitchen counter tops, shower walls, hardware, equipment, and fixtures. It is desirable to ask if each appliance is in working condition. Describe any remodeling or renovation you may find, as well as any abnormal neglect or wear.

Are there any signs of water leakage or moisture inside the house? These may be caused by roof or plumbing leaks, inadequate seals or flashing at windows or doors, or improper ventilation. Look for discolored or peeling paint on the walls or ceilings. Notice recently patched spots, discolored or moldy seams, or a musty odor in bathrooms and kitchens. Any of these conditions may indicate problems, and may need to be noted in the report.

To the best of your ability, note whether additions, major repairs, and remodeling conform to the building codes. Sometimes you will find garage conversions, and even more ambitious structural work, that has been done without a building permit. If you suspect such a condition, in most cases you should investigate and report your findings in the appraisal, possibly with an Extraordinary Assumption that the work is legal.

Every building inspection by an appraiser should include a check for visible indications of structural problems or foundation settling, to the degree that the appraiser is able. Any such problem could reduce both the marketability and value of a property. Therefore, it is important to try to see and report such telltale signs as large cracks or fresh patchwork in the foundation, walls, and ceilings. Structural cracks caused by a sagging foundation most often show up at the corners of door and window openings, as demonstrated in Figure 7-2. Cabinets that have pulled away from the wall or that are no longer plumb (vertical); doors that stick or have been trimmed out of square; or floors that hump, dip, or are not level (see why you needed that marble?) all suggest either a settling of the foundation or a shifting of the structure. Sometimes, evidence of property damage may be found after earthquakes, such as those occurring in 2003 in California.

Part of the appraiser's job can be to estimate the cost needed to cure any deferred maintenance or structural defects. Depending on his or her cost-estimating experience, the appraiser may need to consult contractors or engineers before making a *cost-to-cure* estimate and before completing the report. Appraisers should not try to prepare an

**Figure 7-2
An Example of
Structural Damage.**

Source: Photograph Courtesy of Doug Frost.

estimate that is beyond their competency. Some owners may have already consulted such experts and obtained written estimates of the work needed.

Effective Age

Some residential loan appraisals require the appraiser to estimate the effective age of a building. *Effective age* is usually defined as the relative age of a structure considering its physical condition and marketability. Thus, a very old building that has been extensively updated and now compares in these respects with similar buildings that are, say, 10 years old may be said to have an effective age of 10 years. In assigning effective age, appraisers usually consider the historical age and the degree of maintenance, as well as room additions and remodeling.

Sometimes, the first step in an effective age analysis is to calculate the *average age* of a remodeled structure. This can be done by weighting the old and new components according to their respective age and their proportion of the total structure. For example, if a 30-year-old house was remodeled 10 years ago, and about 80 percent of the original structure remained unremodeled, then the average age (based solely on the physical elements) would be 26 years. Here is how that would be figured:

80%	x 30 years	=	24 years
20%	x 10 years	=	2 years
	Average age	=	26 years

In actual practice, remodeling may or may not actually extend the useful life of a structure. Thus, the effective age assigned by the appraiser need not agree with the calculated average age. There are other issues that the market considers.

It follows that the second step in estimating the effective age of the property is to examine your sales and judge the market reaction to a property's standard of maintenance. For example, if major areas of potential obsolescence, such as kitchens and baths, had been remodeled before the date of sale in any of the sale properties, are their prices noticeably higher? Comparing this price difference to the cost to perform such remodeling can also be helpful!

Measuring Improvements and Preparing Drawings

Most appraisals require some information on the area and/or the volume of the buildings. Necessary dimensions are usually included on a diagram prepared by the appraiser. Whether done by hand, or with one of the appraisal computer programs now available, such a diagram will sometimes include a detailed floor plan of the rooms, doors, and windows. Traditionally, building measurements are rounded to the nearest foot, half-foot, tenth of a foot, or inch. We will discuss this in depth later.

Defining the Building Areas

For detached residential structures, the total or gross *living area* (floor area) is sought. It is calculated using measurements taken on the exterior of the building, so it includes the area of the exterior walls and finish. According to the standard adopted by the American National Standards Institute (ANSI), entryways and protruding fireplace chimneys, as well as bay windows that do not extend down to the floor level, are excluded from the living-area calculations.

However, condominium units are properly measured using interior rather than exterior measurements, since the air space is what is bought and sold. In commercial buildings, interior measurements of useable space are often required. These measurements are also taken between the finished wall surfaces.

According to FNMA and FHA guidelines, the gross living area (square footage) of detached homes should normally include only those areas that are above grade. The *ANSI standard* is consistent with this practice, requiring that all above-grade and below-grade finished areas of a single-family home be presented separately when reporting the total square footage. To be considered as *above-grade* finished area, all of a floor level must be above the outside grade. If one side of a level is below grade, then *all of that level* of the house is considered to be **below-grade** finished area. This is important, because a particular market may have very different preferences for above-grade space compared to below-grade space.

While not yet adopted by all elements of the industry, the ANSI standard further recommends that house measurements be taken to the nearest inch or tenth of a foot, when using English measurement units. The final square footage, however, is reported to the nearest whole square foot, as is the common practice.

It is often easier to record your field measurements on a rough sketch as you work; graph paper of the proper scale can help. Later you can draw a final sketch when you have a better writing surface and your hands are cleaner. (Handling a measuring tape can make them grimy.) One-tenth or one-twentieth inch to the foot are the most commonly used scales, the choice depending on the size of the building. Tenth-of-a-foot scales are becoming more common. Increasingly, appraisers use a laser measuring device (the Disto is one widely used brand). Some models radio the dimensions to a tablet or pocket computer and automatically enter them into a floor plan program. This allows less rounding and much more accuracy, along with fewer errors from copying numbers incorrectly.

Measuring, Diagraming, and Calculating Techniques

Have you ever wondered how to measure a building? It is really quite simple. Just start at one right-angle corner, usually the front left corner, as you face the building from the street. Using the hook on your tape measure to attach it (or an ice pick stuck into a crack or in the ground), extend your tape across the front of the building to the other corner. Write down the measurement. Move your tape hook to the second corner and continue the same procedure along one side, then the back of the house, and the other side, until you return to your starting corner. Remember to pick up any special measurements you might need, such as patio dimensions, while you are there. Be sure to measure separately and clearly label above-grade and below-grade living areas, as well as open or roofed porches, and finished and unfinished basements and storage rooms. Your plane geometry from high school will come in handy if you run across angles that are not right angles.

Be sure the building outline is in *balance*. This means that the horizontal measurements across the front must add up to equal the horizontal measurements across the back; also, the right- and left-side measurements must equal each other when totaled. Example 7-1 may help you understand what is meant by balancing the building diagram.

EXAMPLE 7-1 Example of a Building Diagram

A. Area Calculations:
Floor area:

Shape A:	16 x 18 =	228
Shape B:	6 x 19 =	114
Shape C:	32 x 49 =	1,568
Less Entry:	5 x 5 =	(25)
		1,945 sq. ft.

Garage:

20 x 20 = 400 sq. ft.

B. Proof that the Drawing "Balances":

Front (house and garage): 20 + 29	= 49 ft.
Rear:	19 + 14 + 16 = 49 ft.

Front and rear are in balance.

Left side:	58 + (18 − 6) = 70 ft.
Right side:	50 + 20 = 70 ft.

Left and right sides are in balance.

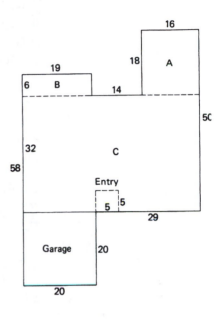

When you have completed your diagram, you must compute the building areas. If you have used a computer floor plan program, it will calculate the areas for you. If you drew a sketch on paper, you must calculate the area yourself. Divide the living area into natural rectangles by sketching light broken lines horizontally or vertically across the diagram. Compute each of the areas separately by multiplying the length by the width of each rectangle. Add all appropriate areas together to calculate the total above-grade living area. (Methods of computing areas of irregular building shapes can be found in Chapter 6.)

Finally, your improvement diagram should separately list and calculate any below-grade living areas and any unfinished basements. Open or covered porches, garages, carports, and other outside structures are also to be figured separately.

Taking Required Photographs

Photographs are a necessary part of the property and building inspection. They serve to document the appearance and the actual condition of the building at the time of inspection, and are generally integrated into the appraisal report.

The standard appraisal report usually contains photographs showing the front and rear of the subject property, along with a street scene. Interior photographs are rarely included in the report, unless unique or unusual features need to be highlighted. Interior photos may be desirable to show any problems. Many appraisers also take extra interior photographs to document features and condition at the time of inspection!

Lenders that use the Uniform Residential Appraisal Report (URAR) generally require that attachments to the form include the standard front, rear, and street scene photographs described previously. However, when only an exterior inspection of the property is to be performed, a front scene of the subject is all that is normally required.

Digital cameras have become the standard tool of appraisers. No film is required, and the images may be viewed as soon as they are taken on the camera's LCD (liquid crystal) display. Poor images may be discarded, and the remainder downloaded and stored in the office computer for inserting into the appraisal report. A number of pictures may be stored in the typical digital camera's smart-media card or chip. After downloading the pictures, the images may be erased, and the card used again.

7.3 Understanding Construction Details

It is desirable for the appraiser to understand the basic principles of construction and be familiar with typical structural details. (Figure 7-3 shows examples of wood framing details.) This section will cover 1) basic *construction classification*, 2) the selection of building materials, 3) typical *building specifications*, and 4) the standards used for judging the quality of a building.

Construction Classification Systems

Historically, most systems for classifying types of construction were based on the structure's resistance to fire. For this reason, buildings are generally classified into four or five classes, according to their particular type of basic frame, wall, and floor construction.

In most building codes and construction cost manuals, basic construction types are classified by either an "A, B, C, D" or a "1, 2, 3, 4" designation system. Details of Class A, B, and C construction are shown in Figure 7-4; Class D details are given in Figure 7.3. The typical specifications for all four classes follow.

Class A buildings have fireproofed structural steel frames and reinforced concrete or masonry floors and roofs. Major institutional

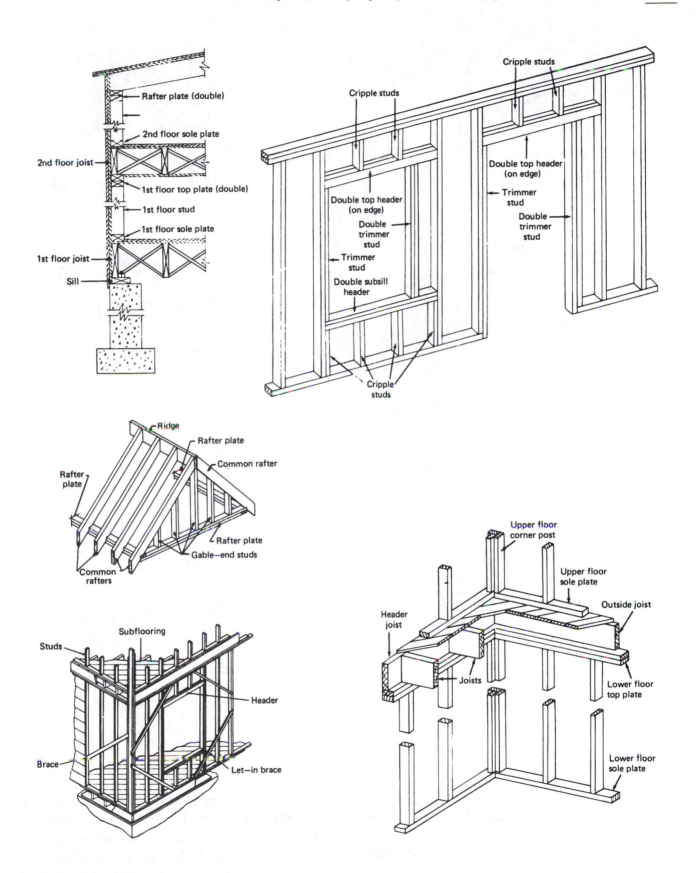

Figure 7-3 Structural Detail: Wood Framing (From Builder 3 & 2, Bureau of Naval Personnel, 1965).

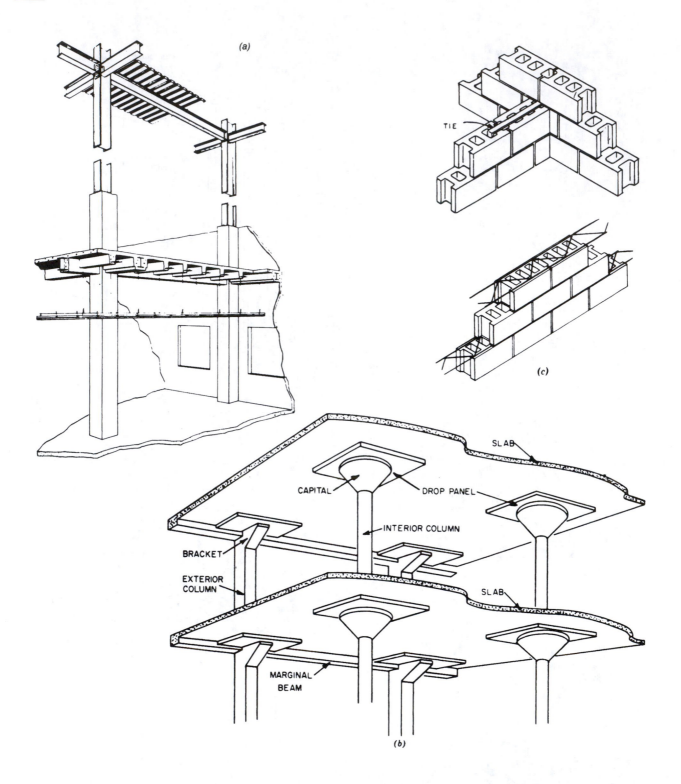

Figure 7-4 Construction Class Details. (a) Class A (Courtesy of Marshall & Swift Publication Company) (b) Class B (From Design Manual Structural Engineering. Department of the Navy, Naval Facilities Engineering Command, October 1970) (c) Class C (From Builder 3 & 2, Bureau of Naval Personnel, 1965)

buildings, as well as high-rise office and hotel buildings are usually **Class A construction**. Class A construction is the strongest for its weight but is the most expensive.

Class B buildings have reinforced concrete frames and reinforced concrete or masonry walls, floors, and roofs. The typical Class B building is a three- to five-story office building or a heavy industrial plant. **Class B construction** is second only to Class A in cost and fire resistance.

Class C buildings have masonry exterior walls, and wood or exposed steel floor and roof structures. Many one- and two-story commercial and industrial buildings fall into the **Class C construction** category. Also, many residential buildings in colder climates belong in this classification.

Class D buildings have wood or light steel frames and roof structures. Most residential buildings in the West and South fall into the **Class D construction** classification. Basic construction features of Class D construction include concrete or concrete-block foundations; concrete slab or raised wood floors; wood framed walls and roof structure; stucco and/or wood siding exterior; drywall or plaster interior; and tar and gravel, composition shingle, wood shingle, or shake roofing. Increasingly, some steel framing is added, especially at large windows, to improve earthquake and wind resistance.

Choice of Materials

Traditionally, the materials used for structural and mechanical components, as well as the finish of buildings, are dependent on the climate, availability, cost, style, durability, and building code requirements.

The climate can dictate the type of foundation, walls, insulation, roof pitch, and finish material. In the moderate climate of America's West and Southwest, stucco and wood structures prevail. Insulation is needed primarily against the summer heat. In colder climates, extensive insulation may be needed to provide better protection from the wind and cold. Heating and air-conditioning systems should be designed to meet climatic conditions. In today's energy-conscious economy, such systems need to be energy-efficient: hence the trend toward solar heating and design features that minimize energy loss.

The selection of materials also depends on their availability. Since the earliest times, mankind has used readily available materials for shelter. Adobe was used in the early Southwest because it was plentiful, easily made into building blocks, and suitable to the hot, dry climate. Wood is used where forests are found, and clay is used where it is readily available and of a quality that is suitable for making into bricks.

Cost is also a factor in the use of materials. Custom homes may still incorporate expensive marbles and rare woods, but the average builder must think twice about the comparative cost of the materials used. As wood is becoming more costly and scarce, some builders are beginning to experiment with plastic, steel, or fiberglass walls, often prefabricated to meet the building specifications. We are already conditioned to the use of fiberglass tub enclosures and plastic counters in bathrooms. Plastics and polymers have also replaced expensive metals in rough plumbing and electrical building components in many areas of the country.

The style of the construction will often suggest that certain materials be used. Traditionally, horizontal wood siding, shingles, and shake roofs go with ranch-style and Cape Cod houses. Tile roofs and textured stucco are typical of Spanish- or Mediterranean-style houses.

The durability of materials must also be taken into consideration when deciding on the materials to be used in a structure. Durability is partly dependent on climate. Most exterior woods deteriorate in areas of high temperature or humidity. One exception to the rule is redwood. Although more expensive than many other types of wood, redwood is much more resistant to weather, does not require paint, and may in the long run be more economical for exterior siding. Durability also depends on usage. Interior finishes that are subject to heavy wear must meet a reasonable durability test. The modern vinyl floor coverings and plastic laminate counter tops that increasingly replace hardwood and ceramic tiles are not quite as resistant to wear, but they are less expensive.

Local building code requirements are also important in determining the materials to be used. The stress and load requirements for wood framing in construction eliminate many varieties of forest products. Douglas fir is most often preferred for its relative strength. Many codes do not allow any wiring except copper for the electrical circuits in a structure. Plastic pipes and sewers are not allowed in some areas. Each locality has its own fairly rigid building code.

Although they often contribute to high housing costs by restricting the types of materials to be used, for the most part, building codes seek to offer the community protection from fire, health hazards, insect and rodent infestation, and unsafe buildings.

Typical Residential Specifications

As already noted, residential structures differ widely in materials and specifications. Examples of the range of choices are shown in Figure 7-5. Typical features found today follow. New materials are introduced frequently. The appraiser tries to keep current by reading construction magazines or visiting construction job sites.

**Figure 7-5
Choice of Materials.**

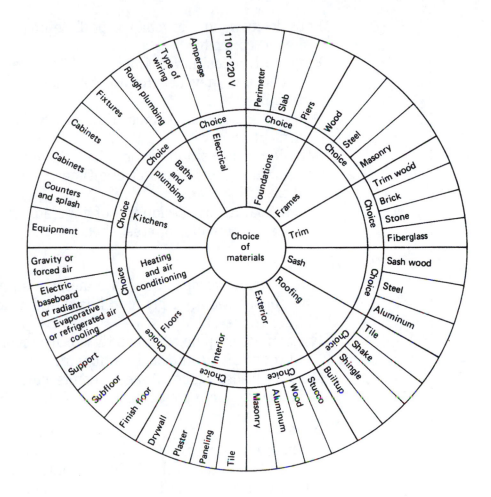

Foundations:

Concrete or block piers.
Perimeter foundation walls of reinforced concrete or concrete block.
Reinforced concrete slab foundation and floor.
Drilled concrete piers and grade beams.

Frames of walls:

Wood, composite, steel, aluminum, or masonry. (Douglas fir, cypress, or hemlock preferred as framing lumber.)
Structural bracing by wood, plywood, or particle board siding; steel moment frames.

Trim and Sash:

Trim: wood, brick, stone, or fiberglass or plastic replica.
Sash: wood, steel, or aluminum (double-hung, casement, or sliding); sliding glass or French doors to privacy areas (such as decks or back yards).

Roofing:

Framing: wood, composite or steel.

Roof deck: wood, plywood, or particle board; aluminum or steel sheets; concrete.

Built-up composition or fiberglass felt, covered with hot-mopped asphalt and gravel. (Asbestos felt may still be found in older structures.)

Growing use of resin composition sheets, bonded at joints, usually with gravel cover.

Shingles: composition, wood, concrete, metal, or clay tile. (Asbestos tile shingles were used at one time.)

Shakes: split cedar.

Other: Spanish or Mission tile of concrete, clay or metal; slate; and copper, aluminum, or steel sheet.

Exterior:

Stucco; wood, composition, or aluminum shingles or siding; hardboard, wood or plywood board and batten siding; or brick or stone veneer.

Types of wood: pine, Douglas fir, spruce, cypress, hemlock, cedar, redwood, or pre-finished hardboard.

Masonry walls: adobe, stone, concrete block, slumpstone, brick, or precast concrete panels (usually reinforced for bearing walls).

Interior:

Wallboard, sheetrock (drywall), or lath and plaster; lath of wood, expanded metal mesh, or drywall button board.

Unfinished or painted masonry walls, sometimes furred out and finished.

Finishes: paint, wallpaper, plywood, hardwood veneer, Douglas fir, redwood or hardwood plank (tongue and groove), ceramic tile, plastic, or marble.

Insulation:

Roof, ceiling, walls, or floor: aluminum foil, cellulose, fiberglass, polystyrene, or other synthetic. (Asbestos-containing materials may still be found in older structures.) Typical R-factor, or rating, varies from about R-10 to R-38 for good ceiling and wall insulation. (The higher number indicates better heat/cold insulating qualities.)

Air sealing: weather-strips; insulated windows.

Floors:

Concrete slab.

Raised (over a crawl space) subfloors of plywood, particle board, or lightweight concrete.

Finished flooring of tongue and groove (or parquet) hardwood, hardwood tile, asphalt tile, linoleum, sheet vinyl or vinyl tile, ceramic tile, terrazzo, marble, or carpeting.

New synthetic or composite materials are becoming common.

Heating and Air Conditioning:

Fuel: natural gas (methane), bottled propane, fuel oil, coal, wood or solar, or a combination.

Heat transfer: hot air, hot water, steam; forced or gravity circulation.

Heating unit: central or individual.

Individual: floor, wall or ceiling; baseboard, radiator, or radiant floor or ceiling.

Fireplaces: wood-burning and/or gas; screens, glass doors, hot air circulators, stove insert.

Air cooling:

Individual through-wall or window unit; central ducted unit.

Evaporative (swamp cooler) or refrigerated.

Combined with heating unit or separate.

Kitchens:

Cabinets: softwood, particle board, plywood, hardwood, plastic laminate veneer, or baked-enamel prefabricated steel.

Counters and splash: ceramic tile, stainless steel, marble, granite, stone composites, laminated wood, plastic, or plastic laminates.

Equipment: sink, garbage disposal, vent-fan and hood over stovetop; built-in oven, microwave, grill, barbecue, dishwasher, mixer-blender, trash compactor, water filter, or instant hot-water faucet.

Baths and Plumbing:

Rough plumbing: of polyvinyl chloride or other plastic, galvanized iron, or copper pipe. Drain pipes may be cast iron or plastic.

Plumbing fixtures: vitreous china toilet and bidet; bathtub of porcelain enameled cast iron, steel, or fiberglass; enameled cast iron or molded plastic sink basin (sometimes integral with counters).

Shower: over tub or stall; surround of curtain, glass, ceramic tile, marble, granite, or plastic.

Enclosures: wood or metal framed cabinets; plywood, laminated wood, hardwood, or steel faces.

Counters: plastic laminate, fiberglass, ceramic tile, cultured marble, quarry marble, or granite.

Accessories: mirrored vanities, heat lamps, exhaust fan, Jacuzzi spa in tub or separate.

Electrical:

Older systems: 110-volt system, with fuse box or circuit-breaker overload control, 70- to 100-ampere capacity, usually not grounded (Figure 7-6a).

Newer systems: 220-volt circuit-breaker system, 100- to 200-ampere capacity, grounded outlets (Figure 7-6b).

Type of wiring varies from "Romex," plastic-coated, with metal or plastic boxes, to metal flex or rigid conduit, with metal boxes.

**Figure 7-6
Electrical Systems.
(a) Old-type Fuse
Box. (b) Modern
Circuit- Breaker Box.**

Source: Photographs Courtesy of Doug Frost.

Outlets vary from one to five or more per room. Electrical Code
  requirements generally call for at least several per room.
Ground-Fault-Interrupted (GFI) outlets, especially in the kitchen,
  bath, garage, and the basement.
Some lighting systems use low voltages for controls.
Specialty wiring: cable TV; alarm and sound systems; computer net.

Building Quality

The published cost-estimating guides most often used by appraisers
provide guidelines for rating the quality of most types of buildings.
Typical **quality rating** standards for single-family residential structures
are as follows:

1. *Good:* To achieve this rating, the building must incorporate better
   than average architectural design, materials, and workmanship. A
   residence receiving this rating usually has at least two bathrooms,
   some form of central heat, and built-in kitchen appliances.

2. *Average:* This rating stands for a medium-quality standard.
   Acceptable to FHA and VA standards with no extras.

3. *Fair:* This refers to a minimum-quality building with limited equipment, plain exterior and interior, and low cost.
4. *Poor:* This quality is assigned to a substandard building with poor structure, interior and exterior finish, and/or inadequate bath-kitchen facilities. Does not meet the building code.

7.4 Functional Utility and Architectural Styles

It is often said that good architectural design is the result of the use of appropriate materials in a proper scale and in harmony with the setting. Good architectural design and functional utility work together.

Defining Standards of Functional Utility

Functional utility consists of the combination of the usefulness and attractiveness of a property. Functional utility measures the livability of a house, in terms of how well it is placed on the site, the general suitability of the floor plan, and the comfort and convenience of the equipment. A functional design provides the most benefits for a given cost. Some design features that contribute to functional utility in homes are contained in the typical minimum property standards already discussed in Section 7.1.

In income-producing properties, functional utility is often measured by using economic standards. Design features that are in demand by tenants, and at the same time help maximize investment return, are the functional ideal. The open and bold styles found in the newest shopping centers, office and industrial complexes, and apartment projects are reflective of these goals. Increasingly, energy conservation, green construction, Internet access and use flexibility dominate functional utility discussions.

Orientation and Floor Plan

Ideally, any residential structure should be oriented, or placed on the site, to take advantage of the view, sun, weather, and natural topography. Such orientation should also provide adequate front, back, and side yards, as well as light, air, privacy, and appropriate access to the street. Provisions for parking, storage, refuse areas, and recreational facilities also contribute to property acceptability.

Inside the residence, the floor plan is considered an important factor in determining functional utility. Easy access to each room, a good flow of traffic, separation of areas for different uses, cross-ventilation, wall space for the placement of furniture, and adequate storage space are sought. Efficient and pleasant layout of the kitchen and a convenient access to yards and utility areas also affect the usefulness and marketability of a home. This is true whether it is a conventional freestanding house or a condominium unit. See Figure 7-7 for typical differences in floor plans.

**Figure 7-7
A Study
in Floor Plans.**

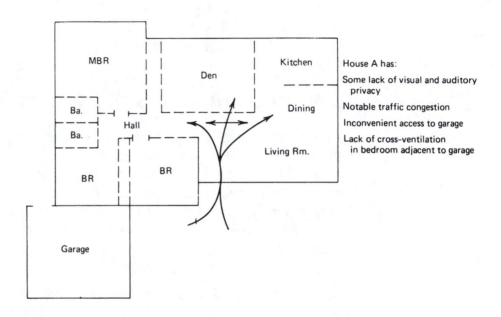

House A has:

Some lack of visual and auditory privacy

Notable traffic congestion

Inconvenient access to garage

Lack of cross-ventilation in bedroom adjacent to garage

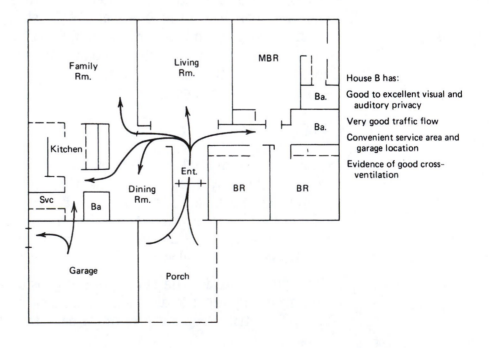

House B has:

Good to excellent visual and auditory privacy

Very good traffic flow

Convenient service area and garage location

Evidence of good cross-ventilation

Architectural Styles

Historically, architectural styles developed in different locations around the world. Now, the traditional styles are often named after the location of their origin or by the historical period during which they were most popular. The combinations and modifications of various styles lend spice and variety to our neighborhoods. Examples of some common styles are shown in Figure 7-8 and described here.

Contemporary styles, sometimes called modern, feature a low, flat roof, a low outline or profile, and a floor plan that is oriented to the

**Figure 7-8
Some Examples of
Architectural Styles
(From Reference
Book, California
Department of Real
Estate, 1989).**

Early English   Early Cape Cod   French Norman

English Tudor   New England Colonial   French Provincial

English   Dutch Colonial   Italian

English   Southern Colonial   Georgian

Early Monterey   Modernistic

California Cape Cod   California Spanish

outdoors. Often, these homes are designed with extensive glass areas. Many residential tracts in the southern California and Arizona areas are of the contemporary style.

The **California ranch style** is related to the contemporary style but precedes it historically. The main elements are a low, rambling profile with a gable roof, wide roof overhang, and lots of heavy wood trim. The ranch style also shows some relationship to the Spanish style of architecture through the frequent use of stone, brick or adobe trim, and design elements.

The **Spanish style** is popular in the western states. It is characterized by its thick-appearing stucco walls (whether adobe or simulated), wood beam trim, and red tile roof.

The **Monterey style** (or Monterey-Spanish) is a modification of the Spanish style. The addition of a wood-beamed, second-story porch or balcony in the front of the house is its distinguishing feature.

The **Colonial style** includes several types of early American architecture, such as New England, Cape Cod, Dutch, Southern, and Georgian. Colonials are usually square or rectangular, stately, and symmetrical buildings with steep gable roofs, shutters, and dormer windows. Each locality added individual variations that set it apart from its neighbors.

The **English half-timber style** looks like many of the squire houses of the English countryside. The key features are the half-timber walls, with masonry or stucco between the timbers, a steep-pitched roof, and casement windows.

Because it was so widely copied at the turn of the century, the **Victorian style** is still apparent in almost every city in America. It is typified by a roof with many gables and a wood exterior. The elaborate wood trim designs around windows, roof eaves, rails, doorways, and ceilings have given this style the description of "gingerbread" architecture.

French Provincial style, also known as French Country, is usually a large house on a large land parcel. It is identified by its very high, steep-pitched hip roof, dormers, and overall formal, balanced appearance.

By no means are today's architectural styles pure. Most modern construction actually incorporates features from two or more traditional building designs. Nor is it always possible to judge the market acceptability of a particular style. The many different tastes in architecture suggest that a variety of styles is more important than purity of styles.

SUMMARY

The inspection and analysis of real property improvements require preparation and planning. The appraiser should prepare to arrive at the field inspection with the equipment and tools needed for an efficient inspection of the building. The most important tool is the checklist or appraisal form for recording data. The amount and kind of data to be collected depend on the intended use of the report, the type of value to be estimated, and the value approach to be emphasized. Therefore, the appraisal should be planned in advance. In this way the appraiser is prepared to note the relevant information at the time of the inspection.

The intended use of the report greatly affects the amount and kind of data required in the inspection and analysis of improvements. The seller of a single-family dwelling might be satisfied simply with a brief description of the building structure, its design, and room count. A lender's appraisal report requirements are usually much more detailed and demanding.

The purpose of most appraisals is to estimate market value. This generally requires a detailed description of the physical structure and a rating for market acceptability. Appraisals made to estimate a different type of value could require more specialized data.

If the cost approach is to be emphasized, the data collected must support the building cost estimate and the rating for age, condition, and utility. If the sales comparison approach is to be stressed, the data required will include items such as the architectural style, number of rooms, and parking accommodations, which can be compared with features of similar properties that have sold. If the income approach is to be emphasized, the appraiser should record the features that most affect the income potential and probable expenses.

Regardless of the approach to be emphasized, the building inspection should accurately describe and rate the physical features of the structure for marketability, quality of construction, and physical condition. Any observed signs of possible problems should be noted and possibly photographed. Measuring the subject property and drawing a floor plan diagram are usually required.

Last but not least, the inspection and analysis of improvements call for some knowledge of structural detail. General industry standards should be understood by the practicing appraiser.

Since market acceptability is the ultimate test of value, it is desirable that the appraiser have a basic knowledge of design principles in construction. Good architectural design incorporates not only the building style but also those features that contribute most effectively to the utility of the building.

IMPORTANT TERMS AND CONCEPTS

Above-grade

ANSI standard

Below-grade

Building specifications

California ranch style

Class A construction

Class B construction

Class C construction

Class D construction

Colonial style

Condition

Construction classification

Contemporary style

Desktop Underwriter Program

Effective age

English half-timber style

FNMA Form 2055

FNMA Form 2075

French Provincial style

Functional utility

Inspection checklist

Living area

Monterey style

Quality rating

Spanish style

Uniform Residential Appraisal Report (URAR)

Victorian style

REVIEWING YOUR UNDERSTANDING

1. During the building inspection, to record data you will need:
   a.   A plat map
   b.   A measuring tape
   c.   A checklist or appraisal form
   d.   A marble

2. The building inspection must be geared to:
   a.   The type of value to be estimated
   b.   The intended use of the appraisal report
   c.   The value approach to be emphasized
   d.   All of the above

3. Minimum property standards may include:
   a.   Ease of circulation and housekeeping
   b.   Adequate sanitation facilities
   c.   Both (a) and (b)
   d.   None of the above

4. Some of the factors usually considered to influence the cost of construction are:
   a.   Design or use type
   b.   Construction classification
   c.   Rating of quality
   d.   All of the above

5. The major items to describe and rate in a structure include:
   a. Foundation, exterior, and roof
   b. List of rooms
   c. Interior and built-in kitchen equipment
   d. All of the above

6. Rating the market appeal of a single-family residence considers:
   a. The demands and tastes of the market in the neighborhood of the subject property
   b. The quality of construction, the materials used, and their finish
   c. General livability and condition of the property
   d. All of the above

7. "Effective age" refers to:
   a. Original age
   b. Average age
   c. Relative age considering the physical condition and marketability of a structure
   d. All of the above

8. The "total living area" of a detached residential structure is measured by:
   a. Exterior measurements including walls and finish
   b. Interior measurements only
   c. House and garage area combined
   d. Exterior measurements less any garage area

9. Classification of basic construction refers to:
   a. Type of use
   b. Type of basic frame, wall, floor, and roof construction
   c. Quality of construction
   d. All of the above

10. The criteria used in the selection of building materials include:
    a. Climate
    b. Availability
    c. Durability
    d. All of the above

11. Good architectural design consists, in part, of:
    a. A unique floor plan
    b. Functional utility
    c. The use of expensive materials
    d. All of the above

12. The architectural style that uses elaborate wood trim designs around windows, doorways, and roof eaves is:
    a. English
    b. California-Monterey
    c. Victorian
    d. French Provincial

PRACTICAL APPLICATIONS

As we will remind you at the start of each exercise, review the exercise at the end of the preceding chapter, and the work that you have performed to date.

The focus for this assignment is on the improvement section of the URAR form, as shown in Figure 7-1. As a starting point, review the form, and review the chapter content. Consider what information you must obtain, and where you might be able to get it.

Some of the information consists of facts that you must research. Start with a careful inspection of the subject property, making notes as you go. Much of the needed information will be gained just from your visual inspection. Note that a good description may call for names for various types of materials or products. Consider reviewing a supplemental text, such as *Houses*, by Henry Harrison, to help you understand what you are seeing and give you the words to correctly describe it. It may be necessary for you to repeat parts of your inspection because you will be training your eyes how to see. Another useful and detailed book on the URAR and 2055 forms is *Using Residential Appraisal Report Forms*, by Mark Rattermann, MAI, SRA, published by the Appraisal Institute, Chicago, 2005.

If your subject property is, as we discussed in the prior exercises, a unit in a condo, co-op, or apartment building, report the number of stories in the unit, not in the building, for the purpose of these exercises only. Answer questions about the roof, basement, foundation, and so on, as if this unit was the only one in the building. Answer questions about parking using the parking that is available for this particular unit. *Never* do this on an actual appraisal! (Please note that you also could use the proper form if you choose. However, if your exercise is for submission in class, check with your instructor to see what should be done, as the instructor may want everyone "on the same form," to allow more efficient review. The Bradford ClickForms software allows you to move your information automatically to whatever form you choose.)

Next, measure the unit, using either the interior dimensions plus six inches for the exterior wall thickness, or else the exterior dimensions. Remember to separate the above-grade living area from any that is below grade, however much. Look at the sample floor plan in the URAR report at the end of Chapter 16 to see how to format your drawing. You will be preparing a good version of this drawing as part of the exercise for Chapter 16, so now is a good time to plan for that step. Floor plans usually are drawn on graph paper, with lines set up at ten to the inch, and drawn as one foot to every line (such as ten feet to the inch). This is a convenient scale for all but very large homes. You can draw your own graph paper, but you might as well go to a stationery store and buy some. When you make your measurements, consider the accuracy of the measuring device that you are using. If it is a tape, marked in inches and feet, down to one-eighth an inch, then that is what you must use, measuring in feet and inches. If the tape is in feet and tenths of a foot, then that will be what you use. Stretch the tape to avoid any sag. And read the measurement to the nearest inch or tenths of a foot—you can always round later! When you have completed your measurement and drawing, verify that your drawing is in balance, as noted in the chapter.

Most of the factual information will be obtained by the inspection and measurement. One key fact will be the year that the unit/building was built. The age may be known already, or you may be able to find out by asking people nearby who might know. You often can find the age on the county (or district, in some states) assessment roll. You might be able to view this at a local title company office, online, at some real estate brokerage offices, or at the county assessor's office. Another source of age information is the building permit department for your community—the city if the building is in an incorporated city, and the county if the building is in an unincorporated area.

All the remaining information calls for you to develop an opinion. For example, what is the condition of the property? Read again the section in the chapter covering this topic. The same issues arise when faced with the question about physical deficiencies or adverse conditions. Consider what you have read and then consider what you know about the subject property.

Finally, start up the software program and open the file that you saved after the prior chapter's assignment. Note that you have already entered the basic information about the property and the assignment, as well as the neighborhood and site description sections. Review this information. Next, enter the information about the site that you have collected.

As we note at the end of each exercise, it is best not to get ahead of yourself. So, do not enter information in the later sections of the report until you have read the chapter(s) that covers that topic. However, it is a good idea to look ahead at the coming sections of the form so that you start thinking about the information that you will need to gather. And it is certainly reasonable, and even desirable, for you to start collecting some of that information early, if you choose to do so.

Reminder: If you have questions about the program itself, please be sure to review the manuals and help information that were included with the program CD. Also, at anytime, you can go to http://www.bradfordsoftware. com, click on "Services" at the upper right of the home page, and then on "ClickFORMS Training Programs" in the middle of the "Services" page. See the free online training section!

CHAPTER 8
THE SALES COMPARISON
APPROACH

PREVIEW

The sales comparison approach is perhaps the most important of the three used by appraisers to estimate value. In brief, this approach involves analyzing properties that sold and comparing them to the property being appraised. This chapter first outlines the steps in the sales comparison approach and then describes the important process of collecting comparable sales data. Finally, this chapter explores the appraisal number or statistical concepts most commonly used in appraisals.

OBJECTIVES

When you have completed this chapter you should be able to:

1. List and explain the four steps in the sales comparison approach.

2. Explain the important concepts behind this approach.

3. Explain how to decide if a sale is comparable.

4. Discuss what information about a comparable sale should be collected.

5. Identify the major sources of market data.

6. Outline the statistical techniques appraisers can use to analyze sales.

8.1 Introducing the Sales Comparison Approach

The **sales comparison approach** (also called direct comparison, sales, or market) is based on the *Principle of Substitution*. It is a process that collects sales of comparable properties that occurred about the same time as the date of value, and compares them to the property being appraised. Simplistic as this may sound, the proper use of this approach requires a good knowledge of the subject property, and an understanding of the neighborhood, city, and region where it is located. A review of Chapters 4 through 7 is suggested if you have any questions concerning this material.

Outline of the Sales Comparison Approach

The sales comparison approach involves four steps, which are summarized in Figure 8-1. *The first step* is to seek out sales of properties that are comparable to the subject property and that sold about the same time as the date of value. This requires understanding the meaning of the word *comparable*, identifying comparable properties, and collecting the necessary information about each property.

Once the necessary information about **comparable sales** has been obtained, *the second step* is to analyze the features of these sales and compare them with the features of the subject property. The purpose of analyzing the sales is to identify which features or characteristics are

**Figure 8-1
Steps in the Sales
Comparison
Approach.**

important in establishing prices. The process has two parts. The first is to identify the ways in which the sales differ from each other and from the subject property. Important differences often include the terms, conditions, or dates of sale. Physical differences such as location, age, and/or size almost always exist.

The second part of sales analysis is to compare the differences in the sale prices of the comparables with the differences in property features. We are trying to find out what causes the price of this type of property to vary, and by how much. If the available sales are essentially identical to the subject property, the prices should be in a very narrow range. However, the sold properties often differ in various ways, with a wider range of prices.

The third step in the sales comparison approach is to adjust for the differences between the sales and the subject property. The purpose of this step is to adjust the price of each comparable, to reflect what the price would have been if that sale property had been more nearly identical to the subject property, illustrated in Figure 8-2. To carry out this step, you will select and use one or more of the adjustment techniques discussed in the next chapter.

After the sales have been located, analyzed, and adjusted, *the fourth step* is to arrive at a value estimate as indicated by the adjusted sales. This final step in the sales comparison approach is also covered in Chapter 9.

Figure 8-2
Adjusting the Sales to the Subject.

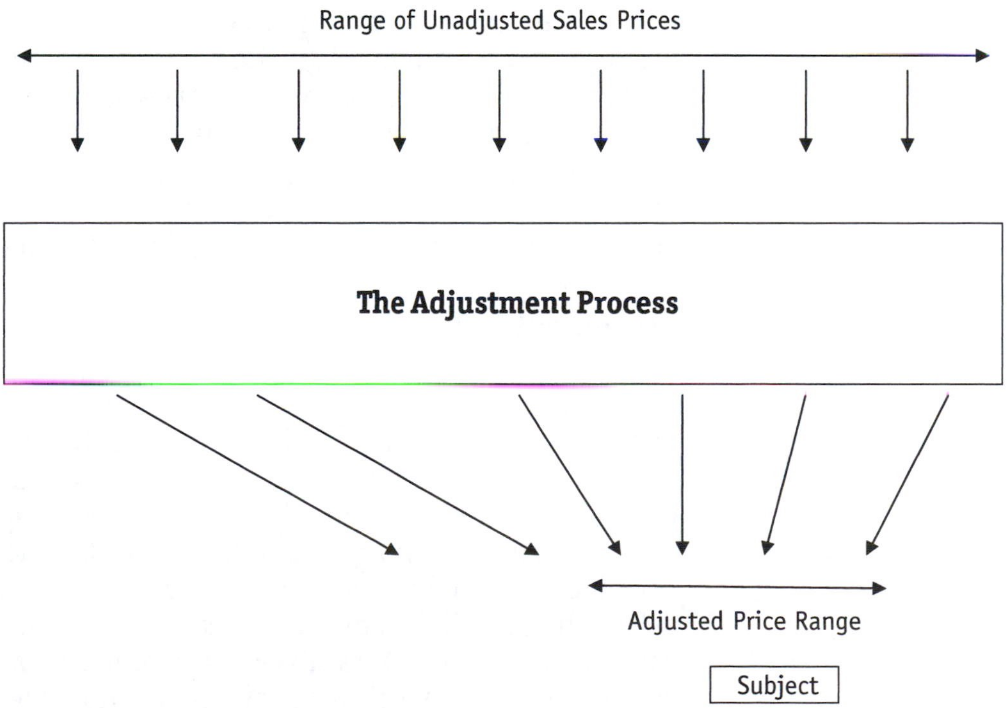

Range of Unadjusted Sales Prices

The Adjustment Process

Adjusted Price Range

Subject

Key Concepts of the Sales Comparison Approach

Several concepts are central to the sales comparison approach. In turn, these explain its significance to appraisers. These concepts are described as:

- *the importance of substitution,*
- *the simplicity of market comparisons,*
- *the relationship to statistics,*
- *the relevance of adjustments, and*
- *the significance of market data.*

The Importance of Substitution

The principle of substitution (see Chapter 5) is particularly important to the sales comparison approach. If a well-informed buyer is interested in a particular property, he or she will generally pay no more than the cost of acquiring another property that is a satisfactory substitute. This process of substitution is commonly used by buyers and sellers: buyers compare a number of competitive listings and select the one that they like best, considering the features and the list prices. Sellers, in turn, often set their list prices by seeing what buyers have paid for similar properties.

Simplicity

Generally, the sales comparison approach is simpler and more direct than the other two approaches, and it often requires fewer calculations. Consequently, there is less possibility of either an error in appraisal judgment or a mathematical error. Since the sales comparison approach is often the easiest approach to understand, it is usually the easiest to explain to clients. In summary, the simplicity and directness of this approach may produce a more reliable value conclusion than could be obtained by the other approaches.

Statistical Connections

Another aspect of the sales comparison approach is its use of concepts from the field of statistics. For example, when we obtain information about sales transactions close in time to the date of value, these transactions represent only a portion of the total activity occurring in the market at that time. Thus, we are making use of the statistical concept called **sampling**. Appraisers seek to find out, through sampling the market activity and then analyzing the sample, how buyers and sellers behave in a particular real estate market. Because appraisers cannot know with certainty what a property will sell for, we speak of estimating market value as "the most probable selling price . . ." The use of probabilities is a task similar to the work of statistical economists. *Bracketing* is another concept employed by appraisers that is derived from statistics. Statisticians try to make predictions only within the range of the data they have studied. For example, a consumer goods marketing study would likely use data that covered both extremes of the market or industry being studied. Gathering data that brackets the known consumption would give an economist a more accurate understanding of the market than just data about the less expensive products (see Figure 8-3). Appraisal statistical concepts are explored further in Section 8.4 of this chapter.

Appraisers apply the same concept of bracketing when selecting market data (such as home sales, rent comparables, or land sale comparables). If the comparable sales differ in any major way from the subject property, it is desirable to select some sales that are better than the subject property and some that are worse. If there are differences in the sales that are important, try to collect sales that are better or worse in this specific feature. For example, if the comparable sales differ from the subject property in building size, comparable sales of both larger and smaller buildings should be obtained. Differences such as age and location should be treated in the same way. By including some sales that are better than the subject property and some that are worse, you develop a better view of the range of market reactions.

Adjustments

As mentioned in Chapter 1, people with expertise in a market can estimate sales prices by intuition. Such appraisals, however, do not necessarily involve any specific analysis of the relevant property differences or their value influences. In contrast, the *adjustment techniques* used in the sales comparison approach enable you to specifically identify the differences that are important in a given market or neighborhood. These techniques can also indicate how much to adjust prices for any particular difference. After adjusting for a major factor, you may be able to identify differences associated with smaller adjustments that you might have missed before. Finally, using specific adjustments allows the appraisal to be objectively reviewed by the client. For these reasons, adjustment techniques are one of the most

**Figure 8-3
The Concept of
Bracketing.**

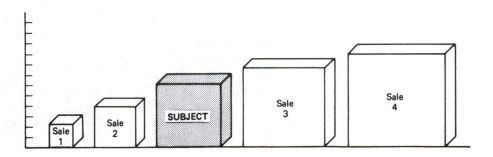

important contributions that formal appraising offers to the broker or salesperson.

Use of Market Data in Other Approaches

When estimating market values, the collection and analysis of market data are essential to each of the three value approaches (see Figure 8-4). For example, the sales comparison approach is used to estimate land value in the cost approach. Similarly, one of the best ways to accurately estimate accrued depreciation in the cost approach is by the analysis of market sales. In the income approach, market rents are estimated by analyzing market rental transactions. Vacancy and expense information for the income approach is often obtained from competitive buildings. Usually, income approach capitalization rates are obtained by analyzing market sales or other market data.

The relationships between the three approaches will become clearer to you as you read the following sections. For now, remember that when you estimate market value, by whichever approach, the market is the support for that estimate. If your opinion of value is to be based on objective analysis instead of subjective intuition, you must obtain and analyze the appropriate type of market data.

8.2 Collecting Comparable Sales Data

As we have already stated, the sales comparison approach depends on comparing the subject property with sales of similar properties. In this section, we discuss the first step in the sales comparison approach, selecting the comparable sales and locating appropriate information about the sales.

**Figure 8-4
Market Data Is Key to
All Three Approaches.**

Selecting the Comparable Sales

A sale must meet three criteria to be considered a valid comparable. First, the property should be a **competitive property**. Second, the sale should qualify as an **open-market transaction**. Third, the sale will have occurred *close in time to the date of value*. Where listings are used, these criteria still apply, with open-market exposure substituting for open-market transaction. Let us take a closer look at these three criteria, which are summarized in Figure 8-5.

The Competitive Property

To be a competitive property, a sale property (or listing) should have been a reasonable substitute or alternative for a potential purchaser who is or was looking at the subject property. A competitive property is located in an area that a buyer of the subject property would also consider. The comparable property must be similar enough to the subject property in size, shape, and features to satisfy the requirements of the buyer. In general, a competitive property should appeal to the same group of buyers. In economics, this group of buyers is called a **submarket**. Thus, you should consider to which submarket the subject property is likely to appeal.

In residential property, the different owner-occupancy submarkets are identified by such important characteristics as family size, age, and economic status. Each group of buyers will have its own housing needs. For example, families of different sizes would seek homes of different sizes. Thus, a two-bedroom home would not usually qualify as an appropriate comparable for a four-bedroom home being appraised. The two-bedroom home clearly would be sought by buyers that were looking in a different submarket, because of family size. Note, too, that in owner-occupied residential property, family incomes of the buyers of the comparable properties should be somewhat similar to those of likely buyers of the subject property. For residential

**Figure 8-5
What Is a
Comparable Sale?**

property purchased as an investment, on the other hand, the buyer submarket will be different because the buyer's motives are different.

In nonresidential property, the submarket may have other characteristics that are important. For example, among potential buyers of small neighborhood stores, one buyer submarket may consist entirely of local investors. Another buyer submarket may be people who intend to have their business occupy the store (owner-occupants). Since the two groups of buyers have different motives for purchasing the property, the factors that they consider important could vary.

Open-Market Transactions

The second criterion for comparability is that a sale must be an open-market transaction. This test seeks to eliminate sales that are not "arm's length" market sales. For example, an income property that has been sold directly to a tenant may or may not have been at the market price. In such a transaction, the sale price might represent either a bargain given by an uninformed seller, or a premium offered by a tenant seeking to avoid the cost and uncertainty of relocation. Adequate exposure to a number of prospective buyers is essential to establish a market-determined price.

Further, when applying this test for an open-market transaction, consider if the sale involved any *unusual conditions*. At times, personal property is included in the sale price, or there is seller financing at favorable interest rates. Transfers between relatives also may result in favorable prices. When markets are weak, sellers often offer *concessions* (for example, paying the buyers' closing costs, or buying down the loan interest rate) to motivate the buyers. Does Figure 8-6 suggest times when appraisers might expect to find more concessions?

In short, you should consider whether there are unusual circumstances about any particular sale that could have distorted its price. In some cases, the appraiser may simply discard a sale where the sale price is not in line with that of the other sales. If the sale is important, however, a careful investigation and an interview of one or more of the parties involved in the transaction may be necessary.

Date of Sale

The third criterion for a comparable sale is that the date of sale must be relatively close to the date of value. Note that the date of sale really refers to the date the parties were *committed to the contract*, as you will see later. The supply and demand of real estate, and thus its value, changes with time. These changes can be rapid, as with a sudden shift in interest rates, or the announcement that a major factory is to be built in the area. If certain sales occur before such a change and you are appraising a property after that time, the earlier sales are unlikely to be as comparable as later sales.

**Figure 8-6
Southland April
Home Sales.**

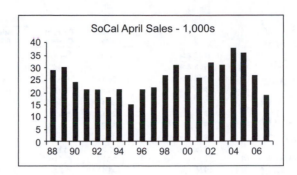

Over a longer period of time, more subtle changes in market attitudes may not shift prices, but may shift the importance of particular property features or locations. For example, a long-lasting gasoline shortage could gradually increase the values of all types of properties close to public transportation routes. Consider any circumstances or events that might have had an effect on market attitudes. Be wary of using comparables that reflect earlier market attitudes toward particular features or locations.

When deciding upon the relevance of earlier sales, the appraiser must also consider general market trends. All sales prices are affected by the underlying inflation, or deflation, in the economy. However, real estate is affected by local influences much more than by national ones. Even during a period of national inflation, prices will be going down for some locations and property types. Similarly, during a depression, prices might still be going up in some locations and for some property types. Real estate price trends are somewhat unpredictable. They may change from month to month or may remain stable for months at a time, in the same manner as general economic price indexes.

How Comparable Must a Comparable Be?

What is the meaning of *comparable*? In practice, it means as comparable as you can find! Every property is unique in some way. As a result, the appraiser may not find very many market sales of completely comparable properties. The appraiser should try to collect sales that are as similar as possible in time of sale, location, and important characteristics. However, the appraiser should try to not use sales that do not meet the criteria for an open-market transaction. On occasion, it may be necessary to widen the standards of comparability, in order to obtain an adequate number of sales. For example, if the subject property is a house built in 1962, we would probably prefer to find comparable sales that were built between, say, 1955 and 1970. As Figure 8-7 indicates, annual price changes can vary for homes of different age categories. However, if we can only find one such sale, then we have to widen the range of acceptable ages to include houses built between, say, 1950 and 1975.

**Figure 8-7
San Francisco Bay
Area Market Trend
Index—by Age of
Home (Source: From
Northern California
Real Estate Report,
Vol. 40, No. 1,
Courtesy of the Real
Estate Research
Council of Northern
California).**

	Overall Index	Percent Change	Price Range in 1967		Year Built		
			Under $27,500	Over $27,500	Before 1941	1941-1955	After 1955
1967 Apr.	100.0	—	100.0	100.0	100.0	100.0	100.0
1968 Apr.	103.2	3.2	103.8	102.2	102.9	103.8	103.1
1969 Apr.	109.1	5.7	110.4	106.9	108.6	109.3	109.6
1970 Apr.	114.4	4.9	116.4	111.7	113.2	115.0	115.3
1971 Apr.	120.4	5.2	123.3	116.3	118.4	122.2	120.8
1972 Apr.	126.1	4.7	129.0	121.8	124.0	126.9	127.5
1973 Apr.	134.7	6.8	137.2	131.2	131.6	136.2	136.6
1974 Apr.	150.0	11.4	152.2	147.2	145.5	152.3	152.7
1975 Apr.	170.2	13.5	172.2	167.8	166.4	173.1	172.1
Oct.	182.1	7.0	183.4	180.7	181.0	183.9	182.9
1976 Apr.	195.4	7.3	195.3	195.8	194.3	197.7	195.8
Oct.	212.7	8.9	212.6	213.0	211.7	216.5	212.0
1977 Apr.	241.8	13.7	240.3	244.0	239.9	243.9	243.2
Oct.	272.5	12.7	272.4	273.1	267.1	276.6	275.2
1978 Apr.	294.8	8.2	296.7	293.0	289.9	298.9	297.2
Oct.	313.5	6.3	313.9	313.5	312.8	315.6	314.4
1979 Apr.	341.7	9.0	340.0	343.9	342.1	348.1	338.8
Oct.	387.0	13.3	382.5	391.9	396.1	386.9	382.8
1980 Apr.	421.6	8.9	415.3	428.3	434.7	426.9	411.1
Oct.	465.0	10.3	462.2	468.1	481.2	469.6	453.4
1981 Apr.	489.2	5.2	486.2	492.5	502.2	494.6	479.2
Oct.	498.7	1.9	498.6	499.1	508.9	504.2	490.5
1982 Apr.	503.7	1.0	502.7	505.0	516.0	505.8	496.5
Oct.	503.6	—	505.5	501.9	522.2	502.9	494.0
1983 Apr.	511.7	1.6	513.1	510.5	536.1	509.9	499.1
Oct.	519.8	1.6	523.1	516.8	548.4	523.9	506.7
1984 Apr.	530.2	2.0	533.1	527.5	561.0	533.5	516.4
Oct.	538.7	1.6	542.5	535.2	574.4	542.2	521.8
1985 Apr.	550.6	2.2	555.0	546.6	593.1	555.4	528.8
Oct.	568.3	3.2	571.9	565.2	615.4	574.5	543.0
1986 Apr.	591.6	4.1	595.9	587.9	649.8	600.1	558.3
Oct.	624.7	5.6	626.3	623.7	696.0	634.8	582.9
1987 Apr.	653.7	4.6	653.9	654.0	734.2	667.3	604.8
Oct.	694.1	6.2	691.0	697.8	783.1	707.8	640.9
1988 Apr.	753.4	8.5	746.4	761.1	865.2	761.2	692.9

Defining the Sales Search Area

How wide an area do you search for comparable sales? The general rule is that the more sales activity there is in an area, the more geographically restricted the appraiser's search can become. In an active market, it is sometimes possible to find an adequate number of comparable sales within several blocks of the subject property, particularly if the subject is located in a residential tract. On the other hand, in appraising a large, new custom home in the middle of a neighborhood of older, smaller homes, the appraiser would have to greatly enlarge the comparable search area. Similarly, when few sales are occurring because of a market slowdown, the appraiser must widen the boundaries of his or her *comparable search area* in order to collect an adequate number of sales.

For some types of property, such as a large leased industrial warehouse, buyers can find satisfactory substitute properties a considerable distance from the subject. In some markets, they will even buy property in another state. To define the search area for comparable sales in this kind of a market, the appraiser must carefully define comparability of location, in order to suggest where a potential buyer would look for likely substitute properties.

Consider the Sales History of the Subject Property

Appraisal tradition at one time did not favor the use of a sale or prior sale of the subject property as a direct market comparable. Now, we see that this **sales history** must not be ignored by the appraiser. The *Uniform Standards of Professional Appraisal Practice* requires that the appraiser consider and analyze any known agreement of sale, option, or listing of the property to be appraised, around the date of value. Prior sales of the subject property must also be considered and analyzed, when they have occurred within three years of the date of value, for all property types, and are available in the normal course of business. (At one time, USPAP required only one year for certain residential properties.) Some appraisers routinely report the last known sale, even if well outside the USPAP analysis time period.

The appraiser should ask the client for any listing or sales agreement, current escrow instructions, any inspection reports, and any preliminary title report (in those states that use them). It is also desirable to note for the file (and report) what was done to investigate these issues. On occasion, the appraiser will not be told of a pending transaction, or accidentally given incorrect information. Often, the listing history will not be clear, leading the appraiser to believe that the property sold soon after it was listed. Would it change your opinion if you found that the property had been listed several months prior, for less money, and the listing had expired after 90 days? Note that some MLS rules allow a listing to be withdrawn and relisted to restart the days on market count at zero!

What Information Is Needed?

Once you have investigated the sales and decided which are relatively comparable to the property being appraised, the next step is to collect the pertinent data. General information is needed about each sales transaction; the property's physical characteristics, its legal status, and its location. If located in a speculative market, a sales history of the comparable also is generally required. For the URAR form, the Certification commits the appraiser to check all sales comparables for a prior sale up to one year earlier.

The Sales Transaction Data

Several items of information about each sales transaction are needed. One is the date of sale. Appraisers prefer the actual date that the sales price was agreed on, rather than the date the sale was recorded. Why? Because the parties sometimes establish the sales price by an option or other agreement, long before the actual recording of the sale. While not always available, the date of the "meeting of the minds" is the theoretical ideal for the date of sale. You can often estimate this date from the recording date, by asking the agent how long the property was in escrow.

You also need to know the correct sales price and the *terms of sale*. By terms of sale, we mean the financing arrangements and any concessions that were made. You should know if the financing was by the seller or by a third party, and whether it was at market interest rates. Where seller financing was at favorable rates, the advantage to the buyer may have been offset by a higher price. Ideally, you should know the actual interest rate, the payment schedule, amortization period, and due date. You should also know whether the mortgage had a due-on-sale acceleration clause, a variable interest rate clause, or any other special provisions. This information is needed to see if the sales price should be adjusted because of the financing. Unfortunately, complete information on sales terms is often not available.

Concessions could be minor: The seller agreed to leave the patio furniture. Major concessions include paying the buyer's closing costs. If there are major concessions, they can impact prices! In a slow market, it is desirable to ask if there were any concessions, and to document what you were told in the file and report.

Depending on the type of appraisal and its intended use, additional sales transaction data may be needed. The property's legal description makes it possible to verify exactly what property was sold. Although usually researched only in the more formal appraisals, obtaining the name of the seller (the grantor) and the buyer (the grantee) is desirable. This helps to determine whether the sale was a family transfer. Sometimes, you may need to contact one or both parties, to verify details of the transaction. Try to find out if there were any items of personalty, such as drapes, kitchen or laundry appliances, rugs, pianos, lawn furniture, and so on, included in the sale price. In large apartment building and large estate home transactions, for example, some personalty is often included with the sale.

Finally, you must consider the **buyer's motives** and **seller's motives**. Was it a family transfer? Was it a sacrifice sale? Was it a tenant purchase? Was it bought by the adjacent property owner? As already indicated, answers to these questions may be very desirable, to help decide whether a sale is a valid comparable. In appraisals of income property, the sale transaction data should also include complete tenant rolls and income and expense information for the property. Sometimes available from sales **data services**, this information is usually requested from the seller, agent, or property manager. It is common for commercial property to be subject to an existing lease. Thus, any sale represents only the value of the leased fee interest. In such cases, the appraiser must consider the nature of the lease, both for the subject and the comparable sales. How attractive is the lease to investors? That is the key!

Physical Characteristics of the Sale

After you have collected information about the sales transaction, the next step is to seek out the *physical characteristics* of the property. Try to identify all of the characteristics that are important to the market being studied. These could include:

1. Land size, shape, topography, soil, and so on.

2. The size and nature of the structure or structures. Above- and below-grade finished areas should be distinguished. Information about garages, porches, and unfinished areas should also be included. Industrial mezzanines and office areas need to be identified.

3. The age of the structures and the quality of their design and construction.

4. Any special features, such as kitchen built-ins, remodeled baths, patios, swimming pools, room additions, air conditioning, electronic air filters, solar heating, insulation, and desirable views.

5. The condition of the structure and the quality of any modernization.

6. Available utilities.

7. Any problems with the property, ranging from small room sizes or poor floor plans to substantial deferred maintenance, inadequate wiring, roof leaks, landslides, and so on.

Legal Data about the Comparable Sale

In addition to the important physical characteristics of the sale property, the appraiser should also be aware of certain legal characteristics. For example, you should investigate the property's zoning category. Are the uses that are permissible comparable to those of the subject property? Next, note the property taxes that are being paid for the property and whether these taxes will likely change upon transfer of ownership. Any special assessment taxes should also be identified, so that you can see if they are similar to those of the subject property. Finally, are there any other public or private restrictions on the property? Any deed restrictions, easements, or leases should be reviewed, to see if they may have affected the sale price.

Location of the Sale

When investigating a comparable property, the appraiser should watch for any differences between the subject property's *location* and those of the comparable sales. Focus on differences that are likely to be important to people in that market. In urban areas, differences in access to public transportation, the cost of fares, and the ability to transfer to other routes may be important. Are freeways easily accessible? How similar is the proximity to jobs, schools, cultural facilities, local shopping, and recreational facilities? Check for detrimental influences, such as traffic noise, incompatible land uses, and/or possible natural hazards. Properties around the sale should be briefly reviewed, to see if their age, value, quality, condition, and/or use differ substantially from the properties around the subject. In short, compare the neighborhood around the sale property with the neighborhood around the subject property (Figure 8-8) to see if there are differences that would significantly affect the attitude of prospective buyers.

Market Conditions

For each comparable sale, you must consider what the state of the market was at the time of the sale. Were market conditions at the time of the sale materially different from those at the date of value? Increased costs of conventional financing or a moratorium on FHA financing in areas using FHA loans are examples of changes in market conditions that usually affect prices.

Using Listings and Offers

In most appraisal assignments (e.g., loan appraisals to FNMA standards), listings and offers are not allowed as substitutes for closed sales. However, in an uncertain market, it is a good idea to cite (in the remarks section, or in a separate attachment if necessary) several listings or escrows (unclosed sales) to show market trends and attitudes at the exact date of value, and to support the value evidence represented by closed sales. (Note that it may be difficult to find out the proposed sale price for a property that is in escrow.) At times, some lenders specifically require this kind of data in appraisals. Appraisals for employee relocation or of lender-foreclosed property (known as REO) also often must consider both listings and pending sales.

**Figure 8-8
Comparing
Locations.**

Listings of property for sale can also indicate the upper limit, or highest probable market value. Sometimes, however, properties will sell at or over the list price. Offers that have been refused are helpful too, because they can suggest the lower limit of the value range. It is important to select listings that are close to the date of value, and have characteristics similar to those of the subject property. When listings are cited, it is helpful to learn from the agent, broker, or other principal party whether there are any unusual conditions in a listing, particularly one where reasonable offers have been refused. Perhaps a personality conflict between the principal parties, not price, was the only reason a particular offer did not become a sale.

For some assignments, the standards set by a particular client or the law of a particular state may block the use of listings or offers. Alternatively, the appraiser might want to be "aware" of them, but not "rely" on them. Again, this would not be expected in a stable market and with good comparable sales. Rather, it is for possible use when the comparable sales may be less reliable.

How Many Sales?

There is no specific number of comparables that is right for every appraisal. The desirable number depends, in part, on how comparable the sales are. For example, if the sales are very similar, located nearby, and close to the date of value, three sales are considered adequate for many appraisal assignments. But where the sales are less comparable or the appraiser has less confidence in the reliability of the information obtained about the sales, a larger number of sales is desirable. Often, a larger number of sales will be needed to justify the adjustments used.

The desirable number of comparables is also influenced by the techniques that will be used in the sales comparison approach. Some statistical techniques, for example, cannot be performed with only three or four sales, and might even require 20 or 30 sales, or more. The intended use of the appraisal report can also influence the number of comparables needed. An appraisal made for loan purposes usually requires fewer sales than an appraisal for court testimony.

Verification of Data

Perhaps the most important aspect of the sale search is the verification of data. As the appraiser, you must consider whether the sales information you have collected is reliable. You may find that one sale has a price that appears out of line with the other sales. It is wise to recheck the key information about that sale. There could be a mistake in your information concerning the price, terms, physical and locational characteristics, or property problems.

Basically, you have two ways to improve *data reliability*. The first is to inspect the sales. For most appraisals, a field inspection of the comparable sales is routine. This customarily consists of viewing the exterior of the property from the street. Such an inspection serves to verify the data collected and to allow a better evaluation of the quality of the property, its condition, and its overall market appeal.

Note that in making this survey, you must try to identify any work that appears to have been done on the property since the date of the sale. The sale price would have been based on the condition of the property at the time of the sale, and not at the time of your field inspection. Such factors as new exterior paint, new roof cover, or visible remodeling would suggest that you should check with a party to the transaction to verify the condition of the property at the time of sale.

In more complex or controversial assignments, the appraiser might want to view the interior of each comparable sale. This may be difficult, since the occupants often resent a stranger knocking at the door. However, a careful explanation of who you are, what is happening, and why an interior inspection is desired can often produce positive results.

The second way to improve data reliability is to cross-check the data already obtained by contacting another information source. When sales data are obtained from a data service (discussed below) or from public records, it may be desirable to verify the price and terms of the sale with a party to the transaction. This could be the real estate broker, a lawyer, the buyer, the seller, or the loan officer involved in the financing.

There is no clear rule as to when this should be done. Generally, it depends on the reliability of the source from which the sale was obtained and the type of appraisal assignment involved. Thus, in preparing a residential loan appraisal in a stable market with ample, consistent sales, many appraisers would not verify the data with a party to the transaction. On the other hand, when appraising a unique property for some type of litigation (such as an eminent domain lawsuit), most appraisers try to verify the price and terms with a party to the transaction. It is also important to consider whether supplemental standards or the contract with the specific client require a particular type of verification. Also, real estate fraud is increasing, calling for more diligence from appraisers.

Sources of Market Data

The appraiser depends upon a broad array of sources for the market data needed in an appraisal. As you will see, such sources range from public records available to everyone, to private data sources available by subscription. Most of the sources we cite here often will be a source of important information about the subject property, as well as the comparable sales. Examples include property maps and the age and floor area of any buildings.

Public Records

Public records are usually located in county offices. They are an important source of market data, because they include copies of local deeds transferring ownership of real estate. These deeds are typically filed by document number or by the date that they are recorded at the office. They are usually kept on microfilm and are referenced either by a document number, the microfilm reel and image numbers, or by book and page numbers. Each deed is indexed both by the name of the grantor (seller) and by the grantee (buyer). In larger counties, the office where the records are kept is often called the Recorder's Office. Small counties frequently assign record-keeping functions to the County Clerk.

Figure 8-9 is a sample grant deed. The exact format will vary. The deed always contains the name of the grantor and the grantee (seller and buyer), a legal description of the property sold, and the date the transaction was recorded. In addition, there usually will be a documentary transfer tax paid at the time the deed was recorded. Often, this tax is a standard $0.55 per $500 of cash consideration. This means that an assumed mortgage, which does not involve new cash, will not be taxed. A new mortgage, however, will be taxed, whether it is made by the seller or by an independent lender. Many jurisdictions "rubber stamp" the deed with information on the transfer tax. They will fill in the amount of the tax and check whether it is calculated on the full price, or whether the tax is on a value reduced by any assumed mortgages or liens (called *less liens*).

Some jurisdictions have a different transfer tax rate, and some calculate it differently. If you are going to use this transfer tax information to calculate the purchase price, you should investigate how it is calculated in that jurisdiction. At times, there is no record of the exact tax on the deed. The record is kept separately at the Recorder's Office, so their tax books can be properly audited and tabulated. This separate record is sometimes available upon request.

In addition to the above-mentioned information affixed to the deed, you can obtain other types of information from the deed. Some jurisdictions will not record a deed unless it has the county assessor's parcel number on it. Sometimes, a street address is placed at the end of the legal description. In California, a "Preliminary Change of Ownership" form must be completed by the seller and forwarded to the county assessor at the time of deed recording. Designed to assist the assessor in the change of ownership reassessment, this form discloses the price and terms of the transaction. Some assessors' offices and private data banks make this information available to private appraisers.

Usually, the recorded deed shows the mailing address where the original of the document is to be returned after it is recorded. Often,

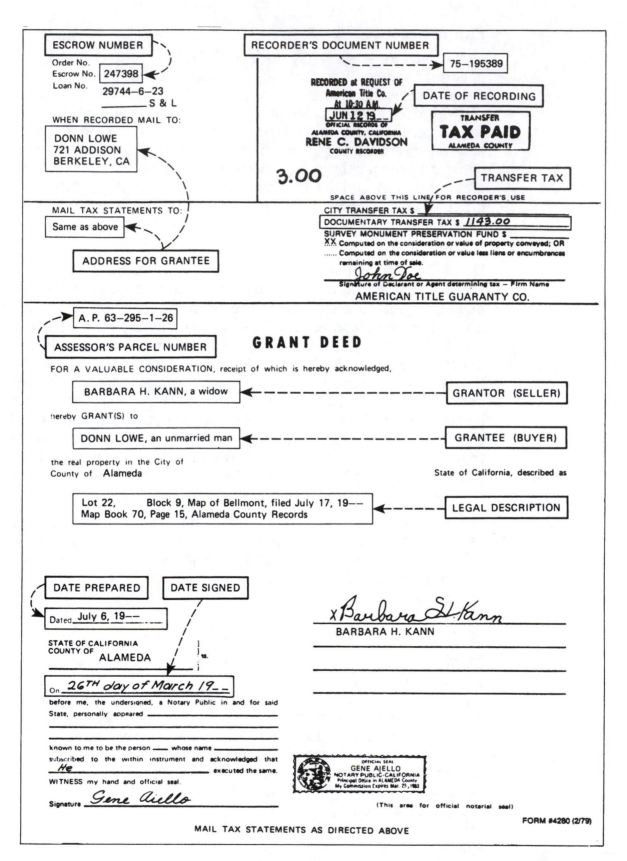

Figure 8-9 Sample Grant Deed.

the mailing address for the buyer or the buyer's attorney or broker is used. Most deeds also contain the new address to which the property tax bill should be mailed. This could be the buyer's address, the buyer's agent (if the property tax is being paid by another party), or the buyer's bank (if taxes are to be paid from an impound account). Either or both of these addresses can lead you to someone who could verify information about the sale.

Most deeds also indicate which party requested that the deed be recorded. This is particularly common when deeds are recorded as part of a title or escrow company closing. Usually, the name of the title or escrow company is on the deed, as well as the escrow account number and the code letters indicating which title company branch handled the transaction. Title companies will not divulge the details of a transaction but will sometimes disclose the name of the broker(s) (or you may be able to get the brokers' names from the MLS). The broker, in turn, can provide information about the property. The name of the notary public who notarized the seller's signature can also be helpful. For example, the notary public's seal will state the county in which the notary practices, which could help you locate buyers or sellers who live out of town.

Finally, you should note that the deed contains dates other than just the date of recording. Often, the date next to the signatures indicates either the date that the document was signed or the date it was prepared. Another date will be on the notary public's affidavit of signatures. This will be the date the individual sellers had their signatures notarized.

When an institutional lender makes a new loan on the property as part of the sale transaction, the lender's loan number is sometimes typed on the deed, or on the mortgage or deed of trust that is the security for the loan. This loan number can prove helpful when discussing the property with the lender or the lender's appraiser, since the loan number enables them to locate the file quickly.

If a new loan was placed on the property at the time of sale, the *deed of trust* (*mortgage* in some states) securing that loan nearly always will be recorded as the document immediately following the deed. This deed of trust will give the lender's name and the amount of the loan. It may also indicate whether it is a variable interest rate loan, and if a clause was included making the loan due in full when the property is resold. The loan number will sometimes be on the deed of trust, as will a mailing address for the borrower, a date of signature, and another notary's signature with the date and county of business. Much of this information may already be on the deed, but occasionally, missing details are found that will be helpful to the appraiser. If the buyer was a partnership or a corporation, the deed of trust nearly always will be signed by one or more partners or officers. These individuals are more likely than a partnership to be listed in a phone book.

Additional documents may also be recorded, such as a chattel mortgage for any personal property, and an assignment of rents if the property generates income. A second mortgage might have been placed by a lender, or by the broker to secure a note for the commission due. This would identify the broker's name and location. There may also be other encumbrances (loans) in favor of the seller or a third party, or there may be requests for a *notice of default*. (The recorder must notify the named party if a notice of default is filed for any deeds of trust listed on the request.) The seller who has a second mortgage from the buyer or some other party (such as a broker with a loan for a commission) may want to be notified of a default on the first mortgage.

Besides the Recorder's Office, a major public source of information for appraisers is the local assessor's office. Although the exact jurisdiction will differ from one location to another, property tax **assessment records** are usually maintained by the county assessor. The primary document to look for is the **assessment roll**. Besides showing the assessed value of all privately owned property, listed in order by assessor's parcel number, the roll shows the owner of record on the date the roll is established and an address for tax bill mailing purposes. Most jurisdictions have a standard series of maps, so that each listed parcel can be described by map reference number. Assessment rolls will often show the date of the most recent transfer of ownership and the document number used by the public Recorder's Office for that transfer. Assessment rolls may also contain a use code (which identifies a category of use for the property, such as residential, commercial, industrial, or vacant land) and may show the age and size of buildings.

The assessor's maps include index maps for the entire county, area index maps, and maps showing each of the parcels in a block. These maps give the dimensions of the parcels and usually show major easements, as well as streets and railroads. Often, the area of larger parcels will be calculated and noted on the map.

There are also usually indexes for the assessment roll. The roll itself usually lists property in parcel number order. One index will list property by address and a second index by the name of the owner. Still another document maintained by some assessor's offices is a list of recent sales. Originally prepared for use by the assessor's appraisal staff, these lists have become, by law, public information in some states.

The assessor's office usually has very detailed information on each property, from its transfer history and building permit history to detailed construction specifications and building perimeter drawings with dimensions. In most jurisdictions, this property record information is available only to the owner. Written permission of the owner is required to obtain a copy. In most appraisals, this is not done. For complex properties or litigation assignments, it can be worth doing.

Multiple Listing Services

In many areas, there are multiple listing services (often called MLS). These are usually sponsored by a local Board of REALTORS® or by local brokers. All the property listings submitted by members are combined and made available to subscribers. These listings historically were published in a weekly or biweekly book. Usually, at the end of the book you would find an index of listings that sold in the immediate past. A quarterly book was published, summarizing all the sales and expired or withdrawn listings that occurred during that quarter. In the past, many multiple listing services restricted the use of such books solely to their members; however, some states have made licensed appraisers eligible for membership. Today, MLS data are usually maintained on a computer and can be accessed by personal computers.

Usually, the MLS data on a property is extremely useful. Of course, the names of the listing and selling brokers and agents are noted, along with phone numbers. The list price, list date, sale price, and closing date are usually shown. There usually is a good description of the number and type of rooms, the equipment, and amenities such as gardens, views, and so on. The age and square-foot floor area, if shown, are usually based on assessor records or are estimates. Many MLS also include one or more pictures of the property.

Data Services

In recent years, the quality and quantity of organized, private sources of market data available for appraisals have dramatically improved. One of the best known of these is Data Express, from the National Collateral Database (until 2006, the Appraisal Institute Residential Database AIRD). This service replaced the well-known SREA Market Data Center and California Market Data Cooperative (CMDC) in 2000.

Data Express sales data is generated largely by cooperating appraisers and lenders and made available to member-subscribers in several formats. A sample page from the monthly book is shown as Figure 8-10. The majority of the sales data are developed from loan appraisals. However, the data incorporates sales transfer information from public records, as well as all available assessors' data.

The National Collateral Database is a part of FNC Inc., http://www.fncinc.com, which provides collateral infrastructure to the U.S. real

Figure 8-10 Single-Family Residential Sales Data/PUD Sales Data (Source: Nationwide property data provided by © 2007 FNC, Inc. All Rights Reserved).

NCD — REMEMBER, YOUR APPRAISAL COPIES ARE THE NEXT BOOK

SINGLE FAMILY RESIDENTIAL / PUD SALES DATA — SGG — SANTA CLARA

Map Code or City Name or Census Tract	Source	Property Address	Assessor's Parcel Number	Lot/Tract	Recording Number	CLSD	Sales Price	Sales Date	Loan Type / Mrtg %	Price per SqFt	Year Blt / Style, Stories	Tot Rooms, Bedrooms / Baths F/H	Sq Feet Liv Area	Kitchen Equipmnt	Air Cond / Fireplace	Utils. / Zoning	Prkg	Quality, Cond, Roof, Ext Wall, Flooring	Lot Size or Area	Flood Zone	Other Improvements / HOA Dues / Comments	Pool/Spa	Prop Rights / Phys Upd
835-D4	H	1750 DEER CREEK CT SAN JOSE	654-32-021	21/4981	19235667	Y	540,000	122106	C V 100%	326	1973 2	5 3 2/1	1655	B	A N G 1	P P P P R1	N A O U	A A C C V	25X83	N	FEN, PATSLB; $175; S		F 0
	H	1798 DEER CREEK CT SAN JOSE	654-32-013	13/4981	19245764	Y	539,000	122906	C V 90%	302	1973 2	7 4 2/1	1784	B	A C G 1	P P P P R1	N O U	A A C C V	25X79	N	DECK, ENPAT; 240 PET P; EE ITM: AUTOTHERM, W-STRIP, FURN-IG		F 0
	H	3626 EASTRIDGE DR SAN JOSE	654-22-010	41/4719	19271215	Y	815,000	011907	C V 90%	377	1970 1	10 4 3/1	2161	D	A C 2	R	V G O N	G G	80X100		S	POOL	0
	H	3565 PLEASANT ECHO DR SAN JOSE	654-67-018	9	19322269	Y	800,000	022807	C V 89%	447	1985 R 1	8 3 2/	1790	BM	A N G 1	P P P P R1	N D O U	G G T C	65X120	N	DECK, FEN, PATSLB; S		F 0
835-D5	P	2174 FLINT AVE SAN JOSE	652-17-018	3/4327	19265516	Y	635,000	011607	C V 100%	431	1968 1	6 2 1/	1472		1			U	61X105		S		0
	P	2233 FLINT AVE SAN JOSE	649-11-011	49/3840	19226956	Y	863,000	121506	C V 100%	372	1965 2	8 5 3/	2317		1			U	60X100		S		F 0
	H	2065 FLINTFIELD DR SAN JOSE	649-28-050	318/6573	19207329	Y	690,000	113006	C 100%	391	1983 1	8 4 2/	1763		1	R-1 SIN	N D A O N	G A A C W	60X100	N	S; CATH CEIL IN FAM RM		F 3
	P	3451 MARTEN AVE SAN JOSE	647-25-075	965	19316693	Y	690,00*	022607	C V 100%	408	1964 2	6 4 1/	1692					U	55X101		S; *P/S 02-06 $720K		F 0
	H	3521 PLEASANT ECHO DR SAN JOSE	654-67-021	12/7018	19223826	Y	1.035M	121306	C V 100%	286	1984 N 2	9 4 3/	3620		A C	SFR	N D O U	A G T C	79X112		S		F 7
	F	3552 PLEASANT ECHO DR SAN JOSE	654-67-033	33/7018	19212006	Y	699,500 / 699,500	111206 / 120506	C	457	1984 1	6 3 2/	1531	RMS	A G 1	P P P P	N D A 1 G A	A A T B C	63X133	N	FEN, PATSLB; S		F 1
835-D6	P	3335 DIAS DR SAN JOSE	649-12-002	53/4078	19208041	Y	770,00*	120106	C V 95%	428	1967 1	8 4 2/	1800		1			U	56X101		S; *P/S 06-06 $680K		F 0
	H	3280 FLORESTA DR SAN JOSE	649-13-019	92	19315473	Y	730,000	022307	C 100%	395	1967 R 1	8 4 2/	1850	RDS	A G 1	P P R	D A O U	A A A W C	054X100	N	CVRPAT, FEN; S		0
	H	3438 GRADELL PL SAN JOSE	652-25-051	11/7629	19221766	Y	695,000	121206	C V 100%	572	1984 R 1	5 3 2/	1216	B	A N G 1	P P P P R1 SFR	N D O U	A G T C V	7000	N	DECK, FEN; S		0
	F	3221 NAPA DR SAN JOSE	649-25-023	293/4431	19237592	Y	700,000 / 700,000	092806 / 122206	C 80%	433	1971 O 1	8 4 2/	1616	S	A N G 1	P P P P R1-8	D A 1 G A	A A W W W	116X58	N	FEN, PATSLB; S		1
	H	3285 PRADO LN SAN JOSE	649-10-024	79	19303881	Y	720,000	021407	C V 100%	483	1965 1	6 3 2/	1492	R	A G 1	P P R1B6	D O U	G X C	64X100		S		0
	H	3261 TREBOL LN SAN JOSE	649-15-023	35	19288220	Y	695,000	020207	C V 100%	331	1968 2	8 4 3/	2097	R	A 1	R	G O N	A A	060X100		S		0
835-D7	P	3229 SAN RIVAS DR SAN JOSE	649-25-007	309	19305488	Y	700,000	021507	C V 100%	426	1971 1	8 4 2/	1644					U	60X103		S		0
835-E5	F	2234 MOUNT PLEASANT RD SAN JOSE	652-01-005	2		N	1.300M	020807	C	803	1955	6 2 1/	1619	RS	A G 2	P P X X	A D A 1 G D	A A C W C	2.721	N	FEN, ENPAT, BRN; S; CTTG	POOL	F 1
835-E6	H	3397 HOITING DR SAN JOSE	652-33-040	1	19308932	Y	691,000	022007	C V 89%	443	1986 R 1	8 3 2/	1559	BM	A N G 1	P P P P R1B6	N D O U	A A C C C	60X100	N	DECK, FEN, PATSLB; S; ADDL 2 O/S PRKG	SPA	F 0
	H	2496 KLEIN RD SAN JOSE	652-09-013	4	19203675	Y	PORTION	112906	C V	642	1964 R 1	6 3 2/1	1869	B	A N G 1	P P P P R1	H D O U	A	1.720	N	FEN, PATSLB, POR; S; *Multi PCL		F 5
	P	2859 RUBY VW SAN JOSE	652-27-079	15	19299009	Y	960,000	020907	C V 90%	416	1997 2	8 4 2/1	2308					U	6098		S		0
	P	3450 VALLEY VISTA DR SAN JOSE	652-21-022	9	19311617	Y	1.200M	022107	C 90%	395	2000 2	11 5 3/	3041					U	5227		S		0
835-E7	H	2758 ALDWORTH DR SAN JOSE	652-31-030	13/6026	19205957	Y	790,000	113006	C V 100%	378	1979 R 3	7 3 2/1	2089	B	A G 2	P P R	V D G O U	G G T C C	065X126	N	FEN; S		F 0
	H	3421 AMBUM AVE SAN JOSE	654-54-014	7/6083	19223852	Y	890,000	121306	C 90%	466	1984 N 2	7 3 2/	1908	BM	A C G 1	P P P P R1B8SF	N D O U	A T C R	9000		FEN, PATSLB; S		F 0
	P	3418 PIN OAK CT SAN JOSE	652-29-017	23/6067	19279651	Y	885,000	012607	C V 82%	398	1978 2	9 4 2/1	2221		1			U	79X151		S		0
835-F5	H	3840 HIGUERA RD SAN JOSE	654-13-035	2	19313511	Y	1.210*	022207	C V 80%	224	1951 S 2	12 6 4/	5391	DMHS	A N G 2	P P X P RES	D 2 G D	G G T C C	1.860	N	PATSLB; S; *P/S 05-06 $1.05M, WT BAR, PANTRY		F 0

THE ABOVE DATA IS BELIEVED TO BE RELIABLE BUT ACCURACY IS NOT GUARANTEED. MAR 2007 – 233 –

MAP / CITY / CENSUS: 835-D4 Thru 835-F5

SINGLE FAMILY / PUD SANTA CLARA

estate loan sector. The database is available by purchase in either print or online format at http://www.collateraldna.com/dataexpress.aspx.

DataQuick Property Finder is another well-known appraisal service, at http://www.dataquick.com, offering tools for both appraisers and lenders. Sales comparables, sales histories, property characteristics, and parcel maps are available, as well as Automated Valuation Models (AVMs).

First American RES (Real Estate Solutions), at http://www.firstamres.com, also offers property data in a broad array of formats and media. Through their well-known RealQuest program, these include online public record property data, as well as CD-ROM data and map disks. First American RES also offers AVMs and a variety of other services.

Fidelity National Data Services, through SiteX Data, is another well-known national provider of sales data. The data is primarily from county transfer and assessment records, and flood and environmental data, and is available by subscription at http://www.sitexdata.com.

Quite a few other local and regional sales data services can be found across the country. Some services may specialize in just one county. In many areas, there are local appraisal cooperative data centers. These can range from a large company to informal agreements between two appraisers to share sales data. In many areas of the country, the publicly available assessment and transfer information is available in both the CD-ROM format and some online format. In addition, many local county assessor offices make some or all of their information available to the public through the Internet.

Now, there are regional data services specializing in apartment rents and vacancy data. Some commercial property listing databases, such as LoopNet at http://www.loopnet.com, now provide data on past listings and sold property.

Title Insurance Companies

Finally, sales data information can be provided by title insurance companies. Many of these companies have extensive microfilm or computer files of all public records affecting real estate. Often featuring a computerized index, each file includes assessment and sales transfer records, deeds, and other recorded documents. Title companies often provide customers with a *property profile*, which may include assessment details of the subject property, along with recent transfers for the surrounding area. Appraisers may be able to obtain copies of such profiles, along with other needed documents. Sometimes, arrangements can be made with a title insurance company to research other specified sales in the area for a reasonable fee. If the research is quite limited, some title companies are willing to provide the information without charge.

The Internet

The Internet has completely changed how appraisers obtain specific property information. The Internet has allowed existing providers of information, from the appraisal data cooperatives to the local, regional, and national providers, to open websites for data access. But other sources also are moving to the Internet as well. More and more county assessors and public appraisers now make their information available. An especially outstanding example is the Harris County Appraisal District in Houston, Texas (http://www.hcad.org/). Be alert for the emergence of additional public records sites, including sites that will feature indexes of recorded documents. A list of some of the resources available on the Internet is provided in Section 8.3.

Parties to the Transaction

As suggested earlier, you should consider the possibility of obtaining information from the parties to the transaction. These parties include not only the buyer and seller, but their respective agents as well. Other parties that could also have relevant information include any brokers who had offers on the property at the same time, or brokers who had prior listings that expired. Any lender involved with the sale can also be a source of information. Sometimes, a particular loan broker's office, or a particular lender's branch, may have been a party to a large percentage of all the transactions in an area, or indeed, may have originated the transaction in question. If so, such an office would be an important resource.

Appraisal Office Data Files

Many appraisers find that the types of properties they appraise will change from time to time, but houses are the most common appraisal assignment. The information needed to complete single-family home appraisals is usually plentiful and easy to find. However, there will be times throughout an appraiser's career when an unusual property will be assigned and the necessary data will not be readily accessible. Keeping this in mind, many appraisers keep on file much of the market data that has been researched, particularly the data collected for unusual assignments. If a similar assignment comes up in the near future, the market data may be of some use. Files of this type are also a useful source of information for other appraisers. One appraiser may have unique information on file that he or she needs for a different assignment. In a cooperative spirit, most appraisers share such information with local professionals if it does not violate the Ethics/ Confidentiality Rule of USPAP. Basically, this rule prohibits the disclosure of confidential data, as defined by USPAP, which was given to the appraiser by the client.

Computer Data Search

The availability of computerized data collections has created a revolution in the data collection process. How do computer data searches work, when comparable sales are being sought via an office computer? Although each data service has its own rules for access and search procedures, there is enough standardization to allow some generalizations.

Access

As mentioned earlier, many data services originally distributed sales and other property data by printed books. Later came disks that are inserted into the CD-ROM drive on your computer. Now, most sales data collections are available via the Internet.

Procedure

Usually, the first step is to connect to the computer where the data is stored, through the appropriate Internet site. Next, the appropriate database is selected from several that may be available. A password is usually required. The database is sometimes chosen by geographical location, type of property (e.g., homes vs. apartments) and type of information sought (e.g., assessment roll vs. sales data).

Within the appropriate database, the next step is usually to define the search to be performed. This is done by selecting the criteria or property characteristics that are considered most important. Location, property use, and specific property features are usually the more critical. A local map reference (e.g., Thomas Bros. or Key Maps), zip code, or street address is used to identify the location, depending on the particular database. Many of the newer databases use a "centroid" search that identifies all of the comparables within a given distance from the subject property.

The property use and acceptable characteristics may be specified next. Physical size (maximum, minimum, or range), the number of bedrooms and baths, age, price, sale date, or any other information stored in the database may be useable as search criteria.

Clearly, selecting the best search criteria, and the best combination of search terms, is important in the sales data search. If the criteria are set in too narrow a range (age plus or minus one year, for example), the search might not produce enough sales; if the criteria are not rigid enough, too many sales may be reported. For this reason, many systems allow the user to do a search and get a report back giving the number of sales meeting the selected criteria. In this way, the user knows whether to change the search criteria before looking at the individual sales more carefully. An outline of both general and specific data resources available on the Internet follows.

8.3 Data Resources on the Internet

The Internet has become a universal source of communication and commerce, serving government, education, and industry alike. Data resources on the Internet are almost limitless, but those that are the most useful to appraisers may be found on websites maintained by government agencies, industry service organizations, and trade associations connected to real estate.

Websites of Government Agencies

Most state and federal government agencies maintain websites, both to offer more efficient public service and to provide networks of information exchange. Appraisers are primarily interested in three types of information to be found on these sites: general data on the economy, regulatory information having to do with real estate and finance administration, and specific property information, such as county assessment records. We have not listed any state or local websites here! Quasi-governmental agencies such as the Appraisal Foundation, Fannie Mae, and Freddie Mac are among those listed that provide regulatory information of use to the appraiser. Appraisers of course also turn to the Internet to find information on equipment purchases, software programs, and solutions to all types of appraisal, equipment, and software problems.

General Data on the Economy

A number of federal government agencies maintain websites that offer general data on the economy. These include current social and economic statistics and indicators, used by both government and industry groups. The following sites are good examples:

> Bureau of Labor Statistics:
> *http://stats.bls.gov/*

> Bureau of Labor Statistics, U.S. Economy at a Glance:
> *http://www.bls.gov/eag/eag.us.htm*

> Census Bureau:
> *http://www.census.gov/*

> Department of Commerce, Bureau of Economic Analysis:
> *http://bea.gov/beahome.html*

> U.S. Congress, Economic Indicators of the Joint Economic Committee:
> *http://www.gpoaccess.gov/indicators/index.html*

> OFHEO, House Price Index:
> *http://www.ofheo.gov/HPI.asp*

Regulatory Information

Regulatory agencies, such as the U.S. Department of Housing and Urban Development, take advantage of the Internet to post their regulations, handbooks, and forms. Much of this material can be downloaded for reference and use by affected institutions, as well as by appraisers. For example, the HUD/FHA *Appraisal Handbook 4150.2,*

Valuation Analysis for 1–4 Unit Homes is available on the HUD website (at http://www.hudclips.org). Fannie Mae, Freddie Mac, and others offer appraisal and related forms, as well as instructions, which can be downloaded for use by the appraiser.

Department of Housing and Urban Development:
http://www.hud.gov/

Environmental Protection Agency:
http://www.epa.gov/

Fannie Mae:
http://www.efanniemae.com/

Federal Emergency Management Agency:
http://www.fema.gov/

Freddie Mac:
http://www.freddiemac.com/

The Appraisal Subcommittee (supervises state appraisal licensing):
http://www.asc.gov/

The Appraisal Foundation:
http://www.appraisalfoundation.org/

Websites of Industry Service Organizations

For many years, real estate research and service organizations have, by their various trade publications, provided the real estate, construction, and appraisal industry with useful data that we could call *tools of the trade*. Specific data provided range from local and national indicators and trends, to industry guidelines for construction cost estimating and property management. Now, many such research and service organizations make their services available on the Internet. Some data are available to the general public, while some data and services are available by subscription only. As mentioned earlier, online data banks for comparable sales have recently been added to the following list. In addition, sites like http://www.zillow.com allow the public to obtain free preliminary value estimates.

Comparable Sales

Fidelity National Data Services—SiteX Data:
http://www.sitexdata.com

DataQuick Property Finder:
http://www.dataquick.com

First American Real Estate Solutions—RealQuest:
http://www.realquest.com/

National Collateral Database—Data Express:
http://www.collateraldna.com/dataexpress.aspx

CoStar Group—COMPS Express:
http://www.costar.com/products/compsExpress

National Association of Realtors:
http://www.realtor.com

Homescout—Listings:
http://www.homescout.com

Cost and Construction

Marshall & Swift Company Group—Cost Data:
http://www.marshallswift.com/

R.S. Means Company—Cost Data:
http://www.rsmeans.com/

Means Quick—Cost Calculator:
http://www.rsmeans.com/calculator/index.asp

General and Other Sites

Building Owners and Managers Association:
http://www.boma.org/

Engineering News—Record:
http://www.enr.com/

Realty Rates:
http://www.realtyrates.com

Mortgage Bankers Association of America—Forecasts:
*http://www.mbaa.org/ResearchandForecasts/
economicoutlookandforecasts*

ULI/PricewaterhouseCoopers—Emerging Trends in Real Estate:
http://www.uli.org

Websites of Trade Associations

Various trade associations with connections to real estate maintain websites for members and the general public. Examples include the following:

American Society of Appraisers:
http://www.appraisers.org/

Appraisal Institute:
http://www.appraisalinstitute.org/

National Association of REALTORS®:
http://www.realtor.com/

Real Estate Educators Associations:
http://www.reea.org/

Society of Industrial and Office Realtors—Commercial Real Estate Index:
http://www.sior.com

AIA—Market Segment Concensus Growth Forecasts:
http://www.aia.org/aiarchitect/

National Association of Industrial and Office Parks—Vital Signs Survey:
http://www.naiop.org/newsroom/pressreleases

The reader should be reminded that the data sources listed above are not intended to be recommended above other sources that may be found on the Internet, but instead, merely representative of those useful to the appraiser. Also, given the high rate of change of the Internet, there is no certainty that any of these addresses (URLs) will still work when you try to use them.

8.4 Appraisal Statistical Concepts

As was suggested in Section 8.1, the use of comparable sales in the sales comparison approach is a sampling process, a technique of statistics. The sales selected for analysis constitute the sample. When applying the sales adjustment methods described above, certain other statistical methods may be useful to validate and interpret data from the sample. However, a fairly large number of comparables are usually required.

One method helps the appraiser discover the central tendency among the sales. *Central tendency* means the numeric value that is suggested as typical, with regard to size, price, or other *variable* studied. Calculating the central tendency can help in several ways. For example, an analysis of the typical square-foot size of the comparables could help interpret their sales prices, or suggest the weight to be assigned them in the adjustment process. There are several different measures of central tendency, including the following:

1. *Mean:* the average numeric "value" of the sample (the average price or average size, for example). Often called the average. It is calculated by adding up the values and dividing the total by the number of observations in the sample. For example, for the numbers 1, 1, 3, 3, 5, 6, 7, 8, 9, the mean is 4.77+.

2. *Median:* the middle value, that is, the value in the sample with as many values that are greater as values that are less. For example, in the same string of numbers, the median number is 5.

3. *Mode:* the most frequently occurring value. In our string of numbers, there are two numbers, 1 and 3, that each occur more than any other numbers, and the same number of times. So, this is a set of numbers with two modes, called a bi-modal distribution!

4. *Range:* the difference, or spread, between the highest and lowest value in the sample. Here, the range is from 1 to 9.

5. ***Standard deviation:*** a measurement of whether the observations are clustered close to the mean, or, instead, scattered throughout the range. It is calculated as the square root of the sum of the squared differences between each observation and the mean of all observations, divided by the total number of observations. Each sale price, for example, would be considered an observation. Many real estate calculators can be used to quickly calculate the standard deviation.

The calculations seem complicated, but can be quickly done with any 6-function calculator (see Example 8.1).

How is this result interpreted? The *average variation* of the sale prices per square foot is just under 9, and is 4.4 percent of the average or mean sale price. This seems to be a fairly tight set of sales. The same calculation could be done for the total sale price, and the price per room, to establish which measure had the least variability.

Linear and multiple regressions represent two additional statistical methods used in valuations, primarily in mass appraisal work and in loan reviews. These methods typically calculate the relationship between a series of numbers, representing property characteristics, and the selling prices of the sample, producing a formula for such a relationship. Hence, the significant characteristics of each sale property (price, square-foot area, age, and so on) are entered into the formula. A statistically indicated value or range of value for the subject property may then be calculated. Linear and multiple regression techniques will be explored further in Chapter 9.

EXAMPLE 8-1 Calculating the Standard Deviation

A. Given:

Three sales, with prices of $180, $200, and $217 per square foot of living area. The mean (average) price is (180 + 200 + 217) ÷ 3, or $199.

B. Calculation:

Sale	Price		Mean		Difference	Square of the Difference
1	180	−	199	=	− 19	361
2	200	−	199	=	1	1
3	217	−	199	=	18	+ 324
Sum of the Squared Differences						686
Square Root of the Sum						26.19
Divided by: Number of Observations						÷ 3
Equals: Standard Deviation						8.73
As a Percent of the Mean						4.4%

SUMMARY

The sales comparison approach is one of the three approaches used to estimate value. The main feature of the sales comparison approach is the process of analyzing sales and comparing them to the subject property, based on the principle of substitution. The sales comparison approach consists of four steps.

1. Research the sales.
2. Analyze the sales.
3. Adjust the sales for differences between the sales and the subject property.
4. Arrive at a value estimate.

When employing the sales comparison approach to estimate market value, an appraiser should consider the concepts that are fundamental to it. These concepts include the principle of substitution, the importance of simplicity, the connections to statistics, the relevance of adjustments, and the foundation: market data. Each of these concepts is important in understanding how to use the sales comparison approach.

The first step of the sales comparison approach, researching comparable sales, consists of two parts: 1) selecting comparable sales and 2) seeking out the appropriate sales information. When selecting comparable sales, three criteria should be met for a sale to be considered a comparable sale: The sale must be a competitive property, be an open-market transaction, and have a sale date close to the date of value.

The ideal is to find comparable sales that meet all three criteria. If you cannot, try to find sales that were open-market transactions and are as comparable and as close to the date of value as possible.

Once you have decided on the sales you are going to study, the next step is collecting the necessary information about the sales transaction, the physical characteristics of the property, its legal status, and its location. It is also important to consider whether there were unusual market conditions at the time of sale.

The number of comparables needed varies with each appraisal situation. How comparable the sales are and which adjustment techniques are used will both affect the number of sales needed to support your conclusion. The area of the sales search will vary as well, depending on the type of property being appraised and the amount of market activity. After deciding on the sales data to be used, you must then decide whether your data are reliable. Inspecting the sales is one good way of ensuring that your data are reliable. Cross-checking your data with data from another source is another.

Since there are many sources of market data, the trick is in knowing where to find the information you need as reliably, efficiently, and easily as possible. There are a variety of sources with which you should be familiar, ranging from public records at the county assessor's office to private firms that provide information on sales for a fee.

Public records include deeds, which contain such needed information as names of grantor and grantee, a legal description of the property, transfer tax information, a mailing address for the buyer, and the transaction date. The assessor's office contains the assessment roll, which lists privately owned property, its value for property tax purposes, and the mailing address for the tax bill. Assessor's maps provide the measurements of parcels and show major easements, streets, and railroads.

Private sources of market data are becoming increasingly valuable to appraisers. In some areas, the multiple listing services (MLS) of local Boards of REALTORS® are now available to appraisers. Many appraisers subscribe to industry services that provide computerized appraisal data. Access to central computer databases is a trend, allowing rapid, inexpensive sharing of data and easier processing of sales analyses and reports.

Whenever needed, the appraiser also seeks out the parties to a transaction, such as the buyer, the seller, or their agents, to obtain or verify sales data and property information.

In recent years, increasing numbers of private data sources have offered appraisal data to the appraiser. One well-known service is First American RealQuest. Other well-known services include Fidelity National Data Services SiteX and DataQuick Property Finder. Their nationwide data incorporate sales transfer information from public records as well as all available assessors' data. In the National Collateral Database Data Express service, the public record sales are supplemented by data generated largely by cooperating lenders and appraisers, and then are made available to member-subscribers in several formats. The majority of the sales data are developed from loan appraisals.

The Internet and World Wide Web have become universal sources of communication and commerce, serving government, education, and industry alike. In recent years, the Internet has become an invaluable source of data for the appraiser. Data resources on the Internet may be found on websites maintained by government agencies, industry service organizations, and trade associations connected to real estate.

The sales comparison approach has a connection to statistics, in that the comparable sales represent a sample from which we can draw certain conclusions. Appraisers use several statistical methods that can help with the analysis of the sample or with data drawn from the sample. The most useful of these mathematical tools are those that can suggest how typical a price or other variable is in the sample, an idea known as central tendency. The mean, or average, is the most common of these statistical measures.

IMPORTANT TERMS AND CONCEPTS

Adjustment techniques	*Mode*
Assessment records	*Open-market transaction*
Assessment roll	*Physical characteristics*
Bracketing	*Public records*
Buyer's motives	*Range*
Central tendency	*Regression, linear and multiple*
Comparable sales	*Sales comparison approach*
Comparable search area	*Sales history*
Competitive property	*Sampling*
Data services	*Seller's motives*
Linear and multiple regression	*Standard deviation*
Location	*Submarket*
Mean	*Variable*
Median	

REVIEWING YOUR UNDERSTANDING

1. The sales comparison approach involves:
   a. Analyzing sales
   b. Comparing sales to a subject property
   c. Both (a) and (b)
   d. None of the above

2. The first step in the sales comparison approach is to:
   a. Research comparable sales
   b. Adjust for differences between the sales
   c. Arrive at a value conclusion
   d. Set up an office data system

3. The sales comparison approach is often simpler and more direct than the income or cost approaches because:
   a. Fewer comparable properties are required, so it is easier to outline the results to clients
   b. There are fewer mathematical calculations, so there is less chance of mathematical errors
   c. Both (a) and (b)
   d. None of the above

4. Appraisers use bracketing in order to:
   a. Apply the cost approach to large mansions
   b. Estimate the upper and lower range of value
   c. Estimate the adjustment for units of comparison
   d. Study properties that are better and worse than the subject

5. Market data are used:
   a.   In the sales comparison approach
   b.   In the income approach
   c.   In the cost approach
   d.   All of the above

6. The criteria used to establish that a property can be considered comparable include:
   a.   It must have sold within five years.
   b.   It must be a competitive property.
   c.   It must be an open-market transaction.
   d.   Both (a) and (b)
   e.   Both (b) and (c)

7. USPAP requires that prior sales of the subject property within three years of the date of value be considered in the appraisal of:
   a.   Residential properties only
   b.   Commercial properties only
   c.   All property types
   d.   None of the above

8. The number of comparable sales needed for the sales comparison approach is dependent on:
   a.   How good the comparables are
   b.   The reliability of the data
   c.   The intended use of the appraisal
   d.   All of the above

9. You need to know all the following information about a comparable property except:
   a.   The sales price
   b.   The date of sale
   c.   The date legal work began on the transaction
   d.   The type of financing involved

10. In order to improve the reliability of the information about a sale, the appraiser should:
    a.   Make at least an exterior inspection
    b.   Identify property changes made since the sale date
    c.   Verify the price and terms of sale
    d.   All of the above

11. Which of the following statistical concepts helps measure central tendency in a sample?
    a.   Mean
    b.   Median
    c.   Mode
    d.   All of the above

PRACTICAL APPLICATIONS

As we will remind you at the start of each exercise, review the exercise at the end of the preceding chapter, and the work that you have performed to date.

This assignment starts the sales comparison approach, which will be reported on the sales comparison approach section of the URAR form, as shown in Figure , and also shown in the forms at the end of Chapter 16. The focus of this chapter is on locating sales that may be comparable and then verifying the information, to decide which sales to emphasize. As a starting point, assume that you want to end up with the best six sales out of however many you identify as possibles. The first step is to locate some possible comparable sales. Review information about your subject property to decide what characteristics about possible sales will be important. Have an idea what you are looking for. Sources of sales include the websites noted in the chapter, as well as sites of local brokerage firms in your area. You may also want to ask agents in brokerage offices, but it is very desirable to do as much research online as possible.

Identify which sales might be good comparables. Often, you will want to start with more sales, so you can easily drop the ones that seem less comparable as you research them. Ten sales or so often is a good target for your initial data collection. The major points of comparability usually would be emphasized, such as sale date, size or room count, and age. However, if your subject property is relatively different from most of the comparable sales in some way—such as a swimming pool, needed repairs, or a rear cottage—then you may want to focus your search more on the unusual feature.

After you have identified the preliminary list of comparable sales, you will start collecting information about each sale. As a starting point, review the form, and review the chapter content. Consider what information you will need to obtain about each comparable sale, and where you might be able to get it. Much of the information may be available on the listing where you located the possible comparable sales.

Some of the information consists of facts that you must research. Start with a careful inspection of each comparable sale property, from the street, making notes as you go. Take a picture of each property from the street. (If asked what you are doing, explain that you are a student appraiser, and you are using the past sale of the property in an appraisal for class.) Much of the needed information will be gained just from your visual inspection. However, the age of the properties may need to be researched, using the same sources that we noted for identifying the age of the subject property. Sometimes, the square-foot area may not be available. If missing, consider checking the county assessment roll or city building permit records, again as discussed in the exercise on inspecting the subject property.

If your subject property is, as we discussed in the prior exercises, a unit in a condo, co-op, or apartment building, you must decide what type of comparable sales to use. For a condo or co-op unit, use sales of the same type of unit. For a unit in an apartment building, treat it as if it were a condo, for the purpose of these exercises only. *Never* do this on an actual appraisal!

The remaining information that you will need about each comparable sale calls for you to develop an opinion. For example, what is the condition of each sold property? Has it been remodeled? Does it have a better or worse view than the subject property? Is its immediate neighborhood better or worse than that of the subject property? Review the information that you gathered, both from the listing and from your field inspection. If necessary, repeat your field inspection in order to focus on these issues.

After you have completed your data gathering, you will need to 1) review all of your information for inconsistencies and missing information, and then 2) decide which of the sales to carry forward to the form. Six is a good number, partly because the form is set up with three sales per page. However, there is no requirement to use a specified number. Consider which sales seem to be the most different from the subject. Because all of the sales should be somewhat similar, the range of sale prices may well be the range of value for the subject property. Consider carefully any sales with prices that are noticeably more or less than the others, and ask yourself why. Also ask yourself if the subject property is more like the sales with the different prices or more like the other sales. It may well be that one group or the other is the better set of comparables.

Finally, start up the software program and open the file that you saved after the prior chapter's assignment. Note that you have already entered the basic information about the property and the assignment, as well as the neighborhood and site description sections. Review this information. Next, enter the information about the sales that you have collected. We will leave the adjustment of these sales for the next chapter's assignment, but take this occasion to look at the sales prices and how they vary. Which ones are high, or low? Is there a clear possible reason, such as date of sale, size, condition, or age? This will get you thinking about the next assignment!

As we note at the end of each exercise, it is best not to get ahead of yourself. So, do not enter information in the later sections of the report until you have read the chapter(s) that covers that topic. However, it is a good idea to look ahead at the coming sections of the form, so that you start thinking about the information that you will need to gather. And it is certainly reasonable, and even desirable, for you to start collecting some of that information early, if you choose to do so.

Reminder: If you have questions about the program itself, please be sure to review the manuals and help information that were included with the program CD. Also, at anytime, you can go to http://www. bradfordsoftware.com, click on "Services" at the upper right of the home page, and then on "ClickFORMS Training Programs" in the middle of the "Services" page. See the free online training section!

CHAPTER 9
ANALYZING AND ADJUSTING COMPARABLE SALES

PREVIEW

We continue our discussion of the sales comparison approach in this chapter. We shall introduce two methods of comparing sales and describe several techniques appraisers use to analyze sales. We will also describe how to make adjustments for differences between the sales and the subject property. Finally, we will explain how to arrive at a value conclusion using the sales comparison approach.

OBJECTIVES

When you have completed this chapter you should be able to:

1. Name the four elements of sales comparison.

2. List the three rules for making adjustments.

3. Name the three types of adjustments most commonly used.

4. Explain how a value conclusion is reached.

9.1 Basic Methods of Comparing Sales

In Chapter 8, we described several key concepts of the sales comparison approach, and we reminded the reader that the approach was based upon the principle of substitution. This principle asserts that any property tends to be worth the cost of, or the price to acquire, an equally desirable substitute property. We also suggested that the sales comparison approach finds its strength in its simplicity; it is a straight-forward, easy-to-understand concept.

There are two methods of comparing sales. The first is the *direct comparison method*, which is the simplest method available for comparing sales in the market approach. It is primarily used when the sales are quite comparable. The second is the *elements of comparison method*, the primary sales comparison tool of the practicing appraiser. Its basis, and a description of its process, will be introduced in this section and further described in Sections 9.2 and 9.3.

The Direct Comparison Method

At the start of the 1900s, there were no appraisers. Local real estate brokers and/or bankers rode in a buggy to the property, stopped, looked it over, discussed its merits and demerits, and settled on a price. This is the origin of the term *curbstone appraisal*. As appraising evolved, brokers and bankers began to debate the value conclusion by referring to the prices of sales with which they were familiar. In essence, they compared sales directly to the subject property. A knowledgeable broker who is working in a territory that he or she has successfully "farmed" over a period of time often does the same thing. Appraisers have a similar technique, called the *direct comparison method*. The central point about direct comparison is that the appraiser does not make any specific adjustment for differences, or even specifically analyze the differences. Instead, the properties are compared as they are, "head-to-head."

Technique

First, locate property sales that appear similar to the subject property and are close enough in time and terms of sale. Next, arrange the list of sales so that they are placed in the order of their relative value or desirability. The list could be in price order, that is, from the highest priced sale on the top to the lowest priced sale on the bottom. However, it is usually better to ignore prices at this stage and rank the sales by listing them in the order of their overall appeal. After completing the list of properties, the appraiser compares the subject

EXAMPLE 9-1 Direct Comparison of Sales

Sale Address	Time Since Sale (months)	Price	Age	Building Sq. Ft.	Comparison to Subject
991 Arlington Ave.	5	$397,000	1925	2,093	W
195 Arlington Ave.	7	$360,000	1924	2,427	W
820 Red Rock Ave.	4	$380,000	1921	1,519	W
1295 Cougar Ave.	2	$390,000	1940	1,776	W
230 Hilldale Ave.	1	$392,500	1930	1,645	W
214 Leroy Ave.	5	$435,000	1935	3,043	?
319 Hemlock St.	3	$455,000	1925	3,300	B
2150 Euclid Ave.	2	$455,000	1924	2,152	?
775 Hemlock St.	9	$462,500	1936	3,400	B
200 Creston	5	$518,000	1937	3,136	B

Note: W = worse; B = better; and ? = questionable.

property to those on the list. Properties that are judged to be more desirable than the subject property could be identified as "Better," those less desirable as "Worse," and those that are uncertain with a question mark. You would expect to find that properties marked with a "B" are the higher priced sales and that those marked with a "W" are the lower priced sales. The sales in between often are a mixture of "Better," "Worse," and question marks. It is within this middle zone or area that the value of the subject property is likely to lie. Example 9-1 shows such a list of sales.

Limitations

The direct comparison technique has several limitations. One limitation is that the sales transactions, dates of sale, and property features should be relatively similar to the property being appraised.

For example, the seventh and eighth sales in Example 9-1 sold for the same price and the buildings are about the same age, but one building is much smaller. Clearly, the two sales are very different in some way besides size. Which one is more like the subject? In fact, are these

Figure 9-1
Direct Comparison of Sales: Which Is More Attractive to Buyers?

sales similar enough to each other and to the subject to allow a good direct comparison? In addition, this technique relies heavily on the appraiser's intuitive ability to judge which sale property is more attractive to buyers (see Figure 9-1).

Sometimes, this analysis will be performed at the same time as the elements of comparison method, if the latter is not leading to a clear solution. The added insight of such a second view can be helpful—a cross-check.

The Elements of Comparison Method

Comparable sales come from the marketplace. Therefore, they reflect not only the value of the property in the market, but also the conditions of the transaction itself. The critical characteristics of both the transaction and the property involved in the sale are referred to as the *elements of comparison*. Once these critical characteristics are identified, the sales comparables can be adjusted for differences. Therefore, the elements of comparison are at the center of the adjustment process.

Elements of Comparison

When the comparable sales have been selected, and all relevant data about them gathered, the next step—an important one—is to identify and compare the *differences* between the sales and the subject property, considering the sales transaction, as well as the property location and characteristics. The appraiser's goal is to pin down which differences cause significant variations in the prices paid in this specific market. The relevant information about each sale is divided into four distinct categories. These are known as the *four elements of comparison*.

The Four Elements of Comparison

1. Terms and conditions of sale.

2. Time of sale.

3. Location elements.

4. Physical elements.

Terms and Conditions of Sale. The *terms* of the sale can influence the selling price. For instance, favorable financing can easily produce a selling price that is higher than typical. In this circumstance, a price adjustment should be made to reflect the advantage. If unfavorable terms are found, the price should be adjusted to show the disadvantage. In condemnation proceedings, as well as in federally related appraisals, legal standards require that appraisals be based on a value assuming conventional third-party financing, at rates and terms in effect on the date of value. At times, it can be very difficult to get the needed information. It is desirable to always ask for a copy of the sales contract and any addenda, to document to the file that this was done, and to state in the report what was asked for and what was received. Situations that call for financing adjustments include:

1. ***Seller financing***: when a loan from the seller is more favorable than the terms of third-party lenders.

2. ***Assumed financing***: where the existing loan is assumed by the buyer and has terms more (or less) favorable than the terms of a new conventional loan.

3. ***Seller-paid points*** or buyer's closing costs: when the seller pays some of the buyer's loan points or other costs, this acts to reduce the *seller's* net receipts in the same way as when the seller sells at a lower price. Sellers who offer to pay loan points or the buyer's closing costs usually try to increase the selling price to help cover the amount paid. Techniques for adjusting for the terms of sale will be discussed later in this chapter. As outlined in the previous chapter, the *conditions* of sale must also be taken into account. Conditions of sale include the following:

1. Property rights conveyed. Is there an unusual easement, or a low lease, that might be impacting the price?

2. Motives of the parties. Is this really an arm's length sale? And is it a market transaction following adequate market exposure?

3. Personal property and/or tenant improvements included.

4. Seller concessions. Has the seller agreed to pay for the buyer's closing costs, or pay down the interest rate on the buyer's loan? Seller concessions are very common when markets are slow, but they cause the real cash price to be overstated!

Date of Sale. Since market conditions and price levels change over time, the date of sale of each comparable should be noted and considered, relative to the date of value for the assignment. Where a specific market price change can be identified and measured, time adjustments need to be made to the sale price of any sale that occurred some time away from the date of value. Changes in market conditions between the sale date and the date of value may make a particular sale less useful as a comparable!

Location Elements. As discussed in the chapters on neighborhood and site analysis, a number of location factors are important elements of the comparison process. Such factors as the condition and quality of nearby properties, the availability of utilities and transportation, and the proximity of nuisances or hazards should be noted and their effect upon the sale price considered. Also, the effects of social, economic, and political forces must be studied to see if any price differences are attributable to them. Different locations, even as little as a few blocks, can have different price levels!

Physical Elements. The property and site characteristics that were discussed in Chapter 8 are important elements of comparison to consider. Key features of a sale include the size, quality, charm, age, and condition of improvements, and the degree of modernization, along with the size, shape, topography, and desirability of the land parcel. Each difference could cause a difference in the sale price. Any observed problems found at any of the comparables should also be noted.

The Process of Comparing and Adjusting Sales

The process of comparing and adjusting sales involves two steps:

1. *Comparison and analysis* of the four elements of comparison described above, and
2. *Adjusting the sales prices* to account for the differences identified.

The Comparison Process

The comparison and analysis step involves using the four elements of comparison, discussed previously, to identify the significant differences among the sales. Then, in turn, identify the significant differences between the sales and the subject property. Most appraisers prefer to identify the differences in the sales terms and the time of sale at the outset of this process. Techniques for this analysis will be covered later in this chapter.

When physical features and location are compared, questions must be asked about market preferences. For example, some of the comparable houses may be built with slab-on-grade, where others may have a raised floor. Will such a difference affect the sales prices? Some of the houses may be one-story, and others of similar living areas may be of split-level or two-story design. Should there be a price adjustment for such features?

In any neighborhood, factors that are most important in affecting market price can often be identified from your own experience in the local market, or by interviewing active sales people who "farm" the area or are otherwise knowledgeable about market preferences here. Clues that can help you identify significant differences can often be found in the sales themselves. For example, you may find sales of two nearly identical homes that sold six months apart. Is there a price difference? If so, perhaps the time difference is the reason. If two similar homes sell at the same time and show a significant difference in price, perhaps these sales reflect a difference in interior modernization, or if they are several blocks apart, in location. Generally, more sales are better than fewer, when performing the sales analysis process!

The Adjustment Process

The second step in the comparison and adjustment process is making the actual adjustment to the sales prices of the comparables. Once you know which property differences appear to be significant, you then estimate the dollar (or percentage) amount needed to adjust the sales price, to make the comparable more similar to the subject. However, there are several precautions needed to obtain good results.

First, *sales adjustments should be reasonable*. In other words, the dollar amount of the adjustment must have a reasonable relationship to the feature being adjusted. For example, it would be unreasonable to use a $30,000 adjustment for an extra one-half bath, if the cost of building a half-bath is only $10,000, and it easily can be done. Second, *the adjustment amount must be consistently applied* to each sale. If there are three sales with similar counts of baths and half-baths when compared to the bathroom count at the subject property, the same amount probably should be added to or deducted from the sales price of each.

Third, *the adjustments must reduce the price spread* between the sold properties by a significant amount. This is a very important check on the adjustment process. *In theory*, if the adjustments are accurate and the sales prices occurred in a perfect market, the adjusted prices of the comparables should all be nearly the same!

Rules for Making Adjustments

The process of adjusting comparable sales for differences cannot be executed in a haphazard manner. A reliable appraisal will result only from a careful analysis of significant differences and careful application of the following *rules for making adjustments*.

1. The sale property (and its price) must be adjusted to be more like the subject property, as shown in Figure 9-2. *Adjust the sale to the subject!* For example, if the sale property has extra features that the subject property lacks, their value must be subtracted to make the sale like the subject. If the sale property is smaller than the subject, the value of the extra space must be added to the selling price. If the sale was made several months ago in a rising market and the date of value for the appraisal is the current date, then the sale price must be raised to account for the increase in prices. Always remember: You must *adjust the comparable sale to the subject*.

2. Use market adjustments. The appraiser's personal reaction to the differences is not what matters. It is the market's reaction that is important. You may like modern houses, but are they popular in this market? You might refuse to buy a house with a view, located 45 steps above the street, but will others?

3. Make adjustments in the proper sequence. Usually, this means that general adjustments are made first, and adjustments for specific

**Figure 9-2
The Adjustment
Process.**

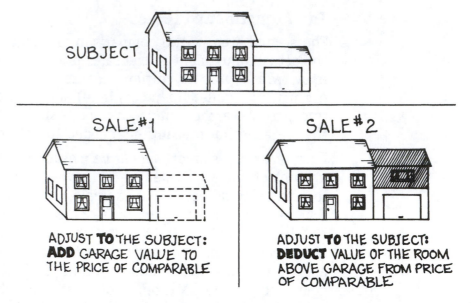

features are made later. A desirable sequence of adjustments is: (1) terms and conditions of sale, (2) time and state of the market, (3) location, and (4) physical features, including quality and condition issues.

Types of Adjustments

The appraiser can select from three commonly used types of adjustments:

- *Lump-sum dollars*
- *Percentage*
- *Units of comparison*

In practice, these methods are often used in combination; however, they will be discussed individually here (see Figure 9-3). Details on how to calculate the dollar amount for sales adjustments are provided later in this chapter (in Section 9.2 for units of comparison and Section 9.3 for dollar and percent adjustments).

Lump-Sum Dollar Adjustment. This type of adjustment uses a specific dollar amount to adjust each sale for the particular property difference. Such an amount is added to, or subtracted from, the price of each comparable sale in order to make it more like the subject. For example, one comparable sale might have a swimming pool, which the subject property lacks. If market study suggests that pools generally add about $15,000 to property values in this area, the appraiser can apply the indicated adjustment by subtracting a lump sum of $15,000 from the price of the sale in question. Here is an example:

Sale price	$405,000
Less: Adjustment for swimming pool	– 15,000
Equals: Adjusted price	$390,000

**Figure 9-3
Types of
Adjustments.**

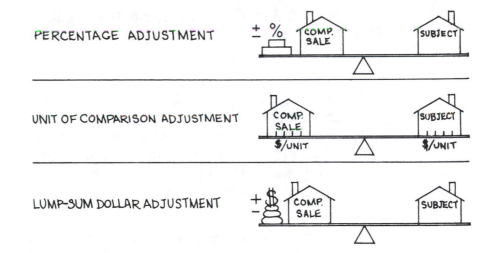

Percentage Adjustment. This second type of adjustment uses a percentage of the comparable's sale price to adjust for a difference between the comparable sale and the subject. For example, in a rapidly rising market, a comparable with a sale date that is four months earlier than the date of valuation might be adjusted up by 4 percent, because the market evidence indicates a 1 percent per month market price change in the intervening time. If the comparable sold for $310,000, then the adjustment would be 4 percent of $310,000, or $12,400 (as shown below).

Sale price	$310,000
Plus: Time adjustment (4%)	+ 12,400
Equals: Adjusted price	$322,400

When two or more percentage adjustments are needed for a particular comparable sale, the appraiser has the option of combining the adjustments by 1) the standard plus or minus method, or 2) by multiplying them together. If the reasons for the adjustment are independent of each other, the plus or minus method may apply. For example, a plus 4 percent time and a plus 3 percent neighborhood adjustment would combine to a total adjustment of 7 percent. However, if both neighborhoods have increased in value, the neighborhood adjustment should apply to the new price levels. This suggests that the two factors should be multiplied. To do this correctly, a factor of "one" must be added first to each "plus" adjustment and then subtracted later. Now, the combined adjustment is calculated as 1.04 × 1.03 = 1.0712. After subtracting "one," the result is .0712, or + 7.12 percent. Compare that to the 7 percent total, if the two adjustments should be added.

When a "minus" adjustment is involved, it must first be subtracted from the factor "one." For example, -5 percent becomes 0.95, that is, (1 – 0.05). When combined with a +7 percent adjustment (i.e.,

1 + 0.07), the total adjustment is calculated as 0.95 × 1.07 = 1.0165. When "one" is now subtracted, an adjustment of plus .0165, or + 1.65 percent, results.

If the adjustments are small, the difference between adding and multiplying percentages will be too small to matter. With large percentage adjustments, however, the difference will be significant, a point to remember! In practice, adjustment percentages are more often added or subtracted, rather than multiplied, because of the complexity of doing the latter correctly. However, this does reduce the accuracy of the calculations!

The Unit of Comparison Adjustment. The third type of adjustment is referred to as the **unit of comparison**. It will be studied in the next section. To use the unit of comparison, first select an important characteristic of the property, such as the square-foot building area, and analyze the sales on this basis. You would convert the sales price of each comparable sale to its price per square foot (that is, divide the sales price by the building area). Adjusting the comparable sales for size differences is accomplished automatically, when the price per square foot from the comparables is multiplied by the square-foot size of the subject. Then, additional adjustments for features such as age, quality, and appeal may be made, using lump-sum dollars or percentage amounts.

Some authors refer to the unit of comparison as an analysis tool, rather than an adjustment tool. However, when applied properly, the method not only serves to analyze the sales; it also has the desired result of adjusting for the variable in question. Note in Example 9-2 that the price per square foot of Sale Two appears to be low. This is not readily apparent from simply looking at the total sale price. This is an example of the benefits of this method as an analysis tool, but it also leads to a more accurate adjustment amount.

Using a Sales Adjustment Grid

It is often difficult to communicate the information in an appraisal report to the reader, especially when a series of sales are involved and a number of adjustments are made. To explain clearly what you have done, it is often useful to show your work in the form of a table. Most form appraisal reports have such a table, called a sales

EXAMPLE 9-2 Calculating a Unit of Comparison

Sale	Building Area	Price	Calculated Price per Sq. Ft.
1	1,877	$311,200	$165.80
2	2,120	320,000	150.94
3	1,795	304,000	169.36

Uniform Residential Appraisal Report

File # SAMPLE

There are	comparable properties currently offered for sale in the subject neighborhood ranging in price from $					to $	
There are	comparable sales in the subject neighborhood within the past twelve months ranging in sale price from $					to $	

FEATURE	SUBJECT	COMPARABLE SALE # 1		COMPARABLE SALE # 2		COMPARABLE SALE # 3	
Address	831 S. Dona Marta St Ventura, CA	896 E. Hyland Ave.		821 E. Sunset Dr.		932 E. Sherwood Dr.	
Proximity to Subject		3 blocks west		4 blocks west		2 blocks west	
Sale Price	$ Re-Fi		$ 321,500		$ 288,000		$ 280,000
Sale Price/Gross Liv. Area	$ sq. ft.	$ 155.46 sq. ft.		$ 145.18 sq. ft.		$ 155.56 sq. ft.	
Data Source(s)		Doc # 182904		Doc # 014815		Doc # 1097024	
Verification Source(s)		Buyer		CMDC		Broker	
VALUE ADJUSTMENTS	DESCRIPTION	DESCRIPTION	+(-) $ Adjustment	DESCRIPTION	+(-) $ Adjustment	DESCRIPTION	+(-) $ Adjustment
Sale or Financing Concessions		Cash		80% Conv.		80% Conv.	
Date of Sale/Time		3/0x		2/0x		11/0x	
Location	Average	Average		Average		Average	
Leasehold/Fee Simple	Fee	Fee		Fee		Fee	
Site	13068	14375	-10,000	11809		15246	-6,000
View	Nominal	Excellent	-10,000	Nominal		Good	-6,000
Design (Style)	Contemp/Good	Mod/Good		Mod./V.Good	-2,500	Mod./V.Good	-2,500
Quality of Construction	Good	Good		Good		Good	
Actual Age	22a/17a	22		24		24	
Condition	Good	Good		Good		Fair	+5,000
Above Grade	Total / Bdrms. / Baths	Total / Bdrms. / Baths		Total / Bdrms. / Baths		Total / Bdrms. / Baths	
Room Count	6 / 4 / 2.00	7 / 4 / 2.00		7 / 3 / 2.50		6 / 4 / 2.00	
Gross Living Area	1,7678 sq. ft.	2,068 sq. ft.		1,970 sq. ft.	-8,000	1,800 sq. ft.	
Basement & Finished Rooms Below Grade							
Functional Utility	Good	Equal		Equal		Equal	
Heating/Cooling	FAU/None	FAU/None		FAU/None		FAU/None	
Energy Efficient Items	None	None		None		None	
Garage/Carport	2 Car Garage Att.	Same		Same		Same	
Porch/Patio/Deck	Cov. Patio	None	+500	None	+500	None	+500
	1 Fireplace	Same		Same		Same	
	Heated Spa	None	+2,000	None	+2,000	None	+2,000
Net Adjustment (Total)		☐ + ☒ -	$ -29,500	☐ + ☒ -	$ -8,000	☐ + ☒ -	$ -7,000
Adjusted Sale Price of Comparables		Net Adj. -9 % Gross Adj. 11 %	$ 292,000	Net Adj. -3 % Gross Adj. 8 %	$ 278,000	Net Adj. -2 % Gross Adj. 5 %	$ 273,000

I ☐ did ☐ did not research the sale or transfer history of the subject property and comparable sales. If not, explain

My research ☐ did ☐ did not reveal any prior sales or transfers of the subject property for the three years prior to the effective date of this appraisal.

Data source(s)

My research ☐ did ☐ did not reveal any prior sales or transfers of the comparable sales for the year prior to the date of sale of the comparable sale.

Data source(s)

Report the results of the research and analysis of the prior sale or transfer history of the subject property and comparable sales (report additional prior sales on page 3).

ITEM	SUBJECT	COMPARABLE SALE # 1	COMPARABLE SALE # 2	COMPARABLE SALE # 3
Date of Prior Sale/Transfer		None	None	None
Price of Prior Sale/Transfer	$250K			
Data Source(s)				
Effective Date of Data Source(s)				

Analysis of prior sale or transfer history of the subject property and comparable sales

1) The site value estimate was abstracted from improved sales in the neighborhood. 2) The square foot area computations and building sketch may be found on the attached Plan of improvements. 3) No functional or external obsolescence is in evidence.

Summary of Sales Comparison Approach

Comp. #1 is the same original tract model as the subject, but it was enlarged before the sale. It has a hilltop view.

Sale #3 is considered to be the most comparable sale, except for its inferior condition. No time adjustment is warranted, judging from Realty Board sales records and current escrows here. We place the most weight on Comparables #2 and #3 because they required the least amount of adjustment.

The subject was in poor condition at the time of its 200x sale. But the historic selling price, adjusted for condition of improvements tends to support the value indicated by current sales.

Indicated Value by Sales Comparison Approach $

Figure 9-4 A Portion of the Sales Comparison Analysis Grid of the URAR Form.

analysis or ***sales adjustment grid***. Filling in this grid (see Figure 9-4) is a common part of appraisal practice. Grids offer the advantage of providing a clear comparison of the sales and how they were adjusted. However, it is important to follow current guidelines available for the specific form used (e.g., URAR) when rating the property features to be adjusted. Sometimes, the adjustment process may be too complex to clearly present in a report, using just an adjustment grid. Also, in many cases, the support for the adjustments is presented as a narrative elsewhere in the report.

Next, Section 9.2 will explore units of comparison in more detail. Following that, Section 9.3 will discuss how to estimate the exact amount for dollar and percent adjustments.

9.2 Selecting and Using Units of Comparison

The unit of comparison technique involves selecting an *important variable aspect* of the sale properties that the appraiser can objectively measure and use to compare and adjust the sales. For example, in doing an appraisal of an apartment building, some sale buildings might be all studios and some all three-bedrooms, making price per dwelling unit too variable. If the number of rooms seems to have a significant effect on the prices of the comparable sales, the price per room can be calculated for each sale and then compared. In order to calculate the price per room for each sale, divide each sale price by the total number of rooms in that property. Where you find a consistent pattern of prices per room, this unit of comparison can be analyzed and then an appropriate price applied to the number of rooms in the subject. In this way, the value of the subject property can be related to the most important market factor. The unit of comparison method "eliminates" the major price differences that were caused by the specific aspect studied, such as the varying numbers of rooms. Once this major property variable is accounted for, you will find it easier to see other influences that are causing additional price differences (see Example 9-3).

How can you tell which unit of comparison to use? The best one is the one with the least variation or irregularity, because it most reliably predicts what the market would do. If we graph the price per unit versus the number of units (discussed next), are the sale points relatively close to a straight line (or a curving one)? Or do they scatter all over the graph? We could also use the linear regression technique or calculate the statistical *variance*, to more precisely compare different units of comparison.

EXAMPLE 9-3 Apartment Prices per Room

Sale	Price	Units	$/Unit	Rooms	$/Room
1	$559,000	4	$139,750	12	$11,646
2	550,000	3	183,333	15	12,222
3	580,000	4	145,000	13	11,154
4	660,000	4	165,000	14	11,786

Types of Units of Comparison

There are three types of units of comparison. These are:

1. Total property
2. Physical units of comparison
3. Economic units of comparison

Each of these measures has its place and is discussed below (see Figure 9-5).

Total Property Comparison

Here, the total property is the unit of comparison! When all the sales are quite similar to the property being appraised, a **total property comparison** may be appropriate. Minor differences between the sales can be accounted for by ranking the sales in the direct comparison method previously described, or by using lump-sum dollar or percentage adjustments. Techniques for estimating the needed amount of an adjustment are outlined in the next section.

Physical Units of Comparison

A **physical unit of comparison** uses any significant, objectively measurable *physical characteristic* that varies among the sales. Most often, the size of the property is used as such a unit. When the sale

Figure 9-5
Types of Units of Comparison.

TOTAL PROPERTY   PHYSICAL UNITS   ECONOMIC UNITS

price of each property is divided by its size, the result is the price per unit of size. Note that highly subjective or unusual property variables, such as view, location, and water orientation, are not readily adjustable using units of comparison.

The most widely used unit of size is the square footage area of land or of buildings. For buildable lots, prices are usually compared by the price per square foot. For larger land parcels, the price per acre is commonly used. In some cases, instead of using the land *area*, you might use the *frontage* of the parcel, for example, the lot dimension facing a major thoroughfare in the case of retail land. (Retail space rental rates may also be compared by the rent per front foot of land or building.)

For improved properties, many different physical units can be used. For example, homes or apartments are often compared by price per room or price per square foot. Apartments and motels may be compared by price per rental unit. Rooming houses or fraternities can be compared by price per bedroom, or price per bed. Truck terminals often are compared by price per truck dock. Convalescent hospitals usually are compared by price per bed and marinas by price per slip or per berth, or by the price per foot of boat dock. In the appraisal of single-family homes, the most common unit of comparison is the selling price per square foot of living area. When the size data are available, and there are only moderate differences in land and building size, the price per square foot method is generally recognized as one of the best ways to compare this type of property.

Using a size-related unit of comparison has two main advantages. First, it eliminates the large sale price variations that commonly result solely from the differences in size. This makes it easier to see other smaller differences that were not previously apparent! The second advantage is that the calculation of value is easily done by selecting the appropriate unit value and multiplying it by the size measurement of the property being appraised. However, when there are large areas of differing quality (such as above-grade versus below-grade living areas in homes), this method may be very hard to use.

Economic Units of Comparison

An **economic unit of comparison** is some *economic feature or characteristic* of the property that closely relates to its value. There are many examples of economic units of comparison. One of the most common is used in appraising vacant acreage. Instead of examining land sales in terms of price per acre or price per square foot of land, the land is studied in terms of its usefulness, or what can be done with it. For residential land, for example, this usually means calculating the price per buildable dwelling unit. The allowable number of dwelling units can be estimated by studying the zoning ordinance in effect.

Zoning ordinances often set restrictions that limit the total building size, as well as the number of units for a proposed apartment building. This is because floor-area to land-area ratios, parking requirements, height restrictions, and other restrictions may apply, particularly in the case of commercial property. Thus, if the comparable land sales are in different zoning categories, the allowable building sizes may vary significantly, even when the lot sizes do not. Here, comparing land sales by price per square foot of land may not be useful. Instead, try the following: First, examine the zoning ordinance to calculate the amount of floor space that can be developed, considering building height limits, parking requirements, and so on. Second, take the total calculated potential building floor area and divide it into the price. This result is the price of the land per buildable square foot of floor area. Using this unit of comparison can often automatically adjust for the zoning differences we have cited. Example 9-4 shows how to calculate such a unit of comparison.

What are some other economic units of comparison? The price per convalescent hospital bed has already been suggested as a physical unit of comparison, but it is also economic. When comparing gasoline stations, you could look at the sale price per pump or the price per 1,000 gallons pumped. Since the gallonage is sometimes used to establish rent, it is also often used to estimate the sale price. With retail stores, there generally is a relationship between the rent that is paid and the sales volume the store generates. Consequently, rent as a percent of sales volume is an economic unit of comparison. This applies to restaurants as well. There is also a relationship between the rental income that a property generates and its sale price. This relationship is mathematically represented by **gross income multipliers (GIM)**. Because of the importance of GIMs, they are discussed as a separate topic.

Economic units of comparison are not much harder to apply than physical units of comparison. For vacant parcels, some additional analysis of the zoning requirements may be necessary. This additional work is worth the effort because economic units of comparison have a big advantage. For complex properties, economic units usually will give you a clearer understanding of the final price than a simple physical comparison will.

In other words, if you adjust ten sales and use a physical unit of comparison, you can expect to find some remaining variation in the price per unit. If instead, you calculate the economic unit that applies, you can expect to find less remaining variation in the price per unit. In other words, another cause of price variation is eliminated when you use economic units instead of physical units. You will then find it easier to see the factors causing the remaining price variation. Such factors as age, date of sale, and location are much easier to understand, when the small differences they often cause are not swamped by the larger differences associated with physical or economic size.

EXAMPLE 9-4 Physical Versus Economic Units of Comparison

A. Assume that there are four sales of land parcels, all zoned for office use. We first analyze by price per square foot of land area, a physical unit of comparison.

Sale	Price per Sq. Ft. of Land Area
1	$ 44.00
2	150.00
3	62.40
4	33.00

Conclusion: A wide range of value indications.

B. The same four sales are next adjusted for differences in the allowable building size, to give an economic unit of comparison. The price per square foot of land area in this example is divided by the building-to-land ratio, which is the building size limit in this zoning jurisdiction. The answer is the land price per square foot of potential building area.

Sale	Sale Price per Sq. Ft. of Land Area		Allowable Building/Land Ratio		Land Price per Building Sq. Ft.
1	$ 44.00	÷	1.00	=	$ 44.00
2	150.00	÷	3.00	=	50.00
3	62.40	÷	1.50	=	41.60
4	33.00	÷	0.75	=	44.00

Conclusion: A narrow range of value indications.

Rent or Income Multipliers

Rent or income multipliers are also economic units of comparison, because they measure an economic characteristic of the property, its income. They are calculated by dividing the price by the rent or income. The result is called a gross income (historically, gross rent) multiplier (GIM or GRM). When multiplied by the income of the property being appraised, a GIM will give an indication of property value.

Multipliers can be calculated by using either the annual or the monthly income. Traditionally, monthly income has been used for single-family residences, while annual income is commonly used for apartments or other income property. Any multiplier should be based on all the income that the property commands and not just its rental income. In the case of apartments, the total income should include any laundry income, parking fees, furniture rentals, and so on.

Note that income multipliers compare the property's income. Why is this part of the sales comparison approach? Income multipliers have traditionally occupied a place somewhere between the income and sales comparison approaches. With single-family homes, multipliers are sometimes considered an acceptable income approach. However, with apartments and commercial property, income multipliers are usually considered part of the sales comparison approach. The distinction is not important; the multiplier is a tool for the appraiser to use whenever it is suitable. Gross income multipliers will be studied further in Chapter 13.

Applying Units of Comparison

Before applying this technique, it is important to review the unit of comparison selected. Remember that it must be a physical or an economic variable that seems to account for much of the price differences found. If your sales are all nine-room homes, for example, price differences cannot be attributable to the number of rooms because they do not vary. However, such differences might be explained by square-foot size differences. So, the sales price per room, graphed against the square foot building area, might be quite revealing. Alternatively, the sales price per square foot of building living area might present a clear pattern.

Once the unit of comparison is selected, the first step is to calculate the unit price. This means the price per square foot, price per bedroom, or price per whatever unit is selected. Once the unit prices for the sales are calculated, these unit prices should be analyzed to identify the causes of any remaining price variation. Are the unit prices for the more recent sales higher than for older sales? Are the unit prices for the larger properties less than for the smaller properties? Are the unit prices for the older structures lower than for newer structures? It is important for the appraiser to identify such differences and take them into account before the units of comparison are applied. If units of comparison are found to vary significantly among the sales for reasons that are not immediately apparent, it is important to try to understand why.

It is very common for the price per unit of comparison to decline as the number of units increases. This means that larger structures usually sell for a lower price per physical or economic unit than smaller ones. In the case of larger homes, the lot value and other fixed value components are spread over more square feet of floor space, serving to decrease the value per unit. Also, the increased floor size often consists of relatively inexpensive bedroom space or larger living rooms. So, in a residential sample comparing similar quality homes, we might find prices of $280/SF at 1,000 square feet, $270/SF at 1,500 square feet, and $260/SF at 2,000 square feet in a particular neighborhood. A note of caution: When the comparable sales that are selected have an extremely wide range of sizes (or other unit of comparison being studied), the sales at each extreme may be less reliable indicators of the price or value per square foot (or other unit) for the subject (unless a graph or linear regression is used, to clearly show where the subject property fits into this declining price pattern)!

Often, appraisers use the sales price per unit as the basis for an adjustment grid. Here, the price per square foot of land area, for example, would be adjusted for time and location, perhaps. Percentage adjustments typically are used for these. This method does not work well for common *dollar* adjustments, such as for swimming pools, added baths or garage spaces, as well as terms and conditions of sale. To handle this common problem, dollar adjustments can be taken first, followed by calculation of the partially adjusted sales prices per unit. Next, prepare an adjustment grid based on price per unit, with percentage adjustments.

Graphing the Sales

Variable units of comparison can easily be analyzed by graphing the sales. This is a *powerful tool* for a set of sales that seem to have a lot of variation. The procedure for preparing a **sales graph** is first to set up the vertical and horizontal scales on the graph paper. Usually, the vertical scale shows the selling price (or the price per unit), and the horizontal scale shows the property characteristic being studied, for example, the square-foot building area. Each sale is plotted on the graph paper by finding the point which matches both the horizontal line through the selling price and the vertical line for the square-foot area. Next, when all of the sales have been plotted, a line is drawn to pass through (or line up with) as many of the sales points as possible. (Statistical techniques that "fit" a line to these points will be discussed later.) Then each of the sales that are above and below the line are analyzed. What is causing each sale price or price per unit to be above or below the line? Finally, the appraiser calculates where the subject property will lie relative to the line (on, above, or below), indicating an estimate of its value.

Figure 9-6 shows a graph of the sale price per square foot versus the total square feet of living area. As previously pointed out, the sales prices per square foot often decline as the houses get larger. Based on the graph, the indicated selling price per square foot of building for a house the size of the subject is $167.50. The subject house contains 1,825 square feet, so the indicated price is 1,825 × $167.50, or $305,688, rounded to $305,000.

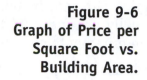

**Figure 9-6
Graph of Price per
Square Foot vs.
Building Area.**

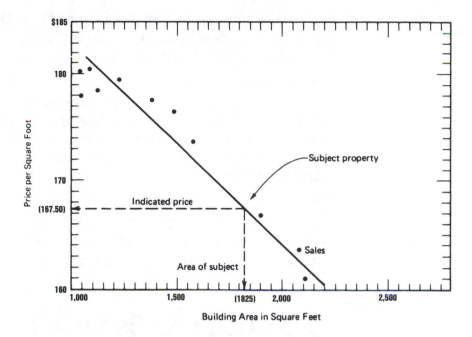

It is important in viewing this graph to note that neither the vertical nor the horizontal scale goes to zero! Always note this when examining any graph, as it dramatically changes the slope of the line and especially changes the apparent variability of the data points!

In some cases, the appraiser might conclude that the subject property is likely to be above the line and in others below it, based on the characteristics of the property as compared with the sales. What do the sales above the line have in common? Are they the more recent sales? What do the sales that are below the line have in common? Are they all older buildings, or closer to the railroad?

Perhaps the date of sale or even the age of the building needs to be analyzed. Here, the appraiser could graph the price per square foot of living area versus the date of sale, or versus the age of the properties. In fact, if the appraiser had plenty of time, he or she could experiment with sales adjustments, *graphing the sales after each adjustment* to see what the effect is. For example, the appraiser could adjust the sales for time at 4 percent, 5 percent, and 6 percent per year and could, by looking at the three graphs, consider which adjustment appears to be a better match to the market. Thus, graphs often can support the selection of an adjustment.

The appraiser also must recognize that the price per unit of comparison can change in a complex manner. Price per room can be influenced by the size of the rooms, or the age of the building. For another example, if you are calculating the price per bed in a convalescent hospital, you must consider the licensing requirements of the state. The license law in several states requires a large increase in the nursing staff for a 100-bed building, as compared to a 99-bed building, increasing the operating expense out of proportion. Thus, the price per bed, instead of changing steadily as the number of beds gradually changes, shifts noticeably at size levels where the licensing staff requirements change.

At the present time, graphing has seen limited use in appraisals, because its importance and usefulness have not always been understood. Also a factor was the time needed to prepare a graph by hand. However, wide use of computerized data services may lead to a greater use of graphs. Graphs are particularly helpful for sets of sales that vary a lot.

Remember that a unit of comparison adjusts for only the one variable selected. The price per unit can still vary widely, depending on other differences such as location and quality. Methods of estimating appropriate dollar or percent adjustments for property differences will be the next topic covered.

9.3 How to Estimate Dollar and Percent Adjustments

Adjusting the sale prices of comparison properties is perhaps the most demanding step in the sales comparison approach. Why? Because it is important that the adjustments be related to the market! The unit of comparison method described previously has this as its major strength. It relies on "reading" the market reaction to some important physical or economic variables. The second reason that adjustment is a demanding step is because proper application usually requires judgment!

Dollar and percent adjustment can be estimated by one of three methods. Two depend directly and one indirectly on market inputs.

Direct Market Method

One of the best methods for estimating adjustments is by the direct comparison of sales. The appraiser searches for sales that differ primarily only in the single property characteristic being studied. When two or more are found, these are often referred to as **matched pairs**. The difference in price between two or more such properties can indicate the appropriate dollar or percent adjustment for the feature under study.

How to Use Matched Pairs

This method is simple. First, find at least two sales (or groups of sales) that are similar in all respects *except* for the type of difference that you want to examine, say, a large age or size difference. Sometimes, the appraiser might adjust sales for one variable, such as date of sale, before using them as matched pairs to study another variable.

Although these sales need not be closely comparable to the subject, they should be similar enough so that the difference being studied is likely to have the same effect on both the sales and the subject property. For example, a swimming pool is likely to have a different value for a home with a very large lot than one with a very small lot.

The second step is to compare the matched pair sales prices, to see how big the difference is. This can be expressed either in dollars or as a percentage of the sale price. With two groups of sales, the comparison might be between the *average* of the price per unit for each group. Often, price per square foot is used when making such a comparison.

The third step is to adjust the sale prices of the comparables to make them more like the subject property, using the amount found by studying the market data. Example 9-5 demonstrates the first two of these three steps, with the ages of the buildings, as well as their sizes, being analyzed (using a limited number of sales to make the comparison simpler).

It is also possible to use the direct comparison method by finding sets of rental comparables. You identify the rental difference that is caused by the feature being studied. This rent difference is then multiplied by the GIM (Gross Income Multiplier) appropriate for that market. The result is the value difference associated with the feature being examined.

Application

When should the direct market method be used? It is the most reliable method when the appraiser needs to adjust for one single major factor, such as terms of sale, date of sale, location, or a major physical factor such as a swimming pool or remodeled kitchen. Adjustments for the date of sale are made by comparing earlier sales and later sales. (Obviously, a resale of the same property might be the most direct evidence of how prices changed with time.)

Here is an example of how this method can be useful in adjusting for location. Assume your subject property is a three-bedroom home and that no three-bedroom homes have sold recently in the subject property's neighborhood, but that some two-bedroom homes have. Look for another nearby neighborhood with sales of both two- and three-bedroom homes of similar age, quality, and amenities. If you compare prices of two-bedroom homes in the subject property's neighborhood with the two-bedroom homes in the other neighborhood, the percentage difference can be your neighborhood adjustment. If, for example, your neighborhood sold for 9 percent more, now you can use the three-bedroom comparables from the other neighborhood and adjust their prices up by 9 percent for the neighborhood difference. One cannot be certain that the price relationship between

---

EXAMPLE 9-5 Calculating Adjustments by Matched Pairs

A. Sales Data Summary:

Value Factor	Sale 1	Sale 2	Sale 3
Price	$270,000	$280,000	$256,500
Size (square feet)	2,500	2,700	2,500
Age (years)	20	20	30

Note that sales 1 and 3 differ only in age and that sales 1 and 2 differ only in size.

B. Analysis Using Matched Pairs:

Age Difference			Size Difference		
Sale	Age	Price	Sale	Size (sq. ft.)	Price
1	20	$270,000	2	2,700	$280,000
3	30	− 256,500	1	2,500	− 270,000
Difference in years:	10	$ 13,500	Difference in sq. ft.:	200	$ 10,000

Price Difference for Age:

In dollars: $13,500/10 years, or $1,350 per year.

In percent: $13,500/$270,000, or 5% difference.

In percent per year: 5%/10 years, or 0.5% per year.

Conclusion: An adjustment at 1/2% (0.5%) per year of age difference is indicated.

Price Difference for Size:

In dollars per square foot: $10,000/200 sq. ft., or $50. Note that the *adjustment* amount per sq. ft. is much less than the *sale* price per sq. ft., a common finding.

Conclusion: An adjustment of $50 per square foot of size difference is indicated.

---

two- and three-bedroom homes will be the same, but it is likely to be fairly close!

It is possible to adjust for many types of physical differences between the subject property and the comparable sales, using the direct market method. The presence or absence of a specific feature, such as a swimming pool, basement, or extra bedroom, or physical differences, such as size, quality, age, or condition, can be measured. The method is also useful in adjusting for the market value benefit of remodeling rooms, such as kitchens or bathrooms.

Matched pairs of sales are sometimes used in combination with other techniques. For example, you can first adjust your sales for specific differences such as swimming pools; then the adjusted sales can be studied further, using a different unit of comparison such as the price per square foot of living area. However, it is well to recognize that as more adjustment methods are used, the probability of individual adjustment errors increases.

The direct market method can also be used to adjust for the date of sale. However, reliable results may require large sets of sales. Such sets are often available to appraisers subscribing to computerized sales data services. For example, an adjustment for time in the market area under study might be estimated by calculating the average price per square foot of *all* the sales each month over the past several months, as shown in Example 9-6. (Using price per square foot reduces the impact of any monthly changes in the average house size.)

Depreciated Cost Method

The second method for estimating dollar or percent adjustments is called the **depreciated cost method**. The adjustment is calculated by analyzing the depreciated replacement costs for the particular property feature. When costs and depreciation amounts are correctly related to the market, the depreciated cost method can be said to represent an indirect market method.

The depreciated cost method involves the following steps: First, select the particular feature or difference between the properties for which an adjustment is indicated. For instance, you might need to adjust for differences in the size of buildings, the installation of special kitchen equipment, or the absence of a garage.

The second step is to estimate the additional cost to include that feature when building a new house as of the date of value. (Techniques for estimating new building costs will be covered in Chapter 11.) The third step, after estimating the new construction cost, is to deduct an allowance (called depreciation) for the age and condition of the feature being studied. (Methods for calculating depreciation will also be covered later, in Chapter 12.) The final step is to adjust the sale price of the comparable sale, by adding or subtracting the depreciated cost amount.

Remember that the purpose of figuring the depreciated cost difference is to modify or adjust the sale price of the comparable sale so that it will better represent the market value of the subject. If the comparable has no garage, for example, and the subject does, then the depreciated

---

EXAMPLE 9-6 Analysis of Monthly Market Price Changes

Month	Number of Sales	Avg. Price per Sq. Ft.	Percent Change
1	67	$150.50	—
2	55	151.25	+0.50
3	86	152.38	+0.75
4	94	153.43	+0.69
5	96	154.66	+0.80

cost of this feature would have to be added to the comparable's sale price. Example 9-7 shows how to prepare this adjustment.

The best use of this method is to adjust for *physical property differences*. The method is particularly useful when adjusting for a specific building feature, such as a spa, swimming pool, covered porch, and so on. The depreciated cost method is also useful when a property has some particular problem that must be corrected immediately, such as a leaking roof or termite damage. The total cost of these necessary repairs as of the date of sale (without any deduction for depreciation) would be the price reduction typically demanded by a knowledgeable buyer.

The depreciated cost method of estimating adjustment amounts is a common tool of the practicing appraiser. Cost manuals are handy and easy to use; the logic of the adjustment process is easily explained. However, it is often difficult to support the depreciation deduction selected. Thus, depreciated cost adjustments are less accurate than they initially might appear to be. Nevertheless, they remain a common and useful tool in adjusting sales.

EXAMPLE 9-7 Adjustment by the Depreciated Cost Method

A. The Problem:

The subject property is an eight-room home, new in 1951, with a double garage. Sale 4 is very similar, *except* that it has no garage.

B. The Solution:

Adjust the price of Sale 4 upward, to reflect the lack of a garage.

The Adjustment Steps:

1. Estimate the garage cost new. The garage area is 20 x 22 feet, or 440 square feet. Replacement cost for a garage of this quality and features, as of the *sale date* (not the date of value), from a local cost handbook is $33.50 per square foot.
2. Estimate the depreciation. The garage's actual age is 29 years, and its total economic life is estimated to be 100 years. Depreciation is believed to be nearly straight line, or 29/100, or 29%.
3. Calculation:

Cost new: 440 x $33.50		$14,740
Less: Depreciation		
Cost new	$14,740	
Times: Depreciation percent	x 0.29	
Equals: Depreciation amount		- 4,275
Equals: Adjustment amount		$10,465
Rounded to:		$10,000

Adjusting for Sale Terms or Conditions

As we discussed earlier in this chapter, the sale price of a property is often affected by the type of financing involved, or other conditions of the sale. If any of the comparable sales had unique financing or sale conditions, an adjustment may need to be made to the sale price of the comparable. The amount of the adjustment can be calculated from a direct market comparison with similar properties that have conventional financing or conditions. However, if such sales are not available, it might be necessary to use a mathematical analysis to calculate a financing adjustment.

One simple financing adjustment arises when the seller pays substantial loan points or other loan charges. In conventional loan practice, the buyer pays the loan points, or fees, that are charged to set up the loan. However, in some types of loans, the interest rate is fixed for a time period and cannot change as market interest rates change. Lenders compensate for this fixed interest rate by charging an extra loan fee, called *points*, which discount the loan and thus effectively adjust the fixed interest rate to the current market interest rate. If the loan points are paid by the *seller*, the effective or net proceeds (or benefit of the sale) to the seller are reduced. To make a proportional adjustment, you might subtract the loan points that were paid by the seller from the stated selling price, as shown in Example 9-8.

A more complicated situation arises when a property is sold with unusually favorable financing. This usually involves the buyer assuming an existing loan that has a lower interest rate than the conventional lender financing available at that time. A desirable loan can materially increase the selling price of the property. Such loans might be either existing assumable third-party loans, or new loans that are taken back by the seller at the time of sale. The favorable loan may have an interest rate that is lower than normal for the market. Or the loan could involve a very low down payment (e.g.,

---

EXAMPLE 9-8 Adjusting for Points

	Sale 1	Sale 2	Sale 3
Sale price	$210,000	$200,000	$225,000
Less: Loan points			
Loan amount	$168,000	$150,000	$180,000
Times: Loan points (percent)	× .04	× .03	× .05
Equals: Cost of points	− $6,720	− $4,500	− $9,000
Equals: Adjusted price	$203,280	$195,500	$216,000

with a seller take-back loan) or a longer amortization (payback) period.

It is also possible (but less common) for unfavorable financing to depress the selling price. Sometimes an undesirable loan with an above-market interest rate must be assumed by the buyer or a stiff prepayment penalty paid. In this case, the sale price could be below the "market value" level.

Estimating the amount of adjustment for favorable or unfavorable loans starts out by estimating market terms for a new loan on similar property. Next is calculating how much less the loan payments would be for the favorable loan than the payments for the market-rate loan —or, how much higher for an unfavorable loan, compared to the market-rate loan. Sometimes, the market price adjustment appears to be based on the monthly payment difference times a time period, such as 20 or 25 months. Other times, especially where the loan cannot be paid off early or refinanced, calculating the adjustment may be done by studying the discount or premium at which mortgages at that interest rate are being sold in the finance markets. It is also possible to analyze these mortgages using mathematical techniques similar to those used by lenders to calculate loan points. Such techniques include what is referred to as discounted cash flow analysis, to be defined and outlined in Chapter 14.

Unfortunately, it is often difficult to estimate accurate adjustments for terms of sale. Judging what buyers and sellers consider to be favorable loan terms in a particular market can be very subjective. Although the mathematical techniques referred to earlier may seem sophisticated and precise, few buyers or sellers understand or use them. As a result, the actual adjustments that occur in the market could differ from what the mathematical calculations suggest. Often, the best adjustment is based upon study of sales with and without such financing.

Statistics—Linear and Multiple Regression

As introduced in Chapter 8, an advanced method of calculating the amount of a sales adjustment uses a statistical technique called regression analysis. There are two techniques of regression analysis currently used in appraising. The first type often is called **linear regression**. This technique adjusts for only one difference or variable, such as the date of sale or the age of the house. As the term *linear* implies, the technique assumes that the relationship between the price and the variable would appear as a straight line if the data were graphed. (A single variable can also be studied using methods that fit a curving line to the points on a graph.) If the variable to be studied is the age of the property, then each year's change in age causes the same constant change in sale price.

Thus, if we graph the sales prices per unit versus the ages of the properties, we would expect the sales points on the graph to form a sloping straight line. The linear regression calculation effectively averages the sales, to find out the average change in price. Figure 9-7 is a graph showing the various sale prices; the straight line across the graph represents the results of the linear regression calculation.

Although the linear regression technique involves a complex mathematical formula, pocket calculators programmed for linear regression make it relatively simple to apply. (Some calculators can also calculate regressions using models other than linear models.) If a single variable, like the date of sale, is being studied, the appraiser merely inputs the price of each sale along with its date (or the number of months since the sale). When all the sales are entered, the program computes the price trend. It is also possible to calculate whether such a trend accounts for most of the differences in price.

For reliable results, linear regression usually requires larger groups of sales than the other sales adjustment methods previously discussed. The growing use of computerized data banks lends itself to greater use of simple regression studies, to support adjustments for age, sale date, size, and other similar elements of a sale that can change in a *continuous linear* (straight-line) manner or a relatively linear manner. Other techniques—the averages of two groups of sales, for example—

**Figure 9-7
Using Linear
Regression to
Analyze Sales.**

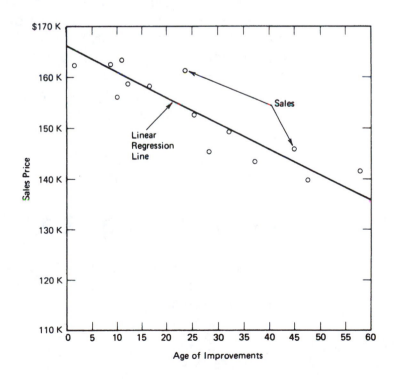

are better for elements that are of a *yes-no nature*, such as the presence of a swimming pool or a remodeled kitchen.

Multiple regression is the second type of regression analysis. The same process is carried out, but you can look at any number of variables. It is usually done with a programmable calculator or microcomputer. For accuracy, you need to have a minimum of 20 to 30 sales and also at least twice as many sales as the number of variables being studied. Some types of statistical flaws can reduce the reliability of the conclusions without the appraiser being aware of them. However, multiple regression is used increasingly by county assessors and by lenders doing appraisal review work. This technique will be used more, as appraisers become familiar with its application and better understand its limitations. A detailed analysis of this technique is part of advanced appraisal study.

Automated Valuation Models

An *automated valuation model (AVM)* is a computer software program that analyzes data using some type of automated process. Some AVMs use a form of the multiple regression analysis described above. Others trend, or time-adjust, the most recent prior sale of the subject. Some use one of the so-called artificial intelligence programs, and some use a combination of these. For many years, AVMs have been used by lending institutions and county assessors as valuation tools. Both in-house and subscription databases are used.

When applied to an individual property, the output of an AVM is not, by itself, an appraisal. However, an AVM's output may become a basis for appraisal, consulting, or review opinions and conclusions, if the appraiser believes the database used and the output to be credible and reliable in a specific assignment. The appropriate appraisal use of an AVM is, like any tool, dependent upon the skill of the user and the tool's suitability to the appraisal situation. A new site, http://www.zillow.com, is an example of a publicly available AVM.

In conclusion, we have discussed thus far in this chapter various topics relating to comparing and adjusting sales. We now turn to the subject of arriving at a value conclusion.

9.4 Arriving at an Indicated Value

The last step in the sales comparison approach is to arrive at a value conclusion. In order to arrive at such an opinion, you need to follow these four steps:

> ### The Four Steps to Arrive at a Conclusion
>
> 1. Review the entire approach.
>
> 2. Review the sales data.
>
> 3. Estimate a value range.
>
> 4. Select a final value.

The First Step: Review the Entire Approach

The first step in arriving at a value conclusion is to consider the limitations of the sales comparison approach and how these limitations apply to the particular circumstances of your appraisal. Taking time to review each step taken in the sales comparison approach provides an overall look at the entire process.

Comparability

The sales comparison approach is most reliable when used to appraise property that is commonly bought and sold. If there are no comparable sales, the approach cannot be applied. Similarly, the more unique, specialized, or rare the property being appraised, the less useful the sales comparison approach will be (see Figure 9-8).

Activity Levels

In any given community, the real estate sales *activity level* will vary from time to time. During a period when few or no sales are occurring, the sales comparison approach may not be very reliable. Similarly, in an

**Figure 9-8
An Historic 1880s
Farmhouse.**

appraisal of a type of property that is rarely sold, such as a major automobile assembly plant, the sales comparison approach is less reliable. Why? Because comparable sales are few and far between. The few you can find may require large adjustments for time and location, but the support for the adjustments may be very weak!

Adjustment Accuracy

Appraisers often say that no two properties are identical. Almost every comparable sale needs to be adjusted for some difference. The final appraisal conclusion is only as reliable as the individual adjustments. When the adjustment amount is large or the amount of the adjustment cannot be based on convincing market evidence, the sales comparison approach may not be reliable.

Statistical Limits

Statistical techniques that are used as part of the sales comparison approach can have serious technical flaws. This is particularly true of linear and multiple regression. Complex mathematical calculations are needed to judge whether conclusions based on these methods can be relied on in any given appraisal. Appraisal judgment may help to reduce the risk of such problems, however.

Lagging the Market

One common problem with the sales comparison approach is that the appraiser often must use sales that occurred prior to the date of value for the appraisal. If the market is changing, all of the sales have a built-in "lag." If values are going up, then the sales prices of the available comparable sales will likely be lower than current values. If prices are going down, the sale prices will likely be higher than the current values.

The appraiser may be able to easily adjust for this time lag, provided that the rate of price change has remained constant. However, if the rate of change in prices has varied since the last sale, the adjustment will be more difficult. When you suspect that price changes may not be fully reflected in your sales comparables, try to solve this problem by also looking for other value evidence that is very close to the date of value. Local brokers could be contacted for listing prices, offers, refusals, expired listings, and sales that did not close escrow, as well as opinions on price trends. When such information is available, the time-lag problem may be resolved. If the date of value is in the past, then look for sales both before and after, to reduce the time-lag issue.

Motivation

The sales comparison approach assumes that the price of each comparable sale is the result of vigorous, arm's-length bargaining by knowledgeable buyers and sellers. As you know, actual sales prices are not always reached in this way. So, try to understand the motives behind the sales. You should eliminate sales that are within a family, and sales for which there is evidence that suggests a panicky seller or buyer. It is difficult to find out whether a particular sale involves rational and aggressive bargaining over the price. Often, however, if the appraiser looks at 6 to 10 sales, ones with unusual motivations will stand out!

When the appraiser has only a few sales or must rely heavily on one or two, motivation becomes an even more important factor to consider. If a particular sale is critical to your analysis and it is defective, the entire market approach is weakened. Therefore, in this review process, you must consider the extent to which your analysis relies particularly on any one sale.

The Second Step: Review the Sales Data

The next step in arriving at an indicated value through the sales comparison approach is to review the detailed data about the actual sales.

Sales Data

First, consider the reliability of the information. What was the source? How reliable is that source, based on previous experience? If certain data are questionable, would an error lead to an answer that is too high or too low? Can that error be cross-checked against other information? If a particular sale is critical to an appraisal, the appraiser should consider whether enough information about that sale has been collected. Is the evidence or information collected adequate? If not, you should cross-check the information with another source or make a second field inspection. The collection of additional information about one sale may sharpen your understanding of all the sales. The option of analyzing additional sales must *always* be considered.

Reviewing the Adjustments

The appraiser next reviews how the sales were adjusted. What type of adjustment was made? Direct market comparisons are usually more reliable than those from statistics or from a cost approach. However, this reliability could depend on the type of adjustment and the quality of the data. At this point, consider the total amount or percent that each sale was adjusted (without regard to plus or minus signs). This gives the best single indication of how comparable a sale is. The less total adjustment needed, the more comparable it is. The more comparable it is, the more weight that sale should be given in arriving at a final value conclusion. The more extreme sales are given less weight and might even be eliminated at this point, or not included in the report.

The Third Step: Estimate a Value Range

The third step in arriving at an indicated value is to estimate the probable range of value. The upper limit of this range is the highest price that can reasonably be concluded, based on the sales study. The lower limit is the lowest price that can reasonably be developed or concluded from the sales. When such a bracket is defined, we are one step closer to selecting a final value indication from the sales comparison approach.

Using the Value Range Produced by the Adjusted Sales

In many appraisals, the *value range* indicated by the sales study can be said to be that range established by the highest and lowest adjusted sales prices. This conclusion is certainly valid where only small, well-supported adjustments have been used in the adjustment process. In such an example, assume that adjusted comparable #1 indicates a market value of $250,750; comparable #2, $260,500; and comparable #3, $265,000. Here, the range of value could logically be suggested at $250,750 to $265,000.

Projecting Upper and Lower Limits for the Sales Adjustments

When the comparables require large and/or marginally supported adjustments, an unacceptably broad range of value can result. To narrow this range, we can apply upper and lower limits to the individual sales adjustments for each sale, and test the reliability of the value indications.

In arriving at the *upper* limit for each adjustment (e.g., the adjustment for time, location, size, etc.), you should select an amount that leans toward a larger adjustment but still appears to be reasonable for the property feature involved. Estimating the upper limit is a question of giving all the benefit of the doubt in one direction—toward a larger adjustment in each case.

To arrive at the *lower* limit for each adjustment, give the benefit of the doubt to adjustments that tend to be smaller. When estimating both the upper and lower limits, also consider and allow for any uncertainty that you may have about the amounts of the adjustments. In practice, this process of estimating limits is usually done by intuition. The concept is displayed numerically in Figure 9-9.

After you total the adjustments used in each sale, to reflect both the highest and the lowest reasonable adjustments, a range of indicated value is produced for each comparable sale. Observe how wide the range is from the lowest indicated price to the highest indicated price. The narrower this range, the more reliable the value conclusion resulting from that particular sale.

Figure 9-9
Estimating the Upper and Lower Limits of Sales Adjustments.

Value Adjustments	Estimated Adjustment	Probable Adjustment Range	Upper Limit	Lower Limit
Sales or financing concessions	0			
Date of sale, time	$1,500	$1,300–$1,600	$1,600	$1,300
Location	0			
Site/view	($4,000)	($1,800–$4,300)	($1,800)	($4,300)
Design and appeal	0			
Quality of construction	0			
Age	0			
Condition	($5,000)	($4,700–$5,500)	($4,700)	($5,500)
Above-grade room count; gross living area	($3,000)	($2,300–$3,600)	($2,300)	($3,600)
Basement and finished rooms below grade	0			
Functional utility	0			
Heating/cooling	$5,000	$2,000–$6,000	$6,000	$2,000
Garage/carport	$5,000	$3,000–$6,500	$6,500	$3,000
Porches, patios, pools, etc.	0			
Special energy-efficient items	0			
Fireplace(s)	($1,700)	($1,200–$3,000)	($1,200)	($3,000)
Other (e.g., kitchen equipment, remodeling)	($4,000)	($3,300–$4,800)	($3,300)	($4,800)
Net adjustment (total)	($6,200)		$800	($14,900)
Indicated value of subject	$143,800		$150,800	$135,100
			(Upper limit of value)	(Lower limit of value)

The Range of Value from the Most Comparable Sales

Finally, your estimate of a value range for the subject property should ideally consider only those sales that appear to be the most reliable value indicators. This should be suggested by the upper and lower limits tested for the sales adjustments. If the adjusted prices of the most comparable sales cluster in a particular area within the total range, the value conclusion should be selected from that narrower range.

The Fourth Step: Select a Final Value

Selecting an indicated value from the sales comparison approach is not a science. There is no mathematical formula for it; to a large degree, it requires judgment. There are, however, some sensible rules. First, usually give the greatest weight to the sale (or sales) that needs the least total adjustment (ignoring the plus and minus signs). This reduces the impact of any errors made during the adjustment process (see Example 9-9).

The second rule is to favor the sales (or the method of adjusting them) that involve the fewest assumptions or the most reliable adjustments. It is possible that the sale with the lowest total adjustment involved one particularly uncertain adjustment. In that case, another sale should be given more weight.

Finally, do not average the sales prices or the adjusted sales prices. Averaging assumes that the difference in price from one sale to the next is the result of pure chance, and that each sale should have equal weight in the conclusion. With real estate, neither is likely to be true. Instead, it is more likely that the variation in the adjusted sales prices is caused by some problem or problems that the appraiser has not yet identified. Since such problems do not occur randomly, averaging will not eliminate the cause.

If the variation in adjusted sales prices is too wide, the best action to take is to go back, reconsider why the adjusted sales still vary, and try to find a logical explanation. It is often useful to examine what the high sales have in common and is missing in the low sales (or vice versa). If that is not fruitful, choose the most reliable sales or where the adjusted sales prices cluster. Using the most reliable sales will reduce the chance that the unknown problem will affect the value con-

---

EXAMPLE 9-9 Which Sale Needed the Least Adjustment?

A. Analysis:

		Sale 1	Sale 2	Sale 3	Sale 4
Price:		$273,500	$246,800	$278,000	$262,900
Adjustments:	Time	+ 7%	+ 3%	+ 6%	+ 5%
	Size	– 4	+ 5	– 4	0
	Location	– 3	+ 3	– 3	0
	Total	0%	+ 11%	– 1%	+ 5%
Adjusted price		$273,500	$273,948	$275,220	

B. Conclusion:
   Sale 4 needed the least adjustment in "absolute" or total terms.

clusion. Relying on the value area where the adjusted sales prices tend to cluster has the same benefit.

In summary, to arrive at an indicated value, make an overall review of the sales comparison approach. Reconsider the data used and verify that they were interpreted in the best manner. Then narrow the adjusted sales prices into a range within which you conclude the value must lie. Finally, within this range, select an appropriate single price based on a careful and thorough analysis of the entire process.

SUMMARY

Analyzing and adjusting comparable sales rely on two main methods: the direct comparison method and the elements of comparison method. The direct comparison method simply compares the overall desirability of each sold property with that of the subject, without any adjustments. Considered too intuitive to be reliable in many instances, the method is not routinely used.

The elements of comparison method compares the sales with reference to the details of four critical elements: the terms and conditions of sale, the time of sale, the location elements, and the physical elements.

In the process of comparing and adjusting sales, the differences in the four cited elements are first studied, in order to establish which differences may have caused the variations in prices. Next, the sales are analyzed, to see how much of a price change the major differences cause. Finally, the prices of the sales are adjusted to account for these differences. Each of the sales is adjusted *to make it more like the subject*.

There are three types of adjustments that can be used, either independently or in combination: the lump-sum dollar adjustment, the percentage adjustment, and the unit of comparison. In order to best explain and display the adjustments selected, a special table called the sales adjustment grid is included in many appraisal reports. However, the sales adjustment grid is only suitable to present a few of the techniques available. Often, some additional comments are needed in order to explain the adjustments used.

The amounts of the adjustments can be calculated in several ways. One, the direct market method, uses the direct analysis of sales to calculate adjustments. This method is often referred to as "matched pairs." The depreciated cost method calculates adjustments using indirect market information: cost and depreciation. It is especially useful when property differences are mostly differences in the physical improvements or when a property has a defect that needs correction. The kind of financing a property has also may affect its sale price;

therefore, adjustments must sometimes be made for the type of financing.

A sophisticated statistical technique called regression can be used to calculate the amount of a dollar or percentage adjustment. Appraisers typically use two of the types of regression, called linear and multiple. A computer software program called an automated valuation model (AVM) analyzes data using an automated process. AVMs may use a form of regression analysis described above, price trending, or one of the so-called artificial intelligence programs. When applied to an individual property, the output of an AVM is not, by itself, an appraisal. However, an AVM's output may become a basis for appraisal, consulting, or review opinions and conclusions, if the appraiser believes the output to be credible and reliable for use in a specific assignment.

The final step in the sales comparison approach is to arrive at a value conclusion. This is achieved by the following four steps:

1. Review the entire approach. Consider and try to account for the limitations of your method.

2. Review the sales data. Consider the overall reliability of your sales data, the adjustments, and each individual sale.

3. Estimate a value range. You should seek to identify a lower and an upper limit of value.

4. Select a final value. You must ultimately select a single value after completing the above steps.

IMPORTANT TERMS AND CONCEPTS

Activity level

Assumed financing

Automated valuation model (AVM)

Comparison process

Depreciated cost method

Direct comparison method

Economic units of comparison

Elements of comparison method

Gross income multipliers (GIM)

Lagging the market

Linear regression

Location elements

Lump-sum dollar adjustment

Matched pairs

Multiple regression

Percentage adjustment

Physical elements

Physical units of comparison

Points

Sales adjustment grid

Sales graph

Seller financing

Seller-paid points

Terms and conditions of sale

Time of sale

Total property comparison

Unit of comparison

Value range

REVIEWING YOUR UNDERSTANDING

1. The four elements of comparison used in the sales comparison approach include all of the following except:
   a. Terms and conditions of sale
   b. Direct elements
   c. Time of sale
   d. Location elements
   e. Physical elements

2. The rules for making sales adjustments include all of the following except:
   a. Adjust the sale price toward the subject property
   b. Use market-related adjustments
   c. Always use dollar amounts
   d. Make adjustments in the proper sequence

3. To use a lump-sum adjustment on a sale that is inferior to the subject property:
   a. Multiply by a percentage of the selling price
   b. Subtract a lump-sum dollar amount from the price
   c. Add a lump-sum dollar amount to the price
   d. None of the above

4. To use the unit of comparison adjustment:
   a. Select the easiest feature to calculate
   b. Select an important property variable
   c. Look for an inconsistent price per unit
   d. None of the above

5. A physical unit of comparison refers to:
   a. Any significant physical characteristic of the sales that varies
   b. The largest physical characteristic of the subject property
   c. Only the building size, expressed in square footage
   d. None of the above

6. The economic unit of comparison is defined as:
   a. The gross income multiplier
   b. An economic measure of the property and its value
   c. The physical characteristic of the property that relates best to the market
   d. The characteristic of the property with the least variability

7. To use the direct market method of estimating the dollar or percent adjustment, you should first:
   a. Calculate the price difference between two matched pair comparables
   b. Calculate the price difference between the comparable sale and the subject property
   c. Select a specific amount and apply it directly to the comparable
   d. Derive the adjustment from older market sales

8. A comparable should be adjusted for terms of sale when:
   a. Conventional financing is involved
   b. It is a cash sale
   c. There is favorable seller financing
   d. Financing equivalent to cash is involved

9. Linear regression, as used here:
   a. Adjusts for only one difference or variable
   b. Adjusts for a number of variables at the same time
   c. Adjusts for two variables at the same time
   d. Is used to calculate the replacement cost new for the subject property

10. In the final step of the market comparison approach, the four actions needed to arrive at a value conclusion include all the following except:
    a. Review the entire approach
    b. Review the sales
    c. Estimate a value range
    d. Average the three best sales
    e. Select a final value

PRACTICAL APPLICATIONS

As we remind you at the start of each exercise, review the exercise at the end of the preceding chapter, and the work that you have performed to date.

This assignment continues the sales comparison approach, which was started with the last exercise. It will be reported on the sales comparison approach section of the URAR form, as shown in Figure 9-4. The focus in this chapter is on analyzing and adjusting the sales, and deriving a value estimate from the sales comparison approach. Previously, you selected the best six or so comparable sales out of however many you identified as possibles. After that, you collected the needed information about each sale, including an inspection of each comparable sale property from the street. Finally, you have entered all of the information into the report form program.

The remaining information that you will need to develop about each comparable sale is the adjustment(s) needed to make it more like the subject property. (Remember the rule: *Always adjust **to** the subject!*) Making these adjustments calls for you to develop a number of opinions. The easiest way to analyze the sales may be at the computer, because the adjustment grid on page 2 of the URAR or 2055 form does the math for you.

So, start up the software program and open the file that you saved after the prior chapter's assignment. Note that you have already entered the basic information about the property, the assignment, the neighborhood, the site, and the sales. Review this information. Now it is time to look at the sales prices and how they vary. Which ones are high, or low? Is there a clear possible reason, such as date of sale, size, condition, or age? Consider which sales seem to be the most different from the subject, and identify the evidence why. You will want to enter an adjustment amount for each significant difference. Remember that each adjustment should have the *effect* of converting each sale into a hypothetical property that is *more similar to the subject*. Therefore, after each adjustment, the spread in the adjusted sale prices at the bottom of the grid should be less. This means that you can try an adjustment, see if it narrows the range of adjusted prices or not, and then try a different amount for that adjustment.

Start with the more objective issues, like house size and age. Notice that the form has already calculated the sale price per square foot of living area for you, at the top of the adjustment grid. Start out adjusting for size with an amount that is one-half of this price; then try one-third. Which narrows the range of adjusted prices the most? Does some other number do better? For age differences, try one percent of the sale price per year of age difference, then one-half of a percent. Which narrows the range the most? Remember to be very careful to make the adjustment so that the sale price becomes the price of a property more like the subject property. It is so easy to adjust in the wrong direction!

When you have selected a tentative adjustment for size and age, study the sales data and the adjusted sale prices. Now which ones are high, or low? Given the characteristics of the sales, what might be the reason? Are the higher sales the more recent sales, or is time not an issue in which are high or low? What about differences in location, as you perceived it when you inspected the sales? What about possible views? Are there big differences in basements or below-grade living area, or condition? Each of these may call for an adjustment. You might select a tentative number for the adjustment, based on the difference that you tentatively believe you see in the sales.

As you move through adjusting for the various differences, keep looking at what is happening to the adjusted sale prices. You may take an adjustment that you know you must make, but it widens the spread. First, recheck that all of your adjustments make the sale more like the subject property. If they are correct, and you are correct that this adjustment needs to be made, accept that. Continue working, recognizing that either something not yet adjusted for is causing the remaining spread, or one or more of your prior adjustments may have been too large or small. Which sales are **now** the low and high ones, and what do they have in common? If the larger sales are now the higher adjusted prices, then perhaps more needs to be taken off of the larger sales.

When you have entered a preliminary adjustment for each significant difference, it is time to start tweaking the adjustments, as just noted, to see if you can narrow the spread. However, note that you *must* be consistent! Do not adjust one smaller sale by $70 per square foot of floor area, and another by $60 per square foot, just to narrow the spread. On the other hand, the adjustment per square foot might well be more for a smaller house than for a large one, (due to the declining price per square foot as houses get larger).

Do not expect to be able to adjust out all of the price difference. In a stable neighborhood of similar homes, you may be able to end up with a 5 percent spread in adjusted sales prices. But in an area where the houses vary a lot, 10 to 15 percent is not surprising. There is one rule that you must not break: The range in *adjusted* prices, as a percent of the lowest price, must end up being somewhat less than the percent range of the *unadjusted* prices. Otherwise, you have failed the adjustment process.

The last step is to select an estimated value for the subject property by the sales comparison approach, and enter it into the form. Consider the adjusted prices: Are they evenly scattered through the range from the low to the high? Or do some or many of them tend to cluster in one area of the range? Is there one or another sale that you simply fought with, trying to see why its sale price was not in line with the others? If so, give it less weight. By now, your subconscious mind may well have a value opinion in mind: Consider what your mind is leaning toward, and why. At the end of the day, you must select one number, and enter it.

As we note at the end of each exercise, it is best not to get ahead of yourself. So, do not enter information in the later sections of the report until you have read the chapter(s) that covers that topic. However, it is a good idea to look ahead, so that you start thinking about the information that you will need.

Reminder: If you have questions about the program itself, please be sure to review the manuals and help information that were included with the program CD. Also, at anytime, you can go to http://www.bradfordsoftware.com, click on "Services" at the upper right of the home page, and then on "ClickFORMS Training Programs" in the middle of the "Services" page. See the free online training section!

CHAPTER 10
VALUING THE SITE

PREVIEW

In Chapter 6, we discussed the main factors that influence the value of land and the techniques used when inspecting a site. In this chapter, we shall outline the four methods used to appraise land and explain how they apply to undeveloped acreage, vacant lots, and sites improved with buildings. Since all land appraisal methods rely on property comparison in some form, understanding the sales comparison approach techniques covered in Chapters 8 and 9 is essential!

OBJECTIVES

When you have completed this chapter you should be able to:

1. Name five different uses of site value appraisals.
2. List the four methods of appraising land.
3. Name five physical characteristics of a site that affect its value.
4. Name three legal and economic considerations in site value.

10.1 Purpose of Land or Site Value Estimates

Land or site value estimates are important, not just in the appraisal of vacant or undeveloped land, but in other circumstances as well. For example, the site is appraised as if it were vacant whenever a separation of land and building value is necessary for improved properties. Also, a separate site value may be needed in performing any of the three approaches to estimate value of an improved property. We shall explore each of these reasons here. In market value studies, we generally appraise land on the basis of its highest and best use, a concept to be reviewed in Section 10.2.

Reasons for Land Appraisals

The appraisal of vacant land usually requires more specialized experience than the appraisal of improved property. The reason for this is that fewer real estate transactions involve vacant land. As a result, sales may not be as comparable as one would like! Bare acreage is also more unique in location, size, or shape than most improved properties. Thus, buyers and sellers often require the services of an expert to interpret for them the physical, legal, and economic factors that determine land value.

In addition, land is frequently leased instead of being sold outright. Whether the lease is for agricultural, commercial, or residential purposes, an appraisal is often needed to estimate either the rental value or the equitable return on investment capital. Land leases can be for very long time periods, so correctly estimating the initial rental amount becomes quite important. Also, appraisers often base an opinion of market rent for land on a market value estimate.

Real estate developers, lenders, and agricultural interests frequently rely on land appraisals to make important decisions on the use and distribution of land. Developers and subdividers need to include the value of the land as one of the costs of the finished product. Thus, many project feasibility studies incorporate vacant land appraisals. Banks and other lenders often furnish construction financing for real estate developments. Since such loans are often based in part on the value of the vacant land, formal appraisals are usually needed.

Many government acts, such as property taxation, eminent domain, and redevelopment, may require estimates of land value, and frequently require formal appraisals. Also, many court actions concern questions of land value. Such actions may arise out of inheritance settlements, divorce actions, and other types of lawsuits.

Allocation of Value for Tax Purposes

Several tax laws require that the value of land and improvements be estimated separately for improved properties. First, **ad valorem** (according to value) property taxes are usually based on separately stated land and improvement values. Also, in some states, property tax areas can apply a different tax rate for land than for improvements. Second, income tax laws generally allow an annual "write-off" or **depreciation** deduction as an expense, when buildings are held for investment purposes. Since this depreciation is allowed only on the investment in the structures, an allocation of the purchase price between the land and buildings is required.

Site Value in the Three Value Approaches

Since land and buildings may be regarded as separate economic parts of the property, site value estimates are sometimes needed in improved property appraisals. Even when the defined purpose of an appraisal is to estimate the total market value of an improved property, the particular techniques used by an appraiser may require an estimate of the value of the land.

The cost approach (covered in Chapters 11 and 12) uses an estimate of the site value as a base figure to which the value of the improvements is added. This means that the site must be appraised separately. Next, the value of the buildings is estimated by using the cost new, less depreciation. (Note that for *appraisal* purposes, "*depreciation*" refers to the difference between the present value of the improvements and their replacement cost new.)

In the income approach, certain capitalization procedures (to be discussed later) split the net income for the property between the two "production agents": land and building. Hence, a separate land value estimate can be required in the income approach, too.

Finally, some sales analysis techniques in the sales comparison approach subtract the land value from the sale price to see what the various buildings "sold for." In order to use this technique, the appraiser must estimate the land value for each sale property and also for the subject property.

Reasons for Estimating Land Value

1. **From One Viewpoint:**
   a. Sale price
   b. Rental value
   c. Feasibility study
   d. Loan security
   e. Property tax
   f. Eminent domain
   g. Income tax basis allocation

Continued on next page

2. From Another Viewpoint:
  a. Cost approach
  b. Income approach—residual capitalization
  c. Sales comparison approach

10.2 The Four Methods Used to Appraise Land

Among practicing appraisers, there are four recognized methods of appraising land (see Figure 10-1). These are:

1. The market or direct sales comparison method,

2. The allocation or abstraction method,

3. The development method, and

4. The land residual method.

As we learned in Chapter 6, the value of land is a function of its highest and best use. Highest and best use is defined as that reasonable and profitable use that will support the highest land value as of the date of value. Before we consider the methods of appraising land, a review of the importance of highest and best use is in order.

Importance of Highest and Best Use

The *Uniform Standards of Professional Appraisal Practice* requires an opinion of the highest and best use of the property in all market value appraisals. This opinion is of the optimum use of the land, both (1) *as if vacant* and (2) *as presently improved*. The first, as if vacant, requires consideration of feasible alternative uses for the land, and therefore it provides the basis for land valuation and for selecting comparable sales. The second, as improved, examines the value contribution of any existing improvements. The appraiser may

**Figure 10-1
Four Methods of
Appraising Land.**

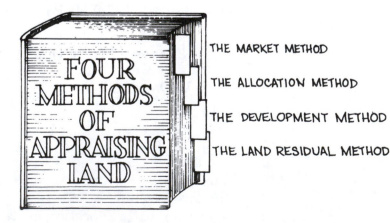

THE MARKET METHOD

THE ALLOCATION METHOD

THE DEVELOPMENT METHOD

THE LAND RESIDUAL METHOD

conclude that they will only have an interim use, if the improvements do not represent the highest and best use as if vacant. In the latter case, the value assigned to the improvements is often referred to as an *interim use value.*

Highest and Best Use Criteria

Any suggested use must meet four criteria, or tests, in order to be selected as the highest and best use. These tests were explained in Chapter 6. The use must be:

1. **Physically possible**
2. **Legally permissible**
3. **Economically feasible**
4. **Most (or maximally) productive**

Appraising Land by the Market Method

The most reliable method of appraising land is referred to as the market, or direct sales comparison, method. In concept, it is little different from the sales comparison approach used to appraise improved properties. However, the *market method* of estimating site value and the sales comparison approach have one important difference—the basis of comparison between parcels.

The Basis and Criteria of Comparison

Whether the land is actually vacant or improved, the market method of site appraisal compares the subject property *as if it were vacant.* When this is understood, it follows that all sales comparisons should be sales of vacant land (see Figure 10-2).

How are the comparables to be selected? Vacant land sales should be similar to the subject land in location, physical characteristics, and potential use. A sale date that is close to the date of value is an important issue. *Location* is important for the many reasons discussed in previous chapters. Close proximity to the subject property contributes to the credibility of the sales since the same value-influencing factors are present (see Figure 10-3).

Physical features also should be similar. Comparing a steep hillside lot with a flat valley lot would probably require unreasonably large adjustments. Such adjustments might need to address the higher site preparation costs (for the hillside lot) and also the value difference often associated with a view.

In the market method of land appraisal, vacant land sales should be chosen for their similarity to the subject land in terms of *potential use.* The most likely use for a parcel is determined primarily by location, zoning (and/or permissible use), and market demand at the

**Figure 10-2
Vacant Land for Sale.**

**Figure 10-3
Four Land Sales
of Varying
Comparability.**

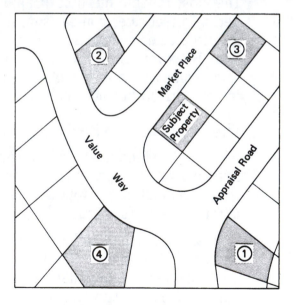

time of the appraisal. Parcels with different likely uses probably have different prices!

Applying the Market Method

Since the market method is the most direct and reliable method of appraising land, it is preferred whenever sales of reasonably comparable vacant land are available. The method is suitable to appraise vacant sites or to allocate vacant land value for improved sites, whether they are zoned for residential, commercial, industrial, agricultural, or recreational use. The application of the market method of site appraisal involves the same sales comparison approach procedures described in Chapter 8 (see Figure 10-4).

**Figure 10-4
Appraisal of Land by
the Market Method.**

Steps in the Market Method of Appraising Land

1. Locate vacant land sales that are similar to the subject site in terms of potential use and that sold relatively close in time to the date of value. Gather information on the sale conditions, the terms of the sale, and the price paid.

2. Compare each sale with the subject property as to the terms and conditions of sale, the date of sale, location factors, and physical characteristics.

3. Adjust the selling price of each comparable site to reflect any important differences between it and the subject site. Adjustments may be made in either dollar or percentage amounts.

4. Arrive at an indicated value for the subject site, placing weight on the more comparable of the sales analyzed.

Specific techniques of comparison and adjustment will be discussed later in this chapter.

The Allocation or Abstraction Methods

When comparable sales of vacant sites are not available, the direct sales comparison or market method cannot be used. As one alternative, land value may be allocated or abstracted from sales of improved property. The allocation, or **abstraction methods,** typically would be used in built-up areas where little vacant land remains. This method can also be useful in the appraisal of portions of a shared land interest, such as those in condominiums, cooperatives, and planned developments.

Since the allocation or abstraction methods are less direct than the market method, they are usually much less accurate. Consequently, if vacant land sales are available, even if not as comparable as one would like, you should not rely on the allocation or abstraction methods.

The first step in the **allocation method** is to identify sales of *improved* properties with site characteristics that are comparable to those of the subject property. Next, allocate a proportion of the sales price to the land and a proportion to the buildings. To do this, you might select the value relationship (percent or ratio) that you have found to be typical for similar properties in similar areas. For example, where your past research has shown that the site represents 35 percent of the total value, a $450,000 sale of an improved property indicates a site value of 35 percent of $450,000, or $157,500. Land and building ratios are subject to constant change, so it is important that your research be related to the date of value. Ratios also vary between communities and between types of property; therefore, you must be cautious in using them.

When there is no well-defined ratio of land value to total value among the sales, you may select an *abstracted site value*. The first step is to identify improved sales, as before. Next, estimate the replacement cost of the building less depreciation (discussed in the next two chapters) and subtract that figure from the total sales price of the improved property. This would leave a value that is attributable to the land (see Figure 10-5). An example is as follows:

Sale price of the property	$340,000
Less: Depreciated cost of the improvements	−156,000
Equals: "Abstracted" land value	$184,000

Instead of using either of these allocation methods, it is sometimes acceptable to use the land value ratio shown on the local property tax assessment roll. If the roll shows a total value of $260,000, broken into a $60,000 land and $200,000 building value, the ratio is $60,000/$260,000, or 23.1 percent land. If the property actually sold for

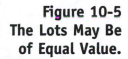

**Figure 10-5
The Lots May Be
of Equal Value.**

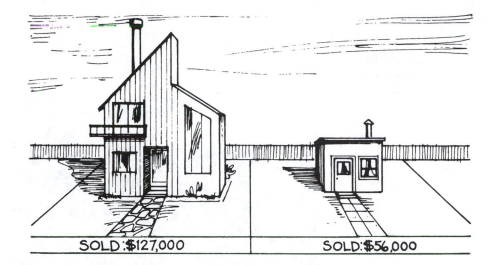

SOLD: $127,000   SOLD: $56,000

$300,000, a land value of $69,300 is suggested by the assessment ratio method ($300,000 x 23.1%).

In jurisdictions where updated market value property tax assessments are not required, or where market-related land and building allocations are not maintained, using assessment ratios is not reliable.

The Land Development Method

As its name implies, this method is used only to estimate the value of vacant acreage that is ready to be subdivided. It is generally used when there are no sales of comparable acreage or when a detailed analysis of the project is desired. The land *development method* shows how the raw land value relates economically to its anticipated market value as developed land. Thus, this method of estimating value requires that we study sales of subdivided lots at the time of value and make a projection of land development costs for the property being appraised (see Figure 10-6).

To estimate value by the land development method, let us assume a residential subdivision. First, estimate the number of lots to be developed, allowing for zoning, lot size requirements, and the land area needed for streets, parks, and any other necessary open space. Next, estimate the typical price that the finished lots could be sold for, as of the date of value, based on sale prices for comparable subdivision lots. Obtain a total dollar amount to be realized from the gross sales by totaling the estimated prices of the lots. Account for all direct and indirect costs of development, including engineering and government fees. Include costs for promotion, sales, and closing charges.

Finally, you must allow for the *developer's profit* (to cover work effort, overhead costs, and return on invested capital), typically either as a percentage of gross sales or a percentage of the capital invested in the raw land. After deducting all these development costs and profits

**Figure 10-6
Modern Land
Subdivision.**

from the gross revenues, the remaining amount constitutes the value of the raw acreage. If the project will take more than a year to build and rent up or sell, a further deduction may be necessary, to adjust for the time that the developer's capital is tied up in the project. There are a number of different methods of performing subdivision analyses, varying in format and in complexity. Example 10-1 displays one method.

The Land Residual Method

This method of estimating the value of the land is based on the principle of surplus productivity, discussed in Chapter 5. The **land residual method** calculates land value by measuring the amount of income (either actual or potential) that is left after deducting the amount of income that should be attributed to any buildings. Hence, the method is one version of the income approach to value.

The land residual method is useful where there are no comparable land sales and newer commercial, industrial, or residential income properties are being appraised. The techniques used in this method will be discussed in Chapter 14.

10.3 How to Use Market Comparison Techniques

The comparison of properties is an essential part of all four methods of appraising land. While the same rules discussed in Chapters 8 and 9

EXAMPLE 10-1 Valuing Acreage Ready for Subdivision

Suppose that you were appraising a 12-acre parcel of land, approved for development into 50 single-family residential lots. Similar lots nearby, ready to build on, are selling for $60,000 each. You project the sales revenues and expenditures as follows. The example allows a developer's return of 30 percent on the raw land investment, which is both a return on the developer's capital investment and also payment for the developer's risk, entrepreneurial skills, and overhead costs.

Projected sales: 50 lots at $60,000		$3,000,000
Less: Development costs		
Direct expenses:		
Design and engineering	$ 20,000	
Clearing and grading	100,000	
Utilities and streets	+500,000	
Subtotal		$620,000
Indirect expenses:		
Studies and reports	$ 10,000	
Legal costs and fees	100,000	
Construction financing costs	150,000	
Property taxes	50,000	
Sales and promotion	+150,000	
Subtotal		+460,000
Total deductions from sales		−1,080,000
Equals: Net proceeds before raw land and entrepreneurial costs		*$1,920,000*

These net proceeds represent the land purchase price plus the entrepreneur's return of 30 percent. Thus, this is12;22 a total that is 130 percent of the land value. Therefore:
Indicated raw land value = $1,920,000/1.30 = $1,477,000 (Rounded)
Note: In this example, the indicated raw land value is just under $30,000 per developable lot, or 50 percent of the finished value. Also, note that just subtracting 30 percent from $1,920,000 gives $1,344,000, an incorrect answer!

apply to the techniques of site comparison, data and techniques that are unique to site appraisals will be emphasized in this section.

Types and Sources of Data

Although the specific types and sources of data needed for comparison of land sales may differ from those required in the appraisal of improved property, the quality and quantity of data to be gathered are essentially the same.

Criteria for Comparable Sales

For vacant land sales to be used as adequate comparables, they must be competitive with both the subject property and each other. They should be located in the same neighborhood as the subject property, or one like it, and be affected by similar social and economic influences. In fully built-up, older neighborhoods, vacant land sales are usually not available. Therefore, sales from a different location may be considered if the sites are relatively similar in physical and legal characteristics and influenced by the same market factors. Similar prices for comparable *improved* properties may be convincing evidence of such similarity.

The comparable sales must be open-market transactions; distress sales and sales where the buyer gains a unique benefit are not usually considered to be valid comparables. An example of such a special benefit would be when a business buys an adjoining vacant property for much-needed expansion. If the alternative to expansion is to relocate to larger premises, the business can often afford to pay a premium to get the adjoining lot.

To be useful, a sale should have sold close to the date of value. This is a relative term! Depending on the intended use of the appraisal and report, the level of market activity at the time and the type of property being appraised, a sale might be considered close enough in time even if it occurred two or three years before the date of value. However, in an active or changing market, sales more than a few months before or after the date of value may be unacceptable.

Current or Prior Sales of the Subject Property

As mentioned in Chapter 8, any known agreement of sale, option, or listing of the subject property close to the date of value should be considered and analyzed by the appraiser. Also, prior sales of the subject property should be investigated. USPAP standards require that such a history include all sales of the subject property that have occurred within three years of the date of value, for all property types. It is important that the appraiser make appropriate comments concerning whether these historical data are relevant to an analysis of the value of the subject property or not, and if relevant, what an analysis of this information indicates regarding the value of the subject property.

What Data to Include

The data collected for each comparable sale should include detailed information about physical, legal, and locational factors, discussed further in the next section. This information helps in judging the comparability to the subject property. The physical data usually include lot size, shape, frontage, slope, and topography. Legal data, including zoning, taxes, special assessments, and public and private restrictions, should also be considered. Sales work sheets are often used, providing the appraiser with a convenient means of recording these and other necessary details, such as street address, legal description, name of grantee (buyer), name of grantor (seller), date, price, and terms of sale. These items will be discussed later in this chapter.

Sales History of the Comparables

If any of the comparable sales are located in an area where there is a lot of speculative buying, it would be advisable for the appraiser to include a *sales history* of these comparable sales for the prior year. Some clients may also require information on prior sales of all comparables. The 2005 revision of the URAR and 2055 forms includes language that suggests reviewing the sales history of all of the comparable sales. Appropriate analysis of and comment on this sales history should be made.

Sources of Data

Data on vacant land sales may be obtained from public records. For example, ownership transfers may be identified by researching recorded deeds in the public recorder's office or the records of the property tax assessor. Checking for demolition and new construction permits, or subdivision map applications, can also point out parcels where a land sale may have occurred, as well as the likely parties to contact.

Buyers, sellers, brokers, land developers, realty board listings, title companies, and lenders are all good private sources of information on market activity involving vacant land. Even newspaper advertisements may be a good data source. Also, real estate professionals are usually willing to cooperate in providing data.

Some cooperative market data banks accumulate land sales information furnished by participating appraisers. Such groups can be helpful sources of data. Although many of these groups have only limited information on vacant land sales, it can help supplement data from other sources. Also, commercial data banks are providing increasing amounts of land sales data.

Verification of the Data

Any information that you collect must be properly verified and interpreted, in order to be of value. Ideally, the total price and the terms of the sale should be verified with a principal party or one of the agents involved in the transaction. This often helps to qualify the sale as an open market transaction. With land sales, it is often especially important to identify the terms of sale. Since institutional loans are less common on vacant land, more seller loans are used. When favorable interest rates or terms are provided, the selling price may be significantly increased to reflect the premium value of the loan.

When direct verification of data is not possible, seek out some of the public and private sources already mentioned. As we suggested earlier, data from public records may not accurately indicate the full purchase price. For example, transfer tax charges shown on recorded deeds may reflect only the cash consideration; the amounts for any existing encumbrances assumed by the buyer are usually not included.

Major Land Features Affecting Value

In the comparative process, it is essential that those features of the property that are important in the marketplace be thoroughly understood. Therefore, we shall review here the major factors affecting land value, previously discussed in Chapter 6. In this chapter, the important *site characteristics* have been divided into **physical**, **legal**, and **location** groupings (see Figure 10-7).

Physical Features

Here are some of the most basic physical features to consider (as illustrated in Figure 10-8):

1. **Size** can be measured in square feet, acres, or hectares (the metric land measure—1 hectare is about 2.5 acres), or just by frontage. The size of a parcel is basic to utility and value. Although its relative importance depends on both use and zoning requirements, size is often the best unit of comparison in the analysis of land sales.

2. **Shape** refers to the general parcel configuration and its relative dimensions. An irregular or long and narrow shape, for example, may reduce the utility of a site.

**Figure 10-7
Important Site
Characteristics.**

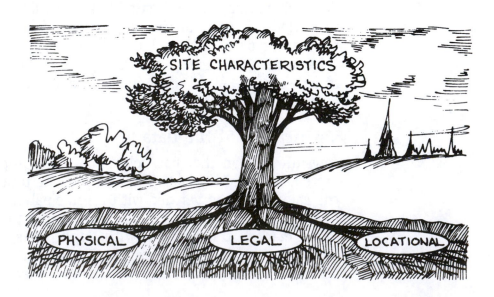

**Figure 10-8
Major Physical
Features Affecting
Land Value.**

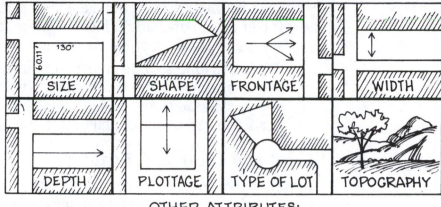

OTHER ATTRIBUTES:
* DRAINAGE *SOIL * CLIMATE * VIEW

3. **Frontage** refers to the width of the lot on the access street. Its importance is a function of the land use and specific zoning requirements. A corner lot, of course, has frontage on two streets. Frontage affects **access** to the property. For example, a gasoline station needs enough frontage for driveways on each side of the pumps. Frontage also affects the exposure of the lot to public notice or view, which is very important for retail properties.

4. **Width** is important to the *effective size* of a lot. Most zoning ordinances not only regulate minimum lot width, but also require side yard setbacks. Hence, for relatively narrow lots, the side yards reduce the net buildable area so that the building might have to be very narrow!

5. **Depth** of the site is also important. Street setback and rear yard requirements of local zoning ordinances can considerably reduce the utility of a shallow lot. On the other hand, extra depth may not contribute proportionally to the value of a lot. In urban single-family residential properties, deep lots may be worth little more than the standard depth, typical for that street or neighborhood.

6. *Plottage value* refers to the added value that is generated when two or more smaller sites can be combined to provide greater utility. For example, two or more commercially zoned lots can sometimes be combined to form the site of a larger, more economically profitable project. However, the assembly of lots does not always result in a plottage value increment! To have added value requires that there be a greater market demand for the larger unit. In some cases, smaller lots may be in demand, leading to lot splits!

7. **The type of lot** may affect its relative appeal and marketability. Preference for different lot types (corner, inside, key, flag lot, and so on) may vary from one location to another, and may vary for different uses.

8. **Topography** refers to the slope and surface features of the site. It can have a dramatic effect on access, drainage, views, the usable area, and the cost of construction.

9. **Other attributes** to be considered include soil and subsoil features, climate, and views. Such off-site improvements as streets, alleys, sidewalks, and street lights also affect the value of the land itself and are therefore important comparative features.

Legal and Locational Features

Although we are accustomed to thinking of a site in terms of its physical characteristics, legal and locational features must be compared in appraisals, too.

First, we must consider the legal form of ownership of the land itself. Would it be possible to compare the airspace and common area interests of a condominium site with a conventional detached lot? Probably not. As we learned in Chapter 6, the legal rights associated with condominiums and planned unit developments make them uniquely different from the site we most commonly associate with "conventional" housing. Compare "like with like" whenever possible.

Zoning and other land-use regulations are also critical legal elements to consider in site comparisons. As mentioned before, the highest and best use of land is limited to those uses that are legal under the zoning in effect on the date of value (or any probable rezoning).

Consider the effect of zoning on the typical lot size, for example. As we learned in Chapter 6, zoning often regulates the number of square feet of land required for each living unit. In single-family residence neighborhoods, the minimum lot size may be only 4,000 square feet under one zoning designation, but one acre or more under another. It follows that sale comparisons should generally be made using sales having the same or a similar zoning designation.

What effect do the many complex federal, state, and local environmental protection laws have on the use and value of land? Such laws usually restrict the legal uses allowable for vacant land, while not impacting a use that is already in existence. When new laws are passed, this means that land that is already improved may not be readily comparable with vacant land now selling under restricted-use laws.

For example, land developed with apartment buildings prior to open-space laws, which reduced allowable density, might now represent privileged, nonconforming properties. In valuing the land under such an apartment, usually it should be appraised as if zoned for the density it actually supports on the date of value, rather than the lower density it would be allowed if it truly were vacant. In the case of commercial and industrial properties, state and federal environmental protection laws may require environmental impact reports before any new development or change in usage occurs.

A number of other legal restrictions that limit land use were covered in Chapter 6 and need not all be repeated here. However, it is important to remember that easements, right-of-way regulations, deed restrictions, and private encumbrances can make the affected parcels unique. Hence, such restrictions must be investigated, for they may detract from the comparability of otherwise similar land.

Many locational factors can affect the value of a site, as was also pointed out in Chapter 6. Negative factors you need to consider may include proximity to earthquake and flood hazard zones and hazardous waste sites. The impact of such locational factors must be carefully weighed by the appraiser.

Utilities and other municipal or public services available to the site are largely a function of the site's location. The level of property taxes and other economic factors also should be considered in making land value comparisons. Differences in the quality of schools, fire and police protection, refuse collection, street lighting, and the level of property taxation are sometimes so important that it becomes difficult to compare land in different political jurisdictions.

Analyzing the Sales Data

As in the sales comparison approach for improved properties, it is necessary to analyze and compare vacant land sales. We must consider the circumstances of the sale and also compare the properties involved. This process uses the four elements of comparison.

The Four Elements of Comparison

Sales should be compared and adjusted by using the same four *elements of comparison*:

1. *Terms and conditions of sale*
2. *Time of sale*
3. *Location*
4. *Physical characteristics*

It is frequently true that the *terms of a sale* determine the price. When vacant land is sold for something other than cash, it is frequently financed by the seller. If the terms of the seller loan are more favorable than outside lenders offer, the buyer may agree to an inflated price. Low down payments, low interest rates, and subordination clauses are often encountered in land transactions. (A subordination clause is an agreement by the lender to subordinate this loan, usually to a later development or construction loan.) It takes a considerable amount of expertise to adjust vacant land sales prices for the effects of unusual financing. (Adjusting for terms of sale was discussed in Chapter 9.) The *conditions of sale* should also be investigated to confirm the real property rights conveyed and to make sure it was an open-market transaction.

The *time of sale* is often the second element of a sale to be compared and adjusted. Changing market conditions usually affect vacant land prices even more quickly and dramatically than prices of improved properties. Changes in zoning, parking requirements, and environmental impact laws are good examples of changing value influences.

Adjustments for *location* are perhaps the most critical and difficult of the adjustments to make in the appraisal of land. That is why close proximity to the subject property is desirable, so that this adjustment can be minimized.

The *physical characteristics* of land were referred to earlier in this section. The characteristics of the subject and the comparables should be compared, with priority given to those differences that affect the potential use of the site. How much do size, shape, topography, and so on, affect the value of a site? These questions can be answered only by an analysis of the market's reaction to them. Several techniques help to interpret the market's reaction to these important physical differences.

One of these is the direct market method discussed in Chapter 9. This technique makes use of matched pairs of sales. For example, if two lots with only one notable difference, say, standard versus excess depth, have sold at different prices around the same time, the adjustment for depth might be "read" from the sales. Or it might be possible to locate a depth table that conforms to the sales data and can serve as a guide. (The use of depth tables to suggest how lot value may vary with relative depth was discussed in Chapter 6.) When a large number of sales are available, graphs or simple linear and multiple regression techniques can assist in the analysis of differences in the sale properties.

Units of Comparison for Land Appraisals

The appraiser normally compares sales by whatever criteria are most significant in the market. Using a unit of comparison helps you to do this. Appropriate **units of comparison** are often determined by the type of zoning and potential use. For example, single-family residential lots are usually sold and compared by selling price per lot or square foot. In the case of land zoned for subdivisions, multiple-residential or condominium projects, the selling price per dwelling unit to be developed is generally the important unit of comparison. Commercial or industrial land is usually sold and compared by the selling price per square foot, but larger parcels are sold per acre. Office and mixed-use parcels sometimes are sold on the price per square foot of potential *building* area. High-valued retail parcels are sometimes sold in terms of price per front foot, where foot traffic is heavy and merchandise display is important.

In the hypothetical sales sample shown in Example 10-2, there seems to be less variability in the price per square foot than in the price per front foot. This implies that the appropriate "market" unit is the price per square foot. (Notice that the price of Sale B does not appear to show any loss of value due to its greater depth!) In any given study, you may need to make several analyses in order to discover the most significant unit of comparison in that market.

EXAMPLE 10-2   Using Units of Comparison in Appraising Land

Sale	Size	Price ($)	Price per Front Ft.	Price per Sq. Ft.
A	50 x 100	250,000	$5,000	$50
B	100 x 120	600,000	$6,000	$50
C	55 x 80	233,200	$4,240	$53
D	75 x 100	367,500	$4,900	$49

The Adjustments

Land prices are analyzed and adjusted as part of the comparison process. To review, the analysis of sales data usually involves adjusting the comparable sales prices to make the comparables more like the subject property, or as close to a substitute in market appeal as possible. These adjustments can be made by adding or subtracting lump-sum dollar amounts from the sales price of the comparable, by adding or subtracting percentages, or by accumulating percentages. You can review these adjustment methods in Chapter 9.

A sales adjustment grid, such as that shown in Example 10-3, is a convenient method of displaying the important sales differences, as well as keeping track of all these adjustments. Often, an appraiser might experiment with adjustment amounts to see which appears to be a better fit to the market.

When you have been able to locate a large enough number of sales, those sales that require very large adjustments are usually discarded. If valid comparable properties have been used and the adjustments are reasonable, the adjusted prices should now fall into a fairly narrow range.

In reconciling the adjusted sales prices to a value conclusion, it is a good rule to give the greatest weight to the sales requiring the least total adjustment. Both the plus and minus adjustments should be considered in this determination. And, as noted earlier, averages are rarely justified in appraising!

EXAMPLE 10-3   Land Sales Adjustment Grid
(Showing Percentage Adjustments)

Sale	Price	Time	Location	Size	Net Percent	Indicated Value
1	$500,000	+ 2	0	− 5	− 3	$485,000
2	450,000	+ 4	− 5	+ 5	+ 4	468,000
3	400,000	+ 5	+ 5	0	+ 10	440,000
4	350,000	+ 10	+ 15	+ 5	+ 30	455,000
5	600,000	− 3	− 5	− 10	− 18	492,000

SUMMARY

Appraisals of vacant or undeveloped land are used for many purposes, including sale and purchase, public actions, and land development. In improved properties, a separation of value between land and buildings is often needed for income and property tax purposes. A separate site value is also required in the cost approach and in several forms of the income approach to value.

Appraisal standards require an opinion of highest and best use in most written appraisals. This optimum use of the land is considered: (1) as if vacant and (2) as presently improved. To be selected as the highest and best use, any use must meet four criteria or tests. The use must be: (1) physically possible, (2) legally permissible, (3) economically feasible, and (4) the most productive.

The four primary methods used by appraisers for arriving at land values are:

1. The market method,
2. The allocation or abstraction method,
3. The land development method, and
4. The land residual method.

The market method is the most reliable for appraising land because it is the most direct. The site is compared to sales of similar parcels of vacant land. The comparison is as if it were vacant and available for its highest and best use. When no comparable sales of vacant land are available for comparison, the site may be appraised by the allocation, abstraction, development, or land residual methods.

The allocation and abstraction methods use sales of improved property and allocate a portion of the sales price to the land. Their use is usually limited to built-up areas where little vacant land remains or areas with no comparable sales.

The development method of land appraisal relates the value of raw land to its potential market value as developed land. It is used to appraise parcels likely to be subdivided or developed in the near future.

The land residual method is a technique of the income approach and applies mainly to commercial and investment projects. It is an estimate of site value based on the actual or potential net income that is remaining after deducting the income attributed to the improvements.

Each of the four methods of appraising land relies on property comparison in some form. The data needed for land sales comparison are basically the same as for improved property. For land sales to be considered valid comparables, they must be somewhat competitive with the subject property and with each other. They must be qualified as open market transactions, and the sales should have occurred around the same time as the date of value.

For the appraiser to compare market sales, it is essential to understand what site characteristics are important. These characteristics are placed in three categories: physical, legal, and locational. The most important physical factors include size, shape, frontage, width, depth, plottage, type of lot, and topography. Legal and locational factors include the most likely profitable use, zoning and other land use regulations, as well as utilities and public facilities available. The four major elements of comparison used in the analysis of sales data are terms of sale, time of sale, location, and physical characteristics. Sales prices should be compared by what the market considers most important.

In the analysis of vacant land sales, the most common units of comparison are those that compare selling price per lot, per square foot, per acre, per front foot, and per unit developed. The sales prices are adjusted from the comparables *toward* the subject property, by adding or subtracting a lump sum or a percentage from the sales price of the comparable. If valid comparables and adjustments have been used and the adjustment process correctly applied, the adjusted sales prices should fall into a fairly narrow range.

IMPORTANT TERMS AND CONCEPTS

Abstraction method	*Elements of comparison*
Access	*Highest and best use criteria*
Ad valorem property tax	*Interim use value*
Allocation method	*Land residual method*
Depreciation (accounting/tax)	*Legal site characteristics*
Depreciation (appraisal)	*Location*
Developer's profit	*Market method*
Development method	*Physical site characteristics*

Plottage value   *Terms and conditions of sale*
Potential use   *Time of sale*
Sales history   *Units of comparison*

REVIEWING YOUR UNDERSTANDING

1. Land or site value estimates are important in the appraisal of both vacant and improved property; thus, such appraisals assist in:
   a. The sale and purchase of land
   b. Land development
   c. Ad valorem and certain income tax situations
   d. Certain appraisal procedures
   e. All of the above

2. The market method or direct sales comparison method of estimating site value:
   a. Does not apply to acreage appraisals
   b. Is the most reliable method available
   c. Is considered inferior to other methods
   d. Is used only when the subject property is a subdivided lot

3. Land value may be abstracted from the sales of improved property. The method is most useful:
   a. In built-up areas where little vacant land remains
   b. As an alternative to the market method when comparable sales are not available
   c. For acreage appraisals
   d. Both (a) and (b)

4. The land development method in appraisal is used only to estimate the value of vacant acreage that is ready to be subdivided. This method requires:
   a. The study of sales of subdivided lots
   b. The projection of land development costs
   c. Both (a) and (b)
   d. Neither (a) nor (b)

5. Many project feasibility studies incorporate vacant land appraisals. If a lot zoned for commercial use is being studied and there are no comparable sales available, which of the following methods would most probably be applicable?
   a. The market method
   b. The subdivision method
   c. The land residual method
   d. None of the above

6. The market method is suitable to appraise either vacant or improved sites zoned for:
   a. Residential use
   b. Commercial use
   c. Industrial use
   d. Any of the above

7. For land sales to be adequate comparables, they must be:
   a. Competitive with the subject
   b. Relatively close in time to the date of value
   c. Open-market transactions
   d. All of the above

8. The unit of comparison for vacant land appraisals is ideally:
   a. The square foot
   b. The total lot
   c. A combination of square foot and front foot units
   d. The unit considered by the market to be most important

9. Land prices are analyzed and adjusted as part of the comparative process. These adjustments could involve:
   a. Adding or subtracting lump-sum amounts
   b. Adding or subtracting percentages
   c. Accumulating percentages
   d. Any of the above

10. From the land sales adjustment grid shown in the following table, calculate the total adjustment and indicated value for each sale, and then choose a logical market value for the subject property. Adjustments are given in percentages, added or subtracted. (Give the most weight to the sale requiring the least adjustment, considering both plus and minus adjustments.)

Sale	Price	Time	Location	Size	Total	Indicated Value
1	$ 38,000	+3	-5	-5	_____	_____
2	40,000	+5	-5	+5	_____	_____
3	35,000	+2	+5	0	_____	_____
4	45,000	+1	-10	-5	_____	_____

   a. $37,450
   b. $35,340
   c. $38,700
   d. $42,000

PRACTICAL APPLICATIONS

As we like to remind you, review the exercise at the end of the preceding chapter, and the work that you have performed to date.

This assignment moves to the task of estimating the value of the site. It will be reported on the cost approach section on page three of the URAR form, as shown in Figure 12-7. The focus in this exercise is on deriving a value estimate for the site by the sales comparison approach. You will need to identify possible sources of land sales information, select reasonably comparable sales, and collect information about each sale. You will also need to inspect each comparable land sale property, from the street, adjust the sales for differences, and select a value opinion for the site.

It will not be easy to perform this exercise. Land sales are often harder to locate than improved sales because there usually are relatively few land sales. And land sales often are made with seller financing that distorts the sale price. Also, there can be issues with the land that are hard to see from the street but impact its usability and price. Finally, because there are often only a few sales, the ones you find may not be as comparable as you would like, making analysis and a final opinion that much more difficult. These problems are typical of a routine land value appraisal.

And, if you have selected a condo, co-op, or apartment unit as your subject property, you must review the earlier assignments, where you selected what site you were going to take as a hypothetical assumption, solely for this exercise. (Remember that you must spell out this and any other hypothetical assumptions in your report.) This assumed site is the one you need to try to value.

To locate land sales, consider all of the possible sources of information noted in Chapters 8, 9, and 10, and in the exercises for Chapter 8. Also consider going to the local building permit office and asking about permits for new homes; often the lot was sold not long before the permit was issued. Individual new home permits are more likely to lead you to a lot sale than a group of permits in a subdivision. Write down all of the names that show on the permit or in the file and the contact information that often is included for when you need to contact people for more information about the sale. Once you have identified a lot where a new home has recently been permitted, try to find the most recent sale of the lot. Check the county assessor's record for the owner at the time of the last assessment and compare that with the owner name on the permit.

Next, research the needed information on each sale. You probably will need to talk to the seller or buyer, or a real estate agent if you can identify them, to determine the price and the financing. (Review the information in the text about handling favorable financing.) After collecting the information, consider what adjustments you may need to make it more like the subject property. (Remember the rule: *Always adjust **to** the subject!*) The URAR form does not provide an adjustment grid for the land sales. However, you can always open a new blank form and enter the land sales data into the adjustment grid, using each line for whichever data you need to adjust for as a temporary worksheet. Or you can use the land comps form included in Click-FORMS, in the Forms Library, under "Land."

Which sales prices are high or low? Is there a clear possible reason, such as date of sale, size, slope, or view? Consider which sales seem to be the most different from the subject, and identify the evidence why. You will want to enter an adjustment amount for each significant difference. Remember that each adjustment should have the *effect* of converting each sale into a hypothetical property that is *more similar to the subject*. Therefore, after each adjustment, the spread in the adjusted sale prices at the bottom of the grid should be less. This means that you can try an adjustment, see if it narrows the range of adjusted prices or not, and then try a different amount for that adjustment.

Start with the more objective issues, such as lot size. The form has a space for you to calculate the sale price per square foot of land, which you usually would do. Start out adjusting for size with an amount that is one-half of the price per square foot. Then try one-third. Which narrows the range of adjusted prices the most? Does some other number do better? Remember to be careful to make the adjustment so that the sale price becomes the price of a property more like the subject property. It is so easy to adjust in the wrong direction!

When you have selected a tentative adjustment for size, study the sales data and the adjusted sale prices. Now which ones are high or low? Given the characteristics of the sales, what might be the reason? Are the higher sales the more recent sales, or is time not an issue in which are high or low? What about differences in location, as you perceived it when you inspected the sales? What about possible views? Often, up-slope lots sell for less than down-slope lots due to higher construction costs and slightly lower prices—*if* the views are the same. And the steeply sloping lots sell for less than more level lots. Each of these issues may call for an adjustment. You might select a tentative number for the adjustment, based on the difference that you tentatively believe you see in the sales.

As you move through adjusting for the various differences, keep looking at the adjusted sale prices. You may take an adjustment that you know you must make, but it widens the spread. First, recheck that all of your adjustments are in the right direction, that is, they make the sale more like the subject property. If they are correct, and you are correct that this adjustment needs to be made, accept that. Continue working, recognizing that either something not yet adjusted for is causing the remaining spread, or one or more of your prior adjustments may have been too large or small. Which sales are *now* the low and high ones, and what do they have in common? If the larger sales are now the higher adjusted prices, then perhaps more needs to be taken off of the larger sales.

When you have entered a preliminary adjustment for each significant difference, it is time to start tweaking the adjustments, as just noted, to see if you can narrow the spread. However, note that you *must* be consistent! Do not adjust one smaller sale by $70 per square foot of floor area, and another by $60 per square foot, *just* to narrow the spread. On the other hand, the adjustment per square foot might well be more for a smaller lot than for a large one (due to the declining price per square foot as lots get larger).

Do not expect to be able to adjust out all of the price difference. With lot sales, a wider range is often unavoidable due to the poorer comparability of the sales. There is one rule that you must not break: The range in *adjusted* prices, as a percent of the lowest price, must end up being somewhat less than the percent range of the *unadjusted* prices. Otherwise, you have failed the adjustment process test!

The last step is to select an estimated value for the subject property by the sales comparison approach and enter it into the form. Consider the adjusted prices: Are they evenly scattered through the range from the low to the high? Or do some or many of them tend to cluster in one area of the range? Is there one or another sale that you simply fought with, trying to see why its sale price was not in line with the others? If so, give it less weight. By now, your subconscious mind may well have a value opinion. Consider what your mind is leaning toward, and why. At the end of the day, you must select one number and enter it.

As we note at the end of each exercise, it is best not to get ahead of yourself. So, do not enter information in the later sections of the report until you have read the chapter(s) that cover that topic. However, it is a good idea to look ahead so that you start thinking about the information that you will need.

Reminder: If you have questions about the program, review the manuals and help information that were on the program CD. Also, go to www.bradfordsoftware.com, click on "Services" at the upper right, and then on "ClickFORMS Training Programs" in the middle of the "Services" page.

CHAPTER 11

INTRODUCING THE COST APPROACH

PREVIEW

The *cost approach* is based on the principle of substitution, and is one of the three recognized approaches to value. It produces an estimate of the total land and building costs that would be needed to create an equally desirable market substitute for the property being appraised.

To introduce the cost approach, this chapter first outlines the approach and then explains the difference between reproduction costs and replacement costs. Examples show how these two different types of costs are used. Next, the chapter covers the four common methods of estimating costs and the direct and indirect elements that make up the total cost of a structure. In the final section, the site, location, and design factors that most directly affect the construction costs of buildings are identified. Chapter 12 will complete the study of the cost approach by listing and describing methods used to estimate depreciation, or loss in the market value of the improvements.

OBJECTIVES

When you have completed this chapter you should be able to:

1. List the five basic steps in the cost approach.

2. Define the terms *reproduction cost* and *replacement cost*, and explain their use in appraisals.

3. Name four methods of estimating costs and explain when each is used.

4. **List the direct and indirect costs that make up a building's total costs.**

5. **Name the important site, location, and design features that influence the construction costs of a building.**

11.1 Use of Cost Estimates in Appraisals

Some are surprised to discover that cost estimates of one form or another are used in all three approaches to value. As we learned in Chapter 3, the cost approach requires an estimate of construction costs, because the value of a property is defined for this purpose as the sum of the land value and the depreciated cost of the improvements. Cost estimates are also used in the sales comparison approach to help us adjust sales, a procedure described in Chapter 9. In the income approach, the cost of the improvements can be a consideration in capitalizing the income of fairly new or proposed investment properties.

The cost estimates that are used in appraisals are what we describe as generalized economic costs. This simply means that they should always reflect:

1. Cost levels as of the date of value, not "book" costs or *historic costs* for the building.

2. Typical costs to build a building, rather than the actual construction costs. These two costs could be the same, of course.

3. Costs that include all the charges to the consumer, not just the cost to the developer or builder. All-inclusive costs are sometimes referred to as "turn-key" costs, where all that the first occupant has to do is to turn the key and move in.

Purpose and Outline of the Cost Approach

In practice, appraisers use the cost approach in market value appraisals for three main purposes:

1. To estimate the market value of new (or nearly new) and economically sound developments, or where land value is much or most of the total value. Here, possible depreciation errors will be the smallest.

2. To appraise institutional or special-use properties, such as a cathedral or a government courthouse, not commonly rented or bought and sold in the open market. In this case, the cost approach may be the only approach available to estimate market value.

3. To check the other value approaches. This option is available whenever appraising improved properties. Using the cost approach can reduce the chance of making an undetected major error in any other approaches used. Even working backwards from a value conclusion that was reached by another approach is a valid cross-check.

The cost approach is also used in appraisals for *insurance* purposes, depending on the definition in the particular policy. Many policies provide *replacement cost* coverage. However, the policies appear to define this term differently than do appraisers. In the past, some policies provided market value coverage, but that is now less common. "Insurable value" coverage was also common, and was defined as a form of depreciated replacement cost.

A recent issue has involved how lenders use the cost estimate in a loan appraisal. Some lenders use this number as the basis for the amount of fire insurance that the lender requires the owner to provide. Accordingly, the appraiser might have become responsible for the accuracy of the insurance coverage, without intending to!

Please note that you have to be careful, when using the cost approach, to consider what property rights are to be appraised. The cost approach, by itself, will not correctly value a property subject to a favorable or unfavorable lease. A separate adjustment, derived from an income analysis, will be needed at the end of the cost analysis.

On the other hand, the cost approach can reflect the value impact of an easement, if it is included in the analysis of land value. It is easy to see why a careful review of the rights that are being appraised should precede performing a cost approach.

Steps in the Cost Approach

The cost approach involves five basic steps:

1. Estimate the value of the land as if vacant and available for use. Generally, this is accomplished by the market comparison approach.
2. Estimate the total cost to reproduce or replace the existing improvements as of the date of value.
3. Decide on appropriate amounts for accrued depreciation (loss in the market value of the improvements).
4. Deduct the accrued depreciation from the cost new of the improvements.
5. Add the depreciated cost of the improvements to the estimated land value, in order to arrive at the property value as indicated by the cost approach.

Since the estimation of accrued depreciation is an important and often complex procedure, all of Chapter 12 has been devoted to this subject. Land valuation was covered in Chapter 10.

Limitations on Using the Cost Approach

The cost approach has certain key limitations. First, some cost elements are difficult to define and estimate, as we shall explain later in this chapter. Second, measuring or estimating accrued depreciation can be difficult and quite subjective. For this reason, the cost approach should not be emphasized in the appraisal of unusual or older buildings, unless no other method is available.

The Choice of Reproduction or Replacement Costs

Real estate appraisal is basically a process of comparison. The cost approach compares the utility of the structure with its economic cost in dollars as of the date of value. It may begin with either an estimate of the **reproduction cost**—the cost of creating a duplicate or identical building—or it may begin with an estimate of **replacement cost**—the cost of constructing a building that would have a similar utility to the subject improvement. Although these two terms are often used interchangeably in casual conversation between appraisers, there is an important technical difference that should be understood.

Defining Reproduction Cost Estimates

Since reproduction cost is defined as the cost of a *duplicate or nearly identical* structure, every physical component must be included. If certain features, such as the intricate design of an out-of-style house, are no longer in demand, their cost is still estimated and included. The reproduction cost estimate is intended to capture the building exactly as it was on the date of value, using the same materials, construction methods, building layout, and quality of work. All of the building's issues are included in the estimate of reproduction cost new on the date of value. These issues might include deficiencies, superadequacies and functional obsolescence. (Superadequacies, remember, are features that are well above the desires of the market at this location.) With reproduction costs, all judgments regarding the relative marketability or the utility of a particular feature are handled in the depreciation portion of the cost approach procedure and not in the cost-new estimate (see Figure 11-1).

Defining Replacement Cost Estimates

Replacement cost is defined as the cost to build a structure of *similar utility*. In this method, you do *not* include every feature of the building in your estimate of cost new. Instead, you examine the utility or

**Figure 11-1
The Choice:
Reproduction or
Replacement Cost.**

Source: Photograph Courtesy of Doug Frost.

usefulness of the improvements on the date of value and estimate the cost to build a structure that provides similar utility. For example, if the subject property had nine-foot ceiling heights, and you concluded that the market considered eight-foot ceilings to provide equal utility, your replacement cost estimate would be of a structure with eight-foot ceilings. Thus, a replacement cost estimate requires a judgment of building utility at the time of estimating cost new, instead of later in the depreciation analysis. Any building features that do not add to the general attractiveness or marketability would not be included in the cost estimate. These features fall into two basic categories:

1. Components of the original building that are no longer being used by builders, because of changes in construction and technology. Common examples include lath and plaster walls and ceilings, knob and tube wiring, gravity furnaces, and cast-iron waste pipes with lead joints.

2. Components that are not consistent with the highest and best use, and/or components that are for illegal uses under current zoning law. An example would be a second residential unit in an area of homes where no second units are allowed. Figure 11-2 points out another example.

**Figure 11-2
High-Cost Features
in a Low-Priced
Neighborhood.**

Replacement Versus Reproduction

Although there is no clear-cut industry standard, replacement cost estimates are probably used much more often than reproduction costs. From the appraiser's point of view, using replacement costs avoids making difficult and time-consuming estimates of the cost of old-fashioned materials found in older construction. Also, appraisers argue that using replacement costs provides a direct rating of the market demand for the quality and design and that this makes the cost approach more realistic. The standard Uniform Residential Appraisal Report form (illustrated in Chapter 16) requires the use of replacement cost estimates, as Fannie Mae has noted (*FAQ # 12*, 11/1/05).

From the client's point of view, however, an appraisal based on reproduction cost is sometimes preferred. Using reproduction cost requires the appraiser to identify and describe the specific existing features of the building whether or not they contribute value and to explain judgments made concerning the amount of utility lost. Any value reductions resulting from such nonmarketable features are thus exposed as specific depreciation allowances, instead of being hidden as they are in the replacement cost method.

In practice, the choice of cost method probably depends primarily on the intended use of the appraisal and if any supplemental standards or contract terms apply. For example, if the intended use of the appraisal is for fire insurance coverage, then it is essential to read the policy to see how coverage is defined. Often, coverage is to rebuild the existing structure. (Sometimes, any costs to comply with new building or energy code requirements are not covered.)

If the appraisal is for a loan, it is likely that replacement cost will be used, because it is simpler and therefore probably more accurate. Where the loan is to be appraised to Fannie Mae standards, then, as noted above, replacement cost is mandatory (as of this writing)! Examples 11-1 and 11-2 should serve to illustrate common usage of both the reproduction and the replacement cost methods.

EXAMPLE 11-1 Appraisal for Insurance Purposes

The subject is a Victorian-style residence built in the 1890s, located in a neighborhood of newer homes. Much of the ornate woodwork would have to be specially ordered, the 12-foot ceilings result in excessive heating costs, wood gutters are no longer used, and so on. Obviously, an insurance policy covering only replacement cost would be inadequate if the owners wanted to be able to reproduce this home.

A. Using Reproduction Cost:

Estimated reproduction cost	$162 per sq. ft.
Less: Lost usefulness (excess quality)	-58 per sq. ft.
Equals: Reproduction cost less utility loss	$104 per sq. ft.

(*Note:* The loss in utility should be estimated by one of the methods outlined in Chapter 12.)

B. Using Replacement Cost:

Estimated replacement cost	$104 per sq. ft.

EXAMPLE 11-2 Antiquated Materials — Loan Appraisal

The subject building is a 1927 custom residence, constructed of hollow-tile walls and other antiquated components not readily available now. It is estimated that construction cost today would be $105 per square foot if we substitute modern construction materials and technology.

A. Using Replacement Cost:

Estimated replacement cost	$105 per sq. ft.

B. Using Reproduction Cost:

Estimated reproduction cost	$150 per sq. ft.
Less: Estimated loss in utility	-45 per sq. ft.
Equals: Reproduction cost less utility loss	$105 per sq. ft.

The reproduction cost method is preferred for the situation illustrated in Example 11-1. Reproduction costs make the actual quality of the house a part of the record and require the appraiser to show how the deductions for superadequacies and functional obsolescence were handled. The replacement cost method is preferred in Example 11-2 because it saves on the amount of time and effort otherwise spent on locating and pricing obsolete materials and construction features that are not likely to increase value.

11.2 Practical Cost-Estimating Methods

Construction cost estimating is considered by many to be a specialized skill requiring a great deal of knowledge about building specifications and construction technology. For routine appraisals, however, reasonable results can be achieved by the appraiser who understands the four basic methods of estimating costs. Although most appraisers use only the first two methods listed, it is important to know the others, for they can be helpful in special situations:

1. The comparative square-foot (or comparative unit) method.
2. The unit-in-place method.
3. The index (or cost service index) method.
4. The quantity survey method.

The Comparative Square-Foot Method

The **comparative square-foot (or comparative unit) method** is the most widely used method of estimating construction costs. It is also the most practical. The appraiser applies this method either by referring to published cost manuals or by citing typical costs that he or she has noted from specific projects. Since cost manuals represent the average cost level at any one time, they are generally preferred over the actual costs for any specific project encountered. The cost of a particular building is estimated by applying the average (or typical) square-foot costs of similar buildings. Differences in building specifications and components that are not included in **base costs** are adjusted by appropriate *multipliers* or adjustment amounts. Example 11-3 illustrates the use of this method. Much of the rest of this section will expand upon this method.

The Unit-in-Place Method

The **unit-in-place method** calculates the separate cost of each component of the building. Typical components would include foundation, walls, floors, roof, ceiling, heating, and so on. The cost estimate for each component includes the cost of attaching or installing the component into the structure. The costs for the various components are added to reach a total cost estimate.

The unit-in-place cost-estimating method is most commonly used to modify or adjust the comparative square-foot method described earlier. Note that in Example 11-3, the basic square-foot cost was refined by using unit-in-place costs for the built-in appliances and air conditioning.

EXAMPLE 11-3 Comparative Square-Foot Cost Estimate for a Single-Family Residence

Assume that you are estimating the reproduction cost of an average quality dwelling with three bedrooms and two baths. It has 2,000 square feet, and there are six perimeter corners. The general specifications of the most nearly similar house in your construction cost manual match those of the subject, except for the built-in kitchen appliances and air conditioning found in the subject house. The adjustments for floor area and shape are obtained from the cost manual. (*Note:* To simplify the example, the local area and time multipliers have been ignored.) Proceed as follows:

Building size		2,000
Times: Cost factor per sq. ft.:		
Base cost factor	$119	
Times: Area and shape multiplier	x 0.973	
Equals: Cost factor, adjusted		x $115.79
Equals: Base cost:		$231,574
Plus: refinements:		
Built-in appliances	$14,000	
Plus: Air conditioning	+12,000	
Equals: Total additives		+26,000
Equals: Building cost		$257,574
Plus: Garage and yard improvements		+32,000
Equals: Total cost estimate		$289,574
Rounded		$290,000

As a primary cost technique, the unit-in-place cost-estimating method is especially well suited for estimating the cost of industrial buildings. Because such buildings often vary widely in size, shape, and height, it can be harder to make an accurate estimate of their cost using comparative square-foot cost calculations.

How It Works

The appraiser refers to one of the various cost-estimating guides that are available, and prices the subject building one component at a time: walls, floors, roof, mechanical, and so on. The figure for each component includes all the necessary costs to fabricate and attach that particular building part to the structure. This usually means that all the direct and indirect costs of labor, material, design, engineering, and builder's profit are included in the component cost figure. The cost guide will spell out what elements of total cost are included. Refer to the details of the cost guide in selecting the correct characteristics of each component. Or study one of the many excellent books that detail construction specifications.

When applying the unit-in-place method, major structural components are figured first. Floors, walls, and roof structures are typically measured and priced by the square foot of surface area. However, walls and foundations might also be priced by the linear foot. Costs for interior and exterior extras and roof cover are then added, along with plumbing, electrical, heating and cooling, and other mechanical components. Example 11-4 will illustrate.

The Index Method

The index (or cost service index) method is sometimes relied on to estimate costs for unique or unusual structures when the original or historic costs are known. The method adjusts the original costs to the cost level on the date of value by a construction cost multiplier, derived from published cost indexes. Year-by-year construction cost information is accumulated and published nationally by several well-known companies. Cost records are cataloged by building design and type of construction, and then indexed to a base year, such as 1926, 1929, or 1940. Regional or area modifiers are also provided to help account for differences in construction costs that relate to location. Use of published building cost services will be further discussed later in this chapter.

The formula for cost estimating by the index method is as follows:

Original cost × (Index on date of value/Historical year index)
= Cost on date of value

EXAMPLE 11-4   Unit-in-Place Cost Estimate for a Small Commercial Building

Floors	5,000 sq. ft. at $7 =	$ 35,000
Walls and foundations	300 linear ft. at $200 =	60,000
Roof structure	5,000 sq. ft. at $15 =	75,000
Interior partitions	100 linear ft. at $40 =	4,000
Ceilings	5,000 sq. ft. at $4 =	20,000
Doors and windows		5,000
Roof cover		10,000
Plumbing lines and fixtures		5,500
Electrical system		5,000
Heating and cooling		20,000
Hardware and all other costs		+10,000
Total direct and indirect costs		$249,500

Note: Before location and time multipliers

To use the index method, follow these steps:

1. Verify that the original cost figure included all of the present building components.
2. Find the applicable cost index figures closest to the date of value and for the original or historic year. Verify that both indexes use the same base year.
3. Divide the date of value index by the historic-year index to derive an adjustment factor.
4. Multiply the original cost by the adjustment factor.

Assume, for example, that you are estimating the cost of a Class D wood frame store building that cost a total of $80,000 to build in 1975. You find that no major remodeling has been done since that time. Your cost index chart for this type of building, at this location, shows a date-of-value index figure of 1760.6, and a year 1975 index of 705.2. Construction cost on the date of value would then be estimated as follows:

$$\$80,000 \times (1760.6/705.2) \text{ or } \$80,000 \times 2.50 \text{ or } \$200,000$$

Some published cost services provide charts of pre-computed cost multipliers. In such cases, the factor for the date of value cost update multiplier (2.50 in this example) may be taken directly from such a chart.

Although not considered as accurate as other methods of cost estimating, indexing is sometimes used as a secondary value tool. For a very unique building, if the historical cost is known, the index method may be the most reliable. When an estimate of replacement cost new is needed merely to indicate an upper limit of value for a building, indexing can eliminate the time-consuming process of a detailed cost analysis. Indexing is also well adapted to computer-assisted appraisal programs, which can use the improvement cost new as a significant variable in the analysis of market sales. Such programs are common in mass appraisal work, particularly for property tax assessment.

The Quantity Survey Method

The *quantity survey method* is the most detailed and accurate of the construction cost-estimating methods. It involves the listing and separate pricing of each of the material and labor components of a project, as well as all of the indirect costs of construction, such as a survey, permits, overhead, and contractors' profit. Written full specifications and drawings are necessary.

Although the quantity survey method is the most precise method of estimating construction costs, it is rarely used by appraisers. Instead, it is used mainly by building contractors when bidding on projects. It is a highly specialized method that requires more technical knowledge of construction than most appraisers have. Also, the great amount of time and detail required by the method is seldom warranted (considering that other cost methods produce reasonable answers in less time).

The main features, applications, and requirements of the four methods are listed in Table 11-1.

**Table 11-1
Cost-Estimating
Methods.**

Method	How It Works	Primary Application	Cost Data Requirements
Comparative, square foot	Uses the average cost per square foot (or other unit) of a comparable new building. Most useful method.	Universally used and accepted for most buildings.	Base costs from published or known sources; refinements made by unit-in-place method.
Unit-in-place	Prices building components by "in-place" cost per sq. ft., linear foot, or lump-sum amounts. More accurate and more detailed than the comparative sq.-ft. method.	Primary method for shell-type buildings and unique projects; most often used to refine the comparative sq.-ft. method.	Component costs from published or known sources.
Index	Trends original (historic) costs to date-of-value cost level.	Unique buildings; mass appraisal applications.	Trend factor from construction cost index service.
Quantity survey	A detailed cost breakdown by each category of labor, materials, fees, profit margins, etc. Most accurate, but least useful for typical buildings because of detail and knowledge required.	Development of detailed construction bid by a contractor.	Prices and amounts of all materials, wage rates and hours, and profit margins, as of the date of value.

11.3 Understanding Direct and Indirect Costs

Have you ever asked a builder or developer what it would cost to construct a house or some other structure? In all likelihood, the answer you got may have confused as much as helped you, because of the different things that people might or might not include when they refer to costs. For appraisals, costs should include all of the expenditures that are required to produce the structure, make it ready for use, and pay for selling costs to get the building to the consumer level. These include not only the builder's **direct costs** spent for labor and materials but also a number of **indirect costs**. The latter are not always reported in informal cost discussions. Interest and property taxes during construction and builders' profits are examples of indirect costs. Failure to take into account all direct and indirect costs of building construction often results in an understated cost approach answer, in relation to market value.

Direct Costs

All of the items directly involved with the physical construction of the structure are classified as direct cost elements. These include the following (discussed below):

1. Labor.
2. Materials and equipment.
3. Design and engineering.
4. Subcontractors' fees.

Labor Costs

Labor costs include all wages and salaries paid for direct work on the construction project. Such expenditures may be paid either by the builder or by any of the several subcontractors involved in the project. All costs of labor, skilled or unskilled, must be included.

Materials and Equipment

The material and equipment costs include all the items that eventually become integral parts of the structure, whether purchased directly or included in subcontracts: the concrete, steel, and lumber used in the foundation and framework, as well as the appliances, finish hardware, and paint that are installed in or applied to the completed project (see Figure 11-3).

Design and Engineering

Engineering and architectural costs are included in the building cost estimate. However, soil grading, compaction, special soil engineering, and retaining walls, on the other hand, are typically included in the *site* value.

Some residential structures require little or no engineering, and many are built from standardized plans and specifications. However, design and engineering can involve substantial expense, particularly for custom and/or unusual construction. This is partly because design or engineering specialists are often required to supervise some or all of the construction work.

Subcontractors' Fees

Much of the construction labor is not provided by employees of the contractor. Instead, subcontractors are used. For example, plumbing, heating, and electrical work are commonly performed by subcontractors. Increasingly, foundation, roof cover, and framing work are performed by subcontractors. Although the amounts paid to subcontractors are not usually broken down between labor, material, and other components,

**Figure 11-3
Typical Multifamily
Construction Project.**

Source: *Photograph Courtesy of Doug Frost.*

any amount paid for such services is included as one of the four direct construction cost elements.

Indirect Costs

Indirect costs include all of the hidden time and money costs involved in a project. Although they are often somewhat proportional to the direct cost of labor and material, indirect costs can vary considerably from one job to another. Here is a list of indirect construction costs to be included in a full cost estimate.

1. Legal fees, appraisal fees, building permits, and licenses.
2. Interest and fees for construction financing and fees for permanent financing.
3. Construction liability and casualty insurance.
4. Property taxes during construction.
5. Construction administration and management.
6. Interest on invested funds.
7. Builder's and entrepreneurial profit.
8. Marketing and selling costs.

Some of the items listed need further definition and discussion.

Interest on Construction Financing

Construction loan funds are usually paid to the borrower in "progress payments," based on the work performed each month during construction. As a result, the amount of principal that has been paid out grows each month, as does the monthly *finance charge*. Usually, the accrued interest is added to the outstanding balance of the construction loan each month.

Calculating the exact total interest amount is quite hard to do. As a rule of thumb, however, interest can be based on one-half of the total amount borrowed, or else calculated for one-half of the entire construction time period. For example, at a 10 percent interest rate, a project that takes two years to develop and has a $500,000 loan would incur approximate interest charges of:

$$(\$500,000/2) = \$250,000 \text{ at } 20\% \ (10\% \text{ per year for two years})$$
$$= \$50,000$$

In addition, the loan fees and points charged for granting the construction financing must be added to the interest charges. For example, the interest on the construction loan and the loan fees and points could be paid in cash by the borrower or, more commonly, included as one of the disbursements to be made from the construction loan funds. In either case, it is a valid indirect cost element. Fees to set up the permanent loan are also included, as these funds will pay off the construction loan. Thus, total loan costs for this example would be calculated as:

Loan fee: three points (3%) on the construction loan, or $500,000 × 0.03	$15,000
Plus: Take-out loan fee: four points (4%), or $500,000 × 0.04	$20,000
Plus: Progress inspection fee at 0.005 (1/2%) of the loan	+ 2,500
Equals: Total fees and points	$37,500
Plus: Interest charges (from above)	+ 50,000
Equals: Total loan costs	$87,500

Property Taxes During Construction

Property taxes during the construction period are included in the construction cost estimate. In many jurisdictions, improvements that start construction after a particular date (such as the property tax lien date) are not assessed until the next year. For this reason, property taxes during construction may consist only of taxes on the land itself.

Construction Administration and Management

These costs are *usually* included in the general contractor's bid and are often referred to as *builder's overhead*. Office rent, office employee salaries, utilities, and transportation costs are examples of such administrative costs. If the builder's overhead costs have been included in an actual contract cost, they should not be added again.

Interest on Investment

The owner's investment in the land and buildings is entitled to a fair return during the construction and marketing period. If the owner has a substantial investment beyond the construction loan funds, then some return to that investment must be accounted for here. For example, if the owner had a $100,000 investment in the site, it could be assigned a 32 percent return rate for the two-year construction and marketing period, or $32,000 interest on investment. This represents a 16 percent annual return. After construction has been completed, sales or rentals provide for a return on investment. However, it often takes from three to six months to sell all the space or to bring a building up to normal occupancy. The lack of return on vacant space during this period is therefore figured as a part of the time period for interest on the owner's investment. Please note that there may be operating costs for the vacant space, after completion of construction. Costs in excess of any rent revenue should be accounted for here.

Builder's and Developer's Profit

These two cost elements are the most variable and difficult to estimate of all the indirect costs of construction. Normal **builder's profit** represents the payment for professional services paid to the general contractor of a construction job. Typical charges for such services are dependent on competition, the predicted construction progress, and other conditions not entirely controlled by the builder. Charges vary from one project to the next, but most depend on the uniqueness of the undertaking. Some information on prevailing contractor profit margins can be obtained from local builders. At one time, 10 percent of the total hard costs was a common profit margin for the contractor. Now, there is much variation. This cost usually is included in a fixed price bid; contractors usually know profit percentages for various types of contracts.

The individual developer who "packages" the project, land, and building is often referred to as the entrepreneur. The **developer or entrepreneurial profit** is the amount required to pay for the "know-how," incentive, and risk involved in speculative development, as well as return on the developer's invested capital. The amount to be charged for this element depends on the amount of funds invested, the likely investment period, economic conditions, and competitive investment opportunities. Many cost manuals try to include a "normal" builder's profit, but very few attempt to suggest the amounts for entrepreneurial profits. However, omitting this amount from a cost approach fails to account for one of the costs that must be paid to get the product into the hands of the consumer.

Entrepreneurial profit can be broken into parts, and is often easier to analyze this way. The major split is between the anticipated return on invested funds, and the reward for time and effort. Generally, development is perhaps the most risky real estate investment, so it will command a yield rate (discussed in Chapter 14) higher than market yield rates for other real estate investments. Accordingly, commercial property permanent loans might be made at 6 percent, sales of leased property at a price to yield 9 percent to the investor, apartment sales at 11 percent to the investor, and development equity funds at 15 percent to the investor. Comparisons with other rates, or developer interviews, are the best sources. The annual yield rate that is selected would be applied to the anticipated equity investment for the time period necessary to complete the construction and marketing process.

When entrepreneurial or developer's profit is split like this, it is important to recognize that applying a return rate to the invested funds may not capture all of the required profit. The key is to understand the meaning of the return rate selected. Sometimes, developers plan projects solely with an eye to that return on funds invested. Other times, they expect both a profit and a certain return rate on invested funds. For example, the invested funds may come from a silent partner, who has an expectation of a return. But the developer in that case might have penciled in a separate profit for his or her time and energy.

11.4 Important Factors Affecting Building Cost

When you make an inspection of the improvements being appraised, your field notes or inspection check-form should contain all of the building information you will need to estimate the reproduction or replacement cost. This section outlines the site, location, design, and construction features that have the greatest effect on the cost of construction. Clearly, these factors should be noted in your inspection. The section also explains how to use published cost data when you are applying the comparative square-foot or unit-in-place methods.

Site and Location Factors

As discussed in the previous chapter, a number of site and location factors have an effect on the value of a site, and most of these also directly relate to the cost of development. The size and shape of the site, and its topography, soil, geology, and climate are the most obvious physical factors that affect the cost of construction. Irregularly-shaped sites may require special design elements in a building. Uphill, downhill, and sidehill lots, as well as those with poor soil or unstable geology conditions, generally require more engineering and foundation work, and often more costly utility service connections for the structure. In areas with severely hot or cold climates, expensive insulation and design elements may be involved. Higher costs can also be expected.

Both direct and indirect construction costs are also affected by location. A remote location will have higher costs for concrete than a central one, for example. Labor, material, and service costs vary from the East Coast to the West Coast, and up and down the country, in much the same way as the cost of living varies from one place to another. Also, as building code requirements for structural, mechanical, electrical, and other components of new construction vary (both from place to place and also from time to time), so will the cost of construction vary. Because urban areas usually have relatively stringent building codes, construction costs are often higher in the city limits than in unincorporated areas.

Design and Construction Cost Variables

On a given site, seven different *building characteristics* affect the total cost of construction as well as the square-foot and unit costs. These can be identified as:

1. Design or use type (type of occupancy).
2. Type of construction (construction classification).
3. Quality of construction.
4. Size.
5. Shape.
6. Height.
7. Yard or site improvements.

Design or Use Type

The design or use category of a structure (sometimes referred to as "type of occupancy") is considered the first cost variable. It defines what features the building is likely to have. For example, single-family homes have entirely different features and cost characteristics than those of stores or factories. In most construction cost manuals, suggested costs consider the following design or use types, grouped into four or five categories:

Auditoriums	Farm buildings
Auto showrooms	Fire stations
Banks	Garages
Bowling alleys	Government buildings
Car washes	Hospitals
Churches	Hotels and motels

Industrial buildings	Residential buildings
factories	apartments
warehouses	condominiums
public storage	detached homes
Lumber yards	duplexes
Mobile home parks	Restaurants
Nursing homes	Rooming houses and
Office and professional	fraternities
buildings	Schools and classrooms
Recreation facilities	Stores and markets
	Theaters

Construction Classification

The second cost variable is the type of construction. Buildings are divided into four or five cost groups, by the type of structural frame (supporting columns and beams), walls, floors, roof structures, and fireproofing. Typical building codes identify four such cost groups: A, B, C, and D construction (or Class 1, 2, 3, and 4, as some codes call them). Such classifications are sometimes based on construction categories in the Uniform Building Code. Specifications for the major classifications are outlined in Chapter 7.

Higher construction costs are typical for Class A and B construction, because of their greater fire protection, better engineering design, and additional component costs. High-rise and institutional buildings usually are designed to meet Class A or B specifications.

Class C and D buildings usually cost less to build than Class A or B buildings. Most residential, commercial, and industrial buildings fit into either the Class C or D category. Class C buildings usually feature masonry walls and wood roof structures. The frame, floor, roof, and wall structures of Class D buildings may be of wood and/or light metal construction. (Light metal buildings are sometimes labeled as Class S.)

A certain amount of knowledge and experience is needed in order to tell in which construction class a particular building belongs. To assist the inexperienced user, most construction cost manuals define the main characteristics of the building classes. It is important to identify correctly the construction class of a building being appraised, because the class significantly affects the cost, and also because typical cost factors are presented in most cost manuals under the respective class headings.

Quality of Construction

For a given use type and construction class, the quality of construction is generally the most important cost variable. In residential appraisal work, quality is usually rated as good, average, fair, or poor. However, in some cost manuals, quality is listed on a scale ranging from "low-cost" to "excellent," with typical specifications usually pegged as "average."

Rating the quality of construction is perhaps the most subjective part of cost estimating. Good detail on the building specifications is the first step. In addition, some knowledge of construction and experience are important in making a valid quality rating. Often, cost manuals will provide specifications or descriptions for the different quality ratings. These may be the best source of quality definitions.

Size and Shape

When estimating construction cost by the comparative square-foot method, it is important to recognize the effect of the **building size and shape** on the square-foot cost.

First, let us examine the effect of size. Nearly all buildings have a foundation and floor, a roof, and outside walls; these we can refer to as the *building shell*. The cost per square foot of such a **shell building** could easily be calculated by adding up the "in-place" costs of these shell components and dividing by the number of square feet in the building. Now, the effect of the floor area on the square-foot cost can be demonstrated by comparing two shell-type buildings of different sizes. Let us assume that, for both buildings in Example 11-5, the floors and foundations cost $7.50 per square foot of floor area; roof costs are $15.00 per square foot of roof; and walls cost $262.50 per linear (running) foot of wall (all calculated as "in-place" unit costs).

Note that doubling the dimensions of the building decreased the square-foot cost by $10.50, or 24 percent! In actual practice, the net effect varies, depending on roof design requirements and the project size. Greater roof spans may increase costs. Generally, however, large projects may often cost less per square foot than smaller ones because of the economies of scale.

In residential buildings (and others that have relatively expensive interior components), the effect of size on square-foot costs may be less predictable than in the examples, but it is still important. The total in-place costs for such things as plumbing, cabinets, and doors are often fairly similar in buildings of different sizes. Consequently, the square-foot cost of such "fixed-cost" components will vary with the size of the building. In summary, *increases* in floor area tend to *reduce* the square-foot costs, and *decreases* in floor area tend to *increase* square-foot costs.

EXAMPLE 11-5   The Effect of Size on Square-Foot Costs (Shell-Type Building)

A. Small building (50 x 50):

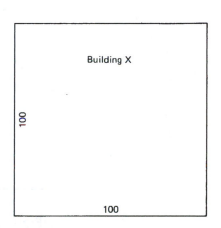

Floor: 2,500 sq. ft. at	$7.50 =	$ 18,750
Roof: 2,500 sq. ft. at	$15.00 =	37,500
Walls: 200 linear ft. at	$262.50 =	+52,500
Total cost		$108,750

Cost per sq. ft.: $108,750/2,500 = $43.50

B. Larger building (100 x 100):

Floor: 10,000 sq. ft. at	$7.50 =	$ 75,000
Roof: 10,000 sq. ft. at	$15.00 =	150,000
Walls: 400 linear ft. at	$262.50 =	+105,000
Total cost		$330,000

Cost per sq. ft.: $330,000/10,000 = $33.00

The effect of *building shape* on square-foot costs can also be somewhat predictable. This can be seen if we compare a 50 × 200 foot building with a 100 × 100 foot building (see Example 11-6). It is important to note that Buildings X and Y in this example have the same square-foot area despite having different dimensions. In Example 11.6, changing the shape from *square* to *long and narrow* increases the square-foot cost by $2.62, or about 7.9 percent. An even more dramatic difference would result if our building Y were scaled down to the square-foot area of Building W in Example 11-5.

In residential buildings, the higher costs resulting from changes in shape can be attributed to several factors. These include:

1. Increase in the number of corners: results in increased costs for foundations and wall framing.

2. Increase in the linear feet of the building perimeter: causes increased costs for walls, doors, windows, insulation, and weather stripping, as well as wiring and the length of plumbing runs and heat ducting.

3. Increase in roof framing and overhangs: adds more valleys, ridges, flashing, gutters, and downspouts to the costs.

EXAMPLE 11-6 The Effect of Shape on Square-Foot Costs

A. Long narrow building (50 x 200):

Floor: 10,000 sq. ft. at	$7.50 =	$ 75,000
Roof: 10,000 sq. ft. at	$15.00 =	150,000
Walls: 500 linear ft. at	$262.50 =	+131,250
Total cost		$356,250
Cost per sq. ft.:		$35.63

B. Contrast with a square building (100 x 100):

Cost per sq. ft. (Building X from Example 11-5):	$33.00

Building Y

200

50

Figure 11-4 shows some of the various shapes that are found in single-family residential buildings.

Height

The wall height, or **story height**, of a building also influences its cost. We can see how height changes the square-foot cost of a building if we use the size and shape examples previously discussed. With a 20 percent increase in wall height, the increase in the square-foot costs of the three buildings W, X, and Y would vary from 6.3 percent to 9.7 percent.

Yard or Site Improvements

Besides the main building, cost estimates made for appraisal purposes usually must include any other improvements to the site. This could mean garage or parking structures, walks, driveways, outside lighting, sprinkler systems, fencing, pools, patios, and landscaping. Published cost manuals provide typical unit-in-place costs for many such items.

Landscaping often varies widely in cost; its contribution to value can vary even more. As a result, most appraisers try to estimate how much landscaping contributes to value rather than what it costs. This is both practical and acceptable in single-residence appraisals.

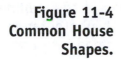
**Figure 11-4
Common House
Shapes.**

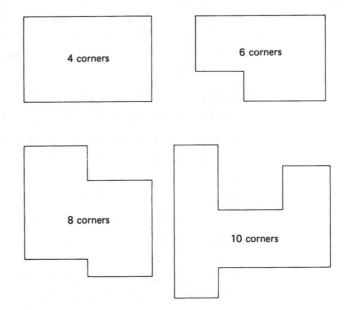

4 corners

6 corners

8 corners

10 corners

Using Published Building Cost Services

As we have already stated, several building cost services are available to the appraiser either by subscription or purchase. The services provide construction cost data in either a published manual, CD-ROM format, or online.

Perhaps the most well-known of the cost services are the *Marshall Valuation Service* and *Marshall and Swift Residential Cost Handbook*, both published by Marshall and Swift Publishing Co., Los Angeles, California, http://www.marshallswift.com. *The Means Building Construction Cost Data* (various editions including Western and Metric), published by R.S. Means Co., Inc., Kingston, Massachusetts, http://www.rsmeans.com, is another highly regarded cost service. Also see http://www.bluebook.net.

Many construction cost services provide both comparative square-foot and unit-in-place costs. While these costs usually include all direct and indirect cost elements, they often exclude entrepreneurial profit, property taxes, interest, and investment return during construction. Of course, the latter should be added as appropriate. It is important to read the fine print, to see what cost elements are included in a particular cost service.

In general, cost services base their published costs on national averages, but regional and/or locational adjustments are usually provided as well.

General Format of Manuals

As a general rule, the published building cost guides are organized and designed around the major cost variables that were just discussed. The usual handling of these elements is as follows:

1. *Design or use type:* usually the main subdivision of the manual. Up to 40 types of buildings may be described, with photographs and general specifications. The types are often grouped into five or so categories.

2. *Construction classification:* given as a separate cost schedule within each design type; four or five classifications are typical.

3. *Quality of construction:* interpreted by pictures and typical specifications for each construction quality level; includes square-foot cost factors for four to six quality levels.

4. *Size, shape, and height:* usually handled by corner count adjustments or by floor area-shape multipliers and then story-height factors. These are used to adjust the manual's base costs. In multiple-residence buildings, adjustments are often based on both the average unit size and the number of units. Both are significant cost variables in such buildings.

5. *Cost refinements:* often given as unit-in-place costs for building components; may be broken down into labor and material components.

6. *Yard or site improvements:* referenced in both the main and supplemental cost sections of most guides.

Suggested Procedure for Cost Calculations

It is very important to read all introductory notes and the instructions for the particular section when using any of the mentioned cost services. They clearly define what costs are included and how to adjust for cost variables.

Once you have selected the cost section to be used, be sure to read the footnotes that often appear on the individual base cost schedules. Base costs sometimes exclude such things as fireplaces and kitchen built-ins, making it necessary to add lump-sum amounts to your initial figure.

Here is a general outline of the steps required in estimating construction costs by the comparative square-foot method, as featured in most of the published building cost services:

1. Select the use-type table appropriate for your building.

2. Select the building construction class.

3. Choose the quality level with the specifications closest to those of the subject property.

4. Read the base cost factor from the table.

5. Calculate any required floor area, shape, corner, story-height, and/ or unit size multipliers; multiply each (as required) times the base cost factor.

6. Multiply the adjusted base cost times the area of the building.

7. Add the unit-in-place costs for any building components and features not included in the base cost.

8. Add **lump-sum costs** for the various site or yard improvements.

9. Apply a **time multiplier** and a **location multiplier** to adjust the published manual costs to the date of value and to local costs. Published cost manuals usually provide such multipliers in a supplement or update section.

Using Online Cost Services

The increased use of office computers and online data services by appraisers has extended to the task of cost estimating. A number of construction cost providers offer online services that can calculate and report building cost estimates upon order, using specifications that are input by the user. As an alternative, the R. S. Means Co. offers an interactive user guide for *The Means Building Construction Cost Data* book mentioned above. Some providers also offer cost-estimating programs to run on the office computer, with periodic cost update disks available. To review the publications and services offered by the construction cost services described in this chapter, you may want to visit the websites maintained by these companies.

SUMMARY

In this chapter, we discussed construction cost estimates: how they are used in appraisals and how they are made.

Cost estimating plays a significant role in each of the three approaches to value. In appraisals, the concept of cost is related to its economic impact. This means that cost estimates are made at price levels as of the date of value. Also, they must reflect the total amount of typical costs that are passed on to consumers. The cost approach is used primarily to estimate the value of nearly new, new or special-use properties. It can also be a check against the other value approaches.

There are four methods commonly used to estimate costs. The *comparative square-foot method* is the most useful, because it is the easiest to apply. The *unit-in-place method* is most often used to refine costs that were estimated by the comparative square-foot method. The *index method* is useful for costing unique structures, or for updating prior cost estimates in mass appraisal applications. The *quantity survey method* is the most accurate method and is used by contractors, but it is too detailed and technical to be of much practical use for appraisers.

When estimating construction costs, it is important to reflect both direct and indirect costs of construction. The contractor's costs for labor and materials are not the only costs involved. Indirect costs such as building permits, interest on loans and on investment, insurance, property taxes, overhead, and profit must also be included.

A number of site, location, design, and construction features affect construction costs. The size and shape of the site and its topography, soil, geology, and climate are the most obvious physical factors that affect the cost of construction. Both direct and indirect construction costs also depend upon location. Labor, material, and service costs vary with location, as do building code requirements for structural, mechanical, electrical, and other components of new construction.

As reflected in published construction cost manuals, design and construction features affecting construction costs include:

1. Design or use type.
2. Construction classification.
3. Quality.
4. Size, shape, and height of the building.
5. Yard or site improvements.

Appraisers often use cost manuals to make cost estimates. Online cost-estimating services are also available. Manuals and cost services provide average cost figures for many types of buildings and can be expected to include photographs, specifications, and cost-estimating techniques as well. Building cost references and computer-oriented services allow appraisers to make relatively reliable cost estimates, using the methods discussed in this chapter.

IMPORTANT TERMS AND CONCEPTS

Base costs

Builder's profit

Building size and shape

Comparative square-foot method

Construction classification

Cost approach

Design or use type

Developer or entrepreneurial profit

Direct costs

Historic costs

Index method

Indirect costs

Location multiplier

Lump-sum costs

Quantity survey method

Replacement cost

Reproduction cost

Shell building

Story height

Time multiplier

Unit-in-place method

REVIEWING YOUR UNDERSTANDING

1. The cost estimates used in appraisals are what we describe as generalized economic costs. This means that they should reflect:
   a. Wholesale costs
   b. Cost levels on the date of value, not "book" costs or historic costs
   c. Typical costs to build such a building
   d. Both (b) and (c)

2. There is an important technical difference between the terms *reproduction cost* and *replacement cost*. Replacement cost refers to:
   a. The cost of constructing an exact replica building
   b. The cost of constructing a building that would have a similar utility to the subject property
   c. The cost of reproducing the subject property
   d. None of the above

3. From the appraiser's point of view, replacement cost estimates are preferred over reproduction cost estimates because:
   a. They provide a direct rating of the market demand for the quality and design of a structure
   b. They are more detailed
   c. They are less time-consuming
   d. Both (a) and (c)

4. The cost approach may be emphasized in a number of appraisal situations. Which is not among them?
   a. Checking the other value approaches
   b. Appraising institutional or special-use properties
   c. Estimating the value of new or nearly new property
   d. Appraising older homes in an active market

5. The most practical and widely used method of estimating construction costs is:
   a. The comparative square-foot method
   b. The unit-in-place method
   c. The index method
   d. The quantity survey method

6. The cost-estimating method that is often used as a supplement to refine the square-foot method is called:
   a. The quantity survey method
   b. The index method
   c. The unit-in-place method
   d. None of the above

7. Estimating costs by adjusting the original costs to the cost level on the date of value with a cost multiplier is a method known as:
   a.   The comparative square-foot method
   b.   The unit-in-place method
   c.   The index method
   d.   The quantity survey method

8. Which method of estimating construction costs is the most precise yet seldom used by appraisers?
   a.   The index method
   b.   The quantity survey method
   c.   The comparative square-foot method
   d.   The unit-in-place method

9. Which of the following do not represent direct cost elements?
   a.   Materials and equipment
   b.   Interest on investment
   c.   Labor and materials
   d.   Design and engineering

10. Using the unit-in-place cost factors provided in Example 11-5, calculate the square-foot cost of a shell-type structure that is 25 feet wide and 100 feet long. Compared with the square-foot cost of building W in the illustration, this represents a square-foot cost that is approximately:
    a. $2.00 lower
    b. $5.25 higher
    c. $2.80 higher
    d.   The same

PRACTICAL APPLICATIONS

As we like to remind you, review the exercise at the end of the preceding chapter, and the work that you have performed to date.

This assignment moves to the task of estimating the cost new of the building. It will be reported in the cost approach section on page three of the URAR form, as shown in Figure 12-7. The first step is to decide if you will estimate the replacement or reproduction cost. Review the text in making this choice. You also may want to wait on the decision until you see what type of cost information you are easily able to locate. Next, you will need to identify possible sources of building cost information, review the specifications of your subject property, and select the needed cost information applicable to your subject property. Finally, you will need to make the calculations and enter the cost information into the spaces on the form.

Notice the information that the form calls for—this is a pretty limited presentation. As a tool, consider using another form as a template or guide to help you process the cost information. One choice would be the Swift Estimator form, in ClickFORMS, in the Forms Library, under "Swift Estimator" and then "Swift Estimator Residential." Another choice would be (in the Forms Library) under the "New AI Forms"; select "Cost Approach." A third possible choice in the Forms Library would be in the "Addendums" heading, and then "Cost Approach."

And, if you have selected a condo, co-op, or apartment unit as your subject property, you must review the earlier assignments, where you selected how much of the building you were going to include in the appraisal as a hypothetical assumption, solely for this exercise. (Remember that you must spell out this and any other hypothetical assumptions in your report.) This assumed building is the one for which you need to try to estimate the current cost to build.

To locate building cost information, consider any possible sources of information noted in the text. Also consider going to the local library, or the nearest college or university library, to see if either has construction cost books. McGraw, Boechk, Means, Dodge, and Marshall & Swift are the major cost publishers, but there are many other cost handbooks. You may find one that is out of date: Consider using it, but updating your costs by a construction cost index. Check the Internet to find one. The major cost publishers all have cost indexes; some are reported in construction industry magazines or websites.

Consider also what cost information is provided. Recall that there are several different cost-estimating methods, so you should review the text to be sure that you understand the several methods and which type of data each source is presenting. In general, you will want to use the comparative square-foot/comparable unit method of estimating costs. Do not attempt the quantity survey method unless you have prior experience using it.

Once you have identified which cost source you will use, review it carefully. Usually, there will be a base cost. Read the notes to make sure you understand what is included in the base cost. Are there adjustments for unit size or number of corners? Are there additive costs for various appliances? And, nearly always, there will be adjustments for time and for the particular location. In addition, you will need to estimate the cost for the garage and any site improvements. The last step is to total the various cost categories into an estimated value for the subject property by the cost approach, and enter it into the form.

As we note at the end of each exercise, it is best not to get ahead of yourself. So, do not enter information in the later sections of the report until you have read the chapter(s) that covers that topic. However, it is a good idea to look ahead, so that you start thinking about the information that you will need.

Reminder: If you have questions about the program, review the manuals and help information that were on the program CD. Also, go to http://www.bradfordsoftware.com, click on "Services" at the upper right, and then on "ClickFORMS Training Programs" in the middle of the "Services" page.

CHAPTER 12
ESTIMATING LOSS IN VALUE: ACCRUED DEPRECIATION

PREVIEW

Estimating the relative loss in the value of improvements, compared to their cost new on the date of value, is a necessary part of the cost approach. Accrued depreciation estimates may also be necessary in the sales comparison and income approaches to value.

What is *depreciation*? Accountants define it one way, but appraisers use another. After explaining the difference, this chapter will explore the types and causes of accrued depreciation in appraisals and explain the major methods appraisers use to measure the actual loss in value.

OBJECTIVES

When you have completed this chapter you should be able to:

1. Distinguish the concept of depreciation as it is used in accounting from that used in appraisal.

2. Name and give the causes of three types of depreciation.

3. Name four methods of estimating accrued depreciation and describe how they may be applied to an appraisal problem.

12.1 Depreciation Defined

Depreciation is a term with two distinctly different meanings, both used by people in real estate. One defines an **accounting** term, used in income tax calculations; the other defines an **appraisal** term, used in the cost approach and also elsewhere in the appraisal process.

Depreciation as Used in Accounting

In accounting practice, all capital assets except land are considered to be *wasting assets*, assets that decline in value over time. These assets may include machinery, vehicles, and other types of equipment, as well as buildings. When reporting income for income tax purposes, owners of assets that are held to produce revenue are allowed to deduct from income an allowance for the annual loss in value that is expected of a wasting asset, just as operating expenses are deducted.

Accountants calculate the allowable depreciation deduction by starting with the historic **book value** of the asset. Book value refers to the original asset cost, plus the cost of any capital additions or improvements, reduced each year by the depreciation deduction taken. Book value is also called **cost basis**. The important characteristic of income tax depreciation as applied to buildings is that it is determined by the property's cost basis at purchase and the legally allowable depreciation period. It does not consider what is actually happening to the building's value (see Example 12-1).

As the income tax depreciation deductions are taken, the building cost basis declines. This declining cost basis is often used in reporting the assets of businesses (on balance sheets). When real estate values are increasing, a company with substantial real estate assets can actually have much higher asset values than that reported to its stockholders. To address this problem, accountants in some situations are now using what is called **current-value accounting**, to supplement the more traditional cost-basis accounting procedure.

EXAMPLE 12-1 Accounting Depreciation

Purchase price and closing costs	$275,000
Less: Land value	− 65,000
Equals: Building cost basis	$210,000
Divided by: Depreciation period (in years)	÷ 40
Equals: Annual depreciation claim	$ 5,250

Accrued Depreciation in Appraisals

The estimate of **accrued depreciation** that is used in appraisals is governed by an *entirely* different set of rules than those used in accounting. In appraisals, first, a dollar or percentage amount is deducted from the estimated cost of the improvements *as if new on the date of value*, rather than from their historical cost basis. Second, the amount of depreciation represents the appraiser's best estimate of the *actual market loss in value* as compared to a new building, whereas accounting depreciation is a theoretical loss. Thus, an appraiser's estimate of depreciation in market value is not dependent *in any way* on the property's historical cost basis, the owner's depreciation schedule, or the loss in value allowable for income tax purposes. As used in appraisals, accrued depreciation is the difference between the cost new of the improvements and the market value of those improvements on the valuation date. This difference is sometimes referred to as **diminished utility**, that is, the total loss in market value from all causes.

As we shall learn in the next section, market value loss can be caused by either physical, functional, or economic conditions. Estimating accrued depreciation is often the most difficult step in the cost approach, and the hardest to support.

Purposes of Depreciation Estimates in Appraisals

You will recall that the cost approach involves, first, estimating the reproduction or replacement cost new of the improvements; then, deducting the total accrued depreciation from this cost; and last, adding this depreciated improvement value to the land value. An estimate of the total property value is the result. (See Example 12-2.)

EXAMPLE 12-2 Appraisal Depreciation

Reproduction cost new			$150,000
Less:	Accrued depreciation:		
	Reproduction cost new	$150,000	
	Times: Depreciation in percent	x 0.10	
	Equals: Accrued depreciation		− 15,000
Equals:	Reproduction cost less accrued depreciation		$135,000
Plus:	Land value		+ 170,000
Equals:	Total indicated value of the property		$205,000

When *replacement cost* estimates are used instead of *reproduction cost* estimates, note that the amount deducted for accrued depreciation should not include any loss of utility from antiquated materials, undesirable design features, and the like. The replacement cost estimate would have already adjusted for such factors, whereas reproduction cost estimates do not.

Although depreciation estimates are of the greatest importance in the cost approach to value, they can also play a part in sales comparison and income studies. For example, the sales comparison approach calls for comparing properties, and this may involve an analysis of their relative loss in value from age or obsolescence. When the comparable sales vary in condition or age, the adjustment for these differences in fact should be regarded as reflecting differences in accrued depreciation.

Also, in the appraisal of land, the abstraction method of calculating land value from improved sales often involves an estimate of accrued depreciation. In this method, the land value is presumed to be equal to the selling price of the property less the depreciated value of all improvements. Last, depreciation estimates sometimes assist the appraiser in the analysis of income properties. When the total net income for the property must be allocated between land and improvements, the market value contribution of each of these agents of production becomes important. As we have seen, the value contribution of improvements can be estimated by calculating their cost as if new on the date of value, and subtracting an estimate of accrued depreciation.

12.2 Types and Causes of Accrued Depreciation

Is any particular building worth the same as another of the same design type, size, and quality? When the location and site are different, different values should be expected. Both cost new and depreciation may be changed. However, even if the site and location are similar, differences in age, condition, and/or utility usually result in different market value contributions from the buildings. Once differences in these influences have been identified, they can be used to estimate the relative loss in building value that they cause. But what are the precise factors involved?

The appraiser's basic task is to recognize specific conditions or features of the property that cause building value losses and then to measure the effect of these conditions on the value contribution of the building. Two steps are involved. First, the loss in building value is identified by the type and probable cause. Second, the depreciation in each category is classified as either **curable** or **incurable**. In other words, the questions are:

1. What is the apparent cause?
2. Can the loss in building value be measured by the cost to correct (or cost to cure) the problem?

Types of Accrued Depreciation

Accrued depreciation is broken into three types, causes, or categories. The three types are labeled:

1. Physical deterioration.

2. Functional obsolescence.

3. Economic (or external) obsolescence.

We shall discuss the question of whether each is economically curable (or repairable) as we describe these three types of value loss. **Curable depreciation** means that the cost to fix the problem is less than the value that would be gained. Such a fix is considered to be economically feasible or curable.

Physical Deterioration

Regardless of location, quality, or design, all buildings deteriorate physically over the years. The **physical deterioration** of a structure describes its wear and tear from use, age, weather, neglect, lack of maintenance, or even vandalism. Since each part of a building is affected differently by these conditions, the loss in value due to physical deterioration is sometimes analyzed component by component. Economically, physical deterioration can prove to be either curable or incurable.

Curable Physical Deterioration

Curable physical deterioration refers to conditions that are economically feasible to correct. This means that correcting the defect would add at least as much to the market value as the cost of the repairs. For example, say it would cost $10,000 to repaint the exterior of a house and it is in a neighborhood where buyers appear willing to pay at least $10,000 more for freshly painted homes. Such a repair or renovation would be judged economically feasible. For an otherwise sound building, painting, replacing a worn-out roof or heating system, or simply making the building more presentable by cleaning can often enhance the market value at least as much as the cost of the work. Thus, such examples of repair would logically fall in the category of curable physical deterioration. These are also called ***deferred maintenance***. Examples are shown in Figure 12-1.

Incurable Physical Deterioration

Incurable physical deterioration, on the other hand, describes building conditions that are likely to cost more to repair than the value that would be added to the structure. Such repairs would not be considered economically feasible. For example, minor damage to the foundation or structural framework of a building would usually be considered incurable physical deterioration. This is because the repair cost might well be substantial and the resulting increase in market value would be relatively small.

(a)

(b)

(c)

(d)

Figure 12-1 Examples of Deferred Maintenance.

Some other types of deterioration are also considered incurable. They involve some particular part of the building that will need to be replaced in the years ahead, but which is too "good" to replace at the date of value. An example would be an older air-conditioning system which will need replacement in five years or so, but which has too much useful life left to be replaced on the date of value. The value loss in such a case is referred to as *short-lived incurable deterioration* (sometimes also called **curable postponed**). In five years, when the remaining economic life of the air-conditioning system has been used up, we would expect the value loss to be curable. Why? Because replacement of the building component probably will at that time be economically feasible, as well as being necessary.

Value losses attributable to the major components of a building, when age is the major contributing factor, are called *long-lived incurable physical deterioration*. These nearly always cost more to repair or renew than the value added by the repairs. Gradual reductions in the value of the foundation, framework, plumbing, fixtures, or electrical wiring, because of age, are examples of long-lived incurable physical deterioration.

Functional Obsolescence

Functional obsolescence describes a type of depreciation that is caused by a relative loss of building utility. **Loss of utility** means that there is some feature of the building that is not as useful as its cost would suggest. This loss of usefulness could be caused by a faulty building design, outmoded equipment, or some other design defect within the structure. A poorly arranged floor plan and a house lacking a typical side yard are examples of functional obsolescence (see Figure 12-2).

Functional obsolescence is often associated with original building design features that are not suitable for the location. For example, a building that is out of place—the wrong type or use for that location—is functionally obsolete (to a degree) and is called a **misplaced improvement**. A building that is too large or lavish for the neighborhood also has functional obsolescence and is labeled an **over-improvement**. (A building that is too small or of too low quality for the neighborhood is called an **under-improvement**.)

Functional obsolescence can also be curable or incurable, depending on whether the cost to cure the problem is less than or greater than the value benefits. In some cases, a kitchen can be remodeled, a room added, or a wall knocked out at a fairly nominal cost, to bring the building up to market standards on the date of value. However, the value loss suffered by a misplaced improvement or an over-improvement is usually considered incurable functional obsolescence (see Figure 12-3).

**Figure 12-2
Functional
Obsolescence:
Nontypical Side Yard.**

Source: Photograph Courtesy of Doug Frost.

**Figure 12-3
A Misplaced
Improvement: Does
It Have Functional
Obsolescence?**

Economic (or External) Obsolescence

Economic obsolescence describes a loss in building value that is caused by factors located *outside* the subject property. It is also referred to as *environmental* or **locational obsolescence.** Environmental hazards, changes in the zoning of a property, inharmonious nearby land uses, dust, and freeway or airport noise are sample conditions that might cause economic value loss to a building. In recent years, such hazards as methane or radon gases or toxic wastes have been specific environmental problems of great concern. Generally, economic obsolescence is caused by some event that has occurred or has been identified in the neighborhood since the property was built.

Note that there is some argument among theorists regarding when economic obsolescence impacts land value and when it impacts improvement value. At the least, the appraiser *must not double-count* a problem, by using land sales that fully reflect it and then reducing building value for it as well.

Economic obsolescence can be curable or incurable, in the same way that physical deterioration and functional obsolescence can be. However, the cause of the problem sometimes is beyond the control of any one property owner. The cost to repair also can be very large. For example, a very expensive sound barrier wall might be needed to reduce the effect on property value created by a noisy freeway. But part of the loss in property value is very likely to be reflected in land values. So, building values might only be reduced to reflect the costs to put in sound-attenuating windows.

Deciding whether to classify a particular loss in building value as functional or economic obsolescence is sometimes difficult. As the demands, wants, and needs of the market change, buildings that were once considered adequate may no longer measure up to current tastes. For example, in some areas, houses or condominium units with fewer than two baths are now considered out of date. Since the cause of such obsolescence is clearly related to external factors (a change in market demand), one might argue that the loss in value should be labeled economic obsolescence. However, the usual practice is to categorize it as functional obsolescence, because it relates to the house as built.

Changes in public control to address general population needs are credited with causing economic obsolescence (e.g., higher density zoning), whereas changes in specific desires of that same population (e.g., one bath or two, as cited above) are usually explained as causing functional obsolescence. No fine line can really be drawn. However, the appraiser should be careful not to account for the decrease in value twice, by counting the same decrease in value as both functional and economic obsolescence.

12.3 Methods of Measuring Accrued Depreciation

There are four basic methods for measuring accrued depreciation. It is important to remember that these methods are not abstract mathematical calculations. Rather, they are attempts to estimate the *actual loss in market value*, compared to a new building. Note that, in practice, it is common to use them in combination. The four methods should lead to the same conclusion, as illustrated in Figure 12-4.

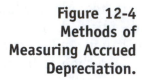

**Figure 12-4
Methods of
Measuring Accrued
Depreciation.**

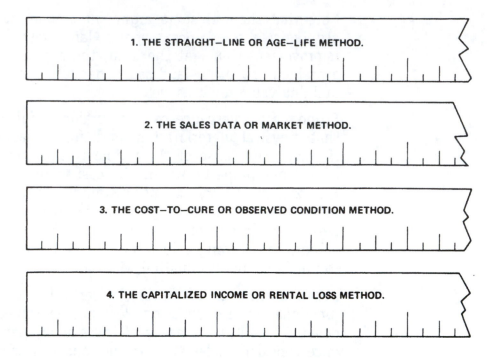

Straight-Line or Age-Life Method

The **straight-line** or **age-life method** of estimating accrued depreciation is based on the theory that all structures have a total useful life that can be predicted or estimated from analysis of sales. This is called the **economic life** of the building. It is defined as:

> "the period over which improvements to real property contribute to property value."

Source: *The Dictionary of Real Estate Appraisal*, 4th ed., Appraisal Institute, Chicago, IL, 2002, p. 92.

Therefore, at the end of a building's economic life, the vacant land would sell for *as much as or more than* the property with improvements! Note that economic life is rarely as long as the physical life of a structure. (See the Highest and Best Use section!)

In straight-line depreciation, loss in value due to age is assumed to be directly proportional to the so-called age life, or useful life, of the structure. With straight-line depreciation, if a residence is considered to have a 100-year economic life but is now 25 years old, it should be given 25 percent depreciation.

Age	25 years
Divided by: Economic life	÷ 100 years
Equals: Accrued depreciation	0.25
In percent:	25%

Buildings of the same age actually vary greatly in their condition and desirability (because of differences in maintenance, modernization, and so on). For this reason, some appraisers base depreciation estimates on the "effective age" of the building rather than the actual age. The *effective age* of a building is the actual age of other buildings that are in similar condition and of similar utility and marketability. For example, a 40-year-old building that has been modernized and well-maintained may be able to compete directly with 20-year-old buildings. Here, the effective age of the 40-year-old building in question would be 20 years. When effective age is used to estimate accrued depreciation, normal functional value loss and some physical deterioration will have been accounted for by the effective age adjustment. If actual age is used in figuring depreciation, however, separate adjustments may be necessary to reflect these factors.

Note that the effective age adjustment is largely a matter of judgment and is very difficult to prove! For this reason, it is often desirable to use the actual age and then make explicit adjustments for any remodeling.

To estimate the loss in value using effective age rather than actual age, you simply divide the effective age of the structure by the total estimated economic life of the structure. Then, convert this figure to a percent of accrued depreciation as before. For example, let us assume that a 45-year-old building with an effective age of 20 years is judged to have a total economic (useful) life of 100 years. Here, the accrued depreciation would be:

Age, 45 years, but effective age	20 years
Divided by: Economic life	÷ 100 years
Equals: Accrued depreciation	0.20
In percent:	20%

Many of the published depreciation tables are based on the age-life concept, although they modify the straight-line idea to a more realistic pattern of loss in value. For example, some of these tables show a more rapid loss of value in the early years, followed by a more gradual loss with age. To use these tables, simply find the correct column for the type of building being appraised. Next, look up the percent of accrued depreciation for the building's age. Finally, multiply this percent times the building cost new on the date of value.

Some published depreciation tables claim to be based in part on studies of actual experience with building demolition or major rehabilitation. Others claim to be based on studies of market sales of old and new buildings. In any case, published tables not relating to the specific market conditions surrounding the subject property would give only a generalized result.

There are a few additional drawbacks to the age-life method of estimating depreciation. The economic life of a structure is difficult to predict because the usefulness and value of a building changes, relative to land values, with both market and zoning changes. Neither can be reliably forecast by an appraiser, investor, or broker. For example, if a community chooses to master plan a neighborhood of old single-family homes for high-density apartment use, the land in time will become valuable for that use, and the homes torn down. Just across the city line, however, the adjacent community keeps the matching homes zoned for low-density homes. Here, demolition of the old homes will be much slower, and more renovation may be noted.

Another disadvantage of the age-life method is that it does not separate curable and incurable loss in value. In a neighborhood with varying amounts of deferred maintenance, common in older areas, an explicit adjustment may be necessary. Despite these issues, the age-life method of calculating depreciation is commonly used, because of its simplicity.

Sales Data (or Market) Method

The **sales data method** is based on the principle that value loss is really determined in the market by buyers and sellers. If old buildings are worth less than new buildings, they will sell for less. In the sales data method, a number of sales are analyzed. This can be done in two different ways. One is simply to study how sale prices (or price per square foot) vary with age. Both graphs and statistical regressions can help with this analysis. The second involves subtracting the estimated land value from the selling prices, to obtain the building's contribution to the sales price. In turn, this amount is compared with the cost of a new building as of the *sale date*. The difference is the loss in value, or accrued depreciation.

To estimate accrued depreciation of a property by the sales data method, follow these steps:

1. *Estimate the land value for each comparable*, by using market sales of vacant land.

2. *Abstract the building portion of the selling price*, by subtracting the land value from the selling price.

3. *Estimate the reproduction or replacement cost new* for the improvements of each comparable sale as of the sale date.

4. *Deduct the abstracted building value from the reproduction/ replacement cost new* for each sale. The difference is the accrued market depreciation estimate for each comparable sale.

Age differences must be accounted for, however, when we compare sales data to the subject property. If we divide the accrued depreciation of each property by the estimated cost new for each property, the result is the percentage of value loss for each sale property. Dividing this answer by the age of the improvements translates into an *annual* percentage loss in value. To complete the analysis, the typical annual percentage loss would be applied to the subject property. Example 12-3 shows how each comparable sale would be analyzed.

The sales data method is the most direct method of estimating accrued depreciation from all causes. It is also the most closely tied to the actual market. If an adequate sample is obtained, the results can be studied by plotting either the total property value, or, better, the building value contributions versus building age on a chart or by using a simple regression analysis program available for desktop computers. (See Figure 12-5 for a study of age and building value loss.)

What about the measurement of value loss resulting from unusual property defects or disadvantages? Although it may be difficult to find sale properties with the same defect as the subject property, either functional or economic obsolescence theoretically can be measured directly from sales. For example, the loss in value from an obsolete architectural style could be estimated by comparing the sales of two similar properties in the same neighborhood, one with the same architectural style as the subject and the other with a different style. The difference in price would be the amount of functional obsolescence caused by the poor style, as estimated by the sales data method (see Figure 12-6).

Cost-to-Cure (or Observed Condition) Method

The **cost-to-cure method** measures the accrued depreciation by the cost to cure or repair any observed building defects. After inspecting the premises, the appraiser tries to identify each building defect, feature,

---

EXAMPLE 12-3 Calculating Depreciation by the Sales Data Method

Reproduction cost new as of the sale date		$200,000
Less: Improvement value:		
Sales price	$240,000	
Less: Land value	– 80,000	
Equals: Improvement value		– $160,000
Equals: Accrued depreciation		$ 40,000
Divided by: Cost new of improvements		÷ $200,000
Equals: Value loss as a decimal		0.20
Value loss as a percent		20%
Divided by: Age of improvements (in years)		÷ 20
Equals: Annual percent depreciation		1%

**Figure 12-5
A Study of Age
and Value Loss.**

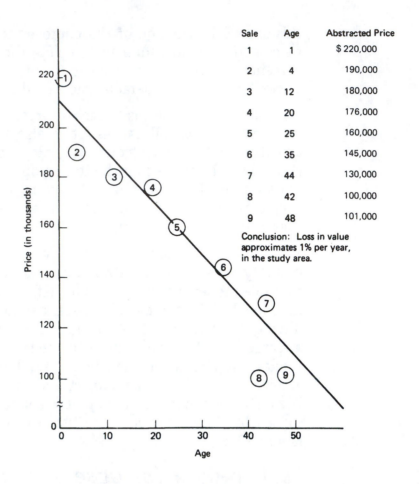

Sale	Age	Abstracted Price
1	1	$ 220,000
2	4	190,000
3	12	180,000
4	20	176,000
5	25	160,000
6	35	145,000
7	44	130,000
8	42	100,000
9	48	101,000

Conclusion: Loss in value
approximates 1% per year,
in the study area.

(a)

(b)

Figure 12-6 Style Difference: Does It Affect Price?

or condition that reduces value. Each is then classified as either physical, functional, or economic. In addition, each defect must be studied to estimate whether it is economically curable or incurable. This method is often used for a specific problem. However, it is rarely used as the sole method, due to its complexity.

Physical Deterioration

When studying physical deterioration, all components of the building belong to one of three categories:

1. *Deferred maintenance*—those components that the market considers to be in need of immediate replacement,

2. *Short-lived components*—those components which will need to be replaced at a future date, and

3. *Long-lived components*—these components are incurable. They will not need present or future replacement; that is, they will last through the economic life of the building.

First, estimate the cost of each item of deferred maintenance work and repairs the market probably will consider necessary to restore the structure to normal condition. Typical items include repainting peeling exterior paint, repairing broken glass, and repairing inoperative building equipment. Larger repairs might include replacing badly worn floor coverings or roofs. Dollar estimates for needed repairs can be derived from contractors' estimates or from cost-estimating services available to the appraiser.

A deferred maintenance item is considered *curable* when the cost to cure or correct is less than or equal to the value added. Also, if the cost to cure is greater than the value added, if the cure allows other components to retain value, it is considered curable. The total estimate of these painting, fix-up, and repair costs is the estimate of the loss in value due to curable physical deterioration.

Next, deterioration in the short-lived components is measured. For example, the building may be 15 years old and have a 35-year remaining economic life estimate. However, the original roof cover has only five years of physical and economic life remaining. So, a buyer would expect to have to replace the roof cover in five years. In order to do so, the purchase price would be reduced to reflect this future cost. Using the age-life method, the roof cover is estimated to be 75 percent depreciated, that is, 15 years of its 20-year life, or 15/20. If the cost to replace the roof cover on the date of value is $10,000, the depreciation would be $7,500.

Finally, the physical depreciation of the long-lived components is estimated by using the data provided above. The 15 years of age is divided by the 50 years of estimated total economic life. Thus, 15 divided by 50 equals 0.30 which is 30 percent depreciation.

In review, by separating components into the three categories—deferred maintenance, short-lived building components, and long-lived building components—the relative loss in value of each can be estimated. Here is how it works:

1. *Estimate the cost new* as of the value date for each building component involved, and separate them into the three categories.

2. *Estimate and subtract* depreciation due to the cost to cure the deferred maintenance.

3. *Estimate and subtract* the depreciation for the short-lived items.

4. *Deduct the cost new* of the deferred maintenance items and the short-lived items from the total cost new. The balance is the cost new for the long-lived components.

5. *For each long-lived component, calculate the percentage of useful life already used up*. Divide the actual chronological age of the component on the value date by its total estimated life.

6. *Multiply the estimated cost new* of the component times the percentage of useful life already used up.

The result is an estimate of the loss of value due to incurable physical deterioration. As you can see, this result will only be as reliable as the estimates of total life and cost of replacement for each component.

Functional Obsolescence

The next category of depreciation to be handled in the cost-to-cure method is functional obsolescence. Functional obsolescence results when there is a problem in the design of a structure or the materials used. The appraiser compares the building being valued with a building constructed in the most cost-effective and functional design as of the date of value. As noted earlier, functional obsolescence may also be divided into curable functional obsolescence and incurable obsolescence. Functional problems can involve either a deficiency in the building, an item that needs to be replaced, or something that is over-built.

This results in five categories of functional obsolescence, three of which are curable and two are incurable.

1. *Curable functional obsolescence—an addition*—some new item must be added or installed to correct what the market considers to be deficient or unsatisfactory.

2. *Curable functional obsolescence—a replacement*—some existing item must be replaced to correct the problem.

3. *Curable functional obsolescence—a superadequacy*—some feature or item is a superadequacy that is economically feasible to correct. *Superadequacy* means that the component is above the standard of quality or quantity that the market considers adequate. For example, a commercial-grade cooking stove in a very small home in a lower-priced neighborhood very likely would cost more than it would contribute to value in the market. The stove could be replaced and sold separately. If it sold for more than its value contribution, the problem is curable and the owner would be prudent to do so.

4. *Incurable functional obsolescence—a deficiency*—where the missing item economically cannot be added. For example, consider a home with a one-car garage and no space for another, in a neighborhood of homes, mostly with two-car garages!

5. *Incurable functional obsolescence—a superadequacy*—for example, if an engineer built a home to live in and decided to build a foundation twice as strong as was customary. Should the house be sold, the market very likely would not pay for the extra reproduction cost amount.

Calculating Functional Obsolescence

The process starts with identifying functional issues that are believed to be a problem in marketing the property, given its market and conditions in that market on the date of value. As noted earlier, in a very hot market, buyers may be more aggressive and less particular. In a very slow market, buyers are able to generate price discounts for any problems. Here are the steps to follow.

1. **Identify the functional problems**. The problem may be general in nature, such as a bad layout or floor plan, or involve specific structural components such as lack of air conditioning, or an inadequate or superadequate mechanical system.

2. **Separate the functional problems into the three categories** of deficiencies (missing components), needed replacements, and superadequacies.

3. **Estimate the market value impact** for each component that has a functional problem; the loss in market value if there is a deficiency, or if a replacement component is needed; and the decrease or increase in value, if any, resulting from a superadequacy. This impact would be based on market or income approach estimates.

4. **For deficiencies, estimate the cost to** install the added component on the date of value (the "cost to cure"). Also estimate the cost new for the added component as if it had been included with the original construction. Compare the cost of the added component with the market value loss. If the value loss without the added component is **greater than** the cost to add it, the problem is *curable*. The depreciation deduction for *curable* functional obsolescence would be the cost to cure, less the cost new if the added component had been installed as part of the original structure.

   If the value loss is **less than** the cost of the added component the problem is economically *incurable*. The depreciation deduction is the market value loss, again less the cost new as if the added component had been installed as part of the original structure.

5. ***For replacements, estimate the cost to replace*** the deficient component on the date of value (again, the "cost to cure"). Also estimate the cost new of the replacement component as if it had been included with the original construction. If the market value loss without replacing the existing component is ***greater than*** the cost to replace it, the problem is *curable*. Conversely, if the value loss is ***less than*** the cost to replace it, the problem is *incurable*.

   The methodology for estimating the functional obsolescence when replacement components are needed is the same as for deficiencies, with one additional step. In order to avoid double counting, the original component's cost remaining after physical deterioration must be added to the functional obsolescence.

6. ***For superadequacies, first consider*** whether it is physically possible to remove the original component, and if the cost to do so (net of any resale or salvage value) is less than the market value impact. If so, the obsolescence is *curable*.

   If you are using ***reproduction cost***, to calculate *curable* functional obsolescence, start with the cost new of the existing component. Deduct any physical deterioration previously charged, add back the cost to cure, and deduct the cost new of the replacement component as if it had been installed as a part of the original building. If the obsolescence is *incurable*, take the cost new of the existing component, deduct any depreciation previously charged, add the market value loss, and deduct the cost new of the replacement component as if it had been installed as a part of the original building, to arrive at the total obsolescence deduction.

   If you are using ***replacement cost*** to calculate the deduction for functional obsolescence, simply use the cost to cure if it is curable, or the market value loss if it is incurable. When replacement cost is used, the cost new does not include the cost of the superadequate component.

Note that the calculation of functional obsolescence depreciation for deficiencies and replacements (and for superadequacies solely when reproduction cost is used) involves deducting the cost new of the added component, as desired by the market, as if it had been installed as part of the original building. Why is this a part of the depreciation calculation? Remember that we are using the cost approach to estimate market value. A comparable building that does not have the problem has the cost of the desired components included in cost new, but the subject property does not. Therefore, the depreciation deduction has to be reduced, to reflect that difference in cost new. In effect, we don't want to have a reduction in value in both cost new and in functional depreciation.

The cost-to-cure method has some very obvious practical limitations. First, individual component life spans that are used to estimate incurable physical deterioration are largely unknown or hard to support. Second, unless component costs have already been estimated by using the unit-in-place or quantity survey method to estimate total costs, it is prohibitively time-consuming! Additionally, the cost-to-cure method cannot measure the loss in value from either incurable functional or economic obsolescence. These losses must be measured separately (by the sales data method or the capitalized income method), adding to the complexity! As a result, as noted earlier, this method is rarely used to calculate total depreciation!

Capitalized Income (or Rental Loss) Method

The **capitalized income method** can be used to estimate either the total loss in value from all causes, or simply the loss in value from a single cause. To estimate loss in value from all causes, a comparison is made between the rent of the subject building on the date of value and the rent of a new or modern building that could take its place. The difference can be called the rental loss attributed to age and/or obsolescence. In practice, a gross income multiplier is normally used to capitalize the rental loss (to convert the rental loss estimate into a value loss estimate). A gross income multiplier (discussed in Section 13.2) would be the typical ratio found between price and gross scheduled rent for similar properties in the area.

To illustrate this method, assume that a single-family residence being appraised suffers from age and functional obsolescence. If its monthly rental is $300 per month less than new competitive properties and a monthly gross income multiplier of 200 is suggested by a market study, the total accrued depreciation could be estimated by the **rental loss method** (see Example 12-5).

The amount of value loss from a single cause or factor can also be estimated. The rental or income loss that results from the unique physical, functional, or economic problem with the building is capitalized. For example, if a poor floor plan results in a $150 per month rent reduction, the value loss from that single cause would be $150 × 200, or $30,000 (assuming that we use the same 200 gross income multiplier as before).

EXAMPLE 12-4 Calculating Curable Functional Obsolescence Deficiency

Cost of enlarging garage on the value date	$30,000
Less: Cost of added garage area if built with the original structure	− 16,000
Equals: Functional obsolescence	$14,000

EXAMPLE 12-5 The Capitalized Income Method

Monthly rental of new competitive property	$ 1,450
Less: Monthly rental of subject property	– 1,150
Equals: Rental loss amount	$ 300
Multiplied by: Gross income multiplier	x 200
Equals: Accrued depreciation	$60,000

When a typical income property is being appraised, the loss in value, or depreciation, can be estimated by a more formal capitalized income method, using net income instead of gross income. The first step is to capitalize the net income that can be attributed to the improvements, after a return for land is deducted. This provides an estimate of the building value. Subtracting this value from the estimated cost to produce the same building will provide the appraiser with the total amount of accrued depreciation for the building. The capitalized income method is actually part of the income approach to value, to be more fully described in Chapters 13 and 14.

12.4 Cost Approach Summary

The cost approach is completed when the estimate of land value is added to the depreciated improvement costs for the property being appraised. Conclusions that might result from the application of the cost approach to a single-family residence are given in Example 12-6.

In practice, how might the cost approach be calculated in a routine appraisal assignment of a home? Figure 12-7 shows the cost approach section that is the same in two commonly used appraisal forms, the URAR and 2055, with numbers filled in. (Note that the 2005 revised form indicates a cost approach is not required by Fannie Mae. However, many lenders still require it.)

The first line in the section indicates that the appraiser is to "provide adequate information for the lender/client to replicate the below cost figure and calculations." This phrase is not very clear. It does indicate that the appraiser is called upon to spell out the basis or source for the cost figures. Certainly, many appraisers will find the best answer will be to reference a published cost manual, as illustrated in Figure 12-7, left section middle. Also, a specific selection of reproduction or replacement cost is now required.

The second line calls for information supporting the opinion of site value. In past decades, appraisers have on occasion used poorly supported land values. The 2005 FNMA form revisions sought to correct this by requiring support for the site value. Ideally, this would require collection and

EXAMPLE 12-6 Cost Approach Summary

Reproduction cost of improvements:

Living area:	1,800 sq. ft. x $75	$135,000
Covered patio:	200 sq. ft. x $25	5,000
Garage:	400 sq. ft. x $30	12,000
Yard improvements:		+ 5,000
Total reproduction cost as if new:		$157,000

Less: accrued depreciation:

Physical deterioration:

curable	$10,000
incurable	5,000

Functional obsolescence:

curable (old-style kitchen)	6,000
incurable (poor floor plan)	5,000

Economic obsolescence: (adjacent to commercial)	+ 10,000
Total accrued depreciation	– $36,000
Equals: Depreciated cost of improvements	$121,000
Plus: Estimated land value from sales comparables	+ 70,000
Equals: Total property value by the cost approach	$191,000

Figure 12-7
Cost Approach Section of the URAR and 2055 Forms.

COST APPROACH TO VALUE (not required by Fannie Mae)				
Provide adequate information for the lender/client to replicate the below cost figures and calculations.				
Support for the opinion of site value (summary of comparable land sales or other methods for estimating site value) The site value was abstracted from improved sales in the neighborhood				
ESTIMATED ☒ REPRODUCTION OR ☐ REPLACEMENT COST NEW	OPINION OF SITE VALUE ....= $			140,000
Source of cost data M & S Residential	Dwelling 1,768 Sq. Ft. @ $ 70.00 ....=$			123,760
Quality rating from cost service Good Effective date of cost data June 200x	Patio 260 Sq. Ft. @ $ 15.00 ....=$			3,900
Comments on Cost Approach (gross living area calculations, depreciation, etc.)	Heated Spa & Deck			9,500
The square foot area computations may be found on the attached	Garage/Carport 484 Sq. Ft. @ $ 35.00 ....=$			16,940
Plan of Improvements.	Total Estimate of Cost-New ....= $			154,100
	Less Physical 17	Functional	External	
	Depreciation 26,197		=$ (	26,197)
	Depreciated Cost of Improvements.................=$			127,903
	"As-is" Value of Site Improvements..............................=$			15,000
Estimated Remaining Economic Life (HUD and VA only) 40-50 Years	Indicated Value By Cost Approach ....=$			282,903

analysis of land sales. It all goes back to the scope of work discussion in Chapter 3. If the client requires a cost approach, or if USPAP requires use of the cost approach in order to reach a credible conclusion, then the scope of work must be expanded, more work performed, and, if performed by a fee appraiser, possibly a bigger fee negotiated.

Notice, too, that the depreciation section of the form calls for a separate amount for each category: physical, functional, and external depreciation! It has not been customary practice to itemize each of the three depreciation categories in recent years, so some change in appraisal practice appears called for. The form does not provide an explicit space for depreciation calculations. Instead, a cost approach comments section is provided, for "gross living area calculations, depreciation, etc."

Finally, notice that the lower left corner entry, for remaining economic life, indicates that it is required for HUD and VA but it is an optional item for Fannie Mae and Freddie Mae, depending on the specific lender client and the client's required scope of work.

SUMMARY

In this chapter, we defined accrued depreciation for appraisal purposes as the estimated loss in market value of the improvements, compared to their replacement or reproduction cost on the date of value. This value loss can be caused by physical deterioration, functional obsolescence, and/or economic obsolescence. Physical deterioration is caused by wear and tear, age, and the elements. Functional obsolescence occurs when faulty design or obsolete features within the property detract from its marketability. This loss in value can be evident from the date of original construction, or it may appear when building styles or features change and the structure no longer meets the desires of the typical buyer in that market. Economic (or external) obsolescence is caused by factors that are outside the property. For example, when rezoning makes existing improvements obsolete (because a more intensive land use becomes legal and is in demand), the resulting loss in building value is categorized as economic obsolescence.

Accrued depreciation may be economically curable or incurable, depending on whether the value increase resulting from the cure is greater than the cost involved. Many types of physical deterioration, such as deferred maintenance, are curable by painting, fixing up, or doing repair work. Some will generate a value increase greater than their cost, making them economically curable. However, certain functional and most economic value loss is incurable.

Accrued depreciation may be estimated by the straight-line/age-life method, the sales data method, the cost-to-cure/observed condition method, or the capitalized income method. Sometimes, a combination of methods can be used.

The straight-line/age-life method relates the loss in value to the estimated life expectancy of the building. Accrued depreciation caused by physical deterioration and "normal" functional and economic obsolescence is estimated by comparing the age of the structure on the date of value with its total projected life. Published depreciation tables are usually based on this method.

The sales data (or market) method measures accrued depreciation directly from the market. This can be performed by analyzing the sale price for the whole property. Also, the price can be broken into components and just the building component analyzed. Here are the steps. First, the land value is subtracted from the sales price of a comparable property, giving the building value contribution. Next, the building value is subtracted from its estimated reproduction or replacement cost, giving the total building value loss. Dividing the building value loss by the new cost gives the percentage of value loss. In turn, the percentage loss is divided by the age of the building, to calculate the annual straight-line depreciation percentage. Functional or economic obsolescence from a single characteristic of a building may also be measured by the sales data method, if sales can be found with the same basic defect as the subject property.

The cost-to-cure method equates the loss in value to the cost of repairs or changes necessary to restore the building to a normal operating condition. Incurable physical deterioration is measured by the observed condition of the components involved. Thus, the cost-to-cure method may be used to measure all types of accrued depreciation except incurable functional and incurable economic obsolescence.

Lastly, the capitalized income method provides an estimate of value loss by relating the value loss to the loss in gross income. A gross income multiplier is usually used to calculate the value loss. The total loss in value may also be estimated by comparing an income-derived building value with the reproduction cost new. Loss in building value because of a single property defect can be estimated by applying a gross income multiplier to the estimated rent loss caused by the particular functional or economic factor involved.

When loss in value from all causes has been estimated, the value contribution of the improvements may be estimated by subtracting the total accrued depreciation from the estimated cost new of the improvements as of the date of value.

IMPORTANT TERMS AND CONCEPTS

Accrued depreciation	*Current-value accounting*
Age-life method	*Deferred maintenance*
Book value	*Depreciation in*
Capitalized income method	*accounting*
Cost basis	*appraisal*
Cost-to-cure method	*Diminished utility*
Curable depreciation	*Economic life*
Curable postponed	*Economic (or external) obsolescence*

Effective age

Functional obsolescence

Locational obsolescence

Loss of utility

Misplaced improvement

Over-improvement

Physical deterioration

Rental loss method

Replacement cost

Reproduction cost

Sales data method

Straight-line method

Superadequacy

Under-improvement

REVIEWING YOUR UNDERSTANDING

1. In accounting practice, depreciation is treated as:
   a.   A theoretical loss in value
   b.   An expense before taxes
   c.   An asset
   d.   Both (a) and (b)

2. In appraisals, depreciation can be defined as:
   a.   A deduction from value
   b.   Actual loss in value compared to cost as if new
   c.   Diminished utility compared to new
   d.   Either (b) or (c)

3. Accrued depreciation is classified into three types or categories. Which of the following should not be included?
   a.   Functional obsolescence
   b.   Economic obsolescence
   c.   Detrimental obsolescence
   d.   Physical deterioration

4. Each category of depreciation can be classified as curable or incurable. This classification is based on:
   a.   The economic feasibility of correcting the condition
   b.   Whether the value loss can be estimated by the cost of needed repair or remodeling
   c.   Both of the above
   d.   Neither of the above

5. A building that is too large for the neighborhood is an example of functional obsolescence, labeled as an over-improvement. Another example of functional obsolescence is:
   a.   A sound building with a worn-out heating system
   b.   A misplaced improvement
   c.   A residence abutting a new freeway
   d.   A building that is likely to cost more to repair than the value added to the structure

6. There are four basic methods for measuring accrued depreciation. Which one of the following would probably be used for estimating the value loss from deferred maintenance?
   a.   The sales data (or market) method
   b.   The straight-line or age-life method
   c.   The cost-to-cure (or observed condition) method
   d.   The capitalized income (or rental loss) method

7. There is a theory that all structures have a total useful life that can be predicted. The method of estimating accrued depreciation based on this theory is:
   a.   The capitalized income (or rental loss) method
   b.   The sales data (or market) method (abstraction method)
   c.   The straight-line or age-life method
   d.   The cost-to-cure (or observed condition) method

8. Occasionally, appraisers base depreciation estimates on the "effective age" of the building rather than the actual age. Effective age is best defined as:
   a.   The average age
   b.   The actual age divided by the age life
   c.   The age of other buildings that are similar in condition and utility
   d.   The chronological age

9. A home was built with only a one-car garage. The lot would allow expanding the garage. Most of the homes in the area have two-car garages. The addition is expected to be about 220 square feet, at a total cost estimated to be $22,000. A new two-car garage should cost, on the date of value, about $60 per square foot. How much is the deduction for curable functional obsolescence?
   a. $13,200
   b. $8,800
   c. $26,400
   d. $22,000

10. An older home had a new roof installed about 15 years ago. However, many of the homes in the neighborhood have new roofs. A roofing contractor estimated the cost of a new roof to be $17,000, but reported the roof was likely to last another five years. What is the deduction for incurable physical deterioration on the date of value?
    a. $12,750
    b. $17,000
    c. $4,250
    d.   There is no incurable physical deterioration.

PRACTICAL APPLICATIONS

As we like to remind you, review the exercise at the end of the preceding chapter, and the work that you have performed to date.

This assignment moves to the task of estimating the depreciation for the cost new of the building. It will be reported on the cost approach section on page 3 of the URAR form, as shown in Figure 12-7. The first step is to review your decision in the last exercise to use either the replacement or reproduction cost. You will remember reading in this chapter that this decision changes how you handle depreciation.

Next, review the information on your subject property, with an eye to the issues that influence depreciation, such as age, condition, layout, and so on. Review the text and the form, so that the depreciation categories are clear to you. Notice that the form calls for you to add site improvements on an as-is basis, which means net of any depreciation. So, the site improvements do not get depreciated with the building and the garage. Consider which depreciation categories may be applicable to your subject property. Finally, you will make the calculations and enter the cost information into the spaces in the form.

Notice that the form is a pretty limited presentation. As you may have done for the last exercise, consider using another form as a template or guide to help you process the depreciation information. The choices include the Swift Estimator form, in ClickFORMS, in the Forms Library, under "Swift Estimator" and then "Swift Estimator Residential." Another is in the "New AI Forms" heading, as "Cost Approach." A third is in the "Addendums" heading, and then "Cost Approach."

And, if you have selected a condo, co-op, or apartment unit as your subject property, you must review what part of the building that you included in your estimate of cost new, as this is the "building" that you must depreciate.

The first step is nearly always to deduct for normal age-related physical depreciation. The amount can vary by property type, size, and location. Developing an accurate number can be done in at least three ways. Consider locating about ten sales of relatively similar homes with wide differences in age. Deduct an approximate value of the land from each sale price. Next, graph the price per square foot on the vertical, and age on the horizontal. You should see the dots indicate declining prices with greater age. Roughly estimate what the drop is over the entire time period, and calculate it as a percent of the sale with the newest building. (Divide the total drop in dollars per square foot by the sale price in dollars per square foot of the newest building.) Then divide that total percentage drop by the number of years between the newest and oldest buildings, to get an annual percent rate of decline in value, or depreciation. Consider using that annual percentage loss in value as the basis for your adjustment for the subject property's normal physical deterioration.

Next, review your subject property and consider whether it suffers from deferred maintenance, in excess of what is typical for a home of that age. If you conclude that some appears to be present, estimate the cost to renovate the property as needed. Do *not* include any remodeling or extensive renovation, as that would more than offset the deferred maintenance. To locate renovation cost information, consider going to the local library, or the nearest college or university library, to see if either has remodeling cost books. Some remodeling cost information is provided on websites focused on renovation issues. Try searching for "maintenance costs" or "remodeling costs" in your browser search bar.

Finally, consider if your subject property may have any loss in value as a result of functional or economic/locational depreciation. Review the material in the text on these subjects. Consider how you might be able to estimate an amount for such a loss in value. There is no consistent method; each case is somewhat different. Remember that your choices are to base the depreciation estimate on analysis of sales, costs, or income impacts.

The last step is to total the various depreciation amounts into a total estimated depreciation, and enter it into the form.

As we note at the end of each exercise, it is best not to get ahead of yourself. So, do not enter information in the later sections of the report until you have read the chapter(s) that covers that topic. However, it is a good idea to look ahead, so that you start thinking about the information that you will need.

Reminder: If you have questions about the program, review the manuals and help information that were on the program CD. Also, go to http://www.bradfordsoftware.com, click on "Services" at the upper right, and then on "ClickFORMS Training Programs" in the middle of the "Services" page.

CHAPTER 13
THE INCOME APPROACH

PREVIEW

The income approach is based on the principle of anticipation. This principle states that the value of any property is based on the *present worth of future benefits*. When an owner's benefits are in the form of money, as is the case with investment or income property, the value of the future benefits may be measured by the amount of income the property is expected to produce. With property such as single-family homes, the future benefits of ownership usually consist instead of such *amenities* as shelter, security, and pride of ownership. Since these benefits are intangible, they usually cannot be valued by the income approach.

In this chapter, we provide an overview of the income approach and outline how appraisers estimate income and expenses. This discussion of the income approach will be continued in Chapter 14, where we explain how a property's income is capitalized. This term means how income is converted into an estimate of value.

OBJECTIVES

When you have completed this chapter you should be able to:

1. Distinguish between the tangible and intangible benefits of property ownership.

2. Name the six steps in the income approach to value.

3. Explain the use of gross income multipliers in the income approach.

4. Define the terms *contract rent* and *market rent* as used in appraisals.

5. Name the three main categories of expenses and give examples of items in each.

6. Outline the procedure used for reconstructing the owner's operating statement.

13.1 Introducing Income Property and Its Appraisal

How is income property distinguished from other types of property? What are the motives and benefits of ownership? These are some of the questions we should consider in order to understand and properly apply the income approach.

Types of Income Property

Any type of real estate may be purchased for income and/or investment purposes. One common reason given for buying a single-family home is that it can easily be converted to a rental property and retained for the possible benefits of long-term value appreciation. However, the term ***income property*** traditionally is reserved for property that is purchased primarily for its income. The properties in Figure 13-1 are good examples of income-producing properties.

Note that most types of income-generating property could also be purchased by an owner-user. Such a buyer would not be as interested in the property's income as an investor-buyer would be. And some investment property (such as vacant land) may be bought to hold and resell, with no or little interim income.

A multiple-family residential property is the most common type of income property. However, income property also includes retail, office, and industrial properties. Thus, a list of property types usually treated as income property should include the following:

**Figure 13-1
Types of Income
Property.**

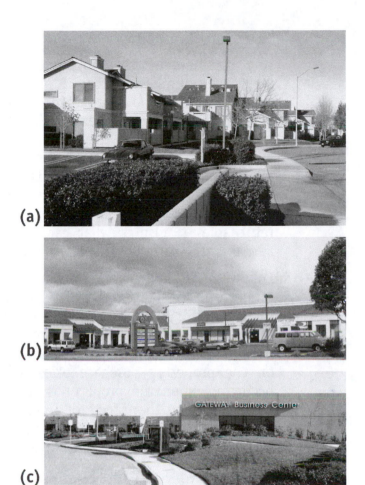

(a)

(b)

(c)

1. *Multiple-family residential*, including large and small apartment buildings.
2. *Commercial buildings*, including stores, offices, medical offices, convalescent hospitals, hotel and motel properties, and shopping centers.
3. *Industrial properties*, such as warehouses and factories.

Motives and Benefits of Ownership

People acquire income property for many different reasons. Some are motivated to invest as a way to "save for a rainy day"; others might consider real estate as either an investment made for a profit or a necessary component of a family business. In other words, the real estate investment market is very diverse and consists of both part-time and full-time investors. As in other investment fields, the small, easy-to-manage holdings are normally sought by the casual or part-time investor, and the large and more complex ones by the full-time professional investor. The benefits of owning income or investment property also vary, in part because they can be either tangible or intangible.

Tangible Benefits

Any income-generating investment can be compared to a personal savings account, where the interest earned on the savings account is the obvious **tangible benefit**. Since the earnings from the savings account are not reduced by any expenses (ignoring personal income taxes for now), we can describe these earnings as a "net" income. Such earnings are referred to simply as the *return on the investment*. The depositor makes the investment, and the interest is the return on that investment. What happens when the depositor needs his or her money back for some other purpose? Since the typical savings account deposit is guaranteed returnable, it insures what can be referred to as the *return of the investment*, also called **recapture** or **capital recovery** (see Figure 13-2).

Following the savings account analogy, the tangible benefits of income property ownership consist of 1) a **return on investment** (which is like interest) and 2) a **return of investment** (allowing the investment funds to be recovered or recaptured). When prices are not changing, the annual net income from an investment property theoretically provides the *return on* the property's purchase price, with *return of* the purchase funds occurring when the property is resold. However, this pattern can be complicated by the effects of financing, income tax, and the inflation or deflation of prices. These two concepts—return on and return of the investment—will be more fully covered in the next chapter.

Figure 13-2 Return on and Return of Investment—Savings Account Example.

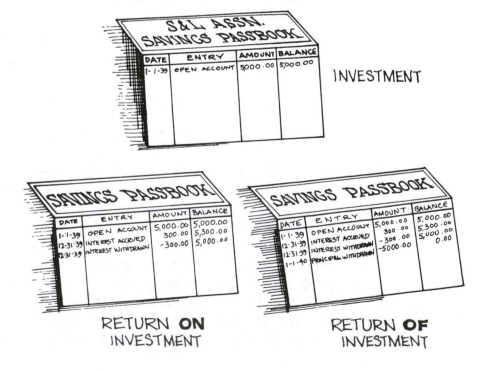

Intangible Benefits

Relatively small income properties, such as two- to ten-unit apartment buildings, are often acquired for both tangible and *intangible benefits*. Retired or semi-retired couples (and in recent years younger employed people) purchase such properties, live in one unit, and rent out the others. Expenses can be kept low by the owner-operators doing their own building maintenance and upkeep. Even so, owners of such properties must often be satisfied with a low return on their investment. They usually settle for less because of the intangible benefits involved. For example, owners who occupy one unit of a small investment property may gain many of the same amenities they would if they lived in a single-family residence. Certainly, pride of ownership and a sense of security can be expected, but there may also be an opportunity for some to develop and apply their management skills.

In summary, the benefits of owning income property may be both tangible and intangible. The mixture of benefits depends on the size and type of the investment. In many cases, the tangible income benefits are enhanced by an opportunity for income tax shelter and for property value appreciation. Such advantages will be more fully explored in the next chapter, in the section entitled "Comparing Investment Property."

The Income-Value Relationship

It is important at this point in our discussion of income property to explore more fully the economic relationship between income and value.

Utility, Income, and Value

Utility is one of the basic characteristics of value. For any commodity to have market value, it must have utility or usefulness. Everything else being equal, the greater the utility, the greater the value. In the case of income property, the utility of a property often can best be measured by the rental income it can produce.

What is income? Income may be defined as the annual money received, or as the flow of funds from an investment each time period. In the case of the savings account mentioned earlier, the expense-free earnings are the income. So are the dividends paid on stocks. With real estate investments, the net rent typically is the income.

The investor usually wants to earn income each year in the future (or whatever time period is being studied). So, the appraiser could prepare an estimate of the income for each future time period. Often, however, the market will use just one year's income, as representative of all the future years.

What is value? In economic theory, value is described as the **present worth of future benefits**. For income-producing properties, value can also be described as the relationship between the amount of net income produced and the rate of *return on investment* required by the typical investor.

Examples of Monetary Relationships

The savings account example clearly illustrates the direct relationship between value, income, and the rate of return on investment. A savings account of $2,000, earning an 8 percent annual rate of interest, would earn $160 in one year—because 8 percent times $2,000 equals $160. If someone told us only the annual earnings and the rate of interest, we would still be able to figure out the amount of money on deposit in the account because of the fixed relationship between the three numbers. The annual income of $160, divided by the 8 percent rate of interest, equals $2,000 that is the amount on deposit.

Let us apply the monetary relationship described here to investment real estate. Assume that the only tangible return on a particular real estate investment is in the form of the annual income. Assume that the income is expected to stay level (the same each year). For a property earning $50,000 per year, if a 10 percent annual rate of return on investment is required, the value would be $500,000. Why? Because $50,000 is 10 percent of $500,000, or $50,000 divided by 10 percent equals $500,000. In both examples, we can again see that value can be described by the relationship between the amount of return and the rate of return on investment (when the income stays the same each year). The amount of value can be expressed by a simple *income capitalization* formula:

$$\text{Value} = \frac{\text{Income}}{\text{Rate of Return}}$$

Alternatively,

$$\text{Income} = \text{Rate} \times \text{Value}$$

However, real estate investments are rarely as simple as deposits in a savings account. For example, the benefits available to the real estate investor are not always limited to just the annual income, as we pointed out earlier. And it is important to recognize that the income each period often changes, either up or down. For this reason, the relationship between income amounts and rates of return on investment is often complex. This topic will be discussed further in the next chapter.

Methods of Appraising Income Property

When the primary benefit of real estate ownership is in the form of monthly or annual income, appraisers most often rely on the income (or **capitalization**) approach as an indication of value. In the following pages of this section, we shall generally describe how the income approach is applied. The next section will discuss a second method of appraising property based on its income, which is known as the gross income multiplier. Introduced in Chapter 9, the GIM method is commonly used as the income approach in the appraisal of single-family residential properties, duplexes, and small apartments.

The Income (Capitalization) Approach

The income approach is always based on the mathematical relationship between value, income, and the rate of return on investment. However, this relationship can be explored in many different ways. One of the simplest is called *Direct Capitalization*. A property earning $40,000 per year on the date of value, at an annual *capitalization rate* of 10 percent, can be said to have a value of $400,000. Dividing the net income by a capitalization rate is one method of income capitalization. Note that the capitalization rate is not at all the same as a rate of return on investment. Future changes in income could make the return on investment more or less than the capitalization rate. We shall return to this important concept a number of times! Here are the six basic steps in the income approach. See the discussion in Section 13.3 about the issues in making these estimates!

1. *Estimate the potential gross annual income* that the property is capable of producing.

2. *Estimate the typical vacancy and collection loss.*

3. *Subtract the estimated vacancy and collection loss from* gross income to arrive at the *effective gross income*.

4. *Estimate annual operating expenses* and subtract them from the effective gross income to calculate the *net operating income*.

5. *Analyze comparable investments* to arrive at a *capitalization rate* and *capitalization method* appropriate for the subject property.

6. *Divide the net operating income by the capitalization* rate to obtain the opinion of capitalized value.

Let us assume that we are appraising a 20-unit apartment house. It has a potential annual gross income of $150,000 and a predicted typical vacancy and collection loss amounting to $8,000 per year. Annual expenses of $45,000 can be expected, including property taxes. Our analyses indicate that an 8 percent capitalization rate is appropriate using the direct capitalization method already discussed. (Other capitalization methods will be explained in Chapter 14.) Our calculations are shown in Example 13-1.

Definition of Terms Used in Income Capitalization

At this stage of our discussion of income property and its appraisal, it is appropriate to define the terms used in income capitalization. Some additional terms will be covered in Chapter 14. Each of these terms is actually more complex than the definition, which is discussed later in the chapter.

EXAMPLE 13-1 Direct Capitalization

Potential gross income	$150,000
Less: Vacancy and collection loss	− $8,000
Equals: Effective gross income	$142,000
Less: Annual operating expenses (including property taxes)	− $45,000
Equals: Net operating income	$97,000
Divided by:	÷ .08
Equals: Capitalization rate	$1,212,500
Rounded: Value estimate	$1,210,000

Potential annual gross income: potential or scheduled rent, plus anticipated service income.

Vacancy and collection losses: amounts of potential gross income that will not be realized because of vacant tenant space, bad debts, and other collection losses.

Effective gross income: the income remaining after subtracting vacancy and collection loss from the potential gross income.

Operating expenses: the expenses required to continue the operation of the property and maintain its income.

Net operating income: the effective gross income less the operating expenses.

Capitalization rate: the rate, percentage, or ratio used to convert income into its value equivalent.

Real estate appraisal using the income approach requires a careful estimate of income and expenses, to be discussed later in Sections 13.3 and 13.4. Section 13.2 continues the discussion of gross rents, as part of the focus on the gross income multiplier capitalization method.

13.2 Gross Income Multiplier Analysis

The gross income multiplier method is one of the most popular income capitalization methods in use by the real estate practitioner. Multipliers are easy to understand and often readily available.

What is a gross income multiplier (often abbreviated as GIM)? As we described in Chapter 9, the **gross income multiplier** is a unit of comparison. It helps the appraiser compare the subject property to the sale properties, by using an economic measurement of the property's usefulness—in this case, the rent. Quite simply, it is the ratio of the selling price to the gross income.

$$\text{Gross Income Multiplier} = \frac{\text{Sales Price}}{\text{Gross of Income}}$$

Using either term—gross income or gross rent multiplier (GIM or GRM) —is acceptable. GRM is the older, and used more by small income-property brokers. GIM is considered to be more precise, so use of this term is increasing. The appraiser must expect to encounter both terms! We will use GIM.

Deriving Gross Income Multipliers

The recommended procedure for deriving gross income multipliers is as follows:

1. *Make an adequate search for comparable sales.* At least three sales, with sale dates close to the date of value, are desired. A larger sample is often preferred.
2. *Estimate the market rents for each comparable* as of the time of sale (discussed in Section 13.3), and add other income, if any.
3. *Divide the selling price for each comparable* (adjusted for any unusual terms) by its gross income.
4. *The result* is called the gross income multiplier and is abbreviated GIM.

Gross income multipliers may be calculated using either the annual or monthly rent. Monthly rent is customarily used in the appraisal of single-family residential property, but the annual rent is customarily used in appraisals of other types of property. One must be careful using the monthly rent if there is much seasonal variation in rents. The GIM using summer rents could be very different from the GIM calculated using winter rents! This topic is explored further in Section 13.3.

The GIM: Calculated with Market Rents versus Actual Rents

Except where rents are controlled by local ordinance, there is a good reason for calculating the gross rent multiplier using the theoretical market rents, rather than the actual rents at the date of sale. When market rents are rising rapidly, some landlords keep their rents moving up with the market, while other landlords lag behind. At the time of sale, then, similar buildings can sell at greatly different multiples of actual rent. Although properties with a lagging rent schedule may sell for less because of the time it takes to bring rents up to market level, GIMs based on their market rents are often more reliable than those based on existing or actual rent. It is desirable to check both, as markets can rely on either. Also, note the discussion in Section 13.3 about using market rents at the date of value, compared with estimating total likely rents for the twelve months after the date of value.

Selecting and Using Gross Income Multipliers

The gross income or rent multiplier can be an effective tool for estimating market value when properties are commonly bought and sold on the basis of gross income. Because the GIM is easy to apply, it seems easy to select. However, selecting the appropriate multiplier requires a good understanding of the property characteristics that cause the multiplier to change.

The gross income multiplier should be based on the actual selling price of the comparable property, adjusted only for unusual financing and other factors affecting its cash equivalent price. Historically, it was considered undesirable to adjust property sales prices for time and physical differences before calculating GIMs. However, the calculated multipliers often vary, and the appraiser must seek the reasons for this variation, just as with all units of comparison. Here are the most important reasons:

1. *Location and neighborhood.* The buyer's impression of risk relative to other investments and the prospects for value appreciation are influenced by the location and neighborhood. Higher multipliers are associated with better locations. Rent control may also be a factor in the considered risk of an investment. Also, if rent control has affected some building's rents much more than others, causing different expense ratios, GIMs probably will not be a reliable valuation method.

2. *Intangible amenities.* Multipliers are typically higher for property bought for owner occupancy or other notable intangible benefits. Examples might be a prestigious address, a famous building, a structure of unusual charm, an apartment building with a superior owner's unit, and so on.

3. *Expense ratio.* Properties with lower operating expenses will normally sell for a higher gross multiplier. Investors are interested in the net, not the gross, income. Thus, a two story walk-up apartment building probably has a different expense ratio, and GIM, than a four story elevator building. Example 13-2 demonstrates the effect a change in the expense ratio has on the GIM.

4. *Number of dwelling or store units.* The number of units (or property size) tends to identify which investment market the property would probably sell in; it also affects operating efficiency. Very small complexes often sell at higher than average multipliers because of the intangible amenities discussed earlier in this chapter.

5. *Size per unit.* Buildings with small dwelling units, offices, or stores can have higher operating costs and often higher turnover rates; multipliers are often lower than average.

6. *Services included.* Utilities, furniture, and other services that are sometimes provided by the landlord will increase the operating costs relative to buildings where tenants pay for them but also increase the gross income. Hence, multipliers can change either way.

EXAMPLE 13-2 Effect of Expenses on the Gross Income Multiplier

Gross Rent	Expenses (%)	Net Income	Capitalization Rate (%)	Price	GIM
$60,000	30%	$42,000	7%	$600,000	10.0
60,000	40%	36,000	7%	514,000	8.6
60,000	50%	30,000	7%	428,500	7.1

Even the most carefully chosen group of sales can produce a wide range of gross income multipliers. Which is right for the subject property? Estimating the appropriate multiplier can be a problem! However, essentially we apply the same techniques that are used in the sales comparison approach when selecting other economic units of comparison. A simple rule is to give the greatest weight to the sales whose characteristics are the closest to those of the subject property. However, where a single factor, such as the number of units or the average square-foot size per unit, varies greatly between the comparable sales, it is a good idea to plot the sales on a graph, or even construct a linear regression equation for the GIM. The GIM can vary with the number of units, as we said earlier, getting smaller as the number of units gets larger. A similar pattern of a declining GIM is sometimes noted as the average apartment unit size declines. In either case, once such a direct relationship between the GIM and the variable is identified, a more intelligent choice of multipliers can be made.

Once you have arrived at an appropriate multiplier for the subject property, the last step is to multiply it times the monthly or annual projected market rent. The result is the indicated value of the subject property. See Example 13-3. (And note the issues involved in selecting the income to use, discussed in Section 13.3!)

EXAMPLE 13-3 Gross Income Multiplier:
Derivation and Use

A. Given:

Assume that you are appraising a ten-unit unfurnished apartment building with a scheduled annual gross rent of $84,000. A rent survey suggests that the schedule agrees with the prevailing market rents in the area. The unit rents are the only source of income.

The comparable sales and their market rents as of the time of sale have been analyzed. The results follow.

Comparable Number	Number of Furnished Units	Number of Unfurnished Units	Price	Scheduled Gross Rent	Gross Rent Multiplier
1	10	—	$729,000	$90,000	8.1
2	—	9	800,000	80,000	10.0
3	—	5	544,500	45,000	12.1
4	4	8	977,500	115,000	8.5
5	—	12	950,000	100,000	9.5

B. Analysis:

Assigning the most weight to comparables 2 and 5 because they are most similar to the subject property, a gross income multiplier (GIM) of 9.75 is indicated. Comparables 1 and 4 were not stressed because they involved furnished units. Comparable 3 is not considered competitive with the subject because it is a smaller project, likely to appeal to a different investor market.

C. Conclusion:

The annual gross is $84,000. Multiplied by the selected multiplier of 9.75 equals $819,000 (rounded).

13.3 Estimating Gross Income and Market Rent

The first step in the income approach is to estimate the **gross income**. This will define the property's potential production, measured in rent dollars. That is why the gross income estimate is sometimes referred to as an *income forecast*. It is also known as **potential gross income**.

The potential gross income of a property refers to the total income that could be generated, assuming 100 percent occupancy. Such income is often composed of two parts: rent for tenant space and payment for services or miscellaneous income. The rent for tenant space is the sum total of all the scheduled rental amounts, including tenant parking spaces. It is sometimes referred to as the **rent roll** in properties with multiple tenants. *Service income* refers to money collected for laundry facilities, vending machines, utilities sold to tenants, and other incidental services.

If market rents are changing, note that the market rents for the property at the time of the date of value are likely to have changed twelve months later. Accordingly, using the monthly rent roll on the date of value times twelve, to estimate the projected gross income for the following twelve months, will not be as accurate as adjusting for the change.

Contract versus Market Rent

Income property is often sold subject to existing leases and other contractual arrangements between the landlord and tenant(s). We define the rent actually being paid in such cases as the **contract rent**. Selling prices are often influenced by the terms of an existing lease, going up if terms are favorable to the landlord or down if favorable to the tenant. In other words, the price tends to reflect the property rights being sold!

In many appraisals, the property is first valued as if it were free from all encumbrances, except for public controls and deed restrictions shown on public records. For this reason, market rent is used to estimate the value of all of the property rights; then, any adjustments relevant to the specific rights being appraised can be made. Appraisal of leased property will be discussed further in Chapter 17. The point here is that estimating market rent for the subject property nearly always is an essential step in the income approach.

Market Rent Defined

Market rent is the rental income the property (or individual dwelling units, stores, or offices) would most probably command, if placed for rent on the open market as of the effective date of the appraisal. This *potential gross rent* is the most common rent figure used in appraisals. It assumes not only that the subject property will be available, that is, unencumbered by any lease, but also that it is being efficiently managed.

(Market rent in the past was sometimes referred to as "economic" rent, but this term is no longer used in appraisal. It has another meaning in economics.)

Understanding Contract Rent

Technically, contract rent means rent being paid under some form of contract that is binding on both owners and tenants. Such rental agreements range from simple oral contracts to complex leases that are beyond the scope of this book. In researching rental information, appraisers need to understand the common types of rental contracts.

A tenant's right to occupy space may result from a month-to-month oral agreement, a short-term written lease, or a long-term lease agreement. Multiple-family residential and commercial tenants usually occupy their space under month-to-month agreements or short-term leases ranging up to three to five years. Tenants of more specialized properties, such as chain restaurants and department stores, are often willing to sign long-term leases of ten years or more. As noted in Section 2.4, agreements for longer time periods generally must be in writing to be enforceable.

Types of Leases

Leases are often described by the pattern that is made by the future rents. The most common types of leases encountered by appraisers are the straight lease, the step-up lease, the CPI lease, and the percentage lease, shown in Figure 13-3. Combinations of these lease forms are common.

The ***straight (or "flat") lease*** is one in which the monthly or annual rent is a fixed amount that stays the same over the entire ***lease term*** (the life of the lease). The ***step-up (or "graduated") lease*** is a more popular type of lease today, because it provides the landlord some protection from inflation while giving the tenant certain or fixed future rents. Such a lease agreement establishes progressively higher rental amounts (rarely, lower amounts) for different segments of the lease term. For example, a lease might call for a rental of $750 per month for the first two years, then $850 per month for the third and fourth year, and $950 per month for the fifth and sixth year.

For the ***CPI lease***, the rentals step up (or down) with the Consumer Price Index (CPI) or some other general economic measure of inflation. Sometimes, a CPI lease will have a cap, or limit on the maximum annual increase. Occasionally, the increase will not be the full CPI percentage change, but rather a portion, such as "two-thirds of the CPI." And indexes other than the national CPI can be used.

Figure 13-3
Types of Leases.

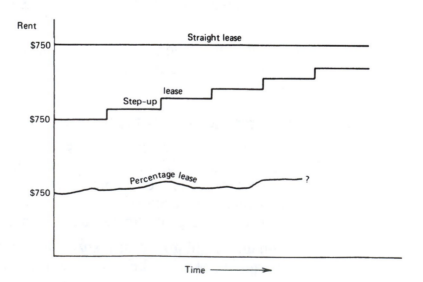

The **percentage lease** fixes the rent as a stipulated percentage of the tenant's economic activity, usually the gross sales of goods and services offered by the tenant. Most percentage leases require a certain *base rent* regardless of sales volume. Typically, this minimum rent is credited against the percentage rent due (rather than the percentage rent being *in addition to* the base rent), but the appraiser tries to verify this. The actual percentage rate generally follows standardized guidelines for each type of tenant, depending on typical profit margins and the volume of business. Percentage rentals range from a low of 2 to 4 percent of gross sales for large-volume department store retailers to as high as 50 to 75 percent for parking lot operators. Most common retail tenancies might pay from 5 to 10 percent of gross sales under percentage lease agreements.

When the existing leases and rental payments are analyzed and compared with past rent payments, appraisers use special terms to describe the various types of rent payments. **Minimum rent** describes the base rent—the minimum amount paid under a percentage lease. **Overage rent** describes the amounts paid over and above the base rent, and **excess rent** is the amount by which the total contract rent exceeds market rent. Most of these terms are of concern only to appraisers performing commercial-industrial appraisals.

When analyzing a lease (whether for comparable data or for the subject property), the appraiser needs to determine who is responsible for paying the various expenses. In apartment rentals, the usual lease terms hold the landlord responsible for all expenses, except for water and gas bills that are separately metered for the tenant's space. However, in commercial and industrial leases, the landlord and tenant may share many expense costs. The trend is to have the tenants pay more or all of the building expenses directly. Operating costs such as maintenance, insurance, and taxes will be discussed later in this chapter.

Review: A Summary of Key Income and Lease Terms

- *Base rent*—a fixed rent, in a percentage lease, to be paid regardless of the sales volume.
- *Contract rent*—the rent to be paid due to a lease.
- *CPI lease*—a lease where the rent increases or decreases, usually each year, according to the change in some economic index, usually the Consumer Price Index.
- *Excess rent*—the amount of contract rent that is above the market rent level.
- *Minimum rent*—see base rent.
- *Overage rent*—the amount of rent paid that is over the base rent amount.

- *Percentage lease*—a lease where the rent is defined as a percent of the tenant's sales volume.

- *Potential gross rent*—the most probable rent that the building can generate, before allowance for vacancy and collection loss.

- *Rent roll*—the actual rent being paid, by unit or space, at a defined date.

- *Step-up (graduated) lease*—a lease where the rent increases or decreases by defined dollar amounts at defined time intervals.

- *Straight (flat) lease*—a lease where the rent stays the same for the entire lease term.

Choosing the Time Period for the Gross Income Estimate

When the appraiser seeks to estimate the market rent for a property, it is necessary to decide what time period the estimate is to cover. Usually, it will be the income for one year—12 months—but which 12 months?

What Are the Possibilities?

Often, the appraiser will obtain income and expense numbers from the owner or the property manager. For larger properties, a sophisticated accounting system may be able to provide data for the 12 months just before the date of value. Owners of smaller properties, however, commonly provide the statement prepared for income tax purposes. This is usually the calendar year that ended before the date of value. For example, if the date of value is in November, the data from the prior year is not very current!

The Rent Roll. The appraiser also may receive a list of the tenants and their rents—called a *rent roll*—as of, say, the first of the month. But the rent roll only reflects what the tenants are paying at that point in time. The manager might have just sent out a notice letter, sharply increasing the rents as of the next month. Also, as noted earlier, when market rents are rising rapidly, some landlords keep their rents moving up with the market, while other landlords lag behind. Some owners will raise the rents on long-term tenants more slowly, or to a lower level, than for new tenants. So, even though the rent roll is as of a time very close to the date of value, it still could fail to give a good picture of the property's income-generating potential.

The Market Rent Roll. Clearly, then, the appraiser must not focus just on the actual financial results, on the date of value and before. In addition, it is very important to consider the market. Usually, the rent schedule should be adjusted to reflect the prevailing market rent (defined below). This means that the building's actual rent schedules should be revised to market rents. (However, if the property is under a city or county rent control ordinance, the existing rent schedule would generally be used.) Remember that this adjustment is needed in estimating the fee simple value. If the property is leased, and the assignment is to estimate the value of the leased fee, then a rent roll as leased must also be prepared.

Another market issue that must be investigated is the trend in rents. The previous year's income and expense statement will be more useful if you understand what has happened to market rents since. And updating the actual rent roll to a market-level rent roll will be performed more accurately and easily if the trend in market rents is established.

The Importance of Future Income. Remember that in Section 13.1, we noted that market value can be described as the present worth of future benefits! Real estate is an investment that usually pays a return over a long time period. So, the buyer really is motivated by the anticipated future income, not the past income, nor the present income.

For example, if market rents are changing, note that the market rents for the property at the time of the date of value are likely to have changed by twelve months later. Accordingly, using the monthly market rent roll on the date of value times twelve, to estimate the projected gross income for the year, will not be as accurate as adjusting for the change. Consciously or unconsciously, the buyer is looking both at the current income and expenses, and also at what is likely to happen in the future.

Ideally, then, the appraiser wants to estimate what the market buyers for property like this believe future rents will be. This statement holds for all income approach values, whether estimated using a Gross Income Multiplier, or capitalized using a single year's income or a year-by-year projected cash flow.

How to Select a Gross Rent Number

Given all of the possible gross income numbers suggested above, what should an appraiser do? Are there any clear rules or concepts that should be followed?

Rule 1—The More Data, the Better. Clearly, the more you know about the past and present income and the market, the better prepared you will be to estimate the future rent. For example, appraisers prefer to have more than one year's income and expense statement, in case there is some unusual circumstance, unknown to you, that distorts the figures. Often, three years' data will be provided. If income or expenses are particularly variable, data for the past five years would be even better (if available).

Just the income and expense statement alone is not as good as also having the rent roll as of the date of value. When each rent was last changed, and by how much, makes the rent roll information even more dynamic and useful.

And, as noted above, it is very important to understand how the actual rents on the date of value compare to market rents. Further, to allow for the investor's view of the future, we need to know how market rents are changing and where the market believes the rents will go in the future.

All in all, it is hard to feel comfortable in performing the income approach unless these several possible rent numbers have been compared with one another. There will be times when only limited past income and expense data are available. The appraiser must try to compensate for that in researching market trends. It is also desirable to note the missing data in the report, and document in the file the attempt to obtain it.

Rule 2—Always Be Aware of the Market. There will always be assignments where the level of market rents will play a small role. Contract rents will appear to be so important that the study of market rents might be minimized or even dropped. However, nearly always, this will be a mistake.

As an example, consider two investment properties that your client is thinking of buying. Both are listed for about the same price and generate about the same net income. Both are leased to a major corporation with excellent credit. The leases started over ten years ago and have another thirty years to run. The tenant pays all expenses for both properties.

Does knowing market rent matter? It could. One property is located in a growing and prosperous community where market rents have doubled since the lease was signed. The other property is located in a depressed area which has seen relatively high unemployment rates and some out-migration. Here, market rents are at least 20 percent below the contract rent. Given the equal list prices, what should your client do?

Rule 3—Be Consistent. This is the critical rule! If you are performing a gross income multiplier (GIM) analysis, and the GIMs were calculated using the rent roll at the time of the listing, you must apply that data to the subject property the same way. Using the projected income for the twelve months after the date of value would be inconsistent and a mistake!

This rule also applies to capitalization of one year's income, using a capitalization rate that was derived from analysis of sales. The appraiser needs to try to determine how the sale capitalization rates were calculated: What was the time period for the income used, and for the expenses as well? The same time period needs to be used in calculating the income and expenses for the subject property. Only then can the market-derived capitalization rates be applied to the subject property's income in a consistent manner.

How to Make a Rent Survey

An estimate of market rent should be based on a survey of the rent charged by competing properties in the neighborhood. When possible, you should choose buildings of the same general age, design, services, and amenities as the subject, so that the rentals can be directly compared with those charged for the subject property's space. For some appraisals, the rental schedules of the comparables used in the sales comparison approach can be incorporated into the rental study.

For each property surveyed, the appraiser should record the location and building description, along with the schedule of existing rents and the vacancy history. The number of units and their size, age, condition, and quality should be noted, along with the specific amenities offered to tenants. For multi-family residential properties, it is very important to note any units subject to either a lease or rent control. Of course, for most retail, office, or industrial buildings, knowing about leases is critical. Also, such features as parking and recreation facilities are important to note and describe (see Figure 13-4).

As shown on the sample rent survey form, apartment units are usually listed by the number of bedrooms and baths, specifying whether each unit is rented furnished or unfurnished. The dates that the spaces were first occupied by the existing tenants and the last date of rent adjustment may also be noted. In a rapidly changing market, this information is needed to suggest when a rental increase might be practical. And it is necessary in order to estimate market rents as of the date of value. If deposits and/or leases are required, record these data, too. Of course, tenant obligations to pay utilities, and/or any rent concessions or free rent agreements made by the landlord, have a direct effect on the rent schedule and must not be overlooked.

In commercial properties, tenant improvements can have a notable effect on the rent schedules of properties surveyed, as well as on the market rent estimate for the subject property. The original rent often depends on who pays the costs of installing items such as partitions, floor covering, lighting, and air conditioning. When these have been installed by the tenant of the surveyed property, the rent will be less than if the

**Figure 13-4
A Sample
Rental Survey.**

MULTIFAMILY RENTAL SURVEY FORM

PROJECT NAME Brookdale Manor   **Address:** 3615 N. Marcus Blvd., Watertown **Map:** 26E4

No. of Units: 150   **Person Contacted:** Grace Scott   **Position:** Ass't. Mgr.   **Ph:** 467-7890

Person Making Survey: B. Neale   **Date of Survey:** 7/4/xx

PROPERTY DATA

Construction: class "D", garden style   **No. of Stories:** 2 **Bldgs:** 1 **Age:** 16 **Cond:** Avg.

Land Area: 2.97 acres   **Density:** 862 s.f. land/unit   **Views:** some city and park

Parking: one covered space per unit; extra open parking spaces available by assignment

AMENITIES

View: some units   **Pool(s):** one   **Recreation Room:** large   **Sauna:** none

Other Recreational Facilities: municipal park nearby has tennis courts and lawn bowling

APARTMENT FEATURES

Utilities: water, trash pick-up provided **Cable TV:** X **Gas, Elec. Meters:** indiv. **Sec. System:** none

Furniture: none   **Carpets:** X **Drapes:** X **Patios:** none

Refrigerators: none **Dishwashers:** built-in **Heating:** gas, wall **Air Cond:** none **Balconies:** X

Range & Ovens: built-in **Fireplaces:** none   **Other Features:** all exterior entrances

RENTAL DATA

No. of Units Unfurn.	Furn.	Apartment Type	Sq. Ft. Area	Monthly Rental Average	Per Sq. Ft.
80	----	1-BR, 1-Ba	675	$655	$0.97
70	----	2-BR, 1-Ba	990	$900	$0.91

Last Rental Adjustment: 5% increase, 9/1/xx **Concessions:** none   **Rent Control:** exempt

Deposits: first & last months rent, plus security deposit of $135 for 1-BR, $150 for 2-BR units

OCCUPANCY

Type: mostly adult; some family units   **Date Opened:** 19xx, after remodeling

Total Units: 150 **No. Occupied:** 135 **Occupancy Rates (Present):** 90% **(Typ.):** same

COMMENTS this project is located within walking distance of schools and shopping

Office Form #32, 4/23/xx

landlord installed them. Therefore, the rent comparable price may need adjustment before comparing it to a space in the subject property that is already ready to occupy.

Industry standards for pricing tenant space usually depend on the type of property. As already indicated, apartment units are usually priced or compared by the number of bedrooms and baths but may be compared by the monthly rent per square foot of living area. Office space may be rented by a monthly or annual price per square foot of *net rentable area,* or by the full floor area occupied. Net rentable area is usually defined to exclude stairwells and elevator and air shafts in the building. Stores and industrial properties are most often rented by the gross square-foot area of the building. However, retail buildings fronting on a busy street or walk may be rented by the front-foot exposure.

Estimating the Market Rent

In most cases, the market rent for the subject property is derived from an analysis of the rental information collected in the rent survey and a comparison of these amounts with the existing rent schedule.

Analysis of Survey Rentals

The rental survey provides data on competitive rental rates. The first step is to analyze the rents to estimate what factors cause rents to vary. Next, the rentals should be adjusted to reflect rental space more like that of the subject property. For example, the following factors should be considered:

1. *Time*: based on the date that the lease was signed or the occupancy began, and the observed trend in rental prices since that date.

2. *Location:* if differences are significant.

3. *Physical features:* such as size, age, quality, appeal, amenities offered, and building condition.

4. *Services, utilities, and personalty (personal property) included in the rent*: Note that furnished apartments should not be compared with unfurnished without adjusting. Any significant furniture or personal property involved in the property being appraised should be described and the rent allocated separately between real and personal property.

5. *Vacancy rates:* abnormally high vacancy, indicating overpricing; or low vacancy rates, suggesting underpricing of units.

6. *Limitations of any rent control regulations in effect:* imposing artificial limits on tenant rents.

Since market rent is commonly understood as the potential legal income of the property, some readers may view a market rent survey as an academic exercise in a rent control situation. However, most rent control ordinances offer some legal opportunity for landlords to appeal rent schedules that are grossly out of line with competing properties, or to apply for supplemental rent increases to cover unusual expenses. The rent survey might be necessary, therefore, to prepare the appraiser to consider such possibilities. If the contract rent is well under the market rent, many buyers would consider that possibility!

Construction of the Market Rent Schedule

The appraiser's final unit-by-unit rent schedule and gross income estimate should result from the analysis of competing property rentals and the history of rentals for the subject property. However, if the existing management is competent and aggressive in pricing and marketing units, the appraiser might well conclude that the existing rent schedule on the date of value represents market rents. On the other hand, any part of the existing rent schedule that appears to be noticeably higher or lower than the competition should be given a second look, and then either adjusted or fully explained.

Existing rent schedules may have other defects. For example, rent for the owner's or manager's unit, as well as income from building services such as laundry facilities, are sometimes omitted. The appraiser's gross income projection should make corrections for such omissions. If the manager is to be provided free rent, it is more appropriate to include the rent from that unit in the gross income and then deduct the rental amount as part of the management expenses. (However, this adjustment may not be appropriate for a GIM analysis, unless the data for the comparable sales can also be adjusted!) Example 13-4 shows how to format a market rent schedule for a six-unit apartment.

The appraiser should consider the past history of vacancy rates for the subject property. Unless there are specific problems with the property or its management, abnormal vacancy rates suggest that a rent adjustment is needed. In an area not affected by rent control, the building with the lowest vacancy rates often has the lowest rents. Efficient management can maximize gross receipts by increasing rental rates to "achieve normal vacancy." For example, an apartment building that has a zero vacancy factor possibly could increase actual (effective) gross receipts if rents were increased, say, from $900 to $950 per month (across the board), as long as less than a 10 percent vacancy factor resulted.

EXAMPLE 13-4 Market Rent Schedule

Unit Number	Unit Type	Existing Rent	Market Rent
101	Two-bedroom	$550	$ 625
102	One-bedroom	480	550
103	Efficiency	400	450
201	Two-bedroom	575	650
202	One-bedroom	Manager	550
203	One-bedroom	460	+ 520
Total monthly rent roll			$ 3,345
Total annual rent roll ($3,345 × 12)			$40,140
Plus: Laundry and miscellaneous income			+ 1,400
Equals: Total potential gross income			$41,540

Allowance for Vacancy and Credit Losses

The *effective gross income* is defined as the market income minus the *allowance for vacancy and credit losses*. It is a projection of the potential income receipts of the property before payment of normal operating costs and capital recovery.

Vacancy rates should always be considered separately for each type of unit. Consider the appraisal of a 20-unit apartment building consisting entirely of two-bedroom units. Your rent survey reveals that buildings in the area with one-bedroom units have much lower vacancy rates than those with two- and three-bedroom units. You would conclude that an appropriate vacancy factor for your building would be higher than that of the typical one-bedroom building.

The allowance for rent or credit losses is estimated next to provide for rents not collected because of nonpayment. In making this calculation, we again assume efficient management of the property and follow the typical experience of the neighborhood. Usually, the figure will represent likely long-term losses, not just last year's actual loss or the next year's projected loss.

In summary, the estimate of effective gross income should result from a carefully worked-out rent schedule reflecting the rental and vacancy pattern of competing properties in its neighborhood. This estimate should not be a mere reflection of the existing operation of the property, but should be a realistic prediction of what maximum income that buyers of the property would anticipate it could reasonably produce under competent management.

13.4 Operating Expenses and Expense Ratios

Annual expenses are deducted from the effective annual gross income to calculate the net income. In turn, annual net income is used in the capitalization process to develop an indicated value of the property.

Expenses to Be Included

For appraisal purposes, expenses are limited generally to the operating costs. These include all property-related expenses necessary to produce the gross income. Owner-related expenses such as loan or interest payments, income taxes, and depreciation deductions are not included. Although such outlays are important to the owner and significant for accounting and income tax purposes, they relate solely to the debt or tax position of one particular owner, rather than to the real estate in question.

One exception occurs when using the equity residual capitalization method, where loan payments are deducted to calculate the cash flow return on the equity investment. This procedure is described in Chapter 14. Another exception occurs in analyses of net income after income tax expenses, which are studied in advanced income capitalization classes.

Operating Expense Categories

Regardless of the type of investment property, **Operating expenses** often are formally classified as either: 1) variable expenses, 2) fixed expenses, or 3) reserves for replacement. There is no requirement that you must separate them in this way, but the categories serve as useful reminders. Increasingly, it seems as if both fixed and variable expenses are becoming more variable! Clearly, however, reserves should be analyzed and reported separately, as will be explained below.

Variable Expenses

Variable expenses are the day-to-day, out-of-pocket expenses required to run the building. These usually include administration and management, maintenance and repairs, and utility costs. Many building expenses may be incurred either as payroll items or as contracted services.

In economics, management is considered to be one of the four agents of production. *Management cost* varies greatly with the type and size of the property. For small apartment buildings, management is often accomplished by the services of a resident manager. Costs vary with the number of units. The resident manager usually collects the rent and takes care of minor maintenance and repair work. Often, the manager's compensation is in the form of free rent and perhaps a small salary.

In larger apartment complexes and commercial properties, professional management companies are often needed in order to oversee the on-site property manager and perform all administrative services for the owner. When all legal, accounting, and supervisory costs are included, such companies usually charge from 3 to 7 percent of the rent collected. In some cases, this includes the payment to the resident manager.

Maintenance and repair costs include all building and grounds upkeep except for the replacement of major building components or equipment. In apartment buildings, monthly maintenance and repair work include grounds and pool maintenance, cleaning, interior painting and decorating, and minor plumbing repairs. Elevator and major equipment maintenance is included and is usually covered by annual service contracts. Outside painting and major building repair is performed at irregular intervals over the years; hence, average annual costs usually should be estimated from the building's history or from industry standards. However, see the discussion on reserves for replacement that follows.

Utility costs include water and power, gas, garbage collection, and so on. In many properties, the owner pays for all garbage collection as well as water, power, and gas for the common areas. The latter include parking lots, and recreation and laundry facilities, as well as central water and space heating. When the rental units have separate meters, tenants usually pay all metered utilities. Again, it is important for the appraiser to research who pays what! Appraisers should compare the actual utility costs of the subject property to those typically experienced by owners of similar buildings. However, it is important to remember that each building is relatively unique. The amount of electricity, gas, water used, and garbage created, varies with the building design and tenant needs. Utility rates also vary from place to place. Also, leases vary concerning who—landlord or tenant—will pay the utility bills. So, utility cost information from competitive buildings must be used cautiously when being compared to the subject property.

Fixed Expenses

Fixed expenses are those paid on a fairly regular basis and are relatively stable from year to year. Insurance premiums and property taxes are the most common examples.

Insurance coverage on income property usually includes fire, extended coverage, and public liability. Special coverages may also apply. Special coverage could include insurance against rent loss, with one type covering rent loss resulting from fires and similar events and another type insuring or guaranteeing against a default for a specified lease (as for a commercial store). Other types of special coverage include flood or earthquake insurance and demolition insurance (insurance against loss resulting from any government order to demolish the property, e.g., because of building code defects). Rates depend in part on the specific coverages. They also vary with the type of occupancy and with the construction classification of the buildings (discussed in Chapter 11). Appraisers often rely on the past costs from the property operating statement to project insurance costs. However, it is a good idea to compare such figures with quotations from local insurance carriers. Note that premiums are sometimes quoted on terms of payment twice per year, or every two years, not on an annual basis. Payment amounts of this type should be adjusted to the yearly cost.

Real property taxes have historically been assessed by an ad valorem, or "according to value," formula. However, in some states, including California, value assessments generally are updated only upon change of ownership. For this reason, the existing taxes on a property are not necessarily a good indication of the anticipated future tax burden for the property. In market value appraisals, the amount used by the appraiser for the property tax expense should be the amount a new owner would probably be charged under the local tax laws. How is this done?

There are two ways to estimate the property tax expense when the income approach is used in an appraisal. The simplest and most commonly used method is to assign a tentative market value for the property based on the best evidence at hand, say, the value indicated by the sales comparison approach. When this is multiplied by the tax rate showing on the assessment roll, a reasonable estimate of the property tax burden can result. Of course, any special assessments (for local bonded indebtedness, and so on) must be added. These may be found on the latest tax bill for the property or obtained from the tax collector's office.

The second and somewhat more accurate method for estimating taxes within the income approach is to project them as a percentage of value in the capitalization of income. Usually, this can be done simply by adding the tax rate to the capitalization rate and capitalizing the net income before taxes with this new rate. (Again, any special assessments or flat charges still must be deducted as an expense.) Referring to Example 13-1, assume that the net income before deduction of taxes was $112,156 instead of the after-tax figure of $97,000. Assume also that the tax rate is 0.0125. Now, our direct capitalization value calculation is:

Net operating income before taxes		$ 112,156
Divided by:		
Capitalization rate	0.0800	
Plus: Property Tax rate	+ 0.0125	
Equals: Composite rate		÷ 0.0925
Equals: Value estimate		$1,212,500

Reserves for Replacement

Certain property components wear out from age and usage and must be replaced from time to time. Although inexpensive replacements are usually accounted for as a maintenance expense, larger costs are most often capitalized (i.e., listed as "capital" improvements). This is why they may not show up on building expense statements. The appraiser must try to find out what the past capital improvements were if these are not listed on the income and expense statements.

An annual reserve allowance is considered a valid way for appraisers to account for these costs, particularly for some types of buildings, and when the items have shorter useful lives than the main structure. When an appraiser encounters a replacement reserve, most often it is for a federally subsidized, low-income housing project or for properties like hotels or convalescent hospitals that have a lot of fixtures and personal property.

When *reserves for replacement* are taken, they could include items such as roof and floor coverings, built-in kitchen equipment, water heaters and boilers, heating and air-conditioning units, and other operating machinery and equipment. In furnished hotels, offices, and apartments, replacement reserves could also be set up to pay for new furnishings as the old ones wear out. However, the expense of furniture reserves is appropriate only if the projected rent includes rent for the furnishings or equipment.

Capital additions to the structure, such as major remodeling and facility enlargement/expansion, do not properly belong under replacement reserves. This is because such work generally alters (increases) the income potential of the property. Replacement reserves are intended simply to maintain the property's condition and income.

How are the dollar amounts for a replacement reserve typically estimated? First, you estimate the cost to replace the building component on the date of value (the roof covering, for example). Next, you divide its replacement cost by the anticipated future useful life of the new item. The result is the annual allocation, or expense, for that component. For instance, if the replacement cost of a drop-in kitchen range and oven is $900 on the date of value and its estimated useful life is 15 years, then the annual reserve for replacement is $60 per year, calculated as follows:

$$\$900 \div 15 = \$60$$

If there are ten such units in the building, the total annual allowance for future replacement of the ranges and ovens amounts to $600 per year (10 × $60 = $600). When the replacement reserve allowance has been estimated for each of the short-lived building components, the separate figures are added together to calculate the full expense for replacement reserves.

Some authorities argue that the replacement of a building component amounts to a capital addition rather than an operating expense; therefore, such replacement costs should not be deducted in the income approach, except to the extent that they are deducted by typical investors for similar properties. In practice, most investors today deduct little or no replacement reserves, and appraisers do not use replacement reserves as often as they did in the past. Please note that when the appraiser has derived the capitalization rate from comparable properties *without* deducting replacement reserves, such reserves should not be deducted from the income of the subject property! As we noted earlier, consistency in applying market data is essential!

Income and Expense Ratios

Income and expense ratios refer to the relationships between the various income and expense categories of income-producing properties. These ratios are used to assist the appraiser in the analysis of income properties.

The **net income ratio** is the **net operating income** (NOI) divided by the effective gross income of a property. First, the net operating income is calculated. For example, a property with an effective gross income of $100,000 and expenses of $35,000 has an NOI of $65,000 (that is, $100,000 – $35,000). Now, the net income ratio can be calculated to be 0.65, or 65 percent ($65,000/$100,000 = 0.65).

$$\text{Net income ratio} = \text{NOI/EGI} = 65,000/100,000 = 0.65$$

The **operating expense ratio** is the relationship of the total operating expenses to the effective gross rent. In the example given above, the operating expense ratio is calculated as $35,000/$100,000, which equals 0.35, or 35 percent. The operating expense ratio is the exact *complement* of the net income ratio. This means that it is calculated as 1 minus the net income ratio. Here, the operating expense ratio is confirmed as: 1 – 0.65 which equals 0.35, or 35 percent.

For specific types, sizes, and locations of properties, operating expenses generally fall within fairly narrow ranges. Thus, knowledge of typical expense ratios assists in the reconstruction of operating expense statements, to be discussed next.

13.5 Reconstruction of the Operating Statement

In written reports, appraisers often include a reconstructed **operating statement** as part of the income approach. This statement shows the appraiser's estimate of stabilized income and expenses for the property, listed category by category. By "stabilized," we mean under economic conditions existing on the date of value, but adjusted to show market rents, average collection losses, and normal expenses for this location. (Recognize that one still might prepare such an estimate even if the property is under rent control, or subject to a long-term lease, in order to emphasize how market income levels compare to the actual income.) Why do we reconstruct the income statement, and how?

Why We Reconstruct the Statement

The owner's actual operating statement for prior years is important because it contains a useful history of the property. Historical income and expenses can help us develop an item-by-item income and expense estimate to use in the appraisal. However, it is important to note that owners' operating statements can be misleading. Quite often, the operating statement furnished to the appraiser is simply the record the property owner has used for his or her annual income tax return. As such, it would reflect the personal income and expenses of the owner. For purposes of the appraisal, many items in such statements are improper, or irrelevant. To illustrate the point, note the following expense items that are reported in the operating statement represented in Example 13-5, and the reason each should be deleted or adjusted by the appraiser.

1. *Depreciation*—This is an owner-related, rather than a property-related, expense. It should be deleted for all analyses (except the infrequent after-income-tax analysis).

2. *Building maintenance*—Actual outlays for building maintenance in any one year may exceed, or fall short of, an annualized estimate; an adjustment is probably needed.

3. *The property tax category only shows one-half year listed*—The appraiser should project the property tax expense for the full year, and, in addition, it should be based on the likely taxes if the property were to be sold.

4. *Interest*—This appears to be interest paid on the existing mortgage loan—another case of an owner-related, rather than a property-related expense.

The purpose of reconstructing the operating statement in an appraisal, then, is to set forth an estimate of the market rents on the date of value, the typical long-term vacancy and collection losses in this location with good management, and the normal annual expenses to operate this property efficiently on a continuing basis.

You should be aware that some advanced capitalization techniques require a year-by-year projection of income, vacancy and collection loss, and expenses. Such a year-by-year series of numbers would probably use different figures from those used in a stabilized statement. As examples, vacancy rates for a new building might be selected to reflect a declining vacancy rate, and replacement reserve deductions could be estimates of the actual replacement amounts for the specific year for which the replacement is anticipated.

Adjustments to Rentals and Vacancy

Reconstruction of the owner's operating statement must incorporate the findings of the income and expense study already described. Reconstruction nearly always involves some rental adjustments. Example 13-6 is a reconstructed statement based on the owner's statement presented in Example 13-5. One common adjustment arises because owners' statements often fail to list the manager's unit in the rent schedule, whereas, in a reconstructed statement, typically all units would be included. Next, the rental rates usually must be adjusted to market rent levels.

The vacancy and credit-loss allowance must be a stabilized estimate. Your analysis should consider the vacancy information developed in the rent survey. You should also consider the effect on vacancy of raising rents to your proposed market levels. Usually, the desired vacancy and collection loss rate is one that represents the long-term rate in the area over the years. One year's abnormally high or low rates (perhaps caused by swings in the business cycle) would be converted to a more typical stabilized rate. (If you were preparing a year-by-year projection, however, you would seek to estimate the rate for each year.)

EXAMPLE 13-5 An Owner's Operating Statement

Receipts:

Rent	$140,000	
Plus: Other	+ 1,000	
Equals: Total receipts		$141,000

Less: Expenses:

Management	$ 4,000	
Utilities	7,805	
Pool service	1,800	
Landscape service	1,700	
Depreciation	10,420	
Building maintenance	5,400	
Property taxes (1/2 year)	5,000	
Interest	+ 20,721	
Equals: Total expenses		− 56,846
Equals: Net		$ 84,154

EXAMPLE 13-6 A Reconstructed Operating Statement

Scheduled Gross Income:			
10 units at $600 per month	$6,000		
Plus: 10 units at $700 per month	+ 7,000		
Equals: Total monthly rents	$13,000		
Times	x 12		
Equals: Total annual rents		$156,000	
Plus: Service Income:			
Laundry facilities		+ 2,000	
Equals: Potential Gross Income:			$158,000
Less: Vacancy and Collection Loss:			
Potential gross income		$158,000	
Times: Vacancy and collection loss (2.5%)		x 0.025	
Equals: Total loss			− 3,950
Equals: Effective Gross Income			$154,050
Less: Expenses:			
Operating expense:			
Management (6%)	$9,240		
Utilities	7,000		
Pool service	1,800		
Landscape service	1,700		
Plus: Building maintenance	+ 7,900		
Equals: Total operating expenses		$27,640	
Plus: Fixed expenses:			
Insurance	$3,000		
Plus: Real estate taxes	+ 15,800		
Equals: Total fixed expenses		18,800	
Plus: Reserves for replacement:			
Carpets and drapes	$4,000		
Kitchen built-ins	1,500		
Roof	1,900		
Plus: Other building components	+ 800		
Equals: Total reserves for replacement		+ 8,200	
Equals: Total expenses			− 54,640
Equals: Net Operating Income			$99,410

Reconstructing Expenses

As noted, there are two typical problems with actual expense statements. The first is the inclusion of expense categories that reflect the owner's particular financing and income tax costs. These expenses are not operating costs and must be deleted. Examples include loan interest, loan principal, income taxes, and depreciation. The only exception occurs when you are using equity residual capitalization, as noted earlier, or an after-income-tax capitalization method.

The second major problem with actual expense statements is the frequent need to adjust the actual expenses reported. One adjustment is to add for expenses not yet paid (e.g., delinquent taxes). Another adjustment is to pro-rate any actual payments for insurance premiums or service contracts that extend beyond a year's coverage. On occasion, property owners will also prepay property taxes so that the payments in that year cover one and one-half years. Still another reason is to add dollar amounts for expenses that do not involve any dollars in this particular owner's operations. One example is the cost of any free living unit provided for the resident manager, mentioned earlier. Another example involves the owner who performs all the maintenance personally so that the only historical maintenance expense was for materials.

Comparing Expenses with Industry Standards

As reasonable as the owner-reported expenses may seem, it is still advisable to compare them, category by category, with amounts reported for similar properties in the area and with industry "norms." Published expense reports that show typical expense ratios are available from the Institute of Real Estate Management (IREM), the Building Owners and Managers Association (BOMA), the Urban Land Institute (ULI), and other management groups. Industry experiences are usually reported either as a percentage of the effective gross income or as a cost per square foot of rentable area. Some expenses, such as management, may best be estimated as a percent of gross income, since that is how they are usually determined. Other costs, such as utilities, may best be estimated by the cost per square foot, since usage is not a direct function of the gross income.

After comparing the actual building expenses with those reported in the area, and with typical industry standards, the appraiser must try to estimate realistic operating expenses for the subject property. The final estimate should reflect not only the prices of labor, material, services, utilities, and taxes in the area, but also the unique characteristics of the property being appraised.

SUMMARY

In this chapter, we provided an introduction to income property and the motives and benefits of its ownership. An overview of the income approach as it applies to various types of residential income, commercial, and industrial properties was also included. The income approach can either analyze income year-by-year, or by emphasizing one year. The latter is by far the most common.

The income approach, using a one-year capitalization technique, consists of the following steps:

1. Estimate the annual potential gross income the (PGI) property is capable of producing.
2. Estimate typical stabilized vacancy and collection losses.
3. Subtract the vacancy and collection losses from the potential gross income to arrive at the effective gross income (EGI).
4. Estimate annual operating expenses and subtract them from the effective gross income to calculate the net operating income (NOI).
5. Analyze comparable investments to arrive at a capitalization rate and method appropriate for the subject property.
6. Divide the net operating income by the capitalization rate to obtain the capitalized value estimate.

The gross income multiplier method is often accepted as a substitute for the income approach in the appraisal of single-family and small investment properties because of the greater importance of intangible amenities or benefits to buyers of such properties. The gross income multiplier is a simple relationship between the selling price and the gross scheduled rent.

The selection of a specific gross income multiplier (GIM) for the subject property should consider the comparability of the location, the building amenities available, and any factors that may affect the ratio of income and expenses. Once selected, the GIM usually is multiplied by the gross scheduled income of the subject property to estimate its market value.

Income property appraisals require an estimate of income and expenses for the property. Gross income consists of the rent for tenant space plus any service income. Since property is often appraised as if "free and clear" of any leases, the rent considered often should be the market rent rather than merely the present rent of the property. Thus, the owner's operating statement serves only as a guide, often requiring both income and expense adjustments. Gross income estimates are based on a rental survey and the past performance of the property being appraised. Effective gross income takes into account vacancy and collection loss projections.

Operating expenses are customarily estimated in three categories: variable expenses, fixed expenses, and reserves for replacement. Variable expenses include such familiar items as management costs, cost of services and utilities, and building and grounds maintenance. Since major building repairs occur at uneven intervals, average rather than actual annual expenditures are usually projected for the building maintenance cost. Insurance premiums and property taxes make up what are commonly known as fixed expenses. A reserve for replacement is the category to cover annual allocations for the eventual cost to replace short-lived building components, such as floor coverings, roof, and mechanical building equipment. These reserves are not usually deducted as an expense in most appraisals.

In written appraisal reports, a *reconstructed operating statement* is often included to support the income approach conclusion. Actual historical numbers for both income and expense may need correcting. The projected rental schedule should reflect the rent level of competing properties in the area, with rent assigned to all units, including the owner's or manager's apartment. Expenses are limited to those necessary to operate the property. Personal expenses, such as interest and depreciation, are deleted for appraisal purposes.

A knowledge of typical expense ratios assists in the reconstruction of operating expense statements. For income property, an expense ratio is defined as the ratio between the total operating expense and the effective gross income. In appraisals, expense estimates should be checked against the amounts reported for similar properties in the area or against known industry standards.

IMPORTANT TERMS AND CONCEPTS

Allowance for vacancy and credit losses	*Intangible benefits*
Amenities	*Lease term*
Capital recovery	*Market rent*
Capitalization	*Minimum or base rent*
Capitalization rate	*Net income ratio*
Contract rent	*Net operating income*
CPI lease	*Operating expenses*
Direct capitalization	*Operating expense ratio*
Effective gross income	*Operating statement*
Excess rent	*Overage rent*
Fixed expenses	*Percentage lease*
Gross income	*Potential gross income*
Gross income multiplier	*Present worth of future benefits*
Income property	*Recapture*
	Rent roll

Reserves for replacement

Return of investment

Return on investment

Step-up (or "graduated") lease

Straight (or "flat") lease

Tangible benefits

Variable expenses

REVIEWING YOUR UNDERSTANDING

1. Which of the following might be classified as a tangible rather than an intangible amenity?
   a. Pride of ownership
   b. A sense of security
   c. Free rent
   d. Work satisfaction

2. Tom Smith has a savings account that just paid a $700 annual dividend. If the declared interest rate was 7 percent, which of the following represents the amount of the deposit?
   a. $1,000
   b. $10,000
   c. $7,000
   d. None of the above

3. An income property renting for $50,000 per year before expenses just sold for $500,000 cash. What was the gross income multiplier?
   a. 1/10 or 10%
   b. 5
   c. 10
   d. None of the above

4. Which of the following property features is/are important in the analysis of the gross income multiplier from comparable sales?
   a. Expense ratio
   b. Services included in the rent
   c. Location
   d. All of the above

5. Market rent can be defined as:
   a. The potential gross rent
   b. The contract rent
   c. The average rent
   d. None of the above

6. Which of the following is an example of a specific expense item rather than a basic expense category?
   a. Reserve for replacement
   b. Property taxes
   c. Variable expenses
   d. Fixed charges or expenses

7. The property being appraised has a 100 percent occupancy rate. What conclusion would you probably draw if the typical occupancy rate in the area were only 95 percent?
   a. Advertising is superior
   b. The rents are too high
   c. The rents are too low
   d. Management is better

8. A rent survey reveals that buildings offering one-bedroom units have a considerably lower vacancy factor than those with two-bedroom units. If the subject property includes only units with two bedrooms, the appraisal should probably project:
   a. An average of the vacancy factors for all units surveyed
   b. A higher factor than found in the one-bedroom units
   c. A lower factor than found in the one-bedroom units
   d. The same factor as found in the one-bedroom units

9. An apartment owner spent $4,000 last year to replace five built-in stoves. In a 10-unit apartment house, what annual expense would be projected for replacement if all the units had stoves? Assume a 10-year life for all replacements.
   a. $800
   b. $4,000
   c. $16,000
   d. $1,600

10. If market rent is less than contract rent, the difference is known as:
   a. Overage rent
   b. Excess rent
   c. Percentage rent
   d. Capital gain

PRACTICAL APPLICATIONS

As we like to remind you, review the exercise at the end of the preceding chapter, and the work that you have performed to date.

This assignment moves to the task of estimating the market rent for the residence, estimating approximate operating expenses, and calculating the value using the Gross Income Multiplier. It will be reported on the income approach section on page 3 of the URAR form, shown as part of Figure 16-9, at the end of Chapter 16. Notice the information that the form calls for—this is a really limited presentation! As a tool, consider using another form as a template or guide to help you process the cost information. There are several good choices, including the FNMA 1025 Small Income Property form, in ClickFORMS, in the Forms Library, under "New FNMA Forms" and then "FNMA 1025." Another choice for just rental comparables and the GIM would be (in the Forms Library) under the "New AI Forms" and then select "Income Approach." A third possible choice in the Forms Library would be in the "Income" heading, and then the "Comparable Rent," "Operating Income Statement," or "Income Approach" forms.

Note that the income approach often will be omitted in appraising single-family homes for loans. Generally, the income approach would be desirable if a lot of the sales in the neighborhood are being purchased by investors and rented out. Consider whether that is true of the sales that you analyzed in the market comparison approach. If it is, an income approach would be desirable. If it is not, please make a hypothetical assumption that it is true, and do this exercise!

The first step is to estimate the market rent of the unit. Consider if you are currently paying rent or if you know about any other rentals in the neighborhood. Check websites such as http://www.rent.com and those of local real estate brokers. Perhaps check an Internet search engine, using "rent" and your town, and "home," to see what other websites might be helpful. Consider talking to the brokers who handled the comparable sales that you identified, as they might manage local rentals for investors.

You will need to research the needed information on each comparable rental. Try to start with at least ten, so you can drop the four or so that are least similar, and end up with four to six good comparable rentals. The key issues will be size and condition, when the agreement was reached, and differences of location, view, amenities, and parking. Try to find out if there was anything unusual about the property or transaction, as a way of catching unusual issues.

Once you have researched the rent comparables, you will need to select the market rent for the subject property. Consider how each compares to the subject property. Calculate the rent per square foot of living area, if at all possible, to eliminate most of the impact from size differences. As with the comparable sales in the market comparison approach, try adjusting the rentals for major differences, based on what appears to be the rental difference from analyzing the comparable rentals. Watch to see that the spread in rent or rent per square foot at the bottom of the adjustment grid is narrowing with each adjustment. If necessary, review the discussion about adjusting sales in the exercise for Chapter 9.

We are suggesting that you also prepare an expense analysis as part of this exercise, even though one is not needed to perform the GIM method of reaching value. Look at the expense categories listed in the text and those shown on the forms. Consider what expenses you already know because you live there. If you rent, explain to your landlord that you are doing a class exercise, and ask what operating expenses seem typical. Check books in the library on small investment properties. Check listings of duplexes and similar small residential properties in the area to see what expenses are listed, and convert them to a per-unit basis. Recognize that the expenses in a listing are often only a partial list. Property taxes are available online from the county tax collector in most counties. Utility costs may be available from the utility company. There is a lot of data out there if you dig for it.

The next step is to collect information to help you select a GIM number, to multiply times the rent, leading to an opinion of value. Consider if any of the sales that you developed, even those you dropped early, were rented. If so, it should be possible to derive a GIM from the transaction. Review the discussion in the chapter. Note that GIM comparables do not need to be as closely similar to the subject as a sale comparable. The key issue is if they are likely to have similar expenses. For example, an elevator building would not be a good GIM comparable for a walkup building because of the elevator expenses. The GIM could be calculated on an annual basis or monthly—it really does not matter. Expect to find variations in the GIMs that you obtain from the sales. This is typical, because the quality of the income information that you have is poor. Review the GIM discussion in the text to see why this might be the case. Consider carefully which information is likely to be more complete or accurate to help you select the GIM to use. Finally, enter the information in the URAR form.

As we note at the end of each exercise, it is best not to get ahead of yourself. So, do not enter information in the later sections of the report until you have read the chapter(s) that covers that topic. However, it is a good idea to look ahead so that you start thinking about the information that you will need.

Reminder: If you have questions about the program, review the manuals and help information that were on the program CD. Also, go to http://www.bradfordsoftware.com, click on "Services" at the upper right, and then on "ClickFORMS Training Programs" in the middle of the "Services" page.

CHAPTER 14
INCOME CAPITALIZATION: RATES AND TECHNIQUES

PREVIEW

In the last chapter, we outlined the basic steps in the income approach, and covered the methods used to estimate income and expenses for investment property. This chapter completes our discussion of the income approach by describing the most commonly used techniques of income capitalization.

OBJECTIVES

When you have completed this chapter you should be able to:

1. Define income capitalization.
2. List the three key characteristics of a future stream of income.
3. List the three methods used to derive interest and/or capitalization rates.
4. Define and illustrate direct capitalization.
5. Define discounted cash flow and describe its use in appraisals.

14.1 Purpose and Theory of Capitalization

We can estimate the value of income property by studying the economic relationship between income and value. Income capitalization is the broad term used to describe this relationship. Income capitalization is the process of converting an *income* estimate into an estimate of *value*.

A number of income capitalization techniques are available to the appraiser; some are relatively simple and direct, whereas others are more complex. In actual practice, the preferred technique depends on the nature of the appraisal problem and the specific kind of market data available. Commonly used techniques of income capitalization will be described in Section 14.3 of this chapter.

Capitalization Defined

Capitalization is the process of converting the projected future net income of a property into its equivalent lump-sum capital value on the date of value. We know that the buyer of an income-generating property often is motivated by the future income to be earned. We also know that value is the present worth of future benefits. And we know that a promised future dollar is worth less than a dollar in hand. It follows that income to be received over a number of years is worth less today than the simple total of the dollars to be received. This recognizes a principle known as the **time value of money**. The capitalization process always reflects the time value of money by somehow reducing or discounting the expected future income to its present worth. The actual mathematics of discounting can be a direct or indirect calculation, depending on the capitalization techniques used.

Income capitalization techniques are all designed to consider three key aspects of the future income:

*   *Quantity*, or the amount of expected future income or cash flow.
*   *Quality*, or the relative *risk* of the income estimate.
*   *Timing*, or the expected frequency and **duration of the income**.

The concept means that the value of an income property does not depend solely on the amount of income that the property produces. The certainty of the income and the length of time it will last are equally important. For example, a large income from a risky investment can be less valuable than a smaller income from a very safe investment. In either case, the value depends in part on the number of months or years the income can be expected to continue (see Figure 14-1).

**Figure 14-1
Three Aspects of
Future Income.**

CAPITALIZATION TECHNIQUES CONSIDER:

QUALITY OF INCOME   QUANTITY OF INCOME   DURATION OF INCOME

Capitalization Rate Defined

As noted in our introduction to the income approach, value results from the relationship between income and value, which is the rate of return. The general definition of a **capitalization rate** is:

> Any rate used to convert income into value.
>
> Source: *The Dictionary of Real Estate Appraisal,* 4th ed., The Appraisal Institute, Chicago, 2002.

There are different types of capitalization rates, reviewed in Section 14.2. Use of a capitalization rate directly or indirectly provides for a return "on" the/8 investment (interest), as well as a return "of" the investment (**capital recovery**). It is important for the appraiser to understand the difference between the *return on investment* and the *return of investment*. "Return on" is the same as interest or yield. It is the profit that the investor seeks. "Return of" is the recapture or return of the invested funds or capital recovery.

The most commonly used capitalization rate is the *overall capitalization rate*, overall rate, or *OAR*, which is calculated by dividing a property's net income by its sale price. Other types of rates are used in appraisals; the type of rate to be used depends on what capitalization technique is used! Generally, these techniques are divided into two families: *ratio capitalization* and *yield capitalization*. The difference is that in yield capitalization, both the future income and the rate of return *on* investment must be specified. This difference will be explored further as the chapter progresses.

Comparing Investment Property

Real estate competes for the use of investors' capital with all other types of financial investments. The appraiser's choice of a capitalization technique and rate should consider the investment criteria that motivate purchasers of investment property. Although such criteria are many and varied, the most important are listed as follows and then defined.

Investment Criteria

1. Safety

2. Yield

3. Liquidity

4. Management

5. Appreciation prospects

6. Property tax burden

7. Income tax shelter

8. Size of investment

9. Hypothecation

10. Leverage

Safety

Investment safety refers to the reliability of the net income estimate and the assurance of getting the original investment back without loss. Well-located property that is leased to strong tenants is generally considered safe, and therefore it attracts investment funds at a lower rate of return than property with inferior locations and tenancies (see Figure 14-2). *Risk* is the opposite of safety; the "flip side of the coin."

Yield

All other things being equal, the investment with the highest yield is the most desirable. Yield refers to the return *on* the investment, equivalent to or the same as interest. This important term is further discussed later in this chapter.

Liquidity

The ease with which an investment can be sold is a factor in its value. Common stocks and bonds are considered more desirable than real estate, if everything else is equal, because they can be bought and sold more readily and quickly, and at less expense.

Freedom from Management Burden

Investments that require the least attention and overall supervision are usually the more attractive ones. Real estate generally requires

**Figure 14-2
Which Property
Is the Safer
Investment?**

(a)

(b)

considerably more management effort than financial investments such as securities.

Prospects for Appreciation

When purchasers of either corporate stocks or real estate can anticipate an increase in the value of the investment over time, they are satisfied with lower current earnings.

Burden of Property Taxes

Ad valorem property taxes decrease the net income of investment property. Thus, such a burden theoretically reduces the attractiveness of real estate, as compared with the types of investments not subject to property taxation.

Shelter from Income Taxes

Tax-free municipal bonds sell for a higher price, for a given income, than similar bonds that have taxable income. This indicates that buyers will accept a lower return on income that is sheltered from income tax. Real estate also benefits from certain income tax shelters. The depreciation allowance for improvements to investment property is an example.

Size or Denomination

Small investments tend to have broader market appeal and greater liquidity than large ones. Until the advent of limited partnerships and syndications, real estate could not compete with investments of moderate and small denominations (see Figure 14-3).

Hypothecation

Hypothecation means using an investment as security for a loan. It provides a practical substitute for investment liquidity. The relative stability of real estate makes it superior to many other types of investments in this respect.

Leverage

Return on investment can often be increased by what is known as "trading on the equity." When property yield rates are higher than the cost of loan money, an investor advantage called *leverage* can result. Here, the investor borrows at a low rate while earning at a higher rate. A similar favorable leverage occurs when there is a fixed loan amount owed on a property that is experiencing rapid market value appreciation. Note that there can be *negative* leverage! If the net operating income declines while the loan payments are constant, the cash flow to the equity will decline and the equity return rate will fall!

**Figure 14-3
Empire State
Building: How Broad
Is Its Market?**

Current and Future Returns

In investment properties, the initial return or profit is the annual (or monthly) flow of net earnings that we refer to in appraisals as the *income stream*. Future, or deferred, return is the payment of dollars available at some future date when an investment is resold. (A future loan refinancing can also provide a future return.) The resale proceeds are called the *reversion* (see Figure 14-4). When real estate is owned free and clear of any loan, the owner's annual flow of earnings consists of the total net operating income produced by the property. However, when real estate is encumbered by a loan, the earnings available to the owner each time period are reduced by the loan payments (interest and principal paid) and are sometimes called *cash flow*, the *equity dividend rate*, or cash return to the equity. It is also referred to as *cash-on-cash* because it is the cash return on the owner's cash investment in the property. The payments to the lender are known as *debt service*—the money needed to service, or take care of, the loan.

In the typical real estate investment, the reversionary returns are the proceeds from the sale of the property, net of selling expenses. With financed properties, the owner's reversion consists of the selling price, less selling expenses, and less any amount owing on the loan at that time. If any loan principal has been paid off over the years, the owner's reversion will be a greater portion of the sale price. This increase in equity reversion due to loan principal payments is sometimes called *equity buildup*. The owner's reversion is also increased by any value appreciation that occurs during the holding period, as shown in Example 14.1. With some investment properties, the loan payments are so large as to eliminate any current cash flow to the owner from the property; in such cases, the return *on* the equity investment, as well as the return *of*, may come entirely from the future sale proceeds.

Income Tax Effects

Income and reversion amounts may be calculated on either a pre-tax or post-tax basis, that is, before or after any federal, state, and local

**Figure 14-4
The Sources of
Investment Returns.**

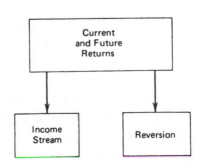

EXAMPLE 14-1 Positive Leverage

A. Given:

Purchase price was $2,000,000. Terms were 25 percent cash down-payment to a new loan for 75 percent of the purchase price, secured by a deed of trust. In five years, the property's value increases by 15 percent. The loan agreement was for only interest payments, so no principal payments have been made. Therefore, the loan balance stays the same.

B. Calculation of Equity Appreciation:

Original price		$2,000,000
Times: Appreciation		x 0.15
Equals: Gross equity gain		$300,000
Divided by: Equity investment:		
Purchase price	$2,000,000	
Times: Down-payment	x 0.25	
Equals: Equity investment		÷ $500,000
Equals: Equity gain		0.60
As a percent		60%

C. Conclusion

Due to the positive appreciation, the 15 percent increase in property value increased the gross equity value by 60 percent (before selling costs).

---

income taxes due. For example, the allowable building depreciation in some real estate investments protects some cash flow from income taxation, increasing the post-tax returns. On the other hand, the taxes due on profits made when the property is sold have the effect of decreasing the future return on the reversion when calculated on an after-tax basis. Note that the income tax rules can change a low pre-tax return to a high post-tax return for some investors. Detailed analysis of income tax aspects of real estate investment is beyond the scope of this book. However, there are assignments where an appraiser has to examine income tax aspects carefully.

Yield versus Recapture

So far, we have pointed out that the financial returns from investments consist of both current income and future reversions. Next, we want to note that such returns consist of various combinations of investment yield (return *on*) and recapture of capital funds (return *of*). Although yield is the return *on* invested capital, yield can be obtained from combinations of current income and capital gain! On the other hand, recapture (the return *of* the invested capital) can also come out of various combinations of current income and future

**Figure 14-5
The Two Types
of Return.**

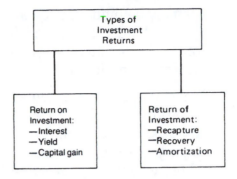

reversions. Figure 14-5 shows the various terms used to describe these two types of investment returns. It should be noted that the term *yield* is sometimes inaccurately used to refer simply to the first-year net cash flow return on invested capital. More accurately, yield refers to the yield-to-maturity, as it is called for bonds. The latter would be a true discounted yield, or **internal rate of return**, as it is often called.

The return of investment capital out of current income can best be illustrated in the field of finance. Lenders are our largest real estate investors: The loan is their investment! In an amortized loan (a loan that is fully paid off over time), the recapture of loan funds is provided for through the principal payments that are a part of the monthly or annual loan payment. The portion of the payment that goes for repayment of the loan principal is providing for loan amortization. Loan amortization (or payoff), then, is the return of the lender's investment capital (see Figure 14-6). And, if the loan is paid off early (by refinancing, a sale with a new loan, or investor cash), the lender receives a future lump sum, similar to a reversion!

In real estate equity investments, recapture of investment capital is not always as clearly defined as it is with loans. However, in certain capitalization techniques, recapture is specifically calculated. What portion of real estate is involved? In traditional thought, recapture is required for only that part of the real estate whose productive

**Figure 14-6
Where the Loan
Payment Goes.**

life may be limited, such as the buildings. This means that the recapture of land value is usually unnecessary. When one land use is no longer in demand, another use usually takes its place, supporting a similar or higher value.

What about improvements? Since they are subject to physical deterioration and obsolescence, it is argued that whatever part of the invested capital went for buildings and structures must be recaptured during their productive life. This will in fact be true in a market where values very slowly decline over time. In the mind of the investor, the recapture of such funds, invested in a "wasting asset," can come out of either the annual net operating income, the proceeds of a future sale, or a combination of the two. When investment recovery comes from the net income, recapture can be thought of either as an expense or as a surcharge on (an addition to) the capitalization rate for the investment (just as property tax could be either a dollar expense or a rate added to the capitalization rate). When capital recovery is to come from future sale proceeds, then recapture is a part of the reversion, which was discussed earlier (see Figure 14-7).

How is recapture handled in appraisals? It depends on the capitalization technique used. There may be a specific dollar or rate allowance for recapture; or recapture may simply be a hidden component of the capitalization rate. Section 14.2 will explain this more fully.

Relating Income Capitalization to Economic Principles

The techniques for income capitalization are derived from the economic principles that were covered in Chapter 5. Here is a summary of the more significant principles: anticipation, agents of production, contribution, and highest and best use.

Principle of Anticipation

Value is equal to the present worth of future benefits. Income capitalization discounts future income to its present capital worth.

**Figure 14-7
The Two Possible
Sources of
Recapture.**

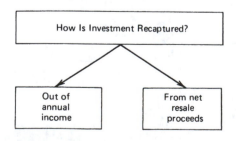

Principle of Agents of Production

All production stems from the use of four agents: labor, coordination, capital, and land. These agents are paid, in the order listed, from available income. Thus, land gets paid all of the leftover income. In practical terms, all operating expenses (variable and fixed charges and reserves for replacement) are subtracted from the gross income, and the remaining net income must be attributed to the value of the land and improvements.

Principle of Contribution

The value of each one of the four agents of production is proportional to that part of the total income that it contributes. This is also true of any one portion or unit of the property, for example, the land or building. Certain residual capitalization techniques apply this principle by isolating the income attributable to a portion of the property (e.g., the land, the building, or the equity investment) and then capitalizing the income into an estimate of value for that portion of the property.

Principle of Highest and Best Use

The highest and best use of property is that use that produces the greatest income return to the land and therefore develops the highest land value. This is why the land residual technique projects the total income available from the highest and best use of the property, and then calculates the land value based on the income left, after allowing for return on the building investment.

The economic principles reviewed above must be kept in mind throughout the appraisal process. In income capitalization, they influence both the choice of capitalization methods and the selection of capitalization rates.

14.2 Selection of the Capitalization Rate

The capitalization rate is the connecting link between an income estimate and a value estimate. Therefore, selecting the appropriate rate is a critical part of the income approach. In this section, we shall define the various rates used in income capitalization procedures and describe the methods for estimating them.

Distinct Types of Rates

For appraisal purposes, there are four distinct types of rates that need to be defined and understood (see Figure 14-8). All are

**Figure 14-8
The Four Types
of Rates.**

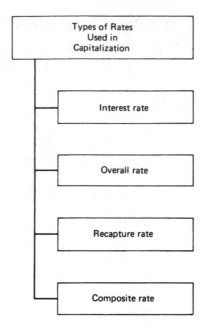

important in the analysis of income properties and the capitalization process. Remember that a rate can be expressed either as a percentage (e.g., 12 percent) or as a decimal number (0.12). Each could be applied to the entire property, the loan or equity, or the land or building.

Interest Rate

The *interest rate* is the rate of return "on" invested capital. The term means exactly the same as *yield rate* and *discount rate*. This rate does not include any provision for the recapture of investment capital. This could be an annual rate, or it could be monthly or quarterly. So it is sometimes called a *periodic rate*.

Overall Capitalization Rate

The relationship between the first-year net income and value for the total property (or the ratio of net income to value) is called the *overall capitalization rate (OAR)*. This rate allows for both return on investment and recapture of investment capital, but the proportions are usually unknown. It is always calculated as an annual rate. This is very commonly used in capitalizing smaller investment properties. The usual symbol is **R**.

Recapture Rate

The rate at which invested funds are being returned to the investor, as a percent of the investment, is called the *recapture rate*. This is usually calculated on an annual basis, and could be applied to the entire property, to the loan or equity, or to the building component. Recapture rates are not commonly used today.

Composite Capitalization Rate

A rate composed of interest and recapture rates in separately selected amounts and known proportions is called a ***composite capitalization rate***. It is an annual rate, in most cases.

The Relationship of Yield and Overall Rates

Nearly always, OARs and interest rates will be the focus of the appraiser's attention. This might be with respect to the total property, the debt or equity components, or, rarely, the land or improvements. Is there any relationship between these two—OAR and interest rates? Obviously, there has to be one, because we know that the rate of return on investment (which is the interest rate) is hidden within the overall capitalization rate.

One of the great conceptual breakthroughs in appraisal theory over the past fifty years is the realization that there is such a relationship. In its simplest form, we can see that when property value is expected to be increasing, some of the return on investment will come from the reversion. Therefore, the overall capitalization rate has to be less than the interest rate.

Of course, when the property value is expected to be declining, the reversion will not be large enough to return the original investment. Therefore, some return of investment (recapture) will have to come from the operating income, on top of the return on investment. In this case, the overall capitalization rate has to be more than the interest rate to reflect the recapture component.

The link between the overall capitalization rate and the interest rate, then, is the expected future change in value, whether up or down. This change is labeled with the Greek letter Δ, or delta. Sometimes, a capital A is used for convenience. We will refer to this value change as ***delta***.

Therefore, interest equals the overall capitalization rate when no value change is expected and thus delta is zero. When values are expected to increase, delta is positive, and so interest equals the overall capitalization rate *plus* delta. When values are expected to decrease, delta is negative and therefore interest equals the overall capitalization rate *minus* delta.

Of course, it's not quite that easy. Delta is the annual percent change in value only when the change will be the same percent each year. Since the overall capitalization rate is applied to only one year's income, if the value change is not expected to occur evenly, the change must be converted to its annual equivalent. This concept is studied further in advanced capitalization courses.

**Figure 14-9
Methods of
Estimating Rates.**

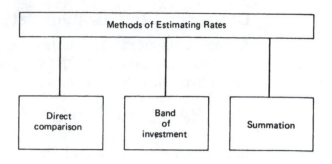

Methods of Estimating Rates

Capitalization rates may be estimated by any of several methods. The direct comparison, band of investment, and summation methods (listed in Figure 14-9) are the ones most commonly used.

The Direct Comparison Method

The *direct comparison method* (or comparative sales method, as it may be called) is generally the preferred method of deriving an overall capitalization rate and is also the easiest to understand. To use the direct comparison method, we simply analyze sales of similar properties that sold close in time to the date of value. In each case, we divide the net operating income by the sale price (after adjusting for non-market financing). The result is the indicated OAR for each sale. Each of these terms has a common symbol, shown here.

Net operating income (I)	$80,000
Divided by: Selling price (V)	÷ 800,000
Equals: Overall rate (R)	0.10
In percent	10%

To select an overall capitalization rate, the direct comparison of market sales is usually the most reliable of the methods available. (R_o refers to the OAR or ratio for the overall property.) However, effort and skill are required when using it. First, an adequate sample of comparable sales is required. Three or four sales are desirable. Even then, three sales might be considered sufficient only if the properties are relatively comparable to the subject property. Comparability is as important here as it was in the sales comparison approach. Location, size, age and condition, number of units (when pertinent), and intensity of land use should be similar to the subject property. Once tentative comparable sales have been selected, the transaction data for each sale should be screened, so that only open market sales that occurred around the date of value are used. Unusual financing terms must be analyzed and the sale price adjusted if indicated. Last, the net income reported for each comparable should be reviewed. Is it based on a current market rent schedule? Have all appropriate expenses been deducted from the scheduled gross? The results of the direct comparison method are only as reliable as the answers to these questions.

In many cases, the appraiser can strengthen the overall capitalization rates obtained from sales. One possibility is to study published surveys of market OARs. Reviewing how the survey rates have changed over time, or how the rates vary by property quality or location, can help in analyzing the sales. Another possibility is to interview active real estate brokers or investors, regarding OARs and the issues that affect them. Such market commentary in some cases could be critical to selecting the rate.

The direct comparison method can also be used to estimate the cash-on-cash or equity dividend rate, which is the overall cap rate for the equity (R_e). The debt service (income to the mortgage, or I_m) of the sold property is subtracted from its net operating income (I_o), leaving the cash flow to the equity (I_e). This is divided by the equity investment (V_e), to estimate the equity overall cap rate (R_e), as shown here.

Net operating income (I_o)	$80,000
Less: Annual debt service (I_m)	− 73,440
Equals: Equity cash flow (I_e)	$6,560
Divided by: Equity investment (V_e)	÷ 160,000
Equals: Equity overall cap rate (R_e)	0.041
In percent	4.1%

Rarely, the appraiser will want to calculate an interest rate for the property (Y_o) from sales evidence. The most reliable method is to use the *delta* relationship, discussed earlier. If the expectation for future value change can be estimated, (by interviews, for example), the annual delta can be calculated and applied to market-derived overall capitalization rates. This is a relatively new concept, not yet commonly used.

Alternatively, the classic analysis could be used, as follows. In order to extract the interest rate from the sale, rather than the overall rate, we must first deduct from the net income the amount required for annual recapture of improvement value, before dividing by the sale price. Such a procedure is most valid when property values are slowly declining over a long time. First, the value of the improvements must be abstracted from the total sale price by subtracting the land value. Next, the annual recapture amount must be calculated. If it is assumed that recapture will take place at a constant rate over the remaining economic life of the improvements, then the annual amount for recapture may be estimated as follows:

$$\frac{\text{Improvement value}}{\text{Remaining economic life}} = \text{Annual recapture amount}$$

What if we assumed that the improvement in the last example represented 80 percent of the total property value and had an estimated remaining economic life at the time of sale of 40 years? The interest rate could be estimated by the direct comparison method, as shown in Example 14-2.

Note that when the interest/yield rate is abstracted from market sales, the appraiser relies on a subjective estimate of remaining economic life and an assumption that the market anticipates recapture out of the income stream. For this reason, the resulting interest rate is best if compared with interest rates calculated by other methods before it is used.

The Band of Investment Method

The real estate market is said to be made up of equity investors on the one hand and lenders on the other. Since both groups may be viewed as investors in income property, they combine to create what is referred to as the "band of investment." The *band of investment method* produces a capitalization rate that is a weighted average. This means that it is an average of two or more rates, adjusted for the percent of property value each source of money represents. The method combines a rate for mortgage loan money and a rate for the investor's equity money. The relative weight or importance of each rate depends on the percentage of the purchase price provided by the loan and the equity down payment.

EXAMPLE 14-2 Interest Rate by Direct Comparison

Total net income		$80,000
Less: Building recapture:		
Sale price	$800,000	
Times: Improvement ratio	x 0.80	
Equals: Improvement value	$640,000	
Divided by: Remaining life	÷ 40	
Equals: Annual building recapture		− $16,000
Equals: Net income after recapture		$64,000
Divided by:		÷ $800,000
Equals: Interest rate		0.08
As a percent		8%

There are two separate versions of the band of investment method. One is used to estimate the interest or yield rate for the property; the other is used to estimate the property overall rate. Of the two, the overall rate calculation is by far the most common.

To estimate a property interest rate by the band of investment method, it is first necessary to estimate the required yield rate for the equity funds. Then, the calculations follow the format of Example 14-3.

In practice, solving for an interest rate by the band of investment method is difficult, because good evidence of the required **equity yield rate** is hard to find. Technically, too, the answer is only correct with an interest-only loan and a level future value. If amortized loans are typical for the type of property you are analyzing, the procedure shown needs to be adjusted for loan amortization and value change. This adjustment step is covered in advanced appraisal courses. This method can be used as a check on market-derived capitalization rates.

The second type of band of investment method calculates an overall capitalization rate (OAR) for the property. This is the more widely used band of investment method among investors and appraisers. It uses the mortgage constant instead of the mortgage interest rate, and the equity cash-on-cash (or dividend) rate instead of the equity yield rate. The **mortgage constant** (R_m) is defined as the total annual loan payment (I_m) divided by the loan amount (V_m), that is, the ratio of the annual loan payment to the loan. The mortgage constant is the OAR for the loan funds. The equity cash-on-cash (or dividend) rate (R_e) is the ratio of the equity cash flow (I_e) to the equity down payment (V_e), or investment. Remember that the equity cash flow is defined as the income remaining from the net operating income after deducting the loan payments. The equity dividend rate

---

EXAMPLE 14-3 Interest Rate by the Band of Investment Method

A. Assumptions:

The prevailing loan terms for a particular type of property include 9 percent interest, with a maximum loan of 75 percent of the property's value. The equity down payment will accordingly be 25 percent of the property's value. For this investment, assume that equity yield expectations are found to be 12 percent.

B. Calculation:

Loan	0.75 x 0.09 =	0.0675
Plus: Equity	0.25 x 0.12 =	0.0300
Equals: Property interest rate		0.0975
In percent		9.75%

EXAMPLE 14-4 Overall Rate by the Band of Investment Method

A. Assume:

(1) There is an 80 percent loan.

(2) The annual total of the level monthly payments on the loan amounts to 13 percent of the original loan amount.

(3) The buyers require a 7 percent first-year cash-on-cash return on the down payment.

B. Calculations:

Loan	0.80 x 0.13 =	0.104
Plus: Equity	0.20 x 0.07 =	0.014
Equals: Indicated overall rate		0.118
As a percent		11.8%

is the OAR for the equity funds. To solve for the overall rate by the band of investment method, follow Example 14-4.

The Summation Method

The *summation method* is nearly always used to estimate an interest rate rather than a rate of capitalization. The rate is calculated by combining, or adding up, amounts for the separate theoretical elements that help determine yield rates. Thus, such a rate is sometimes called a *built-up rate*. The return on a nearly risk-free investment, such as a U.S. government bond, is the starting point and is called the *safe rate*. Penalties are added to the safe rate for the various ways in which the actual investment property characteristics are less than ideal. (In some models, characteristics judged to be better than typical, such as prospects for appreciation, are entered in the formula as negatives.) Some of the investment criteria listed earlier in this chapter will be recognized here.

Safe rate	6.75%
Plus: Investment risk	+ 3.00%
Plus: Lack of liquidity	+ 1.25%
Plus: Burden of management	+ 1.00%
Equals: Indicated interest rate	12.00%

The weakness of the summation method lies in the imprecise and subjective methods available for rating the various investment features involved. However, some very large real estate investors now actively use versions of this concept, and it is useful to illustrate the various investment considerations, even if the exact component amounts are unknown.

Other Methods of Calculating Rates

Several other methods of estimating rates are worthy of mention. An interest rate can be converted to a composite capitalization rate by adding a component for recapture. Adding a recapture component assumes that the typical investor requires that capital recovery be provided for out of current income. This method should be used only when this assumption is a reasonable one for investment markets for the subject property on the date of value.

Capitalization techniques have been developed to allow for analysis of the return of capital from reversion amounts, that is, out of proceeds from the future sale of the property. For example, the so-called *Ellwood method* (named after a well-known mortgage banker, author, and lecturer) suggests methods for adjusting overall rates that were derived from the band of investment method, to reflect both the equity buildup from loan amortization and/or anticipated changes in property value.

Adjusting Rates to Apply to the Subject Property

When capitalization rates are derived from sales of comparable properties, the rates may need to be adjusted to reflect differences in the physical characteristics of the subject property and the comparable properties, as well as differences in the economic conditions as of the valuation date. Although there are no precise methods for adjusting rates, certain techniques of rate adjustment can be borrowed from the rate-finding methods already mentioned. Five key differences need to be considered:

1. Property location.
2. The age, quality, and condition of any improvements.
3. The remaining economic life of the improvements.
4. The ratio of building value to total value.
5. Expenses occurring as a percentage of market value (e.g., property taxes).

Location

Location of the property may have a dramatic effect on interest and capitalization rates, because the property's location can affect the relative risk of the investment, the probable future trend of rental rates and reversion values, and investor motivation in general.

The age, quality, condition, and remaining economic life of improvements are all important too. Although small differences may not merit rate adjustments, significant differences may influence the market attitude about the relative safety and durability of the particular property's income stream.

The ratio of building value to total value may influence the amount of income tax shelter that the investor has available, or it may influence the requirement for capital recovery. As a result, capitalization rates generally should be based on sale properties with building-to-value ratios that are similar to the subject property's ratio.

Expenses

Some expenses vary with the property's value. These also are important influences on capitalization rates. Market-derived capitalization rates may need to be adjusted to reflect the subject property's expenses when they are expected to occur as a percentage of market value. Ad valorem property taxes are the best example. By adding the *property tax rate* to the capitalization rate, property taxes can often be projected more accurately than by estimating taxes as a dollar amount of expense. Note that the net income *before* property taxes is capitalized in this method. An example is given in Chapter 13.

How to Allow for Capital Recovery

In some capitalization methods, the appraiser must explicitly consider capital recovery. Note that these capitalization methods are not commonly used. There are three recognized methods to calculate a specific dollar or percent provision for capital recovery in income capitalization (see Figure 14-10). The straight-line and sinking fund methods specify actual recapture provisions, either in the capitalization rate or in an adjustment to annual income. The annuity method includes recapture within the capitalization technique "automatically." Let us define these three methods and their underlying assumptions. Remember that some capitalization techniques (for example, the direct capitalization method using an OAR) do not specifically provide for capital recovery by any of these three methods. Instead, capital recovery is a hidden component of the overall rate found from analyzing the sales.

Figure 14-10
Capital Recovery
Methods.

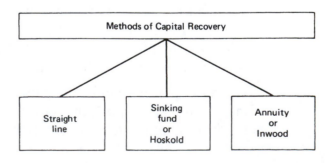

Straight-Line Recapture

The **straight-line recapture method** assumes that annual recapture payments must be provided out of the annual net income and should be the same amount each year. In some techniques, the annual payment is treated as an expense in dollars; in others, it is handled as a component of the capitalization rate. The straight-line recapture method has been a common appraisal tool in the past, but it is conceptually flawed and is not recommended in most cases. It should especially be avoided when reasonably reliable overall capitalization rates (or the components of a weighted-average OAR) can be extracted from the market sales.

The Sinking Fund or Hoskold Method of Recapture

The *sinking fund (Hoskold) recapture method* assumes that the annual investment recapture amounts are deposited into a sinking fund or account, where they earn interest and compound (grow with interest) at a safe rate (usually the savings account interest rate or the going rate for long-term U.S. government bonds). The sinking fund method is conceptually valid. It represents what investors actually did at the time the concept was developed in the late 1800s. Now, the concept is rarely used either by appraisers or investors. However, managers of some large investment funds use analysis methods that are somewhat similar (called the modified internal rate of return, studied in advanced courses) to study the entire fund.

The Annuity or Inwood Method of Recapture

In the **annuity recapture method**, invested capital is recovered from the level annual income in exactly the same manner as a loan is paid off. Annual recapture amounts are assumed capable of earning compound interest at the yield, or interest, rate of the property being appraised, rather than at a safe rate as in the Hoskold method. Because this method also corrects for the flaw inherent in straight-line recapture, a given amount of income recaptures a larger investment than in the straight-line method. Also known as annuity or yield capitalization, the annuity method was in the past reserved for the appraisal of properties under long-term leases to reliable tenants. Now, however, it is considered suitable for any property type if the yield rate is adjusted to reflect the risk involved. This method is another, older, form of yield capitalization, discussed in Section 14.4.

The Recapture Time Period

In any of the three methods mentioned, the recapture of invested funds takes place over a period of time. This period may be either the investor's anticipated holding period, or the estimated remaining economic life of the improvements, depending on the capitalization technique used. The length of the recapture period depends on such influences as the age and condition of the improvements, the risk of building obsolescence, and the specific requirements of the particular investor market.

The Mechanics of Straight-Line Recapture

A few capitalization techniques to be covered in the next section require that you know how to calculate straight-line recapture. Two simple steps are involved:

1. The annual recapture rate is calculated by dividing the capital recovery or recapture time period into 100 percent. The result is the **recapture rate**, expressed as a percentage.

2. The recapture rate is added to the required annual yield, or interest, rate for the property. The total is the **composite capitalization rate** used for that portion of the investment involving the wasting asset.

This composite rate can be used to capitalize the portion of the net income that is earned by the improvements. The result is an estimate of improvement value. Example 14-5 shows how such a rate is derived.

As we have already pointed out, investment capital may be recovered or recaptured out of the current income, the proceeds of sale, or

---

EXAMPLE 14-5 A Composite Building Capitalization Rate

A. Assume:

The market anticipates (1) a 9 percent average annual yield, or average return, on the total debt and equity funds invested in the property, and (2) that the total capital invested in the improvements is to be recaptured over a period of 40 years.

B. Calculations:

Interest rate for improvements	9.0%
Plus: Recapture rate (100% ÷ 40 years)	+ 2.5%
Equals: Composite building rate	11.5%

It is also possible to calculate an overall capitalization rate if, in addition to the above information, you know the building-to-total-value ratio. If we assume that improvement value is 80 percent of total value, then the calculation would be:

Interest rate for the total property		9.0%
Plus: Recapture rate:		
Building recapture rate	2.5%	
Times: Building value ratio	x 80%	
Equals: Building recapture		+ 2.0%
Equals: Overall rate		11.0%

---

some combination. If investors expect value to appreciate in the future, then investment recapture from the income probably would not be a necessary part of the capitalization rate. Remember, too, that in some capitalization methods, the recapture rate is never specifically identified or calculated. Instead, it is simply hidden within the data obtained from the market, as is the case with overall rates derived by the direct comparison method.

14.3 Direct and Residual Capitalization Techniques

As we suggested earlier in this chapter, certain income capitalization techniques are based on the principle of contribution. This implies that any single part of the property can be valued by measuring its contribution to the total net income. Other techniques look at the total property. Four income capitalization techniques are presented here. Their current usefulness and/or their historic importance will be discussed as they are described in this section. The names of the techniques suggest their methods: The value of either the total property, or of a specified portion, is measured by the income that is "residual" to, or accountable to, that portion of the property. Here are the four income capitalization techniques:

1. Direct capitalization technique
2. Equity residual technique
3. Building residual technique
4. Land residual technique

Direct Capitalization Technique

The **direct capitalization technique** is the simplest method of income capitalization, and often the most reliable. It is also the most commonly used. In order to apply the direct capitalization technique, the first step is to estimate an OAR by one of the three methods described in Section 14.2. These were the direct comparison method, the band of investment method, and the summation (built-up) method. The direct comparison method is preferred because it best measures how actual market attitudes affect values. The band of investment technique (using cap rates rather than yield rates) would be second-best in this regard.

The second and final step in the direct capitalization technique is to capitalize the net income that is projected for the subject property. This is done by dividing the net income by the overall rate you have selected.

The direct capitalization technique is always recommended for use when there are adequate numbers of comparative sales to indicate the direct relationship between net income and value (see Example 14-6). This means that the sales should be relatively similar to the subject in size, character, and the ratio of land value to building value. The sales and the subject property should also represent or possess similar risks and value trends. In addition, the sales need to have occurred relatively close to the date of value.

The conclusion reached by direct capitalization is only as accurate as the estimate of income and the overall rate selected. As we learned in the last chapter, income and expenses are not consistently reported by the real estate industry. For example, reserves for replacement are not usually included in the expenses reported in sales and listings. Buildings also differ in the degree of owner management. Appraisal errors can result in both income and capitalization rate analysis when expenses are handled differently for the subject property and the comparable sales. Because of this, it is important to try to establish that the net operating income for the subject property was projected on the same basis as for the sales.

Equity Residual Technique

The **equity residual technique** analyzes the cash flow from an investment. Such a cash flow analysis could also be described as the residual income to the equity investment. The equity residual technique can be used whenever financing terms are a major influence on market prices. However, it is especially useful for analyzing the buyer's equity position relative to a particular proposed or existing loan. The value of the total property is then estimated by adding the loan amount to the calculated equity value (see Example 14-7).

There are three steps in the equity residual technique.

1. Subtract the annual loan payments from the net operating income to estimate the annual cash flow to the investor.

2. Divide the equity cash flow (from step 1) by the estimated equity cash-on-cash rate (equity dividend rate or equity cap rate). The result is the indicated value of the equity.

3. Add the indicated value of the equity to the amount owed on the mortgage. The result is the estimated value of the property.

EXAMPLE 14-6 Direct Capitalization Technique

Net operating income	$ 100,000
Divided by: Overall capitalization rate	÷ 10%
Equals: Indicated value	$1,000,000

EXAMPLE 14-7 Equity Residual Technique

A. Assume:

Net operating income	$ 100,000
Loan amount	$ 600,000
Annual loan payments	$ 70,000
Equity cash-on-cash rate (from sales or interviews)	7%

B. Solution:

Net income	$ 100,000
Less: Loan payments	– 70,000
Equals: Equity cash flow	$ 30,000
Divided by: Equity cash-on-cash rate	÷ 0.07
Equals: Indicated equity value	$ 429,000
Plus: Loan amount	+ 600,000
Equals: Total value estimate	$1,029,000
Rounded	$1,000,000

When the equity residual technique is applied using the typical market financing terms and equity rates, it results in an estimate of market value for the property. However, when it is calculated using unique financing rates (e.g., an assumed existing loan or new seller financing), the resulting value is properly described as "market value as financed." Similarly, if calculated using the desired equity cash-on-cash rate of a particular investor rather than market equity cash-on-cash rates on the date of value, the resulting value is referred to as **investment value**.

Building Residual Technique

The **building residual technique** can be used to capitalize income when the building value is uncertain but there is reliable evidence to support an accurate estimate of the land value. Ideally, the land value would be estimated from sales of land parcels close in time to the date of value and that have similar physical characteristics, location, and zoning.

The building residual technique is most useful when you are appraising older buildings and the sales data are inadequate to estimate overall rates for the direct capitalization technique. Once quite popular, the building residual technique is now considered much less reliable, because it rests on two doubtful assumptions: The first is that future land values will be the same as land values at the date of value; the second is that future building values will decline from the date of value levels so that the investor must recapture the building investment out of annual income. Neither of these assumptions seems warranted in the typical real estate market today.

The building residual technique has five steps, if we assume that straight-line recapture is used.

1. Estimate the interest rate and recapture rate using the methods described in Section 14.2.

2. Calculate the amount of income that is needed to provide a satisfactory return on the land investment by multiplying the land value times the selected interest rate. The resulting income is sometimes referred to as the "land charge."

3. Subtract the land return from the total net operating income to calculate the income that can be attributed to the improvements.

4. Capitalize the income to the improvements by using a composite building capitalization rate that combines both interest and recapture.

5. Add the indicated value for the improvements to the value indicated for the land to obtain the total property value.

An illustration of the building residual technique is given in Example 14-8.

Land Residual Technique

The **land residual technique** is useful when the building value can be reliably estimated but the land value is unclear or unknown. When the improvements are new or nearly new, and are also clearly the highest and best use of the land, the value of the improvements often will equal their cost of reproduction. Now, land value can be estimated by capitalizing that part of the net income that can be attributed to it. Again, we assume that the superior direct capitalization method cannot be applied. Here are the seven steps in the land residual technique (again, assuming straight-line recapture):

1. Calculate the interest rate and recapture rate, as suggested in Section 14.2.

2. Add the two rates to calculate the composite building capitalization rate.

3. Estimate the value of the improvements by using their reproduction or replacement cost less accrued depreciation.

4. Multiply the improvement value by the composite rate calculated in step 2. The result is known as the "building charge," or the income needed to provide the desired return of, and return on, the building investment.

EXAMPLE 14-8 The Building Residual Technique

A. Assume:

Net operating income	$ 91,000
Land value (estimated from land sales)	$200,000
Interest rate (estimated from sales of leased land)	7%
Recapture rate (estimated from the age and condition of the subject)	4%

B. Solution:

Net income		$ 91,000
Less: Return required on land:		
Land value	$200,000	
Times: Land interest rate	x 0.07	
Equals: Land return		− $ 14,000
Equals: Net income to improvements		$ 77,000
Divided by composite rate:		
Interest rate	0.07	
Plus: Recapture rate	+ 0.04	
Equals: Composite rate		÷ 0.11
Equals: Indicated improvement value		$700,000
Plus: Land value		+ 200,000
Equals: Property value		$900,000

5. Subtract the building charge from the net operating income to calculate the net income that is left over and is attributed to the land.

6. Divide the net income that is attributed to the land by the selected interest rate. The result is the indicated value of the land.

7. Add the estimated values for the land and building to calculate the indicated value for the total property.

The land residual technique does not have the importance it once had in the appraisal of developed properties, because this technique involves the same questionable assumptions as the building residual technique. However, the land residual technique is one of the available methods for the appraisal of land, as described in Chapter 10. Perhaps the major remaining use of the land residual technique, or variations of it, is in studies of the highest and best use, and/or project feasibility studies, for vacant or under-improved land. The land residual technique is demonstrated in Example 14-9.

EXAMPLE 14-9 Land Residual Technique

A. Assumptions:

Net operating income	$70,000
Building cost new	$600,000
Interest rate (estimated from the band of investment or summation method)	6.5%
Recapture rate (estimated from the age and condition of the subject)	2.5%

B. Solution:

Net income			$70,000
Less: Income to the building:			
Improvement value		$600,000	
Times composite rate:			
Interest rate	0.065		
Plus: Recapture rate	+ 0.025		
Equals: Composite rate		x .09	
Equals: Income to building			− $54,000
Equals: Income to land			$16,000
Divided by: Interest rate			÷ 0.065
Equals: Land value (rounded)			$246,000
Plus: Improvement value			+ $600,000
Equals: Property value			$846,000
Rounded			$850,000

Other Capitalization Theories

As noted earlier, authorities suggest that all income capitalization techniques fall into two basic groups: direct (or ratio) capitalization and yield capitalization. According to this breakdown, the direct capitalization and equity residual techniques presented above fall into the first group, where the income attributed to the portion of the property being appraised is converted into a value estimate by use of a single capitalization rate, or value ratio. The techniques do not use a yield rate. But the building and land residual techniques would be classified as **yield capitalization** techniques, because each requires estimating a yield rate. Direct capitalization does not explicitly address possible future income and value changes for the property. Therefore, the true investment yield expectations are not known.

Yield capitalization can be a more sophisticated method of analyzing an investment. Either short-term or long-term investments can be appraised. Additionally, true investment yield can be analyzed by factoring in anticipated changes in property or equity income, buildup of equity from loan amortization, and/or property value appreciation or depreciation.

Discounted cash flow (DCF) is perhaps the most common example of yield capitalization. (Other forms are beyond the scope of this book.) The key feature of DCF is the mathematical discounting of specified future incomes or benefits, over a defined holding period. Section 14.4 will analyze discounted cash flow.

14.4 Estimating, Measuring, and Discounting Cash Flows

In appraisals, the value of money to be received in the future must be reduced, or discounted, to its present value (on the date of value), recognizing the time value of money. This section explores how to do that by an explicit projection of all future cash flows.

Nearly always, *yield capitalization* is used to estimate the value of a stream of future cash flows. Remember that yield capitalization requires an *explicit* estimate of:

1. Future cash flows (or their pattern: level, declining, and so on).
2. The time period of the projection—the holding period.
3. The yield rate (synonymous with interest rate, discount rate, or internal rate of return).

Contrast this requirement with ***ratio capitalization*** using an OAR. In that case, whatever the market believes about future cash flows, for however long, is hidden in the OAR selected after study of the market data. It is clear, however, that the market is very aware of possible future cash flow changes and adjusts the OAR accordingly!

The Use of Cash Flows in Appraisals

The analysis of future cash flow lies at the heart of income property appraisal, financing, and management. The cash flow amounts may be in various forms, including annual investment income or profit, cash from a new loan, and/or projected sales proceeds. In the appraisal of new subdivisions or rental properties, for example, a common problem facing the appraiser is how to take into account the time period needed to sell off the units as they are developed or to rent up new and/or vacant income properties. The solution, in both cases, is to view the amounts to be received as cash flows over a defined time period, and to discount these amounts to a value estimate, reflecting the risk involved. Discounting any of the cash flows mentioned above involves the same mathematical tools as those used in yield capitalization.

Yield capitalization can lead to an estimate of market value if market rate and income projections are used. If the cash flows and discount factors are unique to the particular investor, then the appraisal is an estimate of the *investment value* for the property involved.

The cash flows might be those generated by the entire property, the fee simple interest. Or they might be the amounts coming to the investor after loan payments, the equity interest. If the property is leased, the appraiser might be looking at the cash flow from the lease or from the market rents, depending on the assignment.

Any time a property is expected to be purchased for its future income, a cash flow analysis can be used to estimate its value. However, for a relatively simple income-generating property, especially where no material shifts in income over time are expected, ratio capitalization using an OAR is likely to be more reliable and better supported. But where net income is expected to change a lot over time, a cash flow analysis and yield capitalization may be best.

Why would net income change a lot over time? There are many reasons; here are some:

1. Vacant units gradually get rented.
2. A major tenant is expected to leave, creating a large vacancy that will take time to rent up.
3. Tenants on old, below-market leases soon will start rolling their leases over and paying market rents.
4. Market rents have been relatively flat but are expected to increase noticeably in the near future.
5. A restaurant tenant that has been paying only the base rental is finally attracting much more business and is about to start paying percentage rent above the base.
6. Future maintenance expenses may have to increase to meet a new building code requirement.

Estimating Cash Flows

All of the cash flows in a typical investment can be attributed to two primary sources, net operating income each time period (periodic income) and the proceeds from the sale (or refinance) of the property (reversion). As we have already suggested, the cash flow amounts in each case depend not only upon the income-producing ability of the property, but the financing involved and the value of the property upon sale. While cash flows can be measured either before or after income taxes, only pretax cash flows will be discussed here.

Measuring Cash Flow from Periodic Income

To the equity investor, the cash flow from each time period's investment income can be defined simply as the net operating income less debt service. However, cash flows can be even or uneven, depending on the terms of the lease, the amount of expenses, and the amount and type of loan payments.

Even Cash Flow. For an example of even cash flow, assume that an investment property has an annual income of $100,000 from a 30-year net flat lease. There is a $700,000 loan commitment on the property, at 9 percent interest, to be amortized with annual payments over 30 years. From this data, the expected cash flow is calculated as follows (using a financial table or calculator to solve for the amount of the debt service). We will explore the use of tables and calculators below.

Annual net income	$100,000
Less: Annual debt service	− 68,135
Equals: Annual equity cash flow	$31,865

Uneven Cash Flow. Uneven cash flows can be demonstrated using the same assumptions, except here, assume that the lease income steps up after 15 years to $150,000 per year. Notice that the debt service (loan payment) typically does not change. Cash flows would be as follows:

	Years 1–15	Years 16–30
Annual net income	$100,000	$150,000
Less: Annual debt service	− 68,135	− 68,135
Equals: Annual equity cash flow	$31,865	$81,865

If the property is sold at the end of year 30, the net sale proceeds would be added to the cash flow for the 30th year.

Income Projections

To use yield capitalization, the appraiser must select a time period to be analyzed and then estimate the future income each year, or the pattern of future income changes. Often the time period selected is relatively short—5, 10, or 15 years. This reflects the relatively short *holding period* of many real estate investors. Also, because of the time value of money, income changes in the next 5 to 10 years have much more impact on value than income changes in the distant future.

To prepare a good estimate of future annual income is not easy. The first step is to understand market rents on the date of value. Next is to consider what has happened to market rents for this type of property in this location over the 10 years or so *prior* to the date of value. Is the past pattern cyclical? If so, where is the cycle on the date of value? Or have the past changes been a mixture of cyclical and long-term trend changes? The third step is to try to understand what forces in the local economy are behind the past income changes. Was it just inflation, growth in population, or growth in disposable income?

Once the appraiser has made the effort to try to understand the past, it is time to turn to the future. What seems to be the consensus estimate for future population growth? Inflation? Disposable income? After the appraiser understands the likely economic future, consider how market rents are likely to be affected. Also consider what market experts are predicting. Finally, make an estimate of market rents for this property for each year of the projection period.

The next step is to examine any leases, to see when they might end, and if any tenant has an option to extend their lease. The appraiser then modifies the estimate of future income to reflect the impact of the leases on each year's income. A lease that is favorable to the owner could increase the income for some years. A lease favorable to the tenant could reduce the income. And renewal options might be at the then-market level rent, or above or below!

Measuring Cash Flow from Sale Proceeds

The cash flow from the eventual sale proceeds is calculated by estimating the value of the property at the end of the holding period, and deducting from that amount (1) any marketing and title costs expected to be incurred and (2) any loan balance or payoff.

Estimating the Future Sale Price

There are two methods commonly used to estimate the future sale price. The first capitalizes the income at that time, while the second projects the future value as an annual percent change from current values. The capitalized income method is the more common of the two.

You will recall that value is the present worth of future benefits. That is just as true in 10 or 20 years as it is today. Assume that we want to estimate the future sale price, often called the resale price, 10 years after the date of value. We have already prepared an estimate of the net operating income for each of the 10 years. So, we know what we estimate will be the net for the 12 months before the resale. We could estimate the net for the eleventh year, which essentially becomes the resale buyer's estimate of income for the year after the sale! This we can capitalize, using an OAR (or even using a GIM on the gross income). This is called a *going-out OAR*, as it reflects the rate when the owner is projecting leaving the investment. By contrast, the term *going-in OAR* is used to label the rate for the original purchase. Usually, market participants select a going-out OAR that is slightly higher than the going-in rate. However, this can change as the real estate cycle for this type and location of property changes. See Example 14-10.

The second method projects the future value as an annual percent value change, starting with the value on the date of value. It could also be an estimate of the total value change over the projection period. The starting value could be from a market approach or by using direct capitalization. The annual percent value change usually is the same each year, but there is no reason why one could not use a different rate of change every year. The hard part, in either case, is how to tie the value change projection to the market. What does the market think the value change will be? Usually, past experience or interviews will be the only workable sources.

Discounting Cash Flows

Discounting investment cash flows means estimating a value for them, as of the date of value, that recognizes the time value of money and the risk involved. To understand the time value of money, we need to quickly review the theory of discount math.

EXAMPLE 14-10 Calculating Net Sale Proceeds

A. Assumptions:

Referring to the earlier example, assume that the property can be sold, subject to the existing lease, after 15 years. The sale is for cash to a new loan, with the new buyer basing the price on a capitalization rate of 10 percent of the net operating income from the lease. Further, assume that there is no prepayment penalty on the old loan, and that the marketing costs and seller's closing costs total 6 percent of the sale price. We will calculate these amounts as follows, using financial tables or a financial calculator to figure the loan balance.

B. Calculations:

Sale price:		
Annual net income	$150,000	
Divided by: Cap rate	÷ .10	
Equals: Sale price		$1,500,000
Less: Marketing and closing costs:		
Sale price	$1,500,000	
Times: Costs in percent	x 6%	
Equals: Closing costs		– $ 90,000
Equals: Net price before loan payoff		$1,410,000
Less: Loan balance		– $ 549,219
Equals: Cash flow from sale proceeds		$ 860,781

The Theory of "Discount" Math

A given sum that you have to wait for is worth less to you than the same sum today. Placing money in a savings account and taking it out after it has earned interest is a common example. Let us explain. When you place $1.00 in a 5 percent account, you are in fact recognizing that the $1.05 promised in one year has only a $1.00 present value. The deposit is less than the future amount. Hence, $1.00 is the present value of $1.05 when discounted for one year to earn 5 percent.

What is the discount factor in the previous example? Since the ratio of $1.00 to $1.05 is .95238, this is the proven discount factor. The same factor can be used for any sum that is due one year in the future when discounted at 5 percent. For the lump-sum amount of $1.05 due in one year, here are the calculations that show the present value to be $1.00.

Amount due in the future	$1.05
Times: Discount factor	x .95238
Equals: Present value	$1.00

How to Estimate a Factor

Often, using discount math requires that the appraiser use a factor, which is a number that adjusts for the time value of money. Factors can be looked up in a table or can be calculated with a financial calculator. Factors can even be calculated using formulas and a regular calculator!

There are six common factors. We have already noted the need to estimate the present value of a future dollar, which is used to discount the resale reversion amount to its "present value." And there is the present value of a future income stream, for example, the present worth of the next 10 years of annual income. Each of these two factors also has an opposite: the future worth of a dollar today and the future worth of an income stream starting today.

Finally, the last two factors also form a pair, but instead of solving for a present or future value, these two solve for a periodic payment. One is the periodic payment to pay off a present sum, also known as the *loan constant* or *loan payment factor*. The second is the periodic payment to create a future lump-sum value, also known as the *sinking fund factor*, and sometimes used to calculate the annual reserve expense needed in order to be able to replace some item (such as a roof) at a date in the future. The periodic payment could be monthly, quarterly, annually, or any other time interval.

All six factors involve, first, an interest rate, and second, a time period. A set of tables would show different time periods and rates so that the appraiser could select the appropriate ones. Example 14-11

EXAMPLE 14-11 Compound Interest Table

Time	Future Worth of $1	Future Worth of $1/Period	Sinking Fund Factor	Present Worth of $1	Present Worth of $1/Period	Loan Constant
1	1.10	1.00	1.00	0.91	0.91	1.10
2	1.21	2.10	0.48	0.83	1.74	0.58
3	1.33	3.31	0.30	0.75	2.49	0.40
4	1.46	4.66	0.22	0.68	3.17	0.32
5	1.61	6.11	0.16	0.62	3.79	0.26

is a small table excerpt at a 10 percent interest rate. (Published tables usually are to six or seven digits.)

Financial Calculators

Everything that can be found in a table of financial factors can also be calculated in an instant with a financial calculator (Hewlett Packard, Texas Instruments, and others make them). The most widely used is the HP12C, but others have similar keys and capabilities. They are used by keying in a number and hitting the key to identify what the number is—a present value (PV), a future value (FV), a periodic payment (PMT), a time period (N) or number of periods, and a rate (usually i). Once the known numbers are entered, the key for the answer, the unknown, is hit to start the calculation. Financial calculators have essentially replaced all use of printed tables by appraisers.

Discount Formula for a Single Future Payment

Discount factors for a single amount due in one, two, three, or any number of years in the future at any chosen discount or interest rate may be found by the following formula, which is built into discount tables and financial calculators. Note that the single future payment amount is always assumed to be $1.00, so that any dollar amount can be multiplied by the factor to calculate its present worth.

$$\text{Present value of } \$1.00 \quad = \quad \frac{1}{(1 + i)^n}$$

Where: i = discount rate (in percent)
n = number of future time periods

If we use a financial calculator to solve for the single future payment discount factor shown earlier, the variables would be entered and the solution found as follows (FV refers to future value and PV to present value):

Given: $n = 1$; i(in %) = 5; FV = $1.00
To solve: PV = $0.95238

Discounting a Stream of Payments

A stream of payments can be analyzed one at a time, with each discounted as a single payment due at a different date in the future, or the entire stream can be discounted at once. Factors for discounting an income stream may be found in financial tables or calculated with a financial calculator.

To demonstrate how to discount a stream of payments, suppose we solve for the present (discounted) value of the first 15-year income stream given in the uneven cash flow investment example cited earlier. Assuming an investor would require a 12 percent yield, we refer to a 12 percent financial table, in the column referred to as the "present worth of one per period." For 15 years, we find listed the factor of 6.8109. When this present worth factor is applied to the annual income, the present worth of the income stream is calculated as follows:

$$\$31,865 \times 6.8109 = \$217,000 \text{ (rounded)}$$

Using a financial calculator, the variables are entered, and the problem is solved as follows (where PMT is the annual equity cash flow amount):

Given: $n = 15$; i (in %) = 12; PMT = $31,865
To solve: PV = $217,000 (rounded)

Discounting the Sale Proceeds

As explained above, the sale proceeds as a single cash flow amount are projected to be available when an investment property is sold. The following example shows how to discount this cash flow.

We refer again to the investment analysis example cited above. There, the net future sale proceeds were estimated to be $860,781, available in 15 years. To discount to its present value, we refer to a 12 percent "present worth of one" table at 15 years to find the discount factor, and multiply it by the net equity proceeds, calculating as follows:

$$\$860,781 \times 0.1827 = \$157,250 \text{ (rounded)}$$

Using a financial calculator, the same answer is found, as follows:

Given: $n = 15$; i (in %) = 12; FV = $860,781
To solve: PV = $157,250 (rounded)

Summary of Anticipated Cash Flows

Let us summarize the anticipated equity cash flows (a 15-year annual cash flow, and the sale proceeds at the end of 15 years) in the investment example partially solved above.

A. Equity cash flow

Annual cash flow:

Net annual income	$100,000
Less: Debt service	− 68,135
Equals: Annual cash flow	$ 31,865

B. Equity sale proceeds

Anticipated sale proceeds:

Future sale price	$1,500,000
Less: Sale costs	− 90,000
Less: Loan balance	− 549,219
Equals: Sale proceeds	$ 860,781

Summary of Discounted Cash Flows

When we summarize the discounted cash flows shown above, we can solve for the present worth of the equity investment, suggesting the amount of down payment that is warranted for the investment in question, assuming the investor's yield requirement is 12 percent.

Cash Flow	Amount	Times	Discount Factor	Equals	Present Value
Income stream	$3,865	x	6.8109	=	$217,000
Plus: Sale proceeds	$860,781	x	0.1827	=	+$157,250
Equals: Total present worth of equity				=	$374,250

SUMMARY

Income capitalization is a process of translating income into value. By selecting capitalization rates that reflect the types and amounts of return sought in the real estate investment market, the appraiser completes the link between income and value.

Rates may be selected by the direct comparison method, the band of investment method, or the summation method. Briefly, the direct comparison method derives an overall capitalization rate from market sales by using the ratio of net income to the selling price. This method often provides the most reliable estimate of overall capitalization rates. The band of investment method can be used to estimate either the property's interest rate or the overall capitalization rate with the second considered more useful. This method calculates the average of typical loan rates and market equity requirements. Last, the summation method, rarely used now, can be used to build up a rate, by adding investment risk, non-liquidity, and other investment elements to a base rate or safe rate of return.

Some capitalization techniques require a specific allowance for the return of the money invested in improvements on the theory that age and obsolescence will limit their economic life expectancy. This allowance is labeled recapture or return of investment. Three methods of recapture are available. All assume that an annual payment for recapture must be paid from the annual income of the property. The straight-line and sinking fund methods make specific annual provisions for recapture, either in the capitalization rate or by a dollar amount subtracted from the net income. The annuity method provides for recapture in the same way that a mortgage is amortized by use of annuity factors. Selecting the appropriate recapture method depends on the nature, duration, and quality of the income stream.

Four techniques for capitalizing income are noteworthy. Direct capitalization would be used when a market study shows a consistent relationship between net operating income and sale prices. The net income of the subject property is divided by the overall rate to calculate the estimated value. Good comparable sales are desirable for this method. The building residual technique can be used when the land value is known but the improvement value is unknown. Income attributed to the improvements is capitalized and added to the land value to reach a total value estimate.

The land residual technique can be used when the building value is known but the land value is unknown. Income attributed to the land is capitalized and added to the known improvement value. In both the building and land residual techniques, a specific allowance must be made in order to recapture the improvement investments over their estimated economic life. Because of the controversial assumptions required, both methods are rarely used today.

The equity residual technique can qualify as a market valuation technique when typical market loan and equity cash flow figures are used. However, its more common application involves an analysis of a property value from the point of view of a particular investor looking at a specific loan. In either case, the cash flow attributable to the equity investment is capitalized and added to the loan amount.

Many experts suggest that all capitalization techniques can be described as either direct or yield capitalization. Direct capitalization uses a single capitalization rate, or ratio, to convert the income being studied to an estimate of value. It does not matter whether it is income that is attributed to the total property, the building, the land, or the equity. No yield rate assumptions are involved. On the other hand, yield capitalization does require explicit estimates of yield rates, often in a mathematical discounting procedure. This considers anticipated changes in property or equity income, as well as property value changes projected during the investment period. In this way, true investment yield requirements or expectations can be analyzed. In appraisals, the market value of amounts to be received in the future must always be reduced or discounted to their present values, recognizing the time value of money. In this chapter we reviewed the several purposes of cash flow analysis in appraisals. We also covered the subject of discounting cash flows in the context of yield capitalization.

IMPORTANT TERMS AND CONCEPTS

Annuity recapture method

Band of investment method

Building residual technique

Capital recovery

Capitalization

Capitalization rate

Cash flow

Composite capitalization rate

Debt service

Delta (value change)

Direct capitalization technique

Direct comparison method

Discount rate

Discounted cash flow (DCF)

Duration of the income

Equity dividend rate

Equity residual technique

Equity yield rate

Going-in OAR

Going-out OAR

Hypothecation

Income stream

Interest rate

Internal rate of return

Investment value

Land residual technique

Leverage

Mortgage constant

Overall capitalization rate (OAR)

Periodic rate

Ratio capitalization

Recapture rate

Reversion

Safe rate

Straight-line recapture method

Summation method

Time value of money

Yield capitalization

Yield rate

REVIEWING YOUR UNDERSTANDING

1. Income capitalization is the broad term used to describe the process of estimating the value of income property by studying the economic relationship between income and value. This process:
   a. Converts the net income of a property into its equivalent capital value
   b. Reflects the time value of money by reducing or discounting future income to its present worth
   c. Focuses on the present worth of future benefits
   d. All of the above

2. The appraiser's choice of a capitalization technique and rate should consider the investment criteria that motivate purchasers of investment property. Which of the following refers to the ability to use the property as loan collateral?
   a. Size or denomination
   b. Hypothecation
   c. Liquidity
   d. Safety

3. The most commonly used capitalization rate is:
   a. The income rate
   b. The composite capitalization rate
   c. The interest rate
   d. The overall rate

4. Capitalization rates may be estimated by any of several methods. Which of the following is generally the preferred method of deriving a capitalization rate?
   a. Summation
   b. Band of investment
   c. Direct comparison
   d. None of the above

5. There are three recognized methods to provide for capital recovery in income capitalization. In which method is invested capital recovered from the annual income in exactly the same manner as a loan is paid off?
   a. The annuity or Inwood method
   b. The straight-line recapture method
   c. The double-declining balance method
   d. The accelerated method

6. The simplest and often the most reliable method of income capitalization is:
   a. The direct capitalization technique
   b. The building residual technique
   c. The land residual technique
   d. The equity residual technique

7. If a $600,000 property has qualified for a 75 percent loan at a 12 percent mortgage constant and the buyer wants a 2 percent annual cash return on his down payment, what net income would the property have to produce?
   a. $3,000
   b. $57,000
   c. $54,000
   d. $12,000

8. If a particular buyer requires a recapture of the building portion of the price in 10 years, what is the indicated recapture rate for the building, assuming straight-line recapture?
   a. 5 percent
   b. 10 percent
   c. 20 percent
   d. 2 percent

9. Recapture of the investment capital in real estate finance is that portion of the loan payment that is earmarked for:
   a. Interest on money due
   b. Payoff of principal
   c. Interest and principal payment
   d. None of the above

10. A new 10,000 square-foot building has just been constructed at a location where no recent vacant land sales have occurred and competitive investments earn 10 percent interest. The replacement cost is $400,000. Assuming a useful life expectancy of 25 years, an economic rent of $1 per square foot per month, and annual expenses of $30,000 including vacancy, what total property value is indicated?
   a. $740,000
   b. $900,000
   c. $1,200,000
   d. $400,000

PRACTICAL APPLICATIONS

As we like to remind you, review the exercise at the end of the preceding chapter and the work that you have performed to date. This assignment moves to the task of calculating the value using the Income Capitalization Approach. It cannot be reported on the income approach section on page 3 of the URAR form, as the URAR only calls for the use of the GIM in the Income Approach. However, you should consider performing an analysis of value using Direct Capitalization, to help you understand what you have read in the chapter. As a tool, consider using one of the income forms mentioned in the last exercise, as a template or guide, to help you process the capitalization information.

The first step is to develop an estimate of the net operating income for the unit. In the last exercise, you estimated the market rental and the operating expenses. You will also need to make a deduction for the stabilized long-term vacancy and collection loss. Five percent of the gross potential income is often used, unless the property is in a location that averages a lot of turnover or collection loss. Review the format of the examples in the text to see how to process this information into an estimate of net operating income.

The next step is to develop an opinion of the Overall Capitalization Rate to be used to convert the net operating income into a value estimate. Ideally, you want to find comparable sales of somewhat similar properties that were rented at the time of sale. Somewhat similar for the purpose of a cap rate comparable means a property that a prospective buyer of this property might also consider buying—it is a competitive property! It need not be as similar in age, size, and so on, as would be desired for a sale comparable or a rental comparable.

Consider if any of the sales that you developed, even those you dropped early, were rented. Also consider your GIM comparables. You already know the income. If you can estimate the expenses, you can calculate the OAR. (Review the text to be sure that all of these terms are clear to you.) Consider talking to the brokers who handled the comparable sales that you identified, as they might sell properties to investors, and either know of cap rate comparables you can use, or may have an opinion about the market level of cap rates that you can refer to as a source instead of, or in addition to, whatever sales comparables you can develop. As always, you will need to research the needed information on each comparable property. It is not easy to identify capitalization rate comparable sales, so you may not have very many sales to research. It would be lovely to start with ten, so you can end up with four good comparable OARs, but you may not succeed. Once you have collected the information about each sale, you will calculate the OAR for each. There is likely to be some variation in the answers, due to issues with your data on the sales, as well as the imperfections and lack of knowledge notable in the small investment markets. The key issues to think about as you analyze the different OARs from the sales include the following:

- Is the rental information reflecting market rents or the actual history of the property?
- Is the expense information likely to be complete?
- Are there differences of location and amenities?

Try to ask if there was anything unusual about the property or transaction as a way of catching unusual issues. Consider how each compares to the subject property. Finally, enter the information in the form that you have chosen to use.

As we note at the end of each exercise, it is best not to get ahead of yourself. So, do not enter information in the later sections of the report until you have read the chapter(s) that covers that topic. However, it is a good idea to look ahead so that you start thinking about the information that you will need. Reminder: If you have questions about the program, review the manuals and help information that were on the program CD. Also, you can go to http://www.bradfordsoftware.com, click on "Services" at the upper right, and then on "ClickFORMS Training Programs" in the middle of the "Services" page.

CHAPTER 15
RECONCILING THE VALUE ESTIMATES

PREVIEW

After the appraiser has applied each of the three approaches, the several value indications that have been developed nearly always must be reduced to a single opinion of value. The process that the appraiser follows to do this is called *reconciliation*. This chapter will explain that process.

OBJECTIVES

When you have completed this chapter you should be able to:

1. Define the term *reconciliation*.

2. Explain why the appraiser must first review each value approach that has been used.

3. Explain why the appraiser reviews the data used in each approach.

4. Show how to round the final answer.

15.1 General Review of the Appraisal

In order to arrive at a *value conclusion*, the appraiser must first review the appraisal itself. The appraiser must be satisfied that an adequate appraisal was performed, before reconciliation begins. This review can be divided into two steps:

1. Review the overall appraisal process.
2. Review for technical accuracy.

Reviewing the Appraisal Process

The first step is to reconsider the overall appraisal assignment. What was the appraisal to accomplish? Have you (1) precisely located and identified the property, (2) clearly defined the property rights to be appraised, (3) pinpointed the date when the value estimate applies, (4) given a formal definition of the type of value stated, and (5) clearly defined the intended use and user of the appraisal and report? Have you considered if any personal property is necessary in order to obtain the value or income that you have established?

In reviewing the data collected and analyzed, have you considered (1) the type of property being appraised, (2) the agreed scope of work, and (3) the intended user(s) of the appraisal? Depending on the property type, scope of work, and use of the appraisal, one or two of the three value approaches may be most relevant. The appraiser should now go back and apply any important approach that might have been omitted.

Technical Review

The next step in this review process is a clerical check for possible errors. First, all calculations should be checked for accuracy. All critical measurements should be reviewed as well. Are they consistent with the other data about the property? If different sources had varying information, was enough work done to provide reasonable assurance as to which number was closest to correct? Second, all data should be checked for completeness and accuracy. Were the data complete and adequate for the purpose for which they were used?

Third, the appraiser should check for *consistency*. Was the highest and best use of the site used as the basis for its value? Is the property age that was used in the sales comparison approach the same in the cost approach? Were neighborhood ratings applied consistently in the approaches? Were the desirable features that were rated in the sales comparison approach also considered in estimating rents for the income approach? Was any economic or functional obsolescence in the cost approach also adjusted for in the sales comparison and income approaches? A positive answer to these and similar questions will ensure that the data in the appraisal have been processed in a consistent manner.

Finally, the last step in this **technical review** is to reconsider any assumptions made during the appraisal. Now that the appraisal is almost completed and the appraiser has the benefit of added insight into the market, do the adjustments, judgments, and/or assumptions used in each approach appear as appropriate, reasonable, and sensible as they did when first employed? This is another way of checking for consistency.

15.2 Reconciling the Value Approaches

Reconciliation has been defined as:

> The last phase of any valuation assignment, in which two or more *value indications* derived from market data are resolved into a final value opinion, which may be either a final range of value or a single point estimate.
>
> Source: *The Dictionary of Real Estate Appraisal*, 4th ed., The Appraisal Institute, Chicago, IL, 2002.

Appraising the Appraisal

Once an overall review of the appraisal has been made, the process of reconciliation then requires an evaluation of each value approach, to estimate its overall relevance and accuracy, both separately and in comparison with the other approaches. The key questions in this evaluation are:

1. How appropriate is this approach in this case?
2. How relevant, reliable, and adequate were the data used?
3. What range of values do the three approaches suggest, and what does the value indication of each tell you about the others?

How Appropriate Is the Approach?

Having completed the approaches, how accurate and relevant is each? What does each tell you about the importance of the others? The validity or relevance of each approach to value depends first on the intended use of the appraisal. In this book, our emphasis has been on using appraisals to estimate market value. However, there can be intended uses for an appraisal that require something other than estimating market value. For example, appraisals for insurance purposes may call for an emphasis on the cost approach.

The type of property plays a role in determining which value approach is used. It usually makes little sense to use an income approach when you are appraising an owner-occupied unique special use property. The cost approach would be more typical. Similarly, you would normally use the sales comparison approach when appraising a single-family residence or, for that matter, any owner-occupied property in an area where good comparable sales are in ample supply.

The use of the appropriate approach can also depend on the state of the market for this property in this location. In some markets, for example, single-family homes are rarely bought and sold for their income characteristics. In such markets, an income approach would not be appropriate. In other markets, however, single-family homes may be sought for their income advantages; here, the income approach might be the more appropriate.

Finally, you must consider the characteristics of each approach. Each has its strengths. Each has its weaknesses. In a particular appraisal assignment, the strength of one approach may be important; the weakness of another may disqualify it. Your intent throughout is to form an opinion on the relative appropriateness of each approach in this specific appraisal assignment.

Evaluating the Data

The next step in the reconciliation process is to evaluate the relevance, reliability, and adequacy of the data used in each approach. In turn, this step takes you closer to a conclusion about the reliability of the approach itself. Each approach must base its conclusions on evidence that is not only pertinent to that approach, but also reliable enough to support its validity. If all of the GIM comparable sales have such property characteristics that they are likely to have a GIM below the subject, for example, the conclusion is less reliable. Finally, the quantity of data must be sufficient to have provided a reasonable range of market indicators and to have supported the techniques used in making the adjustments required. An old appraisal saying is that "one swallow doesn't mark the arrival of spring, nor does one sale make the market." However, every practicing appraiser has had an assignment where diligent research identified only one or two good items of data, along with other less-relevant data!

As part of this review of the data used, the appraiser should consider the assumptions made in the processing of the data used in each approach. Did the sales require large amounts of adjustment? Were the adjustments well supported? Have replacement costs been based on consumer-level costs of similar buildings and adjusted to this location? Were the conclusions of market rent, and other critical factors used in the income approach, based on well-supported analysis? These are the kinds of questions that the appraiser needs to ask at this point in the appraisal. Finally, the approach that is deemed the more reliable in the appraisal at hand should be given the greater weight in arriving at a final value conclusion. This approach probably would be the most relevant one, and would be supported by adequate and reliable data.

The Value Range

The last step in reviewing the approaches is to develop a **range of values**. It is important to note that each approach to value tells you something about the reliability of the other two approaches. Traditionally, experts have said that the cost approach sets the upper limit of value. Most appraisal theoreticians now say that *depreciated* replacement cost does not set the upper limit. Depending on the types of **judgment or data errors** in the cost approach, it is just as conceivable that, in a particular circumstance, the cost approach will be at the lower limit.

In any particular appraisal, however, the appraiser may have a hunch that one or another approach is likely to result in a value that is high or low. For example, in appraising a home in an area that is primarily owner-occupied, it is possible (but not certain) that the income approach would produce a lower estimate of value than the other approaches. This could depend on how the appraiser came up with the capitalization rate or GIM, among other possibilities. Similarly, in appraising a house that may have some economic obsolescence, the cost approach could be higher than the sales comparison approach, particularly if an economic obsolescence deduction had not been calculated. Here is where the appraiser relies on the economic principles that were developed in Chapter 5. By applying these principles to the region, city, and neighborhood, with facts relevant to a particular appraisal, the appraiser can better judge the reliability of each of the three approaches, to decide whether they have established a reasonable range of value.

After a review of the indications of value reached by the approaches, you will see that there is a highest number and a lowest number. This suggests the probable range of minimum-maximum value. The reliability of each approach influences the reliability of this range. Sometimes, you may conclude that the approach with the lowest indication probably is indeed a low estimate of value. So your own evaluation of an approach may lead you to conclude that it probably is high or low. Comparing its value conclusion to the conclusions from the other two approaches gives you a cross-check. In addition, two of the three approaches clustering at one end of the range could lead you to pick a value toward that end of the range. At this point, then, the appraiser reviews 1) the reliability of each approach, 2) what value each one indicates, and 3) which value indications are or might be high and which low.

Reviewing the Theory of the Approaches

Each approach has its own characteristic strengths and weaknesses. Depending on the type of property and the quality and quantity of evidence considered, a particular approach may deserve more weight or less weight in arriving at a value conclusion (see Figure 15-1).

The sales comparison approach, for example, is often considered to be the most direct approach. When there are ample comparable sales data, it usually should receive the greatest weight in valuing residences. Depending on the quality of the comparable sales, the sales comparison approach is also often considered the best evidence in an appraisal performed for condemnation (eminent domain). However, the sales comparison approach requires that there be comparable sales, that reasonable numbers of sales be available, and, for greatest

Figure 15-1 Reconciliation and Final Value Estimates: Portion of Uniform Commercial- Industrial Appraisal Report Form (UCIAR).

RECONCILIATION AND FINAL VALUE ESTIMATES

Cost Approach Indication	$ 402,000
Income Approach Indication	$ 376,500
Direct Sales Comparison Approach Indication	$ 395,000

Reconciliation: This is the step in the appraisal process in which the relative applicability, significance, and reliability of each value indication is weighed by your appraiser. The final conclusion of value results.

The appraised property is improved with a 25 year old industrial building in good condition. It is located in a close-in suburban industrial park situated near rail lines and major transportation arteries. Light manufacturing and warehousing are the predominant occupancies. We have analyzed the economic and demographic data of the immediate community. We have also collected, confirmed, and analyzed a representative number of industrial sale and lease transactions here, and in two nearby competing industrial parks. The results of these studies have been set forth in the body of this self-contained report within the value approaches demonstrated.

We have concluded that the subject improvements represent the highest and best use of the land, and that the highest and best use of the property is its continued use as rental property in light manufacturing occupancy.

As seen above, three approaches were applied in this appraisal. While good comparable sales were found to support a land value for the Cost Approach, we deem this approach to be the least reliable here because of the lack of market data to reliably indicate the amount of accrued depreciation for this older building. Our Income Approach was based on solid evidence of market rent, stabilized operating expenses, and overall capitalization rates. In the case of the Sales Comparison Approach, four very good comparables were used, with minimal adjustments required. The market data presented in support of both the Income and Sales Comparison approaches in this report were personally verified by this appraiser, and considered to be highly reliable.

Placing somewhat equal weight in this appraisal upon the Income and Sales Comparison approaches, we conclude upon the final market value stated below. As indicated in the body of this report, a market exposure of 3 to 6 months is expected.

Conditions of Appraisal: _____

Per signed statement on page 14.

Effective Date of Valuation		4/2/xx
Market Value of Personal Property		$ 0
Market Value of Other Non-Realty Interests	None	$ 0
Total Market Value of Other Non-Realty Interests		$ 0
Value Estimate - Real Estate (As Repaired)		$ 385,000
Less: Cost of Repairs or Additions		$ 0
Final Market Value "As Is" - Real Estate		$ 385,000

Appraiser #1 Signature   *Samuel Lott Hamilton*
Name   Samuel Lott Hamilton

Property Inspection   Yes [X]

Date   May 2, 20xx

Qualifications Attached   Yes [X]   No [ ]

reliability, that the adjustments to the sales be relatively minor or fairly well supported.

The cost approach is often cited as being especially useful when new, economically feasible buildings are being appraised. In addition, it is considered the only way to appraise building types that do not rent and are rarely bought or sold. Examples could include special-purpose or public buildings, certain factories, newer churches, and so on. Major problems with the cost approach include the difficulty in estimating indirect costs, such as the developer's and builder's profit and overhead allowance.

Another problem with the cost approach is in estimating the amount of accrued depreciation, especially with an older building. Depreciation is also difficult to estimate for misplaced improvements or for buildings suffering from other forms of unusual obsolescence. However, even with its weaknesses, the cost approach is often still useful as a check on the other approaches.

The income approach is particularly useful when appraising types of properties that are usually purchased as investments, based on their ability to generate income. However, for best reliability, the income approach requires adequate comparable market data on such factors as rents, expenses, and capitalization rates and techniques. For example, adjusting the capitalization rate for differences between the comparable sales and the subject property may require documenting changes in rates over time. Other difficult adjustments may be involved. Small errors in some of the data used in the income approach (particularly the cap rate) can cause large errors in the final value conclusion.

Reaching a Final Value Estimate

At the end of this entire process, the appraiser normally reaches a single estimate of value. In a few appraisal assignments, however, a range of value will suffice, if specifically called for by the appraisal assignment and the agreement with the client. There is no magic method to reach a final value conclusion. It is never a mathematical average of the various value indications, but sometimes one could argue that it is a weighted average of them. This means that if there are three indications, they are averaged—allotting, for example, twice as much weight to one approach, an average weight to the second approach, and half a weight to the third approach. However, this often implies a mathematical accuracy that is probably not warranted. In particular, there may be subjective questions that cannot be handled by any weighted process (see Figure 15-2).

**Figure 15-2
Reconciling the
Value Indications on
the URAR Form.**

RECONCILIATION	Indicated Value by: Sales Comparison Approach $ 275,000 Cost Approach (if developed) $ 282,903 Income Approach (if developed) $ 0
	Although not weighted heavily in this appraisal, the cost approach tends to confirm the value indicated by the sales comparison approach. The income approach has not been tested here, because it is deemed to be inapplicable in this predominantly owner-occupied neighborhood.
	This appraisal is made [X] "as is," [ ] subject to completion per plans and specifications on the basis of a hypothetical condition that the improvements have been completed, [ ] subject to the following repairs or alterations on the basis of a hypothetical condition that the repairs or alterations have been completed, or [ ] subject to the following required inspection based on the extraordinary assumption that the condition or deficiency does not require alteration or repair: This Summary Report is intended to comply with the Uniform Standards of Professional Appraisal Practice.
	Based on a complete visual inspection of the interior and exterior areas of the subject property, defined scope of work, statement of assumptions and limiting conditions, and appraiser's certification, my (our) opinion of the market value, as defined, of the real property that is the subject of this report is $ 275,000 , as of June 24, 200x , which is the date of inspection and the effective date of this appraisal.

Of all the steps in the appraisal process, arriving at and explaining the final value conclusion may be one of the most difficult and subjective. However, if the reconciliation process that we have outlined above is carefully followed, the appraiser will have developed a factual basis from which to draw a reliable opinion. The appraiser will then be able to report the factors that were considered, such as the strengths and weaknesses of the approaches and the data that were developed.

15.3 Rounding the Answer

Throughout the appraisal process, we are working with numbers, from calculating the square footage of an area to estimating the value of a subject property. One of the characteristics of a number is how many *significant digits* it has. The significant digits are those that go from the first numeral on the left over to the last figure on the right and that are not a zero. For example, "10" has only one significant digit, while "111" has three. A number calculated in an appraisal might contain all significant digits, for example, $85,319.27. However, a final value conclusion might be presented with differing numbers of significant digits, depending on the appraisal process and the data used. Thus, one appraiser's reconciliation process could lead to a value conclusion of $230,000 (two significant digits). On the same property, another appraiser, perhaps relying on another technique, might conclude a value of $233,495 (six significant digits). To the layperson, this difference might suggest that the second appraisal conclusion is more accurate than the first. In fact, the two appraisals may be of equal accuracy. Accordingly, it can be misleading for the appraiser to use a larger number of significant digits in the final answer than is warranted. In other words, should that second figure, $233,495, be rounded to $233,500, or to $234,000, or to $235,000, or to $230,000, or even to $250,000? Rounding the answer is the last step in reconciliation.

The General Rule

There is a general rule that the appraiser should follow: The answer to any mathematical step should not be reported with any more significant digits than the smallest number of significant digits occurring in any number used. If $36,312.67 is multiplied by 8.7, the answer, $315,920.22, is only mathematically accurate to two significant digits, which would be $320,000. If accrued depreciation in the cost approach is estimated to be 20 percent, this is a number with one significant digit. It follows that carrying the cost approach conclusion to four significant digits implies greater accuracy than is really there.

In the reconciliation process, however, we are analyzing alternate value indications, usually of differing precision. The cost approach might have only two significant digits, whereas the income approach, say, has three. Because these can be argued to be independent of each other, it is acceptable to round the final value conclusion to an intermediate accuracy.

General Practice

There are no standards of practice for rounding. However, few appraisers would report their final conclusion rounded to just one significant digit, for example, $100,000 or $200,000. Instead, appraisers generally round their conclusion to either two, two and one-half, or three significant digits. An answer rounded to two significant digits could be $140,000, $260,000, and so on. When an answer is rounded to two and one-half significant digits, the third digit is either a zero or a five, and no other number. Examples of answers rounded to two and one-half digits would be $145,000, $97,500, and even $220,000. (The last number was rounded from $222,000. Here $220,000 is closer than $225,000.) Answers to three significant digits might be $322,000 or $37,600. Usually, appraisers carry out intermediate answers to more digits than the final answer. Depending on the accuracy of the data, appraisers might round the indicated value of each approach to three or four digits, and then report the final value conclusion with two and one-half or three digits. Ultimately, the rounding choice depends on the accuracy of all of the data and analyses employed.

SUMMARY

After a value indication has been reached for each of the relevant approaches, the appraiser must then reduce these separate value indications to a single estimate. This process is called reconciliation. Before reconciliation begins, a review of the overall appraisal process should be made. Such factors as the intended use of the appraisal, the agreed scope of work, the approaches used, and the data collected should be re-evaluated. The question is: Was the appraisal correctly performed? A check for technical accuracy should also be made. Are your figures, sources, data, and other information correct? Now that the appraisal is completed, do you believe that your initial assumptions, adjustments, and use of judgment are still accurate? These are just a few of the questions you could ask yourself before actual reconciliation begins.

The first step in the reconciliation process is to evaluate the reliability of each approach. Carefully review the intended use of the appraisal. Perhaps the intended use of the appraisal and report naturally calls for greater weight on one approach over others. Such factors as the type of property also can determine if one approach should be considered over others. Next, it is important to understand the strengths and weaknesses of each approach, in order to decide which approach is likely to give the most reliable answer.

The next step in the reconciliation process is to consider if the data used were adequate and reliable. Since each approach is based in part on data, the accuracy of the data used in each approach plays a major part in how you select the final value conclusion. Were enough data used to provide reasonable support for the conclusion of the approach? The approach that has the most accurate and adequate data could have the greatest influence on the final value conclusion.

The last step in reconciliation is to develop a range of values. After reviewing all the approaches, you will probably see that there is a high number and a low number. These two figures can usually be considered as the maximum-minimum range of value. However, many factors, such as the accuracy of the data collected, can influence these maximum-minimum figures.

At the end of this process, a final value conclusion is normally reached. Arriving at a final conclusion involves many considerations. It is not the averaging of the three approaches. It requires the use of judgment—reflection on all of the factors involved in the appraisal and on your subjective or intuitive experience. Combined, these factors should result in a final conclusion.

Once your conclusion has been reached, you will then want to consider rounding your answer. There are no set standards for rounding. Most appraisers usually round to either two, two and one-half, or three significant digits. However, the answer for each appraisal assignment should be rounded according to the limits of the data found in that appraisal.

IMPORTANT TERMS AND CONCEPTS

Consistency	*Rounding the answer*
Evaluating the data	*Significant digits*
Judgment or data errors	*Technical review*
Range of values	*Value conclusion*
Reconciliation	*Value indications*

REVIEWING YOUR UNDERSTANDING

1. Before reconciliation begins, the appraiser should:
    a.   Review the overall appraisal process
    b.   Review for technical accuracy
    c.   Both of the above
    d.   None of the above

2. Briefly, reconciliation is defined as:
    a.   An estimate of value
    b.   One of the three approaches
    c.   The process by which the appraiser evaluates, chooses, and selects from among two or more alternative indications to reach a single answer
    d.   All of the above

3. Reconciliation is important because:
    a.   It is intended to find any possible errors in your appraisal that you may have overlooked
    b.   It can help you to see if the appraisal is accurate and reliable
    c.   It leads to the final value conclusion of the appraisal
    d.   All of the above

4. Appraising the appraisal means asking:
    a.   How appropriate is each approach?
    b.   How much data were used?
    c.   How reliable are the data?
    d.   What range of values do the approaches suggest?
    e.   All of the above

5. In the review of the approaches used, the type of property is:
    a.   Not an important factor
    b.   An important factor
    c.   Important only to the income approach
    d.   The only factor to consider

6. Each value approach has its own strengths and weaknesses. In arriving at a final value conclusion, you should:
   a. Choose the approach that is the most popular
   b. Emphasize the approach that has the most available data
   c. Weigh the strengths and weaknesses of each approach, as well as the reliability of the data collected
   d. None of the above

7. In evaluating the data you used in each approach, it is important to check and see if:
   a. You have collected enough data
   b. The data are reliable and relevant
   c. The adjustments are well supported
   d. Two of the above
   e. All of the above

8. How many significant digits are there in $137,000?
   a. 5
   b. 3
   c. 6
   d. 2.5

9. Which is the correctly rounded answer to $16,280 divided by 11.3 percent?
   a. $144,071
   b. $144,070.80
   c. $144,100
   d. $144,000

10. Rounding the final appraisal answer to three or more significant digits when the numbers used in all the approaches contained as few as two significant digits:
    a. Can be helpful to the client
    b. Is simply a matter of appraisal judgment
    c. Is mathematically justified
    d. Can suggest more accuracy than the data warrant

PRACTICAL APPLICATIONS

Remember to review the exercise at the end of the preceding chapter, and the work that you have performed to date.

This assignment completes the appraisal itself! Here, you will reconcile the several indications of value that you have developed, and decide on your final opinion of value for the property! This will be reported on the Reconciliation section of the URAR form, as shown in Figure 15-2.

The first step is to review the indication of value from each approach. You reached a value conclusion both by the GIM method and also by Direct

Capitalization. So, you actually have two indications from the Income Approach, and four value indications altogether. The Direct Capitalization estimate will not be reported on your URAR form, since there is no place for it. However, you should consider it in the reconciliation process as if it were of equal importance. Note how spread out or clustered the four value indications are. Which is high and which low? Do any of them cluster together, or are they all spread out? If one of the numbers is extraordinarily far away from the others, go back and check that approach for math errors, data errors, or whatever else you can identify. Recognize that it is normal to have some variation in the value indications. A five or ten percent spread from low to high is to be expected. But a wide difference is a clear sign that something has gone wrong! That is why we say that each approach is a check on the others.

The next step is to consider which approach or approaches are likely to be more reliable in this case. Which approach is the one that theory would say to lean on? If you were able to develop a number of relatively good comparable sales, then the Sales Comparison Approach may be the most important. What are the strengths and weaknesses of the data in each approach? It is possible that the Sales Comparison Approach has the best data and may be the most relevant as well. What number did it produce, and where is that conclusion relative to the other three?

Ultimately, you must come up with one single number. After you review the approaches, their conclusions, and the relationship of the answers to one another, move forward. If the Sales Comparison Approach is more or less in the center area of the other approaches, you might select that answer as your final number. But if the Sales Comparison Approach conclusion is to one side of the three other numbers, then you must consider the reliability of the three other approaches, and see if you want to select a final number that is slightly away from the Sales Comparison Approach number, and towards the answers from the other three approaches.

Finally, you need to enter the three approach conclusion numbers into the Reconciliation section of the report, and enter your final opinion as well. As we note at the end of each exercise, it is best not to get ahead of yourself. So, do not enter information in the later sections of the report until you have read the chapter(s) that covers that topic. However, it is a good idea to look ahead so that you start thinking about the information that you will need. Our final step will be to prepare the exhibits to the report, so it might help to preview the full report presented at the end of Chapter 16.

Reminder: If you have questions about the program, review the manuals and help information that were on the program CD. Also, go to http://www.bradfordsoftware.com, click on "Services" at the upper right, and then on "ClickFORMS Training Programs" in the middle of the "Services" page.

CHAPTER 16
REPORTING APPRAISAL OPINIONS

PREVIEW

The appraisal report is a formal communication that conveys the investigation the appraiser has made on behalf of the client. Whether an oral report (nothing in writing) or delivered as a letter, form, or narrative document, the appraisal report must contain certain minimum elements. These are needed to satisfy practical, professional, and legal requirements that have evolved over many years of appraisal theory and practice.

In this chapter, we will first consider the appraisal report choices for appraisers. Next, we examine the reporting options available under USPAP and the minimum required content. The chapter continues with a more detailed discussion of form reports. A discussion and outline of the contents of a formal narrative appraisal report is next. And the chapter ends with a sample form appraisal report using the URAR form set.

OBJECTIVES

When you have completed this chapter you should be able to:

1. **List the three conventional formats of written appraisal reports.**

2. **Describe the three written reporting options provided by USPAP.**

3. **Discuss the eleven required elements of a Self-Contained Appraisal Report.**

4. **Outline the contents of a narrative appraisal report.**

16.1 Appraisal Reports: The Format Choices

In the past, the form and content of appraisal reports were governed simply by good business practice and appraisal tradition. Now, there are legal and professional considerations as well, particularly for appraisals made in connection with federally related real estate financial transactions, such as government-insured loans.

Practical Considerations

Written appraisal reports are a form of business communication. This means that every report should be concise, well organized, and easy to read. In particular, the writer must consider the knowledge level of the intended reader(s) and define any necessary technical terms to ensure understanding. All written appraisal reports should contain only information that relates to the appraisal problem, yet be adequate in scope to meet the client's needs. Extraneous data should be omitted, and the pertinent data should be incorporated in a logical order.

The report must clearly identify who is the appraiser. A signed certification statement is one requirement. Usually, the report is also transmitted with a signed cover letter. At one time, many appraisers used an embossed seal, usually with their professional designation, to establish their identity. Identity theft is a growing problem today; appraisal groups and others are exploring how to be sure that an appraisal report really came from the appraiser that is identified in the report! Also, was the report altered after the appraiser released it? These are issues that appraisers need to consider!

Intended Use and Intended User(s) of the Appraisal and Report

Reporting requirements may differ from one client to another, depending on the intended use and intended user(s) of the appraisal and its report. For this reason, the form and general content of appraisal reports are matters to be agreed on between the appraiser and the client, as part of defining the assignment to be performed.

Reporting requirements also vary from one type of property to another. To address this problem, lenders and government agencies often provide several sets of reporting guidelines to their staff appraisers and to those they retain to do fee appraisal work. One set may apply to residential appraisals, another to commercial and industrial, and so on.

For many loans, there is a federal requirement to estimate whether the property is within a flood hazard zone, as defined and mapped by the Federal Emergency Management Agency (FEMA). Some lenders require the appraiser to make, guarantee, and report that determination! Other lenders assume this particular responsibility on their own.

Method of Transmittal

The appraisal conclusions nearly always must be transmitted to the client. Most often, this will be written, rather than oral. But technology now permits appraisal reports to be transmitted to the client by electronic means, rather than by oral communication or the familiar hand-delivered or mailed report. Several different methods are available. Some lending institutions are now requiring such service, called electronic data interchange (EDI).

Note that an electronically transmitted report is considered by USPAP to be a written report, and must therefore meet the reporting requirements of USPAP for written reports. Appraisers transmitting reports electronically must take reasonable steps to protect the data integrity and security of such reports.

One option is an Internet service, allowing the form report files to be "uploaded" to a website and translated into an electronic form that is compatible with the lender's loan-processing computers. Mortgage lenders promise to benefit the most from the use of EDI appraisal reporting. For example, a program called AppraisaLink was made available to lenders participating in certain Fannie Mae programs. With one click, a lender can order Fannie Mae appraisals and expect electronic reporting on a wide variety of report forms.

Alternatively, some clients now request that reports be emailed as "PDF" files. Sometimes, the PDF file is sent without pictures, maps, and other exhibits, in order to reduce the size of the file. A complete written "printed" report would then be sent, incorporating all of the exhibits. Or the complete report could be assembled into one PDF file, which could either be transmitted as an email attachment or uploaded to a website. The client then signs on to the website with a password and downloads the report file. Uploading to a website avoids the problems of sending an email with a large attachment.

Receiving appraisal orders and reporting them electronically promises to greatly reduce report production cost and time for the appraiser. In addition, turnaround time for the client is often reduced. Over time, the more efficient electronic reports cause an increase in appraiser productivity and income, while also reducing postage costs and express mail fees!

Types of Written Report Formats

Traditionally, written appraisal reports have followed one of three formats: the *letter*, the *form*, or the *narrative* report. Today, these three choices still exist, but we now have a USPAP requirement, discussed later, to use either a Self-Contained, Summary, or Restricted Use report. Thus, the appraiser and the client must agree upon both the physical form of the report, and its classification under USPAP, which heavily influences how detailed it will be.

The Letter Report

Historically, the **letter appraisal report** was simply a short business letter of one to five pages, generally defining the appraisal assignment, with a brief summary of the investigation made by the appraiser, and an opinion of value for the property in question. Now, it must meet the content requirements of one of the three USPAP reporting options described above, and contain all the essential elements of an appraisal report.

The letter format is best adapted to the content requirements of the Restricted Use report. In most cases, the description of the subject property is abbreviated, and only a brief statement of the factual data and its analysis is presented. Exhibits such as a plot plan, floor plan, and pictures may be attached to the report if desired. Usually, supporting data are included in the letter report only by reference. In some cases, a one-line summary of each comparable sale might be in the report, with the specific details about each transaction retained in the appraiser's files. However, the **assumptions**, **limiting conditions**, and appraiser's **certification** must always be included.

The Form Report

Institutions and agencies that regularly contract for appraisals usually require the use of a standard **form appraisal report** for less-complicated properties. Because of its fixed format, the form is best suited to be used as a Summary, rather than a Self-Contained Appraisal Report.

However, in some cases supplements might be required to comply with USPAP.

Forms are often preferred by appraisers and clients because they are usually designed in a standard checklist format on a printed page. The types of data commonly required are presented in a sequence that is easy to review. Most appraisal forms also provide blank spaces for the appraiser to use for additional analysis and comment.

Many variations of the form report are available today. Some agencies and appraisal services develop their own forms for each property type. Written instructions for completion are sometimes prepared. Single-family residential, condominium, multifamily residential, and commercial are examples of standard forms currently available. Most forms are intended for use in loan transactions. However, the Appraisal Institute and others have recently prepared general-purpose report forms.

The increased use of computers to prepare appraisal reports has led to commercial programs that allow easy production of form reports. A number of programs store the most commonly used FNMA, FHA, or relocation appraisal forms, ready to call up and fill out while at the computer screen. Such programs can check math, store and recall comparable sales and/or selected remarks, and prepare plot plans and floor-plan diagrams. Appropriate photographs on file may also be inserted in the report. When the form and its contents are printed out on a laser or ink-jet printer, the report production is complete. Section 16.3 will provide a fuller discussion of form reports. A CD of the Bradford ClickFORMS program is provided with this book, allowing the student to use the program for training exercises.

The Narrative Appraisal Report

The *narrative appraisal report* is the most formal of the written appraisal reports. It is perhaps the ideal format for a Self-Contained report. Ranging from a dozen to a hundred pages or more in length, the narrative format is also suitable for Summary reports, especially of unusual properties. Narrative reports are most often required by large corporations, government agencies, and for unusual properties.

Narrative reports are preferred when the user needs a comprehensive appraisal document, in which all the pertinent facts discovered in the investigation are presented under one cover. Because of the high standards expected of this type of report, the preparation of a demonstration narrative report is often required as a test of competence for the appraiser seeking a professional designation, discussed in Chapter 18.

Over the years, a number of government agencies, lenders, and other users of appraisals have each developed unique requirements for narrative reports. For example, the General Services Administration of the Federal Government has a very long and detailed outline that must be followed by appraisers they engage, as do many other municipal, state, and federal agencies and some courts. *The Uniform Appraisal Standards for Federal Land Acquisition*, second edition, also contains a detailed section on report content. Perhaps the most detailed outlines of narrative reports are those issued by the appraisal societies for demonstration appraisals. These are available to the general public in outline format at nominal cost. Section 16.4 will provide an in-depth discussion of the narrative report.

Format Variations

In actual practice, the formats of appraisal reports often mix the features of the three reports we have described. For example, letter reports sometimes extend in length, to become what could be called short narrative reports. Other written appraisal reports will often mix the features of the letter, form, and narrative appraisal reports, to best suit the needs of the client or the style of the appraisal. Most appraisal offices have developed their own formats as needed for the types of appraisals they perform. Where reports are prepared on a personal computer or word processor, a sample or outline will usually be stored in memory. In this way, the headings, subheadings, introductory sentences, and definitions will be called up and reused or modified to suit the particular assignment.

Federally Related Appraisals

As already noted, federal regulations require that certain real estate appraisals used in connection with federally related transactions be performed in writing, and in accordance with standards that may go beyond the requirements of USPAP. Title XI of the *Federal Financial Institutions Reform, Recovery and Enforcement Act* of 1989 (known as FIRREA) requires that all **federally related appraisals** conform to USPAP, with some exceptions.

"Federally related transaction" is defined in FIRREA as a real estate-related financial transaction which requires the services of an appraiser. In turn, "transaction" is a term covering purchases and sales, as well as loans, which is our focus here. And the "Federally related" part of it is that it applies to transactions that are either insured by a federal agency or made by a financial institution or company that is regulated or insured by a federal agency. The regulated institutions include the banks, savings banks, and credit unions. The agencies that insure loans include the Veteran's Administration and FHA/HUD.

With exceptions to be noted at the end of this topic, the agencies currently require that federally related appraisals performed for institutions under their jurisdiction shall at a minimum:

1. Conform to generally accepted appraisal standards as evidenced by USPAP, unless principles of safe and sound banking require compliance with stricter standards;

2. Be written and contain sufficient information and analysis to support the institution's decision to engage in the transaction;

3. Analyze and report appropriate deductions and discounts for proposed construction or renovation, partially leased buildings, non-market lease terms, and tract developments with unsold units, using market-based data;

4. Be based upon the definition of market value as set forth in the regulation; and

5. Be performed by a state licensed or certified appraiser.

Some federally related transactions are exempt by regulation from the requirements cited; for example, some types of collateral loans. In such cases, federal rules allow lenders to obtain what are referred to in agency regulations as "evaluations" instead of appraisals. Please note, however, that any evaluation that renders an opinion of value is still classified by USPAP as an appraisal!

Each agency has adopted regulations that apply to appraisals performed for the institutions that the agency supervises, or for the agency itself if that is the case. These regulations constitute Supplemental Standards, which USPAP requires the appraiser to comply with. (Review this topic in Chapter 3, Section 3.2, Step 1, element 6.) Please note that a lender or other private institution may have its own requirements that could go beyond those of its regulatory agency. These are contractual requirements, part of what the appraiser agreed to do, in accepting the assignment, not supplemental standards.

Clearly, the appraiser must make a major effort, prior to accepting the assignment, to understand whether it involves a federally related transaction. If so, what agency regulations apply and what is their impact? Of course, as always, also ask what special conditions or requirements the client institution may have.

16.2 The Legal Reporting Requirements

The type of report most appropriate for an appraisal assignment should be decided on in advance, by discussion between the appraiser and the client, as part of defining the assignment. The choice should be based on 1) the intended use and intended user(s) of the appraisal and report, 2) mutual understanding of the differences between the reporting options, 3) any legal requirements, and 4) whether the intended use warrants a detailed or concise disclosure of the steps and information considered in the appraisal process.

One of the most critical issues is meeting the legal requirements of USPAP. Remember that complying with USPAP is required for all nonexempt federally related transactions. And in many states (including California) all licensed and certified real estate appraisers must comply with USPAP for all assignments!

USPAP Reporting Standards

Standard 2 of USPAP is the real estate appraisal reporting standard. It requires that "each written or oral real property appraisal report":

1. "clearly and accurately set forth the appraisal in a manner that will not be misleading";

2. "contain sufficient information to enable the intended users of the appraisal to understand the report properly"; and

3. "clearly and accurately disclose all assumptions, extraordinary assumptions, hypothetical conditions, and limiting conditions used in the assignment." Note that whether these affect the appraisal or not is not an issue as it was in the past. Also, it is no longer necessary for the appraiser to indicate their impact on value.

Source: *USPAP*, 2006.

Types of Written Appraisal Reports

USPAP allows the form, format, and style of the report to reflect the needs of users as well as providers of appraisal services. For this reason, USPAP allows for three different levels of reporting detail: the **Self-Contained Appraisal Report**, the **Summary Appraisal Report**, and the **Restricted Use Appraisal Report**.

You should note that **professional appraisal standards** for both appraising and reporting are in a constant state of change. USPAP in particular is regarded as a dynamic standard, one that is constantly being revised and updated. The Appraisal Standards Board (ASB) has indicated an intent to examine the three report categories. The standards required for federally related appraisals are also subject to frequent change. This means that appraisers whose professional affiliation, state license/certification, or work requires them to conform to these standards must make a major effort to stay current with the changes.

The essential difference between the three types of written reports in Standard 2 is the amount of detail required. This is evident when the common descriptions of these reports are compared.

- *Self-Contained Appraisal Report:* A written appraisal report that presents the required information in comprehensive detail.

- *Summary Appraisal Report:* A written appraisal report that summarizes information for a more concise presentation.

- *Restricted Use Appraisal Report:* A written appraisal report that states the required information with the least detail. It is the minimum reporting format allowed.

Required Elements of Self-Contained Appraisal Reports

USPAP requires that each written Self-Contained Appraisal Report contain certain specific elements. USPAP Standards Rule 2.2 (a) requires that the content "must be consistent with the intended use of the appraisal and, at a minimum":

1. State the identity of the client and any intended users by name or type.
2. State the intended use of the appraisal.
3. Describe information sufficient to identify the real estate involved in the appraisal, including the physical and economic property characteristics relevant to the assignment.
4. State the real property interest appraised.
5. State the type and definition of value and cite the source of the definition.
6. State the effective date of the appraisal and the date of the report.
7. Describe the scope of work used to develop the appraisal.
8. Describe the information analyzed, the appraisal methods and techniques employed, and the reasoning that supports the analyses, opinions, and conclusions; exclusions of the sales comparison approach, cost approach, or income approach must be explained.
9. State the use of the real estate existing as of the date of value and the use of the real estate reflected in the appraisal; and, when an opinion of highest and best use was developed by the appraiser, describe the support and rationale for that opinion.
10. Clearly and conspicuously:
    - State all extraordinary assumptions and hypothetical conditions; and
    - State that their use might have affected the assignment results.
11. Include a signed certification in accordance with USPAP Standards Rule 2-3.

Source: *USPAP*, 2006.

Summary and Restricted Use Appraisal Reports

As we have seen, the Self-Contained Appraisal Report must define the appraisal problem, present the factual data revealed by the study, and provide the analysis that supports the stated opinion of value. The same is true in Summary and Restricted Use appraisal reports. The difference is that the Summary and Restricted Use appraisal reports are allowed to contain much less detail.

The Summary Appraisal Report summarizes the appraisal data in a more concise and less detailed way than the Self-Contained report. Most form reports are Summary reports. And a significant number of narrative reports are also Summary reports.

The Restricted Use Appraisal Report provides a minimal reporting format by stating the required information with the least detail of the three reporting options. The letter format is often used for a Restricted Use Appraisal Report.

If a Restricted Use Appraisal Report is chosen, it must include a prominent *use restriction clause* that restricts the reliance on the report solely to the client. Thus, there can only be the one intended user! Also, the report must contain a clear notice that it cannot be understood properly without additional information that is available in the work file of the appraiser.

16.3 Form Reports: A Closer Look

The URAR Form

The most common form report in use today for loan appraisals is the **URAR** (Uniform Residential Appraisal Report), also known as the **Freddie Mac Form 70** or the **Fannie Mae Form 1004**. Some version of this form often is required by the Federal Home Loan Mortgage Corporation, as well as the Federal National Mortgage Association, the Veterans Administration, the Federal Housing Administration (FHA), and the Department of Housing and Urban Development (HUD). When properly prepared, the URAR satisfies the form and content requirements of USPAP and those of federally related appraisals. Most lenders have adopted the URAR form for many conventional mortgage loans intended for the secondary mortgage market. The most recent version of the form is intended to be used *only* for loan transactions. Prior editions were commonly used for many different appraisal uses!

The properly completed URAR defines the appraisal problem, presents the factual data developed in the appraisal study, and demonstrates evidence of value through the cost, sales comparison, and income approaches, as needed. Typical attachments to the URAR form, depending on the assignment and the agreement with the client, should include a complete legal description (where too long to appear on the form itself), location and plat maps (the former showing the location of the subject property and the comparables), and a diagram or sketch of the improvements. Photographs of the subject property and the comparables complete the report. A sample URAR appraisal, with attachments, is shown in Figures 16-6 through 16-10, which follow the review material at the end of this chapter. The form is also available online and in the Forms Library of the Bradford ClickFORMS program CD included with this text.

Special notice should be made here of the national standards for FHA/ HUD loan appraisals that were adopted by HUD in 1999. In addition to the URAR form, HUD required the completion of a *Valuation Condition* (V.C.) form. This form required a detailed review of the property's condition, code conformity, and any safety problems observed. Appraisals performed on or after January 1, 2006, no longer require use of the V.C. form. Now, any condition issues must be reported on the URAR. To make appraisals for FHA endorsement, the appraiser must be a licensed or certified appraiser, pass the HUD/FHA National Appraiser Exam, and apply and be placed on the FHA Register.

The Federal National Mortgage Association and HUD both publish written guidelines on how to complete the URAR. Such guidelines present detailed instructions for completing these and other required forms. Many lenders publish form completion guidelines. Several excellent textbooks are also available. Changes in statutes, case law, market conditions, technology, and appraisal theory will, of course, necessitate periodic revisions in these guidelines. The appraiser should always review the client's current guidelines before attempting to fill out the selected appraisal form. The forms are also revised periodically! The appraiser usually must use the current edition.

FNMA Desktop Underwriter Forms 2055 and 2070

Lenders are now using two newer residential forms, originally developed by FNMA to be used with an automated risk analysis system called the Desktop Underwriter program. **FNMA Form 2055** is an appraisal form for use only with exterior inspections. **FNMA Form 2070** is used for inspection and reporting purposes only. Both the 2055 and 2070 forms are available online and in the Forms Library of the Bradford ClickFORMS CD.

The 2055 form is considered to be a Summary Appraisal Report. The current version of the 2055 now closely parallels the URAR, primarily varying where needed to reflect the differences between a full inspection and an exterior one. A copy of the first two pages of the 2055 form is shown in Figure 16-11 at the very end of the chapter. Contrast this form with the URAR form that precedes it.

Form 2055 allows the appraiser to make "normal" plus or minus dollar adjustments in the sales comparison process and use the adjusted sales prices to indicate a value for the subject property.

Form 2070 is designed to report either an exterior-only inspection of the subject property from the street or an interior inspection. A state-licensed or state-certified appraiser must be used. Although an estimate of market value for the property is *not* provided, Form 2070 requires the appraiser to comment on how the subject property conforms to zoning regulations and other properties in the neighborhood. The highest and best use of the property *as improved*, as well as any apparent adverse physical deficiencies of the property must also be reported. We note again that Form 2070 is not an appraisal report. And appraisers should expect that new and revised forms will come their way from time to time.

The AI Report Form

The Appraisal Institute and others have recently developed forms flexible enough for a variety of intended uses. A sample AI form can be viewed at http://www.appraisalinstitute.com or in the Forms Library of the Bradford CD included with this book. You should compare this form with the URAR. It is likely to be widely used in the future.

16.4 Content of the Narrative Appraisal Report

Because of the detail and formality that are characteristic of the full narrative appraisal report, this report should have the appearance of a professionally prepared document. Most narrative reports are prepared on a computer, printed out on quality paper, and bound in a durable cover. A carelessly prepared report can be suggestive of inferior effort put into the appraisal itself.

The style of writing, though formal, can be interesting if the writing is succinct and without redundancies. Information on a given topic should be confined to the pertinent subject area and not scattered throughout the narration. To help the client understand, visualize, and remember, topical paragraphs should be sequenced in a logical order. For example, when describing a residential neighborhood, you could cover the location of the subject; a brief history of the general area; identification of the immediate neighborhood; residential quality; land uses; convenience of the subject property to transportation and commercial facilities; and proximity to schools, churches, and parks, approximately in this order.

The contents of the full narrative appraisal report should communicate to the client what the appraiser has done, in a step-by-step logical sequence, describing the data gathered and analyzed and explaining the reasoning that leads to the value conclusion.

Outline of the Narrative Report

One very acceptable format for narrative appraisal reports divides the report into four main sections. Some appraisers combine the two middle sections into one. Remember, however, that for a particular assignment, the report format needs to comply with any specific requirements of the clients that the appraiser agreed to meet.

A. Introduction
B. Description
C. Analyses and conclusion
D. Addenda

These four main subdivisions of the narrative appraisal report include the following items and features:

A. Introduction
    1. Title page
    2. Letter of transmittal
    3. Table of contents
    4. Photograph of the subject property
    5. Summary of relevant facts and conclusions
    6. Standard and special limiting conditions and assumptions
    7. Scope of work of the appraisal

B. Description
    1. Identification of the property
    2. Description of neighborhood and community; current market conditions
    3. Description of land, zoning, community services, and taxes
    4. Description of improvements
    5. Sales history of the subject property; this would include any leases

C. Analyses and Conclusions
    1. Highest and best use analysis
    2. Explanation of and support for the exclusion of any of the usual value approaches
    3. Estimate of land or site value, sometimes placed in the cost approach
    4. Analysis of data by the value approaches
        (a) The Cost Approach
        (b) The Sales Comparison Approach
        (c) The Income Approach
    5. Reconciliation and final conclusion of value
    6. Certification, with the signature of the appraiser(s)

D. Addenda or Supporting Material
    1. Location and plat maps
    2. Plot plan of the subject property

3. Legal description
4. Floor plan of the improvements
5. Photographs of the subject property
6. Sales data sheets, sales photographs, and sale location maps
7. Any relevant cost, income, and market-study exhibits
8. Qualifications of all appraisers signing the report

Introductory Material

Title Page

The first page of the introductory material is the title page. The typical content is: property address, date of value, and by whom the property was appraised.

Letter of Transmittal

The second page of the introductory material usually is the **letter of transmittal**. The format of the letter should comply with standard business correspondence. The letter is usually addressed to the client, unless the appraiser has been instructed otherwise. The purpose of the letter is to formally present the appraisal report and its conclusion to the client. The following elements should be included:

1. Date of the letter.
2. Acknowledgment of the person requesting the appraisal.
3. Identification of the property being appraised and the type of value estimated.
4. The intended use of the appraisal.
5. Identification of the client and intended user(s), by name or type.
6. A statement of the property rights being appraised.
7. A statement that the appraiser has made an investigation and analysis to arrive at an opinion of value, and that the letter is transmitting the appraisal report.
8. Clear statement of any unusual assumptions or limiting conditions.
9. Type of appraisal report, whether Self-Contained, Summary, or Restricted Use. In the case of a Restricted Use appraisal report, a clear use restriction must limit reliance on the report to the client and warn that the report cannot be understood properly without additional information in the work file of the appraiser.
10. The effective date of value.
11. The amount of the value opinion. Some appraisers do not include the value opinion in the cover letter.

12. The signature of the appraiser. The number of the appraiser's state license or certification, if any, and its expiration date should also be given here.

Figure 16-1 is a sample letter of transmittal, with each of the elements identified by number. Other pertinent data, such as a brief description of the property, may also be included.

Table of Contents

The third page of the introductory material is the table of contents. This lists the major topics as they appear in the report and supplies page numbers. Some experts recommend that major tables and exhibits also be referenced here.

Photograph of the Subject

Often, the introductory material next contains a photograph of the subject property or, perhaps, a map or aerial photograph showing its location.

Summary of Relevant Facts and Conclusions

The last page of the introductory material contains a summary of relevant facts and conclusions. Items often included are:

1. Location of the property.
2. Present ownership of the property.
3. Short history of the subject property, discussing any recent construction, rents, or sales.
4. Intended use and user(s) of the report.
5. The effective date of value.
6. The property rights appraised.
7. Type of report (Self-Contained, Summary, or Restricted Use).
8. Any extraordinary assumptions or hypothetical conditions.
9. Type of property.
10. Land size.
11. Improvement size.
12. Age of improvements.
13. Zoning.
14. Present use.
15. Highest and best use.
16. Site value.
17. Value indicated by the cost approach.
18. Value indicated by the sales comparison approach.
19. Value indicated by the income approach.
20. Market value estimate.

The appraiser may include in this summary whatever additional information is considered important.

Burgoyne Appraisal Service
1840 Duval Street
Austin, Texas 77619
Ph. 512-603-1936; FAX: 512-678-2345

(1)
January 19, 20xx

Ms. Martha Harris, Senior Partner
Harris, Grimms, and Shelby
5000 Grand Ave., Suite 250
Fresno, CA 94030

(3) Re: Appraisal Report: 1836 Alamo Street
                              San Antonio, Texas

Dear Ms. Harris,

(2)
(4)
(5)
In accordance with your written request of January 11, 20xx, I have personally inspected and made an appraisal of the single family residence referenced above, for the purpose of estimating its market value. It is understood that this appraisal is to be used in connection with pending litigation. The intended users of this appraisal are defined in the report. This appraisal may not be used or relied upon by anyone other than the intended users, nor used for any purpose other than the intended use, without the written consent of the appraiser.

(6) The property rights appraised are the fee simple ownership, as if the property were free of any leases, mortgages, or other liens. A complete legal description of the property, and the definition of market value used in this appraisal, are provided in the body of this report.

(7)
(8)
Your attention is invited to the enclosed appraisal report, describing the scope of the appraiser's investigation, and presenting the analysis of data supporting the value opinion. The report also includes a statement of the assumptions and limiting conditions that apply to the appraisal. As in all such appraisals, damage from wood destroying organisms, if any, is assumed here to be corrected by the seller, or the repair cost deducted from the stated value opinion.

(9) This appraisal report is intended to be a Self-Contained Appraisal Report, as defined by the current edition of the *Uniform Standards of Professional Appraisal Practice*.

(10)
Subject to the standard and special conditions contained in the attached report, it is my opinion that the market value of the defined rights to the property commonly known as 1836 Alamo Street, San Antonio, Texas, and further described in the report, as of January 13, 20xx, was the sum of:

(11)
FOUR HUNDRED AND NINETY-FIVE THOUSAND DOLLARS
($495,000)

Respectfully submitted,

(12) _____
George Burgoyne, MAI, SRA

TX State Certification AG00xxxx
(Expires 09-12-xx)

GB:inp
(encl.)

Figure 16-1 Letter of Transmittal.

Scope of Work of the Appraisal

The statement of objectives should include the following parts:

1. Property rights appraised.
2. The intended use of the report and the intended user(s).
3. Definition of value to be estimated and the source of the definition. In market value appraisals, the exposure time allowed for in the value estimate should be specifically referenced here.
4. The effective date of value.
5. The extent of the process of collecting, confirming, and reporting data.
6. Type of appraisal report submitted (Self-Contained, Summary, or Restricted Use).

Qualifying and Limiting Conditions

The statement of qualifying and *limiting conditions* serves several important functions. These are to (1) clarify the assumptions made by the appraiser, (2) indicate the limits of the appraiser's expertise and thus limit his or her legal liability, and (3) define the rights of disclosure of information contained in the report. A typical statement includes provisions as follows:

1. The appraiser assumes no responsibility for any legal issues affecting the property.
2. Any sketch in the report is solely for illustration and shows approximate dimensions; the appraiser has made no survey of the property.
3. The appraiser assumes that there are no hidden or unapparent conditions of the property, subsoil, or structures that would render it more or less valuable.
4. Information, estimates, and opinions furnished by others were obtained from sources considered reliable and believed to be true and correct, but no responsibility for the accuracy of such items is assumed by the appraiser.
5. Any distribution of values in the report between land and improvements applies only to the valuation analysis here and may not apply in other contexts.
6. The appraiser is not required to give testimony or appear in court regarding the appraisal unless arrangements have been previously made.
7. Disclosure of the contents of the appraisal report is governed by the Uniform Standards of Professional Appraisal Practice, and the bylaws and regulations of the professional appraisal organizations with which the appraiser is affiliated.

8. Neither all nor any part of the content of the report, or copy thereof, shall be used for any purpose other than the purpose specified in the report without the prior written consent of the appraiser.

Description

This section of the narrative appraisal report is placed right after the introductory material and contains the main descriptive section of the report.

Identification of the Property

The subject parcel should be clearly identified by street address and, usually, the legal description. If the legal description is lengthy, it may be included in the addendum and simply referred to at this point. A map or plat of the property is desirable, especially if the legal description is difficult to follow. Often, a copy of the assessor's parcel map is used, either here or in the property tax section.

Description of Neighborhood and Community; Current Market Conditions

Neighborhood and community data should include a brief history of the area and the prominent physical, social, and economic factors. Such a profile should include the type of neighborhood, its growth rate, the trend of property values, an analysis of supply and demand factors, and the typical marketing time for properties similar to the subject property. To complete the profile, land uses and land-use changes at the time of the date of value should be reported, as well as predominant occupancies, vacancies, and typical rents or prices for property of the same use type as the subject property. The intent is to draw a clear picture of the neighborhood for the reader.

Usually, the quality and general appearance of the homes, main community interests, and sources of employment for the residents are included. Other nearby land uses and convenience to shopping, schools, cultural centers, and transportation routes are also described. When important observations and conclusions are made, they should always be accompanied by supporting facts.

For example, neighborhood improvement or decline, if asserted, should be documented by reference to specific examples of improved or deteriorated property, or by reference to factual studies. Particular attention should be paid when communicating changes in a transitional market. This might mean changes in use, changes in sales volume, or a shift in the direction of price movements.

A reasonable exposure time for the subject property should then be projected, when market value is being sought. This estimate of exposure time must be consistent with your value definition and the value conclusion ultimately reached.

The amount and kind of detail included in this section depends on the purpose it will serve. Neighborhood and community data that are relevant to the type of property under appraisal should be emphasized. In the appraisal of income and investment properties, for example, the report on neighborhood and community should not only include an analysis of current market conditions and the marketability of the subject property, but should also include all market factors that will directly affect projected income or any estimated absorption period (for rent-up or sell-off). Minimum requirements might include an inventory of existing space, a survey of rent and occupancy levels, and data on new construction in progress.

Description of Land, Zoning, Community Services, and Taxes

Land site data, as discussed in Chapter 6, should present the physical characteristics, site location elements, and private and public restrictions that affect the subject property. Any easements or other recorded restrictions should also be described and analyzed. Lot size and shape, street and utility improvements, topography, and soil conditions should be described next, with reference to any maps, plats, and photographs included, either in the report or the addenda.

The precise master plan and zoning classifications of the parcel need to be identified, as well as the municipality that has jurisdiction over the property. (Figure 16-2 is an example of a zoning map.) Also, any special building restrictions or regulations must be described.

The availability of public utilities should be noted, along with any problems regarding their reliability. For example, if a septic tank is used to dispose of sewage, it should be made known to the client. If there are questions about adequate drainage, such questions should be referred to the appropriate expert for study.

Based on the latest information available from the assessment roll, relevant property tax information should also be included in this section. When the appraiser has reason to expect a significant change in property taxes, information on the probable change should be provided here. For example, in some states, property is reassessed upon property transfer or upon signing a long-term lease.

Description of Improvements

Following the inspection guidelines covered in Chapter 7, the description of the improvements should include their physical features and also their condition, general marketability, and appeal. However, if detailed improvement specifications, blueprints, and photographs are to be included, they should probably be placed in the addendum of the report. Any deferred maintenance or apparent structural problems or defects noted during the improvement inspection must also be carefully described in the body of the report. Any personal property or fixtures included with the real estate also should be described.

**Figure 16-2
Example of
a Zoning Map.**

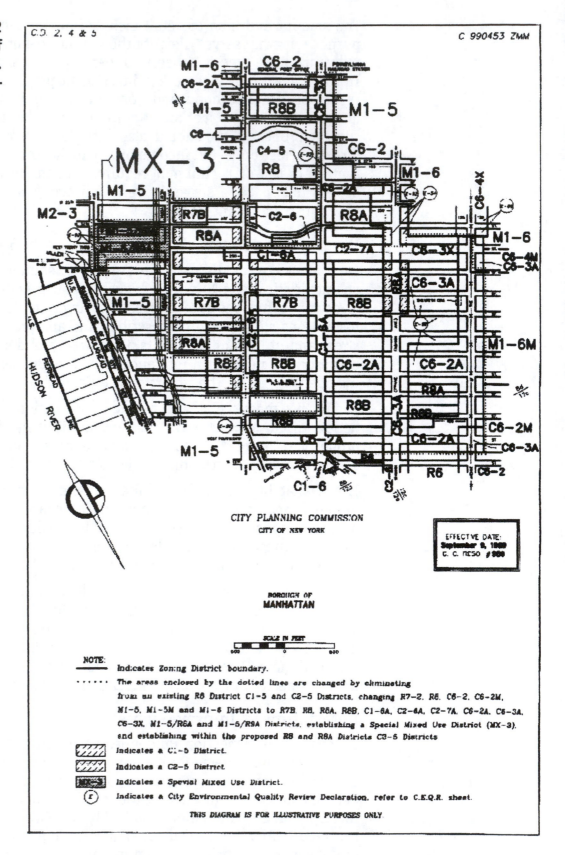

Sales History of the Subject Property

The *sales history* of the property should detail the price and terms of any known sales or transfers of the subject property that have occurred within three years of the date of value for all property types. Any sales option, listing, and/or offer involving the subject property within such time frame should also be included. The relevance, if any, of the described information to the appraisal conclusion needs to be discussed! If the property is leased, often the description of the lease would be in or following this section.

Analyses and Conclusions

Highest and Best Use

The appraiser's opinion of highest and best use must be stated here, along with the analysis that supports the conclusion. The highest and best use statement should cover both the highest and best use of the site as if vacant, and the highest and best use of the existing improved property.

Analysis of Data by the Value Approaches

It is helpful to introduce the value approaches used in the appraisal with a brief description of these methods. Their general strengths and weaknesses and their applicability to the specific appraisal should be explained. Some appraisers refer to this subsection as "methodology."

Estimate of Land or Site Value

When applicable, the appraiser's estimate of land or site value should be presented here. Such value should be based on the recognized methods of appraisal described in Chapter 10. A discussion of the market data leading to the conclusion should be included. Data sheets on each land sale are normally placed in the addendum, along with location, plat maps, and photographs.

The Cost Approach

If structural improvements are included in the appraisal, the cost approach may be presented early or late in the value analysis, depending on its relative importance. The priority of sequence is sometimes interpreted to suggest emphasis. Others suggest one approach or another should be presented first!

As suggested above, land or site value should be based on one of the recognized methods of land appraisal. Reference should be made here to the section of the report that develops the land value estimate and contains the market data leading to the conclusion.

Improvement value should be demonstrated by an analysis of reproduction or replacement cost new, less the estimated total value loss as compared with the improvement as if it were new. A clear explanation of any deferred maintenance and any functional and/or economic obsolescence allowance should be provided.

The Sales Comparison Approach

The basic data to be included in the sales comparison approach are the pertinent facts about each comparable sale and each listing used (the latter to show the trend of the market). In the appraisal of single-family residential properties, these facts usually include:

1. Names of buyer and seller and property address.

2. Date of sale, date of recordation, and document number. In the case of listings, it is desirable to include the type of listing, the date listed, and the dates of any changes in price or terms.

3. Sale price and terms of sale or listing.

4. Lot size and shape.

5. Description of the residence, including number of stories, square-foot size, number of rooms, number of bedrooms and baths, basement or below-ground size and finish, age and condition, type of construction, extent of any remodeling, and character of outside improvements such as landscaping, the garage, and swimming pool.

As already suggested, professional standards also require that the appraiser consider and analyze any agreement of sale, option, or listing of the property being appraised that existed on the date of value, if such information is available in the normal course of business. In addition, prior sales must be considered and analyzed when they have occurred within three years of the date of value (for all property types). If any of the comparables are located in a speculative market, or one with rapid resales, their sales history should also be included with appropriate comments.

Most narrative appraisal reports present comparable sales in an abbreviated chart form (see Example 16-1) in the body of the report.

All the details about the sales are recited in separate sales data sheets in the addendum. A sample sheet is presented in Figure 16-3. The appraiser usually would include the following additional data for multiple-family residential sales:

1. Number, type, and size of units.

2. Sale price per unit, per room, and/or per square foot.

3. Gross scheduled rent; average rent per unit and per square foot.

4. Gross income multiplier.

5. Expense ratio.

EXAMPLE 16-1 Comparable Sales Chart

No.	Address	Price	Sale Date	Quality	Condition	Lot (SF Size)	Building (SF Size)	Age
1	718 Stonewall	$562,000	1/98	Excellent	Good	8,850	4,811	1978
2	3921 Rose	$450,000	7/98	Good	Good	7,250	3,830	1910
3	331 Oakridge	$678,000	2/98	Good	Good	28,793	3,461	1952
4	7792 Crestor	$477,000	2/98	Good	Average	15,000	3,136	1937
5	1864 Walnut	$502,000	10/98	Excellent	Excellent	6,960	2,323	1925
6	8274 Alvarado	$585,000	2/98	Excellent	Good	9,200	5,137	1914
7	Subject	—	—	Excellent	Very good	8,292	5,409	1907

**Figure 16-3
An Informal Sales
Data Sheet.**

FILE NO. 1226

SALES DATA

ADDRESS: 71xx Solano Ave. **PARCEL:** 62-2S72-xx **MAP:** 32F5

CITY: Berkshire **STATE:** Ohio **ZIP:** X98XX

GRANTOR: Lola C. Smith

GRANTEE: James & Lynne H. Jones

DATE SOLD: 1/23/XX **DATE RECORDED:** 2/9/XX

REEL: 2784 **IMAGE:** 26 **DOCUMENT:** XX-149

SALE PRICE: $225,000 **DOCUMENT STAMPS:** $247.50

SALE TERMS: $217,000 mortgage by seller, market rate, 10 year payoff. **CONFIRMED BY:** Buyer; confirmed by seller's attorney.

ZONE: Single family **LOT AREA:** 6225 SF. **LOT SHAPE:** Trapezoid, 65 FF, with diagonal rear line.

IMPROVEMENTS: Wood-frame residence, 1550 SF. **STORIES:** 1 **AGE:** New in 1926.

ANALYSIS:

- Paid $145.16 per S. F. of building.

- Rent was $1,000 per month at sale, raised to $1,125. Another $20 rent increase will go into effect next month because of the anticipated increase in taxes.

- Sold for 200 times new scheduled monthly gross income.

Ofc. Form #623

The Income Approach

In the case of income and investment properties, this section in the appraisal report should report and analyze current revenues, expenses, and vacancies for the subject property. Often, a table showing the past three years' operating income and expenses is provided. Next, the report should summarize the investigation made to estimate market rent and stabilized expenses. A reconstructed operating statement should be provided, along with a discussion presenting the basis for the expense projections.

The report should indicate the relevant capitalization methods. It should explain how rates of return appropriate for the subject property were derived. Specific properties studied should be cited. It is preferred that the income capitalization procedure be clearly demonstrated in formula form, with the process itself explained in a narrative fashion.

Reconciliation and Final Conclusion of Value

This section of the narrative appraisal report should review, in summary fashion, the extent of the process of collecting, confirming, and reporting data. It should also summarize all of the information considered, the appraisal procedures followed, and the reasoning that supports the analyses, opinions, and conclusions.

This section should next review for the reader the findings of each value approach explored and should describe their relevance in this appraisal. If any of the usual approaches have been excluded, reasonable support for this should be offered. The appraiser should also discuss the reliability of the data used and the applicability of each approach, and finally, should provide an argument to justify the final conclusion of value rendered. As suggested earlier, the statement of final value conclusion should reference the appraiser's estimate of market exposure time allowed for in the value estimate.

Certification

This is a signed statement that gives assurance of the appraiser's neutrality and responsibility. In order to comply with good appraisal practice and the *Uniform Standards of Professional Appraisal Practice*, each written real estate appraisal report (and the appraisal file for each oral report) must contain a signed certification that is similar in content to the following form:

I certify that, to the best of my knowledge and belief:

The statements of fact contained in this report are true and correct.

The reported analyses, opinions, and conclusions are limited only by the reported assumptions and limiting conditions, and are my personal, impartial, and unbiased professional analyses, opinions, and conclusions.

I have no (or the specified) present or prospective interest in the property that is the subject of this report, and no (or the specified) personal interest with respect to the parties involved. I have no bias with respect to the property that is the subject of this report or the parties involved with this assignment.

My engagement in this assignment was not contingent upon developing or reporting predetermined results.

My compensation for completing this assignment is not contingent upon the developing or reporting of a predetermined value or direction in value that favors the cause of the client, the amount of the value opinion, the attainment of a stipulated result, or the occurrence of a subsequent event directly related to the intended use of this appraisal.

My analyses, opinions, and conclusions were developed, and this report has been prepared, in conformity with the *Uniform Standards of Professional Appraisal Practice* in effect on the date of this report.

I have (or have not) made a personal inspection of the property that is the subject of this report. (If more than one person signs this certification, the certification must clearly specify which individuals did, and which individuals did not, make a personal inspection of the appraised property.)

No one provided significant real property appraisal assistance to the person signing this report. (If there are exceptions, the name of each individual providing significant real property appraisal assistance must be stated.)

Addenda or Supporting Material

The addenda should contain any relevant data not included in the body of the report. Examples include:

1. Location and plat maps.
2. Plot plan of the subject property (see Figure 16-5).
3. Legal description, as required.

4. Floor plan of the improvements.

5. Photographs of the subject property.

6. Sales data sheets, sales photographs, and sale location map.

7. Any relevant cost, income, and market-study exhibits.

8. Qualifications of the appraiser.

Qualifications of the Appraiser

This is usually a one- or two-page biography of the appraiser, outlining his or her credentials, education, and experience. Any state appraiser license or certification held should be described, as well as professional designations. The list of qualifications often cites important appraisals made, as well as significant leadership activity, any real estate teaching experience, and titles of any published writings. The appraiser must be careful to protect the privacy rights of clients when considering the content of a résumé. The appraiser's qualifications serve not only to suggest the level of confidence to be placed in the value investigation, but also to indicate whether the appraiser would probably be considered by a judge as qualified to testify as an expert witness if such service is ever required. A sample qualifications sheet is shown in Figure 16-4.

Figure 16-4 Sample Qualifications Sheet.

QUALIFICATIONS OF SAMUEL GEORGE

EDUCATION – ACADEMIC
Bachelor of Science and Business Administration Degrees, Real Estate and Urban Land Economics Major, University of Idaho, Moscow, Idaho, 1972 and 1973.

EDUCATION – PROFESSIONAL
Education Seminars and Conferences: University of Idaho Extension; Appraisal Institute, including AI exams or courses 1, 2, 4 & 8; Idaho Real Estate Certificate.

PROFESSIONAL AFFILIATIONS
Member, Appraisal Institute (MAI #CD40); Senior Member, American Society of Appraisers (ASA), in Real Estate.

PROFESSIONAL ACTIVITY
AI: Idaho Chapter Admissions Committee, 1980-82; and other committee memberships
Instructor: Real Estate subjects, University of Idaho Extension Division, Moscow

APPRAISAL EXPERIENCE
Since 1973, appraisals in excess of $100,000.
Expert Witness – Testimony in Shawnee, Clare, and Lowell Counties. Property tax appeals, eminent domain, bankruptcy, income tax, and damage lawsuits.

CLIENTS
Either individually or in association with other appraisers including: Foster City; Bank of Idaho; Union Bank; North Central Bank; First National Bank; Singer Company; SCM Corporation; Newhall Land and Farming Company; Coopers and Lybrand, CPAs; Homequity, Inc.; Executrans; U.S. National Park Service; and numerous private clients.

Figure 16-5
A Detailed Plot Plan
of a Residential
Property.

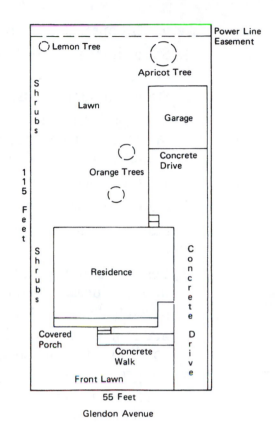

SUMMARY

The written appraisal report is a formal business communication from the appraiser to the client. In the tradition of good business standards and appraisal practice, the report should be concise, well organized, and easy to read.

Both the form and content of appraisal reports are defined by the *Uniform Standards of Professional Appraisal Practice*. To recognize the needs of users and providers of appraisal services, three general types of written reports are defined by USPAP.

Self-Contained Appraisal Report: A written report prepared to describe and present the required information with a comprehensive level of detail.

Summary Appraisal Report: A written report that summarizes its information for a more concise presentation.

Restricted Use Appraisal Report: A written report that states the required information with the least amount of detail. For a Restricted Use Appraisal Report, reliance on the report is limited to only the client.

Every Self-Contained Report must include the following elements:

1. State the identity of the client and any intended users by name or type.

2. State the intended use of the appraisal.

3. Describe information sufficient to identify the real estate involved in the appraisal, including the physical and economic property characteristics relevant to the assignment.

4. State the real property interest appraised.

5. State the type and definition of value and its source.

6. State the effective date of the appraisal and the date of the report.

7. Describe sufficient information to disclose to the client and any intended users of the appraisal the scope of work used to develop the appraisal.

8. State all assumptions, hypothetical conditions, and limiting conditions that affected the analyses, opinions, and conclusions.

9. Describe the information analyzed, the appraisal procedures followed, and the reasoning that supports the analyses, opinions, and conclusions.

10. State the use of the real estate existing as of the date of value and the use of the real estate reflected in the appraisal; and, when the purpose of the assignment is market value, describe the support and rationale for the appraiser's opinion of the highest and best use of the real estate;

11. Include a signed certification in accordance with USPAP Standards Rule 2-3.

Technology now permits appraisal reports to be transmitted to the client by email or **Electronic Data Interchange (EDI)**, rather than by an oral report or the familiar hand-delivered or mailed report. A number of mortgage lenders are now using special software to place appraisal orders and allow electronic reporting of loan appraisals. USPAP reporting standards still apply.

The three traditional formats of written appraisal reports are the letter report, the form report, and the narrative report. The letter report is a short business letter that contains the essential elements of a report, but most often abbreviates the supporting data, referring the reader to the appraiser's files. The conditions, assumptions, and appraiser's certification should always be included or attached, no matter how short the report. Usually, the letter report meets only those content requirements typical of the Restricted Use Appraisal Report.

There are many variations of the form report. The most commonly used is the URAR. Some version of this form is required for most single-family residential loan appraisals by the Federal Home Loan Mortgage

Corporation, the Federal National Mortgage Association, the Veterans Administration, the Federal Housing Administration (FHA), and the Department of Housing and Urban Development (HUD). While best suited for the Summary Appraisal Report, the URAR contains all the basic elements of an appraisal report. Attachments sometimes might be required for the URAR to conform to USPAP.

Some lenders are now using simplified versions of the URAR in conjunction with an automated program called the Desktop Underwriter Program. The latter is used as a method of risk analysis for certain loans involving single-family homes and condominiums. The newer forms are referred to as *FNMA Forms 2055 and 2070*. The latter is an inspection form only.

The ideal format for a Self-Contained Appraisal Report is the narrative report. This report is preferred when the client wants to follow the appraiser's step-by-step logic in arriving at the value conclusion, and needs to have documentation of all the pertinent facts revealed in the investigation.

While various government agencies and appraisal organizations have developed their own requirements for the form and content of narrative appraisal reports, one very acceptable format divides the material into four main sections: 1) introduction, 2) description, 3) analyses and conclusion, and 4) addenda. Such an outline or format is not only traditional, but it also makes it easier for the client to follow, visualize, and remember the facts and conclusions presented.

The narrative appraisal report should meet high standards. The actual writing of this report includes three basic considerations: appearance, form, and content. Obviously, the appearance must be formal, neat, and professional. Narrative appraisal reports should follow a carefully planned outline and form. Of course, the content is the most important of the three considerations. The facts, analyses, and opinions set forth in a narrative report should show the appraiser's best efforts in carrying out the appraisal assignment. Thus, the narrative appraisal report enables the appraiser to utilize all the knowledge, skill, or training at his or her command, and present to the client the required information in a succinct, convincing, and interesting manner.

In practice, appraisal reports tend to mix the features of the basic formats for reports, containing some features of the letter report, some of the form, and some of the narrative report. In federally related appraisals, regulations require that all reports be written, conform to the Uniform Standards of Professional Appraisal Practice, and meet other minimum content standards set by each financial institution of the federal government.

IMPORTANT TERMS AND CONCEPTS

Assumptions

Certification

Electronic Data Interchange (EDI)

FNMA Desktop Underwriter

FNMA Form 2055

FNMA Form 2070

Fannie Mae Form 1004

Federally related appraisals

Form appraisal report

Freddie Mac Form 70

Letter of transmittal

Limiting conditions

Narrative appraisal report

Professional appraisal standards

Qualifications of the appraiser

Restricted Use Appraisal Report

Sales history

Self-Contained Appraisal Report

Summary Appraisal Report

URAR

REVIEWING YOUR UNDERSTANDING

1. Written appraisal reports are a form of business communication. Every report should be:
   a. Concise
   b. Well organized
   c. Easy to read
   d. All of the above

2. The highest level of reliability is found in a:
   a. Restricted Use appraisal report
   b. Form appraisal report
   c. Narrative appraisal report
   d. Well-prepared professional appraisal

3. According to USPAP, the type of appraisal report suggests the level of detail required. Which of the following reports is the most detailed?
   a. Summary report
   b. The Restricted Use report
   c. The Self-Contained report
   d. The form report

4. There are four main subdivisions in the typical narrative appraisal report. Which of the following is not one of these subdivisions?
   a. Introduction
   b. Letter of transmittal
   c. Analyses and conclusion
   d. Addenda

5. Which appraisal form is not an appraisal report, as defined in USPAP?
   a. URAR
   b. FNMA 2055
   c. FHA V.C.
   d. FNMA 2070

6. The short narrative report:
   a. Is best suited for the Restricted Use Appraisal Report
   b. Need not contain assumptions, limiting conditions, and the appraiser's certification
   c. Is the most formal written report
   d. Is required by most institutions and agencies

7. In the form report, it is usually necessary for the appraiser to:
   a. Demonstrate evidence of value through one or more approaches
   b. Describe any significant physical deterioration or functional inadequacy
   c. Rate the neighborhood growth rate
   d. All of the above

8. Sales data sheets in the addenda of a narrative appraisal report contain:
   a. Details about each comparable sale
   b. An analysis of the data by the value approaches
   c. An outline of the investigation made to estimate market rent
   d. All of the above

9. In the reconciliation and final conclusion of value, the appraiser should:
   a. Describe the relevance of each value approach explored
   b. Discuss the reliability of the data used
   c. Provide arguments to justify the final conclusion of value rendered
   d. All of the above

10. The statement of limiting conditions in the appraisal report:
    a. Serves to clarify the assumptions made by the appraiser
    b. Limits the appraiser's legal liability
    c. Obligates the appraiser to appear in court regarding the appraisal at any future time
    d. Both (a) and (b)

11. Most real estate appraisals used in connection with federally related transactions must be performed:
    a. In writing
    b. In accordance with uniform standards
    c. By staff appraisers
    d. To satisfy both (a) and (b) requirements

PRACTICAL APPLICATIONS

This will be the last assignment: to complete the appraisal report! The first step is to review the full URAR report, with exhibits, that is shown at the end of this chapter. You should have completed the first three pages of the form as part of the exercises in prior chapters. Review to be certain that all necessary information has been entered on the form.

The next step is to review pages 4–6, which are now part of the form. You should carefully review the material on these three pages, because when you perform appraisals in real life, you need to be very careful to comply with the requirements set forth. All that is needed to finish these pages is to fill in the remaining material on page 6 and sign the report.

Now it is time to prepare the additional exhibits to the report. First, review the exhibits included with the URAR report presented at the end of this chapter. These include the location map for the subject property and comparable sales, the plat map or assessor's map showing the specific parcel, the floor plan or plan of improvements, and the photos of the subject property and the comparable sales.

You prepared a sketch of the subject property back when you inspected it. Now, insert that sketch on the Floor Plan addendum form. Consider what information you might want to add, as was done with the sketch in your text. You also obtained a copy of the assessor's parcel map prior to inspecting the property. So, insert it into the appropriate sheet for the Plat Map and add labels as needed. Note that if you only have a paper copy of the parcel map, you will need to print out the blank plat map page and paste or tape your paper copy onto the form. You could hand print any needed labels, but it would look more polished to type them into your computer, in Word, WordPerfect, or similar, print them on a sheet of plain paper, and cut and paste the information in blocks onto the form.

Next is the location map. You might print out a suitable map from one of the online mapping sites, such as MapQuest, Yahoo!, Google, or others. Another choice is to select a paper map that covers the area you need in order to show both the subject property and all of the comparable sales. You can cut the paper map to the size needed to fit on the location map page and paste it in place. Add labels as needed for the locations of the subject property and the comparable sales, and for a north arrow. Consider something that you could use to draw neat round circles or perhaps squares for the comparable numbers. A plastic cutout is perfect, but any round, oval, or square object the right size can be used to trace around. An example is the barrel of a round ballpoint pen. And you could print the needed number and subject labels with your computer, cut them out and glue them in place. In an appraisal office, these circles and arrows are often positioned by the mapping program in use, which you are not required to have at this point.

Finally, prepare the photo sheets, as needed. If you used a digital camera and your pictures are on the same computer as your Click-FORMS program, you can just import the pictures into the program and position and label them as needed. If your camera is not digital, you will need to get prints of the needed pictures. (Get two sets so that you can give one to the instructor and keep another to show to future employers.) Paste the pictures on the forms and add labels. The last step is to carefully go over the entire report, looking for typing errors, misplaced location labels, or switched pictures. Make sure that you have entered the hypothetical conditions that we have discussed, as well as any relevant extraordinary assumptions, in the comments block at the top of page 3. Then, your final step is to sign your report at the proper places. Congratulations!

Reminder: If you have questions about the program, review the manuals and help information that were on the program CD. Also, go to http://www.bradfordsoftware.com, click on "Services" at the upper right, and then on "ClickFORMS Training Programs" in the middle of the "Services" page.

Sample Appraisal Report

A sample URAR appraisal report, complete with typical attachments, is provided on the following pages.

Uniform Residential Appraisal Report

The purpose of this summary appraisal report is to provide the lender/client with an accurate, and adequately supported, opinion of the market value of the subject property.

SUBJECT

Property Address 831 S. Dona Marta St.	City Ventura State CA Zip Code 930xx
Borrower Robert Burns Owner of Public Record Same	County Ventura
Legal Description LOt 68, Tract 25xx, Map Book No. 84-81-xx	
Assessor's Parcel # 009-001-xx Tax Year 200x-0y R.E. Taxes $ @0.1026	
Neighborhood Name Mountain View homes Map Reference 48 C-x Census Tract 246xx	

Occupant [X] Owner [ ] Tenant [ ] Vacant Special Assessments $ None   [ ] PUD HOA $ [ ] per year [ ] per month
Property Rights Appraised [X] Fee Simple [ ] Leasehold [ ] Other (describe)
Assignment Type [ ] Purchase Transaction [X] Refinance Transaction [ ] Other (describe)
Lender/Client Sample Savings and Loan   Address 116 San Luis Blvd., Venture, CA 930xx
Is the subject property currently offered for sale or has it been offered for sale in the twelve months prior to the effective date of this appraisal? [ ] Yes [X] No
Report data source(s) used, offerings price(s), and date(s).

CONTRACT

I [ ] did [ ] did not analyze the contract for sale for the subject purchase transaction. Explain the results of the analysis of the contract for sale or why the analysis was not performed. Refinance

Contract Price $ (Re-Finance) Date of Contract   Is the property seller the owner of public record? [X] Yes [ ] No Data Source(s) NDG
Is there any financial assistance (loan charges, sale concessions, gift or downpayment assistance, etc.) to be paid by any party on behalf of the borrower? [ ] Yes [X] No
If Yes, report the total dollar amount and describe the items to be paid.

NEIGHBORHOOD

Note: Race and the racial composition of the neighborhood are not appraisal factors.

Neighborhood Characteristics				One-Unit Housing Trends				One-Unit Housing			Present Land Use %	
Location	[ ] Urban	[X] Suburban	[ ] Rural	Property Values	[ ] Increasing	[X] Stable	[ ] Declining	PRICE	AGE		One-Unit	60 %
Built-Up	[X] Over 75%	[ ] 25-75%	[ ] Under 25%	Demand/Supply	[ ] Shortage	[X] In Balance	[ ] Over Supply	$ (000)	(yrs)		2-4 Unit	05 %
Growth	[ ] Rapid	[X] Stable	[ ] Slow	Marketing Time	[ ] Under 3 mths	[X] 3-6 mths	[ ] Over 6 mths	200 Low	0		Multi-Family	05 %
Neighborhood Boundaries This quiet rural neighborhood is bounded on the N. by the coast mountains;								350 High	30		Commercial	0 %
on the S. by Main St.; on the E. by Foothill Blvd.; and on the W. by the San Jon Barranca.								280 Pred.	22		Other	30 %

Neighborhood Description The neighborhood enjoys an above-average prestige factor. Its natural setting, and overlook of the mountains are the most favorable features. Municipal services are above-average. City parkes and recreation centers are within 1 mile, and slementary schools are within 1/2 mile. Employment centers are within 2 miles, and unemployment rates here are below the state average.
Market Conditions (including support for the above conclusions) After several years of moderate decline, market prices in the subject neighborhood have stabilized. No vacant houses are in evidence, and there are a typical number of "for sale" signs seen. Marketing time has improved from about 6 months, to a present average of 4 months.

SITE

Dimensions   90 X 145.2   Area   13,068 Sqft   Shape   Rectangular   View   Nominal
Specific Zoning Classification   R-1-10, Single family   Zoning Description Single- family detached, 10,000 s.f. minimum lot size
Zoning Compliance [X] Legal [ ] Legal Nonconforming (Grandfathered Use) [ ] No Zoning [ ] Illegal (describe)
Is the highest and best use of subject property as improved (or as proposed per plans and specifications) the present use? [X] Yes [ ] No If No, describe.

Utilities	Public	Other (describe)		Public	Other (describe)	Off-site Improvements--Type	Public	Private
Electricity	[X]		Water	[X]		Street Asphalt	[X]	
Gas	[X]		Sanitary Sewer	[X]		Alley None		

FEMA Special Flood Hazard Area [ ] Yes [X] No FEMA Flood Zone ---   FEMA Map # Not mapped   FEMA Map Date ---
Are the utilities and/or off-site improvements typical for the market area? [X] Yes [ ] No If No, describe.
Are there any adverse site conditions or external factors (easements, encroachments, environmental conditions, land uses, etc.)? [X] Yes [ ] No If Yes, describe.
There were no adverse conditions observed. Site has a steep upslope beginning 25 feet from the back of the house.

IMPROVEMENTS

General Description		Foundation	Exterior Description materials/condition	Interior materials/condition
Units [X] One [ ] One with Accessory Unit		[ ] Concrete Slab [X] Crawl Space	Foundation Walls Concrete	Floors Carpet/Good
# of Stories One		[ ] Full Basement [ ] Partial Basement	Exterior Walls Stucco	Walls Plaster/VG
Type [X] Det. [ ] Att. [ ] S-Det./End Unit	Basement Area sq. ft.		Roof Surface C/Shingle	Trim/Finish Stock/Good
[X] Existing [ ] Proposed [ ] Under Const.	Basement Finish %		Gutters & Downspouts Yes	Bath Floor Ceramic/Good
Design (Style) Contemp.	[ ] Outside Entry/Exit [ ] Sump Pump		Window Type Slid. Alum.	Bath Wainscot Tile Shower
Year Built 1981	Evidence of [ ] Infestation None Vis		Storm Sash/Insulated Yes	Car Storage [ ] None
Effective Age (Yrs) 17	[ ] Dampness [ ] Settlement		Screens Aluminum	[ ] Driveway # of Cars

Attic [X] None
[ ] Drop Stair [ ] Stairs   Heating [X] FWA [ ] HWBB [ ] Radiant Amenities [ ] Woodstove(s) #   Driveway Surface Asphalt
[ ] Floor [ ] Scuttle   [ ] Other Fuel Gas   [X] Fireplace(s) # 1 [X] Fence Wood   [X] Garage # of Cars 2
[ ] Finished [ ] Heated   Cooling [ ] Central Air Conditioning [X] Patio/Deck Concrete [ ] Porch   [ ] Carport # of Cars
   [ ] Individual [ ] Other None   [ ] Pool [X] Other Htd Spa   [X] Att. [ ] Det. [ ] Built-in

Appliances [ ] Refrigerator [X] Range/Oven [X] Dishwasher [X] Disposal [ ] Microwave [ ] Washer/Dryer [ ] Other (describe)
Finished area **above** grade contains: 6 Rooms   4 Bedrooms   2.00 Bath(s)   1,768 Square Feet of Gross Living Area Above Grade
Additional features (special energy efficient items, etc.) Kitchen and master bath have skylights. Master bath has mirrored double pullman basins. The rear yard improvements include a covered patio, and a 7 foot heated spa.
Describe the condition of the property (including needed repairs, deterioration, renovations, remodeling, etc.).   There are no physical, functional, or external inadequacies noted; the kitchen and baths were recently redecorated.

Are there any physical deficiencies or adverse conditions that affect the livability, soundness, or structural integrity of the property? [ ] Yes [X] No If Yes, describe

Does the property generally conform to the neighborhood (functional utility, style, condition, use, construction, etc.)? [X] Yes [ ] No If No, describe

Figure 16-6 Sample Appraisal Report.

Uniform Residential Appraisal Report

There are 3 comparable properties currently offered for sale in the subject neighborhood ranging in price from $ 255,000 to $ 340,000 .						
There are 9 comparable sales in the subject neighborhood within the past twelve months ranging in sale price from $ 250,000 to $ 321,500 .						

FEATURE	SUBJECT	COMPARABLE SALE # 1		COMPARABLE SALE # 2		COMPARABLE SALE # 3	
Address	831 S. Dona Marta St. Ventura, CA 930xx	896 E. Hyland Ave.		821 E. Sunset Dr.		932 E. Sherwood Dr.	
Proximity to Subject		3 blocks west		4 blocks west		2 Blocks west	
Sale Price	$ (Re-Finance)	$ 321,500		$ 286,000		$ 280,000	
Sale Price/Gross Liv. Area	$ 0.00 sq. ft.	$ 155.46 sq. ft.		$ 145.18 sq. ft.		$ 155.56 sq. ft.	
Data Source(s)		Doc #182904		Doc #014815		Doc #1097024	
Verification Source(s)		Buyer		MLS & Seller		Broker	
VALUE ADJUSTMENTS	DESCRIPTION	DESCRIPTION	+(-) $ Adjustment	DESCRIPTION	+(-) $ Adjustment	DESCRIPTION	+(-) $ Adjustment
Sale or Financing		Cash		80% Conv.		80% Conv.	
Concessions							
Date of Sale/Time		3/0x		2/0x		11/0x	
Location	Average	Average		Average		Average	
Leasehold/Fee Simple	Fee Simple	Fee		Fee		Fee	
Site	13,068 Sqft	14,375	-10,000	11,809		15,246	-6,000
View	Nominal	Excellent	-20,000	Nominal		Good	-6,000
Design (Style)	Contemp./Good	Mod/Good		Mod/V.Good	-2,500	Mod./V.Good	-2,500
Quality of Construction	Good	Good		Good		Good	
Actual Age	26 yrs	22		24		24	
Condition	Good	Good		Good		Fair	+5,000
Above Grade	Total / Bdrms / Baths	Total / Bdrms / Baths		Total / Bdrms / Baths		Total / Bdrms / Baths	
Room Count	6 / 4 / 2.00	7 / 4 / 2.00		7 / 3 / 2.50		6 / 4 / 2.00	
Gross Living Area	1,768 sq. ft.	2,068 sq. ft.	-12,000	1,970 sq. ft.	-8,000	1,800 sq. ft.	
Basement & Finished							
Rooms Below Grade							
Functional Utility	Good	Equal		Equal		Equal	
Heating/Cooling	FWA/None	FWA/None		FWA/None		FWA/None	
Energy Efficient Items	None	None		None		None	
Garage/Carport	2 Car Gar. Att.	Same		Same		Same	
Porch/Patio/Deck	Cov. Patio,Deck	None	+500	None	+500	None	+500
Spa	7 ft. heated	Same		Same		Same	
		None	+2,000	None	+2,000	None	+2,000
Net Adjustment (Total)		+ X -	$ -39,500	+ X -	$ -8,000	+ X -	$ -7,000
Adjusted Sale Price		Net Adj: -12%		Net Adj: -3%		Net Adj: -3%	
of Comparables		Gross Adj : 14%	$ 282,000	Gross Adj: 5%	$ 278,000	Gross Adj: 8%	$ 273,000

I X did / did not research the sale or transfer history of the subject property and comparable sales. If not, explain

My research X did / did not reveal any prior sales or transfers of the subject property for the three years prior to the effective date of this appraisal.
Data source(s) NDC, MLS
My research did / X did not reveal any prior sales or transfers of the comparable sales for the year prior to the date of sale of the comparable sale.
Data source(s)
Report the results of the research and analysis of the prior sale or transfer history of the subject property and comparable sales (report additional prior sales on page 3).

ITEM	SUBJECT	COMPARABLE SALE # 1	COMPARABLE SALE # 2	COMPARABLE SALE # 3
Date of Prior Sale/Transfer	Sold 11/0x	None	None	None
Price of Prior Sale/Transfer	for $250K in			
Data Source(s)	poor condition			
Effective Date of Data Source(s)				

Analysis of prior sale or transfer history of the subject property and comparable sales The subject was in poor condition at the time of its 200x sale, but the historic selling price, adjusted for condition of improvements, tends to support the value indicated by current sales.

Summary of Sales Comparison Approach Comp. #1 is the same original tract model as the subject, but it was enlarged before the sale. It has a hilltop view. Sale #3 is considered to be the most comparable sale, except for its inferior condition. No time adjustment is warranted, judging from Realty Board sales records and current escrows here. We place the most weight on Comparables #2 and #3 because they required the least amount of adjustment.

Indicated Value by Sales Comparison Approach $ 275,000

Indicated Value by: Sales Comparison Approach $ 275,000 Cost Approach (if developed) $ 282,903 Income Approach (if developed) $ 0
Although not weighted heavily in this appraisal, the cost approach tends to confirm the value indicated by the sales comparison approach. The income approach has not been tested here, because it is deemed to be inapplicable in this predominantly owner-occupied neighborhood.
This appraisal is made X "as is," subject to completion per plans and specifications on the basis of a hypothetical condition that the improvements have been completed, subject to the following repairs or alterations on the basis of a hypothetical condition that the repairs or alterations have been completed, or subject to the following required inspection based on the extraordinary assumption that the condition or deficiency does not require alteration or repair: This Summary Report is intended to comply with the Uniform Standards of Professional Appraisal Practice.
Based on a complete visual inspection of the interior and exterior areas of the subject property, defined scope of work, statement of assumptions and limiting conditions, and appraiser's certification, my (our) opinion of the market value, as defined, of the real property that is the subject of this report is $ 275,000 , as of June 24, 200x , which is the date of inspection and the effective date of this appraisal.

Figure 16-6 Sample Appraisal Report. (Second Page)

Uniform Residential Appraisal Report

ADDITIONAL COMMENTS

COST APPROACH TO VALUE (not required by Fannie Mae.)					

Provide adequate information for the lender/client to replicate your cost figures and calculations.

Support for the opinion of site value (summary of comparable land sales or other methods for estimating site value)   The site value was abstracted from improved sales in the neighborhood.

			OPINION OF SITE VALUE			=$	140,000
ESTIMATED [X] REPRODUCTION OR [ ] REPLACEMENT COST NEW			Dwelling	1,768	Sq. Ft. @ $ 70.00	=$	123,760
Source of cost data M & S Residential			Patio	260	Sq. Ft. @ $ 15.00	=$	3,900
Quality rating from cost service Good Effective date of cost data June, 200x			Heated Spa & Deck				9,500
Comments on Cost Approach (gross living area calculations, depreciation, etc.)			Garage/Carport	484	Sq. Ft. @ $ 35.00	=$	16,940
The square foot area computations may be found on the attached			Total Estimate of Cost-new			=$	154,100
Plan of Improvements.			Less Physical 17	Functional	External		
			Depreciation 26,197	0	0	=$ (	26,197)
			Depreciated Cost of Improvements			=$	127,903
			"As-is" Value of Site Improvements			=$	15,000
Estimated Remaining Economic Life (HUD and VA only) 40-50 Years			Indicated Value By Cost Approach			=$	282,903

INCOME APPROACH TO VALUE (not required by Fannie Mae.)					
Estimated Monthly Market Rent $ N/A X Gross Multiplier N/A =$ 0				Indicated Value by Income Approach	
Summary of Income Approach (including support for market rent and GRM)					

PROJECT INFORMATION FOR PUDs (if applicable)		

Is the developer/builder in control of the Homeowner's Association (HOA)? [ ] Yes [ ] No Unit type(s) [ ] Detached [ ] Attached

Provide the following information for PUDs ONLY if the developer/builder is in control of the HOA and the subject property is an attached dwelling unit.

Legal Name of Project

Total number of phases   Total number of units   Total number of units sold

Total number of units rented   Total number of units for sale   Data source(s)

Was the project created by the conversion of existing building(s) into a PUD? [ ] Yes [ ] No If Yes, date of conversion.

Does the project contain any multi-dwelling units? [ ] Yes [ ] No Data source.

Are the units, common elements, and recreation facilities complete? [ ] Yes [ ] No If No, describe the status of completion.

Are the common elements leased to or by the Homeowner's Association? [ ] Yes [ ] No If Yes, describe the rental terms and options.

Describe common elements and recreational facilities.   N/A

Figure 16-6 Sample Appraisal Report. (Third Page)

Uniform Residential Appraisal Report

This report form is designed to report an appraisal of a one-unit property or a one-unit property with an accessory unit; including a unit in a planned unit development (PUD). This report form is not designed to report an appraisal of a manufactured home or a unit in a condominium or cooperative project.

This appraisal report is subject to the following scope of work, intended use, intended user, definition of market value, statement of assumptions and limiting conditions, and certifications. Modifications, additions, or deletions to the intended use, intended user, definition of market value, or assumptions and limiting conditions are not permitted. The appraiser may expand the scope of work to include any additional research or analysis necessary based on the complexity of this appraisal assignment. Modifications or deletions to the certifications are also not permitted. However, additional certifications that do not constitute material alterations to this appraisal report, such as those required by law or those related to the appraiser's continuing education or membership in an appraisal organization, are permitted.

SCOPE OF WORK: The scope of work for this appraisal is defined by the complexity of this appraisal assignment and the reporting requirements of this appraisal report form, including the following definition of market value, statement of assumptions and limiting conditions, and certifications. The appraiser must, at a minimum: (1) perform a complete visual inspection of the interior and exterior areas of the subject property, (2) inspect the neighborhood, (3) inspect each of the comparable sales from at least the street, (4) research, verify, and analyze data from reliable public and/or private sources, and (5) report his or her analysis, opinions, and conclusions in this appraisal report.

INTENDED USE: The intended use of this appraisal report is for the lender/client to evaluate the property that is the subject of this appraisal for a mortgage finance transaction.

INTENDED USER: The intended user of this appraisal report is the lender/client.

DEFINITION OF MARKET VALUE: The most probable price which a property should bring in a competitive and open market under all conditions requisite to a fair sale, the buyer and seller, each acting prudently, knowledgeably and assuming the price is not affected by undue stimulus. Implicit in this definition is the consummation of a sale as of a specified date and the passing of title from seller to buyer under conditions whereby: (1) buyer and seller are typically motivated; (2) both parties are well informed or well advised, and each acting in what he or she considers his or her own best interest; (3) a reasonable time is allowed for exposure in the open market; (4) payment is made in terms of cash in U. S. dollars or in terms of financial arrangements comparable thereto; and (5) the price represents the normal consideration for the property sold unaffected by special or creative financing or sales concessions* granted by anyone associated with the sale.

*Adjustments to the comparables must be made for special or creative financing or sales concessions. No adjustments are necessary for those costs which are normally paid by sellers as a result of tradition or law in a market area; these costs are readily identifiable since the seller pays these costs in virtually all sales transactions. Special or creative financing adjustments can be made to the comparable property by comparisons to financing terms offered by a third party institutional lender that is not already involved in the property or transaction. Any adjustment should not be calculated on a mechanical dollar for dollar cost of the financing or concession but the dollar amount of any adjustment should approximate the market's reaction to the financing or concessions based on the appraiser's judgment.

STATEMENT OF ASSUMPTIONS AND LIMITING CONDITIONS: The appraiser's certification in this report is subject to the following assumptions and limiting conditions:

1. The appraiser will not be responsible for matters of a legal nature that affect either the property being appraised or the title to it, except for information that he or she became aware of during the research involved in performing this appraisal. The appraiser assumes that the title is good and marketable and will not render any opinions about the title.

2. The appraiser has provided a sketch in this appraisal report to show the approximate dimensions of the improvements. The sketch is included only to assist the reader in visualizing the property and understanding the appraiser's determination of its size.

3. The appraiser has examined the available flood maps that are provided by the Federal Emergency Management Agency (or other data sources) and has noted in this appraisal report whether any portion of the subject site is located in an identified Special Flood Hazard Area. Because the appraiser is not a surveyor, he or she makes no guarantees, express or implied, regarding this determination.

4. The appraiser will not give testimony or appear in court because he or she made an appraisal of the property in question, unless specific arrangements to do so have been made beforehand, or as otherwise required by law.

5. The appraiser has noted in this appraisal report any adverse conditions (such as needed repairs, deterioration, the presence of hazardous wastes, toxic substances, etc.) observed during the inspection of the subject property or that he or she became aware of during the research involved in performing this appraisal. Unless otherwise stated in this appraisal report, the appraiser has no knowledge of any hidden or unapparent physical deficiencies or adverse conditions of the property (such as, but not limited to, needed repairs, deterioration, the presence of hazardous wastes, toxic substances, adverse environmental conditions, etc.) that would make the property less valuable, and has assumed that there are no such conditions and makes no guarantees or warranties, express or implied. The appraiser will not be responsible for any such conditions that do exist or for any engineering or testing that might be required to discover whether such conditions exist. Because the appraiser is not an expert in the field of environmental hazards, this appraisal report must not be considered as an environmental assessment of the property.

6. The appraiser has based his or her appraisal report and valuation conclusion for an appraisal that is subject to satisfactory completion, repairs, or alterations on the assumption that the completion, repairs, or alterations of the subject property will be performed in a professional manner.

Figure 16-6 Sample Appraisal Report. (Fourth Page)

Uniform Residential Appraisal Report

APPRAISER'S CERTIFICATION: The Appraiser certifies and agrees that:

1. I have, at a minimum, developed and reported this appraisal in accordance with the scope of work requirements stated in this appraisal report.

2. I performed a complete visual inspection of the interior and exterior areas of the subject property. I reported the condition of the improvements in factual, specific terms. I identified and reported the physical deficiencies that could affect the livability, soundness, or structural integrity of the property.

3. I performed this appraisal in accordance with the requirements of the Uniform Standards of Professional Appraisal Practice that were adopted and promulgated by the Appraisal Standards Board of The Appraisal Foundation and that were in place at the time this appraisal report was prepared.

4. I developed my opinion of the market value of the real property that is the subject of this report based on the sales comparison approach to value. I have adequate comparable market data to develop a reliable sales comparison approach for this appraisal assignment. I further certify that I considered the cost and income approaches to value but did not develop them, unless otherwise indicated in this report.

5. I researched, verified, analyzed, and reported on any current agreement for sale for the subject property, any offering for sale of the subject property in the twelve months prior to the effective date of this appraisal, and the prior sales of the subject property for a minimum of three years prior to the effective date of this appraisal, unless otherwise indicated in this report.

6. I researched, verified, analyzed, and reported on the prior sales of the comparable sales for a minimum of one year prior to the date of sale of the comparable sale, unless otherwise indicated in this report.

7. I selected and used comparable sales that are locationally, physically, and functionally the most similar to the subject property.

8. I have not used comparable sales that were the result of combining a land sale with the contract purchase price of a home that has been built or will be built on the land.

9. I have reported adjustments to the comparable sales that reflect the market's reaction to the differences between the subject property and the comparable sales.

10. I verified, from a disinterested source, all information in this report that was provided by parties who have a financial interest in the sale or financing of the subject property.

11. I have knowledge and experience in appraising this type of property in this market area.

12. I am aware of, and have access to, the necessary and appropriate public and private data sources, such as multiple listing services, tax assessment records, public land records and other such data sources for the area in which the property is located.

13. I obtained the information, estimates, and opinions furnished by other parties and expressed in this appraisal report from reliable sources that I believe to be true and correct.

14. I have taken into consideration the factors that have an impact on value with respect to the subject neighborhood, subject property, and the proximity of the subject property to adverse influences in the development of my opinion of market value. I have noted in this appraisal report any adverse conditions (such as, but not limited to, needed repairs, deterioration, the presence of hazardous wastes, toxic substances, adverse environmental conditions, etc.) observed during the inspection of the subject property or that I became aware of during the research involved in performing this appraisal. I have considered these adverse conditions in my analysis of the property value, and have reported on the effect of the conditions on the value and marketability of the subject property.

15. I have not knowingly withheld any significant information from this appraisal report and, to the best of my knowledge, all statements and information in this appraisal report are true and correct.

16. I stated in this appraisal report my own personal, unbiased, and professional analysis, opinions, and conclusions, which are subject only to the assumptions and limiting conditions in this appraisal report.

17. I have no present or prospective interest in the property that is the subject of this report, and I have no present or prospective personal interest or bias with respect to the participants in the transaction. I did not base, either partially or completely, my analysis and/or opinion of market value in this appraisal report on the race, color, religion, sex, age, marital status, handicap, familial status, or national origin of either the prospective owners or occupants of the subject property or of the present owners or occupants of the properties in the vicinity of the subject property or on any other basis prohibited by law.

18. My employment and/or compensation for performing this appraisal or any future or anticipated appraisals was not conditioned on any agreement or understanding, written or otherwise, that I would report (or present analysis supporting) a predetermined specific value, a predetermined minimum value, a range or direction in value, a value that favors the cause of any party, or the attainment of a specific result or occurrence of a specific subsequent event (such as approval of a pending mortgage loan application).

19. I personally prepared all conclusions and opinions about the real estate that were set forth in this appraisal report. If I relied on significant real property appraisal assistance from any individual or individuals in the performance of this appraisal or the preparation of this appraisal report, I have named such individual(s) and disclosed the specific tasks performed in this appraisal report. I certify that any individual so named is qualified to perform the tasks. I have not authorized anyone to make a change to any item in this appraisal report; therefore, any change made to this appraisal is unauthorized and I will take no responsibility for it.

20. I identified the lender/client in this appraisal report who is the individual, organization, or agent for the organization that ordered and will receive this appraisal report.

Figure 16-6 Sample Appraisal Report. (Fifth Page)

Uniform Residential Appraisal Report

21. The lender/client may disclose or distribute this appraisal report to: the borrower; another lender at the request of the borrower; the mortgagee or its successors and assigns; mortgage insurers; government sponsored enterprises; other secondary market participants; data collection or reporting services; professional appraisal organizations; any department, agency, or instrumentality of the United States; and any state, the District of Columbia, or other jurisdictions; without having to obtain the appraiser's or supervisory appraiser's (if applicable) consent. Such consent must be obtained before this appraisal report may be disclosed or distributed to any other party (including, but not limited to, the public through advertising, public relations, news, sales, or other media).

22. I am aware that any disclosure or distribution of this appraisal report by me or the lender/client may be subject to certain laws and regulations. Further, I am also subject to the provisions of the Uniform Standards of Professional Appraisal Practice that pertain to disclosure or distribution by me.

23. The borrower, another lender at the request of the borrower, the mortgagee or its successors and assigns, mortgage insurers, government sponsored enterprises, and other secondary market participants may rely on this appraisal report as part of any mortgage finance transaction that involves any one or more of these parties.

24. If this appraisal report was transmitted as an "electronic record" containing my "electronic signature," as those terms are defined in applicable federal and/or state laws (excluding audio and video recordings), or a facsimile transmission of this appraisal report containing a copy or representation of my signature, the appraisal report shall be as effective, enforceable and valid as if a paper version of this appraisal report were delivered containing my original hand written signature.

25. Any intentional or negligent misrepresentation(s) contained in this appraisal report may result in civil liability and/or criminal penalties including, but not limited to, fine or imprisonment or both under the provisions of Title 18, United States Code, Section 1001, et seq., or similar state laws.

SUPERVISORY APPRAISER'S CERTIFICATION: The Supervisory Appraiser certifies and agrees that:

1. I directly supervised the appraiser for this appraisal assignment, have read the appraisal report, and agree with the appraiser's analysis, opinions, statements, conclusions, and the appraiser's certification.

2. I accept full responsibility for the contents of this appraisal report including, but not limited to, the appraiser's analysis, opinions, statements, conclusions, and the appraiser's certification.

3. The appraiser identified in this appraisal report is either a sub-contractor or an employee of the supervisory appraiser (or the appraisal firm), is qualified to perform this appraisal, and is acceptable to perform this appraisal under the applicable state law.

4. This appraisal report complies with the Uniform Standards of Professional Appraisal Practice that were adopted and promulgated by the Appraisal Standards Board of The Appraisal Foundation and that were in place at the time this appraisal report was prepared.

5. If this appraisal report was transmitted as an "electronic record" containing my "electronic signature," as those terms are defined in applicable federal and/or state laws (excluding audio and video recordings), or a facsimile transmission of this appraisal report containing a copy or representation of my signature, the appraisal report shall be as effective, enforceable and valid as if a paper version of this appraisal report were delivered containing my original hand written signature.

APPRAISER	SUPERVISORY APPRAISER (ONLY IF REQUIRED)
Signature	Signature
Name Richard M. Betts, MAI, ASA, SRA	Name
Company Name Betts & Associates	Company Name
Company Address 25 Agnes St.	Company Address
Oakland, CA 94618	
Telephone Number 510-594-9015	Telephone Number
Email Address richard.betts@bettsandassoc.com	Email Address
Date of Signature and Report June 28, 200x	Date of Signature
Effective Date of Appraisal June 24, 200x	State Certification #
State Certification # AG006703	or State License #
or State License #	State
or Other (describe) _____ State # _____	Expiration Date of Certification or License _____
State CA	
Expiration Date of Certification or License 3/1/07	

ADDRESS OF PROPERTY APPRAISED
831 S. Dona Marta St.
Ventura, CA 930xx

APPRAISED VALUE OF SUBJECT PROPERTY $ ___ 275,000
LENDER/CLIENT
Name   Hector Von Bethofen
Company Name Sample Savings and Loan
Company Address 116 San Luis Blvd.
              Venture, CA 930xx
Email Address _____

SUBJECT PROPERTY
☐ Did not inspect subject property
☐ Did inspect exterior of subject property from street
    Date of Inspection _____
☐ Did inspect interior and exterior of subject property
    Date of Inspection _____

COMPARABLE SALES
☐ Did not inspect exterior of comparable sales from street
☐ Did inspect exterior of comparable sales from street
    Date of Inspection _____

Figure 16-6 Sample Appraisal Report. (Sixth Page)

LOCATION MAP ADDENDUM   File No.   **SAMPLE**

Borrower	Robert Burns				
Property Address	831 S. Dona Marta St.				
City	Ventura	County	Ventura	State	CA	Zip Code	93003
Lender/Client	Sample Savings and Loan	Address	116 San Luis Blvd. Ventura, CA 93900		

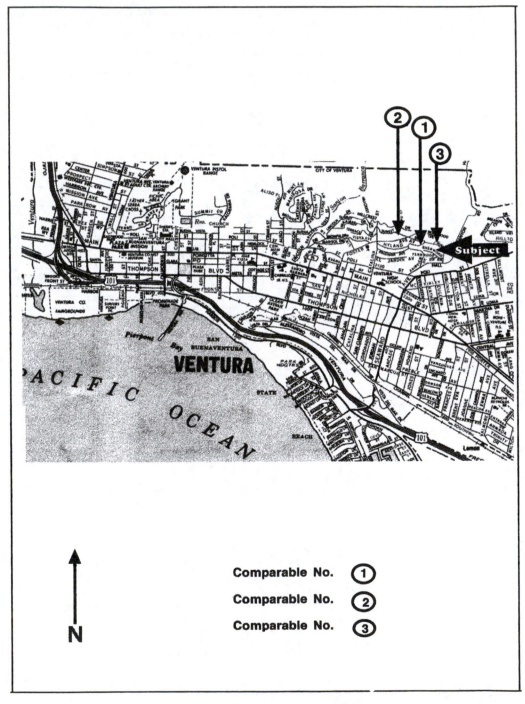

Comparable No. ①

Comparable No. ②

Comparable No. ③

N

Figure 16-7 Location Map.

PLAT MAP

File No. **SAMPLE**

Borrower Robert Burns
Property Address 831 S. Dona Marta St.
City Ventura County Ventura State CA Zip Code 93003
Lender/Client Sample Savings and Loan Address 116 San Luis Blvd. Ventura, CA 93900

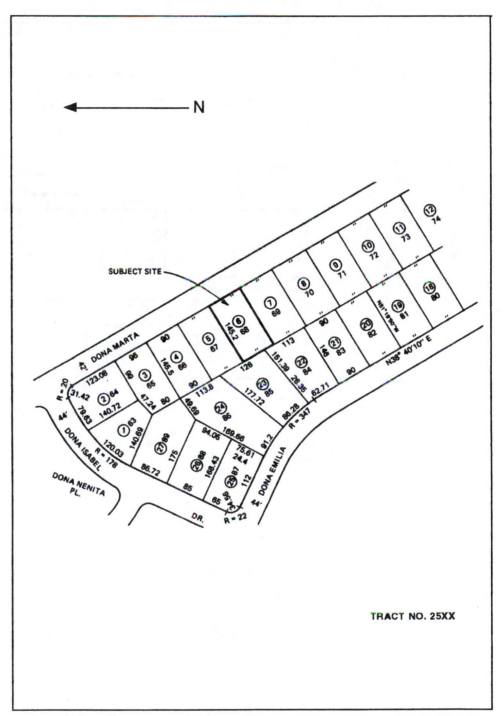

Figure 16-8 Plat Map.

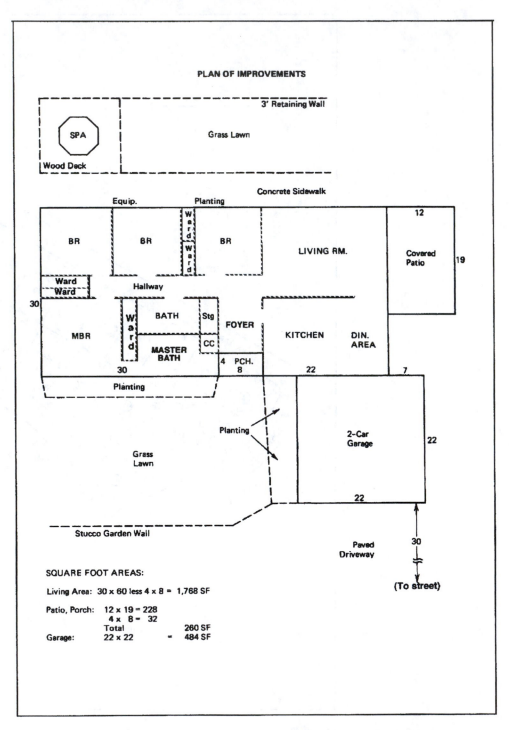

SKETCH ADDENDUM

File No. **SAMPLE**

Borrower **Robert Burns**
Property Address **831 S. Dona Marta St.**
City **Ventura** County **Ventura** State **CA** Zip Code **93003**
Lender/Client **Sample Savings and Loan** Address **116 San Luis Blvd. Ventura, CA 93900**

Figure 16-9 Plan of Improvements.

Front of Subject Property

Rear of Subject Property

Street Scene

Figure 16-10 Photograph Addendum.

Comparable Sale #1

Comparable Sale #2

Comparable Sale #3

Figure 16-10 Photograph Addendum. (Second Page)

Exterior-Only Inspection Residential Appraisal Report   File

The purpose of this summary appraisal report is to provide the lender/client with an accurate, and adequately supported, opinion of the market value of the subject property.

SUBJECT

Property Address		City	State	Zip Code
Borrower	Owner of Public Record		County	
Legal Description				
Assessor's Parcel #		Tax Year	R.E. Taxes $	
Neighborhood Name		Map Reference	Census Tract	
Occupant ☐ Owner ☐ Tenant ☐ Vacant	Special Assessments $	☐ PUD	HOA $	☐ per year ☐ per month

Property Rights Appraised ☐ Fee Simple ☐ Leasehold ☐ Other (describe)
Assignment Type ☐ Purchase Transaction ☐ Refinance Transaction ☐ Other (describe)
Lender/Client   Address
Is the subject property currently offered for sale or has it been offered for sale in the twelve months prior to the effective date of this appraisal? ☐ Yes ☐ No
Report data source(s) used, offering price(s), and date(s).

CONTRACT

I ☐ did ☐ did not analyze the contract for sale for the subject purchase transaction. Explain the results of the analysis of the contract for sale or why the analysis was not performed.

Contract Price $ Date of Contract   Is the property seller the owner of public record? ☐ Yes ☐ No Data Source(s)
Is there any financial assistance (loan charges, sale concessions, gift or downpayment assistance, etc.) to be paid by any party on behalf of the borrower? ☐ Yes ☐ No
If Yes, report the total dollar amount and describe the items to be paid.

NEIGHBORHOOD

Note: Race and the racial composition of the neighborhood are not appraisal factors.

Neighborhood Characteristics			One-Unit Housing Trends			One-Unit Housing		Present Land Use %	
Location ☐ Urban	☐ Suburban	☐ Rural	Property Values ☐ Increasing	☐ Stable	☐ Declining	PRICE	AGE	One-Unit	%
Built-Up ☐ Over 75%	☐ 25–75%	☐ Under 25%	Demand/Supply ☐ Shortage	☐ In Balance	☐ Over Supply	$ (000)	(yrs)	2-4 Unit	%
Growth ☐ Rapid	☐ Stable	☐ Slow	Marketing Time ☐ Under 3 mths	☐ 3–6 mths	☐ Over 6 mths	Low		Multi-Family	%
						High		Commercial	%
						Pred.		Other	%

Neighborhood Boundaries

Neighborhood Description

Market Conditions (including support for the above conclusions)

SITE

Dimensions	Area	Shape	View

Specific Zoning Classification   Zoning Description
Zoning Compliance ☐ Legal ☐ Legal Nonconforming (Grandfathered Use) ☐ No Zoning ☐ Illegal (describe)
Is the highest and best use of the subject property as improved (or as proposed per plans and specifications) the present use? ☐ Yes ☐ No If No, describe

Utilities	Public	Other (describe)		Public	Other (describe)	Off-site Improvements—Type	Public	Private
Electricity	☐	☐	Water	☐	☐	Street	☐	☐
Gas	☐	☐	Sanitary Sewer	☐	☐	Alley	☐	☐

FEMA Special Flood Hazard Area ☐ Yes ☐ No FEMA Flood Zone   FEMA Map #   FEMA Map Date
Are the utilities and off-site improvements typical for the market area? ☐ Yes ☐ No If No, describe
Are there any adverse site conditions or external factors (easements, encroachments, environmental conditions, land uses, etc.)? ☐ Yes ☐ No If Yes, describe

IMPROVEMENTS

Source(s) Used for Physical Characteristics of Property ☐ Appraisal Files ☐ MLS ☐ Assessment and Tax Records ☐ Prior Inspection ☐ Property Owner
☐ Other (describe)   Data Source(s) for Gross Living Area

General Description	General Description	Heating / Cooling	Amenities	Car Storage
Units ☐ One ☐ One with Accessory Unit	☐ Concrete Slab ☐ Crawl Space	☐ FWA ☐ HWBB	☐ Fireplace(s) #	☐ None
# of Stories	☐ Full Basement ☐ Finished	☐ Radiant	☐ Woodstove(s) #	☐ Driveway # of Cars
Type ☐ Det. ☐ Att. ☐ S-Det./End Unit	☐ Partial Basement ☐ Finished	☐ Other	☐ Patio/Deck	Driveway Surface
☐ Existing ☐ Proposed ☐ Under Const.	Exterior Walls	Fuel	☐ Porch	☐ Garage # of Cars
Design (Style)	Roof Surface	☐ Central Air Conditioning	☐ Pool	☐ Carport # of Cars
Year Built	Gutters & Downspouts	☐ Individual	☐ Fence	☐ Attached ☐ Detached
Effective Age (Yrs)	Window Type	☐ Other	☐ Other	☐ Built-in

Appliances ☐ Refrigerator ☐ Range/Oven ☐ Dishwasher ☐ Disposal ☐ Microwave ☐ Washer/Dryer ☐ Other (describe)
Finished area **above** grade contains: Rooms   Bedrooms   Bath(s)   Square Feet of Gross Living Area Above Grade
Additional features (special energy efficient items, etc.)

Describe the condition of the property and data source(s) (including apparent needed repairs, deterioration, renovations, remodeling, etc.).

Are there any apparent physical deficiencies or adverse conditions that affect the livability, soundness, or structural integrity of the property? ☐ Yes ☐ No
If Yes, describe

Does the property generally conform to the neighborhood (functional utility, style, condition, use, construction, etc.)? ☐ Yes ☐ No If No, describe

Figure 16-11 Form 2055 Report.

Exterior-Only Inspection Residential Appraisal Report   File

There are _____ comparable properties currently offered for sale in the subject neighborhood ranging in price from $ _____		to $ _____	
There are _____ comparable sales in the subject neighborhood within the past twelve months ranging in sale price from $ _____		to $ _____	

FEATURE	SUBJECT	COMPARABLE SALE # 1	COMPARABLE SALE # 2	COMPARABLE SALE # 3
Address				
Proximity to Subject				
Sale Price	$	$	$	$
Sale Price/Gross Liv. Area	$ sq. ft.	$ sq. ft.	$ sq. ft.	$ sq. ft.
Data Source(s)				
Verification Source(s)				
VALUE ADJUSTMENTS	DESCRIPTION	DESCRIPTION +(-) $ Adjustment	DESCRIPTION +(-) $ Adjustment	DESCRIPTION +(-) $ Adjustment
Sale or Financing Concessions				
Date of Sale/Time				
Location				
Leasehold/Fee Simple				
Site				
View				
Design (Style)				
Quality of Construction				
Actual Age				
Condition				
Above Grade	Total Bdrms. Baths	Total Bdrms. Baths	Total Bdrms. Baths	Total Bdrms. Baths
Room Count				
Gross Living Area	sq. ft.	sq. ft.	sq. ft.	sq. ft.
Basement & Finished Rooms Below Grade				
Functional Utility				
Heating/Cooling				
Energy Efficient Items				
Garage/Carport				
Porch/Patio/Deck				
Net Adjustment (Total)		☐ + ☐ - $	☐ + ☐ - $	☐ + ☐ - $
Adjusted Sale Price of Comparables		Net Adj. % Gross Adj. % $	Net Adj. % Gross Adj. % $	Net Adj. % Gross Adj. % $

I ☐ did ☐ did not research the sale or transfer history of the subject property and comparable sales. If not, explain

My research ☐ did ☐ did not reveal any prior sales or transfers of the subject property for the three years prior to the effective date of this appraisal.
Data source(s)
My research ☐ did ☐ did not reveal any prior sales or transfers of the comparable sales for the year prior to the date of sale of the comparable sale.
Data source(s)
Report the results of the research and analysis of the prior sale or transfer history of the subject property and comparable sales (report additional prior sales on page 3).

ITEM	SUBJECT	COMPARABLE SALE # 1	COMPARABLE SALE # 2	COMPARABLE SALE # 3
Date of Prior Sale/Transfer				
Price of Prior Sale/Transfer				
Data Source(s)				
Effective Date of Data Source(s)				

Analysis of prior sale or transfer history of the subject property and comparable sales

Summary of Sales Comparison Approach

Indicated Value by Sales Comparison Approach $

Indicated Value by: **Sales Comparison Approach** $ _____   **Cost Approach (if developed)** $ _____   **Income Approach (if developed)** $ _____

This appraisal is made ☐ "as is", ☐ subject to completion per plans and specifications on the basis of a hypothetical condition that the improvements have been completed, ☐ subject to the following repairs or alterations on the basis of a hypothetical condition that the repairs or alterations have been completed, or ☐ subject to the following required inspection based on the extraordinary assumption that the condition or deficiency does not require alteration or repair:

Based on a visual inspection of the exterior areas of the subject property from at least the street, defined scope of work, statement of assumptions and limiting conditions, and appraiser's certification, my (our) opinion of the market value, as defined, of the real property that is the subject of this report is $ _____ **, as of** _____ **, which is the date of the inspection and the effective date of this appraisal.**

Figure 16-11 Form 2055 Report.

CHAPTER 17
APPRAISING SPECIAL
OWNERSHIPS AND INTERESTS

PREVIEW

Appraisals vary in complexity, depending on many factors. Here, we present a group of assignments that are complex because of either the property, the rights involved, or the intended use of the appraisal. This chapter is intended to give you a first look at topics that you will study in advanced appraisal courses or specialized seminars.

The first section provides an introduction to the appraisal of condominiums and other forms of specialized housing, ranging from planned unit developments to mobile, manufactured, and prefabricated homes.

Next, we introduce the appraisal of partial interests in real estate. A partial interest consists of an ownership interest that includes less than the unencumbered fee title. The most common example of this is property subject to a lease.

Finally, we introduce you to the appraisal of property for the purpose of condemnation under the power of eminent domain. This is one of the most specialized technical areas of appraisal practice. The intent of this section is to point out not only the areas of similarity to other appraisals, but also the major differences.

OBJECTIVES

When you have completed this chapter you should be able to:

1. List at least four less-common types of homes, define each, and explain what special problems each presents to the appraiser.

2. Define several commonly marketed types of partial interests.

3. Explain three ways in which the appraisal process is different for eminent domain appraisals.

17.1 Condominiums and Other Specialized Housing

Historically, the typical appraisal assignment has been to value the fee simple ownership in a detached, single-family home. Now, appraisers are routinely asked to appraise several types of shared ownership in what is sometimes referred to as *attached housing*. Among them are a number of new ideas in housing design. Modular and prefabricated homes will also be discussed in this section. All housing types have been grouped by their common elements in order to emphasize their unusual features.

Varying the Type of Ownership

In the conventional detached home, the owner has a fee simple title interest (perhaps subject to a loan and minor easements) that includes both the building and the land under it. However, in the condominium and planned unit development forms of ownership to be discussed here, the person who owns the dwelling unit can hold a fee interest in part of the real estate, and a shared interest in other parts. Finally, in the stock cooperative, the owner is only a shareholder in the cooperative organization that holds the ownership title to the real estate.

Condominiums

In a **condominium** project, the **airspace** occupied by each unit is exclusively owned, but the land underneath is owned in common with the other owners. Actually, in the typical multistory condominium development, the unit owners also share the ownership of the building structure itself, which is the foundation, interior and exterior structural walls, roof, and so on. Each unit owner only owns to the wall surfaces surrounding that unit! Inside the building, common areas such as lobbies, elevators, and hallways are also held in shared ownership. Outside the building, the parking spaces, recreation facilities, and other areas are often owned in common as well (see Figure 17-1).

**Figure 17-1
A Condominium
Project.**

Source: Photograph Courtesy of Doug Frost.

The legal description of a condominium unit, accordingly, is not restricted to just two dimensions on a horizontal plane, as the typical legal description is. Rather, it describes the space as a three-dimensional outline or block of airspace, to include the height of the unit from a given reference point, and the length and width of that space. This explains why the term *airspace condominium* is often used, because each unit consists of a block of airspace. The legal description of condominium units also refers to and describes the common areas, often giving the percent ownership held by each unit.

It is interesting to note that the condominium dates back to ancient Rome. But its active use in the United States is fairly recent, starting with enabling laws passed in the early 1960s. Since then, the condominium idea has been applied to both new construction and to existing buildings converted to this type of ownership. Whether new or old, a condominium building represents a subdivided airspace, with individual ownership of each of the created blocks or units.

A condominium development is usually run by a **homeowners' association.** The basic authority given to such an association is set forth in a recorded document called the **Conditions, Covenants, and Restrictions (CC&Rs).** The association adopts operating rules to minimize conflicts between owners and sets the annual association dues. Normally, the association pays some expenses, such as the building insurance premiums, and maintains the exterior of the building, as well as the common area improvements. Some associations also set up and maintain recreation, child care, and even education facilities.

As in conventional residential properties, the appraisal of condominium units most commonly emphasizes the sales comparison approach to value. However, there are four somewhat unique things to consider when seeking out and analyzing sales in the case of condominiums. The first is the market itself: Have condominiums sold well in this market area? In some areas, neighborhoods, and price ranges, the condominium concept has a mixed sales record. In others, market reception has been very good. In either case, market sales of units in the same project often provide the best comparables. The second aspect is the location in the complex of the subject unit and any sale comparables. What access, privacy, and view amenities are available? Is there adequate sound insulation between units? What are the size, condition, quality, and amenities of the sold units, and how do these features compare with those of the subject unit?

The third aspect is the scope of project amenities available, that is, parking, recreational facilities, and the like. In some jurisdictions, common area facilities can be owned by the developer and leased to the homeowners' association, so it pays to double-check the ownership of the common areas of the project. A fourth aspect for the appraiser to consider is the homeowners' association itself. How much is the annual assessment? How does it compare with that of similar projects? Does the association appear to be competently managed, and is its budget adequate to maintain the project? In many jurisdictions, condominium associations must maintain reserves to fund major repairs and replacements. The appraiser should investigate the status of the reserves, especially when considering sales from other projects. Does the association maintain a good relationship with its members? The continued ability of a condominium project to provide a comfortable and compatible living environment depends on the answer to such questions. Sometimes, an association will charge its members a special assessment to fund some unusual repair. If the assessment is large enough, it will affect sale prices. Be sure to ask about special assessments.

In summary, the appraisal of a condominium unit requires not only a good understanding of the ownership rights involved and the physical differences between individual condominium units, but also consideration of the many factors that affect the tangible and intangible amenities, from one project to another.

Planned Unit Developments

The *planned unit development (PUD)* is classified here as a special type of ownership, because it usually involves shared ownership of recreation and other common areas of the project or community. This is why some state laws classify PUDs as a type of condominium. In many PUDs, however, each building unit and the land under it are both held in fee ownership.

Based on a zoning concept that became popular in the late 1960s, the planned unit development zoning typically allows more flexibility in lot size, density, and variety than is usually allowed in conventional residential zoning, thus encouraging improved project designs. Many PUD projects have been built with townhouse styling (discussed later), so that the two terms, *PUD* and *townhouse*, are often used together. However, some newer housing developments mix the types of units: detached houses, townhouses, zero-lot-line homes (discussed below), condominiums, and sometimes rental housing. Commercial buildings can even be a part of the plan. For this reason, it is better not to use the PUD zoning label to refer to any particular style of structure!

The unique problems in the appraisal of townhouses and planned unit developments often revolve around handling the recreation facilities and other common areas. If the cost approach is applied, a proportional part of the total cost of all common area improvements may be allocated to the unit being appraised. Such a cost may add more to the value of some units than to others. Land value is usually allocated as a percentage of the total property value or else abstracted from sales.

The sales comparison approach may be troubled by a shortage of adequate sales of similar-sized units within the same project. Sales from nearby projects may not be helpful either, if recreation or other amenities are so different that each project forms a different "neighborhood." Subtle differences in the quality and efficiency of homeowners' associations form another reason for trying to have some of your comparable sales from the subject project.

At one time, lenders and the Federal National Mortgage Association (FNMA) created a special category of PUDs, known as a *De Minimus PUD*, with very limited common facilities. Used mainly to qualify certain projects for insured loans, the term and category was discontinued in 1990, expanding the types of projects that could qualify.

Cooperatives

While there are many cooperative ventures in our society, the stock **cooperative** form of housing ownership to be discussed here is rather unique in real estate. For example, in a multi-unit apartment building that is owned by a stock cooperative association, each owner holds a stated percentage ownership in the cooperative association. The association in turn owns the land and buildings, and grants the individual owner the permanent right to occupy the specified dwelling unit, as well as the right to the joint use of the common areas.

Cooperative ownership of real estate has existed in the United States for some years. A substantial number of cooperative apartment buildings were built in New York City during the 1950s and 1960s, for example. A major flaw with the cooperative concept at that time was in the method of financing—the use of one **master mortgage.** Since one master mortgage covered the entire building, the buyer of an individual cooperative unit had to pay for the seller's equity interest (the total unit value less the unit's proportionate share of the balance on the master mortgage) in cash or with an unsecured note to the seller. It was not possible to refinance, unless a majority of the owners of all of the units agreed to refinance the entire master mortgage. When the condominium legislation of the 1960s offered condominiums and other partial ownerships that could be separately financed, the cooperative ownership concept fell into temporary disfavor.

In 1978 and 1979, state and federal legislation greatly modified the cooperative housing concept, allowing individual unit mortgages under some circumstances. In such cases, the cooperative can offer amenities similar to a condominium. In some markets, value differences between the two types are relatively small. In other markets, however, the value difference between physically similar condominium and stock cooperative units may be significant.

Generally, each of the four appraisal considerations that were listed in the discussion of condominiums would apply to the appraisal of a cooperative unit as well. But first, the appraiser must consider whether the unique loan arrangements of the cooperative are important. Does local law allow individual mortgages? If so, when did it become effective? Do the sales prices for cooperative unit sales reflect the amount of equity only, the equity plus master mortgage, or something else? If the appraiser wants to use sales from another building, this information is especially critical. Prior to the cited laws, cooperative units typically sold for substantially less than similar condominium units. Part of the price difference could be explained by the large amounts of cash that were sometimes required to buy a cooperative unit, as compared with a condominium. The local refinancing opportunities for cooperatives should be investigated by the appraiser.

Variations in Housing Design

Several newer types of housing are characterized by the lack of side yards. Eliminating side yards reduces the amount of land required per housing unit and lowers the cost of land. The smaller lot also reduces the per-lot costs for roads, street lights, utility mains, and so on, because the frontage per lot is less. Row houses, townhouses, and zero-lot-line homes are typical of this type of housing.

Row Houses

What is a *row house*? It is a house on an individual lot, which is nearly always owned in fee, built without side yards between it and adjoining houses. The concept of row housing is centuries old and was the tradition in urban housing of the early 1800s in the eastern United States. Many additional row houses were built in San Francisco during the 1920s and in the period following World War II. Lot widths of 25 feet were common. In some areas (for example, in Georgetown in the District of Columbia), lots have been developed with widths of as little as 11 feet. Lot depths of 70 to 100 feet are typical in row house development.

Because of the close proximity of row houses, several potential housing problems must be given more attention by the appraiser in valuing them. One common urban housing problem is obtaining a degree of personal privacy and protection from fire. The limited spacing between neighbors allows row houses less visual privacy than in conventional houses because there is no room for foliage. Fire can be a threat because there is no side yard to function as a firebreak. With row houses, the type of wall between the units may determine the extent of sound insulation and fire resistance. Most commonly, problems arise when two units share a common wall structure, called a *party wall*, instead of two separate walls. This type of construction is now used less frequently, because it is harder to design satisfactorily. In addition, the use of a party wall imposes legal obligations on each owner as to maintenance and repair, which can sometimes lead to conflicts between neighbors.

Townhouses

The *townhouse* is essentially a modern name for the row house. Most townhouses are in projects built since 1970. They are typically designed as two-story units, on fee lots, without side yards. Townhouses are sometimes built in clusters of four or more, creating end units that are separated by side yards from the next cluster of units. A current trend is toward the small townhouse project (as few as three units) on an existing city lot. These are frequently referred to as "in-fill" developments, since they are often "filling in" bypassed vacant lots. Some are built on land where older improvements have been demolished.

The most noticed townhouse projects are the large ones, which are popular in many parts of the country. Sometimes designed as retirement communities, these developments can offer a type of self-contained living environment, complete with recreation facilities such as tennis courts and golf courses. The yard areas and recreation facilities are most commonly owned by all the unit owners. As in planned unit developments, larger townhouse projects usually have a homeowners' association, which takes care of the commonly owned areas and exterior maintenance of the buildings. Homeowners pay association fees to cover common expenses. Effectively, the owners' association is a local government, complete with rules, taxing power, and occasional member conflicts.

Notice that each homeowner usually owns the individual lot on which the home sits. Such an ownership is considerably different from the airspace condominium. In different areas of the country, townhouse projects are called by different names. In California, for example, this type of ownership is usually called a planned unit development and the "townhouse" label, instead, usually refers to the architectural styling that is featured.

Zero-Lot-Line (Patio) Homes

A *zero-lot-line home*, also called a patio home, is based on design concepts developed in California in the 1970s. It is an evolution of the no-side-yard idea. Adjacent homes are built without side yards, as in the row house style. Normally, they are one-story buildings. Instead of being rectangular, as row houses or townhouses often are, the homes usually are L-shaped. Each "L" wraps around a courtyard or patio, as shown in Figure 17-2, forming two of the courtyard's four sides. The side wall of the adjacent house forms the third side of the patio. This wall is usually windowless, to assure the privacy of the patio. The back of the patio may be the windowless rear wall of the house behind, or a high fence or wall. The patio home provides privacy and open space on a very small lot.

In the appraisal of patio homes, it is important to note whether the project design has addressed the sound and fire problems typical of all row houses. The appraiser should examine and note the visual privacy of the outdoor patio, since such privacy is often a major factor to buyers. Because the idea of a patio house is relatively new, it has not

**Figure 17-2
Zero-Lot-Line
Homes.**

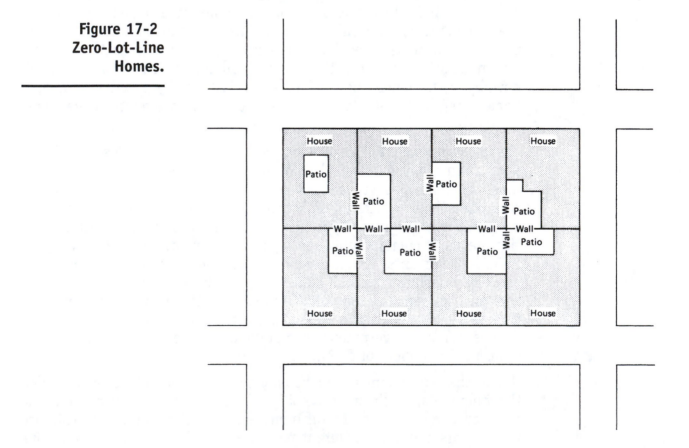

been tested in many markets. The appraiser must consider how it will sell on the local market, usually by comparing the sale prices of patio homes to those of townhouses or detached houses of similar size and amenities.

Varying the Type of Construction

Another type of specialized housing consists of structures that are of unusual construction. Of course, what is unusual construction at any one time may become common a few years later. Two types of similar but unusual construction are of special interest to the appraiser. One is the mobile or manufactured home; the other, the modular or prefabricated home. The number of such types of housing units built and sold over the past several decades has steadily grown, particularly in rural and retirement locations. This increased popularity is due to cost advantages and the decreased construction time usually required, but is restrained by some special problems that appraisers need to understand.

Mobile Homes and Manufactured Homes

According to the U.S. Department of Housing and Urban Development (HUD), *mobile homes* constructed on or after June 15, 1976, are properly classified as *manufactured homes*. When certain design and use requirements are met, such homes can qualify as real property, and their appraisals should follow normal appraisal standards. However, mobile homes that are located in parks where space rent is paid are usually appraised as personal property. Such homes are beyond the scope of this book. (Note that mobile home space rents are controlled in some locations!)

What is a manufactured or mobile home? It is a housing unit that is capable of being moved on the highway in one or more sections. The manufactured home is different from a travel trailer, which is much smaller and designed for part-time living and frequent moving. A manufactured home is also different from a modular home, although the two could have the same floor plan and be built at the same factory. While both fit the general category of "manufactured housing," the modular home has no wheels, undercarriage, or towing arrangement.

Manufactured homes are sold in units of various lengths and widths. Generally, state laws limit the maximum width and length for transporting on the highway. For many states, 12 feet wide by 60 feet long is a practical maximum. Such units are called a "twelve-wide." Often, the manufactured home consists of several units, transported separately and fastened together at the site. Each unit might be the maximum 12 by 60 feet. "Double-wide" homes, 24 by 60 feet, are common, and some "triple-wide" manufactured homes can be found. A modern manufactured home is shown in Figure 17-3.

**Figure 17-3
Manufactured Home
Model.**

HUD Appraisal Standards. In its 1999 Appraisal Handbook, HUD defines a manufactured home as

> . . . a structure that is transportable in one or more sections. In traveling mode, the home is eight feet or more in width and forty feet or more in length. A Manufactured Home is designed and constructed to the Federal Manufactured Construction and Safety Standards and is so labeled. When erected on site, the home is 1) at least 400 square feet; 2) built and remains on a permanent chassis; 3) designed to be used as a dwelling with a permanent foundation built to FHA criteria.

HUD requires that the manufactured home structure be designed for occupancy as a principal residence by a single family. In appraisals for underwriting purposes, the following standards also apply:

The site must be served by permanent water and sewer facilities approved by the local municipal authority, if available at the site. Also:

1. An all-weather roadway must serve the site.
2. The entire property must be taxed as real estate.
3. The towing hitch or running gear must have been removed.
4. No part of the finished grade level under the home can be below the projected 100-year flood level.
5. Structural integrity must have been maintained during transportation, and sufficient anchoring, support, and stability must be evident.

All manufactured homes must have an affixed HUD seals(s) located on the outside of the home. If the home is a multi-wide unit, each unit must have a HUD seal. These seals will be numbered sequentially. If the seals are missing from the property, the appraiser must recommend rejection of the property and notify the lender.

General Appraisal Guidelines. The appraisal of mobile or manufactured homes relies mainly on the sales comparison process. The income capitalization approach is rarely used because very few mobile homes are purchased as income-generating investments. The cost approach is difficult to apply because (1) open market sales of lots zoned for individual mobile homes may be unavailable and (2) the estimate of accrued depreciation is often more difficult than in conventional homes. How is the sales comparison approach applied in the appraisal of mobile homes? Normal single-family residential appraisal techniques apply. If there are no manufactured housing sales within a reasonable distance from the home being appraised, it is permissible to use conventionally built homes as comparables. However, it may be very difficult to support the necessary adjustments. Appropriate adjustments should of course be made for size, location, construction materials, quality, and market acceptability.

Modular and Prefabricated Homes

A major portion of the money spent to build a conventional home goes for labor. Traditionally, each board was cut by hand to the desired length at the house site. Factory-built housing attempts to lower this cost by transferring work from the construction job site to a factory-style operation (see Figure 17-4.). The advantages of a factory operation include the use of machines, to greatly increase the production per person, and an assembly-line style of construction that succeeds with a less-skilled, less-expensive work force. The influence of the factory-style process on housing has been noticeable in the design of both modular homes and prefabricated components for conventional houses.

Most *modular homes* are essentially of mobile home design, but without the running gear and towing assembly. However, some two-story designs have been offered. The biggest handicaps have been public acceptance, the tendency toward a "boxy" look, problems getting building code approval, the high cost to transport units any great distance from the factory, and, occasionally, opposition from construction unions. The advantages are the considerable cost reductions and the reduced construction period, compared with other methods. Within the past few years, more attractive designs of modular and prefabricated homes have reduced the resistance to modular homes among building officials as well as among buyers. In addition, there has been a shift to regulating modular home construction by a *state* building code, superseding the traditional local building codes. Thus, expansion of modular home construction is anticipated in the years ahead.

**Figure 17-4
Modular Homes.**

Source: Courtesy of the U.S. Department of Housing and Urban Development.

Modular homes, based on mobile home designs, are not the only form of "factory" housing. A second category is often labeled ***prefabricated homes*** or housing. Designs are often innovative in both layout and materials. Many experimental ideas have been explored, and some actual buildings have been built. Habitat at the Montreal World's Fair in 1967 was a well-publicized example. Unfortunately, the savings in labor costs are usually somewhat offset by the high capital costs of the factory. Also, buyers have often reacted to such homes as being too boxy, too repetitious, or too unusual.

Market acceptance is the biggest question facing the appraisal of modular and prefabricated housing. Of course, the design must be evaluated to consider unit size, features, and especially the layout. The interior and exterior finish materials and the unit's appearance must then be compared with units that are selling in the local area. When the units are quite different from housing sold locally, the appraiser might want to get a consumer panel's reaction to the units if the appraisal is being made prior to actual sales of any units in this area.

As noted earlier, the use of ***prefabricated components*** is the second major example of factory-built housing. Roof trusses were an early prefabricated component. As a form of prefabrication, many larger home builders now precut and package all the lumber needed for a particular model of a home. Many fireplace-chimney units are prefabricated. Plastic tub and shower combinations are now common; full prefabricated plastic bathrooms are available, but less common. Some builders now preassemble nearly all of the complex plumbing, drain, and vent pipes into one wall section. Increasing numbers of firms supply preassembled wall panels, or structural shear wall panels. Precast concrete floor or wall assemblies are especially common. The use of prefabricated components is clearly a growing element in construction, spurred on by the high costs of on-site labor and the appeal of some new energy-saving wall assemblies now being offered.

17.2 Valuation of Partial Interests

Partial ownership interests are created when deeds or other legal instruments divide or limit the fee simple title to the property.

Concepts and Definitions

The most familiar **partial interests** in real estate are those listed here. Brief definitions are included.

1. Interests created by a lease.
   Leased fee: the owner's interest in a leased property.
   Leasehold: the tenant's ownership interest in a leased property.
   Sub-leasehold: the sub-tenant's ownership interest in a leased property.

2. Other partial ownership interests:
   Life estate: Consists of an ownership interest that conveys the right of occupancy, like a lease, but concludes upon the death of the named person, who usually is the owner-occupant.
   Undivided interest in commonly held property: Created when two or more persons share the ownership and each owner has a nonexclusive right of use. Such rights are often coupled with the sole ownership rights of an adjacent property, as in condominiums.
   Mortgaged property: Property subject to a mortgage or deed of trust.
   Time-share: The right to an exclusive use or occupancy of a property for a reoccurring time period, for example, the tenth week of each year.
   Easement: Rights or interests held by one party allowing them the specified use of the land of another. An easement may be created by a grant deed or other means.

While appraisals can involve many different types of partial interests in real estate, the most common involve undivided interests in commonly held property. These were already discussed in Section 17.1 under the topics of condominiums and specialized housing. Leased property and other types of partial interests will be covered in this section. Please note that this discussion is only an introduction to the unique appraisal problems these ownerships can present.

Leased Property

A familiar appraisal situation involving a partial interest is the leased property. Any lease of real estate subdivides the rights to the property, because the tenant gains possession of the property in return for agreeing to pay the owner the contracted rent. If the contract rent is less than the market rent (which might happen in a rising market), the tenant keeps the difference. The benefit of such a rent difference creates a value that belongs to the tenant. The amount of this leasehold value depends on the size of the rent differences, as well as how long the lease is to continue.

Defining Leased Property Interests

As you can see, the difference between the contract rent and the market rent divides a leased property into two partial interests. The first is the owner's interest (lessor's interest, or *leased fee*), and the second is the tenant's interest (lessee's interest, or *leasehold*). Theoretically, each can be sold; therefore, each can be valued. In practice, sales of leased fee interests are much more common than sales of leasehold interests. In the appraisal of partial interests, the combined values of the two interests are generally considered to add up to equal the value of the fee simple interest. However, it is very clear that this is not an exact and/or constant rule. Note that leased property interests may involve any type of real property, and not just the typical income-generating property. For our examples, we shall talk about an income-generating property (such as a store), because we can more easily show how the benefits of ownership are split up by using dollars of income.

Who Gets What?

The primary question in appraising leased property (and every other partial-interest situation) is: "Who gets what?" How are the rights to the property split up? What are the obligations of owner and tenant? The lease conveys possession of the property for a limited time in return for a rental. Thus, it is essential to know what property is conveyed. Is the basement included? Does the owner retain use of a locked storeroom? Was the furniture included in the lease? Did the tenant pay for any remodeling or other work?

We must also know what the time period is, that is, the time remaining until the lease expires. This means we must know the exact starting date of the lease. Many leases give the tenant an option to extend or renew the lease when the expiration date arrives. Such options sometimes are at a different rent, or even at a rent to be agreed on. Thus, we must read lease renewal option clauses carefully in order to try to understand their real effect on the owner's and tenant's respective rights.

Finally, we must know what rent terms have been agreed on. The rent could be "flat"—the same amount throughout the lease; or the rent might be projected to vary, as in a step-up lease, where the rent increases by a stated amount at predetermined periods. Some leases set the rent as a percentage of the tenant's business, usually in terms of the gross volume of sales. Percentage rent can be combined with a minimum flat rent, or it may be calculated only on sales volumes over a stated amount. Sometimes, percentage rent is reduced by stated categories of expenses paid by the tenant. More and more, we see leases in which it is agreed that the rent is increased as the cost-of-living index increases. The index used could be the national index, or the index for a particular city. The rent increase resulting from increases in the index is sometimes calculated annually, although every five years is also a common interval. There may also be a maximum, or "cap," to the allowable cost-of-living rent increase. In short, rental terms agreed on between owner and tenant can be almost as varied and complex as the human mind can make them.

The tenant's responsibility for expenses is another factor in the analysis of leased property interests. This is significant, because the rental alone may not completely define what amount the tenant has to pay. Each lease may vary, from a "gross" lease, which stipulates that the landlord must pay all building operating expenses, to a true "net" lease, where the tenant pays everything. Indeed, in shopping centers, leases often require the tenants to pay operating expenses, plus a contribution toward a center promotion budget, plus separate payment for all the special partitions, storefronts, and so forth in the store. As a result, the key question the appraiser must answer about lease compensation is: "Who pays what?"

Valuing Interests in Leased Property

The lessor's and lessee's interests in leased property usually are appraised by the income approach. Separate valuations of the two interests are typically required. The cost approach does not provide a way to separate the interests. When market sales of leased property are available, the sales comparison approach might be considered. However, an income analysis is generally required to interpret the sale and apply income criteria to the property being appraised.

The value of the leasehold (the lessee's interest) can be estimated or measured by capitalizing the favorable rent difference over the life of the lease. By favorable rent difference, we mean the difference between the contract rent and market rent. This difference is a net annual benefit, similar to annual incomes from other real estate, and can be capitalized and converted into an estimate of value today. In contrast to other real estate income flows, however, this income benefit is scheduled to end at a known time in the future. For this reason, the capitalization procedure is more complex.

If leasehold estates were commonly bought and sold, the income to the lessee (the net rent savings) could be capitalized by using an overall capitalization rate derived from an analysis of sales. However, only those sales of similar tenant interests would be relevant. In practice, appraisers use annuity capitalization, a technique that was presented in Chapter 14 of this text. (The annuity capitalization techniques are more fully covered in advanced appraisal courses.) Briefly, annuity capitalization makes use of special factors, or multipliers, usually from calculators or financial tables. The length of the lease and the relevant interest (discount) rate determine the factor selected. The appropriate factor is then multiplied times the annual income to calculate the "present value" of the annual income as of the date of value. If the tenant's rent advantage is not the same each year, more complex methods can be used. The rent advantage is a cash flow, as discussed in Chapter 14. It is capitalized as shown in Example 17-1.

The more common appraisal problem involves the appraisal of the landlord's interest, the leased fee, which could also be labeled the value of *the property subject to a lease*. As suggested above, the sales comparison approach may sometimes be used here. However, the appraiser using this approach must first investigate, for each sale, what interests were conveyed. If these are similar to the subject property interests being appraised, the appraiser must still compare the market and contract rents and the terms of the lease with those of the subject prop-

---

EXAMPLE 17-1 Capitalizing the Leasehold Advantage

A. Given:

Lease term: 19 years
Contract rent: $1,220 per month, escalating with the C.P.I.
Market rent: $1,670 per month, escalating with the C.P.I.
Market yield rate for leasehold investments: 18 percent per year
The market considers the contract escalation clause to effectively be at market.

B. Analysis:

Tenant's rent advantage:

Market rent	$ 1,670
Less: Contract rent	− 1,220
Equals: Rent advantage	$ 450
Times: Present worth factor	x 64
Equals: Value of the leasehold	$29,000

Note 1: The factor is the present worth of $1 per period, for 228 periods (19 years times 12), at a yield rate of 1.5 percent per month (18 percent divided by 12 months). In a financial calculator, n=228; i=1.5; PMT=1; and solve for PV.
Note 2: The factor and the answer are rounded.

erty, and make adjustments for differences. A sale of a property that is subject to a poor lease is a difficult comparable to use, because the adjustments for differences in the lease term and the reversion are very difficult to perform correctly.

The valuation of the leased fee interest involves analyzing the lease income for a known time period, generally the term of the lease. The present value of this income is estimated in the same manner as is the present value of the leasehold income. However, in addition to the lease income, the lessor gets back possession of the property when the lease is up and gains the right to sell the fee interest, or rent it at full market rent. This return of the full ownership is called the *reversion* (discussed in Chapter 14).

To summarize, the value of the leased fee interest is measured by the economic benefits that the lessor obtains from the lease. These can be described in terms of these two types of cash flows: (1) the annual income from the lease and (2) the market value of the fee simple rights at the end of the lease. Reworded, the value of the leased fee interest on the date of value equals the value at that date (the "present value") of the income from the lease, plus the value at that date (again, the "present value") of the reversion of the fee simple rights.

How is the present value of the reversion calculated? The first step is to estimate what the market anticipates the fee simple value of the property will be at the time the lease ends. Review how to estimate the reversion, in Section 14.4. This future value is translated into an estimate of present value, using another form of discount factor called the *reversion factor*, or the present value of one factor. The appraiser looks up the proper factor in the financial tables or a financial calculator, using the lease length and the relevant interest/discount rate. Then, the factor is multiplied times the appraiser's estimate of the future value of the reversion. The answer is the present value of the reversion. It is added to the present value of the income stream, and the total is the estimated value of the lessor's interest. (For a review of discounted cash flows, refer to Section 14.4.) Since the combined value of the lessor's and lessee's interests approximates the value of the undivided fee *in some cases*, appraisers might choose to value the lessor's interest merely by subtracting the value of the lessee's interest from an estimate of the undivided fee value. This issue is explored further in advanced appraisal classes.

Valuing Other Partial Interests

Life Estates

Another way of breaking up the fee simple interest is to split it into the **life estate** and the **remainder estate**. This unusual breakdown nearly always involves a residence. The owner of the life estate controls the right of possession and use of the property during the lifetime of some specifically named person. While the named person usually also is the owner of the life estate, he or she need not be. The named person need not occupy the property either, since the owner of the life estate may rent the property or sell the life estate and its right of occupancy. The life estate owner usually must pay all the operating expenses, but does not pay rent. A life estate is different from a lease, in that no rent is paid and the term is not a fixed number of years. The owner of the remainder of the estate has no rights to the real property, except the right to gain full fee simple ownership upon the death of the named person by whose life the estate is defined.

No one can reliably forecast when a named individual will die. However, there are studies of the average remaining life for people of various ages. These studies are called actuarial studies and were developed to calculate necessary life insurance premiums. The most common reason to value a life estate is when the remainder interest is given to someone, triggering a gift tax return. For this reason, from the actuarial studies, the Internal Revenue Service calculates the breakdown of a property's total value into the life estate and the remainder, based on the age of the person holding the life estate. Appraisers are rarely, if ever, involved with these since the IRS procedure is commonly used.

Mortgaged Property

When someone borrows money and signs a mortgage or deed of trust on real property as security for the loan, he or she has split up the fee simple interest into two parts. The lender's interest in the real property is the right to have the real property as security for the amount owing on the promissory note. The borrower's interest is the right to full use of the property but with the obligation to make the payments.

In one sense, the value of the mortgage at any point in time is its principal balance, or the amount owed. However, if mortgage interest rates for new loans at that time are considerably different from the interest rate being paid on the existing note and mortgage, then there is a problem. No one would buy the promissory note at its outstanding balance because the interest return they receive would differ from the going market rate of interest at that time. Thus, the market value of the note at that time is a price that will yield for the buyer of the mortgage the market interest rate at that time, given the dollar payments that the borrower has promised to make. Calculating this value involves another aspect of annuity capitalization. First, the annuity factor for the required yield rate and time is looked up or calculated. Note that if the loan payments are received monthly, a monthly-payment factor or calculation must be used. The table, or calculator factor, is then multiplied by the payment amount to find the market value of the promissory note. The value of the note can differ from the value of the lender's interest in the real estate itself. This topic is explored more fully in advanced appraisal courses.

The value of the borrower's interest in the real estate (also called the *equity interest*) is calculated most accurately by capitalizing the net income that the owner will have left after making loan payments. A number of capitalization techniques are available; one, described as the equity residual technique, was discussed in Chapter 14 of this text.

Time-Share Ownership

Time-share ownership is a recent example of the increasing complexity of real estate. Most often applied to resort or vacation housing, it is a subdivision of the fee interest into individual units and also into blocks of time, with each time block for each unit owned by a different owner. The usual division is made by weeks. Thus, Owner A might own the right to occupy the particular unit during the second and third week of July of each year. Owner J might purchase the last three weeks of each even year, and so on. Most commonly, the project developer not only sells the units but manages them as well. Unoccupied units are rented out to non-owners, and the unit owners are credited with the revenue after deducting expenses. Note that in some cases, the particular unit is not fixed, but floating among all units of that classification!

The individual time blocks sell for varying prices. In or near ski areas, the Christmas and Easter blocks sell for a large premium, but the summer periods may sell for a *seasonal discount*. The developer's most critical decision is to select a sale price for each block, with these premiums and discounts carefully balanced. The goal is to generate the maximum total revenue and the most rapid sell-out of all the time blocks. Prices for the individual units usually vary as well, because of differences in views, exposure, and other locational influences. As a result, there is no fixed formula for valuing individual time blocks. Valuation of the time-block ownership basically involves estimating (1) the value of the unit in fee simple and then (2) the bonus/discount for each time block. The appraiser must carefully study the locational differences of each unit and the seasonal bonus/discounts found in the market for time-share projects that can be compared with the subject. Only by doing such research can the appraiser hope to value these interesting partial rights in real property. It is also important to identify if each comparable sale is one of the original sales by the developer, or a resale. Some projects have had very weak resale markets. In others, the management firm takes a very active role in promoting any units available for resale!

17.3 Valuation for Eminent Domain

We said earlier that valuation for **condemnation** action under the power of eminent domain is one of the most specialized areas of appraisal practice. The power of eminent domain is one of the four rights to real estate that are retained by the government (see Chapter 2).

Defining Eminent Domain

Eminent domain refers to the government's right to take private property from its owners for public use (whether the owners want to sell or not), upon payment of just compensation. Generally, the term **just compensation** has been interpreted by the courts to mean the fair market value of the property.

From this introduction, you can see that appraisal for eminent domain has the same general purpose as most other appraisals: the estimation of market value. There are other similarities, as well as some differences. Valuation for eminent domain is a complex subject; this section is intended to be an introduction.

The Appraisal Process

Eminent domain valuation involves the same appraisal process as we detailed in Chapter 3. The four steps of the appraisal process were listed as:

1. Identify the appraisal problem to be solved.
2. Identify appropriate solutions—the scope of work.
3. Execute the appropriate scope of work.
4. Report the findings and conclusions reached.

Let us explore these steps as they apply to eminent domain appraising.

Step 1: Identify the Appraisal Problem to be Solved

In Chapter 3, we listed the six critical factors that must be identified to define the appraisal problem. These factors are also vitally essential to condemnation appraisal:

1. Identify the client and other intended users.
2. Identify the intended use of the appraiser's opinions and conclusions.
3. Identify the type and definition of value to be developed.
4. Identify the effective date of the appraiser's opinions and conclusions.

5. Identify the subject of the assignment and its relevant characteristics.

6. Identify any assignment conditions.

1. Identification of the Client. As in other appraisal work, defining the appraisal problem in a condemnation setting requires the appraiser to first identify the client and other intended users of the appraisal. This will clarify his or her development and reporting responsibilities. In condemnation appraisals, the client may be the condemning agency, the owner of the property being taken, a tenant, the lender, or other interested parties.

2. Intended Use of the Appraisal. The appraisal and the report may be intended for use by the **condemnor** (the public agency) or the **condemnee** (the property owner). If the public agency is the client, the value opinion might be for budget planning, or used as a basis for the dollar amount offered to the property owner. Often, the condemnor will furnish the property owner with a copy or a summary of the appraisal report. When the appraisal is for the condemnee, it is most commonly for use in challenging the value assigned by the condemnor. Normally, the identification of the intended use of the appraisal allows the appraiser and the client to select the scope of work to be completed and the level of information to be provided in the appraisal report. However, in condemnation appraisals, the rules of the court can govern.

3. The Type and Definition of Value. In eminent domain appraisal, the type of value is always market value. The appraisal report must contain the correct market value definition and its source, as set forth in the applicable law or court rules.

4. The Effective Date of the Appraisal. Deciding on the effective date of value can be a significant problem in condemnation appraisals. It will usually be the date that the formal court documents are filed, but it can also be a different date. The appraiser usually will have to rely on the client's attorney to indicate the legally correct date of value. Sometimes, too, the appraiser will have to reappraise the property as of a later date, such as the trial date.

5. The Subject of the Assignment and Its Relevant Characteristics. Identifying the property to be appraised can be a special problem in condemnation appraisal work because the government does not always acquire the entire property. However, the appraiser must consider the concept of the *larger parcel*, even if only a portion of the property is to be acquired. In commercial appraisals, the ownership and value of *fixtures* are also common problems. We shall explore these two topics further under the heading "Problems in Condemnation Appraisals."

The property rights to be appraised in condemnation are an important relevant characteristic. Most commonly they involve the fee simple rights. On occasion, however, the property being condemned can be limited to an easement, a leasehold estate, or some other partial interest. The appraiser will usually be provided with a clear statement of the rights to be taken.

In addition, other important characteristics of the subject property must be identified. These could include the key information about the site and any improvements, issues impacting the highest and best use of the property, and so on.

6. Assignment Conditions. As explained in Chapter 3, every appraisal must comply with various conditions. *Compliance with USPAP* is the most common, followed by *Supplemental Standards.* Often in eminent domain appraising, there will be Supplemental Standards imposed by the law or court rulings. Remember that a Supplemental Standard only adds to and cannot diminish the purpose, intent, or content of the requirements of USPAP. A common Supplemental Standard when performing appraisals for a federal agency is to comply with the *Uniform Appraisal Standards for Federal Land Acquisitions*, noted in Chapter 3. In rare cases, eminent domain appraisals will be subject to *Jurisdictional Exceptions*, where a law or court ruling or order blocks or modifies a provision of USPAP. (See the discussion on this topic in Chapter 3.)

Extraordinary Assumptions for eminent domain appraisals could include reliance on the opinion of engineers, attorneys, or others in arriving at the value conclusion. Such opinions should be specifically documented and cited.

Hypothetical Conditions are rare in eminent domain appraisals. A hypothetical condition may be used in an eminent domain appraisal only if it is allowed by the court rules, and, under USPAP, necessary for reasonable analysis or comparison. In any case, the use of a hypothetical condition must result in a credible analysis. The one standard hypothetical condition in essentially all eminent domain appraisals is to ignore the effect—positive or negative—of the government project upon the property's value. We will discuss this issue later.

Assumptions and Conditions of the general sort would typically be no different in an eminent domain appraisal than when performed for another intended use. *Contractual Conditions* imposed by the client are very common, especially for assignments where the condemnor is the client. Many government units are very knowledgeable about appraisals and have specific requirements to be met. Remember, however, that no contract can require the appraiser to violate USPAP, any jurisdictional exceptions, or any supplemental standards.

Step 2: Identifying Appropriate Solutions: The Scope of Work

An appraisal plan for eminent domain appraisals should follow the same well-organized plan, called the scope of work, used for other assignments. However, each element of the plan may be more complex to execute than in other assignments. Also, it is common for the scope of work to change as the assignment progresses. As discussed in Chapter 3, the scope of work refers to:

- The extent of the property identification.
- The extent of property inspection.
- The type and extent of data researched.
- The type and extent of analysis employed to reach a conclusion.

If the property has already been taken (acquired), and a retrospective appraisal is being made, considerable research may be needed to describe the property as of the date of value. The "inspection" of the property may be limited to such a description, what remains of the improvements, and the present use of the land. Historical aerial or satellite photography also can help. As mentioned above, identification may also pose some special problems if there is a partial taking.

As will be pointed out below, the courts often define the kind of data that will be allowed, and therefore the kind of data the appraiser will need in a given eminent domain appraisal.

As in other appraisals, an outline may be needed to plan the sequence of points to be covered in the appraisal and the report. Such an outline should include known dates of client briefings, depositions, and court appearances.

Step 3: Execute the Appropriate Scope of Work

In the third step of the appraisal process, executing the appropriate scope of work, there is a major difference between condemnation appraisal assignments and others. The difference is that the courts (rather than the appraiser) make the final decision as to an appropriate scope of work. For example, the law may influence what types of data are admissible, that is, can be used in testimony. Indeed, some jurisdictions by law exclude some types of market data that an appraiser might otherwise consider relevant to a particular appraisal. Note that listings and offers are not usually admissible in some courts. Sometimes, a particular court will establish its own definition of comparability, as to acceptable time limits for the date of sale or the distance of comparable sales from the subject property. However, the great majority of condemnation appraisals rely on the same kinds of sales, rents, costs, overall rates, and so on that are required for loan appraisals or other common appraisal purposes.

A major issue in data collection in eminent domain appraisals is the usual requirement to disregard the influence of the government project on value. Often, the closer and more recent comparable sales and rents may well reflect that influence. This could lead the court to rule that these comparables cannot be used, forcing the appraisers on both sides to rely on old sales and sales from far away!

Special rules in condemnation appraisal also affect applying the appropriate value approaches. Certain possible methods of analysis, such as the development method of land appraisal, may not be allowable in some jurisdictions, or are given less weight by the courts. The appraiser will want to know this in planning the appraisal in order not to rely on a method that the court will exclude. However, there are no special approaches to value, just the time-tested sales comparison, cost, and income approaches you have met before. Thus, most condemnation appraisals will rely on the same appraisal techniques and methods you would use for any other appraisal assignment.

Arriving at a value conclusion is no different for eminent domain appraisal than appraising for other purposes, except that the value conclusion may have to be given in several parts, as detailed later under the heading "Problems in Condemnation Appraisals."

Step 4: Reporting the Conclusion

The fourth step in the appraisal process, reporting the value conclusion, is also modified for eminent domain appraisals. The major difference between condemnation and other appraisals is that the format for such appraisal reports varies a great deal. In some cases, as in appraisals made for the condemnee, you might be asked to prepare only an oral report, leaving the expense of preparing a written report to a time closer to trial. If the parties can settle the case without a trial, the written report will not be needed. In some cases, only a file memo will be prepared. In preparing an appraisal for the condemnor, however, a written appraisal report is usually required. The report will often be a long, documented narrative. The condemnee will sometimes be given a copy. A well-written report may play a key role in convincing the property owner to accept the government's offer.

Problems in Condemnation Appraisals

Condemnation law is different for real and personal property. Thus, for condemnation appraisals, it is often necessary to carefully identify and appraise only the real property.

Fixtures and Personal Property

One problem area is fixtures: objects that were once personal property but have been attached or joined to the real property. Fixtures may be classified as either real or personal, depending on a series of complex rules. You may want to review the earlier coverage of this topic in Chapter 2. On occasion, the appraiser will have to prepare sets of values including and excluding particular fixtures, and wait for the court to rule which are real property and which are personal property.

Related to the fixture problem are the possible issues involving personal property. Usually, the condemnor only acquires the real property, so the condemnee retains and takes the personal property. However, there may be times, depending on the law involved, where a personal property appraiser (perhaps a machinery and equipment appraiser) and/or a business valuation appraiser will also be involved. In these cases, it is important to coordinate who is appraising what, so nothing gets omitted but nothing gets counted twice!

The Legal Setting

In condemnation appraisal work, the appraiser may end up as an expert witness, testifying to the judge and jury and being cross-examined about qualifications, comparables, and methods. The appraiser must be aware of this possibility and prepare for it from the early moments of talking to the prospective client. The fixture issue, discussed above, is one of a number of issues that are decided by the rules of the courts. Eminent domain appraisal is different from most other appraisal work, precisely because it is prepared for, and presented to, the courts and is performed according to the special rules established by the courts and legislature.

Often, the appraiser will have to rely on an attorney hired by the client (whether condemnor or condemnee), to provide needed legal advice concerning both the appraisal and the testimony. This could involve many issues, such as establishing the probability of rezoning, what value date to use, what property to appraise, which data and approaches will be admissible in this court, and so on. If the attorney for the other side has a different view of the law and prevails, your appraisal and your testimony could be tossed out. It is prudent to try to understand the basis for any legal advice and to ask the attorney again if the advice is not understood. A written letter from the attorney detailing the position the appraiser is to follow on any vital issues is often desirable.

Another key aspect of the legal setting is the usual requirement, noted earlier, to ignore any positive or negative influences on value created by the proposed government project for which the property is being acquired. Assume that the government is building a new airport and this fourplex is just off the end of the runway and right in line with it. Because of the expected noise, it is very likely that rents and value will fall. The owner should be paid what he/she could have sold it for, absent the airport. The government has no right to force a bargain price.

Also consider if the government is building a new freeway, and a farm in a very poor rural area becomes the location of the only on/off ramps within ten miles! The farmer should be paid for what he/she could have sold it for, absent the freeway. The government should not have to pay for the increase in value that its own freeway expenditure is creating.

This requirement can have major effects on the appraisal and the data to be selected. It is an issue that needs to be considered and probably discussed with the attorney.

The Partial Taking

Perhaps the most unique aspects of appraising for eminent domain are those that stem from a *partial taking*: when the government agency is acquiring only a portion of the property, called the ***take parcel***. The owner is to be left the rest, called the ***remainder parcel***. The total parcel is called the ***larger parcel***. Figure 17-5 portrays such a partial taking.

The Larger Parcel

The appraiser must first determine what the larger parcel is. What if the same owner owns the two adjacent houses? What if he or she has a 99-year lease on the warehouse behind? What if her brother and she jointly own the property across the street? This issue is important in evaluating whether the remainder parcel has been hurt (lost value) as a result of the "take." The courts have evolved three tests to determine which parcels make up the larger parcel, based on the theory that the larger parcel consists of a coherent functional economic grouping.

First, the parcels must be contiguous. Increasingly, the courts have interpreted this to include across the street, or even up the street, if economically joined together. Second, they must be under the same ownership. The appraiser may need to review the many court cases examining this issue, or explore the issue with the attorney. Third, the parcels must be put to the same use. The courts have tended to

**Figure 17-5
A Partial Taking.**

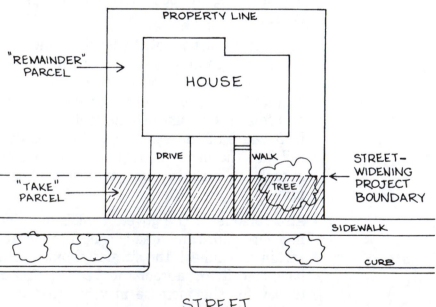

interpret this rule rather strictly. Again, it may be wise for the appraiser to ask an attorney's opinion on this legal issue.

Take, Damages, and Benefits

The courts have interpreted just compensation in a partial taking to include the following three elements. Some courts require that each element of the three be calculated in turn, separately. Other courts combine all three elements by appraising the value of the larger parcel and then just subtracting the value of the remainder parcel. The key is to use the procedure approved by the court involved.

The first element to consider is the value of the part to be taken. The part to be taken is usually valued as if it were a separate parcel. In some courts, however, it is valued as a fraction (by area, for example) of the larger parcel.

The second element is the possible damage to the remainder parcel as a result of the government project, called *severance damage.* For instance, a parcel might no longer front on a road, so the owner must now build a $500,000 access bridge over an irrigation canal in order to regain access to the property. The $500,000 cost might be a measure of the damages. A government project could harm property in many other ways. Not all damages, however, are compensated for under the power of eminent domain. Some damages are the result of actions legally authorized under the government's police power, and no compensation or payment to property owners is required. For example, the government, in widening a commercial boulevard from two to four lanes, could also install a center barrier, or median. This would prevent drivers from turning left (in the middle of the block) into shopping area driveways. Customers would have to drive to the next intersection, make a U-turn, and come back. They might shift their business to another store on that side of the street, hurting the business and the value of stores on this side of the street. Contrary to certain logic, such limited "circuity of travel" is rarely ruled as a *compensable damage.* In many partial-taking appraisals, the appraiser will need to research carefully which damages are compensable and which are not. A legal opinion will often be necessary.

The third element of just compensation in a partial taking is the possible benefit of the government project to the remainder parcel. The courts have defined two kinds of benefits: general and special. Only special benefits affect the calculation of just compensation in most courts. General benefits are those that are shared by the community at large, or at least by more than just a few adjacent property owners. Special benefits, on the other hand, are those that benefit only the remainder parcel (or perhaps only a few more parcels). An example of a special benefit could arise when a larger parcel is swampy land and too wet to build on. As part of a government project, the low corner of the parcel is taken and extensive drainage put in. After the project, the remainder parcel is well drained, fully developable, and much more valuable. If other land in the area has not been similarly benefited, the remainder parcel has obtained a special benefit.

The courts differ on how to apply the value of special benefits. Some courts simply value the larger parcel and then deduct the value of the remainder parcel in its improved state. In this case, extensive special benefits could reduce the total payment by the condemnor to zero. Some states allow recognition of special benefits only to the degree that they offset damages. Thus, the appraiser must first decide if benefits to the remainder exist. Next, are they special benefits? Third, how are they to be appraised? And, fourth, how are they to be applied in calculating the final estimate of just compensation?

As you can see by this brief overview, appraisals for use in eminent domain actions are complex and often very difficult. As a result, most appraisers are not selected to perform this type of work until they have some experience. Usually, total takes are the initial assignments. After some experience is gained, partial-take assignments will come next.

SUMMARY

Today, appraisers are faced with a growing variety of appraisal assignments. Many of these assignments now involve unusual concepts in ownership, design, and construction. Such types of housing include:

Condominiums

Cooperatives

Manufactured homes

Mobile homes

Modular homes

Planned unit developments (PUDs)

Row houses

Townhouses

Zero-lot-line (or patio) homes

In contrast to the undivided fee interest held in a conventional detached home, the owner of either a condominium or PUD may hold a fee interest in part of the real estate, and a shared interest in other parts. In the airspace condominium, the fee interest is held in the airspace defining the unit, while ownership of the building structure and common areas is shared with the other owners. In PUDs, a fee interest is usually held in the home and the land directly under it, with the recreation and open space areas held in common ownership. Finally, in the stock cooperative, the owner is but a shareholder in the cooperation that holds title to the real estate.

The appraisal of cooperatives, condominiums, and PUDs requires a good understanding of the ownership rights and common facilities involved, as well as the physical differences to be found in individual units. Such appraisals also require a look at the financial and management structure of the homeowners' association of the unit being appraised, as well as that of any comparable sales. The continued ability of such a project to provide a comfortable and compatible living environment is often an intangible factor that varies from one project to another.

Several newer types of housing design were also discussed in this chapter. Some are characterized by the lack of side yards and the amount of land required per housing unit. Row houses, townhouses, and zero-lot-line homes are typical of this type of housing.

The appraisal of mobile and manufactured homes was also discussed. According to HUD, mobile homes constructed on or after June 15, 1976, are properly classified as manufactured homes. When certain design and use requirements are met, such homes can qualify as real property. Their appraisals should follow normal appraisal standards. However, mobile homes that are located in parks where space rent is paid are generally appraised as personal property.

A common appraisal situation involves estimating the market value of the lessor's and/or lessee's interests in a given property. Other partial-interest appraisals include those involving the property interests of lender and borrower, and the valuation of time-shared ownerships.

One of the most specialized areas of appraisal practice involves valuing property for eminent domain. This type of appraisal follows the same steps in the standard appraisal process; however, a few areas need special attention. For instance, unlike the regular appraisal process, eminent domain cases often require the appraiser to testify as an expert witness before the courts. Therefore, the data collected and analyzed should be selected based on the applicable court rules, well prepared, and documented for such testimony. Eminent domain cases also differ, in that the value definition, date of value, and methodology are defined by the courts. The classification of property fixtures is also much more critical.

Finally, eminent domain often involves acquisition of only a portion of the property, called a partial take. Here, the appraiser must consider the concepts of the larger parcel, the remainder parcel, severance damages, and general and special benefits, in order to reach a final value conclusion.

IMPORTANT TERMS AND CONCEPTS

Airspace

Compensable damage

Condemnation

Condemnee

Condemnor

Conditions, Covenants, and Restrictions (CC&Rs)

Condominium

Cooperative

Eminent domain

Fixtures

Homeowners' association

Just compensation

Larger parcel

Leased fee

Leasehold

Life estate

Manufactured home

Master mortgage

Mobile home

Modular home

Partial interests

Partial taking

Party wall

Planned unit development (PUD)

Prefabricated components

Prefabricated homes

Remainder estate

Remainder parcel

Row house

Severance damage

Take parcel

Time-share ownership

Townhouse

Undivided interest in commonly held property

Zero-lot-line home

REVIEWING YOUR UNDERSTANDING

1. Which of the various forms of housing units are characterized by the lack of side yards?
   a. Mobile homes, standard detached single-family residential
   b. Apartment buildings, condominium buildings
   c. Row houses, townhouses
   d. None of the above

2. A condominium is:
   a. A type of building description
   b. Like a cooperative
   c. A legal concept of ownership
   d. A type of physical design of a building

3. A zero-lot-line home is also known as:
   a. A duplex
   b. A modular home
   c. A patio home
   d. A condominium

4. Homeowners' associations are often found in:
   a. PUDs
   b. Condominiums
   c. None of the above
   d. Both (a) and (b)

5. Partial interests are created by:
   a. Deeds or legal instruments
   b. Transfer of the fee interest
   c. The termination of a lease
   d. None of the above

6. The lessor's interest in leased property is referred to as the:
   a. Leasehold
   b. Leased fee
   c. Fee simple
   d. Remainder

7. A gross lease is:
   a. A lease under which the tenant pays for all expenses
   b. A lease under which the landlord pays for all operating expenses
   c. A lease that applies only to commercial properties
   d. None of the above

8. The benefits that belong to the leased fee interest include:
   a. The lease income
   b. The reversion
   c. Both of the above
   d. None of the above

9. Generally, the courts have determined that just compensation in eminent domain cases means:
   a. The fair market value of the property
   b. Market value plus compensation for anticipated future benefits
   c. The market value at the time the property was bought by the current owner
   d. All of the above

10. Eminent domain cases are commonly referred to as:
    a. Condemnation
    b. A take
    c. Both (a) and (b)
    d. None of the above

CHAPTER 18
THE PROFESSIONAL APPRAISER

PREVIEW

In this last chapter, you meet the appraisers, the people whose craft you have been studying. The first section looks at their education and experience. The second section outlines the typical requirements for state licensing and certification. The third section covers the major professional appraisal organizations: their purposes, membership criteria, and professional designations. In the fourth and fifth sections we examine the standards of appraisal practice and discuss appraising as an occupation.

OBJECTIVES

When you have completed this chapter you should be able to:

1. List the five key elements to becoming a competent appraiser.

2. Define the typical state requirements for *appraiser licensing and certification*.

3. List two major organizations of professional appraisers.

4. Outline the first two standards of the Uniform Standards of Professional Appraisal Practice.

5. Discuss the different positions open to appraisers.

18.1 The Appraiser's Background

What are the backgrounds of people who do real estate appraising? What kind of training is necessary? Are there minimum educational requirements? The qualifications of appraisers vary widely. A few states now require that *all appraisers* meet minimum requirements of education and experience and be licensed or certified. However, most state laws require only those involved in federally related appraisals to meet such standards. The typical requirements for state licensing and certification will be outlined in Section 18.2.

The five key elements to become a competent appraiser are covered below. Each is essential! These are:

1. *Education*
2. *Experience*
3. *Knowledge*
4. *Judgment*
5. *Integrity*

Education

Most appraisers find that a state license or certificate is essential, whether mandatory or not. As a result, nearly all appraisers must complete the course work required for a license. However, most practicing appraisers also have some college-level training, and the majority have college degrees.

Reasons for Education

Formal education helps the would-be appraiser gain valuable general knowledge and skills. Most college courses help an individual learn to reason clearly, which is an aid in figuring out appraisal problems. The appraiser also must learn to write clearly. The appraisal report, even if on a form, must succinctly communicate the appraiser's findings.

Mathematics is also an important skill to master, since all three approaches involve working with numbers. Algebra is helpful in handling formulas in the income approach. Plane geometry is helpful in calculating areas of odd-shaped parcels. Computer skills now are also essential!

Appraisers also need to have a good understanding of the many factors that affect real estate. Taking courses in finance, real estate law, economics, taxation, city planning, city and county government, and urban geography are very helpful in expanding one's understanding of real estate. The series of real estate courses taught at many community colleges is particularly helpful in expanding the appraiser's knowledge of real estate markets and brokerage. Other courses, such as beginning geology, blueprint reading, architecture, accounting, transportation geography, and statistics, may also be helpful. Some take courses in business appraisal (or other specialties) in order to widen their practice.

The third area in which appraisers seek formal education is in their own field. Theories, ideas, and techniques that are learned in an accredited appraisal course will enable future on-the-job training to be much more meaningful.

General Educational Trends

An increasing number of appraisers have college degrees. The largest professional appraisal group, the Appraisal Institute, requires a college education for its professional *designations*. Growing numbers of employers are requiring appraisal trainees to have college degrees. Nearly all trainees must take real estate courses. The concern is with making the trainee a productive appraiser in the shortest possible time.

A growing number of colleges and universities offer degrees in real estate or in business with a real estate field of emphasis. The University of Wisconsin at Madison, Indiana University, and the University of California at Berkeley and at Los Angeles are among the colleges and universities that are well known for their real estate curricula. In recent years, several universities have announced master's degree programs in real estate appraisal. Programs at over seven universities have been endorsed by the Appraisal Institute. Credit is earned for certain Appraisal Institute courses and experience requirements by fulfillment of the degree requirements there. In the absence of a degree specializing in real estate, preferred fields of emphasis include economics, business administration, finance, urban geography, or city planning.

The American Society of Appraisers offers a certificate program in personal property appraisal at four leading universities, as well as a certificate program in machinery and equipment appraising at another university.

Real Estate Courses

Many appraisers have taken the series of real estate courses for brokers that community colleges offer (see Figures 18-1 and 18-2). Typically, these include courses in real estate principles, practices, finance, law, appraisal, and economics. Additional courses may cover real estate investment, exchanges, remodeling, escrows, and other specialized topics. In several states, the student can earn a Certificate in Real Estate by attending a required series of courses. Real estate certificates are gaining recognition as a sign of a well-rounded real estate education. Many of these appraisal-related courses meet both the requirement for the certificate and the content requirements toward licensing and certification.

**Figure 18-1
The Classroom
Experience.**

Source: Photograph Courtesy of David Lloyd.

Nearly all the appraisal courses sponsored by the major **professional societies** have been state-approved for licensing and certification credit. Such courses may be more advanced than the community college appraisal courses. Some appraisers take the community college course at the very start of their career and the first course of either the American Society of Appraisers or the Appraisal Institute after six months or a year on the job. An additional course might be taken every six months or a year after that, depending on course availability and the appraiser's work experience.

Appraisers may also rely on professional societies for specialized education. Appraisal groups offer seminars and courses on such subjects as appraising industrial property or condominiums, and introduction to money markets. In addition, numerous workshops, special seminars, and dinner speeches can further the education of appraisers who participate.

**Figure 18-2
The College Campus.**

Source: Photograph Courtesy of David Lloyd.

Shared Ideas

By nature, appraisers have to be inquisitive. As a result, casual meetings between appraisers are often filled with shoptalk about this or that new house design, theory, trend, and so on. It is a form of self-improvement education!

The body of appraisal theory could be learned by self-instruction. Numerous texts, journals, books, and case studies are available. The number of online courses is expanding rapidly. However, appraisal classes in a classroom setting offer you the opportunity to exchange ideas with your peers. For example, your fellow students in advanced classes may hold a variety of jobs in real estate appraising, and thus have different experiences to share. Shared ideas are a significant part of the learning experience and often become a springboard for continued learning after the class is finished.

Experience

Education alone will not create a competent appraiser. The second element is applying the ideas and skills learned in class. You will not really know if you understand an idea—the sales comparison approach, for example—until you have tried to use it a number of times. Real estate appraisal involves many bits of knowledge that can only be learned through experience. Rating the quality and condition of houses in a field assignment is an example. Despite what we have said on these subjects in this book, you will find that much of your skill in such areas will be gained in the field.

Do not expect to be able to make good appraisals upon completing this book or any other. It usually takes six months of full-time experience before an appraisal trainee can produce reliable appraisals of a variety of single-family properties without close supervision. For work requiring a state license, of course, trainee-produced appraisals must usually be supervised and signed by a staff member who is state licensed or certified. And after the end of 2007, all trainees must be supervised by a *certified* appraiser, with a limitation on the number of trainees per supervisor. With this in mind, the importance of experience in appraising can be understood.

With more complicated appraisals, the appraiser needs more experience than just counting off the number of years. The experience also needs to be varied as to the type of property and the intended use of the appraisal. The appraiser learns from each new assignment. This accumulated experience is very helpful in performing complex appraisals.

Knowledge

One measure of an appraiser's qualifications is the extent of his or her knowledge. The general areas of knowledge most important to a real estate appraiser are real estate markets, property operations, and market data.

Markets

Real estate appraisers try to understand how real estate markets function, from the role of the broker to the interaction of supply and demand. This means that appraisers try to be aware of the forces that affect prices and trends. A practical understanding of markets can be extremely valuable to the appraiser.

Operations

Appraisers have to be somewhat familiar with the characteristics and management procedures of the various types of real estate they appraise. For instance, what are the day-to-day problems of convalescent hospital buildings? What is the current practice in writing tax escalation clauses in office leases? Which lenders customarily make loans on retail store buildings? How common are net-net-net leases on office space? What is the typical depth of an office space from center hall to outside windows? In what locations are walk-up, three-story apartments feasible?

Market Data

One reason for hiring appraisers is that they know how to find market data. On occasion, a client will hire an appraiser solely to work up a list of relevant sales or rents. Market information is not widely circulated, even in today's computer world. The knowledgeable appraiser will have developed sources for particular kinds of data. Few people realize the amount and variety of data that the expert appraiser can uncover.

Judgment

One of the most important components of the appraiser's art is judgment, an elusive concept. One definition is:

> . . . . the operation of the mind, involving comparison and discrimination, by which knowledge and values and relationships are mentally formulated.

Source: *Webster's New International Dictionary*, 2nd Ed.

Note that this definition uses the word *discrimination* to mean "recognizing differences." The essential elements in this definition of judgment are to: (1) compare, (2) distinguish differences, (3) recognize relationships, and (4) arrive at opinions. Such a description is so general, it sounds almost like the appraisal process itself. What makes the use of judgment different from the overall process that appraisers follow? Judgment for an appraiser means the ability to develop an understanding of the complex relationships among factors, events, and so on. Figure 18-3 suggests the difficult task of weighing and balancing these diverse elements.

Judgment is the ability of human intuition to process a mass of data and develop a reliable opinion from it. It is the ability to draw good conclusions. A knowledgeable broker (working in a well-known sales territory with which he or she is familiar) is using judgment when he or she walks through a home and can judge what it will probably sell for. This also holds true for investment brokers. In short, judgment is what gets us from the market data, and any mathematical or graphic analysis of it, to an opinion about market value.

There is no simple method for developing good judgment. Taking classes can show what factors to consider. Experience gives you practice in applying analytical techniques to practical situations. Developing good judgment, however, may require a third step: self-review. You may need to follow up on your appraisal to see if your opinions turned out to be true. If not, why not? You may also want to see what others think of your opinion and what reasons they offer for their differences. In a broker's open house tour, for example, how do your estimates of probable selling price compare to those of others and, equally important, to the final price? We believe that good judgment is developed by education, experience, reviewing one's mistakes, and considering the comments of others.

Integrity

Another critical characteristic of a professional appraiser is integrity. **Integrity** is defined as:

1. ....complete, undivided, or unbroken....
2. Unimpaired; soundness; purity....
3. Moral soundness; honesty; freedom from corrupting influence or practice....

Source: *Webster's New International Dictionary*, 2nd Ed.

**Figure 18-3
Appraisal Judgment.**

We noted earlier (in Chapter 1) that one of the most important reasons for obtaining an appraisal is because it is an impartial answer to the question of value. In order to be relied upon, then, every appraisal needs to be performed by someone "free...from corrupting influence or practice...." Otherwise, the appraisal is not *credible*!

Nearly always, the client has an interest in the appraisal answer: It will make or lose him/her money. Thus, appraisers often are encouraged to make the value (or rent) opinion as low (or high) as practical. And if they do not want the number changed, then they want the assignment completed unreasonably soon, or for too low a fee for the work that needs to be done! The practicing appraiser must learn to say "no" and have the integrity to not let pressure influence the conclusions.

The appraisal profession was first developed in the 1930s, due to the problems valuing property during the depression and issues that emerged at that time regarding the value of real estate securities. And the current licensing system was created in response to the great savings-and-loan collapse of the 1980s, caused in part by poor appraisals and appraisers without integrity. Now, the home price boom in the recent past has partly been fueled by poor loan standards and accommodating appraisers!

Integrity of the appraiser is a key issue. It is essential if you want to develop a lasting career in appraisal!

18.2 State License and Certification Requirements

Title XI of the *Financial Institutions Reform, Recovery, and Enforcement Act of 1989 (FIRREA)*, generally effective in 1993, requires that most appraisals involved in a federally related real estate financial transaction be performed by a state licensed or certified appraiser. (Certain regulated exemptions apply.) **Federally related transactions** are transactions involving financial institutions that are under federal supervision, such as banks and credit unions, or where the transaction involves federal loan insurance or assistance. While some states require that every appraiser have a license, most require no license or certification for (1) appraisals not involving federally related real estate financial transactions and (2) opinions given by real estate licensees, engineers, or land surveyors in the ordinary course of business. All state appraisal regulations are subject to the approval and oversight of a federal committee established by FIRREA, the Appraisal Subcommittee of the U.S. Federal Financial Institutions Examination Council (FFIEC), at http://www.asc.gov. Under FIRREA, the minimum license and certification requirements are set by the Appraisal Qualifications Board of the Appraisal Foundation.

Please note that FIRREA only established requirements applicable to real estate appraisers. Appraisers in other specialties, such as business valuation, machinery, and so on are not covered by FIRREA, and are not licensed by most states. Those who belong to one of the major professional organizations are obliged to comply with USPAP; others are not, but may choose to do so.

Parameters of Practice in Federally Related Appraisals

While federal regulations allow some variation in the levels of licensing and certification established by state law, the typical levels and parameters of practice are as follows:

1. *Trainee License:* Appraisal of properties that the supervising appraiser is permitted to appraise, under close supervision.

2. *License:* Appraisal of noncomplex one- to four-unit residential properties, up to a transaction value of $1 million; complex up to a transaction value of $250,000. Defining "complex" is an issue!

3. *Certified Residential:* Appraisal of all residential properties, regardless of transaction value or complexity. Federal guidelines limit this practice to property with one to four dwelling units. Appraisal of nonresidential properties with a transaction value up to $250,000 is also authorized.

4. *Certified General:* Appraisal of all real estate property transactions, without regard to property type, transaction value, or complexity.

Basic Education and Experience Requirements

State and federal laws require specific amounts of qualifying education and experience for the license and certified appraiser designations. In recent years, the minimum hours have generally increased.

Education Requirements

The minimum amount of appraisal-related education required for license and certification depends on the qualification level. The following chart shows the minimum course hours typically required for each classification at the time of writing, and the new levels that become effective on January 1, 2008.

	Hours	
Classification	Before 1-08	As of 1-08
a. Trainee License	90	90
b. Licensed (Residential)	90	150
c. Certified Residential	120	200
d. Certified General	180	300

In addition, the 2008 hours must involve instruction in specific subject modules for specific numbers of hours. There appears to be some flexibility in meeting the hours for a specific module from several different courses or seminars. It is highly recommended that those seeking more information on this topic either check with their state appraiser licensing agency or with the Appraiser Qualifications Board of the Appraisal Foundation. Please note that the AQB gave the states several options in making the transition to the new requirements. Check carefully what your state requires!

The College Education Requirement

Effective on the same January 1, 2008 date, AQB has added college education requirements for the Certified Residential and Certified General Licenses. This is in addition to the specified hours of appraisal-related education. For the Certified Residential License, the requirement is for an Associate Degree (usually a two-year, full-time program) from a Regionally Accredited College. Alternatively, the license applicant can complete 21 college semester credits in courses covering some or all of seven specific subject matters.

For the Certified General License, the requirement is for a bachelor's degree (usually four years). Alternatively, the license applicant can complete 30 college semester credits in courses on eight specific subject matters plus two elective courses from five topics.

Check with your state appraisal license agency to see exactly how they interpret the AQB standard and when it might be applicable to you.

National USPAP Course

1. For basic (or qualifying) education (that education used to obtain an initial or upgrade license), all applicants must successfully complete the 15-hour "National USPAP Course" or its equivalent (as determined by the AQB).

2. For continuing education (that education used to renew a license), all licensed appraisers must successfully complete the seven-hour "National USPAP Update Course" or its equivalent (as determined by the AQB) *every two years*.

3. For both basic and continuing education, USPAP credit can only be awarded when the class is instructed by an AQB Certified Instructor, *and* at least one instructor is a residential or general state-certified appraiser.

Experience Requirements

Experience in real estate appraisal and/or appraisal assistance is required, as follows (states may vary). Please note that the listed number of hours of actual experience must be accumulated over the minimum number of months or longer! Also, all experience must comply with USPAP to be accepted: Check that your work as a trainee complies!

Classification	Hours*	Min. Months
a. Trainee License	None	None
b. License	2,000	12
c. Certified Residential	2,500	24
d. Certified General	3,000	30

*State laws may vary

Acceptable appraisal experience may include fee and staff appraisal, ad valorem tax appraisal, condemnation appraisal, technical review appraisal, appraisal analysis, real estate counseling, highest and best use analysis, feasibility analysis/study, and/or teaching appraisal courses. In California, those holding a valid California real estate broker license had been awarded 1,000 hours of experience toward the appraiser licensing requirement, but the Appraisal Subcommittee has determined this does not comply with FIRREA.

As part of the AQB-mandated changes effective January 1, 2008, trainees will be allowed to earn experience credits by completing special case studies classes. Only 50 percent of the total required hours of experience can be gained in this fashion! The course is being called a "practicum." At the time this edition was written, it appeared that both the practicum courses and the instructors would need to be approved by the Appraisal Foundation, based on guidelines being developed by the AQB.

Gaining the first year's experience has been the most challenging step in becoming an appraiser for many decades. It is widely hoped that the practicum course will have a material effect on this problem. Recognize, however, that real estate is a very cyclical industry—when times are slow, there still will be few entry positions.

Other Requirements

Applicants for appraiser licensing or certification must pass a qualifying exam and pay all appropriate fees. Most states will issue a trainee license to applicants lacking the necessary experience. In general, the term of licensing or certification is either two or four years, depending on the state, with renewal requiring the completion of 14 hours of approved, appraisal-related continuing education courses for each year during the period preceding the renewal.

Please note that certain types of appraisal assignments require additional qualifications of the appraiser. To make appraisals for FHA endorsement, for example, the appraiser must apply, pass the short exam on the application form, and be placed on the FHA Appraiser Roster.

18.3 Appraisal Groups

The majority of appraisers are either designated members or member candidates of one of the various appraisal organizations. Many non-members regularly attend appraisal group meetings. What do appraisers gain from being associated with such groups?

Benefits

One benefit is that most groups award professional designations to their members who have achieved the required standards. These designations provide a means for the general public to rate the competency of appraisers. Until recently, licenses have not been generally required for any appraisal activity. When licenses were required, the qualifying education and experience requirements were minimal (compared with those today). As a result, the public has come to rely on the better-known professional designations as an aid in selecting appraisers.

A second benefit is that these groups provide a major source of *formal* and *informal training* and for appraisers. As already mentioned, these groups sponsor regular courses, one-day seminars, afternoon workshops, and dinner speakers for the benefit of members. The various groups also publish periodical journals, texts, research monographs, and newsletters. Beyond this type of formal education, the groups' meetings offer informal education. People ask their peers how to handle a particular problem. They ask who may have researched a particular type of property sale. They may ask the group's leaders to arrange for a speaker on some new, troublesome problem (mini-warehouses, for example, when this type of property was first developed).

Major Organizations

There are two nationally recognized appraisal organizations with a membership encompassing all areas of real estate appraising. Both (or their legal predecessors) were founded in the 1930s and now have chapters throughout the country, and both offer more than one professional designation. A summary of these designations and their requirements is presented here.

Appraisal Institute

The Appraisal Institute (http://www.appraisalinstitute.org) was formed in 1991 when the American Institute of Real Estate Appraisers merged with the Society of Real Estate Appraisers. Both groups had been founded in the 1930s, with the original members being real estate brokers or residential lenders, respectively. The membership of the Appraisal Institute now includes real estate appraisers of every occupational background. Appraisers first apply and are accepted as candidates for a professional designation. Candidates must then complete a series of courses (or successfully challenge the course exam), submit written demonstration appraisal reports for grading, and have samples of their actual appraisals reviewed for experience rating. Once designated, members must complete a continuing education program every five years. However, this is voluntary for people designated many years ago.

The Institute has an extensive educational program, involving many course titles taught at locations across the country. Courses are taught either in an intensive fashion, lasting for several days to one week, or in an extended fashion, such as one day or one or two nights per week. Courses may be either nationally or local chapter-sponsored. Some courses are also available online. The Institute's publishing program includes the major reference text, *The Appraisal of Real Estate*, as well as a number of other texts, research monographs, and the quarterly journal, *The Appraisal Journal*.

Member, Appraisal Institute (MAI) is the designation granted by this group to an appraiser qualified to appraise income property, complex realty, and all real estate interests generally. Members who earned the similar *SRPA* designation from the Society of Real Estate Appraisers may still use this designation. The requirements for the MAI designation include at least 4,500 hours of experience appraising a variety of types of income-generating properties. There are approximately 5,600 active holders of the MAI designation. This designation probably has the widest public recognition.

Currently, people who want to receive the MAI designation must attend a total of at least 380 hours of classes (or successfully challenge the eleven related examinations) and pass a two-day, four-module examination. While there are other options, most candidates submit a narrative demonstration appraisal report, around 100 pages in length and quite thorough in coverage. A college degree or equivalent is required.

Senior Residential Appraiser (SRA) is the designation granted by the Institute to an appraiser qualified to appraise single-family and duplex to fourplex residential properties. The *Residential Member (RM)* designation formerly awarded at this level by the prior group, American Institute of Real Estate Appraisers, may still be used by those who earned it. The SRA must have passed six examinations that reflect 200 hours of classroom instruction. In addition, the SRA must receive credit for 3,000 hours of residential appraisal experience over at least 24 months, appraising one- to four-unit residences. At the time of this writing, an associate college degree or equivalent is required. The applicant must also submit a satisfactory demonstration appraisal report. There are about 2,500 holders of the SRA designation.

The *Senior Real Estate Analyst (SREA)* designation, formerly granted by the Society of Real Estate Appraisers to an appraiser with substantial experience in real estate analysis and consulting work, may still be used by those Institute members who earned it before the two professional groups merged.

American Society of Appraisers

The ASA (http://www.appraisers.org) differs from the Appraisal Institute in one primary way: Membership encompasses the appraising of all types of property, not just real property. The membership of ASA is composed of appraisers whose individual specialties range from ceramics to chemical plants. Total membership is about 5,000 including designated and non-designated. The breakdown by specialty is:

Business Valuation	42%
Machinery and Technical Specialties	21%
Real Property	20%
Personal Property	13%
Gems and Jewelry	4%

The group is headquartered in Washington, D.C. It is the successor, by merger in 1952, of two earlier groups, the American Society of Technical Appraisers and the Technical Valuation Society, which were both founded in 1936. The Association of Governmental Appraisers, the Society of Governmental Appraisers, and the Association of Federal Appraisers also merged into ASA in the early 1980s.

The educational program of ASA features a four-part series of courses in the Principles of Valuation, offered in four disciplines (Business Valuation, Machinery and Equipment, Personal Property, and Real Property). ASA publishes textbooks, a quarterly journal, and monthly technical journals. In addition, the society sells professional reference books for appraisers at a discount.

The ASA awards its professional designations based on competency to appraise a specified type of property; the holder of the designation must indicate the specialty on any qualifications list. Appraisers may be designated in six major property categories: business valuation (1,109 designees), real property (894 designees), personal property (297 designees), machinery and technical specialties (581 designees), gems and jewelry (74 designees), and appraisal review and management (18 designees).

The ASA awards three levels of designation, described below. All designees must fulfill requirements related to ethics and the Uniform Standards of Professional Appraisal Practice. Everyone must also pass all four courses, or pass a comprehensive exam. Once designated, all must complete continuing education requirements every five years.

1. *AM*, or *Accredited Member*, is the first professional designation or level. The candidate's technical appraisal proficiency and understanding of the fundamentals of appraisal ethics, principles, and concepts are evaluated by intensive written and oral examinations. Copies of the candidate's appraisal reports are reviewed and must meet professional criteria. The candidate is interviewed. In addition, the candidate must have a college degree or its equivalent and two years of full-time appraisal experience. There are about 200 holding the AM designation.

2. *ASA*, or *Accredited Senior Appraiser*, is the designation awarded to appraisers who have met the requirements for Accredited Member and also have five years of appraisal experience. In addition, Accredited Senior Appraisers must be recertified every five years. There are approximately 2,700 designated ASA.

3. *FASA* stands for *Fellow of the American Society of Appraisers*. It is awarded to holders of the ASA designation who have distinguished themselves in their appraisal activities. This can be through teaching or writing, or by activity as a National Officer. ASA has about 50 Fellows.

Specialized Groups

A large number of other nonprofit appraisal groups exist; some are nationwide, others are regional or local. The national groups tend to have a particular area of interest as opposed to the two general groups that were summarized earlier. Of the large number, several will be mentioned here.

International Right of Way Association

This group, usually abbreviated as IR/WA (http://www.irwaonline.org/), is headquartered in Los Angeles and was founded in 1934. As its name indicates, membership orientation is toward those involved in the appraisal and acquisition of rights of way. This includes utility company power lines, oil company pipelines, and public highways. All three involve the acquisition of property by condemnation under the power of eminent domain. As a result, other appraisers active in condemnation appraisals may also join IR/WA. Examples include county public works department employees, city real estate officers, flood control district land representatives, and so on. Fee appraisers and attorneys who do contract work for all these organizations also join. The IR/WA awards several professional designations.

American Society of Farm Managers and Rural Appraisers

This society (http://www.asfmra.org) is headquartered in Denver, Colorado. Founded in 1929, it awards professional designations for farm managers (AFM), rural appraisers (ARA), review appraisers (RPRA), and agricultural consultants (AAC). There are area chapters in most major farming regions.

International Association of Assessing Officers

Membership in the IAAO (http://www.iaao.org/) consists mostly of governmental property tax assessment staff, private firms who contract in some states to do periodic reassessment work, and private tax representatives for major retailers and manufacturers. The group is headquartered in Chicago and was founded in 1934. There are local chapters in some parts of the country. The IAAO awards two real estate designations: (1) CAE (Certified Assessment Evaluator), denoting competence in all real estate appraisal/assessment work and (2) RES (Residential Evaluation Specialist). There are also two specialty designations offered: PPS (Personal Property Specialist) and CMS (Cadastral Mapping Specialist). The listed designations are available to all members who meet the requirements of the designation, whether regular members (government employed) or associate members (privately employed).

National Association of Independent Fee Appraisers

The NAIFA (http://www.naifa.com/) accepts as members fee appraisers of real estate and other interested appraisers. The group was founded in 1961 and is headquartered in St. Louis, Missouri. The NAIFA awards three professional designations: IFA (Member), IFAS (Senior), and IFAC (Appraiser-Counselor). There are local chapters around the country.

Institute of Business Appraisers

Founded in 1978, IBA (http://www.go-iba.org) is headquartered in Boynton Beach, Florida. Its members are involved in the appraisal of businesses. The group awards the designation CBA (Certified Business Appraiser).

Association of Machinery and Equipment Appraisers

Membership in AMEA (http://www.amea.org) consists of machinery and equipment appraisers. Candidates must have a minimum of three years of experience, pass a written exam, and submit a sample appraisal report.

18.4 Standards of Professional Appraisal Practice

In a cooperative effort to elevate the standards of professional appraisal practice and to better serve the public, the *Uniform Standards of Professional Appraisal Practice* (known as USPAP) were adopted in 1986–87 by nine leading appraisal groups. Now maintained by the

Appraisal Standards Board (ASB) of the Appraisal Foundation, USPAP standards are, by federal law, the minimum acceptable standards for most appraisals made in conjunction with federally related financial transactions. All state-licensed and certified appraisers are required to follow USPAP. In the past, an updated version has been released each year. Starting with the 2008 edition, an update will be released every two years.

It is important to note that the overview of professional standards provided in this section is intended to be introductory in nature. Those who intend to pursue a career in appraisal or finance are urged to purchase a complete and current copy of the *Uniform Standards of Professional Appraisal Practice* (USPAP) from the Appraisal Foundation, at http://www.appraisalfoundation.org.

Ethics and Competency Standards

Ethics Rule

The Ethics Rule of USPAP covers four general areas of practice and is binding. These are grouped below. For the specific details of these important requirements, the appraiser should refer to the most current issue of USPAP.

1. *Conduct*—requires that the appraiser perform all assignments ethically and competently in accordance with USPAP and any supplemental standards that apply, and do so with impartiality, objectivity, and independence, and without accommodation of personal interests.

2. *Management*—prohibits the payment of any undisclosed fees, commissions, or things of value in connection with the procurement of an assignment. Any compensation for developing an opinion of value that is contingent upon the value conclusion or result is also generally forbidden. And false, misleading, or exaggerated advertising is also forbidden.

3. *Confidentiality*—requires that the appraiser not reveal confidential factual data obtained from the client, or the results of an assignment, to anyone other than: (1) the client and those he/she has authorized, (2) state enforcement agencies and third parties authorized by law, and (3) a duly authorized professional peer review committee.

4. *Record Keeping*—requires that the appraiser prepare and keep a comprehensive workfile for each assignment, for at least five years after preparation, or at least two years after final disposition of any judicial proceeding where testimony was given.

The Competency Rule

Competency requires that appraisers accept only that work that they have the knowledge and experience necessary to perform (either individually or, if needed, in association with others).

The Scope of Work Rule

For each assignment, the appraiser must identify the problem to be solved, determine and perform the scope of work necessary to develop credible results, and disclose the scope of work in the report.

Other Rules

The other rules imposed by USPAP are the *Jurisdictional Exception Rule* and the *Supplemental Standards Rule*. Both were extensively discussed in Chapter 3. (The ASB has proposed to merge the Supplemental Standards Rule into the Scope of Work Rule.)

Standards of Practice

The standards relating to the development and communication of a real estate appraisal are broadly stated as:

Standard 1. In developing a real property appraisal, an appraiser must identify the problem to be solved and the scope of work necessary to solve the problem, and correctly complete the research and analysis necessary to produce a credible appraisal.

Standard 2. In reporting the results of a real property appraisal, an appraiser must communicate each analysis, opinion, and conclusion in a manner that is not misleading.

USPAP contains additional standards covering appraisal reviews and other specialties. Each standard is expanded into a series of *Standards Rules*, usually with comments. The appraisal practices presented in this text are intended to be consistent with these standards.

Impact of Professional Standards

Recognized by government and industry alike, uniform standards of conduct and practice among appraisers serve to protect three distinct groups. First, they protect the interests of the public at large. Second, they specify actions to protect the interests of the appraiser's clients. Third, they establish standards to protect the interests of other appraisers and the profession in general.

The Public

The appraiser should have no financial or undisclosed interest in the results of the appraisal assignment. This has three subcategories.

Impartiality

1. The appraiser should not have an undisclosed interest in the property being appraised.

2. The appraisal fee should not be contingent on the amount or direction of value concluded, or on the occurrence of any event.

3. The appraiser should not directly pay or receive referral fees, so that referrals will be objectively considered.

Disclosure and Methodology

The appraiser should report his or her findings in a non-deceptive form. In particular, every report should fully disclose any assumptions relied on, provide a summary of the scope of work, a statement as to whether the property was inspected and by whom, and identification of who takes the responsibility for the conclusions in the report.

The early codes of practice used to say the appraisal report should include all the data and reasoning used to reach the value conclusion. Today, the common view is that the report can be a summary of the total appraisal effort, if specifically requested by the client, as long as the report contains the minimum content defined by USPAP, clearly identifies the extent of the appraisal process performed, and is credible.

Support for the Conclusion

The appraisal conclusions should be based on data and analyses, rather than solely on judgment or intuition. Supporting data and analyses should be contained in the report, or otherwise retained in the appraiser's file for a reasonable time defined in USPAP.

The Client

Competency

Appraisers should take on only those appraisal assignments that are within their ability. Some assignments, or parts of assignments, may need to be referred to a business valuation or machinery and equipment appraiser. If necessary, the appraiser should enlist the aid of a more experienced appraiser to be sure that a competent job is being performed. Appraisers should only agree to prepare appraisals that they anticipate can be completed within the agreed-on time period.

Finally, once an appraiser accepts an assignment, he or she should perform it competently and adequately, regardless of whether the agreed-on fee will cover the necessary time. Unexpected problems with property, personality differences, and overtime pressures do not waive this standard, unless clearly covered by the agreement with the client.

Confidentiality

The appraisal report is not a public document. Therefore, the appraiser should keep the value conclusion completely confidential from everyone, except as directed by the client, required by order of a state license board or a court, or required for authorized professional peer review committees. Confidential information provided by the client, or by others, and clearly labeled as such, should also be held confidential.

The Profession

Competitive Activity

The appraiser may compete for business with other appraisers but should do so in a professional manner. This competition precludes trying to block others from practicing as appraisers. It also precludes attempting to take business away from other appraisers by casting unsupported doubts on their capabilities. The appraiser should base every major appraisal conclusion on the analysis of data, and this analysis should be retained in a file.

Cooperative Activity

The appraiser should work with other appraisers to establish a code of behavior agreed to by all. Once established, each appraiser should try to comply with the code. The appraiser should also support and assist any investigation of possible violations of the code of behavior.

The appraiser should share available market data with other appraisers (to the degree legally possible in adversary cases). However, confidential data provided by the client is restricted by the Confidentiality section of the Ethics Rule of USPAP. At the least, the appraiser should not try to hide important market data or mislead other appraisers about the particulars. The appraiser should also indicate when and how others have played a part in the value analysis of a particular report.

18.5 Appraising as an Occupation

There are various ways to look at the occupation of appraisal. For example, we could compare people with professional designations to those without, or compare beginning appraisers to experienced appraisers. For many years, the major breakdown within the industry was between those who work for a salary, and those who work for themselves and get paid a fee for each assignment. Another common separation is between those who perform appraisals for loan purposes versus those for other purposes. Increasingly, this last viewpoint is what people talk about!

Starting Out

The First Few Years

Many appraisers start with a salaried position in a financial or governmental institution or a larger appraisal company. The starting position is usually as an assistant or trainee appraiser. The industry rule of thumb is that the first six months of employment are a net loss. After that, the trainee can work alone well enough so that the amount of supervision falls off, and appraisal production (or assistance) and quality of work climb. Only larger institutions or companies can usually afford this cost burden for an appraisal trainee.

Another avenue into appraising is to work in a related area and gain valuable experience ahead of the trainee stage. One example is the person who works as an appraisal researcher, secretary, or office manager, and gradually learns research skills. Over a period of time, a researcher who is intelligent and interested can develop good appraisal skills. A second example is the real estate broker or salesperson who gradually works into an appraisal career over a number of years.

Often, obtaining the initial employment as a trainee will be the hardest step. Getting acquainted with appraisers in your community can help. Taking professional courses also develops your skills, your resume, and your contacts. Work as a researcher sometimes is an excellent entry path. And some government institutions (county assessors' offices and some state transportation departments in particular) hire trainees on a regular basis. No one path is best. No one path is guaranteed to work all of the time. The openings occur when and where they occur!

The Second Year

By the end of the first year, most people have learned enough that they are an asset to the organization. Nearly always, they will have obtained a Trainee License as soon as possible so that they can try to earn experience credits for their subsequent work.

Remember that, effective January 1, 2008, the trainee must work under the supervision of one specific Certified Residential or Certified General Appraiser, and the supervisor is limited in the number of trainees supervised. Check your state for the exact number, generally no more than three or four. In most states, that trainee will need to register the name of the supervisor with the state licensing agency. Also, the work will only be acceptable for experience credit if it is in compliance with USPAP. Accordingly, it is important for trainees to select a supervisor carefully and consider changing if they have concerns!

Typically, trainees in their second year will be paid in proportion to the number of appraisals produced, if they work for a loan institution or an appraisal company. Trainees working for a government institution will be paid a salary.

The Third Year

By now, some trainees will have received the Residential License and most others will be close. This may be a time when appraisers change where they work. Some go to a salaried position, some move to an appraisal company, and others open their own office. Often, the choice is heavily influenced by where the appraisal occupation is in its business cycle.

When loan volume drops (usually due to higher interest rates), loan appraisal assignments also drop. Many trainees working for appraisers with a loan practice are let go. Both trainers and licensed appraisers may apply for any salaried government positions that become available. But when loan volume is high and loan appraisal assignment numbers are soaring, people are more likely to move to an appraisal office or open their own, when they obtain the Residential Appraisal License.

Who Do You Work For?

Appraisal positions vary in job security as do many other jobs in real estate, but appraisers have been changing where they work more frequently in recent years. One reason is that lending institutions and appraisal companies tend to hire and fire staff appraisers with changes in the volume of loans. These are the positions that often provide the initial experience, knowledge, and industry contacts that make it possible for appraisers to earn a license, leave their positions, and open their own appraisal businesses. But many wait to obtain a professional designation or an opportunity to contract for appraisal assignments. Some wait for retirement, and soon thereafter open a part-time practice to supplement retirement income.

The Institutional Position

There are many public and private institutions that hire appraisers. Some may have only one or two appraisers on their staff, while others have hundreds. Those with small staffs are usually less known to the public. Most appraisers have worked for an institution during some point in their career.

Among the public institutions with appraisal departments, county or district property tax assessment offices are perhaps the best known. Some county schools and county public works departments also maintain appraisal staffs, as do most state public works departments and highway or transportation departments. Salaried appraisal staffs are often part of state water, parks, and general services departments, along with some state housing and real estate appraisal licensing departments, and state bank and savings and loan regulatory bodies. Regional park and transportation districts may have an appraisal staff. At the federal level, appraisal staffs are located in the Corps of Engineers, Navy and Air Force Departments, National Park Service, Forest Service, Bureau of Land Management, Bureau of Public Roads, Internal Revenue Service, Department of Housing and Urban Development, Federal National Mortgage Association, Postal Service, General Services Department, and others.

The role of the appraiser in a public institution varies. Establishment of property tax values is the role of the tax appraiser. Another institutional role is to estimate market value of parcels to be acquired by condemnation under the power of eminent domain. This function involves the second largest group of governmental appraisers, after property tax assessment valuation. A third role is to review or audit appraisals made by private parties or institutions such as banks or savings and loans, lenders who submit loans to FHA and FNMA, and individuals making income tax or estate claims based on private appraisals, and so on. In some cases, government appraisers are staffed to value surplus, publicly owned parcels, for the purpose of estimating a listing price and probable selling price.

Many private institutions also have appraisal staffs. Banks, savings and loans, life insurance companies, mortgage brokers, mortgage bankers, and similar lenders are among the best known. But many appraisers also work for real estate investment trusts (REITs), larger pension funds, and real estate investment management firms.

Some appraisers work as real estate analysts or managers for large developers, real estate departments of larger national corporations, and for franchise firms. Major oil companies have appraisal staffs, as do pipeline firms, railroads, electric, gas, water, and telephone utility companies, and major mining companies. Often, such appraisal personnel perform related real estate functions as well, from marketing research to site acquisition negotiations, construction supervision, and property management.

What is it like to be an *institutional appraiser*? The varied list of institutions reveals that the positions themselves vary. The majority have regular hours, five days a week. Because you could spend much of your time on the road inspecting properties and sales and confirming market data, you often work out-of-doors with unpredictable working conditions. Some of these assignments have substantial overtime and travel, but this is usually understood at the start.

Salaries for institutional appraisers tend to be mid-level in the total range of salaried jobs; that is, they are fairly good. Positions with longer hours and/or more travel tend to be higher paid. Starting salaries for novice appraisers are considerably lower than for experienced persons, and the salary increase for experience is greater than for many other occupations.

The greatest demand is for salaried workers with at least two or three years of experience and a state license or certification. Beginning or trainee positions are relatively few. Trainees are usually hired only when the employer's workload is expanding. However, if there are too few experienced appraisers looking for jobs, trainees are occasionally hired to replace appraisers who have retired or resigned.

The Fee Appraiser

The term *fee appraiser* is used in the industry to refer to one who performs appraisals and is nearly always paid on an assignment basis. Some institutional appraisal employees are also paid on a fee or commission basis, but this is not considered to be "fee appraising."

Fee appraisers are also sometimes referred to as "independent appraisers." However, this description is offensive to some salaried appraisers, because to them it implies that only fee appraisers arrive at an independent conclusion, that is, one that is not imposed by the employer.

To be successful, the fee appraiser must be competent both in making appraisals and also in running a small business. This includes managing files, keeping financial records, marketing one's skills effectively, making proposals, collecting money owed, hiring and firing, arranging for space and equipment, and training a staff.

Fee appraisal offices are usually fairly small. Many consist of just the appraiser and a part-time assistant. A smaller office may be operated out of the appraiser's home, with typing hired out or performed by the appraiser. Offices of three (appraiser, assistant, and secretary) or four people are also common. Not too many offices are much larger. An office of 30 people is currently considered very large. Offices of this size are found in large metropolitan areas, and it is likely that there are less than fifty such offices in the country.

There is a clear trend towards the small office, usually one appraiser working at home to minimize overhead. There is also a clear trend towards groups of larger offices. Some of these are affiliated with major commercial brokerage companies and concentrate on commercial properties. Some are affiliated with major lenders or title insurance companies and concentrate on home loan appraisals. These two trends indicate an underlying weakness or relative decline in the traditional model of a two-to-four appraiser office in rented office space.

Partly, this is tied to another trend—the steadily growing importance of the Internet for communication and for data access. More and more appraisers work at home at least part of the time. This is true whether their pay is a salary or an assignment fee, and regardless of whom they work for.

Loan versus Other Assignments

As noted above, this is becoming the major focus of appraisers talking about the fee-based side of their occupation. Loan appraisals may be performed by independents working out of their home, or in larger firms, or working for a lender. Nearly all receive much or all of their compensation on a per-assignment basis. The past decade has seen a sharp increase in the pressure to speed up the process. There also has been pressure to minimize the sales adjustments taken in order that appraisal reports would sail through any review process. This pressure also was applied to minimize negative descriptions or even ignore actual problems. Pressure has also increased to "meet the number" or "make the deal"—appraise the property high enough that the loan will close. Most of the pressure has been in home loans, not commercial.

All of these issues, and others as well, have led to a substantial erosion in the quality of the average loan appraisal. Turn-around time became critically important and pressure to keep fees low increased. Because of these changes, appraisal of houses for loans has evolved into a high-volume, low-profit, lower-quality business, especially when compared to the work of decades past. However, quality complaints have grown!

Meanwhile, the fee appraisals performed for other intended uses have seen much less pressure, whether on delivery deadlines, property problems, fees, or the final opinion. These types of assignments are essentially not cyclical at all, and grow in number every year. In many ways, this work is relatively unchanged in quality and professionalism from 10 or 20 years ago.

One key characteristic of an appraisal for these other (non-loan) intended uses is that they are all different! Each is an appraisal following the same process, and it might be reported on a similar form. But there will be issues associated with each type of intended use that will be relatively unique. And none of the intended uses of an appraisal requires a volume of appraisals remotely as large as loan appraisals. Few appraisers specialize in only one or a few types of appraisals.

As a result, each appraisal is a relatively unique assignment. It could be described as a relatively high-quality, custom-made product, contrasting with the lower quality high-volume or mass-production characteristic of today's loan appraisals.

This difference—custom versus volume production—has widened substantially in the recent decade. It is a topic of increasing discussion among appraisers. Will the difference narrow or continue to widen? Is this difference simply a neutral response to the market's needs for different qualities of appraisals in different circumstances? Or is this a sign of a problem?

Time will tell which is correct. In the meantime, however, you as a beginning appraiser need to be aware of this key difference in appraiser occupations. You will need to consider it many times, as you ponder what path to take.

What Is It Like to Be an Appraiser?

The previous discussion has focused on some of the objective aspects of appraisal as a profession. However, the work of appraisers is enjoyable enough for us to offer the reader some additional thoughts about the occupation.

1. Our work is varied. We not only meet people of all ages, occupations, and backgrounds, but we also see the varied and interesting ways that people live or work, and how they invest their money.

2. Our work is challenging, since no two properties are alike. There are stimulating problems to solve, even when studying routine properties. The more difficult assignments often require a high degree of professional skill and determined effort.

3. Our work involves us with what is going on in our town. We might be making the construction loan appraisal on the large new store in town, or an acquisition appraisal for a new redevelopment project. Our education in real estate economics strengthens our ability to understand these events. As a result, we often have a good grasp of current trends.

4. For some of us, we can perform appraisal inspections at our own convenience to an extent. Some clients want inspections performed during evenings or weekends, so we can work extra hours if we wish. Because our knowledge and judgment will continue to grow as we get older, there will be no mandatory retirement!

5. We know that there are a number of related areas in real estate where our knowledge is also useful. While some appraisers go on to other fields such as property development, mortgage banking, brokerage, and so on, most of us continue to enjoy the challenge and stimulation of professional appraisal work.

SUMMARY

For those not performing federally related appraisals, there are no standard educational requirements for becoming an appraiser. However, having a formal education in real estate can only improve your career options, as well as your income. Many employers in real estate require that appraisers have a college degree. While a growing number of universities offer a degree program in real estate, you can usually do about as well with a degree in a field related to real estate, such as economics, finance, or business administration. Many community colleges and appraisal societies offer courses in real estate.

Becoming a competent appraiser requires many different skills. Besides pursuing a formal education, you also need to develop your knowledge of markets and real estate operations. This kind of knowledge is more often gained in the field than in the classroom. Having sound judgment is also an important skill for an appraiser. Developing good judgment usually comes from a combination of experiences: in the field, in education, and most important, as a result of self-review. Integrity is also essential! Appraisers must be able to say "no" in order to succeed!

Effective in 1993, state and federal laws required that most appraisals involved in federally related real estate financial transactions be performed by state licensed or certified appraisers. Qualifying education and experience requirements vary according to the scope of practice, with 150 hours or more of appraisal-related coursework required and at least 2,000 hours of appraisal experience. Please note that the education requirements cited here increase as of January 1, 2008.

There are a number of appraisal organizations, societies, and groups. Many specialize in particular appraisal areas, such as the American Society of Farm Managers and Rural Appraisers. Joining such a group can offer many advantages: the chance to meet and talk to other people in your field, special courses and workshops on important appraisal topics, and professional designations.

The two main appraisal organizations are the Appraisal Institute and the American Society of Appraisers. Each group offers several designations. The *Uniform Standards of Professional Appraisal Practice* were adopted in 1987 by leading appraisal groups to maintain a high standard of appraisal practice. Now, USPAP comprises the minimum acceptable appraisal standards for most appraisals involved in federally related financial transactions. Because integrity is a basic requirement of appraisers, standards codes seek to protect the general public, the client, and the appraisal profession.

Appraisers may be divided into two categories: those who work for a salary and those who work on a per-assignment basis. Many appraisers begin in a salaried position as a trainee or researcher. This initial employment might be with a financial or government institution or larger appraisal firm. Many private and public institutions hire appraisers. Fee appraisers, on the other hand, usually work for themselves in a small office or as contractors for a larger office. They must have a good sense of business management to be successful.

Appraising is an interesting and varied profession. It is a field that can offer many benefits to those who enjoy its variety and challenge.

IMPORTANT TERMS AND CONCEPTS

Appraiser licensing and certification	*Fee appraiser*
Competency	*Impartiality*
Conduct	*Institutional appraiser*
Confidentiality	*Integrity*
Designations	*Management*
Disclosure	*Professional societies*
Federally related transactions	*Record keeping*

REVIEWING YOUR UNDERSTANDING

1. To become an appraiser generally requires:
   a. A college degree
   b. A high school diploma
   c. No specific educational requirements except where licensing or certification is required
   d. None of the above

2. New state and federal laws generally require the appraiser to be licensed or certified to perform appraisals that are:
   a. In support of any loan
   b. Over $250,000
   c. Involved in federally related financial transactions
   d. Not made by a designated appraiser

3. The Certified Residential appraiser is typically eligible to appraise:
   a. All residential (one- to four-unit) properties
   b. Noncomplex properties only
   c. Complex one- to four-unit residential properties only
   d. All properties

4. Ideally, a prospective appraiser should be knowledgeable about:
   a. Economics and advertising
   b. Professional appraisal groups
   c. Income and commercial properties
   d. Real estate markets, operations involving real estate, and sources of market data

5. Joining an appraisal group or society has many advantages. These include:
   a.   Educational seminars and workshops
   b.   Professional designations
   c.   Both of the above
   d.   Neither of the above

6. Of the several smaller groups mentioned, which one specializes in appraising property for property tax purposes?
   a.   International Association of Assessing Officers
   b.   International Right of Way Association
   c.   National Society of Real Estate Appraisers
   d.   None of the above

7. The American Society of Appraisers differs from the Appraisal Institute in one important way:
   a.   ASA members appraise various types of property, not just real property
   b.   ASA members appraise real property exclusively
   c.   ASA members work primarily for the government
   d.   None of the above apply

8. Which professional group offers the "MAI" designation?
   a.   Appraisal Institute
   b.   Institute of Business Appraisers
   c.   American Society of Appraisers
   d.   None of the above

9. Which of the following areas of appraisal practice is (or are) covered by the *Ethics* provision of USPAP?
   a.   Conduct
   b.   Management
   c.   Confidentiality
   d.   Record keeping
   e.   All of the above

10. A fee appraiser is:
   a.   An appraiser who works for an institution for a fixed salary
   b.   An appraiser who is paid on a per-job basis
   c.   An appraiser who works for a percentage commission
   d.   An appraiser who specializes in the appraisal of leased fee estates

ANSWERS TO REVIEWING YOUR UNDERSTANDING

Answers by Chapter

Question Number	1	2	3	4	5	6	7	8	9	10	11	12	13	14	15	16	17	18	
1	c	a	b	d	b	d	c	c	b	e	d	d	c	d	c	d	c	c	1
2	b	b	c	d	c	a	d	a	c	b	b	d	b	b	c	d	c	c	2
3	a	*	b	e	b	b	c	b	c	d	d	c	c	d	d	c	c	a	3
4	c	b	b	a	c	a	d	d	b	c	d	c	d	c	e	b	d	d	4
5	a	c	d	b	c	c	d	d	a	c	a	b	a	a	b	d	a	c	5
6	c	*	d	b	d	b	d	e	b	d	c	c	b	a	c	a	b	a	6
7	a	a	b	e	d	c	c	c	a	d	c	c	c	b	e	d	b	a	7
8	e	*	b	b	b	a	d	c	d	b	c	b	b	b	b	a	c	a	8
9	e	*	c	b	b	b	b	c	a	d	b	b	a	b	d	d	a	e	9
10	c	b	c	d	b	a	d	d	d	*	b	a	b	a*	d	d	a	b	10
11		b				b	d						a			d			11
12							c						a						12
	1	2	3	4	5	6	7	8	9	10	11	12	13	14	15	16	17	18	

*Answers/Solutions

Chap.#	Ques.#	Answer/Solution
2	3	Intent, Annexation, Adaptation, Agreement, Relationship of Parties.
2	6	Building Codes, Coastal Preservation Zones, Master Plans, Rent Control, Subdivision Requirements, Zoning Ordinances, etc.
2	8	One square mile; 640 acres.
2	9	Square of 6 miles per side; 36 sections of 640 acres each.
10	10	$35,340, $42,000, $37,450, $38,700. Answer is (a), but median value around $38,000 may be preferred.
14	10	Solution follows.

Annual gross income:

Rent per square foot	$ 1.00
× Floor area	× 10,000
= Monthly rent	$ 10,000
× Annualizer	× 12
= Annual gross income	$120,000
− Expenses (given)	− 30,000
= Net income before recapture	$ 90,000
− Building charge: $400,000 ×(.10 + .04)	− 56,000
= Net income residual to land	$ 34,000
÷ Capitalization rate	÷ 0.10
= Land value	$340,000
+ Building value	+ 400,000
= Total property value	$740,000 (Answer)

GLOSSARY

A

Absorption Period The estimated time period required to sell, lease, place in use, or trade the subject property in its marketing area at prevailing prices or rental rates.

Abstraction Method Method of appraising vacant land. The allocation of the total sale price or appraised value of a property between land and building, either by using a ratio or by subtracting a figure representing building value from the total price (or value). Also called Allocation Method.

Access Right The right of a property owner to have a means of entry and exit from his or her property to a public street.

Accrued Depreciation Loss in value from the replacement cost of new improvements; the difference between the cost new as of the date of the value and the market value; diminished utility.

Ad Valorem Tax A property tax based upon the value of the property.

Adjustment In the sales comparison approach, a dollar or percentage amount that is added to or subtracted from the sale price of a comparable property, to account for a feature that the property has or does not have, which is different than the subject property. Also used with rental comparables or capitalization rate comparables.

Age-Life Method of Depreciation See Straight-Line Method of Depreciation.

Agents of Production See Principle of Agents of Production.

Allocation Method See Abstraction Method.

Amenities Qualities that are pleasing and agreeable; generally, intangible benefits of property ownership.

Amortization The repayment of a financial obligation on an installment basis; also, recovery of any investment over a given period of time.

Annuity A series of relatively reliable payments, anticipated over a period of time.

Annuity Capitalization An income capitalization method, a form of yield capitalization; usually discounts the projected future annual income to an estimate of value, by multiplying by an appropriate factor. The factor provides for both return on and return of investment capital.

Anticipation See Principle of Anticipation.

Appraisal An estimate or opinion of value as of a certain date. *Complete Appraisal.* The act or process of estimating value, or an estimate of value, performed without invoking the Departure Rule of USPAP. Eliminated in 2006 and replaced with the Scope of Work Rule. *Limited Appraisal.* The act or process of estimating value, or an estimate of value, performed under and resulting from invoking the Departure Rule of USPAP. Eliminated in 2006 and replaced with the Scope of Work Rule.

Appraisal Foundation, The An entity created by the appraisal profession to regulate its own industry. Empowered by the Financial Institutions Reform, Recovery, and Enforcement Act of 1989 to set minimum standards and qualifications for performing appraisals in federally related financial transactions.

Appraisal Process An orderly procedure that appraisers use to solve a valuation problem.

Appraisal Report Communication of a formal appraisal. *Self-Contained Appraisal Report.* Contains all information needed for solution of the appraisal problem. *Summary Appraisal Report.* Contains only a summary of the information used to prepare the appraisal. *Restricted Use Appraisal Report.* Contains only a brief statement of the information used.

Appraiser One qualified by education, training, and experience to estimate the value of real or personal property, based on experience, judgment, facts, and use of formal appraisal procedures. *Certified Real Estate Appraiser.* An appraiser certified by the appropriate state agency to value real estate. With *de minimus* exceptions, federal law allows only licensed or certified appraisers to appraise property in a federally related real estate transaction. Generally, Certified Residential Real Estate Appraisers may appraise one- to four-unit residential transactions without regard to property use, transaction value, or complexity; Certified General Real Estate appraisers may appraise all real estate transactions without regard to transaction value or complexity. *Licensed Real Estate Appraiser.* An appraiser licensed by the appropriate state agency to value real estate. With *de minimus* exceptions, federal law allows only licensed or certified appraisers to appraise property in a federally related real estate transaction. In general, the licensed appraiser is allowed to perform appraisals only of non-complex one- to four-unit residential properties up to $1 million transaction value, and complex one- to four-unit residential units up to $250,000. See also Federally Related Transaction.

Appreciation Increase in the value of property.

Appurtenance That which has been added or appended to a property and which then becomes an inherent part. Contrast with Fixture.

Appurtenant Right A right that belongs to the owners of one property that gives them the right to use another property (which they do not own), in a specific way that benefits their property (an easement for example).

Area The space or size of a surface, defined by a set of boundaries.

Assemblage See Plottage.

Assessment The valuation of property for the purpose of levying a tax; assessed value. Also, a single charge levied against real estate, to defray the cost of public improvements that serve it.

Assignment Conditions In USPAP, all of the assumptions, conditions, standards, and exceptions that apply to a specific assignment.

Association Agreement Set of private conditions, covenants, and restrictions applying to all properties in a planned unit development, condominium, or other community project.

Assumption of Mortgage The taking of title to property wherein the buyer

assumes liability for payment of an existing note secured by a mortgage against the property.

Automated Valuation Models (AVMs) Computer software programs that analyze data using automated systems, such as regression analysis and/or so-called artificial intelligence.

B

Balance See Principle of Surplus Productivity, Balance, and Contribution.

Band of Investment Method of estimating either interest or capitalization rates, based on a weighted average of the mortgage interest rate (or other measure of the cost of borrowed funds), and the rate of return on equity that is required.

Base Costs Average or typical building costs, usually from cost manuals; used, with appropriate refinements, to estimate cost of construction.

Base Line In U.S. government surveys, the east-west reference line through the base point.

Base Rent See Minimum Rent.

Book Value The capital amount at which property is recorded or listed for accounting purposes; cost basis.

Bracketing When using the sales comparison approach, selection of market data so that the subject is contained within a range of data (that is, some properties larger and some smaller).

Building Code Municipal, county, or state ordinance that regulates the type and quality of building materials and methods of construction permitted. Many jurisdictions share Uniform Building Codes.

Building Residual Technique Technique of income capitalization; the net income to the building (after deducting the income required for the land) is capita-

lized into an estimated value for the building.

Bundle of Rights The rights that accompany the ownership of real estate.

C

Capital An agent of production; construction and equipment costs; investment money.

Capital Gain Profit on the sale of a property.

Capitalization The process of converting an estimate of future income into an estimate of value, as of a specific date.

Capitalization Rate Any rate used to capitalize income. Often referred to as a "cap rate." The rate of return, percentage, or ratio used to convert income into its value equivalent.

Capitalized Income Approach See Income Approach.

Cash Flow (1) The income or loss arising from an investment in a specified time period; (2) net operating income minus debt service. (It can be calculated before or after income tax.)

Cash-on-Cash The investor's return to the cash equity investment, based on the actual cash invested; cash flow as a percentage or ratio to equity (the investor's cash invested, divided by investor's annual cash flow).

Cash Return to Equity Equity dividend; cash flow to the equity investment.

Central Tendency In statistics, the tendency for data to cluster; measurements of central tendency include the mean, median, and mode.

Central Town A town that performs a variety of services for the surrounding area.

Certification A signed and dated statement declaring that the appraiser has performed an appraisal in an unbiased and professional manner and that all assumptions and limiting conditions are set forth in the report. See also Certified Real Estate Appraiser.

Certified Real Estate Appraiser See Appraiser.

Change See Principle of Change.

Client Defined in *USPAP*, 2006, as "the party or parties who engage an appraiser (by employment or contract) in a specific assignment."

Comparable Sales Property sales used for purposes of comparison in the appraisal process; ideally, relatively similar to the subject property, open market transactions, and with a time of sale close to the date of value.

Comparative Square-Foot Method Method of estimating construction costs, based upon the construction cost per square foot.

Competency In USPAP, having adequate knowledge, experience, and ability to perform a specific assignment competently.

Competition See Principle of Competition.

Complete Appraisal See Appraisal. Now considered obsolete in USPAP since 2006.

Composite Rate A capitalization rate composed of interest and recapture in separately estimated amounts.

Compound Interest Interest paid on principal and also on the accrued and unpaid interest.

Condemnation The taking of property by a governmental agency through the power of eminent domain. Also used to refer to the authority, under the police power, to order a dangerously neglected or damaged building destroyed without reimbursement to the owner.

Conditions, Covenants, and Restrictions (CC&Rs) Recorded deed restrictions that run with the land, usually initiated by the original subdivider. Also see Association Agreement.

Condominium A form of legal ownership; each individual owns the airspace in his/her unit in fee simple, plus an undivided interest in the structural supports, building systems, and all common areas.

Conformity See Principle of Conformity.

Consistent Use See Principle of Consistent Use.

Construction Classification Type of construction; a system that rates the structural frame, walls, and roof of a structure according to their relative fire resistance (for example, Class A, B, C, or D Construction; Class A being the most fireproof).

Contract Rent Amount of rent being paid, under contractual commitments, binding owners and tenants.

Contribution See Principle of Surplus Productivity, Balance, and Contribution.

Cooperative A form of legal ownership; each owner holds a stated percentage ownership in the cooperative association, which owns the land and buildings and grants each owner the permanent right to occupy the specified dwelling unit, as well as the right to the joint use of the common areas.

Coordination An agent of production; management.

Corner Lot Lot with frontage on two intersecting streets.

Correlation See Reconciliation. Now an obsolete term.

Cost See Replacement Cost; Reproduction Cost.

Cost Approach One of the three classic approaches to value. It involves estimating the replacement (or reproduction) cost new of the improvements, deducting the estimated accrued depreciation, and then adding the market value of the land.

Cost Basis Original price paid for a property, plus capital improvements, less allowable depreciation deductions (an accounting term).

Cost Multiplier Factor used in adjusting published construction cost figures, to adjust for time and for local cost differences.

Cost-to-Cure Method of Depreciation Method of estimating accrued depreciation (loss in value), based on the cost to cure or repair observed building defects.

Courtyard Home See Zero-Lot-Line Home.

Credible Appraisal Worthy of being relied on.

Cul-de-sac Lot Lot located at or near the end of a dead-end street.

Curable Depreciation Items of physical deterioration or functional obsolescence that, if repaired, would add at least as much to the market value of the property as the cost of repairs.

Curbstone Appraisal A slang phrase, implying an informal valuation of a property based on observation and experience.

D

Debt Service The periodic payments, usually of interest and principal, required by a loan agreement.

Decline Phase Third phase in the cycle of a neighborhood, generally marked by delayed repairs and deterioration of buildings.

Dedication A voluntary giving of private property to some public use by the owner, as in the dedication of land for streets in a subdivision.

Deed Restrictions Private limitations, set forth in the deed to a property, that dictate certain uses that may or may not be made of the property.

Demand The desire to possess plus the ability to buy; an essential element of value.

Demography The study of human populations (for example, size, density, growth rate).

Depreciated Cost Method Method for adjusting comparable sales; adjustments are calculated from an analysis of the depreciated replacement cost for each feature that is different.

Depreciation Loss of value in property, brought about by age, physical deterioration, and/or functional or economic obsolescence.

Depth Distance from the frontage of a lot to the rear lot line.

Design Type Classification of buildings, based on the use for which a structure is designed.

Development Method (Land Development Method) Method of vacant land valuation; development costs are subtracted from estimated gross sales and, finally, developers' profits are accounted for. The results provide an estimate of raw land value.

Development Phase First phase in the life cycle of a neighborhood, consisting of the initial construction of improvements on vacant land.

Diminished Utility See Accrued Depreciation.

Direct Capitalization Method Income capitalization technique; value is estimated by dividing the net operating income by the overall capitalization rate.

Direct Costs All of the costs that are directly involved with the physical construction of the structure, including labor, materials and equipment, design and engineering, and subcontractors' fees.

Direct Market Comparison Approach See Sales Comparison Approach.

Direct Market Method Method of adjusting comparable sales; two or more comparable properties with one differing feature are used to estimate the amount of the adjustment for that feature (also called the matched pair method).

Discount Rate See Interest Rate.

Discounted Cash Flow (DCF) Technique of income capitalization; estimated future investment cash flows or returns are mathematically discounted to their present value.

E

Easement Right, privilege, or interest that one party has in the land of another, created for a specific purpose by grant, agreement, or necessity.

Economic Base For a community or defined geographic area, the portion of its economic production that is sold or exported outside its boundaries.

Economic Life The total number of years of economically useful life that may be expected from a building.

Economic Obsolescence Loss in value that is caused by factors located outside the subject property; locational or environmental obsolescence.

Economic Rent See Market Rent. (An obsolete term.)

Economic Trend Pattern of related changes in some aspect of the economy.

Effective Age Relative age of a structure, considering its physical condition and marketability.

Effective Date The date of value; the date when the opinions of the appraisal are valid.

Effective Gross Rent Gross rent roll minus an allowance for vacancy and credit losses.

Effective Interest Rate The percentage rate of interest that is actually being paid by a borrower for the use of money; distinct from nominal interest rate.

Electronic Data Interchange (EDI) Computer-linked system that allows the transmission of appraisal reports and other data by electronic means; increasingly replaced by email.

Elements of Comparison Four categories of information about sales: terms of sale, time of sale, location elements, and physical elements.

Elements of Value Four prerequisites that must be present for an object to have value: utility, scarcity, demand, and transferability.

Ellwood Technique A mortgage/equity method of capitalization; now rarely used.

Eminent Domain The power of a government to acquire property for a public purpose by paying just or reasonable compensation.

Environmental Impact Report (EIR) A formal report designed to assess the results or impact of a proposed activity or development upon the environment. Environmental protection laws generally require EIRs for major public or private developments and other activities posing a potential threat to the environment.

Environmental Obsolescence See Economic Obsolescence.

Equity Interest or value that an owner has in real estate, over and above the liens against it.

Equity Buildup Increase in the investor's share of the total property value, due to the reduction of debt, through payments applied to the loan principal, and/or through increases in property value.

Equity Capitalization Rate Factor used to estimate the value of the equity in the equity residual technique of capitalization and other mortgage and equity techniques; the equity cash flow divided by the equity value; also called the equity cash-on-cash rate.

Equity Residual Technique Technique of income capitalization. The net income remaining to the equity investor (after mortgage payments) is capitalized into an estimate of the value of the equity.

Escheat The right of the state to take back title to property, if the owner dies or disappears and leaves no relatives or heirs.

Estate A person's ownership interest in real property.

Ethics Rule In USPAP, the obligation of an appraiser to comply with professional practice requirements regarding conduct, management, confidentiality, and record keeping.

Evaluation An analysis of a property and/or its attributes in which a value estimate is not required.

Excess Rent The amount by which the total contract rent exceeds market rent.

Expense Ratio See Operating Expense Ratio.

Export Production Goods and services produced for sale or use outside of the town or area in which they are produced.

Exposure Time How long the property would have been marketed, in order to sell for the appraised value.

External Obsolescence See Economic Obsolescence.

Extraordinary Assumption Defined in *USPAP*, 2006, as "an assumption, directly related to a specific assignment, which, if found to be false, could alter the appraiser's opinions or conclusions."

F

Farmers Home Administration (FHmA) An agency of the Department of Agriculture that is primarily responsible for providing financial assistance to farmers, and others living in rural areas where financing is not available on reasonable terms from private sources.

Federal Home Loan Bank Board (FHLBB) Former administrative agency that exercised regulating authority over the FHLB system. Its functions are now performed by the Federal Deposit Insurance Corporation and other federal agencies.

Federal Home Loan Mortgage Corporation (FHLMC) A quasi-federal agency, now a private corporation known as Freddie Mac, that provides a secondary market for mortgages originated by savings and loan associations.

Federal Housing Administration (FHA) An agency of the federal government that insures mortgage loans.

Federal National Mortgage Association (FNMA) A quasi-public agency, now a private corporation known as Fannie Mae, whose primary function is to buy and sell mortgages in the secondary market and to sell securities backed or secured by blocks of mortgages.

Federal Reserve System The federal banking system of the United States. Under the control of a central board of governors (the Federal Reserve Board), it includes a central bank in each of twelve geographical districts, with broad powers to control credit and the amount of money in circulation.

Federally Related Transaction Any real estate-related financial transaction involving a federally regulated lender or federal insurance, and that requires the service of an appraiser. See Financial Institutions Reform, Recovery, and Enforcement Act.

Fee Absolute See Fee Simple.

Fee Simple An estate or ownership interest in real property, where the owner has title that is limited only by the four government powers (escheat, taxation, police power, and eminent domain).

Financial Institutions Reform, Recovery, and Enforcement Act (FIRREA) A federal law passed in 1989 to provide guidelines for the regulation of financial institutions. One part of the law requires a state license or certification for the performance of federally related real estate transaction appraisals (with *de minimus* exceptions). See also Federally Related Transaction.

Fiscal Policy Actions by the federal government to influence economic activity by changing government expenditures or taxation.

Fixed Expenses Operating costs that are more or less permanent and that vary little from year to year.

Fixture Personal property that is considered part of the real estate, because it has become attached, physically or legally, to the real estate.

Flag Lot Rear lot, behind other houses or lots, with a long, narrow access road (like a flagpole).

Flat Lease See Straight Lease.

Form Report Written appraisal report, presented on a standardized form or checklist.

Formal Appraisal An estimate of value that is reached by the collection and analysis of relevant data. A formal appraisal is usually reported in writing.

Frontage Boundary line or lot side that faces a street.

Functional Obsolescence Loss in value that is caused by a relative loss of building utility or usefulness.

Functional Utility The combination of the usefulness and attractiveness of a property for its intended use.

Future Value The estimated value of money or property at a date in the future.

G

Government National Mortgage Association (GNMA) A federal corporation, known as Ginnie Mae, mainly involved in the secondary mortgage market and in issuing federally insured, mortgage-backed securities.

Government Survey System See Rectangular Survey System.

Graduated Lease See Step-Up Lease.

Gross Domestic Product (GDP) The value of all domestic goods and services produced in the country.

Gross Income Total income from property, before any expenses are deducted.

Gross Income Multiplier (GIM) The ratio of the selling price (or appraisal value) to the gross income of a property (that is, value divided by gross income). May be multiplied by the gross income of a property to produce an estimate of the property's value. Also known as the Gross Rent Multiplier (GRM).

Gross Lease Rental agreement under which the landlord pays all expenses.

Gross Rent Multiplier See Gross Income Multiplier.

H

Highest and Best Use The reasonable and probable use of a property that will support the highest present value of the land. See also Principle of Highest and Best Use.

Historic Cost Original cost of a property at the time it was constructed or purchased.

Hypothetical Condition Defined in *USPAP*, 2006, as "that which is contrary to what exists but is supposed for the purpose of analysis."

I

Improvement Permanent structure or other development that becomes part of the land.

Income Approach One of the three classic approaches to value, where the expected net income from the property is capitalized into a value estimate.

Income Forecast Gross or net income estimate.

Income Property Property that is purchased for its income-producing capabilities.

Income Stream Actual or estimated flow of net earnings over the time period being studied.

Increasing and Decreasing Returns See Principle of Increasing and Decreasing Returns.

Incurable Depreciation Building defects or problems that would cost more to repair than the anticipated value increase if the repair were made.

Index Method Method for estimating construction costs; adjusts the original costs to the cost level on the desired date by a multiplier, obtained from a published cost index.

Indicated Value Value estimate calculated/produced by an appraisal approach.

Indirect Costs All of the time and money costs involved in a construction project that are not directly involved with construction itself. Examples are loan fees, interest, property taxes during construction, legal fees, and marketing costs.

Informal Appraisal An estimate of value that is reached by using intuition, past experience, and general knowledge.

Intangible Property Rights to something other than tangible, or physical, property.

Intended Users Defined in *USPAP*, 2006, as "the client and any other party as identified, by name or type, as users of the appraisal, appraisal review, or appraisal consulting report by the appraiser on the basis of communication with the client at the time of the assignment."

Interest Charge for the use of money for a period of time.

Interest Rate The rate of return on capital; usually expressed as an annual percentage of the amount loaned or invested. Same as yield rate or discount rate.

Interior Lot Lot with frontage on only one street.

Internal Rate of Return The rate of return (profit, yield or interest), generated by an investment over the holding period; considers all future benefits, discounting them to equal the value of the initial investment. See Interest Rate.

J-K

Jurisdictional Exception Defined in *USPAP*, 2006, as "an assignment condition that voids the force of a part or parts of USPAP, when compliance with part or parts of USPAP is contrary to law or public policy applicable to the assignment."

Just Compensation Payment for private property that is obtained by a government agency by condemnation through the power of eminent domain.

Key Lot Lot that has several other lots backing onto its sideyard.

L

Labor An agent of production; cost of all operating expenses and wages except management.

Land The surface, the soil and rocks beneath, and the airspace above that the landowner can reasonably use and enjoy.

Land Residual Technique Technique of income capitalization; the net income remaining to the land (after income attributable to the building has been deducted) is capitalized into an estimate of value for the land.

Landlord Property owner who rents property to another.

Larger Parcel Total parcel of property from which a government body is acquiring only a portion through condemnation.

Law of Fixtures Five tests to determine whether an object is a fixture or personal property.

Lease A written contract between the owner and the tenant, setting forth the terms and conditions under which the tenant may occupy and use the property.

Leased Fee Property owner's interest in leased property.

Leasehold Tenant's interest in leased property.

Lessee Tenant; one who rents property under a lease contract.

Lessor Landlord; owner who enters into a lease with a tenant.

Letter Report One- to five-page written report, summarizing the appraisal and its conclusions.

Leverage Use of borrowed funds to purchase property, with the expectation of increasing the rate of return to the equity investment; sometimes called "trading on the equity."

Licensed Real Estate Appraiser See Appraiser.

Life Estate Holder controls the right of possession and use of a property during the lifetime of some specifically named person.

Limited Appraisal See Appraisal. Now obsolete; in USPAP until 2006.

Limiting Conditions All of the conditions, general or specific, imposed by an appraiser that limit the use of an appraisal or report.

Linear Regression Statistical technique for calculating value or adjustment amount; assumes that the unknown changes in a constant or straight-line manner; the line of "best fit," usually for two variables.

Liquidity The ease with which property can be converted into cash.

Living Area The area of a house that is fully finished and heated.

Local Production Goods and services produced for sale or use in the town or area in which they are produced.

Long-Lived, Incurable Physical Deterioration Loss in value attributable to the major components of a building, when age is the major contributing factor and the cost of repair exceeds the value that would be added by the repair.

Lump-Sum Dollar Adjustment Type of sales adjustment; specific dollar amount is added or subtracted for each differing feature.

M

Manufactured Homes Homes built in a factory; may include modular homes, as well as mobile homes constructed on or after June 15, 1976, according to the U.S. Department of Housing and Urban Development (HUD). See also Mobile Home, Modular Home.

Market Approach See Sales Comparison Approach.

Market Exposure Making a reasonable number of potential buyers or tenants of a property aware that the property is available.

Market Method of Depreciation See Sales Data Method of Depreciation.

Market Rent The rental income the property could command, if placed for rent on the open market as of the effective date of the appraisal.

Market Value The most probable price in terms of money that a property should bring in a competitive and open market under all conditions requisite to a fair sale, with the buyer and seller each acting prudently and knowledgeably, and assuming the price is not affected by undue stimulus.

Marketing Period The typical time required to sell or lease a property.

Mature Phase See Stable Phase.

Mean Measure of central tendency; the average price or numeric value of a group of data. See Central Tendency.

Median Measure of central tendency; the middle value, that is, the one with as many higher values as lower values, in a group of data. See Central Tendency.

Metes and Bounds Description Legal description of land that describes the length and direction of each boundary line, in sequence, starting at a defined point of beginning.

Minimum Rent Base rent, which is the fixed minimum amount to be paid, usually in a lease where there also is percentage rent. See Percentage Lease.

Misplaced Improvement A building that is the wrong type or use for its location; an example of functional obsolescence.

Mobile Home A housing unit that is capable of being moved on the highway. According to the U.S. Department of

Housing and Urban Development (HUD), mobile homes constructed on or after June 15, 1976, are properly classified as *manufactured homes*. See also Manufactured Homes.

Mode Measure of central tendency; the most frequently occurring price or value in a group of data. See Central Tendency.

Modular Home Building composed of modules, each constructed on an assembly line in a factory. See also Manufactured Homes.

Monetary Policy Programs by the Federal Reserve System that increase or decrease the supply of or demand for money, in an effort to achieve designated economic goals. Contrast with Fiscal Policy.

Mortgage Legal instrument by which property is used to secure the payment of a note, evidence of a debt or obligation.

Mortgage Equity Analysis An income capitalization technique used to separately analyze the return or yield requirements of the debt and equity investors.

Mortgage Equity Capitalization Income capitalization, using one of several techniques which focus on the relative importance of borrowed funds and investor equity, and the annual income required by each.

Multiple Listing Service (MLS) An association of real estate agents, providing for pooled listings and shared commissions.

Multiple Regression Statistical technique used to analyze data to estimate the probable sale price (or other desired unknown), involving study of more than one known characteristic of the data.

N

Narrative Report A detailed, formal, written report of the appraisal and the value conclusion.

Neighborhood An area whose occupants and users share some common ties or characteristics.

Neighborhood Cycle The process of neighborhood change, involving four phases: development, maturity, decline, and renaissance. See also Principle of Change.

Net Area See Useful Area.

Net Floor Area The occupied area of a building, excluding air shafts, stairs, and elevators.

Net Income Gross annual income, less income lost due to vacancies and uncollectible rents, less all operating expenses.

Net Income Ratio Net income divided by the effective gross income.

Net Lease Lease under which the lessee pays all property expenses.

Net Operating Income See Net Income.

Net Rentable Area See Net Floor Area.

Nominal Interest Rate A stated (or contract) annual rate of interest; may not correspond to the true or effective annual percentage rate (for example, when payments are made monthly).

O

Observed Condition Method of Depreciation See Cost-to-Cure Method of Depreciation.

Obsolescence Loss in value due to a reduced desirability or usefulness of a structure. See Functional Obsolescence; Economic Obsolescence.

Open-Market Transaction Transaction in which the property was exposed to many prospective buyers, and both buyer and seller act willingly, with full knowledge of all details of the property and the transaction, and under no pressure.

Operating Expense Ratio The ratio of total operating expenses to the effective gross rent in an income property. See Net Income Ratio.

Operating Expenses Expenses required to run a property (that is, to maintain its income). Typical categories include fixed expense, variable expense, and reserves for replacement.

Operating Statement Written record of a property's gross income, expenses, and resultant net income for a given period of time.

Overage Rent Amounts paid over and above the base rent, under a percentage lease.

Overall Rate (OAR) The relationship between the net income and value of the total property (that is, the net income divided by value); used to capitalize income.

Overimprovement A building that is too large or has excess quality for its neighborhood and therefore suffers from functional obsolescence; also called superadequacy.

P

Partial Interests Interests in real estate that represent less than the fee simple estate (for example, a leased fee or leasehold estate).

Partial Taking The process by which a governmental agency acquires only a portion of a property through condemnation.

Patio Home See Zero-Lot-Line Home.

Percentage Adjustment Type of sales adjustment; the estimated difference caused by the specific characteristic is calculated as a percentage of the sale price of the comparable, and then applied as an upward or downward adjustment to the price.

Percentage Lease Lease agreement by which the tenant pays a stipulated percentage, usually of the gross sales of goods and services offered by the tenant; most percentage leases require a certain base rent regardless of sales volume.

Personal Property Property that is movable; any property that is not real property.

Physical Deterioration Wear and tear from use, age, the weather, neglect, lack of maintenance, and/or vandalism.

Planned Unit Development (PUD) A project consisting of individually owned parcels of land, with a common area and facilities owned by an association of which the owners of all the parcels are members.

Plottage The combining of two or more parcels together for increased utility; also referred to as assemblage. The term *plottage* is also used to denote plottage value. See also Plottage Value.

Plottage Value The increase in utility or unit value (for example, price per square foot) that is created by joining two or more parcels together into one larger ownership.

Points Amounts paid by the borrower or the seller that increase the effective yield for a lender; each point equals 1 percent of the loan amount.

Police Power Power of a governmental body to regulate property for the health, safety, morals, and general welfare of the public.

Prefabricated Home House manufactured (and sometimes partly assembled) before delivery to the building site.

Present Value The current value of some future income or benefits, discounted for the future time period and for the

need to earn interest on the original investment, at a defined interest rate.

Principal Meridian Line In U.S. government surveys, the north-south reference line through the base point.

Principle of Agents of Production All production or income can be said to be the result of the four factors of labor, coordination, capital, and land.

Principle of Anticipation Value is the present worth of future benefits, whether income or intangible amenities.

Principle of Balance See Principle of Surplus Productivity, Balance, and Contribution.

Principle of Change Real estate values are constantly changed by social, economic, and political forces in society. See also Neighborhood Cycle.

Principle of Competition Market demand generates profits; profits generate competition; and competition stabilizes profits.

Principle of Conformity Maximum value results when properties in a neighborhood are relatively similar in size, style, quality, use, and/or type.

Principle of Consistent Use Requires that land and improvements be appraised on the basis of the same use.

Principle of Contribution See Principle of Surplus Productivity, Balance, and Contribution.

Principle of Highest and Best Use Maximum market value of a given parcel of land, vacant or improved, is created by development or utilization at its highest and best use.

Principle of Increasing and Decreasing Returns Income and other benefits available from real estate may be increased by adding capital improvements only up to the point of balance in the agents of production, beyond which the increase in value tends to be less than the increase in costs.

Principle of Progression and Regression Lower-valued properties generally benefit from close proximity to properties of higher value, and higher-valued properties tend to suffer when placed in close proximity with lower-valued properties.

Principle of Substitution When a property can be easily replaced by another, the value of such property tends to be set by the cost of acquiring an equally desirable substitute property.

Principle of Supply and Demand Prices and rent levels tend to increase when demand is greater than supply, and tend to decrease when supply exceeds demand.

Principle of Surplus Productivity, Balance, and Contribution Income that is available to land, after the other economic agents have been paid for, is known as the surplus of productivity; a proper balance of the agents maximizes the income available to land; the value of any agent is determined by its contribution to the whole.

Promissory Note An agreement signed by the borrower, promising to repay the loan under stipulated terms.

Q-R

Quality of Construction Classification or rating that considers the basic structural integrity, materials, finishes, and special features.

Quantity Survey Method Process for arriving at a cost estimate for new construction, involving a detailed estimate of the quantities of raw materials used, the current price of each material, and installation costs.

Range Measure of central tendency; the difference (or spread) between the highest and lowest value in the collection of data. See Central Tendency.

Range Line In U.S. government surveys, the series of north-south lines, six miles apart, parallel to the principal meridian line.

Ratio Capitalization Describes any capitalization method that uses the typical ratio of income to value to convert projected income into a value estimate for the property (or property component) under appraisal. Includes direct capitalization, as well as land, building, and equity residual capitalization methods when sales price-income ratios are used.

Real Estate The land and everything that is permanently fastened to the land; real property.

Real Estate Cycle Periodic pattern of changes in the amount of construction and volume of sales in the real estate market.

Real Property Real estate.

Recapture The return of investment capital. May come out of periodic income, or future resale and/or refinancing, or some combination.

Reconciliation The process by which the appraiser reviews and analyzes the indicated values developed by the applied approaches, to arrive at a final value conclusion.

Recorded Lot, Block, and Tract Legal description of a parcel of land, by means of reference to the recorded plat of a subdivision.

Rectangular Survey System System for legal description of property, using base points, principal meridians, base lines, and a grid system.

Regression Analysis See Linear Regression; Multiple Regression.

Remainder Estate An estate that takes effect after the termination of a life estate.

Remainder Parcel The portion of a property left to the owner, when a government agency has acquired a portion of

the property (called a partial taking) by the power of eminent domain.

Renaissance Phase Fourth phase in the cycle of a neighborhood; the transition to a new cycle through the demolition, relocation, or major renovation of existing buildings.

Rent Consideration paid for the use of real property.

Rent Multiplier See Gross Income Multiplier.

Rent Roll Total of all scheduled rental amounts for all tenant spaces, services, and parking.

Replacement Cost Cost of constructing a building or structure that would have a similar utility to the subject improvement, but constructed with modern materials and according to current standards, design, and layout.

Reproduction Cost Cost to build a near duplicate, or replica, structure.

Reserves for Replacement Annual allowances to fund the future replacement of particular building components and equipment. In some cases, deducted from annual income.

Residual Techniques of Capitalization Income approach methods that separate the net income into amounts that are assigned to a particular component of the property, such as land or building, or debt or equity, for purposes of analysis of its value contribution to the total property.

Restricted Use Appraisal Report See Appraisal Report.

Return of Investment Recapture or repayment of the funds that have been invested in a parcel of real estate, either in cash or other valuable assets.

Return on Investment Profits produced by the investment in real estate.

Reversion Return of the investor's capital, and/or added profits, through a sale

of the property; also, the return of rights in real estate to the lessor at the end of a lease.

Row House See Townhouse.

S

Sales Analysis Grid Table of relevant data on comparable properties.

Sales Comparison Approach One of the three classic approaches to value. It involves comparing similar properties that have recently sold to the subject property.

Sales Data Method of Depreciation Method of estimating depreciation. Building values abstracted from sales are compared to costs new on the sales date.

Scarcity A condition where demand exceeds supply; one of the four elements of value.

Scope of Work Defined in *USPAP*, 2006, as "the type and extent of research and analysis in an assignment."

Section In U.S. government surveys, a one-mile square block of land, one of 36 in a township.

Self-Contained Appraisal Report See Appraisal Report.

Severance Damage Damage to the value of the remainder parcel (the part not acquired) as a result of a partial taking (acquisition of part of a property) by eminent domain.

Special-Function Town A town whose employment emphasizes one special service or purpose.

Stable Phase Second phase in the cycle of a neighborhood, marked by stability of the existing buildings and occupants.

Standard Deviation A measure of how variable a sample is, that is, whether the observations are clustered near the mean or scattered throughout the range.

It is calculated as the square root of the sum of the squared differences between each observation and the mean of all observations, divided by the total number of observations. In an appraisal, each sale price of a comparable, for example, could be considered an observation.

Step-Up Lease Lease agreement that establishes progressively higher rental amounts for different segments of the lease term; graduated lease.

Straight Lease Lease agreement in which rent is a fixed amount that stays the same over the entire lease term.

Straight-Line Method of Depreciation Method of estimating depreciation, in which the loss in value of a building is assumed to be the ratio of its age, on the date of value, to its total useful or economic life. The loss in value will be the same dollar amount each year.

Subdivision The division of real property, as shown on a surveyed map, into lots or plots, with streets and other improvements suitable for development.

Summary Appraisal Report See Appraisal Report.

Summation Approach See Cost Approach.

Superadequacy See Overimprovement.

Supplemental Standards Defined in *USPAP*, 2006, as "requirements issued by government agencies, government sponsored enterprises, or other entities that establish public policy which add to the purpose, intent, and content of the requirements in USPAP, that have a material effect on the development and reporting of assignment results."

Supply and Demand See Principle of Supply and Demand.

T

T-Intersection Lot Lot facing the dead-end street at the T-intersection.

Take Parcel The portion of a property acquired, in a partial taking, by a governmental agency using the power of eminent domain.

Tangible Property Physical objects and/or the rights thereto.

Tax Money legally collected by a government to fund government needs.

Tenant One who occupies and/or leases property.

Terms of Sale Financing arrangements and conditions of a sale.

Time-Shared Ownership Subdivision of the fee interest of a property, or of one dwelling unit, into blocks of time, with each time block owned by a different owner.

Time-Value of Money The financial principle that a dollar in the present is worth more than a promised dollar in the future, because the present dollar can earn interest between now and the future date.

Topography Nature of the surface of land.

Townhouse Row house; a house on an individual lot, owned in fee; usually built without side yards between adjoining houses; an architectural style.

Township In U.S. government surveys, a six-mile square block of land, bounded by township and range lines.

Township Line In U.S. government surveys, the series of east-west lines, six miles apart, parallel to the base line.

Transferability Capable of change in ownership; one of the four elements of value.

Transportation-Service Town A town that is selected to provide services along a transportation route, usually located at transportation nodes.

Turn-Key Costs Costs that include all of the charges to the consumer, not just the costs to the developer or builder.

Type of Construction Building classification, based on a structure's basic frame, wall, and floor construction.

Type of Occupancy See Design Type.

U

Undivided Interests in Commonly Held Property Where two or more persons share the ownership of property, each having a non-exclusive right of use. Undivided interests are sometimes coupled with the sole ownership rights of an adjacent property, as in a condominium.

Undoubling In good economic times, when the occupants sharing a housing unit decide they can each afford a separate unit, thus increasing demand.

***Uniform Standards of Professional Appraisal Practice* (USPAP)** A set of standards and ethics, originally developed by nine appraisal associations to guide members in the development and reporting of appraisals; now maintained by the Appraisal Standards Board of the Appraisal Foundation.

Unit-in-Place Method Method of estimating the replacement cost of a building, by estimating the installed cost of each component part.

Unit of Comparison Adjustment Sales analysis tool, wherein the sales prices of the comparables are converted to price per physical or economic unit that is found to be closely related to selling price or value. The value of the subject property is suggested by multiplying its number of units by the price per physical or economic unit of comparison found to be appropriate.

Units of Comparison See Unit of Comparison Adjustment.

Use Type See Design Type.

Useful Area That portion of the gross area of a site that can be built on or developed for parking and so on.

USPAP See *Uniform Standards of Professional Appraisal Practice.*

Utility Usefulness; in economics, one of the four elements of value.

V

Value The worth, usefulness, or utility of an object to someone for some purpose.

Value Conclusion The final opinion or estimate of value in an appraisal.

Value in Exchange The value of an item or object to the general public; an objective view of value.

Value in Use The value of an item or object to a particular user; a subjective view of value.

Variable Expenses Operating expenses that vary with occupancy level or intensity of use of a property (for example, utility costs and maintenance).

Variance In zoning, a legally allowed exception to the normally permitted development or use of a specific site; in statistics, a measure of how much the data varies or spreads from the mean.

Veterans Administration (VA) A federal agency which, among other things, guarantees approved lenders against financial loss on loans made to eligible veterans.

Volume Measurement of the amount of space that a three-dimensional object occupies. In real estate, volume is normally measured in cubic feet or cubic yards.

Y-Z

Yield Total net profit earned by an investor on invested capital.

Yield Capitalization Capitalization method with an explicit estimate of the future income or income change pattern, holding period, and yield rate. It mathematically discounts future benefits for the holding period at appropriate yield rates.

Yield Rate See Interest Rate, Discount Rate, Internal Rate of Return.

Zero-Lot-Line Home House built without a sideyard; may be wrapped around two or more sides of a courtyard or patio.

Zoning Local laws that control the use of land under the police power of government. Zoning regulations apply to the type of use (for example, residential, commercial), density, height of buildings, parking requirements, and so on, permitted in a specific jurisdiction.

INDEX